D0948539

THE WORLD IS
WHAT IT IS

ALSO BY PATRICK FRENCH

YOUNGHUSBAND
The Last Great Imperial Adventurer

THE LIFE OF HENRY NORMAN

LIBERTY OR DEATH
India's Journey to Independence and Division

TIBET, TIBET
A Personal History of a Lost Land

PATRICK FRENCH

THE WORLD IS
WHAT IT IS

The Authorized Biography of V. S. Naipaul

PICADOR

First published 2008 by Picador
an imprint of Pan Macmillan Ltd
Pan Macmillan, 20 New Wharf Road, London N1 9RR
Basingstoke and Oxford
Associated companies throughout the world
www.panmacmillan.com

ISBN 978-0-330-43350-1 HB
ISBN 978-0-330-45598-5 TPB

Copyright © Patrick French 2008

The right of Patrick French to be identified as the
author of this work has been asserted by him in accordance
with the Copyright, Designs and Patents Act 1988.

All rights reserved. No part of this publication may be
reproduced, stored in or introduced into a retrieval system, or
transmitted, in any form, or by any means (electronic, mechanical,
photocopying, recording or otherwise) without the prior written
permission of the publisher. Any person who does any unauthorized
act in relation to this publication may be liable to criminal
prosecution and civil claims for damages.

1 3 5 7 9 8 6 4 2

A CIP catalogue record for this book is available from
the British Library.

Typeset by SetSystems Ltd, Saffron Walden, Essex
Printed and bound in India by
Gopsons Papers Ltd., Noida - 201 301

This book is sold subject to the condition that it shall not,
by way of trade or otherwise, be lent, re-sold, hired out,
or otherwise circulated without the publisher's prior consent
in any form of binding or cover other than that in which
it is published and without a similar condition including this
condition being imposed on the subsequent purchaser.

Visit *www.picador.com* to read more about all our books
and to buy them. You will also find features, author interviews and
news of any author events, and you can sign up for e-newsletters
so that you're always first to hear about our new releases.

MG

Contents

PART TWO

List of Illustrations

SECOND SECTION

Introduction

When V.S. Naipaul won the Nobel Prize in Literature in 2001, each country responded in its own way. The president of the Republic of Trinidad and Tobago sent a letter of congratulation on heavy writing paper; an Iranian newspaper denounced him for spreading venom and hatred; the Spanish prime minister invited him to drop by; India's politicians sent adulatory letters, with the president addressing his to 'Lord V.S. Naipaul' and the Bollywood superstar Amitabh Bachchan sending a fax of congratulation from Los Angeles; the *New York Times* wrote an editorial in praise of 'an independent voice, skeptical and observant'; the British minister for 'culture, media and sport' sent a dull, late letter on photocopying paper, and BBC *Newsnight* concentrated on Inayat Bungla-wala of the Muslim Council of Britain, who thought the award 'a cynical gesture to humiliate Muslims'.[1] At this point in British history, when the sensational and immediate mattered above all else and fame was becoming more important than the achievements that might give rise to fame, Naipaul's half-century of work as a writer seemed less significant than his reputation for causing offence.

'My background is at once exceedingly simple and exceedingly confused,' he suggested in his Nobel lecture.[2] When slavery was abolished across the British empire, workers were still needed for the sugar plantations, and in India his destitute forebears were sent to the Caribbean as bonded labourers; it was slavery by another name, slavery with an expiry date. Vidia Naipaul, born in rural poverty in colonial Trinidad in 1932, would rise from this unpromising setting to become one of the great writers of the twentieth century. This achievement does not mean that all his writing was good, or that his behaviour was exemplary, but rather that his cumulative accomplishment outstripped his contemporaries, and altered the way in which writers and readers perceived the world. Using simple sentences, he would look at complex modern subjects: extremism, global migration, political and religious identity, ethnic difference, the implosion of Africa, the resurgence of Asia and the remaking of the old European dispensation in the aftermath of empire. His achievement was an act of will, in which every situation and relationship would be subordinated to his ambition. His public position as a novelist and chronicler was inflexible at a time of intellectual relativism: he stood for high civilization, individual rights and the rule of law.

This was not an unusual position for someone of his background to be taking, but in Europe in the early twenty-first century it became extraordinary, aided by Naipaul's tendency to caricature himself in public, outside his books. He said, or was said to have said, that Africa had no future, Islam was a calamity, France was fraudulent and interviewers were monkeys. If Zadie Smith of *White Teeth* fame – optimistic and presentable – was a white liberal's dream, V.S. Naipaul was the nightmare. Rather than celebrate multiculturalism, he denounced it as 'multi-culti', made malign jokes about people with darker skin than himself, blamed formerly oppressed nations for their continuing failure and attacked Prime Minister Tony Blair as a pirate who was imposing a plebeian culture on Britain. The only Blacks he associated with now were Conrad and Barbara. For a successful immigrant writer to take such a position was seen as a special kind of treason, a betrayal of what should be a purely literary genius. The critic Terry Eagleton complained 'Great art, dreadful politics' while the reggae poet Linton Kwesi Johnson said, 'He's a living example of how art transcends the artist 'cos he talks a load of shit but still writes excellent books.'[3] Naipaul's outrageous denunciations were less interesting than the work which preceded them. A parallel might be drawn with Albert Einstein when he discoursed on socialism rather than concentrating on science, or with Aleksandr Solzhenitsyn, who identified the crimes of Soviet communism at a time when serious people were seeking to ignore them but in old age took to railing against amorphous ills, like consumerism. Solzhenitsyn once commented: 'In the West, one must have a balanced, calm, soft voice; one ought to make sure to doubt oneself, to suggest that one may, of course, be completely wrong. But I didn't have the time to busy myself with this.'[4]

Naipaul was initially unwilling to take the call from Stockholm, since he was cleaning his teeth. When the secretary of the Nobel committee got him on the line, he enquired, 'You're not going to do a Sartre on us, and refuse the prize?' Naipaul accepted, and put out a statement that the Nobel was, 'a great tribute to both England, my home, and India, the home of my ancestors.' There was no mention of Trinidad. Asked why not, he said it might 'encumber the tribute', which provoked the Barbadian writer

George Lamming, an ancient rival, to suggest Naipaul was 'playing ole mas', meaning he was masquerading or making trouble for his own entertainment, a Trinidadian trait. I noticed that when he was being rude or provocative in this way, Naipaul was full of glee. Creating tension, insulting his friends, family or whole communities left him in excellent spirits. He might for instance, on the basis of a photograph in the *Daily Mail*, denounce Queen Elizabeth's granddaughter Zara Phillips for having a 'criminal face', or say that a friend's daughter was 'a fat girl, and she did what fat girls do, she married a Zulu', or accuse a journalist of 'doing disreputable things like mixing with Bengalis – and other criminals.'[5] Later, after I had visited Trinidad, I realized this style of conversation was not rare in the Caribbean. It was what Trinidadians call 'picong', from the French 'piquant', meaning sharp or cutting, where the boundary between good and bad taste is deliberately blurred, and the listener sent reeling.

Around this time, I was asked to write V.S. Naipaul's biography. I was hesitant; I was finishing another book, and saw it would be a big and potentially fraught project, perhaps the last literary biography to be written from a complete paper archive. His notebooks, correspondence, handwritten manuscripts, financial papers, recordings, photographs, press cuttings and journals (and those of his first wife, Pat, which he had never read) had in 1993 been sold to the University of Tulsa in Oklahoma, a place famous for its hurricanes and the worst race riot in America's history.[6] The archive ran to more than 50,000 pieces of paper. I told V.S. Naipaul that I would only want to write a biography if I could use material at Tulsa that was closed to public access, and quote from it freely. I would need to interview him at length. My intention was to end the biography in 1996 as he entered his sixty-fifth year, a few months after Pat's death, rather than come too close to the distorting lens of the present. There was silence; then some months later a letter of acceptance came, written as if unwillingly in a fast, cramped hand, in violet ink. Over the five years since that letter, Naipaul has stuck scrupulously to our agreement; I have had no direction or restriction from him. He had the opportunity to read the completed manuscript, but requested no changes. When he was in Tulsa in 1994, Naipaul said in a speech, 'The lives of writers are a legitimate subject of inquiry; and the truth should not be skimped. It may well be, in fact, that a full account of a writer's life might in the end be more a work of literature and more illuminating – of a cultural or historical moment – than the writer's books.'[7]

I had met Naipaul a few times before this, once in England and later in Delhi while writing an article for the *New Yorker* magazine. Tarun Tejpal, a friend who worked as a journalist, telephoned and invited me to a press conference, saying he would collect me from my hotel in ten minutes. His car, shabby against the grand hotel limousines, drew up under a colonnade. I climbed into the back and noticed that I was sitting beside Sir Vidia Naipaul. He was wearing many layers of clothing and a tweed jacket, despite the heat. He held a trilby hat carefully in his lap. A roll-neck sweater merged with his beard, completing the impression that he was fully covered. Nadira, the second Lady Naipaul, was sitting in the front beside Tarun. She asked me about the article I was writing, and I mentioned some trouble I was having with the magazine's celebrated fact-checkers. 'Don't let the *New Yorker* worry you,' said Naipaul, enunciating each syllable of each word in his modulating voice, part West Indian, part Queen's English. 'The *New Yorker* knows nothing about writing. Nothing. Writing an article there is like posting a letter in a Venezuelan postbox; nobody will read it.' He paused, and continued, 'We were talking about the funeral of Princess Diana.' The princess had died some months earlier. 'What were your thoughts about it?'

From everything I knew of Naipaul, I imagined he would hate the sentiment swirling around the dead princess, and view her as another Evita Perón. He was watching me through narrowed eyes with a would-be benign smile – 'playin' dead to catch corbeau alive', to use the Caribbean phrase. We were in a Delhi traffic jam by now, horns honking. I was jet-lagged; I thought I might be honest.

'I found it moving. I liked seeing the British express their emotion in public.'

There was silence.

'Oh,' he said in a distraught voice. His face went dark. 'Patrick, Patrick, Patrick.'

Tarun looked at me nervously in the driver's mirror.

'Why, what did you think about it?' I asked.

He contemplated the question before answering.

'It filled me with shame – shame and disgust. The sort of disgust one feels after visiting a prostitute, if you know what I mean. They had a man, Mr John, doing the singing.' (I realized later that he was referring to Elton John.) 'I had to walk across Kensington Gardens to my flat before the funeral. I saw the flowers for her, wrapped in plastic, rotting in the sun. I saw shrines. There were Negroes at the shrines, weeping, openly. Why were they weeping? Why? Why were they weeping?'

He was almost shouting. Tarun was trying to stop himself from laughing. Nadira seemed both amused and exasperated. She turned and held her husband by the arm.

'That will do.'

She spoke to him as if he were a mischievous boy, and she were his mother.

It was, I came to see, a typically Naipauline performance: outrageous, funny, impossible.

If you reject the land that formed you, as Naipaul began to do actively in his thirties, you become defined by that rejection. It provides you with a struggle. 'You were born in Trinidad?' Bernard Levin asked in an interview in 1983. 'I was born there, yes,' came the reply, 'I thought it was a great mistake.'[8] Naipaul's dismissal of his homeland became part of his persona, a persona he invented in order to realize his early ambition to escape the periphery for the centre, to leave the powerless for the powerful, and to make himself a great writer. I sometimes thought of him as a man running up a beach with the advancing tide behind him, managing to stay a bare step ahead of the water. In order to become what he wanted to be, he had to make himself someone else. He could not remain regional. His ambition was linked to fear, as it often is in an author or creative artist: fear of failure, fear of not being able to write, fear of disappearance, fear of mental or physical breakdown, fear that people were trying to do him down, fear of being faced down, fear of losing face, fear of being found out. Repeatedly he had to re-create or mask himself, clearing away his past, in order to become the apparently stateless, hyper-perceptive global observer who could, as a book reviewer once put it, look into the mad eye of history and not blink. This took its psychological toll. In 1971 he told an interviewer that he had made a vow at an early age never to work for anyone. 'That has given me a freedom from people, from entanglements, from rivalries, from competition. I have no enemies, no rivals, no masters; I fear no one.'[9] Everyone has entanglements and rivalries, and Naipaul was to have many during the 1970s: his attempt to avoid them and become solely 'the writer' was itself an act of pre-emptive rejection, which arose from anxiety and fear.

His attempts to separate himself from the consequences of his own behaviour, and to present himself not as a person but as solely 'the writer', a figure who could in theory be studied objectively, was what made this biography possible. Opposing others, following his unique vision, apparently convinced his literary calling was hereditary and noble, was central to his idea of himself. It may have begun as a pose, but it was a mask that had eaten into the face. He once said to me, 'I was not interested and I remain completely indifferent to how people think of me, because I was serving this thing called literature.'[10] This remark was, in one sense, true. Intellectually he believed the truth should not be skimped in a biography, yet personally he felt obliged to guard himself. Even when speaking frankly about intensely personal subjects, he wore a shield of self-protection. During these interviews, his replies alternated between statements of absolute self-belief and defensive emotional fragility. Of all the people I spoke to for this book, he was outwardly the frankest. He believed that a less than candid biography would be pointless, and his willingness to allow such a book to be published in his lifetime was at once an act of narcissism and humility.

In Trinidad, V.S. Naipaul appeared to be admired as someone who had got ahead, who had taken on the outside world on his own terms, and won. This is not to suggest that admiration for him in the Caribbean islands was unmitigated. One man described him to me as a 'failed calypsonian'; a woman in a business centre threatened to attack me when I said I was writing about him; Anthony Petit, describing himself as 'aspiring author and head of the Triniwriters group', wrote to the *Trinidad Guardian* in 2003 to say the Nobel Prize winner did not deserve any respect from Trinidadians since, 'Anyone can write like Naipaul.' Petit thought that because 'the role model in question rejects his heritage, while using said heritage for advancement and accolade, we cannot but shake our heads sadly and turn elsewhere for solace and inspiration.'[11]

Despite this, and reciprocal barbs over the decades, Naipaul's achievement was a source of national pride. In Toco, at a hotel by the sea, a pair of calypso singers from Port of Spain were singing fast, funny songs with the aid of a small guitar to entertain the tourists. I asked one of them, Keith Eugene Davis, how he kept his material fresh.

'You feeling for some rum?'

I took the hint and bought him a drink.

'I tell you how. I read the newspapers.'

'Have you heard of a writer called V.S. Naipaul?' I asked.

'Man, course I heard of him.'

'Can you do a song about him?'

At once the guitar was in his hands, and he sang spontaneously:

> Now I must tell you after all,
> People know about V.S. Naipaul,

But is very sad to explain,
That man don't live in Trinidad again,
So now the facts I must unfold,
One of the best writers in the world,
But then I give you my view,
He was very international too,
So I think it very wise,
When they give him the Nobel Prize.[12]

Quotations from my interviews with V.S. Naipaul are threaded through this book. Where his statements are self-serving or eccentric, I have often let them stand without authorial intrusion, figuring the reader should be able to make a judgement. These conversations, conducted on an occasional basis at his house in rural Wiltshire over several years, were the strangest experience of my professional life. He could be angry, acute, open, self-pitying, funny, sarcastic, tearful – but he was always intense. I tended not to contradict him, preferring to let him talk. Early on, I realized that I risked being cast as the house liberal, a role I did not want. I found that a confrontational interview with Naipaul was apt to induce a fruitless hardening of his position or elusive generalization, which was in itself a form of game-playing or manipulation. I have left in his conversational repetitions, what has been called the Naipaul 'bis', after a term used in music (and modem protocols) to denote a repeat. It is not easy to describe the effect of this verbal tic. It has become part of his speech, and can be compelling and comic, arising from his resonant voice and the certitude with which he speaks, until refuted. I remember at a formal dinner after a conference seeing Naipaul being presented with a plate of what appeared to be meat (it was baked endive, hiding beneath a crust of melted cheese) and as the waiter attempted to set it before him, he said: 'That is *not* my food. That is not *my* food. *That* is not my food. That is not my *food*.' Each time he said the words, he altered their implication. When the confusion was explained to him, he accepted the plate meekly, saying 'Ah.'

My approach to writing biography is as it was when I began my first book. I wrote then that the aim of the biographer should not be to sit in judgement, but to expose the subject with ruthless clarity to the calm eye of the reader. Since writing about a writer for the first time, I have become more doubtful about the notion that an artistic creator should be expected to explain himself. Anyone who has written imaginatively will know that the process remains mysterious, even to the author, however hard you try to unpick it. Would Conrad, were he alive to answer, be able to say quite what Kurtz meant by 'The horror! The horror!'? The best writing can be examined only in its effect. Sometimes, a critic or biographer can see things the author cannot. In his Nobel lecture, V.S. Naipaul said that a writer's biography can never fully reveal the source of his books: 'All the details of the life and the quirks and the friendships can be laid out for us, but the mystery of the writing will remain. No amount of documentation, however fascinating, can take us there. The biography of a writer – or even the autobiography – will always have this incompleteness.'[13] I would go further: a biography can never fully reveal the source of its subject. The commonplace that a biographer has found the 'key' to a person's life – usually something arbitrary like the death of a sibling, or moving house – is implausible. People are too complicated and inconsistent for this to be true. The best a biographer can hope for is to illuminate aspects of a life and seek to give glimpses of the subject, and that way tell a story.

PATRICK FRENCH
London, December 2007

PART ONE

PART ONE

CHAPTER ONE

THE NEW WORLD

THE ISLANDS OF THE Caribbean dot and dash their way through the sea, linking different worlds. Central America joins the southern and northern hemispheres, taking you up through Colombia, Panama and Nicaragua by the land route until you reach Mexico, or down through the shallows of the Atlantic from Florida to the Bahamas, skirting Cuba and Jamaica, passing Haiti, the Dominican Republic and Puerto Rico, until you find yourself in the sprayed arc of islands known as the Lesser Antilles, some no more than a few miles across: Anguilla, Sint Maarten, Guadeloupe, Saint Lucia, Martinique, Grenada. At the tip of the chain lies a larger island which, beneath the sea or geologically, is part of the South American mainland. Almost square, with a low promontory at its south-western corner pointing to Venezuela, this is Trinidad.

In the summer of 1498, three ships approached the shores of the island.[1] The men on board were exhausted and burned by the sun, surviving off raisins, salt pork and sea biscuits, their supply of water running low. They were led by a white-haired voyager in his forties named Christoforo Colombo, known also as Christóbal Colón or Christopher Columbus. He was ill, his body inflamed and his eyes bleeding. It was Columbus's third voyage in search of Asia, and the one on which his future depended. A few months earlier, Vasco da Gama had reached Calicut, opening Europe's sea route to India. Renowned for his acute sense of smell, Columbus would have drunk in the lush, flowering vegetation of the island with its easy, humid, tropical climate, home to rainforests of bamboo and hardwood, flashing birds like the silver-beaked tanager, rivers, waterfalls and an array of caymans, snakes and beasts such as the nine-banded armadillo. There were no cocoa estates, no sugar-cane plantations, no breadfruit trees; Captain Bligh had yet to bring them from Tahiti. The only inhabitants were families of Amerindians who lived by farming and fishing, having paddled across the sea from the Orinoco river delta many centuries before.

Seeing three ranges of mountains running across the island, Columbus named it La Isla de la Trinidad after the Holy Trinity, in the Christian way. Later that day his sailors landed on the south coast to take on fresh water – the moment of first contact. Over the following weeks they navigated neighbouring waters, and became the first Europeans to see the mainland of South America, the fresh green breast of the New World. Columbus suspected as he charted the wide mouth of the Orinoco river that he was on the edge of a continent rather than another island. With his health failing, he ordered his ships to sail north through the stretch of water between Trinidad and the mainland – the Gulf of Paria – until they reached the island of Margarita.

The outbreak of the sixteenth century brought adventurers to the island of Trinidad, who enslaved the indigenous Amerindians and sent them to work in Spanish colonies overseas. The old world disappeared: land was stolen, new settlements were made. The English, Dutch, French and Spanish all battled and schemed for supremacy in the islands of the West Indies. Using the legal formalities of the time, local chiefs lost their inheritance and power. Sir Walter Raleigh, an English marauder who raided Trinidad in 1595, found five desperate, dispossessed men in the custody of the Spaniards. They turned out to be 'the last aboriginal rulers of the land, held together on one chain, scalded with hot bacon fat, and broken by other punishments.'[2]

Nearly three centuries after the appearance of Columbus, Trinidad had barely been colonized. By 1783 it had 126 whites, 259 free coloureds, 310 African slaves and 2,032 Amerindians.[3] To encourage settlement, King Charles III of Spain offered land and tax breaks. Roman Catholics of French descent moved from neighbouring islands, accompanied by their slaves, and started farming cocoa, tobacco, cotton and sugar. By 1797, when the Spanish surrendered Trinidad to the British during the French Revolutionary Wars, the population had risen to just under 18,000. In the nineteenth century, migrants flooded in, and by 1900 there were around 300,000 inhabitants. Unlike most other islands in the West Indies, the people of Trinidad came from many different places: there were Africans who spoke French creole or Yoruba, sailors and indentured labourers from China, neighbouring Venezuelans, German and French labourers, Syrian and Lebanese business families, wanderers from Grenada and Barbados, residual Amerindians, visitors from Madeira, demobbed black British army veterans, Portuguese and Spanish-speaking farmers of uncertain ethnicity and free slaves from the

United States. Most Caribbean islands were homogenous by comparison, with white planters and black slaves, but Trinidad was uniquely and enduringly ethnically complex. Even its place names were various: Amerindian (Chaguanas), Spanish (San Fernando), French (Sans Souci) and British (Poole).

When slavery was formally abolished across the British empire in 1834 and cheap labour was needed for the sugar-cane plantations, malnourished Indians were shipped over from Calcutta and Madras. While the white planters of the West Indies had grown rich on sugar cane, their cousins in India had made fortunes from land revenues; and many beautiful houses were built in the English countryside. North India, under British control, was awash with dislocated, landless peasants. A voyage across the oceans and a stint as a bonded or indentured labourer was an alternative to destitution. In Trinidad, the newly arrived East Indians were nervous of the alien society in which they found themselves. They feared the island's black majority: Negroes seemed physically stronger, had rough manners and their dark skin identified them with the lower castes of Hinduism. The Negroes, for their part, came to regard these East Indians as heathens with peculiar customs who kept to themselves, were mean with money, cooked strange food and were servile to the plantation owners. Black agricultural labourers found their wages being undercut. They looked down on the Indians, who had to work long hours in the cane fields, as the 'new slaves'.

*

Christmas 1894: Picture the tropical island of Trinidad with its sandy beaches, bursting coconuts, leaping howler monkeys and freshwater mangrove swamps teeming with scarlet ibis. A ship approaches Nelson Island, a parched limestone islet overlooking the capital, Port of Spain. The passengers who have survived the three-month sea voyage from Calcutta are loaded into open rowing boats. Quickly, the holding barrack is filled with men, women and children, their names recorded in a ledger under the supervision of a government official, the Protector of Immigrants. Their possessions are fumigated. They are housed, both sexes, in a long shed lined with wooden bunks filled with hay, infested with mosquitoes and sandflies. Most are Hindus, driven to flight by starvation or debt or trickery. All are desperate. They do not even know where they have come to; all they know is the name of the hot place to which they have been shipped, transposed into Hindi as 'Chinitat'. Soon, an overseer will come from a plantation and indenture them as estate labourers, or coolies. The *Handbook of Trinidad and Tobago* states that when visiting the colony, 'Elaborate tropical outfits are not necessary . . . For ladies, the same clothes as would be worn during a hot English summer are suitable all the year round.'[4] Photographs of these new arrivals from India show them dressed almost in rags: a kurta and dhoti and light turban for the men, or a sari with the *pallu*, or tail, of the sari draped over the head in modesty for the women. These broken-down, thin-limbed immigrants with their tiny bundles of possessions can only have made the journey to Trinidad as a last resort.[5]

One man among the many – his name recorded as Kopil – is a Brahmin, from a family of hereditary pundits in a village near Gorakhpur on the Nepalese border with India. He has pretended to be from a different background, since the recruiter back in India told him he might not be accepted as a labourer if he admits to being from the highest caste. For thirteen generations, Kopil's family have presided over the religious destiny of their neighbourhood, reading the Sanskrit texts and lecturing on spiritual practice to those who seek enlightenment. Wishing to study, he had walked south to Benares, the sacred Hindu city on the banks of the Ganges, where he met a recruiter who told him stories about the Caribbean, and how in this far-off place he would be given a gold coin each day as a reward for sifting sugar. If Kopil emigrated, he might even want to have a broad canvas belt made in which to store the gold coins. He is brought to a depot in Calcutta, and taken aboard the ship *Hereford*. At once, he feels his difference from the other immigrants. On board ship, he finds a piece of beef in his food. Although the voyage is terrible (forty people die from an outbreak of cholera, their corpses thrown overboard) Kopil starves himself for two days in horror at this contamination by cow meat, until the surgeon-superintendent intervenes and he is given a separate daily ration of raw potatoes and rice, which he cooks himself.

He reaches an island far from the large country and ancient civilization he has left behind. It is Kopil's misfortune to be indentured to Woodford Lodge in Chaguanas, an estate in central Trinidad where the regime is especially severe. Each morning, to preserve his caste identity, he sets his own pot of *khitchri* – rice and spiced lentils – on an earthen oven before going to work. Kopil is assigned to the shovel gang, to digging and planting. It breaks him. He is put on the weeding gang with the women and children, and later made responsible for clearing the dung from the animal pens, a sweeper's job. Kopil's health breaks. He is twenty-one years old, alone, a minority within a minority in the most fragmented place on earth. Then, by chance, an Indian *sirdar* – a driver or overseer – learns that he is a Brahmin and can read Sanskrit. Kopil might have some use; he can read the scriptures. The sirdar, a Bengali called Govinda, has a fifteen-year-old daughter, Soogee. A marriage is arranged, and Kopil is saved from extinction. Govinda 'cuts' Kopil – he pays the government a fee to buy him out of his indenture, and installs him in a small house near the Catholic church in Chaguanas. With Soogee, he will manage a general store for his father-in-law.

The shop does well. Decades pass. Kopil adjusts his name to the regal-sounding Capildeo Maharaj. He becomes renowned as a pundit, explaining sacred texts and duties at impromptu services, and conducting pujas or ceremonies. Sometimes he takes his congregation on a pilgrimage to the sea for religious bathing, the Atlantic standing in for the Ganges. With Soogee, he has nine surviving daughters and two sons, but spends much of his time alone, reading the scriptures and meditating. He is conscious of his status; once, when an illiterate pundit tries to officiate beside him at a wedding, he has the man sent away. Capildeo Maharaj is a good businessman too, trading goods on a return trip to India. He buys land in Chaguanas and employs labourers to grow rice, peas and eddoes, an edible root. Soogee persuades him to send the children, girls as well as boys, to a local school run by Canadian missionaries, despite his misgivings about Christianity. To display his new wealth, Capildeo Maharaj has a heavy gold necklace made for his son Simbhoonath, and builds a solid white house on the main road in Chaguanas with thick walls and pillars at the front, close to the railway station, the police station and the court house. It has a blank facade, blocking the view of any outsiders on the passing road, and is modelled on a building he remembers from Gorakhpur. He calls it Anand Bhavan, or the Abode of Bliss, after the family mansion of the Nehru family back in Allahabad. In 1926, Capildeo Maharaj sails to India to arrange a holiday for his family. While travelling back to his ancestral village, he is struck by a stomach ailment, and dies.

Not long after this Seepersad Naipaul, a twenty-two-year-old Brahmin from a poor family, is employed to paint a sign at the general store on the ground floor of Anand Bhavan. He likes the look of the sixteen-year-old girl behind the counter, Droapatie Capildeo. Not realizing she is a daughter of the house, he passes her a note. It is discovered, the formidable Soogee intervenes, and on 28 March 1929 Seepersad and Droapatie are married at the warden's office in Chaguanas.[6] They have a daughter, Kamla, the following year, and on 17 August 1932 their son Vidyadhar is born. He is named for a Chandela king, the dynasty which built the magnificent Hindu temples at Khajuraho in northern India. His name means 'giver of wisdom'. Back in the early eleventh century, King Vidyadhar had fought against Mahmud of Ghazni, the first of the infamous Muslim invaders of India. It was an apposite name for the boy. Years later, as V.S. Naipaul, he would say, 'It's such a grand name, a very special name – I cherished it for that reason. I think great things were expected of me.'[7]

*

How much of Capildeo's personal story, passed down as family lore, is true? Would this small, shrewd man have been so easily duped by the recruiter? Were his forefathers revered as pundits in their village? Were they even Brahmins? The name Capildeo sounds like a dialect rendition of Kapil Dev (he would have spoken in Bhojpuri, a language similar to Hindi used around Gorakhpur), a name which gives no indication of caste, and the suffix Maharaj was certainly bogus. How would he have cooked rice and potatoes on board ship, where the fire regulations were so strict? Why was Govinda so concerned that Capildeo was a Brahmin, and able to read Sanskrit, when he himself was a convert to Roman Catholicism? Might the marriage to Soogee have been essentially a practical arrangement, a recognition of Capildeo's talent for business? Was he really planning a holiday in India for his family when he died? Shortly before sailing he had mortgaged much of his land and left Soogee and his children; he was accompanied on the voyage by another woman, Jussodra, who was the wife of a man named Phagoo. Was the story that Seepersad Naipaul told his family about his accidental courtship (which his son Vidyadhar would one day fictionalize in *A House for Mr Biswas*) an elaboration or the reality?

The British imperial obsession with records and taxonomy means that a few facts about Capildeo Maharaj can be fixed. A man named Kopil arrived in Trinidad on the ship *Hereford* in 1894, and was indentured as a coolie at Woodford Lodge estate; someone paid for him to be 'cut' from his indenture. He gained a reputation as a pundit, and was an office-holder in the East Indian National Congress, a fledgling organization inspired by the rise of nationalism in India.[8] In 1913 he was listed on his daughter Droapatie's birth certificate as 'Capildoe Maraje, Hindoo Priest'.[9] He or his wife Soogee owned agricultural land around Chaguanas. Astonishingly, some lines of Capildeo's actual conversation survive, spoken in creolized

English and recorded by a member of his congregation, a man named Shiva: 'Siewah, just as a man haveam own mudder, man mus haveam own lan. You na have am own lan and house, you na own man at all. [Shiva, just as a man has his own mother, a man must have his own land. If you don't have land and a house, you are not a man.]'[10] It was a sentiment that might have been spoken, in standard English, by Mr Biswas.

In a society where everyone has been uprooted and people can invent their own past, many things become unstable. It is possible, though, to build up some sort of picture of the world in which Capildeo and Vidyadhar's other three grandparents lived. Caste had given a structure to Indian society for thousands of years. It was based on the Hindu idea of karma, where past actions in previous lives determined a person's status in the present. Pundits, learned Brahmin men with a knowledge of the Sanskrit teaching traditions, performed ritual duties in order to safeguard social order. At its best, caste gave a sense of identity and community; at it worst, it condemned people to a degraded life based on an inherited social position, and provided an excuse for inhuman cruelty. British classifications of the people of India in the eighteenth century gave rigidity to an ancient and flexible concept. The principal categories – Brahmins (priests, scholars), Kshatriyas (warriors, rulers), Vaishyas (traders), Shudras (labourers) and Untouchables (outcastes) – disguised fluidity between regions, centuries and subcastes. Local cultural variants, focusing for example on a particular deity, now appeared to be part of a larger, graded philosophy called Hinduism. Nor was caste an exclusively Hindu phenomenon: Indian Muslims, Sikhs and Christians all came to use it as a form of social stratification.

The first indentured Indian immigrants docked in Port of Spain in 1845. They were unpopular: a creole town councillor collected a petition against 'immoral heathens', saying they would be a drain on the taxpayer and might discourage Negro migration from neighbouring islands and the USA.[11] Trinidad's superintendent of prisons wrote that many coolies were guilty of 'gross idolatry' and cruel to their wives: 'As a general rule they have few good qualities, and are faithless, unprincipled, immoral, lazy, and fond of wandering . . . they are filthy in their habits, and have little care in regard to clothing.'[12] As an undeveloped plantation colony, the island needed labour if the sugar industry was to survive. The island's African slaves had moved to the towns and set up as tradesmen, dockers and domestic workers after emancipation.

Most indentured Indians came from parts of north India that were

suffering famine, drought or social upheaval, such as Bihar, Punjab and
the United Provinces (Awadh). The spread of European manufactured
goods and changes in land-ownership after the decline of the Mughal
empire meant that agricultural labourers, weavers and potters were often
left destitute, particularly on the plains of the Ganges. In these uncertain
times, caste affiliation became a means of securing a position. After their
role in the Mutiny of 1857, Brahmins came to be perceived by the British
as clever but pernicious, and less malleable than other groups.[13] At the
time Capildeo was recruited, around 15 per cent of immigrants were from
higher castes (Brahmin, Thakur, Rajput and Khatri), 34 per cent were from
farming or artisan castes, 37 per cent were from lower or backward castes
and 14 per cent were Muslim.[14] Whatever a person's background, migration
overseas was never an easy choice: it would mean the end of village or
community life, possible death during the three- to four-month sea voyage
and theoretical loss of caste caused by crossing the 'kala pani', or black
water.

A recruiter would pass through poor villages looking for those with no
future; many recruits had stories of being coerced or drugged. They would
be transported either on foot or by train to the Indian capital, Calcutta,
where they would be sold to a sub-agent, who was often a Muslim or
Jewish shopkeeper. The recruits were mustered at a high-walled depot by
the Hooghly river, fed, inspected for disease and given clothes and a red
woollen hat for the sea voyage. Often they would not understand each
other: speakers of Marathi, Kashmiri, Telugu, Punjabi had no common
tongue. Most single women who chose to emigrate were recruited from
urban areas rather than villages, and in many cases they had already run
away from home or a bad husband, or been expelled for a social
transgression, and were seeking to avoid prostitution. At the dock in
Calcutta a registering officer, usually a junior magistrate, recorded the
migrant's name, sex, caste, village and occupation. It was a casual act of
lasting significance: the name, written in roman script probably for the first
time, would provide a label for their descendants. Each migrant would sign
or thumbprint a document agreeing to be indentured. Their names were
written down as they spoke them, and since there were no standard
transliterations for Indian names, the spelling might indicate the regional
pronunciation of the speaker or the ignorance of the registering officer. To
someone with a knowledge of Indian names, these transliterations now
seem bizarre and anglicized: thus (some of this is guesswork) Lutchman
was Laxman, Beharry was Bihari, Gopaul was Gopal, Permanand was

Prem Anand, Teeluck was Tilak, Ramkissoon was Ram Krishna, Sammy was Swami, Gobin was Govinda, Capildeo was Kapil Dev and Seepersad was Shiv Parshad or Shiv Prasad.

Life on board the three-masted sailing ship meant a hundred days of torment. Leaving everything they knew, this first wave of the modern Indian diaspora sailed through the Bay of Bengal, round the rough sea at the Cape of Good Hope, past St Helena and through the Doldrums towards the West Indies. Hundreds of passengers might die from a contagious disease during a single voyage. They lived below decks in three compartments – men, women and couples – lit by fixed coconut-oil lamps, and in the daytime were allowed to come to the upper deck to walk, wrestle or engage in stick-fighting. Flogging was the standard punishment for disobedience. Discipline was enforced by the surgeon-superintendent, a British medical officer who was also responsible for supplying food, protecting the passengers' health and making sure the sailors, most of whom were Indian, did not molest them. The surgeon-superintendent received 'head money' for each migrant landed alive, and was answerable to the protector of immigrants.[15] On the plantation, coolies would start work at six in the morning, stop for breakfast at ten-thirty and continue work until four in the afternoon. They were paid a token wage of two to four shillings a week. At Woodford Lodge estate they would cut sugar cane, a rough, sharp, brutal crop, haul it to the refinery on ox-carts and move casks of sugar by barge to the road. Lack of women during the early days of indenture led to fights between men, often involving a cutlass, and rum-fuelled violence against women – including murder – became known as an Indian trait. Daily life was controlled by the sirdar, usually a physically imposing figure who spoke a little English and doubled as a moneylender. The barracks had wooden partitions: a 10 by 12-foot room was expected to house a married couple and children. Cooking was done out on a step. The plantation was a discrete world, without privacy or individuation. Wandering more than two miles from your designated estate was a criminal offence punishable by imprisonment. The Indian government retained a duty of care for indentured labourers, and the protector of immigrants issued an annual report on their condition. Although he was meant to represent their interests, court records show that the protector's loyalty usually lay with the planters, particularly regarding the brutal way in which discipline was enforced on the estates.[16]

Indenture differed from the formally defunct African slave trade in several vital respects. It was theoretically voluntary, and it was time-limited: after a period of five to ten years, the recruit would be given a small plot of land or a return passage to India. Crucially, families stayed together: under an ordinance from the Indian government, they were not allowed to be split up when they landed. This gave Indians a monumental historical advantage over Trinidadians of African descent. The emphasis in Indian culture on strong family and caste ties enabled them to retain and build a sense of community abroad. When their period of indenture expired, many Indians preferred to remain in Trinidad and take a grant of land, even if it was swamp. They worked the land and grew rice, sugar cane and coconuts; some kept cows, some sold milk. One witness at a Royal Commission in 1897 said the ambition of Indians in Trinidad was 'to buy a cow, then a shop, and say: "We are no niggers to work in cane fields." '[17] The agent of the Tennant family estates complained that a time-expired Indian employee would seek work wherever wages were highest: 'you cannot rely upon him with the certainty that you can rely on the indentured labourer.'[18]

When Capildeo Maharaj set sail for Trinidad in 1894, British rule was less than a hundred years old and Queen Victoria, the Empress of India, was approaching the end of her reign. In the crisp words of the *Handbook of Trinidad and Tobago*, 'The Colony does not possess responsible government. The government is administered by the Governor advised by an Executive Council, which consists of three *ex officio* members and such other members as may from time to time be appointed by the Governor.'[19] Security was provided by the paramilitary Trinidad Constabulary and the Trinidad Light Horse, which consisted of managers and sirdars from the estates. J.H. Collens, a British school superintendent who published *A Guide to Trinidad*, wrote that 'the Coolie is well shaped, with regular features, wiry, though not over-muscular, and possessing considerable powers of endurance. He is frugal and saving to a fault, living on the plainest and coarsest of diet, often denying himself sufficient even of this fare to gratify his love of hoarding.'[20] This emphasis on planning for the future was contrasted by colonial writers with the Negro tradition of living for the moment. Remarkably in 1889, a year after Collens published his guide to Trinidad, 12,549 Indian savers had between them deposited over £250,000 in local banks.[21]

Shortly before the First World War, the Indian government commissioned a survey on the condition of indentured labourers in Trinidad, British Guiana, Jamaica and Fiji. It found that barracks were made of wood with corrugated-iron roofing, and that the only drinking water was rainwater collected in tanks. There were few latrines, and people had to defecate in nearby fields. In rural Trinidad, disease was rife, particularly hookworm, malaria, dysentery and skin infections.[22] There was already growing opposition in India from Mohandas Gandhi and others to the practice of indenture. In a speech to the Indian National Congress, the nationalist politician G.K. Gokhale observed that indentured labour had been banned elsewhere, and asked: 'Why should India be marked out for this degradation?'[23] In 1917, after sending 144,000 people to Trinidad, the Indian government ended the system of indenture. Ethnic tensions grew now as their descendants asserted themselves economically and politically. Black soldiers had returned to Trinidad after the First World War inspired by the Universal Negro Improvement Association, founded by the Jamaican campaigner and racial separatist Marcus Garvey; Indians were stirred by Gandhi's freedom movement. From 1925, there was some elected representation on Trinidad's Legislative Council.

At the time of Vidyadhar's birth, the population of Trinidad stood at a little over 400,000, of whom about one-third were Indians, employed as agricultural labourers, merchants, spirit-vendors, clerks and shopkeepers. Few were lawyers, teachers or in government service. Indians had a higher death rate and a higher birth rate than any other social group. Unlike Chinese immigrants, they did not intermarry. The number of 'Indian Creoles' – meaning people with one Indian parent – was minuscule outside Port of Spain. Literacy in Trinidad stood at 57 per cent, balanced almost evenly between men and women; among Indians it stood at a pathetic 23 per cent, and among Indian women at 13 per cent. Only Christian converts had average levels of literacy, thanks to a Canadian Presbyterian mission which had the aim of 'Christianizing and educating' the Indians of Trinidad.[24] In popular legend in 1930s Trinidad, Indians were depicted as poor, mean, rural, heathen, aggressive, ethnically exclusive and illiterate. This, then, was the rough world into which Vidyadhar Naipaul was born.

CHAPTER TWO

IN THE LION HOUSE

VIDYADHAR'S EARLIEST MEMORIES were imagistic, fleeting, possibly imagined: the mauve uniform of a Negro nurse at the colonial hospital in Port of Spain as he was treated for pneumonia at the age of two, his hand held before an oil lamp with his young cousins to make the solid flesh turn transparent in the light, walking with his mother outside Anand Bhavan and seeing chickens in a ditch, pointing to them and saying, too young to pronounce the words, 'Mama, chiti!' Where, if anywhere, did he live as a child? After they married, his parents had moved to the market town of Tunapuna where his father worked as a sign-painter. Now, there was a hut behind his father's shop in Chase Village, but it was scarcely a home. Solidity was provided by Anand Bhavan, his birthplace, known as the 'Lion House' by the family because of the beastly sculpted shapes on the front balcony. Since the death of the patriarch Capildeo Maharaj, Soogee had made it a base for her nine daughters and their husbands and children, and for her two sons, Simbhoonath and Rudranath, of whom much was expected. Vidyadhar remembered moving between the shop in Chase Village and the Lion House in Chaguanas, standing by the roadside with his sister Kamla listening to a bus, wondering from the sound of the engine whether it was coming or going.

As he moved into comprehension, his memories became more complex. He was now known as Vido (pronounced vee-doe). Someone offered him a sweet. It looked like one of the glass marbles used to stop soda bottles in his father's shop, and he said no; but it was a real sweet. An image: friends of his father playing with loose gravel on a country road, squatting and pretending to find coins in the gravel; Vido knew the men were playing, and was captivated. Or: Vido and Kamla taking a length of sugar cane; he asked her to cut him a piece, and held the cane while she took a sickle or 'grass-knife' and cut. She nicked his thumb, blood flowed, and Kamla was punished by their father. Why did Pa punish his big sister when she had been doing what he asked?

'It was completely unfair.' Another memory: after visiting his father's 'peasant relations', Vido was laughed at by his cousins for speaking in dialect when he came back to the Lion House: 'I did bin there,' he said. Vido had an immediate sensitivity to language. Men were building a hut near his father's shop. 'They are treading the clay or earth for the walls. I think the clay would have been trodden with a mixture of grass to bind it, I'm not sure, and it was in a pit next to my father's house and one of the men said that he was very tired, he was feeling mashed up. And I associated that with the mashing that he was doing that day, with the treading of the clay.'[1]

'To Vidyadhar,' Pa wrote in a book of sentimental poetry for children, inscribing it self-consciously like a Victorian paterfamilias: 'From his <u>father</u>. Today you have reached the span of 3 years 10 months and 15 days. And I make this present to you with this counsel in addition. Live only to the estate of man, follow Truth, be kind & gentle and trust God.'[2] But Pa was not himself; he was in the midst of a breakdown. Four months after giving his son *The School of Poetry*, he took a copy of *Lessons in Truth: A Course of Twelve Lessons in Practical Christianity* (designated 'No. E.2' in 'The Naipaul Library') and drew a sketch of himself in the front of it, looking strange. 'Among deeds that man counts for greatness and nobility, there is none greater than being a man,' he wrote to himself in biblical prose. 'Why should one be vexed with anyone else?' Mystical quotations from Epictetus, Kabir and Plotinus followed, and a line from Tagore: 'O fool, to try to carry thyself upon thy own shoulders! O beggar, to come to beg at thy own door!' Seepersad was wrestling with mental disturbance, trying to find a way forward from the village Hinduism of his childhood with its poorly educated pundits and half-understood rituals. As well as Christianity, he studied the texts of the late nineteenth-century reform movement the Arya Samaj, which rejected superstition, animal sacrifice and the caste system in favour of a modern, rational Hindu philosophy based on dharma or duty. What, after all, did caste amount to but an accident of birth? He read widely: J.S. Mill, Gustave Flaubert, Mulk Raj Anand, Mary Wollstonecraft and J.S. van Teslaar on psychoanalysis. He corresponded with a Scottish woman called Margaret Sheldon, the wife of an estate manager, about religion and theosophy. 'I am God's child and He loves me. All my health and strength and intelligence are from God,' Seepersad concluded.[3]

At the age of five, Vido joined Kamla at the school in the country town of Chaguanas, a simple establishment where discipline was strict. He said years later in his Nobel lecture, 'I walked from my grand-mother's house – past the two or three main-road stores, the Chinese parlour, the Jubilee Theatre, and the high-smelling little Portuguese factory that made cheap blue soap and cheap yellow soap in long bars that were put out to dry and harden in the mornings – every day I walked past these eternal-seeming things – to the Chaguanas govern-ment school. Beyond the school was sugar-cane, estate land, going up to the Gulf of Paria.'[4] He liked his teacher, Miss Hotaing, 'a Negro lady, so kind and nice'.[5] One of his first lessons concerned the coronation of Trinidad and Tobago's new monarch, King George VI. Vido took to schoolwork, and was captivated by the rhythms of *Nelson's West Indian Readers*, influential books with distinctive blood-red covers compiled by the local inspector of schools, Captain James Cutteridge. He learned pages of the *Readers* by heart. 'Dan is the man in the van. A pan is in the van.' The pictures were plain and elegant, done in red, black and white: A was for apple, Q was for queen, Y was for yam. The illustrations showed a pair of white children, Tim and Tot, making sandcastles on a beach with a bucket and spade. 'The ox is big. Tim is not so big. Tim is on a box by the ox. A dog is by the box.' In the second primer, more children appeared, looking most unlike the chil-dren of the West Indies: Jim, Jack, Jane, Dick, Pam, Peggy, their names chosen, according to Captain Cutteridge, because common West Indian names were too long. 'The ox gives meat too, said the cow. He gives beef,' a statement that might have given pause to the more orthodox junior Hindu students of *Nelson's West Indian Readers*.[6] Later, in *A House for Mr Biswas*, a boy reads aloud from a level-four *Reader* about an escape from a German prison camp in 1917. 'This education is a helluva thing,' says the proud father. 'Any little child could pick up. And yet the blasted thing does turn out so damn important later on.'[7]

One day Vido saw a teacher from his school, Mr Sinanan, pushing a stacked box-cart along the road outside the Lion House. Mr Sinanan said to Pa, who was at Chaguanas for the day, 'Well, you know, I'm moving. I'm moving and instead of getting a cart or some van or jitney [shared taxi] to come and move and pay all that money, I'm moving it myself. Let people look at me. Let them laugh that I'm moving it myself.'[8] It was, for Vido, an early lesson in social gradation and the humiliations of poverty.

Seepersad and Droapatie had more children, rapidly. By the time he

was five years old, Vido had another two sisters: Sati and Mira, spaced
at two-year intervals. Pa, though, remained tormented: his dreams of
being a journalist had fallen apart when he was in his late twenties, and
now he was stuck in the middle of nowhere, unable even to support his
family. He shifted between his shop in Chase Village, the Lion House
and his relations. The shop was, in Trinidad parlance, a 'parlour' – a
store selling refreshments. Kamla remembered it as 'a shop that looked
more like it was going out of business than in business, because so few
things were in the shop. All the shelves weren't solidly packed with
stuff.'[9] Pa kept a cow for milk. He preferred to read or wander off and
do some sketching, or fly kites with Vido and Kamla rather than work.
In retrospect, the children realized he had been mentally disturbed. Ma
held everyone and everything together, aided by her own family, the
Capildeos, whom Pa despised even while he relied on their charity.
When he was prescribed Sanatogen tonic for his breakdown, his
mother-in-law refused to give him money to pay for it, a slight he
always remembered. In Kamla's view, 'While he lavished love and
affection on his children, as a husband he left much to be desired. My
mother took the brunt of his bad tempers which took the form of
scathing attacks on her family, making her accountable and even
responsible for all that he regarded as their shortcomings. Occasionally
she did answer but more often than not she ignored him . . . Temperamental, impractical, facetious, he gave her no emotional support.
Fiercely independent, she made no attempt at compromise. She neither
saw nor supported his point of view about anything.'[10] Despite their
conflict, Seepersad was not violent to Droapatie. His depictions of
casual, almost ritualistic violence in his writings drew not on his own
behaviour, but on what he had observed during his childhood.

Seepersad Naipaul was intelligent and ambitious, but he had lost his
way. Unlike Droapatie, he came from a family that had barely thrown
off the shackles of indenture: his siblings were Hindi-speaking cane-
cutters. Family tradition suggests that his grandmother had brought his
father to Trinidad in the 1870s as a baby, fleeing disgrace or abandon-
ment in the area around Ayodhya. She said she came from a Brahmin
family with the name of Parain, Parray or Panday. The boy, known as
Naipaul Maharaj, was apprenticed as a pundit in the village of Diego
Martin, and became an agricultural labourer and dealer in religious
goods. He was a tough man, and kept his wife and three children –
Ramparsad, Seepersad and Prabharan – on a starvation diet. His

brutality led his wife to repeatedly run away to her family in Chandernagore (including when she was heavily pregnant with Seepersad), and she finally left him to live with another man, also violent, with whom she had a third son, Hariprasad. Young Seepersad was shunted between relations, and lived for a time on El Dorado Road in Tunapuna with his mother's sister and her husband, Sookdeo Misir. He had to tend cows and goats before going off to school, barefoot. There was talk of him becoming a pundit, and he learned some Sanskrit. Sookdeo Misir, who ran a successful private bus company plying the route between Port of Spain and the north-east of the island, became Seepersad's mentor. He taught him how to paint the livery on the side of the buses – like the Ramdin Special Number One – and gave him a basic education, but no more.[11] Vido remembered, 'My father's people were physically quite different from my mother's. They had this slightly Nepali cast of face. One of my father's grandparents was Nepalese. I have a clear memory of my father's mother's sister. She was very much someone from the hills.'[12]

The remarkable thing about Pa, so remarkable as to be almost incredible, is that by the time he was in his late teens, he had escaped from a likely future as an agricultural labourer in the grim depths of the rural Indian community. He had taught himself how to read and write English, and had conceived the idea of becoming a journalist, a profession that was open usually to whites and Negroes. He began with some stilted but opinionated articles in the *East Indian Weekly*, an intermittent paper published by a Chaguanas man. In 1928, a prominent Muslim barrister, F.E.M. Hosein, had spoken out against those Indians who thought it 'the highest piece of wisdom to seek as suitable life partners ladies of a lighter hue and of a different race.' The idea of racial annihilation and miscegenation became a theme for his generation of young, nationalist Indians. Seepersad Naipaul wrote that mixed marriages were a 'perversity responsible for race-dissolution' and that if they continued, the Indian community in Trinidad would 'waste its identity in the universal throng of an alien population.' The outer self reflected the inner man: he complained about the adoption of Western dress, a trend known then in Trinidad as 'Bobism'. Wearing trousers, jackets and ties was, Seepersad believed, one of the 'many symptoms of demoralization among westernized Indians.' Almost the only person to publicly oppose this view was Krishna Deonarine, who wrote in the same paper that intermarriage was good, Bobism was to be applauded

as a sign of modernity and that India was still ground down by social
tradition and 'excessive religiosity'.[13] The following year Deonarine
went a step further and, delving into Roman history, changed his name
to Adrian Cola Rienzi; he would become an influential figure in
Trinidad politics in the 1930s and 1940s.

In 1929, the year of his marriage, Seepersad began work as a
freelance reporter on the *Trinidad Guardian*, one of the two principal
newspapers in Port of Spain, on a salary of $4 a week, or around £34
in today's terms.[14] In this new, urban setting he succumbed to Bobism,
dressing in a tie, shirt and cotton blazer, sometimes even wearing an
ostentatious bow tie. It was an unusual job for an Indian to be doing:
the heads of department were white and the rest of the staff were black
or mixed. The *Guardian* office was a busy, masculine environment at 22
St Vincent Street in the heart of the little city. Wireless operators took
down news from the Associated Press and Reuters in Morse code;
editorial and advertising were based upstairs, linked to production and
the press room on the ground floor by a spiral staircase; edited copy
was sent by a wooden chute to the composing room, to be set in hot
metal on a linotype machine. The paper's editor, Gault MacGowan, had
been a respected foreign correspondent on the London *Times*. Since his
arrival in Trinidad, the thrill of news had chased the heavy advertisements off the front page, and the layout of the paper was now modelled
on the London *Daily Express*. Political and social events in Britain and
the West Indies were covered in detail, as were sports, illustrated by
half-tone photographs. The *Guardian* was surrounded by the competitive hum of the capital: a lawyers' office, a rum shop with separate
'salons' for professionals and street people, Trinidad's chamber of
commerce, some brothels and a little cafe which sold sugar-cakes –
coloured confections of grated coconut, redeemable against the tram
tickets that came with the job of reporter. A jangling tramcar ran the
length of St Vincent Street.[15]

Intrigued, perhaps, by the ambitions of a rustic Indian from the
sugar belt, Gault MacGowan gave Seepersad a weekly column on
Indian affairs. In later years, Pa would say that MacGowan had taught
him how to write. The endearing relationship between the two men
was closely fictionalized in *A House for Mr Biswas*. Here is Mr Burnett,
editor of the Trinidad *Sentinel*, offering Mr Biswas the sort of advice
that every writer needs but rarely gets: ' "Considerably" is a big word
meaning "very", which is a pointless word any way. And look.

"Several" has seven letters. "Many" has only four and oddly enough has exactly the same meaning.'[16] Seepersad's buoyant column, cheekily signed 'The Pundit', soon stirred up resentment among his fellow Indians. The idea of the feuds, fights, festivals and private quirks of the community being revealed to a public beyond Chaguanas was a new and disturbing notion. At first, Seepersad reported the activities of his in-laws and their local political activities in a complimentary way, but inevitably his professional obligations caused problems. He was obliged to mention the conviction of two of his brothers-in-law for violence during an election.[17] The rapidly expanding Capildeo clan disliked the activities of this young son-in-law; his nom de plume looked like a mocking reference to the late Capildeo Maharaj, whose Brahminical stature was rising with each year that passed, his scandalous elopement with Jussodra now consigned to silent memory.

MacGowan liked the sensational, and Seepersad delivered. He was soon writing under his own name about buried treasure, boys stealing oranges, a revolt by young Hindu men against matchmaking, and despair in Chaguanas at the arrest of Mahatma Gandhi on his salt march in India. 'CENTRAL T'DAD HUNT FOR CARONI DEATH TRAGEDY CLUE' ran one headline, and underneath it, 'INDIAN SHOT DEAD WHILE READING A HINDU EPIC. By S. Naipaul, Trinidad Staff Correspondent.' He milked this story: the island was being 'combed' by police who were 'on the alert'. The dead man, Sagan Maraj, 'was shot while he was reading the Hindu epic – the Ramayan – which tells of a fierce battle between Rama, an Indian prince and a King of Ceylon ... Sagan began reading aloud, when suddenly in the lone still silence of the night three shots rang out in rapid succession ... Who shot him and why was he shot?'[18] He told of violence at a Muslim festival in the village of Charlieville, and of the distress of a group of Indians who had visited their homeland: 'Khemraj told me yesterday ... "A bull that has fallen by the wayside will be given quick aid, but a real colonial-born Indian will be shunned. A maze of conventions rule the heart of the Hindus."'[19] A powerful reformist social message underlay Seepersad's writing. In June 1933 he described the 'amazing superstitious practices' of rural Indians who interpreted outbreaks of smallpox and rabies in animals as 'an unmistakable sign of the wrath of Kali, a female deity'. To propitiate the deity, women would collect alms and purchase a goat to be sacrificed, rather than treat the livestock, and the disease would continue to spread.[20]

This report was his undoing. Like a good newspaperman, he became part of the story. 'GUARDIAN REPORTER THREATENED WITH DEATH UNLESS HE MAKES A GOAT SACRIFICE — ALLEGED VILIFYING OF A HINDU GODDESS — GRUESOME LETTER. By S. Naipaul' was the headline. 'Next Sunday I am doomed to die. Kali, the Hindu deity and a species of Indian ju-ju will cause the end of me. I am to develop ptomaine poisoning on Saturday, will die on Sunday and will be buried on Monday. The amazing prophecy is contained in an anonymous letter written in Hindi and addressed to me.' Seepersad was full of scorn and excitement about the letter: what was his response to those who demanded goat-slaughter to satisfy the local 'Kali cult' (which he linked to African 'ju-ju' or witchcraft)? 'Briefly and explicitly I say bunkum. Frankly I don't believe in Kalis, deities or ju-jus, and so, I won't sacrifice a goat.'[21] Two days later, the joke went bad. The story made the front page, though this time it had to be reported by a colleague. 'WIFE OF THREATENED REPORTER URGES SACRIFICE TO HINDU GODDESS — POLICE PROTECTION OFFERED TO MR S. NAIPAUL — MORE LIGHT ON SANITARY INSPECTOR'S END — YOUNG JOURNAL- IST SLEEPS WELL DESPITE "SENTENCE OF DEATH" — ALL TRINIDAD IS TALKING OF THE SENSATIONAL DEATH THREAT TO MR S. NAIPAUL, CHAGUANAS CORRESPONDENT OF THE "GUARDIAN".'

Soon after the original story about smallpox and rabies had run in the paper, the resident sanitary inspector for Chaguanas, Mr H.L. Thompson, fell ill. In the blackmailing letter, the author blamed Thompson for giving the story to the press, and suggested Seepersad might suffer a similar fate. Now Thompson was dead, probably poisoned. The police put Seepersad under guard and relocated him to another district. The *Guardian* pursued the story, discovering that Mr Thompson had been prosecuting men who were selling milk from smallpox-ridden cows. The paper reported that the previous year Seepersad had been the victim of 'foul play' when 'he was ambushed and beaten because he published the truth regarding a local Indian dispute. Chaguanas and surrounding villages are notorious for gang violence and sinister conspiracies frequently resulting in injury to persons.' Droapatie wanted her husband to back off. 'In an agitated tone and with visible signs of worry and anxiety on her face, Mrs S. Naipaul, the pretty Indian wife of the Guardian reporter said this . . . "For his own sake and the safety of his family, I have advised my husband to make the goat sacrifice to appease the wrath of the goddess.

But he believes that ju-ju – to use his own words – is all bunkum."'
The report concluded: 'Mr and Mrs Naipaul's two children [Kamla and
Vidyadhar] are aged four and 18 months.' Creative as ever, Gault
McGowan ran an accompanying piece asking whether any local com-
pany would give his reporter life insurance: two would, two would not,
and one 'refused to express any opinion except to Mr Naipaul himself'.[22]

Before the week was out, Seepersad's world had been undone; he
undid it for himself. Under intense pressure from his wife and her
extended family, he agreed to execute a goat. The rationalist, the
reformer, the Arya Samajist, the dapper journalist, the modern man, the
scorner of ju-ju, succumbed to a Hindu tradition linked to sacrifice that
even in India was associated with the more extreme Tantric prac-
titioners. It went against everything that Seepersad believed in and,
inevitably, was reported in lurid detail in the *Guardian*; the story was
even picked up by the *Herald Tribune* in New York as a piece of
exotica. One of his colleagues, clearly appalled, described the scene: the
improvised altar in a backyard, the flower garlands, the offerings of
sweet bananas and coconuts for the goddess, the blameless little white
goat, the cutlass resting on a tree stump, Seepersad squatting beside the
pundit who was dressed 'in a loincloth, with the shining mahogany of
his skin uncovered', the goat anointed with oil and vermilion powder
and suddenly beheaded, its legs convulsing even as the severed head
was placed on a brass tray and offered to furious Kali. At the centre of
the ceremony crouched the sorry figure of Seepersad Naipaul, dressed
all in white, bedecked like the goat in a garland of scarlet hibiscus
flowers, throwing cloves on a fire and dutifully following each muttered
command of the pundit.

Seepersad wrote his own piece for the newspaper about what had
taken place. It contained flashes of rebellion, but was the work of a
broken man. He would 'rather believe in a single God, than a thousand
Kalis . . . Kali may again threaten my life, but I am certain I will never
again make a sacrifice.' The former scourge of Bobism even boasted
that, after representations to the pundit, he had been allowed to keep
wearing his shirt and trousers rather than dress in a dhoti or loincloth.
'More than once during the ceremony', he wrote, 'I asked myself
whence came the moral feebleness in Hinduism?'[23] The next day he
wrote a jaunty front-page story which began, 'Good morning everybody! As you behold, Kali has not got me yet.'[24] But it was a false or
failing bravado now. Seepersad was profoundly, even fatally, humili-

ated. The sequence of what followed is unclear, but his byline disappeared from the paper, and he stopped reporting from Chaguanas. Some months later, Gault MacGowan left the *Guardian* after a dispute with the management; Seepersad was taken off the staff by the new editor, and made a stringer. He broke down. Helped by his in-laws, he started the 'parlour' in Chase Village; it failed. In late 1935, the Capildeos sent him to be an overseer on a cocoa estate in nearby Cunupia, where he had a mental collapse.

Nearly forty years later, when Vido discovered the complete story of the goat sacrifice by looking through back copies of the *Guardian*, he asked Ma, 'What form did my father's madness take?' She replied, 'He looked in the mirror one day and couldn't see himself. And he began to scream.'[25]

*

Soogee Capildeo, now called Soogee Capildeo Maharaj, though she had been born and baptized Rosalie Gobin, was known to her forty-odd grandchildren as Nanie (the Hindi and Bhojpuri word for a maternal grandmother) and behind her back as Queen Victoria. A Roman Catholic of unspecified caste, she became a born-again promoter of her late husband's Brahminism. Nanie hoped that through their developing status, the Capildeo clan might reach a commanding position within the island's Indian community. Ma and her siblings endorsed these attitudes. As Vido realized later, 'We were given in the Lion House which my grandfather built, some idea of a kind of caste inheritance. The [family members] who came afterwards, they can't understand that. They wouldn't understand my concern and my pride in India or my interest in Indian art and architecture ... Growing up in these conditions, I was full of self-esteem. I think it came from many contradictory sources. It came from the very strong caste sense in my grandmother's family.'[26]

In the New World, caste had become a bulwark against the dominant religion of the other ethnic groups: Christianity. Hindu temples were constructed, and coloured flags erected on bamboo poles outside a building after a puja, a common practice at the time in parts of north India. Religious customs evolved and transmuted just as the Indian diet began to incorporate the yam and sweet potato. Relations between Indian Muslims and Hindus were good; from the 1850s, Trinidad's Hindus had taken part in 'Hosay', the annual Shia festival commemorating the martyrdom of the Imam Hussein, known demeaningly locally as the 'coolie carnival'. With few high-caste Indians in Trinidad, those who carried the scriptural knowledge of the old world were valuable. Families of Brahmin descent took to using an identifiable Brahmin name such as Panday, Mishra or Tewari as a surname, while others appropriated such names out of social ambition. When pundits were called to plantation villages to perform marriage and death rites, there were rumours about the ones who were less ascetic or plausible than they claimed to be. A supposedly pukka pundit who ate meat in secret would be called a 'Pork Brahmin', while a man who clearly knew nothing about the tradition he was supposed to be propagating was known as a 'Brahmin-by-boat', meaning that he must have acquired his caste during the sea voyage from India.

The three surviving photographs of Capildeo Maharaj show him looking distinctly Brahminical. In one picture he ostentatiously carries a book; in another he stands with Soogee by his side, her hand resting on his shoulder in Caribbean informality; in the third he sits with his little son Simbhoo standing beside him. Capildeo's fair skin, sharp nose, shaped moustache, plump cheeks and high forehead all mark him as a Brahmin of the United Provinces. He wears white clothing befitting his caste, his shoes are unlaced to indicate that he has not touched leather with his hand, his dhoti is tied in a respectable way, and around his neck is what looks like a japmala or 108-bead rosary. This physical evidence, combined with the certainty that he knew Sanskrit, make his claimed family lineage highly plausible. The region around his home town of Gorakhpur had many poor Brahmins, so many that merchants would sometimes employ them as talismanic companions when travelling.[27] Without this caste background, it would have been impossible for Capildeo to have obtained his linguistic and scriptural knowledge by the time he sailed for Trinidad in 1894.

Seepersad Naipaul's antecedents are vaguer; he never liked to discuss his childhood. His rejection of orthodox Hinduism and its superstitions matched his uncertainty about his origins and his antipathy towards the memory of his violent father. Did his grandmother, a wronged woman of high birth, leave India with a baby boy, Naipaul Maharaj? There is no record of these two in the archives in Trinidad. A Nepaliah arrived on the indenture ship *Essex* in 1875, a Napaul on the *Foyle* in the same year, a Nepaul followed on the *Jura* in 1878, and a Napaul sailed on the *Sheila* in 1879.[28] On Seepersad's birth certificate (which states that he is illegitimate – only in 1945 were informal Indian marriages conducted 'under bamboo' recognized as legal) his father is given as 'Nyepaul, labourer'. Instead of a signature, he has marked the birth certificate with an 'X', suggesting that

he was illiterate and had not been educated as a pundit.[29] There is no way
of knowing whether this man – Nyepaul, X – was a Brahmin; like Kopil
or Capildeo, his name gives no indication of caste. The strongest assertion
of his status comes from the deathbed recollection of his daughter
Prabharan, recounted in solemn tones by V.S. Naipaul in his 'Prologue to
an Autobiography':

> She wanted me to know now, before the knowledge vanished with
> her, what she – and my father – had come from. She wanted me to
> know that the blood was good ... Her father was a pundit, she
> said. And he was fussy; he didn't like having too much to do with
> the low. And here – since her face was too old to be moulded into
> any expression save one of great weariness – the old lady used her
> shrivelled little hand to make a gentle gesture of disdain. The
> disdain was for the low among Hindus.[30]

Vido's account of his aunt's terminal conversation may be accurate, but
it does not make his paternal grandfather a Brahmin. Nyepaul may have
been a pure Brahmin, a Brahmin-by-boat, or he may have come from
another caste background altogether. Since caste is patrilineal, and
traditionally a Hindu woman takes on the caste of her husband at
marriage, Vido and his siblings may not have been Brahmin either. V.S.
Naipaul never addressed this inconsistency, preferring to embrace the
implied 'caste sense' of his mother's family, the Capildeos, whose legacy
he otherwise claimed to reject. 'My father's background,' he admitted
later, 'is confused in my mind.'[31]

*

Soogee, the powerful matriarch of the Lion House, was a small, stout,
fierce, dark-skinned woman who spoke rarely and was listened to with
awe. After Capildeo Maharaj's death, penniless because he had mortgaged
much of their land in order to elope with Jussodra, she arranged the
marriage of her teenage daughters without paying a dowry; the chosen
husbands (each known to Vido as Mausa – the Hindi word for a maternal
aunt's husband) were said to be Brahmins from poor families. Using the
Mausas as her workforce, she grew and traded rice, sugar cane and later
cocoa. Each daughter (Rajdaye, Ramdoolarie, Dhan, Koonta, Ahilla,
Kalawatee, Droapatie, Tara and Binmatie – known as Mausi, the word for
a maternal aunt) had a room of her own at the Lion House, where she
could sleep with her husband and children: the husband in the bed, the

children on the floor. Vegetarian food from their own land – pigeon peas, okra, rice, pumpkin, potato, spinach, green fig, chick peas, breadfruit, all spiced with masala in an approximation of north Indian cuisine – was cooked communally by the Mausis in a dingy, blackened kitchen. Men and boys dressed in shorts and shirts, the shirts usually made from flour bags, and wore long trousers when working in the fields. Barefoot around the house and yard, outside they wore 'washekongs' – Salim collects a pair in *A Bend in the River*: 'from *caoutchouc*, the French word for rubber, being patois for canvas shoes.'[32] The women wore long white or yellow cotton skirts with a bodice. Kurta pyjamas and saris were worn only for religious ceremonies and festivals, or when the in-house pundit Hargovind Mausa publicly read sacred texts such as the *Ramayana* in the large hall downstairs.

What Nanie said, went. 'At the Lion House,' Kamla remembered, 'we were just told what to do, and we did what we were told to do, whatever was commanded. There was no encouragement of a thinking process. It was an emotionally restricted way of bringing up children.'[33] Her cousin Brahm saw Nanie as 'very demanding, very strict. Nanie believed in the Hindu way of life but the irony of it is, she would help with the churches and celebrate all the Catholic festivals because she didn't believe in putting all your stones in one basket. She told us that she wanted us to speak in English, not Hindi, because we had to be educated.' Nanie made it clear in graphic terms to her children and grandchildren that they were not part of a wider Trinidadian community. Brahm remembered: 'When I went to school I was told by my grandmother, "You can't associate with niggers." Only Indians were accepted. She had bright, piercing eyes – she could see through your soul with one glance.'[34]

During the 1930s, Nanie navigated her family's financial position by buying and selling real estate. The land registries of Trinidad contain no fewer than twenty-eight transactions involving Soogee Capildeo Maharaj during the period 1929 to 1946, mainly in land in the sugar belt such as Cacandee, Endeavour village and Chandernagore. Some deals were simple, and some were complex; it appears that during the early part of the Second World War she made a healthy profit by dividing her agricultural land into parcels and selling it to small farmers, most of whom appear to have been Indian (with names like Seemungal Mahabir, Dukhanee Rambhoras and Dhanradge Mungaree).[35] She also negotiated with some of the larger colonial estates. In 1933, she sold a large field in Carapichaima in west-central Trinidad to Stephens Ltd., and three years later purchased a similar-sized plot from them near Chaguanas.[36] In 1934 she sold ten acres of land to Woodford Lodge Ltd., and in 1940 bought a large agricultural structure in Charlieville from J.G. Henriques & Company.[37] No figures are recorded to show the value of these sales and purchases, but it can be presumed that Soogee kept a tight grip on the profits. However much wealth she had tied up in land, she still had to pay off mortgages and loans, and to run a large family. The importance of money was instilled in all her grandchildren at an early age.

Although many of her transactions would have been fronted by her two favoured sons-in-law, and by her son Simbhoonath when he grew older, Nanie retained control of the family's finances. The sons-in-law who worked for her directly were not paid, and had to come to her if they needed money for clothing, shoes or household goods. One Mausa would be played off against another, and the family seethed with bitter feuds. Furious arguments between the adults would be conducted in the Bhojpuri-inspired Hindi that was common among descendants of Indian indentured labourers across the region, half-understood by the children. Sahadeo Mausa, an uneducated man who worked a regular fourteen-hour day as a farmer for the family, challenged Nanie about being treated like a coolie; he got nowhere. Knowing he faced greater poverty if he left the extended family, he took out his frustration on his son Brahm, slapping and punching him for the smallest misdemeanour. The sisters would compete to see who could discipline their children most forcefully. Relationships in the household were often callous, and Vido learned an early lesson that remained with him for life:

> Children were beaten with a strap or with a stick. Outside, we were surrounded by language that came from the days of slavery. Parents would say: 'I will peel your backside. I will beat you till you pee. I will make you fart fire.' You can hear the language of the plantation. I think there is a lot of violence in Indian peasant families. But my father and mother didn't punish people too often, though we were surrounded by people being punished . . . What happens in that kind of awful set-up is that lots of quarrels break out between people, and those quarrels were my training for life, my training in life and society – propaganda, alliances, betrayals – all these things. So, in a way, nothing that happened later ever really shocked me.[38]

For the first six, formative years of Vido's life, his father was often absent, mentally and physically. The central figures in his early days were women: his grandmother, his mother, his aunts, his teacher and his big sister. The men in the Lion House, with the exception of the two pampered sons of the family, were emasculated, having been chosen for the role of son-in-law because they were nominally of high caste but poor enough for their parents not to expect a dowry. Although Ma was conscious of her role and duties as a traditional Hindu woman, cooking and caring for her husband and children, she was tough; her mother was powerful in a way that can have been matched by few Indian women in Trinidad at this time. Kamla remembered Ma being 'a strong woman with a strong personality. Vain, proud and conceited, she needed all of these qualities for her survival.'[39] Their brother Shiva noted that she had rigid ideas about history: 'my mother has always found it hard to forgive the Muslims for their numerous invasions of India and for forcing the partition of the subcontinent.'[40]

In his own presentation of the past, Vido would concentrate subsequently on the virtues of his father, with the result that Ma's voice can be hard to hear. An academic who interviewed her in 1988 for a study of Trinidadian Indian women noted: 'Her answers are always alert, sometimes aggressively so; she is a confident and self-assured woman.' When asked why her mother had sent her daughters to school at a time when other Indian women were illiterate, Ma replied, 'Don't ask me that question again. She decided to educate them and I think she was very correct in educating them.' To an enquiry about her non-Indian neighbours, she answered: 'Don't ask me anything about other people, ask me nothing about other people . . . my husband can't come home and see me gossiping on the street . . . You see a woman has a place in this world and when she abuse that place, she has lost the thing they call womanhood because she is no more that woman.'[41] Ma's bright, certain, robust, slightly mocking tone of voice would be inherited by Vido; without the impetus of Ma and her family, his later achievements would have been impossible.

CHAPTER THREE

'LIKE OLIVER TWIST
IN THE WORKHOUSE'

THE NEAR HALF-MILLION people of Trinidad were given three scholarships each year to a university in Great Britain. Innumerable children would compete for the chance to have a free education overseas, and to change their own and their family's future. In a colonial society where the opportunities for advancement were so restricted, island scholarships, like places in the better cricket teams, were fought over fiercely. Success marked you as a person of intellectual ability, part of a new group that was being groomed for the day when Trinidad gained self-government.[1] Jean-Paul Sartre put it this way: 'The European elite undertook to manufacture a native elite. They picked out promising adolescents; they branded them, as with a red-hot iron, with the principles of western culture, they stuffed their mouths full with high-sounding phrases, grand glutinous words that stuck to the teeth. After a short stay in the mother country they were sent home, whitewashed.'[2] In 1938, Ma's younger brother Rudranath won an island scholarship to study medicine, an achievement that had the potential to shift the status of the Capildeo family from being big in Chaguanas to being big in Trinidad. He was one of the first Indian winners, defying expectations. Half a century earlier, the Governor of the newly united colony of Trinidad and Tobago had told a group of Indian school-children: 'Now all you children, all of you little boys and girls can never hope, of course, can never hope to occupy any very high social position in life – it would be very foolish and over-ambitious on your part to expect to do so.'[3] With nationalism flourishing after strikes and riots the previous year in the oilfields of Fyzabad, led by the splendidly named Tubal Uriah "Buzz" Butler, a Grenadian small-church preacher, the prospect of constitutional reform was imminent. Butler's 'British Empire Citizens and Workers Home Rule Party' – backed by the trade-union leader Adrian Cola Rienzi – was attracting popular support.

In order to give her son Rudranath a home near his school while he was studying for the scholarship, Nanie had bought a house, 17 Luis Street, in the Port of Spain suburb of Woodbrook, a mixed-race area distinct from St James, the down-at-heel quarter known as 'coolie town' which was occupied mainly by people of south Indian descent who had left Hinduism far behind. During the week, Nanie would stay in Port of Spain to look after Rudranath and make sure he did his school work. She bought other properties too, and needed a family member to administer them and collect the rents. This coincided with Seepersad's recovery from his breakdown, and his success in 1938 in regaining his job as a *Guardian* journalist. It was decided that the Naipaul family, now including a baby girl named Savi or Savitri, would move to Luis Street. With Trinidad in a state of unrest and the Second World War looming, Ma, Pa and the children had a moment of respite. The family took the steam train from the station at Chaguanas for the slow twenty-mile journey to Port of Spain, and began afresh.

Pa's confidence revived, and he began to write stories for his own entertainment. George John, a young black sports reporter on the *Guardian*, found Seepersad to be 'a very quiet man who didn't mix very much. He was basically a rural Indian, not a town Indian. He came from the sugar belt. Naipaul would not go drinking with other journalists.' Although there were now two other Indians working on the paper, their community was still associated by the citizens of Port of Spain with low status activities such as street-vending, carrying head-loads and collecting garbage. Indians were looked down on. In all professions, according to John, 'There was a definite bias in favour of the lighter-skinned. Not only in newspapers. It was like that in the civil service, in the higher ranks of the police. You entered the banks and all the people you saw, the tellers and so on, were white girls or white men.'[4] 'White' or 'lighter-skinned' in this context in Trinidad in the 1940s might mean British expatriate, Portuguese, 'French creole' (some-one of European appearance, usually descended from plantation own-ers), 'Spanish' (mixed ethnic descent with fair skin and 'good' – meaning straight – hair) or 'Red' (African features with light skin and hair). The gradation was strict and instinctive, part of a way of think-ing that was instilled early in this ethnically diverse colonial setting, although people might try to 'pass' as something they were not. There was even a Bajan rhyme about skin shades: 'white, fusty, dusty, musty, tea, coffee, cocoa, black, dark black'.

In Luis Street, Vido came to know and appreciate the qualities of his father. These were, in retrospect, idyllic days for him. Woodbrook had been built on an old sugar estate near the harbour owned by the makers of Angostura Bitters, the Siegert family, with its streets laid out on a grid and named after members of the family such as Alberto, Luis and Ana. For the first time, Vido encountered electric lights, pavements and running water. The capital had cinemas, rum shops and cricket pitches, and on Sunday afternoons the police band would play for the crowds near the Queen's Park Savannah. The Naipaul family appeared to have a home of their own. The house was a three-bedroomed wooden building raised on pillars, with a verandah, a yard and an outdoor latrine. A Negro carpenter lived in the 'servant room' in the yard; when Vido asked him one day what he was making, he replied 'the thing without a name'.[5] At the end of the road was the harbour and the reclaimed area of land known as Docksite. Vido's uncle Rudranath, preparing for his departure for England, had one bedroom, and another was rented to a mulatto couple, Mr and Mrs Guy, who were friendly to Vido. The children usually slept out on the verandah. For Vido, 'This whole thing unrolled every day in front of my eyes: the life of the street.'[6] It would give him the material for his first book, *Miguel Street*.

For a term, he went to Woodbrook Canadian Mission School, where his teacher was Mr Dairy. Vido liked 'the writing and the paper and the pencils and shaping letters. It was at Mr Dairy's school that I began to make the letter J, the capital J, endless curls in my J, you know, out of pleasure indeed in the shape of letters. And I took this one day and showed it to my father, and he told me, "No, no, too many curls." So I lost that little bit of style.' In 1939 he joined his cousin Boysie at Tranquillity, which had a strong academic reputation. Former students included the pan-African theorist George Padmore and the sprinter McDonald Bailey, who would be the first black athlete to win an Olympic medal for Britain. At Tranquillity Boys' Intermediate School, Vido made friends across cultures, despite Nanie's racial injunctions: Winston A.G. Springer, known as WAGS, Kenneth Cazabon, related to the painter Michel Jean Cazabon, and Yip Young, a 'very bright and delicate boy who was half-Negro and half-Chinese.'[7] He would swap his morning snack with a Negro boy named Tanis. 'He was excited by the food I brought to school. I was a ready swapper. I gave Tanis my stuff. There would have been curried potatoes, in a little tiffin carrier.

He gave me a kind of parlour cake, with coconut inside. I have a clear memory of that.'[8]

In the middle of the day, Tranquillity children walked home for lunch. Kamla went to the girls' branch of the school. One day Vido stopped to read a street sign, Cipriani Boulevard. 'Cipriani Boul Edward,' he said, 'and a Negro man there, he was very amused and he told me how to pronounce it. Big word and I'm quite young.' Most of the pupils and all the teachers were black or mixed, and it was a new experience for Vido to be surrounded by many people who came from a different culture. He stood out: 'I was an object of great curiosity to people. I was very small, and they couldn't have been nicer. There were few Indians, almost no Indians in the school. It was the first time we were coming out [of the countryside]. If I had gone to a rough place, it might have been different. I have to record how nice people were to me, as an unprotected little boy.'[9] He was now called Vidia on paper, a shorter and more modern version of Vidyadhar, and he was placed second out of thirty-six in the class at the end of his first term. His teacher Mr Romilly noted in the school report that he was 'an intelligent pupil'.[10] At Tranquillity he was given a solid grounding in grammar, spelling, vocabulary, arithmetic and geography, and on Empire Day the children all sang 'God Save the King' and 'Land of Hope and Glory', including the immortal line 'Britons never, never, never shall be slaves.'[11]

At home, Vido made friends with Mr Guy, the lodger, who 'made the world very, very exciting. I was six or seven. He must have had some talent for getting on with children.' One day the two of them were standing on the verandah at 17 Luis Street when a decrepit Indian man came past pushing a handcart packed with steaming ice, selling ice lollies or palettes at a cent each. He was calling out 'Palette! Palette!' Vido wanted to run out and buy an ice lolly. But: 'Mr Guy said to me, "No. He will bring it to you."' To Vido, this was no simple message: 'It was an important kind of instruction to me, meaning, once you're spending money, you have certain rights. It was a training in the ways of the world – you don't run after that barefoot man in the street; he must come to you. I remember it to this day.'[12]

The idyll could not last. In 1940, Seepersad and Droapatie were told by Nanie that they would be moving to a new family commune at a place called Petit Valley.

*

Cool and shady, with savannah and plenty of snakes, Petit Valley was unfamiliar land, an estate of three hundred acres to the north of Port of Spain. An old colonial house built by one of Trinidad's respected 'high brown' families, the Maillards, stood on a verdant, forested hillside. Around it were oranges, shaddocks (a citrus fruit, like a grapefruit), cacao trees, nutmeg, zabocas (avacado pears), tangerines and mangoes. The people in the village near the house were 'panyol' or 'cocoa panyol' – coming from the word Español, or Spanish, meaning they were of mixed ethnicity, although probably their ancestors would have come from Venezuela. The local patois had many French words, from the days when the owners of the cocoa estates had brought slaves from neighbouring islands. The long-established overseer at Petit Valley was called Metti, from the French 'métis', meaning half-caste, a name Vido would use when he came to write *A Bend in the River*. The Mausis, Mausas and cousins all moved there, although some would travel back and forth to Port of Spain or to Chaguanas, where Nanie remained in the Lion House. Her elder son Simbhoonath, now aged twenty-six and studying to be a lawyer in the town of San Fernando, was the guiding force behind the project. The family would develop the land at Petit Valley. When Vido heard about the move, he was distraught: 'I think I must have made a great scene about it, and my grandmother began to talk to me. I don't know why she took the care. She told me how beautiful it was, how lovely the house was, how lovely the big trees were – so I was primed to love these things.'[13]

Coming from the cane fields and rough dwellings of Chaguanas, the Capildeo family led by Simbhoo had little idea what to do with their new domain, which had been sold to them cheap by the Maillards because it was unprofitable. To the dismay of people in the local village, the area around the house became squalid, in its beautiful setting. 'They did a kind of peasant agriculture,' said Vido later, 'burning down the hillsides and planting corn, maize and peas. They pillaged the oranges from the orange trees, took the avacadoes. They planted nothing. They were camping ... It was all so improvised, all so dreadful. We were given a very low idea of human needs. I think without anybody knowing, this was coming from Mother India, from a beaten-down, broken-down people.'[14] Trees were uprooted and the house reworked. A big, unfamiliar brick oven was taken apart, and the area beside it roofed over in corrugated iron and tree branches. The verandah was used to store crops and old bread, which Nanie would buy in bulk from a baker in Port of Spain. The indoor water closet with its European cistern and chain was dismantled, and an outdoor latrine built in the woods, to which a sodden path was soon worn. 'I think the WC offended the Hindu sense of cleanliness and so it was destroyed. It became a room where people sewed ... I am talking about people who were close to immemorial peasantry.'[15] An ornamental cherry tree by the tennis court on the side of the main drive was turned into logs. 'There was no reason to chop it down. It was just something to do, something to chop down. Where we come from ancestrally, there are no trees – they think spirits hide in trees.'[16] While the children watched in excitement, Uncle Simbhoo supervised the destruction of the electricity generator, the leaves of lead being melted in a large pot and tipped into Ovaltine tins; pipes were put between the tins and the molten metal hardened, creating dumb-bells for the Mausas to use for exercise. 'I think they played with them for a while and then forgot them.'[17] The house was lit by oil lamps now, like the Lion House. Vido's retrospective cynicism was matched by the memory of Margaret Maillard, the granddaughter of the vendor, who visited. 'It was a roomy house. The Capildeos were very gracious to us when we came but we were horrified by the way they had partitioned it.'[18]

Ma and Pa were given a space in the servants' quarters to the back of the house, overlooking the hillside. Seepersad hated being part of the extended family again, and took to demanding meals in his bedroom. There were frequent, angry disputes with his brothers-in-law. Vidia noted later that his father avoided touching the ground at Petit Valley, and linked it mentally with his supposed Brahminism. 'I don't think my father ever let his foot touch the ground. He couldn't go to have a shower barefoot. He always had to wear wooden sandals. He never let his foot touch the ground.'[19] The children had little contact with their uncles, aunts or cousins on the Naipaul side of the family. Ma cooked, cleaned, washed and looked after the five of them with the occasional help of her sisters. Vido took his mother's care and support as his right, in the manner of a boy in a Hindu joint family. In Kamla's opinion, 'Our vanity, our conceit, our resilience, our tenacity, our strength – these things we got from our mother. Words, the sound of words, our love of books, our sense of humour, our passion, our occasionally neurotic behaviour, our physical frailties – these things we got from our father.'[20] Vido's own view in later life was: 'My mother would cry because she thought my father was being awkward. Her loyalties were really to her clan, her sisters. She was part of the mess, you know.' When pressed, he said, 'I adored her as a child. She was a beautiful lady. Carried herself very well ... I think my father was a weak man, a suffering man who could only work when people loved him. My mother was very tough and strong. I think I got my strength from her.'[21]

As the atmosphere at Petit Valley worsened, Pa built a plain, pretty timber house for himself in the forest, standing on stilts. When he burned heaps of leaves and wood that he had cleared, a fire began and lingered in the undergrowth. At night it flared up, as Kamla remembered:

Vidia and I were awakened and told to run to the big house to get help. There was a forest fire at the back of the house and it was spreading. A patch of forest separated us from the big house. In the daytime it was no problem to run through it, following a path we naturally made going from one house to the other. But it was night and it was dark. Vidia and I were terrified of the fire, of the dark and of the forest on either side of the lonely road. Stories of forest spirits became very real in that setting, of La Diablesse, the enchantress with the cloven hoof who led men astray, of Soucouy-ants, who were women who could turn themselves into balls of fire [and become vampires]. Holding each other's hands, Vidia and I took the road. I was calling upon the name of Rama, the only name that came to me at that time and I was encouraging Vidia to do the same as a means of keeping these evil forest creatures at bay. Once aroused the family came immediately to our assistance.[22]

They beat down the flames with branches, and Pa was left without a house again.

The cousins – boys and girls of all ages – were not encouraged to associate with people who lived nearby, such as the mulatto family who lived by the road and worked on the estate, or the Indian Muslim family who kept a parlour and had a pretty daughter. There were no friends, only family. Although the status of the Naipaul children was complicated by Pa's chronic disputes, they were in a stronger position than some of their cousins, such as the children of the widowed Tara Mausi, whose husband, Ramjattan, had been gored to death by a bull. Tara's daughter Phoola remembered being entirely dependent on the goodwill of Nanie and Simbhoo. 'We had to respect the aunts and uncles, even when they were wrong. The aunts were smart people. On reflection, I would say anyone who had a father had more security than us.'[23] More unfortunate still were the children of the oldest Mausi, Rajdaye. Her husband, Aknath, had been the overseer on the family sugar-cane plantations in Chaguanas and Nanie's enforcer in many of her business ventures. When Rajdaye died, there was a feud which led to Aknath Mausa being purged. His children became virtual orphans, living in a shack in Petit Valley. One of them, Jai, remembered: 'We were 200 yards from the main house. I was twelve, my brothers were nine and six. I had to cook for them and look after them. My grandmother wouldn't allow my father's name to be spoken. I feel we were really, really badly treated. There was no compassion from her.'[24]

The children made their own entertainment, outdoors and indoors. Each morning each child would take the crushed end of a fresh stick to use as a toothbrush, then split it and use it as a tongue-scraper. They husked corn and harvested coffee, cocoa, oranges and bananas for market. One day they put on a play of the trial scene from Shakespeare's *The Merchant of Venice* in the drawing room, and Vido was struck by the beauty of his female cousins. In later years, he 'found it very hard to think of making love to an Indian girl. It had an incestuous sense to it.' A little before this he had his first sexual experience, when he was seduced by his cousin Boysie. The encounter was unwanted. As he put it: 'I was myself subjected to some sexual abuse by an older cousin. I was corrupted, I was assaulted. I was about six or seven. It was done in a sly, terrible way and it gave me a hatred, a detestation of this homosexual thing. I never went through a period of liking the same sex.'[25] Molestation continued intermittently over the next two or three years, usually in the area where the boys slept. Vidia never mentioned it to anyone, at the time or later. He insisted he was never a willing participant, although his denial is not wholly convincing given the similarity in age of the two boys. He feared the idea that he was a participant in sexual experimentation between male cousins. 'It was an outrage, but it was not a defining moment. I was very young. This thing was over before I was ten. I was always coerced. Of course he was ashamed too later. It happened to other cousins. I think it is part of Indian extended family life, which is an abomination in some ways, a can of worms . . . After an assault one is very ashamed – and then you realize it happens to almost everybody. All children are abused. All girls are molested at some stage. It is almost like a rite of passage.'[26] The Mausis were alert to any hint of burgeoning sexuality between male and female cousins. 'If we sat boy and girl in a hammock together, it was a grievous thing. An aunt would come and say, "What are you doing there?" ' Savi remembered.[27]

Vido spent much of his time at Petit Valley with Pa, who would read to him and sometimes to the other children: extracts from *Julius Caesar*, *Nicholas Nickleby*, *Three Men in a Boat*, Charles Kingsley's retelling of the Perseus myth in *The Heroes*, and later from Gandhi's *Autobiography*, Conrad's *The Lagoon*, Maupassant's *The Necklace* and Maugham's *Cakes and Ale*. Although such authors described unfamiliar worlds, the stories lingered: 'I still remember *Cakes and Ale* begins with the narrator going back to his lodgings, and there is a message from his landlady Mrs Fellows saying Mr Kear rang up twice. "He says it's important." And Maugham observes in the Maugham-like way, which stays with me to this day, "I know that when people say things are important, it doesn't mean it is important to you; it's important to them." So one was being trained early in this way. The effect was to introduce me to the romantic idea of this world outside, and to the romantic idea of writing.'[28] Representations of the West Indies were to be found mainly in books by white visitors, like Alec Waugh writing of indolent bellboys and 'the inevitable negroes' in *The Coloured Countries*, or Edmund Whitman using chapter titles like 'Banana Escapades' and 'Jamaica Ginger Snaps' in *Those Wild West Indies*.[29]

Pa and Vido positioned themselves in an ordered fantasy world derived from European literature, far from the noise, squalor and their own powerlessness in Petit Valley. At school, Vido might read an extract from *Martin Chuzzlewit* in his *New Royal Reader*, containing place names that would one day become familiar: 'The coach was none of your steady-going, yokel coaches . . . It cared no more for Salisbury than if it had been a hamlet. It rattled noisily through the best streets, defied the cathedral, took the worst corners sharpest . . .'[30] Aspiration and ambition became an alternative to daily life in Petit Valley. 'I suffered like hell in this place,' Vido said later. 'It has given me all kinds of things [for my writing]: my understanding of the ease with which civilizations can be destroyed. When I was in Africa [in 1975] and saw in the Congo the ruins of Belgian cities, when I saw the same thing in Rwanda in 1966, I knew about people camping in houses and not knowing what to do with the things, just stripping it apart.'[31] At Petit Valley, Vido began to keep a diary, written in pencil in a *Guardian* reporter's notebook. He wrote about the death of his paternal grandmother and Pa's distress, but after a while the diary 'became very affected and melodramatic. I was melancholic, and I had a slight wallow, as a child. I remember writing, "I feel like Oliver Twist in the workhouse." I knew it wasn't true, but I had no other means of expressing what I felt.'[32]

At Christmas 1941, the local school in the village at Petit Valley held a concert. The family walked through the tropical night to the school, which was full of lights and people singing songs. Vido was excited by the glamour of the occasion. 'One of the songs had a little Negro boy, nattily dressed in a suit. Clearly his parents had dressed him up for this occasion. Whether he did a little dance or whether he just came out dressed in this way, he looked so cute in that suit. But he sang, "Oh, I'm a happy little nigger." It was the most successful number of the evening. I remember people laughing till they almost cried with pleasure at the little boy. "Oh, I'm a happy little nigger and my name is John." The chorus was, "I can sleep on a cotton bale or roost up a tree, tell you what it is boys, nothing hurts me." I think it goes: "I like cake, I like honey, I'm not the boy to refuse any money. Once I went a courting with my little black sioux" – or it might be, "my saucy black sioux" – "her brother Tom insulted me and peppered me too." It was only years later that I understood what we'd heard. Clearly it's written by an American white man, out of a kind of love for the little black boy, but within this love is complete contempt.'[33] The song would stick in Vido's formidable memory, to be pondered over subsequent years, and used to show the way in which culture and meaning change in a different historical setting: the American south, a 'panyol' village in colonial Trinidad, the independent Caribbean. It resurfaced in 1967 in *The Mimic Men*, where Browne is humiliated to have been a 'singer of coon songs' as a child, and indirectly in *A Way in the World* in 1994, where Lebrun tells a similar story and concludes, ' "Every educated black man is eaten away quietly by a memory like that." '[34] This was how V.S. Naipaul's fiction would work: a moment would be stored, remembered, examined and retold through the decades.

At weekends, Simbhoo would arrive and take command of the family. Each Sunday evening, he gathered the children and taught them Hindu mantras, or gave a talk on Indian civilization and the epics. They had to learn the Hindi alphabet and some vocabulary, but never learned how to connect the words and speak the language. Later, as 'Pandit Simbhoonath Capildeo', he would self-publish *100 Questions and Answers on the Hindu Religion*, a book that his nephew Vido would proceed to satirize in *The Mystic Masseur*.[35] He expected deference from his nephews and nieces, and his brothers-in-law were always aware that he held the purse strings. According to Brahm, 'Power corrupts – and it was an accepted fact in the family that Rudranath and Simbhoonath were the gods, so [as children] you had to bow down to them and literally put your hand down to their feet, so they could bless you. Simbhoo was given full reign to do anything and everything he wished to do. From my point of view, he was a tyrant. Our grandmother would always defer to him, to both her sons.'[36]

For Vido, Kamla and their cousins of a similar age, travelling the five miles to and from school each day was a complicated manoeuvre. Like her brother, Kamla worked hard and was an academic succcess at Tranquillity. Sometimes they would take the Sam Super Service bus, at other times they would travel in an old Ford motor car with running boards which Nanie had bought, but it broke down and nobody knew how to repair it. Pa would cycle to work at the *Guardian*, and sometimes stay in Port of Spain overnight. When the Americans came to Trinidad in 1941 and built the Churchill–Roosevelt Highway and a deep-water naval base at Chaguaramas (under the Lend-Lease agreement, which exchanged British empire bases for American ships) an uncle bought a truck to rent. It had to be at the new base that was being built at Docksite by six o'clock each morning. The truck was driven by Sahadeo Mausa, known as Power Mausa by the children because of his interest in mechanics, who would drop them at Luis Street with an aunt to wait for school to start each day. He continued to assault his son Brahm. 'He would punish me with strapping, slapping, depriving me of food, he would hit me with whatever was at hand. My father was mentally and emotionally unstable.'[37] Vido remembered this period as a time of unhappiness and hunger. He started to get asthma, gasping for missing breath, sucking in air, wheezing his way through the long, hot nights. Often, there would be no proper food available, and he would go to school or to bed on an empty stomach. In Kamla's view, this was the result of wartime food shortages rather than neglect, and she thought Vido's claim of being starved was 'a ridiculous memory, it is a damn stupid memory'.[38]

Full-bellied or hungry, he kept up his studies at Tranquillity, encouraged by Nanie, who would appear in Petit Valley from time to time for an inspection, usually accompanied by her black servant Miss Blackie. When classes ended, Vido would remain behind for extra tuition with a teacher from the school. In 1942, although ranked fifth in

a class of forty-five, he won an exhibition to his Uncle Rudranath's old
school, Queen's Royal College, where the government now paid his
fees and gave an annual grant for the cost of books.[39] Although
physically weaker than his contemporaries, he was marked out as an
achiever, one of twenty children across the island who had won an
exhibition. 'He was brilliant,' said his cousin Jai, a view shared by
Brahm: 'Every day for school we had to learn twenty Latin words. So
we'd come from school and study, and after five, ten minutes he would
say, test me and everything was bang on. Amazing. He said to me at
Petit Valley he would like to become a writer.'[40] Vido's own view was
that his cousins had been told to revere academic success, 'I suppose
because they respected my brightness. I was always treated with regard.
And I could make jokes. Very good jokes too.'[41] He never felt
completely part of the world of his cousins. 'There was a distant relation
who came to stay with us in order to go to school, an elegant boy, and
he was mocked and mocked. They told terrible stories about his
personal habits, eating the scabs of his sores. I was horrified. Reason
told me it was wrong. I couldn't run with them.'[42]

In the vacation, Pa would take Vido to Tunapuna to stay with his
old mentor Sookdeo Misir, now a rich man from his Arima Bus
Company. Vido liked the atmosphere at Sookdeo's more wealthy
household, and the food that came from its kitchen. A cousin there had
a less affectionate memory of the precocious scholar. Sookdeo's grandson Romesh recollected Vidia, aged about ten, lording it over the other
children: 'Instead of joining us playing cricket, he would stay reading.
He would wait until my grandfather came home from the estate, and
would sit there on the back porch and read newspapers very impres-
sively. He was able to pronounce and understand every word in the
newspaper. The old man was very enamoured with him because of his
brilliance.' Sookdeo was himself uneducated. 'Of course we were pitted
against Vidia by our grandfather saying, "See what you all are doing,
playing football and cricket. Why don't you learn to read and write
properly, like Vidia?"'[43] Margaret Maillard, who went to school with
Kamla and would marry another future Nobel laureate, Derek Walcott,
remembered his academic talent. 'We knew he was bright. He had to
do a French exam, and he learnt in full the answer for a question – in
French.'[44]

In 1943, Seepersad could stand it no longer at Petit Valley and the
Naipaul family moved in desperation to 17 Luis Street. Once again, Pa

was relying on Nanie's network of support, even while he railed against it. Over the next year they were joined by more family members, and the little house became crowded. Each branch of the extended family used its own kerosene stove to cook. For Vido, school seemed to be an alternative world where he could find a footing. Queen's Royal College or QRC had been set up in 1859 by the colonial government to counter 'French' influence on the island. It was a substantial late-Victorian colonial building done in multicoloured stone and fringed by palm trees, located on the edge of the Queen's Park Savannah by the Anglican bishop's residence. QRC was modelled on an English boys' public school, and offered a high standard of education. It was rivalled by St Mary's or the College of the Immaculate Conception, which was run by Roman Catholic priests. No other Caribbean island had the same rivalry between two schools of such academic excellence.[45] Like Tranquillity, QRC had few Indian pupils, and they were mainly Christian or Muslim.

Although Vido was brought up like many Hindus to be aware of his difference from Muslims, there was no obvious communal divide in Trinidad. Watching newsreels of events in India at the cinema, he felt they were engaged in a common struggle: 'I thought of Muslims as being part of us, one people. Some Indian Muslims went to school with me. I never thought about it ... We were fed Indian nationalism by people [such as Simbhoo] who were doing nothing about it in real life – imagine us as village big-shots. There was a man called Chandra Bahadur Mathura, who ran a wretched little rag of a magazine called *The Indian*. We were schooled in it: we knew about Gandhi, we knew about Nehru, we knew about Azad [the Muslim president of the Indian National Congress]. I remember seeing the newsreels of the Cripps Mission in 1942, Stafford Cripps talking to the Mahatma ... I felt proud.'[46]

At school, he made no deliberate effort to associate with other Indians. 'My friends at QRC would have been black people,' he recalled.[47] From Tranquillity came Yip Young and WAGS, who liked his humour. He made friends with Charles John, whose father was a Woodbrook policeman, and William Demas, a tall, gangly, flat-nosed black boy who got free textbooks because his father was a DPO, or deceased public officer. The boys called each other by their surnames, in British style. Each morning Naipaul would walk to school early and run home to Luis Street for lunch, accompanied to the end of the road by Charles John. He never brought friends home, preferring to keep the two worlds separate. 'It seemed natural to have the friendship outside the house. You wouldn't want another boy to see your poverty,' he said later.[48] To his sister Savi this seemed odd, particularly as Vido grew older: it appeared to represent a separation arising from social, ethnic or cultural embarrassment.

The school buildings at QRC were 'very beautiful' to Vido. 'I liked the ritual of the school life. I liked the formality. I liked the spaciousness of the grounds. Every form had its form master, and he did the roll every morning. For me, the school was immeasurably exciting.'[49] He enjoyed classes in Latin, French, Spanish and Science. Still small, he was conscious that he was one of the youngest boys in his year. Since it was wartime, many of the British teachers had been called up to fight and replaced by West Indian teachers, making the staff as racially diverse as the pupils. The principal, Mr Hamer, was English. It was a highly competitive school, with metropolitan values. Caribbean dialect was ironed out in favour of standard English, although the pupils remained bilingual – outside class, they might still say, 'Higher monkey climb, more he show he ass', or, 'Cutlass don't leave mark in water', or 'Play jackass, they go ride ya'. At home, a boy might have a third language, deriving from his parents' country of origin: Portuguese, Bhojpuri, French, Cantonese. Selby Wooding, who was at QRC a couple of years ahead of Vido, considered it 'an honour school. Boys could be depended on to be trustworthy. It is a world that has vanished now.' The happy few were expected to behave like English schoolboys in the tropics. According to Wooding, 'You had to wear the mask of the master in order to advance.'[50]

*

When Seepersad Naipaul conceived of becoming a writer, in emulation of authors he admired like O. Henry and W. Somerset Maugham, he had few indigenous examples. Herbert de Lisser, a Jamaican, had published a couple of books in London during the First World War, and was followed in the 1930s by Alfred Mendes, a Trinidadian who placed two novels with Duckworth of London, one with a blurb by the writer Anthony Powell.[51] Jamaican-born Claude McKay had moved to America and achieved some literary prominence as part of the Harlem Renaissance, and W. Adolphe Roberts published detective novels in the USA. Jean Rhys, a woman from a white creole family in Dominica, had published stories and novels. The nearest thing Pa had to a homegrown model was C.L.R. James, a former QRC student and one of its earliest black teachers. His realistic street novel *Minty Alley* was published by Secker & Warburg in 1936 after he sailed to London to try his luck in the imperial capital. James wrote a series of letters for the *Port of Spain Gazette* in the year of Vido's birth: they told how he liked the 'intellectual ferment' of Bloomsbury, enjoyed reading 'the delightful Miss Rebecca West in the *Daily Telegraph*' and claimed he had bested Edith Sitwell at an evening lecture with a clever reference to William Faulkner. Parodying the manner of the European visitors who wrote about the West Indies, James observed that since 'the English native is so glum and dull and generally boorish in his manners . . . any man of colour who is not repulsive in appearance, has good manners, and is fairly intelligent, is a great favourite with the girls.' The habitations of the English he found glum, owing to 'the terrible habit of joining all the houses one to another for hundreds of yards.'[52] Apart from these rare achievers, aspiring Caribbean writers like Pa faced self-publication, a haphazard activity that was taken less than seriously in this busy, verbal, storytelling culture.

Pa knew he had written good stories, and wanted to see them in print. He needed money, and in 1943 turned to Simbhoo. 'My father paid for the publication of his stories,' Simbhoo's son Suren remembered. 'Without that book, Seepersad would have been nothing.'[53] A thousand copies of *Gurudeva and other Indian Tales* were printed at the *Guardian* commercial printery, selling at $1 each. Pa brought home the proofs in his jacket pocket each evening. Not realizing the extent of his literary ambition, most people assumed this was a venture to make money. The publisher was listed as Trinidad Publications of 17 Luis Street, and an advertisement to the left of the title page asked for submissions of short stories, essays and novelettes. *Gurudeva* was like a booklet, seventy-two pages long with a soft blue cover showing the veiled head of an Indian woman above a rural scene: palm trees, the sun, an ajoupa hut, a Hindu temple and prayer flags high on bamboo poles, drawn by a local artist, Alfred Codallo.[54] Devotedly, Kamla and Vido stuck an errata slip to the flyleaf of each copy of their father's treasured book. Over time, the entire print-run sold. There were complaints from Indians who thought the book insulted their community.

In linked short stories, *Gurudeva* described the picaresque progress of its title character, a rogue who starts out as a juvenile husband, becomes a boastful but cowardly village stick-fighter, gets sent to jail, and ends up as a phoney pundit before sacking his wife, Ratni, in favour of Daisy, who bobs her hair and dumps him. Set in the 1930s and 1940s, it shows the

Indian community in Trinidad cut adrift from its origins, coming to terms with a confusing, changing world. Seepersad based Gurudeva on his former brother-in-law Dinanath Tiwari, a gangster and pundit who had given the name 'Vidyadhar' to his son, and who was now divorced from Ma's sister Ramdoolarie.

Gurudeva and other Indian Tales might be dismissed as a literary curiosity, the work of a famous writer's father, but is a book of rare quality in its own right, an early text in the tradition of Indian diasporic fiction that was to develop vigorously later in the century. At its best, the writing has a classical quality. Here is Gurudeva collecting and preparing sticks for fighting:

> He would take himself into the high woods up in Chickland, three miles away, and cut the pouis that flourished abundantly on the high lands, and gathering them in a bundle, he would tote them home. Out in the yard he would make a blazing fire of dry leaves and bake the sticks in it and beat the barks off them on the ground. Then he would cut each stick into the desired length – from ground level to his lower ribs – and then with cutlass, with broken bottles with razor-sharp edges, and finally with sandpaper, he would impart to each stick the smoothness and uniformity of a ruler. Then he would go to the giant bamboo clump near by and bring forth a length of bamboo, stout and ripe and roomy in its hollowness, and an inch or two longer than his stick; and he would punch out all the compartments but the last, and order Ratni to make enough oil from coconuts and fill the bamboo vessel with it to the very top . . . Into the bamboo he would immerse as many of his precious sticks as it could hold. Then he would stand the vessel in a corner of his room and would not bring out the sticks from it till ten days or a fortnight when he would let off a whoop of joy. For the sticks would be found to have taken on a rich brown colour and almost twice the weight they had before their protracted bath.[55]

The prose is economical and illustrative, giving the reader a rapid, intimate glimpse of a completely alien world. Unlike other Caribbean writers of this period, Seepersad Naipaul wrote only about what he knew. Part of his achievement was to shift between rival forms of the English language in order to show his world. The narrative is in standard English. Gurudeva speaks in dialect. When Ratni asks why he needs quite so many sticks, 'Gurudeva promptly silenced her with a slap. "Mind you' own business," he said. "Don' put goatmouth." '56 Mr Sohun the schoolmaster, who stands in for Seepersad in the narrative, speaks in educated English. He tells a baffled Gurudeva that Trinidad's pundits are more concerned with wearing sandalwood paste caste-marks than with learning how to read the scriptures: 'Not caste, but the shadow of caste remains in the West Indies,' he tells him. 'Its only use here is to inflate some people's ego.'57 In the final scene, where Gurudeva is hauled before the village council or panchayat for taking a second wife, the proceedings are conducted in Hindi. When a man accuses him of beating Ratni, Gurudeva stands up and shouts, ' "Why you don' keep you' dam mouth shut? Why you 'terrupting?" Pundit Shivlochan raised both hands to heaven and said: "No *Angrezi*, please! I do not understand *Angrezi*." '58 The shift in language and tone through these stories, written by a man who had taught himself English in early adulthood, is done effortlessly. The humour too is gently done. When fighters from a rival village arrive during Hosay, Gurudeva wraps a handkerchief around his jaw in a pugnacious manner and says he has toothache and a sprained wrist. Scowling in the direction of the enemy, he mutters, ' "It is lucky for them, though, that I get sick today. Odderwise I woulda show them." '59

Some writers spend a lifetime finding a style. They experiment, reject their forebears, imitate their contemporaries. Reinventing language is part of their literary ambition. Samuel Beckett, born in the same year as Pa, squeezed words in order to see what they might do. Modernist writers, and the deconstructionists and critical theorists who came in their wake, believed language is necessarily fictive and that its rupture might lead to creation; sometimes, in the work say of Ezra Pound or Virginia Woolf, they were right. Apart from a slight shift around the time he wrote *The Mimic Men*, V.S. Naipaul never went through a process of linguistic experimentation. He would circumnavigate Modernism, even as he absorbed its implications. His writing style formed early. At the age of only eleven, he was given his own private epic by his father, and took it as his model; his later achievement came out of this restriction. When he was asked – fifty-seven years on – by the Indian website *Tehelka* for some rules for aspiring writers, V.S. Naipaul's response owed much to Pa's instruction:

1. Do not write long sentences. A sentence should not have more than 10 or 12 words.

2. Each sentence should make a clear statement. It should add to the statement that went before. A good paragraph is a series of clear, linked statements.

3. Do not use big words. If your computer tells you that your average word is more than five letters long, there is something wrong. The use of small words compels you to think about what you are writing. Even difficult ideas can be broken down into small words.

4. Never use words whose meaning you are not sure of. If you break this rule you should look for other work.

5. The beginner should avoid using adjectives, except those of colour, size and number. Use as few adverbs as possible.

6. Avoid the abstract. Always go for the concrete.

7. Every day, for six months at least, practise writing in this way. Small words; short, clear, concrete sentences. It may be awkward but it's training you in the use of language. It may even be getting rid of the bad language habits you picked up at the university. You may go beyond these rules after you have thoroughly understood and mastered them.[60]

Seepersad's idea of literature, conceived in colonial isolation and arrived at by rejecting the florid Victorian tomes that had impressed him early on, became Vido's. Language was to be plain; where it became beautiful, it was through simplicity. To describe the process by which Gurudeva might turn a length of bamboo into a vessel for soaking sticks, Pa took only ten words: 'he would punch out all the compartments but the last'.

Gurudeva and other Indian Tales was the prequel to *A House for Mr Biswas*, and gave V.S. Naipaul the picaresque character of Ganesh for his first published book, *The Mystic Masseur*. In old age, he believed his father's book was under-appreciated, particularly by Indian critics, despite his attempts to promote it: 'No one in India knows that it's good writing. They think it's purely my sentimentality ... They wouldn't be able to compare it with Tolstoy's later writing, *Master and Man*. They wouldn't be able to compare it with *The Odyssey* or Gogol. They would think this is just peasant writing about peasant details. The more I look at it, the more I [can] see the actual way I write – very pictorial, very fast, the details. I knew that I had been given a feeling for language, and it was very beautiful, and it was my own epic.'[61]

CHAPTER FOUR

TO THE MOTHER COUNTRY

BY THE START OF 1945 the liberation of Europe was under way and the Second World War was coming to an end. Many West Indians had volunteered to fight, including thousands in the Royal Air Force and the Royal Canadian Air Force. The presence of American and British servicemen in Trinidad had precipitated social adjustment. Films, gum and raised hemlines came to town. As peace loomed, so did political change; the British empire was bankrupt, and decolonization was being discussed freely. Elections to the Legislative Council were planned for the following year, the first to be based on a universal franchise; Simbhoo would run unsuccessfully as a United Front candidate in Caroni.[1] In V.S. Naipaul's novel *The Suffrage of Elvira*, Mrs Baksh says, 'Everybody just washing their foot and jumping in this democracy business. But I promising you, for all the sweet it begin sweet, it going to end damn sour.'[2] Old conventions changed; where Droapatie and the Mausis wore clothes modelled on Indian fashions of centuries ago, they put their daughters in dresses. Some thought of trying to establish their own households outside the joint family. At the far end of Luis Street, a man named Tubal set up a brothel; when walking past, the cousins were instructed to cross the road and not look inside. Vido wrote later, 'The American soldiers loved a fat back-street whore, the blacker the better; they packed them into their jeeps and raced from club to club, throwing their money about ... Beside them the British soldiers were like foreigners ... they spoke this strange English; they referred to themselves as "blokes" ... not knowing that in Trinidad a bloke was a term of abuse; their uniforms, their shorts in particular, were ugly.'[3]

During the school term, the three-bedroomed house in Luis Street would be filled with children, sometimes more than two dozen staying overnight. At first they slept on the verandah, but then the verandah filled and the foul-smelling downstairs area beneath the house was used for accommodation. Nanie bought tables which were lined up in the basement to make a sleeping area. The boys slept on the north side of the house, the girls on the south. Each cousin would be given a pillow and a blanket made from stitched rice bags. To passers-by, it was a hilarious sight, the rows of Indian children stacked up on the tables under the house like peas in a pod; for the children, some now in their teens, the public mockery was humiliating. Nanie had Pahl cocoa bags sewn together and strung along the side of the house to protect them from view. Poker, the roguish descendant of an indentured labourer who had been on the same ship as Capildeo Maharaj, lived in the 'servant room' in the yard. More relations arrived, and at its high or low point, 17 Luis Street was inhabited by up to forty people. For Ma and Pa, the situation was complicated by the unforeseen arrival in February 1945 of another child, a boy named Shivadhar Srinivasa, known as Sewan or Shivan. One day when Vido was coming home from school he took shelter from the rain. 'It was a custom of the place, if it begins to rain, you can go to the verandah of any house – just one of these civilities which we took for granted and didn't fully understand. So I went to a house. It was a Negro house, not far from where we lived and I heard them talking about us. About how we were all crowded in that little house, and I was so ashamed.'⁴ He protected himself by imagining a life elsewhere.

In August, his uncle Rudranath returned after more than six years away in England on his scholarship. He had forsaken medicine for mathematics, and there was talk that he would be offered a place on the faculty at London University, where he was doing a PhD on 'the flexure problem in elasticity'. Rudranath was treated as a conquering hero, an expert on all things, the new head of the family, displacing his elder brother Simbhoo. He was particularly friendly with his young female relatives. Mira remembered him on his return as 'very charming. He liked to flirt with the girls, with the nieces, he was like the darling uncle, playing tennis with everyone.' He took it upon himself to educate them in mathematics, and if anyone failed to understand, he would go into a fury. Mira recalled him beating Sati with his belt. 'She couldn't do some mathematical problem he had asked her. I remember being very upset because she was my sister.'⁵ Rudranath's son Rudy remembered his father as 'a great intellect but a restless soul. He used sarcasm all the time, the one-line quip that would cut you off at the knees. He thought of the Naipauls as the lesser side of the family.'⁶

Naturally, Rudranath was given a room of his own at Luis Street, and the rest of the family had to squeeze tighter. Pa was riven by distress at his own impotence, although his situation was improving. *Gurudeva* had been noticed by Dora Ibberson, a British woman who was starting a new social welfare department for the Trinidad government. She asked Seepersad if he would like to make a survey of the rural Indian community. A car came with the job, and a salary twice that of the *Guardian*. He accepted, but as he prepared to go to Jamaica for six months of training, he fell ill with nerves. Dora Ibberson arranged for the whole family to be taken by car to the sea at Toco, their first and only family holiday, and one of many events that would later be fictionalized in *A House for Mr Biswas*. While Pa was away in Jamaica, it was decided by Nanie and her sons that the extensive Capildeo landholdings and properties would be divided. Nanie took a firmly patrilineal view: the boys would inherit. Each Mausi was given a small plot of land, and the more influential sons-in-law were ousted, creating a lasting family rift. Pa dismissed the gift of land as a con, calling the agricultural plots, 'swamp lands, lagoon lands, rice lands, big deal!'[7] For him, the Capildeo brothers were now a pair of gangster bosses: Capo S. and Capo R.

Still, Pa had a new job and a Ford Prefect – licence plate PA1192. What he lacked was a place of his own. Port of Spain with its 100,000 inhabitants was full of people, and little new housing had been built there during the war. He did not even have space for his few pieces of furniture. In his little room at the back of Luis Street, Pa railed against Capo R., his words being carried through the air vents to other rooms. Ma tried to maintain the peace. Capo R. responded, and unforgivable insults were hurled around the little house. The children were shocked by the things the adults were saying, swearing at each other viciously across the partitions between the rooms. Vido remembered the obscenities and the sense of entrapment, while he was meant to be revising for his Senior Cambridge exam: 'In the crowded place below the floor [where the children slept] the air was bad and I suffered terribly from nausea. People were cooking on kerosene stoves. I had asthma. I really felt pushed to the limit there. My schoolwork suffered, and the report of my form master for 1946 says, "Has gone backwards rapidly." And indeed I had.'[8] He disliked the communal food at Luis Street: fried breadfruit, curried vegetables, concoctions made of chatagne (a local chestnut), and the ubiquitous roti, a Trinidadian reworking of the Indian flatbread, rolled up into a parcel with a filling of spiced chickpeas or goat meat.

Mira remembered the tension between Pa and Ma: 'There were times when he would say horrible things to her, and would actually throw china and food. I remember he would throw things at the wall out of anger.'[9] In desperation, Seepersad approached his only wealthy relative, Sookdeo Misir, and asked for a loan to buy a property. He only had the first $1,300 of the purchase price. Without collateral, he was lent $4,000 or £833 (the Trinidad & Tobago dollar was pegged at £1:$4.80, and both sterling and the US dollar were legal tender). It was a substantial debt, but it enabled Pa to buy a house in the run-down Indian district of St James, to the north-west of Woodbrook. Number 26 Nepaul Street was a box, a hot, rickety, partitioned building near the end of the street, around 7 square metres on two floors with an external wooden staircase and a corrugated iron roof.[10] On the last day of 1946, the Naipaul family moved in. The upper floor sagged in the middle, but as Kamla said, 'It was our home, the first home we ever had.'[11]

At once, the dynamic between the parents and the children shifted: they became a unit, a nuclear family, a father, mother, brothers and sisters. Seepersad was just forty, Droapatie thirty-three, Kamla sixteen, and Vidia, Sati, Mira and Savi descended in two-year decrements; Sewan was ten months old. They had greater freedom now to do as they liked, without the sanctions of the joint family. Kamla and Vido could travel around Port of Spain on foot, or ride one of the new trolleybuses that had replaced the trams. The house was rarely locked, and one day they returned to find it ransacked: the 'thief' was Pa, playing a practical joke, which the children did not find amusing. He would dress up and take them and the cousins on excursions to the sea in the Prefect. 'Seepersad would drive us down to Dhein's Bay for a sea-bathe,' his nephew Suren, Simbhoo's son, remembered. 'He was a lazy, easy-going character, always chain-smoking. All these sons-in-law were lazy sons-of-bitches who specialized in not working. Any needs that [Droapatie] Mausi had, she would come to us.'[12] Brahm saw the situation in a different light: 'Seepersad was very kind taking us to the beaches. Looking back, I think he was ostracized by the family, especially Simbhoo and Rudranath because he could match them with his intelligence, he didn't feel inferior to anybody. He was very calm in his own way, and always had a sense of orderliness. Plus Seepersad had a heightened white colour, he stood out. Some of the neighbours on the street when we were playing would call him pale white.'[13]

'To try to put it in a moral context,' said Savi later, 'my father always disliked the way the Capildeos did things, and therefore we were taught to question the way things were done. I would describe them, the Capildeo boys, as pretty rotten: their jealousies, their selfishness, their pettiness to anybody who showed any sign of any ability. I remember Simbhoo's comment when Kamla wore lipstick for the first time: "Is your mouth bleeding?" These were the types of comments that were made . . . I remember Sewan going to Simbhoo one day as a little boy and they invited him to eat and he didn't want to sit on the floor or eat with his hands. Simbhoo's comment was, "And you haven't even gone to Oxford as yet." [My husband] did not like Simbhoonath because when he got married to me, an ordinary lowly niece, we went to a function at his house and he asked us whether we would eat in the kitchen. That's the man.'[14]

Mira remembered Capo S. during the years after they moved to Nepaul Street as 'very intimidating, serious. He was always prowling in the car looking for the nieces and the nephews who might be breaking the rules of the family. I remember seeing his car pass by and being actually scared even though I had permission to go to the movies with this guy.'[15] The girls and Ma did all the ironing, washing, polishing, cooking and cleaning at Nepaul Street. Savi felt that, as the son, 'Vidia was always catered to in the household from when he was a young child – by my mother, my father, all siblings without exception. He has always expected people to support him.'[16]

As well as developing an interest in film at this time, and visiting the Port of Spain cinemas – the Rialto, the Deluxe, the London – Vido sent letters around the world, seeking some sense of what was happening elsewhere. Enid W. Schuette of *Time* magazine in New York told him that most *Time* readers were indeed American, and sent a batch of stamps for his collection. The secretary general of the Royal Empire Society in London informed him that he had received an 'honourable mention' in that year's essay competition. A New Zealand postmaster put him in touch with a penfriend, although he already had one, Gordon Peterson of Taunton School in England, who wrote saying that the cross-country run had been rained off, and asked whether there was an ice-rink in Trinidad. Vidia's favoured penfriend, however, was a girl named Beverly in Hawaii. A fortnight before leaving Luis Street, aged all of fourteen, he had written her a letter in his best courtly style:

My Dear Beverly,

I have looked in vain for my pen, and so I have been forced to write this letter in pencil, imitating the example set by you in your first letter.

I have received your charming letter, the more charming postcards and the yet more charming photograph of yourself. I guess that sums up what I feel about you, especially when we consider how beautiful the postcards were . . .

We have much in common with Hawaii – tropical scenes, the allure of a moonlight night, etc. Perhaps you have heard about our calypsoes. They are world famous. It was a Trinidadian – a Negro – who made up the calypso about 'Rum and Coca-Cola'. If you have not heard it you certainly have missed something. The best part of it runs like this:

'The Andrews Sisters and Bing Crosby
Should make a trip to the West Indies,
Siddong (= sit down) under de (= the) silvery moon
Lissening (= listening) to dem (= them) calypsonian croon.'

It would be very amusing to tell you how native Trinidadians speak English – the uneducated ones, of course.

'Marnin' me darlin'. And how is de baby? 'E still got the fever? Why you don' try geeing (= giving) 'im some shinin' bush.'

'Po' me! De amount a t'ings I try to send 'way dat fever, me eh know what to try again. Ah go tek him to the Healt' Office.'

Now here are the ways a word 'lick' is used.

'Ah go lick in she features wid a rock stone' = I will smash her face with a stone.

'This road lickin' up me tire, man' = But this road is eating up my tire.

'Lick the stamp' = Literal meaning . . .

Friday I went to see the 'Hurricane' – quite an old picture.
I can't think of any more to write, so
Cheerio,
Vidia.[17]

Beverly's reply does not survive, so there is no way of knowing whether she was able to distinguish between Trinidadians, native Trinidadians and Vidia Naipaul.

*

Vido was not alone in trying out a new style or identity, in presenting himself as a sophisticate. It was not rare in Trinidad for people to remake themselves, to change their name or adjust their background. The 'smart-man' who managed to deceive others cleverly was much admired in Trinidad, like the hustler in *The Middle Passage* who sold tickets for a fictitious Sam Cooke concert, and disappeared:

> Three youths were talking about this affair one afternoon around a coconut-cart near the Savannah.
> The Indian said, 'I don't see how anybody could vex with the man. *That* is brains.'
> 'Is what my aunt say,' one of the Negro boys said. 'She ain't feel she get rob. She feel she pay two dollars for the *intelligence*.'[18]

With so little common heritage between communities, attributes could be borrowed and people could 'play themselves'. Adrian Cola Rienzi had once been Krishna Deonarine; Mr Ramprasad became Mr Ablack; Mr Meighoo became Mr Mayhew; Ganesh Ramsumair in *The Mystic Masseur* would become G. Ramsay Muir; Pa sometimes signed an article Paul Nye or Paul Prye. It was necessary to have a public face, since whatever your ethnicity you could be sure that aspects of your home life, the familiar indoor world, would be culturally alien to those you met outside. Lloyd Best, a black boy two years younger than Vidia at QRC who was sponsored through school by Sookdeo Misir, expressed it this way: 'The most important single feature of Trinidadian culture is the extent to which masks are indispensable, because there are so many different cultures and ethnicities in this country that people have to play a vast multiplicity of roles, each of which has got its own mask depending on where they are. It's true of the whole Caribbean, and Trinidad is the extreme case in my view.'[19]

Almost nobody knew their real personal history. They might come from West Africa, or Venezuela, or Madeira, or south India, or from some complicated intermingling of ancestry, travels through different places; only in exceptional cases would the family journey be clear. Each community was divided and subdivided. Among Indians there were Hindus, Muslims and Christians; among the Hindus, there were caste divisions; among Indian Christians, there were Anglicans, Presbyterians and Roman Catholics. People of African descent followed a multiplicity of Christian faiths, and had little sense at this time of African brotherhood, or of a united black heritage. At the heart of Trinidad lay the void, the void of dispossession and extermination: the unexpressed knowledge that the land had once belonged to someone else, the Amerindians who had been killed or chased away. The spirit of the dispossessed could be felt, as it can be in parts of the American West. Even Trinidadians of probable Amerindian descent had no way of knowing whether their forebears had lived there at the time of Columbus's arrival. For everyone, Trinidad was a borrowed island; only after independence was there an active attempt to create and shape a shared 'Trini' identity.

A pupil at QRC might come from a background that belied his physical appearance, like Hok in *The Mimic Men*, a boy who owes something to Yip Young. Passing his mother while walking with other pupils, Hok ignores her, until he is sent back by his teacher to greet her: 'She was indeed a surprise, a Negro woman of the people, short and rather fat, quite unremarkable.'[20] Vido strove to keep his home and school lives discrete, and tried not to be perceived merely as another offshoot of the Capildeo clan. He wanted to be himself, and himself alone. In Savi's recollection, 'He never invited a schoolfriend into the house. We never understood. He stood at the gate talking to them.' Nor did he like other guests. 'When people came to visit, even when family came, he would leave the books downstairs because he studied on the dining table and race upstairs to tell us that people were downstairs. He would not go and open the door and say come in. I guess he was shy. He couldn't cope with it.'[21] Vido claimed later to have had no friends at QRC, although others considered him a popular boy. 'At school I had only admirers; I had no friends.' This is disingenuous; he had friends, but kept much of himself hidden from them. Later in life, he would deliberately avoid friendship for fear it might make him less distinctive, less singular. 'It is important not to trust people too much. Friendship might be turned against you in a foolish way, and you must not impose yourself to that extent on anyone. Burdening them with your trust. It is a burden. Friendship has not been important to me.' The tensions and double-crossings of Petit Valley and Luis Street made him permanently wary and protean, a trait that would become more extreme and self-referential as the years passed: 'I profoundly feel that people are letting you down all the time.'[22]

Pa had reacted to the complexities of his own background by embracing Indianness while rejecting orthodox Hinduism, or what in Trinidad was known as 'Sanatanism'. In August 1947 India gained independence, and like its new leader Jawaharlal Nehru, Pa believed in religious and cultural reform. Hinduism had regulations on all things: clothing, ritual pollution, caste distinction, bodily functions, diet. The Naipaul family were not vegetarian, as most Brahmins are supposed to be; they sometimes ate meat, and treated chicken as a vegetable. At Christmas they would celebrate with baked fowl, dalpuri, nuts and fruit. Following the principles of the Arya Samaj, Pa believed in Hinduism as a philosophical system and thought that old rituals should be swept away. He particularly disliked the island's orthodox Brahmin pundits, whom he knew were often phoneys and hustlers. Hindu missionaries from India visited Trinidad, and a divide developed between 'Sanatanists' and 'Samajists'. Vidia, as a rationalist and his father's son, rejected the group activities linked to caste. His grandmother would hold public readings of the scriptures at the Lion House and 17 Luis Street, at which her grandsons would sit at the front and be fed first, displaying their caste status. When other teenage boys in the Capildeo clan had their heads shaved as part of the sacred thread ceremony, to show they were Brahmins, Vidia refused to take part. At the same time, he maintained the pride in caste that was the identifying force in his mother's family. He wrote later that during a science class at school he had refused to put his mouth to a length of tubing, and 'an Indian boy in the row behind, a Port of Spain boy, a recognized class tough, whispered, "Real brahmin". His tone was approving.'[23]

Like Nanie, Pa and Ma believed in education as the route to progress. Kamla and Vido, both gifted academically, were encouraged to study for foreign scholarships. At first, Vido's commitment was tentative. At the end of the second term of 1947, his school report said he was being slack, and that although a pupil of 'real ability . . . he is not giving of his best'. A term later his form master wrote: 'There is still much room for improvement, however, and in the literature he must show greater balance in his judgements if he is to gain the double distinction he seeks.'[24] Balance was never to be his strong point, but he would achieve distinction. The turning point in his attitude came during a conversation in the cricket nets with William Demas, his senior by two years, who had just won an island scholarship to Cambridge University in England. Vido remembered: 'I told him that I wanted to win the scholarship too, and said I'm going to start working soon. He said, you mustn't say that, what you must say is, I'm going to go home now and start working. I followed his advice. I have always remembered his advice. He did economics at Cambridge and later became governor of the Central Bank of Trinidad.'[25] From the summer of 1947, Vido concentrated on the scholarship, specializing in French and Spanish literature and Roman history. He thought the emphasis on learning at QRC arose from 'the general atmosphere in the colonial world: it was a special school and we owed something to our school, we owed it to ourselves. And you see the rewards were so few. There was only one scholarship in each subject. So you had to come tops. So it bred a lot of neurosis too as a result.'[26]

To Mira, four years his junior, Vidia seemed to be a solitary, scholarly figure, less sociable than other members of the family. His books were kept at one end of the dining table in Nepaul Street, on a section that was made of lighter wood. For her, 'that was like his little desk, his study. He was definitely privileged. We were just pesky little sisters. We regarded him as being very bright. Eggs were very hard to come by, and I always remember that Vido would get the scrambled egg and not us because he had to study for his exams. It was very important. I think it was because he was the boy who might go somewhere. He needed the nourishment of the eggs and I think I love eggs because Vido got the eggs!'[27] Savi remembered him working hard and exercising hard, and often going swimming. Indoors he talked to her, but outside the house it was as if she did not exist: 'The only time Vidia spoke to Mira and I was the day Gandhi died. He said, "Gandhi was assassinated." I am not too sure we knew the meaning of the word assassinated at that point. We got the message. Otherwise he rode past us on his bicycle almost every day. We were little girls, nuisances.'[28]

With or without the benefit of eggs, and while also helping to care for little Sewan, Kamla was the first winner of a new scholarship for the island's Indian girls to study at Benares Hindu University in India. It was an exceptional achievement; and she looked good too. While Kamla prepared for her departure in summer 1949, she took a temporary job at the *Guardian*. Melvyn Akal, who came from an Indian Presbyterian family and would later marry Savi, said Kamla was renowned as a beauty by the boys at QRC: 'I knew of her because at school boys would be teasing Vidia and saying, "How are you brother-in-law? How is Kamla today?"[29] Too glamorous for schoolboys, Kamla began a romance instead with Sam Selvon, a handsome man in his mid-twenties who had been a wireless operator during the war, and was now working as a news reporter at the *Guardian*. Although he came from an Indian family, Selvon had a Scottish grandfather and was creolized in a way that was anathema to the Naipauls and the Capildeos. Besides this, he was a skilful aspiring writer, and Kamla had to make sure the relationship remained hidden from Pa and the family.

Vido became increasingly serious as he worked for his exam, the Higher School Certificate: he believed his future depended on it, and asserted later that without a scholarship abroad he would have been doomed. 'By the time I was about twelve, I had decided to get away, to leave. The scholarship protects you, gives you money for some years. It is protection.'[30] To succeed, he would need to beat not only his talented contemporaries at QRC but pupils from good schools such as St Mary's and Naparima College in San Fernando. There were only four scholarships available for the whole island — two more than there had been during wartime. In March 1949 the results were published: Vidia Naipaul had failed to win a scholarship. The family were depressed, and silent. Vido was tormented. At this point, it turned out that QRC had misread the new guidelines for the exam, and he had sat the wrong combination of papers. He had, however, achieved a distinction in both French and Spanish. His uncle Rudranath wrote from England offering congratulations and condolences.

A front-page story in the *Guardian* headlined 'Special "Schol" Urged for QRC Student' stated: 'Government will be asked by the Education Board to grant a special scholarship to V.S. Naipaul of Queen's Royal College who took Modern Studies in the last year's Cambridge Higher School Certificate Examination. At yesterday afternoon's meeting of the board, Mr R. Hamer, principal of the college said that, owing to a lack of understanding of the regulations at Q.R.C. very few pupils in the modern studies group were eligible for a scholarship ... Mr Hamer proposed that the Board ask the Government to grant him a special scholarship ... Unanimous approval was given to Mr. Hamer's proposal.'[31] Since they were already planning to increase the total number of foreign scholarships, the Trinidad government concurred. Vidia said, 'There were articles in the press, and there were letters from Negroes who didn't like the idea of me getting a scholarship. The thing about being sixteen and having letters against one – I got used to criticism at an early age. I got used to being attacked in the press. It was an early baptism.'[32] Looking back, conditioned by a sense of his own destiny, he claimed to see his victory as a grand moment of survival. 'It's one of these lucky things in my life which I just squeaked through.' Without a scholarship, 'I think I would have gone crazy. I would not have accepted it and I think that is why my friend Yip Young killed himself shortly after I left. He thought he had no future. I could have been destroyed at many stages. If I lost, I would have collapsed. The stakes were always big in my own mind ... In these primitive societies the main talent is intrigue. Shall we say the Negroes of Trinidad excel only in intrigue, in government department intrigue? They excel in that. I would never have done it well.'[33]

At the end-of-year Sixth Form party, held in the gym at QRC, Vido was on lively form, displaying a talent that was not purely cerebral. His cousin Jai watched him show off before a female audience, the sisters and friends of his classmates. 'He was in front of a line of girls enjoying himself, doing acrobatics, doing flips, bending right back onto his hands. It was fun for everybody. He was very much the joker, very much the acrobat.'[34] He also had a reputation for being cynical and acerbic, and for taking a line that was different from everyone else. One boy, labelled 'banal' by Naipaul, had to go home and look up the word in a dictionary. Lloyd Best recalled how he would 'hold court' in front of other boys at QRC, expressing his views on cricket or the world, or pillorying any contemporaries who did not come up to scratch. 'He always saw society from one angle, different from everybody else, even when he was in school. That's why I say that he was always holding court. Because he had a point of view that was very different from everybody else.'[35] A schoolboy pose, an attitude intended to distinguish himself from others which had initially been borrowed from his father and his uncle Rudranath, was to become integral to his personality.

Vido wanted to go to Britain that autumn to study English literature, but the education board decided he was too young, and should wait until 1950. His chosen destination was Oxford University, but a college had first to accept his application. Although he had it retouched, he was worried the photograph that accompanied his entrance forms made his face look fat. His application was circulated around the Oxford colleges and picked up by Peter Bayley, a Fellow in English at University College who was impressed above all by his photograph and his ethnicity. Bayley recalled: 'A dossier, with photograph, smiling Indian boy, you can imagine, charming little Indian boy he looked ... a very distinguished achievement from his big grammar school in Port of Spain. And because I loved India and had many Indian friends, because of being there for nearly four years in the war, I just didn't hesitate, just took him ... I don't remember any references. I was terribly pro-Indian, and in fact I very deliberately used to take Indians in the college ... In those days you admitted your own people for your own subject. Vidia, when he came to me, had been turned down by five or six colleges.'[36]

William Demas, studying in Cambridge, sent 'My dear Naipaul' a letter: 'I must offer you my sincere congratulations both on your Schol. and on your double distinction. That's quite a feat ... You must be feeling exhilarated at the prospect of escaping from the "hole" and seeking "freedom" in the Mother Country. I think you will enjoy Oxford, for if conditions here apply to Oxford, there will be quite a lot of "arty-crafty" people, discussing the latest Art exhibition, and what not.'[37] Demas's words are interesting: the idea of wanting to escape, of referring to Trinidad as a 'hole' and believing there was no future for an ambitious person in the Caribbean, was common at this time, and by no means restricted to those of Indian descent. He followed up with a second letter advising Naipaul to bring woollen underwear, grey flannel or corduroy trousers, a sports jacket and a tweed suit to England. An overcoat could be purchased on arrival. 'My allowance of £60 was not sufficient. But I think you will find it sufficient, as you wear much smaller sizes than I.' Demas had visited Oxford, and found it to be like a miniature London, though with a medieval atmosphere. As for himself, he was working hard and had met several 'frivolous Continental girls' at the International Club. He concluded: 'A word of warning. Cynicism is no longer in fashion among students. I think your stay here will cure you completely of yours.'[38]

In the meantime Vido needed a job, since Pa was about to lose his. After his survey of Indian villages was complete, Dora Ibberson's department was abolished and Pa was taken on by the probation service. He was supposed to monitor released prisoners in the Chaguanas area, but it was not a success. Now he was applying high and low for another position, and the family was seriously short of money. Eventually, after several months out of work, he was hired again by the *Guardian*. Despite looming political change, the paper still concentrated on British and imperial news. A front page might be headlined 'Britain Will Not Revalue Pound' or 'Eire To Break Free From Empire' or even 'King's Health Improves'. A picture would show white people setting off from Port of Spain on a ship bound for England, or 'debutantes' in the Queen's Park Hotel ballroom, or a British MP arriving in Trinidad. Inside, there might be a large photograph of an English aristocrat walking through Hyde Park, for no apparent reason, or a headline such as 'Late Baronet Praised'. Politicians and titled people from England fulfilled a function that would later be taken by celebrities.

On his seventeenth birthday, Vido was given a job at the Red House where his cousin Owad worked (it had been painted red as a patriotic gesture to mark the diamond jubilee of Queen Victoria). He copied out birth and death certificates in the Registrar General's Office on a salary of $75 a month, or around £370 in modern terms. Using his first earnings, he bought his mother a set of bamboo wall vases, which touched her. For several months, an acting second-class clerk, he had to sit at a table facing a wall painted in green distemper surrounded by hefty ledgers that smelled of fish glue. In 1994 he would publish a redolent account of this period, 'History: A Smell of Fish Glue' in *A Way in the World*. It was a 'very dull job', Mr Hamer said in a letter, and he deserved something better; he would put in a word at the Caribbean Commission, which was supposed to be planning the region's future.[39] Nothing came of it, and in January 1950 Hamer gave him a temporary post as 'secretary and relieving master' at QRC on a salary of $139.96 a month. 'Good, isn't it?' Vido suggested to Kamla. 'Teaching is fun. I enjoy it very much and everyone remarks how well I look, not pale and sickly as when I used to copy out certificates.' The pupils liked him. 'When I came into the hall last Friday – boxing night, all the boys cheered me as one man.'[40]

He also gave tuition to some of his cousins such as Jai and Sita, Simbhoo's daughter, and taught English to older pupils at Tranquillity with WAGS, Winston Springer. Each day he and WAGS would go for lunch together and smoke cigarettes. Vido got on well with Johnny Chen-Wing, a tall, orphaned fourteen-year-old, the only Chinese boy in the class. Chen-Wing's uncle kept a grocery store, and he would take packets of Raleigh cigarettes and give them to his teacher. He found Mr Naipaul 'small, very interesting, handsome, an inspirational teacher. Instead of teaching the syllabus, he would teach what he was interested in ... He had holes in his shoes I remember, when he put his feet up on the desk. He would read prodigiously: Maugham, Forster, V.S. Pritchett, G.B. Shaw as well as French and Spanish writers, Molière and Baudelaire, two books a night.' Chen-Wing thought that by going to Oxford, Naipaul missed out on the period of ferment that led to independence. '[In the 1940s] you could walk freely in the streets of Port of Spain. The unrest, the discontent between Negroes and Asians became much worse, more pronounced, after the 1950s.'[41]

In his spare time, Vido went to art classes at the British Council, where he was complimented on his 'bold' style of painting. He did accomplished sketches. At home he would try to hone his literary skills by writing descriptions of landscape or Port of Spain scenes in turquoise ink in a notebook. He reviewed a book by Somerset Maugham in the QRC *Chronicle*, and another by an Indian author for a four-page monthly magazine called *The Hindu* that Simbhoo was publishing. He tried doing a tough street story, but despite its arresting opening – 'Carlos Antonio was buried today' – it soon became confused.[42] For several weeks Vido worked on 'How They Made a Queen', a description of a beauty pageant he had attended at the Rialto cinema. It attempted to be light and sophisticated, but became wordy and lapsed into cliché: 'The general hum was punctuated by bursts of applause which greeted the entry of well-known local characters.' He tried to ridicule the compère, but was more interested in the beauties, although he did his best to hide this. One was deemed to be 'a short, plump thing who could have been the model for Maupassant's Boule de Suif.' Another was 'a not displeasing blend of contradictory racial types. Her eyes and cheekbones proclaimed her Chinese; but her nose and lips belied that influence. Her colour was of appetizing ginger-bread.'[43] Looking back, loftily examining his own trajectory, he thought the beauty contest had been 'a shabby occasion' and he lacked the knowledge to write about it: 'What was the basis of the writer's attitude? What other world did he know, what other experience did he bring to his way of looking? How could a writer write about this world, if it was the only world he knew?'[44]

*

Kamla's departure for the east in the summer of 1949 had caused Ma and Pa great distress, knowing it would be years before they saw her again. Mira remembered the journey to the docks as being like 'a death in the family. It was so sad. The whole family, millions of us, went to the wharf to wave goodbye and send her off to India; and India was truly an unknown land.'[45] Afterwards Vido went upstairs at 26 Nepaul Street and cried silently with his face buried in the pillow on Kamla's bed.

She soon had news for him from England, secret news about Rudranath. 'Mamoo [mother's brother] is married. He has an intelligent, healthy looking son, 4½ years old. His wife is typically English. She is not ugly.'[46] Kamla was staying with him in his house in Surrey; he had been hospitable, and lent her money in case of disaster in India. Everything was unfamiliar. She advised Vido to borrow a book from the library and learn table manners before coming to England. Excited by her trip, he wrote back, 'Britain is a civilized country and safe. People don't have to boast about Ancient Culture; they have their culture and don't seek apologies for the lack of it in boasting about past achievement . . . Don't worry. This is Adventure . . . Don't let those damned Indians get you into any fancy arrangements – their luxury passages & luxury hotel accommodation. Find out the price of everything.' He admired her ability to be 'a favourite . . . I cut a pretty ridiculous figure wherever I go – a rather comic little boy, amusingly precocious, whose ideas and whose habits are only amusing and have little weight. I don't think I make friends; and I am too light to influence other people. I want to write; but I doubt if any writer had a poor imagination as I.'[47] Kamla was doing an interview on the BBC West Indian service, and Pa wrote her words of advice: 'Don't say scholarship to make Indians more Indian. Don't say Indians and non-Indians culturally apart. Say they are merging their cultures into one. We know it isn't true, but don't worry.' As for Vido, Pa reported to Kamla, 'He is nauseatingly rude to me, of course, as he has always been, but that is all.'[48]

Away from his older sister, Vido maintained the closeness of their relationship by telling her news from home, and trying out his opinions. 'Jane Austen appears to be essentially a writer for women; if she had lived in our age she would undoubtedly have been a leading contributor to the women's papers. Her work really bored me. It is mere gossip.' Still on the attack, he praised Beverley Nichols's controversial book *Verdict on India*. 'He went to India in 1945, and saw a wretched country, full of pompous mediocrity, with no future. He saw the filth; refused to mention the "spiritualness" that impresses another kind of visitor. Of course the Indians did not like the book, but I think he was telling the truth. From Nehru's autobiography, I think the Premier of India is a first-class showman with a host of third-rate supporters. I don't know whether I could agree with Nichols' condemnation of Gandhi as a shrewd politician, using his saintliness as a weapon of rule. But I am sure it has a certain basis in fact.'[49] He knew that Kamla would be entertained and interested by what he thought, and that he could write freely. The result was a vigorous, contentious prose that streaked ahead of the prissy writing in 'How They Made a Queen'.

Her letters back to him were often admonitory. When he reached Britain, she advised, 'Try your best & keep out of the company of West Indians . . . And I beg of you Vido do not get yourself mixed up with any English girl. I don't have to tell you the consequences.' She found Benares Hindu University to be ill-disciplined, and the food there 'spiced to the highest'. As for India, 'Once you get accustomed to the dirt, everything is just fine.'[50] With her Caribbean dresses and shorter hair, Kamla Naipaul was different from the other girls at Benares Hindu University, and viewed as fast and vociferous. When she spoke out on behalf of the students over a problem at the hostel, the vice-chancellor told her she should keep quiet because she was not Indian. The little Hindi she spoke was derided as 'dehati' or rustic, her language influenced by the Bhojpuri spoken by Indians in Trinidad; she said 'tharia' for thali (a metal plate) and 'murai' for mooli (the vegetable).[51] In October, after a cousin sent her a gossipy letter, she advised Vidia against drinking alcohol and smoking excessively. He was angered. 'My dear little fool, You are the damnedest ass. Your letter amused me as I read the first few lines; then it became grotesque. You are a silly stupid female, after all. I fancy you rather enjoyed writing that plea to a wayward brother. It made you a heroine à la Hollywood. Listen, my dear "very pretty" Miss Naipaul . . . For three weeks past, I have been smoking. As much as with Springer and Co. when you were here. That is bad, isn't it? I have been drinking excessively? Well, yes, water.'

The force and vigour of their conversations by letter reflected the way they spoke at home, and Vido could talk to Kamla with greater honesty than anyone else. 'My stay in Trinidad is drawing to a close,' he wrote. 'I only have nine months left. Then I shall go away – never to come back, as I trust. I think I am at heart really a loafer. Intellectualism is merely fashionable sloth. That is why I think I am going to be either a big success or an unheard-of failure. But I am prepared for anything. I want to satisfy myself that I have lived as I wanted to live. As yet I feel that the philosophy I will have to expand in my books is only superficial. I am longing to see something of life.' It was grand, it was ambitious, but Kamla understood his dreams. He offered to find her a publisher if she wrote an account of her stay in India. 'Pa can put me on to Rodin, the star-writer of England's *Daily Express*.' By the end of the year, he was assailed by a 'feeling of fatigue – both mental and physical . . . You may laugh, but I am in love. That is why I have not read or written you or written anything into my book. And can you guess who is the female? – Golden . . . She never let me go far. To date, she hasn't even allowed me to kiss her . . . You won't tell any of the people home any of this, will you? . . . I promise you I won't let anything improper take place . . . I want to get away from this stagnating atmosphere into something more vivacious and stimulating. A sane man, if placed in a lunatic asylum, soon goes mad.'[52]

Golden, or Golon, was his mother's cousin. She lived in San Fernando in the south of the island, but since Trinidad was so small he could go there and back at weekends. Pa and Ma knew of the infatuation, but did not take it seriously. Golden was a few years older than Vido, and the relationship never progressed. He described the experience later as 'calf love, hopeless adolescent love. I thought she was very beautiful.'[53] While his black friends such as WAGS were having teenage sexual adventures, Vidia remained a virgin. Later, he would blame his slow sexual start and inability to seduce on Indian or Hindu culture, rather than on his own secretive, fastidious personality. Younger than the other boys in his class at QRC and coming from a different cultural background, he was not sure how to get started. Most of his knowledge of love affairs and intimacy came from reading books, and he despised his more adventurous contemporaries for their sensuality even while he envied them. Around this time, or possibly after Vido's departure for England, Pa began an affair with a woman he had met through his work on the *Guardian*, who lived in the heart of Port of Spain. 'I know there were stories about him having girlfriends,' said Mira. 'My father liked to take care of himself, to look nice and all that.'[54] According to Suren, quoting old family gossip, 'Seepersad had a woman in Pembroke Street, a Red woman, and Droapatie found out about her. I think she gave him a beating. Droapatie exuded a power, like her sisters. She was the boss.'[55]

As he prepared to depart for England in August 1950, aged not quite eighteen, Vido was highly educated, intelligent, ambitious and emotionally immature. He had been brought up on the idea that boys deserved special treatment by virtue of their sex, but his life so far had been influenced by strong women: Nanie, Ma and Kamla. Vido disliked his maternal uncles, even though he was obliged to respect them. His father was depressive, literary and bad at holding down a job. The other men in the Capildeo clan were castrated by their subordinate position, perceived by those in power to be lazy sons-of-bitches. In his writing, Vido would revere his father, elevating him as an exemplar and applying a degree of sympathy and compassion to him that was lacking in his treatment of other people. He attempted to depict Pa as a special and deserving case because he was serving the cause of literature. His practical failings and his involvement in the Trinidad hustle were set aside. Only in old age would Vidia begin to wonder whether his father was to blame for many of the deprivations of his childhood. In 2007 he said, 'I feel great rage against my father for having all these children, and not protecting them.'[56] In his later writing he would blank the role of his mother, who together with her family was central to the opportunities he was given to better himself. Mira remembered Ma as being particularly fond of her elder son. 'I know my mother adored Vido. She really did. It was this thing about the male. I felt that she was such a caregiver and a good mother because we didn't have the money – it was subsistence living really – and yet we had meals every day.'[57]

Vido was setting out for a country that had been presented to him as the epicentre of civilization. Each aspect of his education had emerged from overseas, yet he had no personal knowledge of Britain or the British. There were a few English boys and white Trinidadians at QRC, but as Eddoes says to Hat in *Miguel Street*, ' "You ain't know what you talking about, Hat. How much white people you know?" '[58] Vido was schooled in a way of working that should assure his success at Oxford, but he had no first-hand experience of social customs in post-war Britain or of the reality of life there for an Indian or West Indian. Lloyd Best would later popularize the term 'Afro-Saxon' to describe people of his generation who were able to flourish in British institutions by adopting the mask of the master, with the consequence that they were deracinated from the culture that gave birth to them. Vido, following in the footsteps of Rudranath Capildeo and a few other Indian island scholars, was an early Indo-Saxon. At the end of the scholarship process, what would he do – stay in Britain or return to the West Indies, or get a job with the government of independent India, as Pa suggested? At Oxford, what would be expected? Were his manners good enough? Would he have to restrain his opinions, and speak quietly in public places? Would he be lonely? Chekhov had written, after travelling to the penal colony of Sakhalin, that longing for the homeland was sufficient reason for a man with broken nerves to go insane. Would the natives of London behave like the white people in books and cinema newsreels? In the days before commercial television and the internet, the opportunity to comprehend or even see how another culture operated was minimal. For Vido, everything that lay ahead would be alien, although seemingly familiar.

On 1 August 1950, the day of his departure, he woke early and hardened his heart. He would not show distress. Since no ships were sailing for England on a suitable date, he would be flying to New York to sail from there. At Luis Street, saying goodbye, he heard that the aeroplane was delayed. He waited in anxiety for three hours, talking and not talking. Finally, he put his luggage in the Prefect and Pa drove him away from Port of Spain, away across the sugar belt to the airport at Piarco. Members of his extended family were assembled there in the little wooden building at the side of the runway to say farewell. Shortly after midday, the plane left the ground and took Vido above Trinidad for the first time. He would never see Pa again. As he receded towards America and England, he saw the island as he had never seen it before, the pattern of the fields and the roads and the houses, while his family looked up at him suspended in the sky in a cross, at a right angle to Columbus, leaving the New World.

CHAPTER FIVE

'DE PORTU HISPANIENSI
IN TRINITATIS INSULA'

BRITAIN IN 1950 WAS in a bad condition. Clement Attlee's Labour government had been narrowly re-elected, food was still rationed and sterling was weak. The welfare state was costing too much, financed by borrowed American money, and it was becoming apparent, particularly since India had declared itself a republic, that Britain's days of empire were ending. Despite this, and although most British colonies had stopped turning a profit in the 1920s, the Colonial Office staff had tripled in size since before the war. London remained damaged by wartime bombing, and the air smelled of coal smoke. Clothes were drab, nylons were available only from black marketeers and utility clothing was still in use. Immigration had started, although at this time nobody could foresee how fundamentally it would alter British society. Two years earlier, the ship *Empire Windrush* had docked at Tilbury with passengers from Jamaica including the calypsonian Lord Kitchener (otherwise known as Aldwyn Roberts from Arima). The Colonial Office accommodated them in an old air-raid shelter at Clapham Common; jobs were available in nearby Brixton, and a new community was born. The recent British Nationality Act specified that any citizen of the Commonwealth – every fourth person on the planet – could live in Britain. At the time of Vidia's arrival, the immigrant population stood at 25,000. Half a century later, the non-white population of Britain would reach 4.6 million, or 7.9 per cent.[1]

In *Miguel Street*, Vido would fictionalize his departure from Trinidad. The narrator's mother gives a party, 'something like a wake', and in the morning his uncle takes him to the airport in his broken-down van. The book ends with the line: 'I left them all and walked briskly towards the aeroplane, not looking back, looking only at my shadow before me, a dancing dwarf on the tarmac.'[2] In *The Enigma of Arrival*, a mixture of memoir, essay and fiction published in 1987, he offered an

account taken from life, presenting himself as an epic figure destined
for what lay ahead. The author is on a small plane and asks the
stewardess, 'white and American and to me radiant and beautiful and
adult', to sharpen his pencil. She does so, and he makes notes: 'I had
bought the pad and pencil because I was travelling to become a writer,
and I had to start.' He realizes, in retrospect, that he ignored many
things: the gathering of family who came to say goodbye at the airport,
the cousin who advised him to sit at the back of the plane for safety,
the shift in his personality as he supposedly became conscious of himself
as a writer, setting out. Once in New York, a taxi driver fleeces him.
Alone in his room at the Hotel Wellington, the author sees a tap
marked HOT for the first time in his life, and eats a whole baked chicken
his mother has packed for him, 'over the waste-paper basket, aware as
I did so of the smell, the oil, the excess at the end of a long day ... the
writer of the diary was ending his day like a peasant.'³

In a letter written on Hotel Wellington paper dated 2 August 1950,
Vidia extolled the decadence of New York to Sati. He had been served
orange juice, eggs and coffee for his breakfast. 'In about 2 hours I will
be going to the boat. Tourist class on an American ship is sheer class
... For the first time in my life people are calling me sir at every turn.
I am enjoying myself and – pardon me! – am not missing home.' To
Kamla, a few weeks later, he was more vulnerable: 'I was scared. I had
never been on my own before. The idea of passing a night in a strange
city and boarding a boat was terrifying ... But the plane did come on
time and at about 12.50, V.S. Naipaul was cut off from all family ties.'
In New York, 'I took a taxi, felt like a lord at the hotel when a black
porter took my luggage in, calling me "sir" every two or three words.
It quite took my breath away. I was free and I was honoured.' He
revealed to Kamla that he had eaten Ma's chicken over the waste-paper
basket; 'my darling mother looks after her children with all the poor
little love she can dispose of.' The sea voyage had gone swimmingly,
and he had considered kissing a married German woman. England was
'proving very pleasant'. His cousin Boysie had installed him at Rudranath's lodgings in north-west London. Vido had met a girl and taken her
'to St Paul's and Regent's Park' – how familiar he made these places
sound! – 'but she has packed me up'. She was followed by a Norwegian
he met on a train while going to look at Oxford. 'We did some
sightseeing together and I paid her the wildest compliments in French
... I think I will go to Norway this Christmas. She was very nice.

Your ever loving Vido.'[4] He liked the buses and milk bars and the lettering on the London Underground but, like Willie Chandran in *Half a Life*, found Buckingham Palace disappointingly small. The city's geography appealed to him. 'I liked the feeling of being sheltered, the light being so much softer than the light of the tropics,' he said years later.[5]

In *The Enigma of Arrival*, he reconstructed and lightly fictionalized this period. The account is much more solemn: no mention of Boysie paving the way, or chasing girls around St Paul's and Oxford, or using Capildeo hospitality. He takes a train from the coast to Waterloo station, and stays in a dingy lodging house in Earls Court where he contemplates his literary destiny. The Earls Court lodgings in fact come from a later period, starting with his first Christmas in London. Boysie took him there to meet his girlfriend Carmen Johnson, the housekeeper. In *The Enigma of Arrival* she becomes Angela, and her real boyfriend is an absent and violent man, possibly in prison. The narrator notices the refugees from Europe, 'Asiatic' students and north Africans who are staying in the house. Only later does he see their significance; at the time, wishing to be a writer in the mould of Somerset Maugham, Aldous Huxley or Evelyn Waugh, he does not consider them 'material' for his fiction. 'Because in 1950 in London I was at the beginning of that great movement of peoples that was to take place in the second half of the twentieth century – a movement and a cultural mixing greater than the peopling of the United States . . . Cities like London were to change. They were to cease being more or less national cities; they were to become cities of the world, modern-day Romes, establishing the pattern of what great cities should be, in the eyes of islanders like myself and people even more remote in language and culture.'[6]

While he waited the six weeks for term to start, Vidia wrote a story that he hoped would be published by Penguin, and attempted to follow his father's advice to meet 'big shots in the film and writing business'. He made little progress. His attempts to establish contact with Rodin, confidently flagged to Kamla as Pa's associate and 'the star-writer of England's *Daily Express*', came to nothing. Was Pa bluffing? 'I am sorry Rodin was not too helpful,' Pa responded. 'I shall write him. Really, I ought to have given you a letter of intro. It's the right way to go about these things, I suppose. He must be a big shot.' In *Half a Life*, this encounter and similar rebuffs would be fictionalized and treated with a greater degree of honesty than the moving but monumental self-representation of the same period in *The Enigma of Arrival*. The protagonist Willie – named after Somerset Maugham – meets a prominent journalist in the lobby of a newspaper office, but finds they have nothing to talk about. Willie is 'unanchored' in London, unsure how to behave. 'He had to learn how to eat in public. He had to learn how to greet people and how, having greeted them, not to greet them all over again in a public place ten or fifteen minutes later.' Over time, he realizes his past is unknown to these foreigners; he is 'free to present himself as he wished ... The possibilities were dizzying. He could, within reason, re-make himself and his past and his ancestry.'[7] The implication, always unexpressed, is that Vidia was thinking of his own emphasis on dignified Brahminism and its importance in his literary self-representation.

Rudranath's flat was far from central London, and Vidia spent some of his days there under the eye of its owner, an elderly German refugee named Mrs Wolf, who hated Africans but tolerated Indians. Rudranath himself, now a lecturer in mathematics at London University, was away in Trinidad and Vido was embarrassed to tell him where he was staying, as Pa complained to Kamla: 'he is all nicely fixed up with Boyzie [sic] at Rud's London lodgings. Nothing to pay. But I must say Vido is rather tactless: he wrote Rud, not giving even the address he wrote from, and without a word of thanks ... Rud drew my attention to this in a mildly reproving and disappointed way.' Boysie introduced Vidia to Ruth, Rudranath's English wife, and he disliked her on sight, calling her a 'stupid, arrogant, shrewish, self-pitying woman' in a letter home. Nor did she take a liking to him; she wrote to Kamla: 'I saw Vido a fortnight ago. It was a dreary sort of day and I was in such a dull mood, that I'm afraid he thought I was an absolute horror.' He visited Carmen in Earls Court with Boysie several times and met a Frenchman, Yves Leclerc, who was lodging in the house and making a living by translating thrillers into French at high speed. 'He was a giant of a man, but wonderfully encouraging to me at our first meeting, when there was little to encourage. He was born in Morocco, or had lived there. He had been in the French underground during the war and when I knew him he still had his Maquis name, Coulon.'[8] Yves Leclerc would recur, in life and in fiction. Carmen, who came from Italy, tried early to knock the rough Caribbean corners off Vido's behaviour. 'I had to learn manners,' he recalled, 'closing a door behind you, saying please. She was shocked that I would just say, "Carmen give me some lunch."

I should say, "Carmen, give me some lunch, please. Can you please give me some coffee?" [9]

Already, then, Vidia felt the gap between the England of his imagination and quotidian life there, and between Pa's literary aspirations and his lack of connections in London. His father's most useful guidance would not be about star journalists or men of letters, but about how to live. From the start, Pa's weekly or fortnightly aerogrammes to his son contained wise words mixed with redundant advice. 'Good reading and good writing go together . . . Self-confidence is a very valuable asset and I am glad to know you feel confident; but don't underestimate people and problems . . . I have no doubt you will be a great writer: but do not spoil yourself . . . No harm in kissing a girl, so long as you do not become too prone for that sort of thing.' Above all he emphasized, knowing his son's latent instability, 'You keep your centre.'

*

Oxford was the oldest English-speaking university in the world, founded soon after the Battle of Hastings. Ever conscious of its own antiquity and status, its buildings were largely unmarked, their dirty yellow sandstone walls merged with the fabric of the town. Kings, archbishops, scientists and statesmen had studied there, and newcomers and outsiders were expected to know their way around, geographically and culturally: a quad was a courtyard, a hall was a dining room, a don was a teacher, a bulldog was a university policeman (who wore a bowler hat) and a scout was a cleaner. The academic year was divided into the Michaelmas, Hilary and Trinity terms; the summer holiday was the long vac, or vacation. The university worked on a federal system. Each college was self-governing, with its own customs and identity. Only in the late nineteenth century were men who were not members of the Church of England permitted to receive an MA degree, opening the way for Jews, Methodists and Roman Catholics, and conceivably for Hindus and Muslims. Academic halls were established for women in 1878, although they were not yet able to take a degree. With its cobbled roads, biting winds and chiming clock towers, Oxford had a medieval, ecclesiastical feel. A street bounded by tall sandstone walls and metal gratings would lead to a narrow passageway which bulged with age; an ancient studded door guarded by a gruff college porter would open within a larger wooden door, revealing a quad quartered by dark archways leading to a staircase, a chapel or another quad.

University College, off the High Street, had been established for the study of theology more than two centuries before Trinidad was named. Previous inhabitants of 'Univ' included the poet and atheist Percy Bysshe Shelley, who reclined in white marble in a large funerary monument inside the college, the rising politician Harold Wilson, the literary socialite Stephen Spender, the prime minister Clement Attlee, the reformer William Beveridge, the fantasy writer C.S. Lewis and Prince Felix Yusopov, who assassinated Rasputin. The seventeenth-century chapel had a relief sculpture of the great Orientalist William Jones, a graduate of the college, revealing that he had 'Formed a Digest of Hindu and Mohammedan Laws'. Vidia's room was on a noisy staircase above the Junior Common Room, with a shared bathroom down the corridor. Although he might meet women undergraduates at lectures or through activities such as student journalism, much of university life and particularly college life remained staunchly male. One contemporary said, 'If you were female and didn't have a face like the back of the bus, you could do very well at Oxford. On the other hand, the women's colleges, they protected their young charges and we had curfews – we were supposed to be in by eleven at night. It was like the kind of thing you read about American high schools, that people would talk about girls. It was very easy to get a reputation for being easy, though there was more "making out" than actual sex.'[10]

The behaviour of the undergraduates and graduates at Univ was monitored by the head porter, Douglas Millin, who made sure students were signed in and the college gates were locked behind them each night. A wartime battery sergeant-major in the Royal Artillery, Millin combined an abrasive manner with devotion to Univ, and was described in the college magazine as 'a master of spoken English, embellished with just a smattering of rich Anglo-Saxon'.[11] He said in an interview when he retired after thirty-three years in the post that, 'my jobs stretch from cutting a bloke down who's hung his bloody self to finding a safety pin for a lady's elastic knickers that's fallen down.'[12] According to Ravi Dayal, an Indian student at the college in the early 1960s, Millin disliked Vidia: 'Douglas said, "There've been lots of Indians in Univ, all fine people, all gentlemen, but not Naipaul. He used to take the mickey out of people." He remembered Naipaul making some rather pretentious person weep in the quad.'[13]

A more gentle pastoral role was taken by the dean, Giles Alington, a popular bachelor don who was less interested in academic life than in the well-being of the college, and exerted discipline lightly. The *University*

College Record noted that he was known for his 'not uncultivated eccentricities (the foot-long pipe with the tiny bowl, in summer the daisy between the teeth)', one of which was the frequent use of double negatives.[14] Supporting the Master, Dean, Head Porter and dons were around thirty college servants: scouts, messengers, butlers, gardeners, even a college waterman to look after the river boats. Peter Bayley, who had spotted Vidia's photograph and accepted him at the college, was immediately welcoming. Only a decade older than Vidia and shortly to be married to the daughter of a don, he specialized in sixteenth- and seventeenth-century English literature and had served in the Far East and India during the war. Bayley's first impression of Vidia was positive. 'Well, he was very small and he had this infectious smile and laugh, a rather asthmatic laugh – an asthmatic laugh can often seem more mirthful. He was extraordinarily responsive and bright. He very quickly got involved in things, he wanted to get involved. I never saw him look unhappy. He was made a member of the Martlets, the college literary society, very early. Vidia has got this legend going about his unhappiness there and how he disliked Oxford. It's not my impression at all. He did suffer from asthma and he felt the cold desperately. I think that college rooms were not very well heated in those days.'[15]

The 1950 freshmans' college photograph, which Vidia missed, showed nearly eighty young men standing in neat rows, hair brushed and parted, dressed in the style of the era in a suit or tweed jacket, collar, tie, V-neck jersey, baggy trousers and dark shoes. Some, maybe the older ones who had done National Service and in a few cases fought in the war or served as Bevin Boys, had a loose scarf thrown over the shoulder. There were three non-white freshmen in the photograph: Pillai, Holder and Al-Barwani. They were part of a tradition that had begun in the 1890s of students coming to study in the mother country from across the empire, usually intelligent young men from ambitious families who were setting themselves up for a prominent career back home.

Each Freshman at Univ had to sign the admissions register beneath a Latin inscription prepared individually by the Classics Fellow, a tradition dating back to 1674, the year in which Chhatrapati Shivaji was crowned king of the Marathas and John Milton died. Most of the entries are alike, but in Vidia's case the Classics Fellow had to think hard while preparing the text: 'Ego Vidiadhar Surajprasad Naipaul e collegio reginae sanctae in Trinitatis insula filius natu major Seepersad Naipaul de Portu Hispaniensi in Trinitatis insula lubens subscribo sub tutamine magistri Bayley annos

XVIII natus.'[16] It showed his difference. 'I, Vidiadhar Surajprasad Naipaul of Queen's Royal College in the island of Trinidad elder son of Seepersad Naipaul of Port of Spain in the island of Trinidad willingly assent to study under the tutorship of Master Bayley, in my eighteenth year.'

*

Pa's first letter to Vidia after he arrived at Oxford in early October set the tone for what was to follow, passing on news from Trinidad and giving encouragement that was aimed partly at himself. 'Don't be scared of being an artist . . . One cannot write well unless one can think well.' Would his son send a copy of *Mr Sampath*, a recent novel by the increasingly well-regarded Indian writer R.K. Narayan, and some special photographic paper? Only at the close of the letter did Pa let reality intrude, and look at his own situation squarely. 'This is the time I should be writing the things I so long to write. This is the time for me to be myself. When shall I get the chance? I don't know. I come from work, dead tired. The *Guardian* is taking all out of me — writing tosh, what price salted fish and things of that sort.' Vido was moved. 'What a delight to receive Pa's excellent letter from home. If I didn't know the man, I would have said: what a delightful father to have.' He felt he had been accepted at the university and at his college, and had made 'quite a number of acquaintances'. As for England, it was teaching him 'to say thank you and please'.

Vidia thought that the quality of education he had received at QRC put him ahead of his contemporaries. At his first tutorial with Peter Bayley, he was asked to read some work aloud, but was hesitant. Another undergraduate, Nicky Baile, whom Vidia admired for his ability to walk outdoors wearing only a shirt in winter, began instead. Vidia remembered, 'I was so nervous about what I had written, and there was Nicky Baile reading his piece which was so juvenile and childish, reading this rubbish quite shamelessly, and I said, "As a matter of fact, I have got something here", and read it out. For me, Oxford never recovered from that.'[17] Peter Bayley remembered Vidia reading a later essay on Milton's *Paradise Lost*. 'He sat in an armchair and said in that really polished English voice, "In *Animal Farm*, it would be remembered all animals are equal, but some animals are more equal than others." Then he sort of whinnied a bit and said, "The same is regrettably true of Milton's angels", and I knew I had a winner. I should explain that *Animal Farm* had only been out a few years by that time. Now everybody says "all animals are equal" whereas he was the first.'[18] In later life, Vidia would assert that he had learned nothing at

Oxford; and each time he said this in an interview, a slew of headlines would appear, expressing surprise.

While he adjusted to Oxford, Vidia confided in his family in Nepaul Street, and like other students in the college would usually write a letter home on a Sunday evening. Pa's response was enthusiastic. 'Your letters are charming in their spontaneity. If you could write me letters about things and people – especially people – at Oxford, I could compile them in a book: LETTERS BETWEEN FATHER AND SON ... You must aim to say only what you have to say and to say it clearly.' Pa was full of ideas, rather too many ideas for Vidia at times as he tried to go about his business as an Oxford undergraduate, far from Port of Spain. Where was the R.K. Narayan novel? Vido would shortly be receiving a parcel of sugar, pickles and tins of grapefruit juice and orange juice, packed by his mother. Might Vido be able to place an article in the *Sunday Express* that Pa had written about the cricketer Sonny Ramadhin? And if he met the philosopher and diplomat Dr Radhakrishnan, he was to tell him his father regarded him as 'one of the greatest minds of modern India ... And you would have broken the ice, as they say. Contact, Vido, contact all the time. Let me go on. Suppose you had a fairly good chat with this great scholar, you could have described the experience or the incident to me in a letter.'[19]

'Write Vido,' Pa suggested to Kamla in Benares Hindu University, 'but don't say anything to hurt him. You know, at heart he is not a bad fellow; only a bit erratic & thoughtless and callously unconventional.' Vidia soon became disconnected from home. He was overdeveloped and underdeveloped all at the same time, intellectually advanced and emotionally restricted, alone in an alien world, an engaging, attractive young man from a distant island, who stood five feet six in his stockinged feet. Outwardly, Vidia seemed to be one of the crowd. 'I would say he was positively popular in the college, that is my view,' said Peter Bayley. 'I thought of him as the little Indian boy in *A Midsummer Night's Dream*. [Puck refers to Titania's pageboy as, 'A lovely boy, stolen from an Indian king.'] He was exceptionally charming ... completely natural and very unselfconscious. He fitted in. He wanted to be an Englishman. For example his friend Peter Roberts who eventually became Canadian ambassador in Moscow, he once said Vidia was rather lordly. Sometimes he would say, Peter, come on let's go out and walk the streets of the town. We'll go and have a cup of coffee at the Randolph – the grandest hotel in Oxford. I wouldn't have dreamed of going to the Randolph. Peter Roberts said, he would go in and he would sit down in the lounge and he'd summon a waiter and he would say, "A pot of coffee, please, for one and would you please bring two cups." Well, there is confidence.'[20]

This was Trinidadian poise, or style, and it did not indicate tranquillity. Vido found it easier to explain his situation to Kamla than to Pa or Ma. In late November, as the English winter closed in, he wrote, 'A feeling of emptiness is nearly always on me. I see myself struggling in a sort of tunnel blocked up at both ends. My past – Trinidad and the necessity of our parents – lies behind me and I am powerless to help anyone. My future – such as it is – is a full four years away.' He had written eight chapters of a humorous novel that was 'bound to sell'. He told Kamla about a failed relationship with a beautiful Belgian girl he had been pursuing, Claude Golfart. She said she was in love with someone else, and had written him a letter suggesting that he was too forceful and intense for the English. He quoted it to Kamla. 'My dear Vidia . . . Because you are intelligent, you rush this slow country's atmosphere and people – perhaps compromise, though hateful, is still best.'

Kamla, in her letters back, sought to offer support. She did not want Vido to be placed in the same category as 'them West Indians'. His rule for girls should be: ' "Would Kamla think her a fool?" . . . You are too young to have any particular girl. I say, don't you go and get yourself hitched to anybody. Boy, I hope you'd have some room in your heart and home for me when I get back. Save a little corner for me, will you?' She felt in retrospect that her brother's sexual frustration and awkwardness with girls came less from the strictures of Hindu family life than from his ambition, and the work that came with it. 'In his Oxford years, Vidia didn't have the know-how to court a girl because he had spent his entire life just studying for exams. It was something which he put himself under because he had to win this scholarship to get out of Trinidad. There was no time to think about girls if he was trying to win one scholarship after another. Remember he won the first scholarship at ten.'[21] Savi thought her brother's hesitation was a trait that grew not out of Indian culture but from his personality, combined with the peculiarities of Ma's clan: 'All the Capildeo men as far as I was concerned as a female, they were all wimps. They never approached girls in a normal way. They were always withdrawn, shy – as if approaching a girl was a wrong thing. The Capildeos never ate in anybody's house. They would visit but never eat. So it was all part of this Hindu restrictiveness.'[22]

Money both in Oxford and in Trinidad was a constant concern. Ma had asked 'very humbly' if Vidia and Kamla might be able to pay Savi's school fees; Kamla thought she would be able to spare $18 a month; Vidia could spare nothing. At Univ, he had to adjust to the stodgy, restricted, post-war English diet. Each person would be given a butter ration at the start of the week. Although he was not vegetarian, Vidia avoided beef and pork. He ate lamb at first, but gave it up during the 1950s. Subsequently, as he became more concerned about his Indian heritage and apparent caste origins, he would continue to eat fish and from time to time chicken, although a Brahmin would ideally eat neither. He liked to believe his sensitivity to the smell and appearance of food and his antagonism towards certain kinds of meat and fish was inbuilt, almost genetic, arising from the background of his grandparents. 'I hated the idea of mussels and things like that crossing my mouth. Chicken would be terrible because of the oiliness. The thought of eating something that had been living was painful for me. I think that my vegetarianism was a personal thing . . . it is probably a peasant throwback in me. I am essentially a vegetarian peasant when it comes to food.'[23]

He had good news when the BBC paid him a guinea (one pound and one shilling) for a poem broadcast on *Caribbean Voices*, an influential half-hour weekly radio programme on the BBC. It was to be his only poem. 'Two Thirty A.M.' is a solemn, adolescent cry of anguish. It was read by John Figueroa, an extensively bearded brown Jamaican:

> darkness piling up in the corners
> defying the soulless moon . . .
> it is neither today's tomorrow
> nor is it tonight's last night
> but now
> and forever
> and you are scared
> for this is forever
> and this is death
> and nothing
> and mourning[24]

In the Christmas vacation, he went to London and took a room in Carmen's lodging house near the underground station at Earls Court, where he felt homesick but was glad to have space of his own at a cut-price rate. Ma warned him to look after himself, writing in telegraphic style, 'Vido I am nervous about your smoking again please remember there is a limit to everything health is first.' He told his parents about the sight of floating ice. 'Last week I had my first snow. It came down in little white fluffs; you felt that a gigantic hand had punched a gigantic cotton wool sack open, letting down flurries of cotton shreds,' he wrote home beautifully, the Caribbean boy in London. 'If you went out your shoulders and your hair were sprinkled with the fluffs. The closest thing I have seen to it in Trinidad is the stuff that gathers in a refrigerator – not when it gets hard though.' He was studying Shakespeare and Virgil and Anglo-Saxon. 'I want to come top of my group. I have got to show these people that I can beat them at their own language.' It was a lasting ambition.

Over Christmas he met up with Boysie, who was spending much of his time with Carmen in Earls Court, and with his uncles Simbhoo and Rudranath, who were making plans to purchase a house in south London for £5,000. Yves Leclerc said to him of the British: 'Their women can't cook, can't dress and are invariably plain.' He saw a group of prominent West Indians: Sam Selvon, Carlisle Chang, a Trinidadian artist who was in London on a scholarship, and Gloria Escoffery, a Jamaican writer and painter. Vidia set out to make a spectacle of himself. When Gloria said that she wrote in order to explore, he cut in, paraphrasing Pa, 'Surely you're starting from the wrong end. I always thought people understood before they wrote.' When she passed around a short story which touched on racial issues, and Sam suggested 'the colour problem' could not be explained in something as short as a short story, Vidia saw his opening: 'My dear Gloria, why not write a little pamphlet on the colour question, and settle the whole affair?' He was relieved to be telephoned the next morning by Carlisle Chang and told the party had talked about him after he left. 'Gloria, he said, had infinite faith in me. They all thought me a little queer, but that, I thought, was because I spoke a bit of sense, and told these culture-creators where they got off. The queerness, they discovered, was due to my reaction to England. How I enjoyed that evening!'

After Christmas, he returned to Oxford and took a room in a house in Richmond Road in Jericho that had previously been occupied by a young chemistry undergraduate, Margaret Roberts, later Thatcher.[25] He did not meet Margaret until many years later, when she had become prime minister. When term began, the landlady, Mrs King, allowed him to return occasionally for a hot bath. He was still unimpressed by the intellectual abilities of his fellow undergraduates. In an exam, writing about 'the ugliness of the theology of *Paradise Lost*', he used the phrase

'Prayer, the incense for the incensèd God' in an essay which was marked by Professor J.R.R. Tolkien, the professor of English language and literature at Oxford who in his spare time wrote about hobbits. 'Now I knew exactly what I was doing. "Incensèd" meaning angry, it's the same word. And Tolkien said to me, "it's good, did you intend it?" And I was ashamed and I said no. And so I lost points in Tolkien's mind, I suppose, and the witticism yet was my own. I was too well prepared for Oxford, I suppose.'[26] Some of this remembered response to Oxford was retrospective superiority, Vidia's reaction to the university's cultivated sense of exclusivity. For despite his talent and hard work, he never achieved the level of academic success that he had expected of himself.

Vidia told Kamla he had few friends and less money, his isolation expressing itself in arrogance: 'You would be surprised when I tell you that the majority of the students here are very stupid, and that the average intelligence is much lower than that of the sixth form of my years at QRC.' Too many students were on state grants, he told his parents conceitedly: 'Gone are the days of aristocrats.' The English were a curious people: 'The longer you live in England, the queerer they appear. There is something so orderly, and yet so adventurous about them, so ruttish, so courageous. Take the chaps in the college. The world is crashing about their heads, about all our heads. Is their reaction as emotional as mine? Not a bit. They ignore it for the most part, drink, smoke, and imbibe shocking quantities of tea and coffee, read the newspapers and seem to forget what they have read.' Not that Trinidad was any better. 'I never realized before that the *Guardian* was so badly written, that our Trinidad worthies were so absurd, that Trinidad is the most amusing island that ever dotted a sea.' For all his cynicism, he hated being excluded and wanted to succeed. Oxford had been presented to him as the pinnacle of achievement, but now it was failing to give him what he wanted. The past, meanwhile, was receding as Trinidad was rendered absurd.

*

'I am a feature reporter on the staff of the university magazine *Isis*,' Vido told Kamla in January 1951. 'It doesn't mean much, but if there is fair play I should become at least assistant news editor by the end of the year.'[27] Fair play, however, was by no means assured at the *Isis*, an independent student paper run by a clique of well-heeled young men from the university. 'I will tell you something about Oxford,' he wrote to his parents guilelessly, 'intelligence is not all that one requires to get along. One has to know "the boys" ... To get on, you must throw sherry parties, take the editor out to dinner.' Writing to fourteen-year-old Mira, Vido played the elder brother: 'Have you developed a taste for reading now? My dear girl, if you have, I have a great pity for you. One must devote all one's life to reading and the pursuit of knowledge, or never begin at all ... I trust you will pardon the didactic tone of this letter ... Goodbye, my dear Ranee [Queen]!'[28] Touchingly, Pa sent Vido $10 to hold a sherry party. 'I know full well what this thing means and how necessary it is. Meanwhile be a man and cringe to none,' Seepersad told his son.

After earlier complaints that he was not writing home frequently enough, Vido had fallen into a pattern of regular correspondence with Pa. Bored by much of his work under Master Bayley, he felt he was 'improving intellectually' thanks to a close reading of Aristotle's *Poetics*. 'He was such a clear, intelligent thinker. Every sentence adds something new. That is the best type of criticism.'[29] A shared interest in literature united father and son. They discussed newspaper design and compared notes about journalism. Pa was reading John Galsworthy and Rudyard Kipling; Vidia was reading Leo Tolstoy and E.M. Forster. 'I am beginning to believe I could have been a writer,' Pa wrote sadly, and Vidia praised him, sincerely: 'I have always admired you as a writer. And I am convinced that, were you born in England, you would have been famous and rich and pounced upon by the intellectuals.' He himself had been told he was 'gifted' by Yves Leclerc in Earls Court, and advised to finish his novel.

Vidia complained that an interview he had done for *Isis* with the film producer Emeric Pressburger had been mangled by an editor, which left him in 'a white-hot temper'. And 'When Palme Dutt, the half-Indian boss of the British Communist Party, came to Oxford, I gave him so much hell that the Communists rang up the editor and cursed him. I think a man is doing his reporting well only when people start to hate him.' Pa, significantly, did not agree. He advised his son not to be concerned if an editor tried to improve his work, or 'at least not yet'. He should be patient. 'And as to a writer being hated or liked – I think it's the other way to what you think: a man is doing his work well when people begin liking him. I have never forgotten what Gault MacGowan told me years ago: "Write sympathetically"; and this, I suppose, in no way prevents us from writing truthfully, even brightly.' Pa believed in Vido. 'You don't have to worry about us – so long as I keep going. Give yourself all the chance.'

But Vidia did worry. 'You must realise,' he wrote to Kamla, 'that without us, the family has lost its heart. The responsibility is mighty, I know, but it is not depressing.' His idea of himself as the writer was the way forward. The BBC might accept two of his stories, he told her in the same letter, one a rewritten version of 'How They Made a Queen'. 'If they really have, it means that for two weeks' work, I shall have raked in more than fifteen guineas. Not bad! And I am only eighteen!' He was only eighteen, precocious but precarious, writing fluent letters and hoping to write great books. In *A House for Mr Biswas*, Vidia would characterize his correspondence with Pa harshly: 'Anand's letters, at first rare, become more and more frequent. They were gloomy, self-pitying; then they were tinged with a hysteria which Mr Biswas immediately understood. He wrote Anand long humorous letters; he wrote about the garden; he gave religious advice; at great expense he sent by air mail a book called *Outwitting Our Nerves* by two American women psychologists. Anand's letters grew rare again.' When Mr Biswas fell ill, 'He continued to write cheerful letters to Anand. At long intervals the replies came, impersonal, brief, empty, constrained.'[30]

Both men felt their talent was being stifled. Vidia had been shown around the Morris Motors works 'as a member of the Press, and treated to the most wonderful lunch I have ever had in England so far.' When his report was published in *Isis*, his name 'in biggish capital letters,' he thought it would be the 'first and only big article' he wrote for them: 'It is really impossible to get ahead in that paper.' The article itself, run over several pages under the headline 'When Morris Came To Oxford', covered traffic congestion, industrial diversification and ideas about pressed steel.[31] *Isis*, in practice, had little to offer V.S. Naipaul. The magazine ran worthy articles about subjects like Morris cars but was filled mainly with pert undergraduate humour, self-referential university news and polite photographs of female undergraduates – 'EDWINA, the most beautiful sight in Town' – amid advertisements for sherry, Brylcreem, snap brim hats and the latest Hillman Minx. A daring contributor might write an article about the evils of apartheid or the need for tolerance towards 'maladjusted individuals' – meaning homosexuals – or he might try to be amusing on the letters pages, like Edgar Farquarson: 'I have discovered, after investigation, that of the members of your staff listed in your first issue, three are Negroes, four homosexuals, two are frequently to be seen in public-houses, and one is a woman. All this is unspeakably revolting to the Freshman's conscience.'[32] An undergraduate might advise his contemporaries on social matters: 'It is "smart" for parents to stay at one of the large hotels in town, or to motor in daily. It is not "smart" to stay with relatives in North Oxford.'[33]

A rising star among them would feature as the '*Isis* Idol', illustrated with a carefully staged black-and-white photograph. The Idol's early triumph was presumed to mark the beginning of an exhilarating career in politics or the arts. Idols included Jeremy Thorpe, the Liberal Party leader who would later resign over a sex scandal involving an assassinated dog, Godfrey Smith, the future editor of the yet-to-be-launched *Sunday Times* colour supplement, and Robert Robinson, who would become the waspish invigilator of BBC daytime radio quiz shows. Of Jeremy Thorpe, *Isis* wrote presciently that though he had much talent, 'some feel that as a future politician, he would be wiser to be more discreet.'[34] Other figures who appeared in the pages of the *Isis* at this time included Robin Day, Norman St John-Stevas, Michael Heseltine, George Carman and the president of the Oxford University Conservative Association, William Rees-Mogg, who was already making his name as a comic figure: 'Anyone thought of a new joke about William Rees-Mogg?' the paper enquired.[35]

The weekly gossip column 'Roundabout' told languidly of goings-on at various colleges. At a party 'next Saturday in LORD STORMONT's rooms, we gather that gatecrashers will be welcome.' Plans were afoot for a production of *Twelfth Night* at New College: 'The parts of the messengers, hautboys and tuckets have been entrusted to the college haughties, led by ANTONIA PAKENHAM. But who cares?'[36] A future diplomat whose girl-friend had recently been snatched by a wealthy Egyptian student lamented the presence of dark faces at Oxford: ' "I can't bear Wogs," moaned genial JOHN SHAKESPEARE, as he submitted the Magdalen students to a keen scrutiny. "One thing about Trinity," he went on, gravely eyeing CHRIS-TOPHER FETTES, "at least we're all homogenous . . . if that's the word I mean?" (N.B. – No more Shakespeare boosts until further notice. – ED.)'[37] 'Americans-and-Colonials' such as the Indian cricket blue Ramesh 'Buck' Divecha usually made it into the magazine only via a sporting triumph: 'This fine specimen of Hindu manhood is equally at home theorising on the secrets of his successes in Vincent's or fingering his native chapattis in the Taj . . . He returns to the jungle in August to study for his Bar Finals.'[38]

Vidia was all at sea in this cliquey, smirking, undergraduate atmosphere;

there was little chance of his parents coming to stay in one of the large hotels in town. His articles for *Isis* were not impressive. Only one contains a hint of literary talent, the report on the visit of R. Palme Dutt, whom he described 'holding his slender arms parenthetically at his sides, then slowly wagging a right index finger at the audience.'[39] A letter arrived for him from WAGS in Port of Spain: 'My dear "Paul" . . . Do send me a copy of *Isis*. Have you met with any colour-prejudice in Oxford?' Before long the magazine became too much for him. Peter Bayley remembered Vidia arriving one day at his rooms 'in great distress. He said he found a note in the office of the *Isis* which implied that because he was a foreigner, he should piss off. "Keep out Vidia," or something like that. He showed me the note and I said, "Well, this is all a joke, isn't it?" He said, "I don't think it's a joke." He was bitterly upset. He felt rejection, whether justified or not I just don't know. I assume not, because undergraduates are not beastly; it may have been a badly timed joke.'[40]

Like Vidia, Pa felt that racial prejudice underlay his own lack of advancement. He had been on the *Guardian* for 'sixteen months now, but they haven't given me a raise. A thing that is making me bitter – I suppose that's how a Communist comes into being – is that a third-rate English boy . . . is getting a far bigger salary than I am getting.' His particular enemy was a senior editor, Mr Jenkins. 'They are capitalist exploiters,' Pa wrote to Kamla. 'Imagine fat, goofy Jenkins being my boss. You know, I have often imagined the man coming to work with rouged lips, and to carry the imagery a bit further, in a frock. Short, fat Jenkins!' He was annoyed that Sam Selvon's forthcoming first novel, *A Brighter Sun*, had been mentioned on the BBC: 'I'd be a liar if I didn't admit that far from feeling well about it, I felt peeved with myself . . . The fact is I feel trapped.' The sheer unfairness of his position ate at him. As he wrote to Kamla, oblivious to her past connection with Selvon, he was writing some of the best news stories in the paper, as well as sub-editing the *Guardian Weekly*, 'yet the white man who does no more on the same job, gets damn near double the salary I get.'

In April, Vidia was invited to visit the home of John McConville, another 'Univ man', for the vacation. 'I have never spent a more congenial four days in England,' he told his parents. 'Blackpool is the big northern seaside resort of England. It is a big machine made to extort money from the people on holiday, full of fortune-tellers, gypsies, all named Lee, and all claiming to be the only Gypsy Lee on the front . . . The beach is pleasant, as pleasant as Trinidad's east coast, minus the coconut trees, but the water and wind are hellishly cold, and the water is always the colour of mud.' In retrospect, he perceived the trip to the McConvilles differently. 'They had a strange accent. Northern. It didn't sound right. The father was a doctor, and told a story about seeing D.H. Lawrence at a bus stop. I felt an outsider; I rather liked being an outsider; it was not in our tradition to stay with people. I suppose I was a bundle of nerves.'[41]

Vidia was aware of his tendency to cynicism. As he told his 'darling sister' Kamla, 'I was seriously thinking this morning how people could ever put up with me . . . The boys who like me, like me because mine is a "cynical flamboyance", because I pose as an "enfant terrible". Yet I sincerely am never aware of POSING. I suppose the reason is that in the W[est] I[ndies] we lived so completely within ourselves, we grew to despise the people around us. But the people ought to have been despised! A friend told me the other day that people don't like me because I made them feel that I knew they were fools.' He wished to assimilate, at least socially, and told Kamla he still spoke in 'a foul manner' although his pronunciation was improving 'by the humiliating process of error and snigger'. In the Trinity term examinations he almost got a distinction, and had the best results of any English Literature student in his college. He threw a party in his room for ten guests, serving tea and beer. Boysie turned up in the middle of it and 'the boys enjoyed his company' he told Ma and Pa. When the term ended, he was at a loss. For days he was 'literally penniless' and had to cadge meals off friends, particularly Ian Robertson, an assistant curator at the Ashmolean Museum to whom he had been given an introduction by the British Council in Trinidad. He was helped a few weeks later by earning eight guineas from *Caribbean Voices* when his first short story, 'This is Home', was broadcast; a damaged version of the manuscript survives on microfilm in the archives of the BBC.

*

During Pa's early years as an aspiring writer of fiction, he had no market for his work, only a few non-paying local magazines such as the *Beacon*, published by Albert Gomes, which printed stories by himself, C.L.R. James and Alfred Mendes. After the Second World War, things had changed. The Jamaican poet Una Marson broadcast a morale-boosting BBC radio show from London during the war for West Indians in the armed forces. Marson was the first black woman to make programmes at the BBC; there is a photograph of her in a studio with William Empson, George Orwell, Mulk Raj Anand and T.S. Eliot, among others. In 1946 the show *Caribbean*

Voices took a fresh turn under a new editor, Henry Swanzy: it became a weekly half-hour display case for new writing and poetry. Swanzy liked Seepersad Naipaul's stories, and broadcast six over four years. The first was 'Sonya's Luck', about a rural Hindu bride who elopes with her lover on her wedding night, only for the couple to discover that their parents have already betrothed them to each other. Another was a non-fiction account of going to a meeting of Christian 'shouters'. *Ramdas And The Cow* was a story about a Brahmin who wants to sell a barren cow to a butcher, but dare not for fear of his neighbour Gurudeva; Ramdas refers to the cow 'by all sorts of crazy names and cuss-words, the most common of which was "bitch".'[42] He hatches a plan to get the cow to the butcher, only for it to fall down dead. In the evolving intellectual and political climate, with the prospect of self-rule sweeping the region, Swanzy's show had a catalytic effect, linking writers and critics from across the territories of the English-speaking Caribbean from British Honduras to British Guiana. Radio was the perfect medium to create such a virtual community. Contributors would send a story or poem to a BBC agent in Jamaica who sifted the material and sent it by boat to Swanzy for consideration at his office in Oxford Street. Back in the West Indies, they would cluster around a wireless or Rediffusion set and listen for the legendary opening: 'This is London calling the Caribbean.' During the life of the programme, there were 372 contributors, of whom about one-fifth were women.[43]

Outwardly, *Caribbean Voices* was a classic assertion of imperial authority: the colonized produced writing which after scrutiny and critical assessment by their masters in London was broadcast back to them. In practice, the process was highly collaborative and creative, as writers and manuscripts travelled back and forth across the Atlantic, leading to the flowering of talents such as Andrew Salkey, Edgar Mittelholzer, Samuel Selvon, George Lamming, Edward Brathwaite, Derek Walcott and the Naipauls, père et fils. The impetus lay with Henry Swanzy, a short, plump, musical man of Irish origin who despite his booming upper-class voice was more concerned with dismantling the British empire than building it. He said later that 'one had the sort of left-wing view of encouraging people who had had a raw deal.'[44]

Born in 1915 in Ireland, Swanzy had graduated from Oxford and worked as a ministerial private secretary in the Dominions Office before joining the BBC's Empire Department. A paternalistic but critically acute figure, he took Caribbean writing seriously. When authors such as Selvon moved to England, he offered them personal support, holding discussions at his house in Hampstead and introducing them to literary editors and critics. He worked closely with the small journals of the West Indies, particularly *Kyk-Over-Al* in British Guiana and *Bim* in Barbados, whose inspiring editor, Frank Collymore, became a close collaborator. Only *Focus* in Jamaica stood out against Swanzy's charm, for nationalist reasons, seeing the British Broadcasting Corporation as the tool of a failing colonial power. Henry Swanzy's taste was for the local rather than the derivative: he said his listeners had 'sat with the fishermen hefting sea-eggs, gone with the pork-knockers into Guyanese jungles, followed the saga-boys and the whe-whe players, heard the riddles, the digging songs, the proverbs, the ghost stories, duppies, La Diablesse, Soukivans, zombies, maljo, obeah, voodoo, shango.'⁴⁵ His favourite material was unsentimental: after broadcasting a Runyonesque short story by Sam Selvon about Indians pimping girls to Yankee sailors in Port of Spain, he faced furious complaints from listeners in the Caribbean, many of whom had a strong, conservative Christian faith. Henry Swanzy was to be a crucial figure in Vidia's successful development as a writer.

Vido's first story, 'This is Home', was based on the memory of his father building the house in the woods at Petit Valley. In the fictionalized version, a young couple reach their new home in a lorry which 'whined like a kicked puppy'. The man is handsome but 'seared somehow, with sorrow' while his wife moves 'calmly and deliberately, with all the charm of a woman in her first pregnancy.' Soon, however, 'He was seized with distaste for her, for her methodical, ritual approach to ordinary things . . . He saw the tasks of the world split into two. Man the author, man the worker. Woman the anvil for man's passion: the feeder and lover of her master . . . It was the idea of fitting into a primeval universal pattern of living to mate, and mating to create that filled him with dread. Sex was the whole works and he knew it; and it hurt him.' The woman turns her face to him. 'He kissed her. "This is home," he said. I am not ashamed any more, he was telling himself. And yet he could feel that he was lying.'⁴⁶ V.S. Naipaul's first short story is ponderous and laden with uneasy symbolism. It carries a teenager's idea of how people a little older than himself might behave. Yet it contains certain key themes – dislocation, homelessness, anxiety about the relationship between men and women – that he would write about repeatedly in his later work.

In July, Vidia joined an agricultural camp, working eleven hours a day. 'Believe me, you can keep manual labour. I don't care for it at all,' he told his parents.⁴⁷ His mother sent him some tins of fruit juice, a bottle of guava jelly and a tin of sugar. 'Look for 3 packs of cig[arette]s in sugar,' his father warned. Snippets of news reached him from abroad. 'Today the Tewaris are here. Nigger Betty and her mother,' Mira reported, referring to friends from Jamaica. WAGS told him that he had fallen in love with 'a not bad-looking girl of 20 . . . She proved, however, to be of rather easy virtue and I repeatedly dashed her.' Kamla said she was spending her summer holidays with a family in Benares where her Naipauline irreverence had caused an upset: 'I made a slip of the tongue . . . We were having a few religious discussions when Hanuman came into the conversation. One of the girls asked me if I knew Hanuman. And, without thinking, I promptly replied, "Yes, a monkey." Boy, I am sure the mother was scandalised. She spends her whole day praying.'

Vidia went on writing, and kept encouraging Pa, telling him in July, 'YOU HAVE ENOUGH MATERIAL FOR A HUNDRED STORIES. FOR HEAVEN'S SAKE START WRITING THEM . . . The essential thing about writing is writing . . . You are the best writer in the West Indies, but one can only judge writers by their work.' He was making an obvious but astute point, and one that he himself would never forget: there are many would-be great writers, but the only ones who become great writers are those who sit down and write. Vidia promised to have Pa's stories typed up, and to help him find a publisher. From the BBC offices in Oxford Street, Henry Swanzy had praised Pa to Vidia as 'a natural writer'. The manuscript of his own novel was now complete. He showed it to Peter Bayley, a large typewritten manuscript. Bayley thought later – wondering whether his memory might be playing tricks on him – that it contained the seeds of Vidia's first four novels. 'I found there *The Mystic Masseur, The Suffrage of Elvira* and of course quite a lot of *Miguel Street* and indeed anticipations of *Mr Biswas*.'[48] It was read by a friend, Ronnie Eyre, later a film and theatre director, and by Ian Robertson. Vidia felt confident he would find a publisher. 'As soon as your novel is accepted, write me,' Pa told him. But despite Vidia's best efforts, nobody wanted to publish his book. He said later, 'I began when I was about seventeen, much influenced by Evelyn Waugh, writing a farce set in Trinidad, and I worked at that for two years. Now, nothing happened to that; I was heartbroken.' It taught him 'how to take a book to the end'.[49]

At the start of September, using money that he should have been saving for the coming academic year, Vidia went to Paris. Flamboyantly, greedily, he bought a taste of the world he aspired to by travelling by air. He was taken by coach from Kensington Air Station to London Airport, and flew in style across the channel, sipping complimentary champagne. 'The month's tour of France is so cheap – $180 – that I suspect that something must be wrong somewhere,' he wrote to Pa, who supported a family on $165 a month. 'Anyway, I have remarkable luck wherever I go. And, the Colonial Office is granting me $60.'[50] He defrayed a fraction of the cost some years later by writing a version of the flight for *Caribbean Voices*. Later still, he wrote, 'Air France used to run an Epicurean Service between London and Paris. The advertisements taunted me. Poverty makes for recklessness, and one idle day in the long summer vacation I booked.' In the earlier account, Naipaul or 'Narayan' writes of a conversation with an Indian journalist he meets on the flight; by the time of the second article, 1965, his travelling companion has become a stock 'Indian' character who chucks him under the chin saying, '*Hin-du wege-tar-ian!*' By this time, his view of himself had shifted: 'To be a colonial is to be a little ridiculous . . . To be an Indian from Trinidad, then, is to be unlikely and exotic. It is also to be a little fraudulent.'[51]

From Paris, he told Kamla he had met an attractive Finnish woman, 'and we spent three delicious days together.' Vidia could not work out how to proceed, and so retained his virginity. Her name was Dorrit Hinze; he took a photograph of Dorrit wearing flat shoes and a shapeless post-war dress, squinting buxomly in the sunlight outside Notre-Dame cathedral. He said later, 'I bought her chocolate and I took her to my hotel. I was immensely stirred but I didn't know how to seduce her; I was so ashamed of my incompetence.'[52] While Vidia wrestled with the Finn, the BBC broadcast his story 'The Mourners'. Like 'This is Home', it is melancholic. A girl, Ann – this was V.S. Naipaul's first and last use of a female narrator – visits a relation whose son has died, and listens unwillingly to an account of the dead boy's qualities. The attempt to convey the affect of grief is melodramatic. In 1967, Naipaul would publish a revised version in the collection *A Flag on the Island*. The story has improved, showing how he could turn a dud into a success by making precise changes. The opening becomes taut; Ann becomes Romesh; clichés are cut. In the first version, the mourning mother is described incidentally, but in the second she is fixed immediately: 'She was in a loose lemon housecoat; she half sat, half reclined on a pink sofa.'[53]

At the start of the new term, admiring his literary ambitions, Peter Bayley asked the Dean to give Vidia a grant of 30 shillings from college funds to repair his typewriter, which he had dropped. 'Indians', the Dean told him in the manner of the time, handing over the cash, 'are very charming, very poetical; some are even geniuses. But you are so startlingly incompetent.' To Kamla, Vido wrote, 'Ruth and Capo R have invited me to spend Xmas with them at Brighton. I am not sure whether I shall accept or not. I don't like that woman. She has got a filthy mind. Capo R and I, on the other hand, have been hitting it off rather well. He has got so far friendly as to tell me that his marriage was the biggest mistake in his life.' Kamla urged her brother to be more diplomatic: 'For goodness sake, don't openly show your dislike for Ruth. Learn some of the silly conventions of society and practice smiling before your mirror even if you don't want to.' In late December, Vidia wrote home, 'I have just returned from Brighton where I spent Xmas with Rood Mamoo. I spent a really enjoyable time, and I am sure that I could not have spent Christmas better anywhere ... This afternoon I paid a call on Owad. He lives with a tiny colony of St James Indians in a shabby quarter of London ... I have just heard that someone suggested at home that I was hurried away from T'dad because I was carrying on with negresses!! Did you hear that one? It is rather thrilling to find oneself the object of baseless slander ... I have been thinking about what I shall do after Oxford and I have come to the conclusion that I shall come back to Trinidad for a bit at least if I can get a job at QRC.'

In the New Year of 1952, having given up on *Isis*, he started designing the Oxford *Tory*, a freshly established paper of the Oxford University Conservative Association. He enjoyed the work, although he had no political affiliation to the Conservatives. He admitted to his parents that for several months he had 'been prey to the gravest emotional upset I have ever experienced'. Mira wrote: 'I hardly know what to say, except ... to assure you, if assurance is necessary, that we are all looking forward to the day when V.S. Naipaul will have become a famous name in the world of letters.' Underneath her words, little Sewan had written, 'Dear Vido, I send you a kiss.' In late January his mother wrote, 'Well this is one thing I am begging you not to do, don't marry a white girl please don't ... I suppose there are plenty Indian girls in England studying. If you marry one of them only when you are through with your education, I shall be very pleased.' Pa agreed with Ma; he believed 'that by far the majority of intermarriages end in failure.' Soon, though, he was reconsidering, forced to admit that things might be more complicated: 'Who you should marry is entirely a matter for you; though for my part I should be more happy to see you marry an Indian, in the end it must be as you yourself choose. But give yourself plenty of time for this.'

On 9 February, only a few days after Ma's letter arrived, Vidia happened to meet a girl named Patricia Hale at his college play. Like most undergraduates, she was white.

CHAPTER SIX

'I LOVE YOU, MY DEAR PAT'

PAT HALE WAS A SLIM, small undergraduate with a kind, pretty face. She was a member of the Oxford University Dramatic Society, and Vidia first glimpsed her holding a stack of programmes on the final night of the Univ play, Jan de Hartog's *Skipper Next to God*. He had designed the poster and helped to organize the publicity for the play. They chatted, and he invited her to tea. Pat was seventeen days older than Vidia, reading history at a women's college, St Hugh's. Like him, she came from a poor background and had reached Oxford University on intellectual merit, in her case on a state scholarship. Over tea, they talked some more, and a tentative romance began. In March 1952, Pat went home for the vacation. Her parents and sister lived in a decrepit two-bedroom flat above the Birmingham Municipal Bank in Kingstand-ing, a drab suburb of the great nineteenth-century city of Birmingham in the English Midlands. Her father worked in a local firm of solicitors as a managing clerk, a position similar to a legal executive. Mr and Mrs Hale both came originally from Gloucestershire.

Vidia sat down to write to Pat. His tone was that of the would-be romantic lover. He was trying out a role, for he had never written a proper love letter, and did not know where to begin. Each sentence, each sentiment, seemed insincere, as if someone else might already have written it. 'Yes, darling, I am missing you very much. At odd moments, I seem to smell you (don't be angry: it's a pleasant smell) . . . I think of your room tonight – at St. Hugh's – robbed of you, robbed of all its charm, its warmth, its cosiness. I cannot go there and relax in your chair or sofa or have you steal eggs to make me a decent tea. How I love you for all that! No, no I am not drunk. Allow me to be utterly un-British & to wallow in my sloppiness. I love you, my dear Pat, and I feel it grow stronger every day. Promise me one thing, though – read & destroy. I should hate to think that next term in one of your peevish moods, you should read this letter to me mockingly. A man who writes with sincerity usually sounds silly.'[1]

He made it plain he was depressed: 'For the past 3 months I have been through a mental hell-fire. Nothing like it ever happened to me before, & I hope nothing like it ever happens again.' He made it plain he was a writer: 'The novel is going slowly – very slowly. This always happens to me. But loneliness will eventually force the thing out on paper – if it really wants to come out.' He made it plain that other people were doing better than him, in particular Guy Lorriman, who had a room on the same staircase at Univ and was being praised around Oxford for Vidia's work on the *Tory*: 'Well, you know that if the circulation has doubled it was because of me. Nearly every idea was mine. Now, I don't mind getting only peanuts for my pains, while friend Lorriman gets the credit for being a journalistic genius ... Lorriman was made a member of the Press club. I wasn't. L[orriman] was invited to the *Isis* term party. I wasn't.' Vidia knew he was making himself look ridiculous, and concluded, 'No, there ain't no justice. Do you mind terribly if I remain buried in obscurity at Oxford?'

Pat, correspondingly, was simpler. She wrote unaffectedly of life in Kingstanding, of her parents going out to buy their first television set after the death of King George VI, of paying a visit to her good friend Sheila Rogers, of her annoyance at her boisterous younger sister Eleanor charging around the cramped family flat, and of going to watch Alan Guinness in a play called *Under the Sycamore Tree* in Birmingham. In a round, girlish hand, she told him:

> There is something very exciting about the first letter received from someone. I'm glad you didn't write straight away. It gave me time to look forward to it. I'm also glad you didn't write a clever letter, a sort of literary piece of art, you know ... Vidia, you've been very good to me. Since I've been home I've realised how much I enjoyed being with you, how interesting you make things, how in fact you've stimulated me.

There were, though, immediate and lasting problems: 'My father has told me that I must not let you write me letters here. He has fits like this when he suddenly does things that put me in the most ghastly positions. Generally I disregard his wishes in the best western and decadent manner but he has caught me. If I don't make it plain he will insist on reading your letters, etc ... I apologise for him. He gets these fits and he's not perfect but he isn't really prejudiced, Victorian or anything else.' The themes were set: Patricia was moved and stimulated by Vidia, her father objected to the possibility of a foreigner in their midst, and Pat's reaction was to blame herself: 'I just feel sick and more deeply convinced than ever of my general worthlessness.'

He responded with formality, with a letter for family consumption, and waited until the holidays were over. 'Dear Miss Hale, The Modern History Prelim Results will be out tomorrow, and, as I promised, I shall telephone them to you. Some people are so eager to get bad news. I shall call at 11:30 am, shortly before I leave Oxford for the day. Yours sincerely, V. S. Naipaul.' They spoke on the telephone, and Vidia paid her whispered compliments. He was unstable now. He felt increasingly homesick, and wondered about booking a passage home to Trinidad for the summer vacation. He asked his father to investigate dates and prices, and suggested he might obtain a cheap passage on a merchant tanker. 'Stress that I am a student at Oxford, not a Negro going to play the fool in London. Wonderful snob-value.' Pa moved fast, delighted at the prospect of seeing Vido again, booking a passage and borrowing money to make a downpayment of a quarter of the fare. Pa was writing less now, growing orchids and sleeping in the afternoons. Although he was only in middle-age, he felt old.

Vidia presented a paper to the Martlets on 'The Use of the First Person Singular in English Fiction', and offered it unsuccessfully to Henry Swanzy for *Caribbean Voices*. He told his parents of sitting in the Dean's rooms, drinking port. 'I had the group laughing whenever I wanted them to laugh. This morning someone told me that my paper was by far the brightest he had ever heard at the society.' He parodied Henry James, praised Daniel Defoe and 'quoted a bit of Cecil Hunt, about the telegraphic style. "A shot rang out. A man fell dead. Two more shots rang out. Two more men fell dead."' He described a typical meal in hall, 'a long, high room, with an enormous fireplace that is never used. The roof is timbered, and some of the windows have stained glass. Pictures of past great men of the college hang on the walls.' After eating, Vidia would proceed to the Junior Common Room to sit beneath sporting pictures and crossed rowing oars drinking coffee, eating a doughnut and reading the newspapers. 'English food is a calamity and a tragedy,' he wrote later. In the evening he would have half a pint of stout in the college beer cellar. It was a traditional, English, clubbable, unreal way for a young man from the Caribbean to be living, and it left him feeling lonely and unfulfilled. He wrote a luminous panegyric to Trinidad:

I feel nostalgic for home. Do you know what I long for? I long for the nights that fall blackly, suddenly, without warning. I long for a violent shower of rain at night. I long to hear the tinny tattoo of heavy raindrops on a roof, or the drops of rain on the broad leaves of that wonderful plant, the wild tannia. But, in short, I long for home, or perhaps, the homely atmosphere. And I miss my bicycle rides, and the sea, and the pit at Rialto, and the sort of cigarettes I used to smoke, to every one's scandal.

It was a time of desperate longing for Vidia, and by the end of March he had moved beyond Wertherism; he was going off the rails.

'This is a desperate plea for help,' he wrote to Kamla in a scrawled hand. 'I am broke, broke, broke. Can you send me £5–£10.' He wrote home from Málaga in southern Spain a fortnight later, now on the rails, sounding manic: 'Since March 30 I have been travelling constantly. Take out a map of Europe and follow me . . . steamer for Calais . . . Paris the following day. Austerlitz Railway Station. Romantic name – romantic journeys. Huge locomotives pulling expresses bound for all over Europe . . . Did not sleep that night. Next morning, at Narbonne, decided to be luxurious and have breakfast in the dining car, just as the sun was rising. Beautiful. Paris – Châteauroux – Toulouse – Carcassonne – Narbonne – Perpignan . . . Four armed police go past the railway coach corridor in Port Bou. Later, passport inspected – 3rd time in Spain. My temper rises and I swear loudly in English . . . Barcelona at 3 – travelling constantly, then, for 19 hours. Ordinary station, nasty and blackened with smoke. At the exit hordes of touts trying to sell you their taxis and their hotel . . . Have coffee in a room that overlooks one of the beautiful avenues of Barcelona; speak to my hostess and her daughter – a slim, pretty little thing of 22 who had been playing the piano while I was eating. Presently I find that I am flirting with both mother and daughter . . . Tomorrow I leave for Cordoba or for Madrid.' On the way back, he had an intense but embarassing encounter with a woman on a train. 'A Spanish lady came into the coach,' he remembered. 'We talked during the night and I embraced her. That was very comforting.' He explained to her in less than perfect Spanish that he was not feeling well, but 'she misunderstood. I was telling her about my mental condition. She thought I was telling her that I had syphilis or something.'[2]

When Vidia got back to England, he was in a bad state. Trinidad was off. 'The fact is,' he admitted, 'I spent too much money in Spain. And, during the nervous breakdown (yes, it was that) I had, I grew rash and reckless and threw money about with a don't-care-a-damn inconsequence. My only opportunity of recuperating from my present chaos is to remain in England this summer and live very cheaply.' Pa, as ever, was loving and tolerant; he offered no reprimand but, like Mr Biswas, sent his son a copy of *Outwitting Our Nerves* by sea mail and pressed him not to be downcast. 'Lose yourself in the throes and thrills of your creative work,' he suggested, 'and write on E[ast] I[ndian] or EI-Negro themes. We must not let Selvon alone get away with it.' As for himself, 'In this struggle for existence I feel just hemmed in by hard, unescapable facts and forces.' Vidia responded blandly: 'The grass is green; and the wind is not too sharp. It is agreeable to go for bicycle rides into the country around Oxford or for walks.' He had made new friends, played cricket, done a painting in oils and been paid eleven guineas by the BBC for a story called 'Potatoes', its Caribbean setting giving him an opportunity to dream of home. He had held a bring-a-bottle party in his rooms attended by forty people, including women and the Dean, and been elected secretary of 'the Martlets (the College Intellectuals).' This, he murmured loudly to Sati in Trinidad and Kamla in India, was, 'Not an honour to shout about.'

Vidia thought he understood what had gone wrong. 'Of course I know the reason for my breakdown: loneliness, and lack of affection. You see, a man isn't a block of wood that is sent abroad and receives two notches as a sign of education. He is much more. He feels and he thinks. Some people, alas, feel more, and think more than others, and they suffer. It is no good thinking that the sensitive man is happier or greater. No one cares for your tragedy until you can sing about it, and you require peace of mind to do this.' Pa was worried about Vidia, writing to Kamla, 'I have sent him some money. I am really very, very sorry for him. He is so impulsive, so unpredictable.'

Afraid of what might lie ahead, Vidia found the name of a psychologist in the pages of the *Oxford Mail* and made an appointment. The man came from central Europe, and gave him two free consultations. Vidia said later: 'He told me that I was just racially insecure, and I rejected this, then later I saw that it was the great solitude which was leading to that feeling of insecurity. Probably he was getting it right, but I hated him because if you go and expose yourself to someone at a moment of your greatest weakness you do hate them. But it's one of

the great triumphs in my life that without having any further connections with psychologists and doctors I was able to deal with it ... I
took hints from the psychologist and worked on it and that means just
as before I was questioning myself all the time internally, regardless of
where I was, whether I was in a café, or in a bus or talking to people,
I was now fighting back, I wasn't surrendering to it. And I won
through.' In later years, when life was going badly and he had sealed
himself off against his own emotions, 'I measured everything by the
unhappiness of those eighteen months. So I always felt good, nothing
could be as bad as that ... It was a great depression verging on
madness ... Pat was a great solace to me at that period; probably I
clung to her because of that depression.'[3]

*

During the summer of 1952, Vidia and Pat's relationship became closer.
He could reveal his state of mind to her in a way that was impossible with
others. Only she, he suggested, would be able to save him from himself.
Writing from his room in Univ, he told her, in a profound admission, that
beneath his impossibility, his complexity and his rages, he had a clear
moral vision, or an integrity. The clarity of Pat's letters to him and her
approach to life had made his own writing less opaque.

> You first met me when I was in the grips of a long and suicidal
> depression. I suppose I am a depressive. I observe this, not in
> pride or in horror, but simply as I would observe that it is
> raining and that tropical skies are usually boringly blue.
> Whether the depression causes the fatigue or fatigue the
> depression I don't know. But both are causeless and both scare
> me; and both make me a difficult man to live with ... I am
> telling you this so that you will be a bit more patient with me
> whenever you sense that I am sinking to the depths. You saved
> me once, and it is from that rescue that I have been able to keep
> going – from Feb 9 to today. I love you, and I need you.
> Please don't let me down. Please forgive my occasional lapses.
> At heart I am the worthiest man I know.

Realizing the strength of their connection, he prepared her a reading
list to reveal the world of his childhood: Hinduism, as mediated
through Western eyes. He suggested several Indian epics and dramas,
Christopher Isherwood and Swami Prabhavananda's translation of the

Bhagavad Gita, 'Intro by Aldous Huxley. (ESSENTIAL)' and '*The Hindu View of Life* by Prof. Radhakrishnan (INTERESTING).'

When the long vacation came, things fell apart again. Penniless, Vidia had to lodge with Rudranath and Ruth at their new house in Balham in south London. Their son Rudy, who was seven years old, remembered Vidia being treated with condescension. 'My father had great intellectual arrogance, and he was tough on Vidia. He had a teacher-student attitude to his nephews and nieces. He was like a lord of the manor ... A lot was happening: his nephew Devendranath was suffering an acute schizophrenic illness and thought he was Christ ... My father would have gone at Vidia. He didn't like his affected pseudo-Oxford accent, and Vidia was an angry, mixed-up young man. I can remember him singing "Ol' Man River" and darning his socks.'4 Nor did Ruth like Vidia's behaviour. She was a university graduate – she had met Rudranath when University College London was evacuated to Bangor during the war – and objected to being treated like a housekeeper. Vidia quickly deduced that 'a campaign of humiliation' was being conducted against him by his extended family. The trouble began with a familiar kitchen stand-off. Vidia, a Univ man and secretary of the Martlets, was asked to wash the dishes, but continued to read a newspaper before sauntering to the sink, where he was told to sit down again by Owad's wife, Jean. 'Don't pamper him at all,' insisted Ruth, trying to convert her displaced Hindu in-laws to a modern English approach to household chores. 'He must learn to do these things.' Vidia wrote a letter to his parents in a tight, angry hand, including a diagram of his bedroom to show how visitors to the bathroom had to pass through its cramped confines. 'I asked for a chair for the bedroom in which they had so kindly put me up for £1 a week ... Ruth said that I was to take one and bring it down every morning.' Then she asked him not to drop his cigarette ash on the floor. For Vidia, this was 'the last straw'. He told her he would not allow his spirit to be broken, and left.

It did not occur to him that his uncle might be doing a favour by renting him a room, or that his aunt might expect him to wash-up or not drop cigarette ash; he saw the encounter only in terms of the slight to his dignity. 'I am very homesick,' he admitted to Kamla. 'I am scared to be alive. For the past six months an air of unreality has hung about the things I have done.' It was not easy at this time for someone with brown or black skin to find accommodation in Britain, although East

Indians tended to fare better than West Indians; a survey of 300 London landladies in the early 1950s found that only 26 per cent would accept 'lightly-coloured non-European' students, while a mere 10 per cent took black people; some charged a sliding 'colour tax' on foreigners.[5] In Sam Selvon's book *The Housing Lark*, a character called Syl says his name is Ram Singh Ali Mohommed Esquire and mutters 'aloo, vindallo, dansak, and chutney' in order to get a room. The landlord rumbles him. ' "You look like an Indian, but you are from the same islands as those immigrants . . . you are not from the East."

"I used to live in the East End," Syl say hopefully.

"That is not far enough East," the Englisher say, "Take a week's notice as from today." '[6]

Vidia travelled to Harrogate and lodged unhappily with the 'upper class, but poor' parents of a friend from his college, John Fawcett. He wanted to be part of another world, but with the Fawcetts he again began to feel uneasy. Looking back, he thought, 'They were anxious to be nice to me, but I felt awkward. There was something about the food. I didn't like the ritual of napkins and napkin rings in John's house. I just felt it wasn't me. So I was rather primitive. And the thing about 1952, I was mentally disturbed. I was very, very disturbed, very melancholy, I had a degree of clinical depression. It had to do with lack of money, solitude, sexual deprivation.'[7]

The grace he displayed at Oxford was not enough to carry him through, or give him security. Peter Bayley had been impressed by Vidia's confidence, but it was skin-deep. When he and his wife, Patience, invited a group of undergraduates from Univ to lunch, 'there were one or two dumbstruck Freshmen who were very awkward and shy . . . Vidia was much more socially at ease and of course he was full of ideas and conversations. We had a very nice dinner service, Limoges, and the gravy-boat was all in one. I remember Vidia going to pour gravy. He meant to pick it up and it wouldn't come loose on the saucer and he looked about and then he put his hand down and I said, "It's all in one Vidia." Silly, trivial story. He was socially an extraordinarily composed person. He would come sometimes to the house in winter, when it was cold . . . My wife used to make cinnamon toast and he loved cinnamon toast.'[8] Vidia, then, was able to adjust and compose himself in a social, formal setting.

*

Pa was glad Vido had abandoned the Capildeos, but had worrying news of his own: more family responsibility: 'This will pain you: but your Ma will be having a baby – in September or October ... I know it's a mess, but there we are.' Vidia was not happy, but he wrote to Ma that he thought it would make 'little difference, except perhaps for you'. Ma was surprised herself. 'I myself never was thinking that I am going to have another baby,' she wrote in fractured English. 'I got very discourage and mindsick to know that it will be true. I am just telling myself that the Lord knows best, and there must be a reason why.' Vidia responded warmly to his mother 'that nothing will ever make me stop having all the respect and love in the world for you ... Frankly, whenever I think about you and Pa, I think that you have been noble.'

Vidia communicated with Patricia intensely by letter, but the dispute with his uncle, his lack of money and the plight of his parents were shown to her in partial glimpses. He felt embarrassed. Pat had returned to Birmingham in early July and taken a job on a farm near Kingstanding. Each day, she had to bicycle ten miles through the suburbs and country lanes, hoe weeds or pick potatoes in the fields, and then bicycle home again before trying to write a few lines to Vidia. 'This will be a terrible letter as I am so tired I just don't know what I'm doing,' she wrote on 10 July. 'You doubtless will shudder at the thought of me working with labourers' wives, getting my hands caked with mud.' She had grown fascinated by one of the farm workers, Peter Petch.

> I should say he knows or rather has read more English
> literature than you even. He is completely self-educated – by
> that I mean he reads purely for pleasure. He is not completely
> unselfconscious, if you get what I mean, but his approach to
> literature is absolutely unaffected. I think you'd find it
> fascinating for people like that are so hard to find. His life is a
> rather tragic one. His wife was quite nice looking and was an
> enthusiastic cyclist. A couple of years ago she became suddenly
> paralysed. She is now on her back all the time – suspended and
> strapped – it's awful. He looks after her in addition to his farm
> work. Don't imagine he is an indifferent farm worker either. He
> wins prizes for ploughing and things – quite extraordinary.
> Everything centres upon his wife who lies in a downstairs room.

Vidia was immediately jealous of the 'not completely unselfconscious' Mr Petch, with his skill at the plough and his apparent erudition and virtue, and conscious of the likely sexual need generated by an incapacitated wife. Lodging with John Fawcett's family and feeling like 'a hopeless intruder', Vidia was conscious only of his own insecurity. Unlike his friends, the fellow undergraduates with whom he blended so seemingly easily, he had nowhere to go. He made plans to meet Pat at the theatre in Stratford one evening later in the month, concealing his intermittent letters to her in disguised envelopes to deceive Mr Hale. 'My financial position is hopeless. I will starve after the end of August ... If the BBC accept my story I may get some cash.'

Not enamoured by the idea of doing farm or manual work, Vidia was caught 'in an agony of love and frustration. I want you so badly ... I suppose what has really got me down is the utter solitude in which I now find myself and the prospect of ten more weeks of it.' Pat made detailed plans for their meeting: 'Sheila tells me that the theatre bus leaves Stratford twenty minutes after the performance ends so there should be plenty of time ... You might get a cheap day return even if you do go back late if the guard on the train is indulgent.' She fretted over his health: 'For all your talk about working and feeling better during the winter I'm sure that coming from the tropics, you're liable to get run down during the winter even though you don't realise it.' Crucially, she had not yet told her father that she was going to meet him. 'I feel so weary by the time evening comes that I shirk it. This week-end, or perhaps to-night, I really will ... All my love Pat. P.S. I love you 6^2.' The squared six referred to a joke between them about love; when Sewan was a little boy and his sisters asked him how much he loved them, he would answer numerically, 'I love you six.'

When Pat broke the news to her father, the reaction was explosive. Stratford was off; she suggested Vidia might go with a friend rather than waste the chance of a night at the theatre, and sent him the tickets for seats P25–26, price nine shillings and sixpence. The squabble with her father, a common intergenerational and transcultural dispute that was now escalating badly, caused Pat to wonder in the language of the time whether she should leave home.

> I have worked like a nigger all day trying to drive out all the unpleasant weights that have settled on my inside ... I can't write you the whole nasty little altercation. I don't think it will serve any useful purpose besides. Amongst other things my father was determined to have it out with you if I went to

Stratford . . . It is 'Indians or University – You can't have
both!' Incredible, isn't it? I don't think he would carry out the
threat of next term being my last. I hope he would be too
ashamed. I'm screwing up my courage to face the music.

Vidia, staying with Guy Lorriman in Kent despite an earlier promise
never to accept the hospitality of his acquaintances again, was horrified.
'I need hardly say that such a step, in addition to being extremely
foolish, will also prove calamitous,' he informed her drily. 'You know
how I stand. Besides I am convinced that one ought to do all in one's
power to maintain cordial relations with one's parents.'

Pat calmed down, and they resolved to see each other later in the
summer. She wrote about Laurence Sterne's discursive novel *Tristram
Shandy*, which she loved, and about her frantic little sister Eleanor, with
whom she had to share a bed: 'You should see her! She's racing around
the garden wielding a rifle. She alternates two headgears. Sometimes a
homemade Red Indian head dress made from coronation (1936) ribbon
and yellow feathers, sometimes Mummy's A[ir] R[aid] P[recautions]
helmet (1940–46) and a pair of goggles.' Home life was not inspiring.
Each evening the family would eat at six o'clock, and afterwards her
father would go 'over the way' to the Kingstanding pub, where he
would drink quietly with the local butcher, newsagent and builder until
closing time. Meanwhile, at the farm, the estimable 'Mr. Petch offered
to lend me "The Communist Manifesto" on Wednesday. That man
gave me a further shock yesterday by talking quite knowledgeably
about Rowlandson and Hogarth.'

In August she travelled south to Gloucestershire to stay with Auntie
Lu, her favourite aunt, her mother's elder sister, Lucy. Free from
parents, correspondence was easier, and they managed a snatched
meeting in Gloucester, where Pat had been to school. Later she wrote,
'I received your letter this morning. I can't describe my feelings as I
read it. I stood at the bottom of the stairs clutching the milk bottle and
feeling alternately as great as the whole world and as humble the
smallest speck of dust on it . . . I have just breakfasted on a huge peach,
brown bread and butter and three cups of coffee. You are the only
thing wanting. But wanting is a pleasant way, nevertheless. I suppose it
is because I saw you on Monday but I feel very peaceful – as if I'd
known you for a couple of centuries.' She told him about meeting Ella
Wallen, an old schoolteacher.

> She first made my acquaintance at the age of eight when she
> was new and had to teach the small "advanced arithmetic" class
> of the second form . . . She was toiling through fractions when
> suddenly she saw my hand waving about. I was a conscientious
> child in those days and with a kindly smile she waited for me to
> ask for mathematical enlightenment. I looked at her coldly and
> asked, "Why do I have to learn arithmetic when I'm going to
> be an actress?"

Back in Oxford now, scraping his landlady Mrs King's breakfast into
the bin each morning rather than admit he could not eat greasy sausages
and bacon, Vidia wrote Pat a long, confessional letter by return. He felt
able for the first time to express a petty personal secret which made him
feel ashamed. He described an experience of literary rejection, how his
novel had been sent back to him.

> It was in the middle of December – a Sunday. I had come back
> from London, and had found my returned novel resting
> mockingly in my pigeon hole . . . I drank gin heavily. After that I
> remember three things. One, screaming for more gin. Two,
> feeling hopelessly drunk and lost, and wishing to beat my head
> against a wall. I stumbled down the stairs and opened a door. I
> wanted a bed to lie down on. There was a woman in the room,
> making herself up or getting ready for bed. I ignored her, said,
> 'Excuse me', and flopped down on the bed. When I got up she
> was gone. I crossed the road, couldn't find No 12 for a long time.
> Mrs. King must have heard me prowling around. She opened the
> door & put on the light. 'Up here Mr. Naipaul,' she called. It was
> only yesterday that she reminded me of that disgraceful incident.
> I was never drinking man. When I came to Oxford, I was a
> teetotaller; but very shortly I found that 'the real Oxford'
> consisted of smart young men who drank heavily. In three terms
> I got drunk about 6 times. Then I went to the agricultural camp
> in the vac. And got drunk every day I was there. Surprisingly, I
> found that this had made me a sort of hero with a group of
> Welsh miners . . . I wonder whether it is right telling you all this.
> But who else can I tell? You are the only one who ought to know
> me completely and wholly, and I must hold nothing back.

He had been through an even more humiliating experience with drink
when he first arrived at Univ. After a surfeit of port, he had vomited

over his clothes. 'I didn't rinse them out or anything. I took them just as they were to the Oxford valet service which is just next door to University College and the man was shocked beyond words. He said, "I can't accept this. I have to think of the staff." And I was with him, I agreed with him.'[9]

Vidia's letter to Pat also contained a rare statement of his own philosophy. Private ideas that had been forming inside him slowly and would expand over the years into an intellectual and literary programme could now be communicated. He complained about the hypocrisy that came from revealed religion, using Guy Lorriman's social Catholicism as an example.

> The Rosary is chanted (in itself a most primitive incantatory magic) and Lorriman is convinced he is good; and convinced that his desire to rise will be blessed. What shall I think about the mind that can tolerate and praise this: willing to praise his own speeches in his magazine, willing to contravene all ethics, even journalistic ones, to delay the date of publication to print his own praise, and only restrained by the fear that such praise, appearing in his own magazine, might not do him good. And, then, seriously wondering how I, a pagan, could have any sense of what is right! This isn't an isolated freak of behaviour. It betrays the entire make-up.

Rationalist, culturally Hindu with a dose of Trinidad's practical Christianity, having grown up in an island society where each religion and race had to exist in parallel private and public spheres, the son of a questioning father and a morally upright mother, Vidia had formed his own ethical notions and applied them stringently. He did not want to reform, convert or emancipate; he was a watcher, a writer:

> I think that we have in us a cumulative conscience, a sort of birthright of the human race. We do know what is right and what is wrong: stealing, adultery, infidelity, killing a member of one's own people or tribe (you can kill as many of the opposite types as possible!), lying and dishonesty. The cliché virtues are common to all races, and their observation in the breach is common to all races, too. Now don't feel that I want to reform the human race. I am the spectator, the flâneur par excellence. I am free of the emancipatory fire. I want to create myself, to work

out my own philosophy that will bring me comfort. I want to see the good and the bad.

He shared two formative moments of his childhood with Pat:

> My first memory of sadness – cosmic sadness – came in 1941
> or thereabouts. We were living in a small house in the country,
> far away from everybody. It was late tropic evening, rapidly
> growing dark. I looked out of the window to the kitchen that was
> downstairs and began to cry. I had seen my mother and some of
> my sisters. I suddenly felt that we were all hopelessly lost,
> without any purpose. My mother saw me crying and asked why.
> Naturally I couldn't say. Then it was, too, that I came across
> some of my mother's girlhood possessions and the futility and
> waste of her life struck me. I was nine at the time. When I was
> twelve, I went to the seaside. Three people – a brother & 2
> sisters – had been drowned. They could have been saved, but the
> fishermen had wanted to know how much they would be paid!
> Oh, the terror I felt then. The fishermen pulled in the seine
> [fishing net] and brought in the bodies and caught an
> extraordinary number of catfish, always anxious to get at the
> helpless. The three bodies relaxed in the sand. The sun going
> down. And, from a cheap beach café, a gramophone: 'Bésame
> mucho" – Kiss me often, my darling, and say that you'll always
> be mine. I don't know what people of 12 feel, but I have never
> forgotten that.

Pat reassured him of his literary potential, but told him he should not write only about futile and miserable people. 'Your stories have humanity but not in the full sense. You stop too often with the tired and turgid mother, the insignificant clerk, the second rate school teacher. You realise the futility, stupidity and misery. But that's not all, you know it isn't.' There was nothing unusual about the depression he might feel,

> You tell me you are frantically lonely and miserable because you
> can't see me and can't work because of it. I won't take the
> responsibility for you getting a Second [class degree] . . . And
> don't start flattering yourself that your state is unique, your
> feelings and sufferings incomparable. You may have had a
> breakdown a little while ago but it was to yourself that you had

to look for remedy. You know the power of mind over matter.
You are quite an ordinary mechanism, my love. The only
difference between it – the mechanism – and another is that I am
in love with it and I can't bear to see it run down.

Vidia was attracted by Pat's sympathy and by her perception. 'My letters
are so dull. I would like to write brilliant letters – the type that people
publish,' he apologized. 'My theories about emotion and the written
word are mildly exciting, though. And, despite the fact that you never
agree with any of my literary judgements (a big source, I assure you, of
future squabbles), I shall expound them to you one day.'

*

Pat's comment that Vidia's stories had 'humanity but not in the full sense'
was right. The first story to break through to something fresh was
'Potatoes'. He found his own voice for the first time, poignant and funny.
He introduced his first non-Indian character, adjusting the dialogue
accordingly, and brought in sly comedy. The setting of the story overlaps
old and new, Hindi and English, traditional Indian life and 'this cosmo-
politan hotch-potch where nothing was sacred'. Mrs Gobin, a young
widow, tries to gain independence from her powerful mother. ' "Ever
since you have been living in the town, you have been playing the white
woman," ' says her mother. Spotting a gap in the vegetable market, she
visits a merchant who sells her two hundred pounds of potatoes at an
inflated price. 'An obsolete cash-register was operated by a venerable-
looking man with a beard, who could pass for a religious prophet, but
who was, in fact, merely a Hindu of mediocre caste. Mrs Gobin sets up a
stall where her son sits 'blackening in the sun, and selling nothing'. The
local jeweller buys five pounds of potatoes, and the rest go bad in the
heat. So Mrs Gobin 'put on her going-out outfit and went to her mother,
to collect her allowance.'[10]

Back in Oxford during the long, hot summer, Vidia's depression
worsened, even as his intellectual understanding and his literary ability
grew. He did not tell Pat when he made a half-hearted attempt to kill
himself. 'It was a very bad period, the long, long summer with my
questioning myself internally night and day, every waking minute, that
great depression,' he said later. 'I tried foolishly once to put an end to it.
It didn't work.' Vido dressed in the suit he had worn on the day he left
Trinidad to fly to New York and start his new life. Then he went to the

gas fire in his room and turned on the gas, but did not light it. He lay down on the bed, wearing the suit, a stately would-be corpse. 'I dressed for the occasion.' He had decided to play a poor man's Russian roulette: the gas fire worked on a coin-operated meter, and he would lie there until it ran out. If he lived, he lived; if he died, he died. As he lay there in his suit, the gas ran out. He took this as an omen. Afterwards, he forced himself to postpone his suicide, reasoning that there was no point in doing it that day. 'I used to put it off, day to day, saying, "Pat is coming to see you next week." '[11] He did not try to kill himself again.

He met Pat in Oxford, in Gloucester and in the old Cotswold village of Chedworth, with its oak-timbered buildings that she loved for their beauty. They met again in Northleach, among the quaint houses of yellow Cotswold stone. Vidia's landlady told him he had done well for himself. 'Mrs King went into raptures over you. "She is a good girl, Mr. Naipaul. You stick to her, and you'll be all right." And don't I know it.' After one romantic meeting, Pat wrote: 'I do think our behaviour in cafes etc. is rather wonderful. We have world-shaking arguments, you read histrionic poetry, we quarrel fiercely, I drink milk, you don't eat meat (but are obviously no true vegetarian) . . . we are having a rather wonderful love affair, don't you think?'

Vidia's family found out about Pat by accident. 'By the way,' Pa wrote in August, 'some girlfriend of yours named Pat sent you a letter.' It had been forwarded to Trinidad by the college by mistake and read by the whole family. Vidia was humiliated, but knew he had no choice but to explain. In formal, stilted tones, he expressed his 'displeasure' that the letter had been opened. Appreciation of Pat was confined to a peroration in pained double negatives, a stylistic tic he claimed to have copied from the Dean.

> But I shall satisfy in everything your curiosity. Patricia Ann Hale is a girl of 20. She is a member of the university, not unintelligent, nor altogether unattractive. I met her in February and have been thankful ever since. She befriended me at the height of my illness, put up with all my moods – my coarseness and my fits of anguish. The relationship between us, while not a platonic one, is so far virtuous. The talk about being 'netted' is rather cynical, and I do trust that you will not make things doubly difficult for us. Her father is making a terrible fuss about it, and I hope that the same narrowness will not be found in you. About her character: she is good, and simple. Perhaps a bit

too idealistic, and this I find on occasion rather irritating. She
insists on looking at the good, and chooses to shut her eyes to
the bad. She shares my literary tastes, and I have found my
friendship with her most stimulating.

He told Kamla about her too, who wrote Pat a generous letter at his
request: 'Dear Miss Hale . . . Vidia's is not an easy nature to deal with
– he is more than a handful. What lies on the surface is in exact
contrast to what lies at the bottom and when once you have realised
this, then everything is just fine . . . I have no objection whatsoever and
I am sure you would find my parents as amenable and co-operative.'
Seepersad, though, was not pleased. 'The girl, I have no doubt, is
everything you say of her, and we are deeply grateful to any whose
understanding and solicitude helped you so much when you most stood
in need . . . But, as you say, her father disapproves of the relationship
between you; and here at home no one is happy over the idea of your
marrying any but an Indian.' Vidia's reply to Pa was cruelly discour-
aging. 'I don't want to break your heart, but I hope I never come back
to Trinidad, not to live, that is, though I certainly want to see you and
everybody else as often as I can . . . I have really been suffering from
an abnormal mental condition. I was depressive. I have seen the
psychologist twice and there is now no further need to see him . . . Of
course, I don't intend getting married for at least two years.'

In early September, only three days after the assurance that the
relationship with Pat was 'so far virtuous', they had sex for the first
time, Vidia having bought a contraceptive gel from a chemist with great
embarrassment. The 'rather wonderful love affair' had become a real
love affair. They were both virgins, both physically reticent and neither
was a natural seducer. The mental implications were substantial. Vidia
tried in his mind to convert the consummation of his powerful sexual
desire into an act of purity, and to convince himself that he would from
now on be instinctively faithful. He wrote Pat a disturbed letter which
exhibited feelings of guilt, jealousy and self-justification alongside
promises of love, honour and devotion. Awareness of the power of his
own latent lust was converted into a fear of her possible infidelity, and
marriage seemed a solution.

> I merely wanted to tell you that I loved you completely and
> that Tuesday formed a lasting bond between us because you
> had surrendered something to me which ought to be

surrendered only to the man whom you loved and who loved you and who wanted to marry you. You see, I also felt that I had aroused you sexually and I know how dangerous this can be and I felt terribly responsible. Essentially it is an act of love, not of lust. I wanted you to know that I had thought at length before doing what we did. I was prepared for a showdown with your parents and mine. And yet I was worried. I didn't feel sure how you felt. I was tortured by memories of Mr. Petch and realized that on that Thursday you had written me a long letter that concerned itself almost wholly with the man. I was also worried about losing you, because that would ruin Schools [final exams] for me. I shall be perfectly frank with you. I feel myself capable of lasting love because now, you see, I am really not drawn to other women. I just say to myself 'she hasn't got a quarter of what my Pat has.' I know I am capable of this and I wanted some similar assurance from yourself. I was also worried because I know that you had such a high view of human nature that it would be easy for a smooth-tongued person to hurt you – you know in what way I mean. And you know, too, how much I worship purity . . . Somerset Maugham is right when he says that deep requited love is one of the rarest things in the world. So I feel and I am anxious to keep everything that way. I feel I have been luckier than I deserve.

In larger handwriting, he added, 'I feel a thorough ass writing this. Frankly, I don't know whether it is an expression of love or of stupidity . . . In other words, if you decide to be faithful to me, and if you want me, I want to marry you.' Later still, forty-nine years later, he wrote a troubled note on the letter: 'The relationship consummated. The jealousy over Peter Petch. Disingenuous talk of the purity of love.' At the beginning, Vidia felt 'sex with Pat was fumbling and awful for both of us. Pat was very nervous. I wasn't trained enough or skilled enough or talented enough to calm her nerves, probably because I didn't want to calm her nerves. It didn't work.'[12]

CHAPTER SEVEN

TO THE EMPTY HOUSE

AT THE START OF the Michaelmas term of 1952, Vidia moved out of college to lodge in an ugly brick building near some university offices in Wellington Square. His attempts to become a writer continued. Like all would-be achievers, he raged against mediocre types who were having greater success. Hearing the hack crime novelist Ernest Dudley broadcasting on the Light Programme, he felt obliged to write a letter of complaint to the BBC: 'I have just listened to tonight's *Dudley Nightshade*, a programme for "listeners who don't scare easily". Such a humourless, horrorless jumble of cliché snippets, introduced with such pompousness . . .' Then he thought better of it, turned the paper over and began a letter to Pat instead. News about himself from *Caribbean Voices* was more interesting: 'I hear that the BBC man, in a review of the work he has broadcast, speaks of "V. S. Naipaul's corrosive satire." Don't you want me to keep on being a corrosive satirist? It is my nature. If I write otherwise I shall cry as I write, like Dickens. I can't write about sadness sadly. It would kill me . . . Oh, darling, I love you from the bottom of my corrosively satirical heart. Your own Vidia.'

They saw each other whenever possible. In the days before mobile phones, email or texting, everything had to be done by hand. Pat would scribble a note in the morning ('No time for anything more as the hatch closes at a quarter to nine and I haven't been to breakfast yet') and send them to Univ, where they would arrive in his pigeonhole addressed to 'Mr Napail' or 'Mr Naipoo', the two syllables of his surname defeating, deliberately or otherwise, Douglas Millin and the college servants. Vidia would take a bus up the Banbury Road to St Hugh's, find Miss Hale absent and write on a scrap of file paper under the watchful nose of the uniformed porter ('My dear Pat, Good news. The BBC is giving me 11 guineas for the story. I got the contract today. Yrs Vidia'). Other students encouraged the relationship. Pat's friend Pluto told her 'the nicest thing at breakfast'. When someone said 'you can't have deep and lasting friendships at Oxford "it's so artificial",

Pluto said "Nonsense" as usual and that she could think of several friendships that would (she thought) outlast Oxford – for instance us!' This was an important compliment, since Pluto was afraid of Vidia, having had a scary experience with Sikh soldiers while interned in the Far East during the war.

In October, Ma gave birth to a baby daughter named Nalini, or Nella. At the same time, to add to the action, Kamla sent news: 'You might be very surprised when you hear that a few days ago I became engaged to an Indian chap who comes from Fiji,' she told Vidia. 'He is Christian, though, and with the most awful name of Vincent Richmond, yet I don't think I can get the ideal person.' She seemed uncertain about her emotional commitment. Marriage was years away; she might come home and become a school principal; or she might leave Benares without completing her degree because people were spreading vicious rumours about her; or she might go to Fiji and marry Vince. Pa tolerated Christianity, writing to Kamla: 'If a fellow is a decent Indian, it doesn't matter if he is a Christian; but he should <u>never</u> be a Mohammedan.'[1] Next, news reached Vidia that the diabetic, blind matriarch who had held the family together – Soogee Govinda, Rosalie Gobin, Soogee Capildeo Maharaj, Queen Victoria, Nanie – had died at the age of sixty-five. 'Nanie kicked the bucket on the 23rd of last, and my! she had a wonderful funeral,' wrote Sati irreverently.

Vidia's jealousy and insecurity continued. Finding a friendly letter from Peter Petch lying on Pat's desk, he was driven into a fury. 'I feel <u>a fool</u> ... I don't know what to do or think or say. Perhaps I am stupid, but I think this is well – I asked you not to deceive me. Well, if Mr Petch is just being friendly!' Pat tried to soothe him, but he would not be soothed. No Iago poisoned his mind against fair Patricia; he poisoned himself with imaginary sexual fears about men who might offer her something he could not. He was worried she was acting in a college play. 'Darling, I have been a fool,' he wrote, 'and I am terribly ashamed of myself. I should be encouraging you – but you know the meanness and the fears that made me do otherwise. But nothing will make me cease detesting those wretched acting men of Oxford. I have managed to work all the gall out of my system. Please act; you have my blessing and you can be assured of my support – whatever I can give ... I feel unspeakably brutal when I make you cry ... Please, please – never stop loving me – your own Vidia. 6[1000].'

Pat was shocked by his anger, railed against it, but was finally

acquiescent, blaming herself and the force of his love for what had
happened, setting a cage that would catch her for the rest of her life. 'I
think this evening was probably irreparable,' she told him:

> Darling, remember my agony when you lose your temper and
> say those frightful things. I do half understand that it wouldn't
> happen if you didn't love me. But you see I couldn't say those
> things to you ever and I am or can be very brutal. If – God – if
> I did know you for the rest of my life they would never cease
> to tear me in two . . . I fear you must despise me at last. I have
> nothing but contempt for myself . . . I think this might alienate
> you further. I nearly gave myself once before. But the
> realisation that my love was not complete stopped me. I could
> not have given myself to you if I had not loved you completely.
> I have made my decision. I realise that one cannot have a
> second chance. I could not love or live with another man.

Vidia's love to the power of a thousand was a momentary respite. Two
months later, over Christmas, he returned to the assault in a piece of
confessional prose done half for himself and half for Pat. The restrictions of Mr Hale meant that he was unable to send it, so it became a
gradual diary. It was a rare example of internal, exploratory, idealistic
writing, of a kind that he never did again after his early twenties.

> I have decided, my life, that since I cannot write you, I shall
> hold this one-way talk with you & present it to you when I see
> you. In it I shall enter all the thought I think – and I shall be
> honest . . . What knifes me into acute agony is your acting. I
> think of you painted & wearing gaudy clothes not your own
> and I feel afraid. Afraid that you may change & stop being the
> woman I love . . . You see, I have a little bit of Hindu left in
> me and this cannot stand my wife painted & performing before
> people. And it is the <u>being away from me</u> that I fear.

A few days later he continued, becoming emotional, even melodramatic.
'Most of what I wrote last night is stupid, especially the Hindu bit . . .
Darling, you have filled me with a new strength. I feel stronger than
ever. I feel the great novels being written, I feel the urge to do great
things – for YOU. Please believe me, when I say that in all my plans,
you are the centre. Everything I do is for you. I just want to be yours,
to be the vessel for the creation of works that shall be monuments to

YOU.' Then he turned unusually soppy. 'I can carry you on my back and take you to the springs of love – pure and crystal. I can take you to the pot of gold under the rainbow and to the heart of a dew-drop.' He saw the future, their future:

> I cannot belong to India for the simple reason that I don't know the language. Language is so important in belonging. Not the superficial knowledge I have, say, of French, or Spanish – but a language one has grown up with. And, for me, that language is English and that spells Oxford, and Patricia, and Birmingham and Snow Hill and Kingstanding and your hands pressed against mine as we walk down to the Bull Ring (where Birmingham's politicians hold <u>socialistic</u> meetings, I bet). And it means coming back to Oxford and after 14 hrs hitch-hiking and saying that Birmingham is beautiful and being laughed at. It means getting your permission to go to Paris and getting a telegram saying NO. It means going to London lonely and returning and getting a telegram saying GO. It means YOU. We shall be a good & successful partnership. I shall make your parents glad that you married me. I shall make my parents exultant that I married you. We shall make the world aware of us and love us. We shall never part. We have become one often and that has riveted us together. Kill me the day I am unfaithful. For then I shall have grown cheap & worthless.

He concluded with a few lines from *Othello* and a let-out for his display of sentiment. 'If it were now to die, | 'Twere now to be most happy; for, I fear, | My soul hath her content so absolute | That not another comfort like to this | Succeeds in unknown fate . . . My dear Pat, Am in awful rush to get train. These letters are no good. I was ashamed of them; and still am. They may amuse you. All my love, Vidia.'

Patricia, at home in Kingstanding in the cold and the snow, working in a Birmingham tax office to get money, said she found life 'meaningless' and 'unutterably dead' without him. She read the Sanskrit epic the *Mahabharata*, wrote letters in sneaked moments and did her best to tolerate Eleanor, 'mercifully quiet at the moment trying to make a hand-puppet with a burst rubber ball and some bits of paper'. They had brief telephone calls, arranged days ahead, and managed to meet for an afternoon in Cheltenham. Pat made 'stern arrangements' for their parting at the bus station, in case anyone was watching. 'It was funny in the end,' she wrote afterwards. 'I was looking at you to see you light your pipe and shake out the paper . . . I keep thinking of you carrying cups in one hand and Yorkshire pancakes in the other looking so marvellous. I just want to take you to me – scarf hanging down, shoulders slightly slouched.' Vidia felt just as passionately. He could not envisage life without her, and hoped they would have children together. 'Oh my darling I wish you were here,' he wrote from Oxford at the end of December. 'I want so much to look at you and feel you and smell your breath and feel that you are alive and with me, feel that you love me and we have become indissolubly one. For, alone, I am weak and feel half a person. You are the stuff of my existence . . . I wish to give you my children. The desire to have a child by you is greater than ever. It would be the crowning act of our union.'

*

In January 1953, Seepersad Naipaul was taken ill at the *Guardian* and admitted to hospital with a coronary thrombosis; he remained there for six weeks, and when he was released rested at home because he had trouble walking. His chronic indigestion had turned out to be heart disease. Sati told Vido the news, and Kamla wrote her brother a harsh and emotional letter: 'Pa's greatest worry is that he cannot get his stories published. Sati wrote saying that he sent you one but you have done nothing about it so far. Now something immediate regarding the publishing of his stories means life or death for him and consequently life or death for us, especially those poor little children at home . . . Write something encouraging to Pa immediately . . . Carelessness about this means Pa's death.' Vidia said he would, but did nothing.

Far from home, aware that he could do little to help his father, he showed flashes of family feeling to Peter Bayley. 'When my little boy was born, my first child, it was February 1953 on a Tuesday morning, and Vidia and his friend Lawrence O'Keefe both turned up to my room. I'd just rung to the hospital and heard that it was a son and I was very surprised by Vidia's reaction – almost touchingly overjoyed, as if to say how marvellous you have a son. Maybe that was the old Hindu in him. I was really touched and they both said, "Well you won't want to have a tutorial now." So off they went. He talked later about flying a kite with my little boy, so I have always been surprised that he had no children. It was just exceptional human affection.'[2] It was around this time that Vidia met Jill Brain, an undergraduate studying history at St

Hilda's College, who would nearly supplant Pat in his affections some years later.

Vido told his father he should not worry; he would leave Oxford in June. 'If I try to hawk your book around, I wouldn't be doing you a favour. I would be trying to sell stuff that deserves to be published.' Rather than tell Pa that he thought the stories had no chance of being taken by a London publisher, he opted for inertia and silence. 'The manuscript was in a bad state. I didn't think the work was ready for publishing. I didn't want to wound him by making it explicit,' he said later.[3] Vidia investigated employment. The omens were not good. 'The Dean thinks the prospect of my getting a job in this country is a pretty bleak one, and I never thought otherwise,' he told Pa. 'He thinks, however, that I can perhaps represent a firm in some country – or something like that.' Vidia remained a foreigner in a foreign land; he had a footing only at Oxford University. Meanwhile, his examinations were approaching, 'and I must step up the work'. His father replied in a shaky hand, writing in pencil, in bed, thanking him and telling him he was 'the last hope of England' and should not take on the responsibility of his siblings or a wife: 'First, make your way in the world.'

Vidia's relationship with Pat endured through 1953, the year in which Mount Everest was climbed, Queen Elizabeth II was crowned and Winston Churchill was somehow awarded the Nobel Prize in Literature. Pat said they should not be formally engaged. 'We don't need things like that,' she wrote to Vidia. During the term-time they were together, and in the holidays they met whenever they could. 'I always imagined myself having a love affair with a man who possessed a great soul. I imagined earnest, exquisite conversations. Yet I don't want you to talk in those very precious moments. I just want to drift – lose myself in that nearness,' she wrote in March. 'I live through you. Goodnight my love. I'm just living for Tuesday and can't think of anything else.' Afterwards, on Easter Sunday, she wrote passively, 'Vidia, I have known ever since Tuesday that we are more in love, that I am more a part of you and you of me. I felt that you gave yourself more completely than ever before and that I received you more fully than ever before.' She accepted that her dreams of acting would have to be abandoned because of his anxieties. She embraced the idea of sacrifice in the cause of his possible greatness. 'You know I could not do anything without your real consent and I have proved to you that the pain of not doing it because of you is as nothing beside the pain of doing it without your support: I just can't.' Dependence was, underneath everything, what he wanted and needed; it would enable him to reinforce his idea of himself, and pursue much larger ambitions.

In April, another of his stories was broadcast on the BBC, his family sitting around the crackling Rediffusion set in Nepaul Street trying to hear each word. 'Old Man' tells of a Chinese family who find themselves stuck in Trinidad while trying to return home and, 'to use their mother's words, "do good" for the Chinese people' by welcoming the Communist leader Mao Zedong. The voice of the author intrudes: 'When we are abroad, you see, we realise that Trinidad, with its blending of peoples, and with its burning political problems of no significance, is really the world in small.'[4] It was a proficient and amusing story, but Vidia told his mother it was 'a pot-boiler, and I am quite ashamed of it. But I think it is what Swanzy wants. It is vaguely about Mary in Luis St. I have added a lot of pure lies.' He was working hard now, knowing he would be sitting his final exams for his Bachelor of Arts degree during the summer. 'The world, which hasn't been to Oxford, places perhaps an unjustified esteem on the place,' he told Pat, and listed his timetable for the Easter vacation:

> 8.00 Rise. 8.30 In Library. 8.30–9.30 Anglo Saxon. 9.30–10.30 Middle English. 10.30–11.00 Break for coffee & rolls (no breakfast). 11–12.30 Literature. Lunch. 1.30–4 Literature. Tea. 4.30–7 Literature. Dinner. 8–10 Literature. Leave College at 10. 10.30–11.30 French Drama.

Literature meant English, or at least British literature: the canon of dead white male poets, playwrights and novelists from the sixteenth to the nineteenth century: Edmund Spenser, William Shakespeare, George Herbert, John Dryden, Jonathan Swift, Alexander Pope, Henry Fielding and finally William Wordsworth. Twentieth-century writers were seen as untested, and suspect, and were excluded. Modernists, in the form of James Joyce, T.S. Eliot and Virginia Woolf, for instance, formed no part of his Oxford education. 'I met their work accidentally,' he said later. 'I was not interested in Modernism as a movement. It bypassed me. I couldn't get on with [Woolf's] *The Waves* – writing should never draw attention to itself.'[5] In a letter to Henry Swanzy, he denied that Eliot's themes had influenced his own writing at all. 'As a matter of fact, *The Waste Land* determined me to read no more Eliot for the rest of my life.' He added, to Swanzy: 'The future is as black as ever. Nobody loves me, nobody wants me. In England I am not English, in

India I am not Indian. I am chained to the 1000 sq. miles that is Trinidad; but I will evade that fate yet.'[6]

Although he was busy with revision, Vidia had time to worry about his elocution; after all, his education was not restricted to studying texts, and he did not want to stand out as a colonial. 'Can you pronounce "bourgeois" properly?' he asked Pat, whose own accent had adjusted from Midlands to Received Pronunciation as a result of elocution lessons. 'I used to say "boo-jwah". This, according to a man called Walker-Heneage (public school) is hopelessly wrong. Phonetically I think it is spelt (bu 'dzˇwa). I tried for two hours, but I couldn't get the pronunciation right. It is one of those things I must get used to not being able to do – like dancing.'

Vidia had other thoughts, too. Might Pat be able to make her letters a little erotic, he asked politely and obliquely? 'I do wish you could make your letters really "lurid" – if you know what I mean. I would like everything to be mentioned. I would like to hear about the more intimate things about you which no one else knows about; just as now I, without wishing to be shocking, would like to tell you how soothing &, at the same time, "maddening", to taste your mouth and feel your breasts.' There was little chance, as Pat did not even like to mention underwear. When she responded with a story of Eleanor racing about the flat with stones stuffed into a borrowed bra, the bra became, 'the garment I dislike mentioning – we both dislike the name'. She thought more of having children than having sex. 'I hope you realise that our children would be just like Eleanor and your brothers and sisters. We should loathe them half the time. I was thinking yesterday maybe I would like to have them at home because I'd want them all the time afterwards and nursing homes seem so horrible about that ... I am very much in love with the fundamental purity and honesty in you. I have a terrible, overmastering desire to throw myself at your feet.' Despite the extent of her commitment, a passing reference to Peter Petch in a letter still caused Vidia agitation.

In the summer of 1953, life looked better. Vidia had an interview with Burmah Oil, only '£625 a year starting, but they provide free furnished houses'. During their last summer days together at Oxford, he and Pat watched an outdoor performance of *Troilus and Cressida* by the university dramatic society. Sad not to be performing, Pat saved a copy of the programme with its harshly lit period photographs of the smartly dressed young actors, her contemporaries: Alasdair Milne as

Troilus, Sheila Graucob as Cressida and Patrick Kavanagh as Pandarus. Then the young lovers parted.

Back in Birmingham, Mr Hale spent the evenings 'over the way' at the pub; Eleanor ate beetroot and onion sandwiches, kept a bucket of tadpoles and screamed whenever she was made to have a bath. 'As she was carried from the bathroom I heard her singing for some unaccountable reason "I'm going to Westminster Abbey to be buried".... Eleanor is a little beast. She's been being horrible about "fat chests".' For the first time in a year, Vidia was mentioned in Kingstanding. 'Just after lunch to-day by the way Mummy asked if "that Indian" was still at Oxford. In spite of my agitation I still managed to feel resentful at the terms of reference. Anyway I said you had just taken Schools.' Pat listened to piano recitals on the radio, and yearned to be with Vidia. 'I'm not being melodramatic . . . What would I do if there was no cause to worry about your possible failure to do the washing up, or having babies in a hot climate? The mere thought makes me desolate. Please don't take your babies elsewhere.' She wanted a son. 'I had a crazy notion that Humphrey — a name I've never had any particular attachment for — would go with Naipaul.'

In a letter laden with anticipation, she made further plans. 'When our little girls are little they're going to have plaits except when they have very fat faces when I think fringe and bob will be rather charming — especially of course if the "Mongol strain" in you comes out.' Remaining in the Himalayan region, she told him she was following the story of Tenzing Norgay, who had recently climbed Mount Everest with Edmund Hillary.

> May I take this opportunity to say that much as I am attracted by Mrs Tensing I am not going to be a Hindu wife . . . Oh by the way, Mummy doesn't like India and Nehru! 'Nasty little hypocrite,' is her opinion of the latter, 'who wants to put his own house in order before he tries to dictate to other people.' He 'Shanghaied' Mountbatten over Cashmir . . . P.S. I found a completely white hair the other day. I yanked it out and put it in my French Dictionary. If it's still there I shall put it in the bottom of this envelope so that you'll see how you're driving me to an early grave!

In July the degree results were published. They both got a Second, or what Vidia called 'just a bloody, damned, ***** Second'. It was a slight consolation to learn that J.R.R. Tolkien had said his Anglo-Saxon paper was the best in the university. Pat's old teacher Ella Wallen, a spinster who disapproved heartily of Vidia, sent him a patronizing letter of congratulation: 'You must be feeling that an Oxford Second is a very pleasant thing to have achieved and worth coming halfway across the world for. I must say I think it's pretty bright of you; the change of climate would probably have addled my brain completely.'

Might he join the Indian diplomatic corps, Pa wondered? Might Kamla join, Vidia enquired? His sister sailed to England in June. Vidia had asked her to bring 'Gandhi's autobiography (sold only in India): *The Story of My Experiments with Truth*' and 'A good, readable, authoritative and exhaustive History of India (does any such exist?) and English translations of the Hindu epics and dramas.' Vidia was overjoyed to see Kamla again, introducing his glamorous elder sister to Pat and to Peter Bayley. Kamla rented a room next door to his lodgings in St John Street for a few days. 'Pat liked you very much; thought you pretty and considered that your personality was charming. She is glad that you are saner than me. I suppose that you liked her; but I can't be too sure,' he wrote to Kamla later. Pa sent her news of a possible job offer from St Augustine Girls' High School. 'Do come home as early as you can. Wish I could send you some money,' he concluded, deleting the remaining sentences with a string of XXXs.

The deleted text ran as follows:

> Believe me, Kams, we were never so hard up in our whole life. I am not working. The Guardian (because of the nature of my illness) is terminating my service at the end of the month. [The editor Courtenay] Hitchins told me so yesterday. Just think . . . but do, Kamla, do not say a word of this to Vido. I don't know [how] he has done in his exams, and if he has more work yet in front of him, better don't tell him anything of what's happening here. Let's wait until he has finished his studies. Now, please remember not to tell Vido a word just yet.[7]

Mr Hitchins had written giving Pa 'formal notice' that his services were no longer required after July, leaving the family in a fatally precarious position.[8] Pa told Vidia later what had happened. 'They pay my salary to the end of the month. But I don't want you to worry over these things.' Vidia responded warmly but impractically. 'As soon as I have got a job, you are to come and live with me and fulfil an ambition of mine to have you idle, content, and I shall certainly see that you have some whisky to hand.' Pa was taken by the prospect, young Sewan reported: 'All of us at home except Nalini is calling Pa the Englishman because he says that he is going to England.' Might Vidia try to get his stories published, Pa asked? He enclosed a list of names and addresses of authors' agents. Could *The Adventures of Gurudeva* be turned into a book, he asked again? 'If you cannot manage it, try getting it published through a good agent; but see that you pick an honest one. I understand many of these fellows are crooks.' Vidia did nothing, while pretending that he was doing something: 'I am working on your stories; so don't complain about my indifference.'

*

In the summer, Vidia had moved to a tall, narrow, flat-fronted Georgian house in St John Street, off St Giles'. Other lodgers there included Stephan Dammann, a half-French student who had read history in Vidia's year at Univ. He spent an enjoyable few weeks staying with Stephan's family in Somerset. They all liked Vidia, and Stephan's brother Rickie remembered him as 'a very nice and rather shy person, certainly a great deal more shy than Stephan's other Oxford friends.'[9] In late July, Kamla went to stay with Rudranath while she waited for her passage home. It was a disaster. Capo R. 'was filled with bitterness, hate and contempt and all directed against his family,' Kamla wrote later.[10] Rudranath raged against his own family, and when he began to rage against Pa, Kamla returned the insult. She was thrown out of the house in Balham. She stayed with a cousin, and then with Vidia. 'In the last week or so,' Vidia reported home, 'Capo R. was becoming more and more unpleasant and Kamla eventually did the proper thing. She left.' He revealed a little more in a letter to Pat: 'I have only just returned to London after taking care of my sister (she was in trouble with my uncle: driven out from his house at midnight). I got the news in a telegram, after getting your telephone message. Then – back to Oxford and further distressing news: my father ill, and dismissed from his job. The repercussions of this are important, & I must see you before you go away. But wishing you a happy birthday is still very much in my mind. So happy birthday, Mrs. N.' He was trying for a job at the Oxford University Press, and writing a story, 'Rosie'.

Kamla travelled home on the same ship as Capo R., the *Colombie*. 'Last night there was a grand ball and I was the Captain's guest,' she wrote to Vidia from Guadeloupe. 'I danced with him and had to dance with many others. I had two glasses of champagne . . . About Capo R., well he was always on deck and I in my cabin. We never met. But there are a few persons who know that we are related and at times it becomes embarrassing.' Back home, the stand-off with the Capildeos continued. The Mausis were displeased by Kamla's confident new India-derived attitude. 'They would have been infinitely more pleased,' Pa wrote, 'if she had come down the gangplank twiddling a mala [Hindu rosary] or singing a couplet of the Ramayana.' She took a job at St Augustine teaching English and geography at a salary of $180 (£38) a month, only days after her return. Remembering this time later, Kamla said, 'Pa was driving me to school and back each day, and then he wanted to teach me [to drive]. Every time I did something stupid he began laughing so hard until he began coughing. I remember I got my first pay. I gave him $5 as his pocket change and he began to cry. Some things you don't forget. First time he's taking money from his daughter. First time his daughter has had money to give him.'[11] Sookdeo Misir offered Pa a job in one of his stores as an act of charity 'just to sit and watch the goods', and offered to write off what he was owed on the mortgage, so that Pa could buy a house where he did not have to risk his heart by climbing upstairs.

Vidia returned to writing, telling Pat about a planned short story inspired by the title *The Fall of a Titan*, a novel by the Russian defector Igor Gouzenko.

> The titan is Mr. Teughnsend. He has, you may know, a fatal
> flaw, like Hamlet. He – I hardly dare whisper it – he,
> Teughnsend, the great, the breeder of boy scouts, freeman of
> Oxford, the erstwhile host of E.W. Swanton, the man who saw
> 'Aile Selassie on the platform of Swindon Station, Townsend the
> good citizen, good Tory, the cultivator of hallotments, and the
> owner and driver of a shootin' braike – this paragon, I shudder to
> say, drinks! Secretly. Can you see the story? Teughnsend (I
> assume he will spell it that way) – his rise; training his children to
> say 'writing-paper' and not 'note-paper'; putting poor Roger in
> his shootin' braike; voting Conservative, dressing in suits all the
> time; and then the fall – slow but perceptible.

It was never written. This was the kind of story – limited, backward-facing, concerned with gradations of English social class – that V.S. Naipaul would never write.

Pat thought he needed to hurry up. 'Contrary to you sweet heart I think leisure kills a writer unless he's about sixty and has led a very active life. If you haven't written in amongst all the hurly burly you never will and what you write will never be really good. Look at your beastly "Willy" [Somerset Maugham]. I'd leave you if you were ever like that.' She advised him not to get into debt, and asked him to send £1 that he owed her. Her affection was undimmed. 'I'm an absolute fool when you're concerned and (not to be told to your enormous ego) I really adore and worship that stupid expression of dove-like harmlessness you put on for photographs.' In August, she went off to Austria on a school trip with Ella Wallen and her pupils, despite finding her old teacher thoroughly tedious: 'I carefully ration her out in doses.'

Vidia had not found a job, and decided he might continue his studies at Oxford as a postgraduate. Short of money, he considered becoming a temporary dishwasher at a local hospital, although 'I look forward with extreme disgust to scraping off the loathsome remains of other people's meals.' Nervous about what lay ahead, he took refuge in illness, and had his worst asthma attack since his arrival in England. 'The doctor was altogether pleasant. He gave me an inhaler that looks as if it could be the popular conception of a death-ray gun ... I was hoping they would send me to a hospital, where I would be saved the bother of having to dress and go out for meals.'

He started a holiday job on a farm near Oxford at £4 a week (around £75 in today's terms), working 'preposterously long hours'. Before long, he was concerned that the regular farm workers were not making good use of their time. Pat was despatched a letter, complete with diagrams of chutes, trailers and sacks of wheat:

> The more I see of farm labourers and farmers, the more I am convinced that the labourers are the nearest things to pure animals I have yet come across ... A sack of wheat weighs between two and three hundredweight. What they do is this. One ass drags this sack to the end of the trailer and places it on the back – yes, 3 cwt on the back – of another ass who staggers to the spot where he has to deposit the load. When I saw this I suggested – purely as a makeshift – that a smooth bit of board could be used as a chute from trailer to ground – the board moveable so that you could drop your sacks where they wished. No, they said; they had been doing it this way for years. But today the carpenter began building a chute ... I try to preserve my sanity by reading set amounts every night – 150 pages. But I am so tired that I give up.

His writing was not going well, 'Rosie' being turned down by Henry Swanzy. Too often, he thought, 'my stories remain merely ideas for stories'. What would he do if his inherited dream of becoming a writer could not be fulfilled? He wanted to be an Indian diplomat, he wanted to be wealthy, he wanted to succeed.

> I don't want to reform the world, but I would like to do something. Oh dear! This is sounding so pompous that I am ashamed to continue. Frankly I do not wish any notoriety at all; but the trouble is that it is extraordinarily difficult to do anything constructive. Would joining the Indian Foreign Service – if they would have me – help at all? Getting embroiled in politics seems to me too messy. But enough of this rot. You see, writing has lost its glamour. I have been asking myself quite often recently about the value of the man who spins tales. He becomes a flaneur, like your pet antipathy Willie Maugham. The man who reports is not half the man who acts and is reported about. And on the other side – there is the desire for suits and beautiful dresses for you and a pleasant home and gardens and horses and children. I like luxury. I take to it easily, and feel it is mine by right. And, in this mood, damn the bloody Africans in Kenya and South Africa. It is so easy, you say, to label yourself humanitarian, socialist, liberal. Kingsley Martin can do it in his paper [*New Statesman*]. He can praise the disobedience campaign in South Africa; but would he forego even a meal for the sake of the people he defends?

Come September, Vidia was still thinking and worrying rather than doing and writing. 'I hope you now realise that my asthma is having a record run: an attack normally lasts three to four days. This one is almost a week old,' he wrote proudly to Pat. Unable to decide how to proceed, he blamed her for causing him to be 'a failure'. She was not cowed, writing him her angriest letter yet in response:

> You managed to pack into one short letter all the silly notions – 'women's college attitude', 'elderly virginal counsellors', 'your mother has ruined you' – that try my patience to the uttermost. They are shallow, rather conceited and the mental equipment of the young man. But they indicate something which I would very much like you to lay aside for my sake: the belief that the mere fact of having a man is all-sufficient to a woman's

happiness, that a woman should make the man's life her own without, it seems, a reciprocal action on the man's side and in short the idea that marriage should entail selfishness on one side and annihilation on the other . . . The union of two real people is nobler than one-sided submission. Notice I say one-sided submission. I think the submission and revelation of love is the most glorious thing. But to be really complete love must enter into everyday life. It must entail the acceptance of each other's ambitions and respect for each other's beliefs.

She berated him once more for shattering her ambitions to be an actor:

'Stage struck' is your dismissal of something which was exactly parallel to your wish to write . . . But you won't make the effort to jerk your head out of the sand, put yourself inside me, try to understand. If I'm unhappy you just say you can't bear other people being miserable and that I'm more or less driving you to drink. How would you fare if I behaved like that . . . I'll admit that what I want from you is an admission that you were wrong to stop me acting, that you will make a real effort to enable me to do so if the chance comes again and that you love me – women's rights, feminine acting and all . . . The difference between man & woman is not that big where mind and hope is concerned. I've got my Thibet too and loving you ought to put me a step closer to it not deny it to me altogether.

Vidia did not like being reprimanded. 'I only know one thing – I am a beast and a cad and a fool and an egotist because you didn't appear before Oxford audiences. I suppose I must be. I wish you could just sit down and outline your grievances – equal pay etc.' He knew he was being unfair. 'I paint myself as the wronged innocent. Of course this is silly. I realise that I have been often silly – but being silly is only one of "my ways".' Only many years later did he fully acknowledge his regret at stopping Pat from acting. In 2001, he wrote some tragic, broken notes: 'I wish I had encouraged her. Too late, alas . . . My wretchedness about that now . . . My great grief.'

*

In the autumn, Vidia began work half-heartedly for a postgraduate research degree, a B.Litt. in English literature, with a specialization in Spanish literature. It would give him an extra year in which to coast. He was constantly short of money, and took a job selling the *Home Encyclopedia* at a 15 per cent commission. He sold a copy to Peter Bayley's wife, Patience, and another to a waitress at the Kemp Cafeteria in Oxford. 'She probably bought it out of sympathy for me,' he thought. 'I couldn't go knocking on doors. I didn't have the face to do it.'[12] He was assailed by fears of mental or pulmonary breakdown. Pa sent him tins of salmon, some socks, shirts and a vase, and implored him not to marry. 'If you get a well-paid job, some one of us will be able to join you in England or wherever you are, and, on the whole, we would try to make things as home-like for you as we possibly can . . . it is felt by everybody at home (not excluding myself) that if you get married at all you will be lost to us. We cannot afford losing you; I am not good any longer for hard work.' Vidia responded that there was no need to worry. 'About the business of marriage, I myself am rather unsure; and I can understand your reasoning.' To Pat, though, he expressed no doubts.

As he thought seriously about what he wanted to do next, Vidia tried to detach himself from what had come before. He knew that he did not want to return to Trinidad, and felt tainted when he was reminded of what he might have been, or might still be, or might yet become. Fellow Trinidadians with their would-be stylish clothes, strange names and quaint pronunciations aroused his anger and contempt. Sitting in an Oxford coffee shop with a college friend, he was approached by a man 'too elaborately dressed to be a member of the University', he told Pa. 'Noble Sarkar! Smaller than me; darker than I remembered; uglier than I remembered; stupider than I thought,' he wrote in priggish tones. 'That is the W.I. intellectual, I am afraid.'

He could not help commenting on the 'ignorance and stupidity' of any Trinidadians he met: they reminded him of everything he did not want to be, and hoped to escape from. An encounter in Oxford in early October with an eminent old boy of QRC, Solomon Lutchman, left him in a frenzy. 'I never realised the man was so utterly ugly, so utterly coarse – low forehead, square, fat face, thick lips, wavy hair combed straight back.' He mispronounced words and, fatally, wore a sky-blue club blazer. 'Wearing the blazer of a Caroni Cricket Club in Oxford. I ask you – can you conceive anything narrower and stupider?' This disproportionate rage, though, was provoked by ideas as well as by appearance; Vidia's rage against these individuals arose in part from his view of the world, and a conviction that his own future lay at the centre, not the periphery. He was enraged by what he saw as Lutchman's insularity, and by his failure to see his own larger position. 'His lack of vision, his impregnably stupid preoccupation with the 500,000 inhabitants of T'dad as being the hub of the universe, annoyed me. He ignores the bigger things ("Why should I care about Dominica or the starving Jamaicans?"). He does not see the injustice done to the Africans in Kenya or South Africa; the fact that 12 years ago Indian troops were being killed in the desert by the Germans and today – Indian immigration to Kenya stopped, Germans invited.' Why, in 1953, should Germans rather than Indians be allowed to enter a British colony, except for reasons of racial prejudice? 'And S. Lutchman is an educated Trinidadian.' Pa, one of Trinidad's 500,000 inhabitants, never read this letter.

Back in Port of Spain on 3 October 1953, the family had been to a puja in Luis Street to commemorate Nanie's death. Pa remained in bed at home, having had chest pains in the morning. A message reached Ma that he was feeling ill, and she, Kamla and Mira returned. He needed the doctor. They summoned Dr Mavis Rampersad, a family friend, and Pa was displeased because he thought he should be attended by a male doctor. When she arrived, he was looking better, and soon they were joking and laughing with him. Then as evening neared, Pa cried out in pain. His heart was in agony. Pa shouted at Mira when he heard her laugh, not knowing that it was a laugh of pure shock: Dr Rampersad had just told her that Pa was dying. An injection stilled him. The other children, and more family members, were in Nepaul Street now, and they watched in disbelief as Pa foamed at the nose and, in Dr Rampersad's words, 'went out like a candle'. At the age of forty-seven, Seepersad Naipaul, the writer, who had lifted himself out of nowhere and tried to make his way in the world, was dead.

His body was dressed in clean clothes and laid out upstairs at 26 Nepaul Street, and families of mourners trooped in and out of the little box of a house. Mira remembered two cousins arriving. 'I didn't care for them but they came and began crying. I thought I was duty bound to cry, so I did a little crying too.'[13] A pundit recited prayers and purification rituals were performed, befitting Seepersad's hereditary status as a Brahmin. Sewan, the eight-year-old son of the house, the only son in Trinidad, was so disturbed by what had happened that he refused to take part in the funerary rituals. The following day, on baby Nalini's first birthday, Pa's body was taken to the banks of a stream at El Socorro, a small village outside Port of Spain. The regulations covering death had changed, and Seepersad Naipaul was one of the first Hindus to be legally cremated in Trinidad. A pyre was made of wood and ghee, and lit as the clan watched. The next day his ashes were immersed in the stream at El Socorro. When Ma and the six children reached Nepaul Street they found the house had been cleaned in their absence by some friends, ready for their return. But Pa was not there.

In the months that followed, the family were left in desperate straits, dependent on Kamla's earnings. In order to repay Sookdeo Misir's loan on the house, Kamla had to take out a mortgage with Hamel-Smith, a Trinidad law firm. As Savi remembered, 'After my father died, everything fell apart. I honestly do not know how we managed. We were pretty much left to the wind. Vidia could not come back; he had his own life, his own problems . . . I know that for Mira and I to get shoes and clothing, I sewed clothing for my friends and they would pay me, that's how we outfitted ourselves. The nuns were very kind to us. They called us and said, you don't have to leave school. When you leave you'll pay us the fees.'[14]

Pa's death reached Vidia gradually; Kamla wrote to Peter Bayley asking him to break the news, but before her letter had arrived he received a telegram from Sookdeo Misir's daughter, Bas Mootoo. It read: 'DISTURB- ING NEWS COME TO LONDON IMMEDIATELY.' He guessed what had happened, and boarded a train. At her house in Paddington, his fears came true. Bas told him what had happened. He saw a vase sitting in the house which he knew Pa had sent him. 'It was a brass vase and I was young and didn't know how to deal with this. I eventually had the courage to say, "I think that vase is mine. I think it was sent by my father." It's been with me in all my moves, in every place I've lived, all the little flats and everything,' he said later.[15] Vidia went to the post office and sent a telegram home. 'HE WAS THE BEST MAN I KNEW STOP EVERY- THING I OWE TO HIM BE BRAVE MY LOVES TRUST ME VIDO.' He followed it with a letter to Ma: 'Please don't worry about me . . . everything that I am is directly due to him . . . He worked for all of us; what we are he has made us. And when you think from what he started, you ought to feel proud.'

Eight years later, Vidia published his own version of Pa's death in his loving, fictional tribute to his father, A House for Mr Biswas. The book ends like this:

> The furniture was pushed to the walls. All that day and evening well-dressed mourners, men, women and children, passed through the house. The polished floor became scratched and dusty; the staircase shivered continually; the top floor resounded with the steady shuffle. And the house did not fall.

The cremation, one of the few permitted by the Health Department, was conducted on the banks of a muddy stream and attracted spectators of various races. Afterwards the sisters returned to their respective homes and Shama and the children went back in the Prefect to the empty house.[16]

Pa was dead: now Vidia tried to cut away from Trinidad.

CHAPTER EIGHT

'THEY WANT ME TO KNOW MY PLACE'

VIDIA REFUSED TO DISCUSS his father's death with his cousins or his uncle in London, despite their efforts to draw him out. He talked about it a little with Pat but otherwise kept silent. He said to Lawrence O'Keefe, ' "My father has kicked the bucket." He was surprised by the words. I didn't mention it to anybody else. I had come out of my great depression and then my father died.'[1] For a fortnight, Vidia felt frozen, unable to write to Ma, but when he did he told her he hoped his life would be a continuation and a fulfilment of Pa's: 'It hardly seems necessary for me to tell you how lonely and unprotected I feel.' He sank lower and lower in November, and was reduced to begging for money from Kamla. 'I have tried eating cheap food, but that was nothing but masses of boiled potatoes, and it made me ill and weak. I have now decided that I cannot risk losing my health, and so I have a good meal twice a day ... Whatever happens, though, we must see that Shivan [Sewan] and anyone else who so wishes have a university education. These days I think of home nearly all the time.' Writing to his mother, he admitted that he was 'very ashamed' to have asked for money and pleaded with her childishly, 'I am not really a bad boy and I asked when everything else I could do failed.'[2] In December, he failed the examination for his B.Litt.

In the summer he had been given a travel grant of £75 (£1,400 in today's terms) by the Colonial Office to go to Spain and pursue his studies. He spent Christmas 1953 in Madrid, from where he wrote to Pat in disingenuous tones:

> By the time this letter reaches you I suppose you shall have told your father everything. I am behind you all the way & I want you to know this! ... Will you forgive me if I say that you are the best woman in the world? That you are a vision of <u>purity,</u>

cleaner & purer than anything that has crossed my life . . .
Today I went to the British Institute to see [the translator and
'Raggle Taggle Gypsy'] Walter Starkie. As I was climbing up
the steps of the British Institute, my right foot was trapped in a
bit of carpet. I fell down the stairs and fainted. My foot was
sprained & I have a bad orange-sized bump on my ankle now.

A few days later he wrote again: 'My only vision of you now is the one
I preserve of Feb 9, 1952 at the Univ Play . . . All the qualities I
dreamed of in my wife you possess. You have changed me more than I
really care to admit and, from a purely selfish point of view you are the
ideal wife for a future G[rand] O[ld] M[an] of letters.'[3]

When writing to his family, Pat's purity was not his only consideration. In Madrid, 'at least two Spanish girls made passes at me. England
is by comparison dead and the English are made of wax. They are the
most immoral people I have yet known; yet they set about the matter
with a grimness and a sense of determination that is frightening . . . By
the way, can I have a picture of Meera [sic] and Savi together. I have
pictures in my wallet of everyone except those two.'[4] Pictures came,
and he told Sati he treasured them. 'I like Nalini – you know the
picture in which she is looking with trusting delight into Ma's face. I
also like the group of you five. I was so proud of you that I showed it
to a number of my friends.'[5] A couple of years later he did a version of
the trip to Spain for *Caribbean Voices*. A Spanish man accosts him and
asks if he will translate a letter from a girlfriend; they go to a cafe,
drink together and the piece ends with the narrator being treated to a
trip to a brothel. The first part happened, but the conclusion was
invented to impress his contemporaries at the BBC. The story was
reprinted in the *New Statesman* in 1958, and his friend Francis Wyndham
told Vidia he found it 'scabrous'. Later, he admitted forlornly: 'The
scabrous element was made up. I was scratching myself, it was not part
of my real work, I didn't have enough experience. I had to make a little
money here and there.'[6] While in Madrid, he bought a kimono for Pat
which she was to keep for many years; wearing it made her feel sensual,
and it became a sexual indicator between them.

The early part of 1954 found Vidia staying in London with his
cousin Owad 'in great dirt & discomfort' at a run-down house at 70
Bravington Road in West Kilburn. 'I am looking very hard for definite
employment,' he told his mother.[7] To wash, he would go to the public

baths. He had given up on a project called *The Mystic Masseur* and begun writing a story for the BBC. 'It is called *My Aunt Gold Teeth* and begins: "I never knew her real name, and it is quite likely that she did have one, though I never heard her called anything but Gold Teeth,"' he told Pat. 'I find writing very difficult & sometimes I fear that I may lose my grasp of English altogether and be left languageless!' For the second and last time, he made an attempt at poetry:

> I have thought & thought but I can't rhyme
> Besides I haven't time
> In five and twenty seconds I go to dine
> And confound this wretched Valentine![8]

Staying in the 'slum basement' of Owad's house, he found his extended family ceaselessly irritating. 'I am afraid I am years and ages away from these people – but then I always was,' he wrote in angry, pompous desperation, aware he was depending on their charity. He feared losing the gains of Oxford and being absorbed back into Port of Spain. 'I find their English coarse & acidulous. I have spent a number of days fearing that I was going to speak like them if I stayed on here much longer. Finite verbs are discarded; verbs never agree with their subjects; solícitor becomes sólicitor, marble arch mabble atch. Downright bad English does not worry me, but the stressing of wrong syllables is a damned insidious thing.' In April he sent Sati a telegram: 'BEST WISHES YOUR MARRIAGE WHY NO INVITATION FOR ME LOVE VIDO.'[9] Aged twenty, she was marrying Crisen Bissoondath, whose family kept a dry goods store in Sangre Grande. Later that month they married, and Ma gave a midday wedding dinner for the two families at 26 Nepaul Street.

Willy Richardson, a tall, elegant black Trinidadian who knew the Naipaul family and had covered Queen Elizabeth's coronation for the BBC, booked Vidia to broadcast a story on *Caribbean Voices*. Vidia remembered him as 'a lovely man' whose wife, Lesley, had a job in the Colonial Office: 'They were an attractive couple. I used to go to his flat in Notting Hill.'[10] The story was *A Family Reunion*, in which he fictionalized the aftermath of Nanie's death. A powerful Indian grandmother is dying. Her servant, 'called, graphically, Miss Blackie (her real name was Geraldine Green)' and widowed daughter are making preparations for Christmas. 'It never struck them as strange that, although they were Hindus, they celebrated Christmas. In Trinidad, Christmas and Easter are celebrated by everyone, just as everyone celebrates the Muslim festival of Hosein.' The house is decaying; it rains. 'The bush around the house had a new smell – a fresh smell, as of fish. This meant that snakes were about and it was dangerous to let the children go outdoors.' After initial harmony, the family degenerates into feuds. The old lady, ill in bed, shouts abuse at her noisy grandchildren. 'But her obscenities were harmless: she spoke Hindi, and the children spoke only English.' Nobody knows how she intends to divide up her property until her two sons write a cheque for $500 to each of their six sisters; the rest will be theirs. 'They considered that they had no obligation to their sisters; indeed, because of their superior education and position, Suruj and Krishna looked down on them.'[11]

Then came the news that Vidia's postgraduate academic studies were at an end. He had returned to Oxford to take a further examination for his B.Litt., but despite a satisfactory result in his written paper was turned down after an interview or 'viva' with a retired professor of English, F.P. Wilson, who was renowned for being taciturn and socially awkward. 'I wish you to know that I was failed deliberately,' he told Pat. 'I was viva'd – not on the paper – but on the Spanish theological temper. No one last term was subjected to that sort of thing. Wilson's attitude was just one big sneer from beginning to end; and, of course, he did ask me once more where I came from . . . It is just another one of the hundred & one insults that make my life in England hell – that also gave me my breakdown.' Half a century later this perceived discrimination still upset him: he noted on an old letter to Pat that Wilson had failed him for the B.Litt 'quite deliberately, & out of racial feeling'. He remained at Oxford, the staff at the college library having given him an administrative job to tide him over. Come the summer, Vidia was back with Owad in Bravington Road, and desperate. He had little encouragement bar a testimonial from Peter Bayley saying he was 'a sympathetic and delightful person, with a most attractive sense of humour [and] outstanding literary gifts' who deserved a job. 'More than most I think he could be said to be a citizen of the world. He is a British subject of Indian descent domiciled in the West Indies.'[12]

*

Without the protection and distinction of Oxford University, Vidia floundered. 'It is wrong for you to think that I do not wish to come home,' he told Ma in confusion in May. 'I think I shall die if I have to spend the rest of my life in Trinidad. The place is too small, the values are all wrong, and the people are petty. Besides, there is really very little for me to do there ... Do not imagine that I am enjoying staying in this country. This country is hot with racial prejudices, and I certainly don't wish to stay here ... Now that the time is drawing near for my day of departure from Oxford, I am discarding all my English friends and acquaintances. I shall spend the rest of my life trying to forget that I came to Oxford ... The world is a pretty awful place, but our star will shine bright yet. Love to all, from your silly son, Vido.'[13]

He tried writing to John Grenfell Williams, the head of colonial broadcasting at the BBC, who had invited him to dinner in Hampstead two years earlier. Might he help him find employment? 'I very much want to go to India. But there are many difficulties. I cannot be employed on the Indian side because I am British, and on the British side, I cannot be employed because I am Indian ... if you can reveal a glimmer of hope I will be very grateful.'[14] Grenfell Williams asked Vidia to see him and offered support, but said there were no positions available at the BBC. Vidia made a request to Henry Swanzy: would he recommend him for a job in America as a 'television apprentice' which required 'the ability to communicate ideas'?[15]

A week after he departed finally from Oxford, Vidia discovered he had been turned down for a job in Dehra Dun in India and another post in Darjeeling. The Colonial Office would shortly be cutting off his grant since he was no longer a student, and his financial situation was impossible. He wrote to the *Manchester Guardian*, to the *New Commonwealth*, whose editor was 'a Univ man', and to the J. Arthur Rank Organization, all without success. He thought about applying to work with the British Council overseas, or joining the civil service. He approached two dozen advertising firms. The American television company sent him 'a long, personal letter of rejection'. A friend of a friend who worked for Orson Welles told him there were no possibilities in the world of film. A classified advertisement in *The Times* newspaper promoting his talents yielded no response. He secured a meeting with the Advertising Appointments Bureau, where a representative informed him frankly that he was the wrong colour for the advertising industry. 'He told me I was banging my head against a brick wall. I had an unfortunate name & face. He could do nothing for me. This is the official appointments bureau, run by the advertising agencies themselves.'

The Indian High Commission, the embassy of the Indian government and Pa's ideal place of work for both Kamla and Vidia, told him there were no openings available. Vidia would fictionalize this rejection in *A Bend in the River*. Indar, an East African of Punjabi origin who has graduated from a good English university, visits India House in London and is shunted from official to official before being shown 'into the inner office, where a fat black man in a black suit, one of our black Indians, was sitting at a big black table, opening envelopes with a paper knife.' The official asks, ' "How can you join our diplomatic service? How can we have a man of divided loyalties?" ' Indar wonders to himself, ' "How dare you lecture me about history and loyalty, you slave?" ' and leaves India House 'full of rage.'[16]

Vidia considered living with Pat and trying to write full time. 'It is risky, but I know I have talent & am bound to succeed sooner or later,' he told her. Pat's response to his stories of rejection was remorselessly English: practical, fussy, naive and in its way right; he had to make an effort to appear more like everyone else. 'I must be cruel to be kind. If you have been wearing that sports jacket and/or a blue shirt to your interview you need look no further for the reason you were rejected . . . Don't ever ever wear that blue shirt of Owad's again for you honestly "lose caste" in it! Oh dear, how incorrigible you are.' The sports jacket would metamorphose into the 'one jacket, a light-green thing that didn't absolutely fit and couldn't hold a shape' worn by Willie Chandran in 1950s London in *Half a Life*. Like Vidia, 'He had paid three pounds for it at a sale of The Fifty Shilling Tailors in the Strand.'[17]

In the autumn of 1954, Vidia began to write a serious novel based on his experiences working as a clerk at the Red House in Trinidad. It was provisionally entitled *The Shadow'd Livery*. He was keeping his father's prized letters in a tea chest in his basement room at 70 Bravington Road. The noise and the squalor made him angry and sarcastic. There always seemed to be a baby crying next door; his ties got lost and his shirts were torn; his books disappeared; a rat bit him during the night – 'I still have the bump on my head,' he told Pat, using the Poste Restante at the Birmingham GPO as their point of contact. He was conscious of the success of other West Indian writers. Earlier, WAGS had written, 'You felt hurt when Mittelholzer was so highly praised in John O'London's but do you know that the Penguin reviewer regards his as one among 50 good novels of the decade?'[18] Vidia was obliged to share a room with his cousin Brahm, 'an illiterate, gross man,' he decided hastily, who had recently arrived from Trinidad and seemed to represent everything Vidia was seeking to escape: 'He walks like a dachshund, grunts like a pig, doesn't spit in the road like other beings of Bravington Road, but spits into people's yards.' In time, he got used to his cousin and drew a sketch of him sitting squarely in a chair, 'in a deceptively pensive mood'. He considered going back to Queen's Royal College as a teacher and trying to write 'a good novel or two', constantly aware of his obligation to his widowed mother and siblings. 'My family commitments are so over-powering,' he told Pat, who had taken a holiday job at a reformatory school in the Cotswolds and was visiting Anglo-Saxon churches. 'A mother and four children, and I am only 22.' He had received a letter from home 'that tore my heart. Their trust, their faith, their love – never mentioned, but underlying every word. My little brother needs me now. I can feel it.' What could he tell them that would make things seem all right? 'I have been turned down for 26 jobs so far: this sort of news one doesn't like to write home about,' he told Ma. 'But even English boys from Oxford have had worse luck than that.'[19]

Ill-equipped, emotionally and practically, to look after himself, Vidia was unable to give any useful advice to Pat when she had the inevitable, long-awaited showdown with her father. The spark came when Vidia sent a telegram asking her to come down from Birmingham to London for the weekend. She wrote to him with clarity, dignity and honesty to explain what had happened. Her father had returned from the Kingstanding pub at closing time: 'I began by merely saying I was going to London, very humbly & apologetically for he had brought a chicken for Sunday lunch & I was very conscience-stricken about it. I even thought of sending you a telegram "Father has brought chicken for Sunday. Can't come."' Mr Hale responded that Pat would certainly not be going to London, and that if she did he would accompany her and tell the young man in question 'just what he thought. I think he would be more politic than to use the "wog" language he employed with me. What he would do is to tell you: that he would never admit you to our family circle; the obvious disadvan-tages of mixed marriage and the steps – drastic – he would take to prevent such a marriage taking place.' Unwilling to put Vidia in such a situation in front of gawping cousins at Bravington Road ('I knew your propriety would forbid you receiving my father, whatever his intentions, in a sparsely furnished basement!'), Pat remained at home. She was not, though, cowed by her father's threats, legal or otherwise. They could be married by special licence. 'Alternatively we can part. As far as I am concerned the last is not an alternative.' Later, she wrote movingly, 'I have absolute faith in your ultimate ability to do something great. I am convinced that we are going to be a distinguished couple.'

Vidia's response was equivocal, lacking empathy. 'I do indeed feel for your hardship at home . . . I have been thinking that even when things are blackest the love of a good woman is enough to give a man courage and confidence. I told this to Owad this morning, in my disjointed non-sequitur fashion, and he replied, "It is all you really have." And it is true. Things could have been much worse. There could have been no you.' In the language of the time, Vidia was 'in too deep' to get out; he loved Pat, he needed her, but he was not sure whether he wanted to be married. His solution was to allow his body to take over where his mind had stopped. 'I really don't know what is going to happen,' he wrote. 'Something must break soon or I'll die. The attack of asthma that began last Friday is still with me, developing, like the summer grass, fastest by night.' Stress about his predicament combined with the damp and mould of Owad's basement to give him one asthma attack after another, leaving him weak and depressed, having to go day by day to the hospital for an adrenalin injection. He was reduced to sending desperate pleas to a worried Pat. 'ASTHMA AGAIN PLEASE COME TOMORROW' was one message, and she came, down from Birmingham on the train, and took him to the hospital at St Mary's, Paddington, where he proceeded to have a tantrum at being kept waiting, and walked out. Pat was left to soothe the hospital staff. 'Try & think of the humiliation you caused me then first in the casualty department and then back in the office when I had to hand them back their documents and thank them with all the dignity I could muster,' she wrote to him. He was sorry. 'I really did behave atrociously yesterday and the surprising thing is that at the time I had no idea I was behaving badly.' His excuse, looking back, was illness: 'When you can't breathe, you become enraged and sometimes that anger can give you the breath to move.' He remembered it as a time of incapacity and 'asthma, asthma, asthma. Things were bad. Everything had gone wrong at this stage and I was very young, there was complete solitude, no vision of writing or how to move, knowing that what I was doing was rubbish.'[20] Through all this, the demands of home were constantly with him. In August, young Shiva wrote a letter which contained the line, 'You must not waste your money because you must remember we are not rich, but poor.'[21]

*

Pat decided unilaterally that it would be best to leave her family and move to lodgings if she were to continue both her studies and her relationship with Vidia. In August, the University of Birmingham awarded her a research scholarship with free tuition and a grant of £285 for the academic year.[22] Leaving home was a brave move for a twenty-two-year-old woman in a precarious position to be making at this time, but she did it with panache. 'I hope to leave home (oh dear) tomorrow & luggage books & furniture by taxi at 3.30.' She would lodge with a Miss Gilson in the Birmingham suburb of Moseley. Vidia, consumed by his own anguish, poverty and asthma, was of no help, using his preferred method of abdication rather than involving himself in a testing situation. 'I have no indication of what your feelings are about me going into lodgings & have taken this decision entirely on my own,' she wrote to him anxiously. Within a few weeks, Pat's father had sent her what she called 'a heartrending letter'. In a sloping, barely legible hand, Ted Hale begged her to come home, and offered to pay her landlady 'a month's rent in lieu of notice . . . Although I shall never be able to agree with you on this matter which has caused this dreadful upset I promise that I will never refer to it again and that you may please yourself what you do . . . It's playing on my mind and I can't seem to think about anything else. Please do come back at once. Your loving Daddy.' Pat, however, knew where her loyalty lay. 'Here I can be of use to you whereas at home I cannot,' she told Vidia. 'Here I can offer you hospitality and comfort. I have also found in Miss Gilson a mutual friend.' When he had money, Vidia went to Birmingham for the weekend to be with Pat. It was just over a guinea if he travelled by bus, but it took six hours.

Occasionally, he saw Oxford friends. Lawrence 'Lol' O'Keefe and his wife Suzanne invited him to dinner. 'They live at a place called Black Heath: suburbia.' He saw another old Univ friend, James Sutton. 'He wants me to come to a small party he is giving tonight. It is pure South Ken[sington], and I well remember the agony I went through at his last invitation.' Above all, he saw Jill Brain. She was his age, privately educated, with a father in the RAF. Now she worked as an editorial assistant at the Cement & Concrete Association and shared a basement flat in Chelsea with Brenda Capstick, another Oxford graduate. Jill was pretty, funny and good company – and Vidia was strongly attracted to her. He showed her his most buoyant side, and she was mildly aware of his desire, although since she was engaged to someone else, thought little of it. She remembered: 'He was clever, witty, ambitious. The guy I knew was cheerful and funny. I wouldn't have hung out with someone who was miserable. I don't remember a lot of angst . . . He did talk about being a writer. I greatly enjoyed being with him. I remember we had a joke about what we called "fellow countrymen". It was clear to me that he didn't regard all his fellow countrymen as precisely equal.' Jill lent Vidia her typewriter and often invited him to supper at her flat in Oakley Street in Chelsea. 'I remember stuff about food – what he wouldn't eat. I could handle vegetarian, but I hadn't quite carried it through to the stock in the soup. I remember a lecture about cows.' Looking back, she wondered whether Vidia's wit and ease had caused her to misconstrue him. 'He was very, very articulate and well read and fluent in English. Looking back, I think that I always took him as less foreign than he was, because he spoke such good English, and that was a mistake. I may have taken him to be a psychologically simpler person than he was.'[23]

Finally in September Vidia got a temporary job at the National Portrait Gallery with the aid of his Oxford friend Richard Taylor, 'working gentleman's hours' on a salary of a guinea a day. He had to catalogue Edwardian caricatures from the magazine *Vanity Fair*, and was entertained by the social commentary and skill of the cartoonists. Writing to Pat, he imitated the famous signature of 'Spy', 'Leslie Ward: old Etonian', and 'Ape', 'a wop called Carlo Pellegrini'. His asthma continued, and at times he would have to leave work and go in search of an adrenalin injection. The food at 70 Bravington Road appalled him. Pat, always compassionate, suggested he might cater for himself and sent food parcels, which she called 'morale raisers'. Vidia remained inert. Sometimes he did not even bother to open her parcels to remove the fruitcake or the tin of sardines. Instead, he complained about being given no breakfast and disgraceful, low-grade plantation food for supper by Owad's wife, Jean: boiled rice with curried potatoes, or pancake and curried cauliflower.

When Owad was in a friendly mood, he told Vidia to invite Pat to spend the weekend in London. In the cramped confines of 70 Bravington Road, she would share a bed with Jean, to ensure propriety. Vidia had to squeeze in beside his cousins Brahm and Owad: 'if one is going slumming, one had better do it in style, don't you think?' If visits to London were difficult, trips to see Pat in Moseley were as fraught. Miss Gilson allowed him to stay in a room in her house, though his first visit there was marred by an incident when Vidia thoughtlessly woke the neighbours. 'Sweetheart you could not have made a worse impression if you had tried (well, I don't know about that really),' Pat wrote next day. 'What I mean is we can't really blame Miss Gilson for being rather disconcerted. Dear, there was one thing you did which upset her, quite justifiably, on Monday. You woke the neighbours without telling us so that she was bombarded by questions, etc. without warning . . . I know you were very disturbed & all over the place. Miss Gilson was rather decent about it . . . But dear try & think carefully of the impression you are creating – without being servile.'

By November the weather had turned cold and the National Portrait Gallery let him go. Vidia took to attending news cinemas to pass the time. He was penniless, failing and increasingly bitter. Pat suggested he might return to Trinidad and try his luck there. Only anger animated him. 'Ever since I was twelve I swore to get away from Trinidad,' he responded. Later, he recalled that people would 'say to me, why don't you go back home and serve your country. What country? A plantation? How was one going to serve it?'[24] Now, Vidia became philosophical. He saw his predicament, passionately and dispassionately, as the product of complex historical circumstances. He was an East Indian West Indian who had been pulled out of his own society by a superior British education, leaving him a double exile, a deracinated colonial who was legally prevented from migrating inside the new Commonwealth. He told Pat:

> You tell me I talk a lot of rot about history. But I wonder whether you ever consider that my position has been caused by several complex historical factors: the slave trade, its abolition; British imperialism, and the subjection of Indian peoples; the need for cheap labour on the Caribbean sugar plantations; Indian indentured immigration . . . So today, you have me – disowned by India. Well, I belong to the Commonwealth. It is true that I cannot go to Canada, New Zealand, Australia, South Africa, Kenya, Uganda, Tanganyika, the Rhodesias, Nyasaland; but then I ought to know my place in the Free World . . . You see, it is all right to get worked up about the (admittedly frequent) acts of physical repression; but the more insidious form of oppression is the spiritual one. I am an example of that, whatever you may say . . . You will say that I am free. Of course I am free. I have freedom of speech (in England, anyway); freedom of worship. All these of course are quite useless to me without freedom of opportunity.

It was a rare and direct statement of his own plight, and contains the themes and anxieties that would be played out in the writings of V.S.

Naipaul over the next fifty years. His predicament would become both his handicap and his opportunity.

He tried to write about his deracination for the BBC, and in October submitted a script, 'A Culturally Displaced Person', which was turned down as 'exaggerated' by Gordon Waterfield, head of the Eastern Service. What was Mr Naipaul worrying about? 'The reference to being educated in an alien tradition and speaking its language and thinking in it, surely this is a rather out-of-date form of nationalism . . . Mr Naipaul could, it seems to me, equally write a good talk saying how lucky it is that he knows English since it enables him to keep in touch with Indian thought, Indian novelists, etc.'[25] Half a century later, Vidia had a defensive memory of Waterfield's response: 'His reaction was rather foolish, a pretty pompous thing. What I was saying became a commonplace of thought. I was enraged by it. I thought he was trying to do me down. I needed the money; I assure you it left no mark on me.'[26]

While assuring him of her love in 'these perilous days' Pat suggested he might 'start making concrete enquiries after a clerical temporary job. There are loads. Don't be angry.' She enclosed a 2½d stamp so he could reply, which he did in a furious, acute, self-pitying analysis of his position, describing the everyday racial humiliations he faced in London and his epic uncertainty over his future, displaying raw wounds to her that he would afterwards try to keep hidden from the world for the rest of his life:

> Go out & get a clerical job, you write, adding, there are heaps of those. I hate to spring a surprise on you . . . but the people in authority feel my qualifications fit me only for jobs as porters in kitchens, and with the road gangs. My physique decrees otherwise . . . It is my own fault. Why don't I go back where I came from, and not be a nuisance to anyone? Niggers ought to know their place.

He described an interview at the Colonial Office, at which he was kept waiting for more than one hour before being told, 'Come on, stop feeling sorry for yourself and go back home. You will find something.' But Vidia did not want to go back to Trinidad, '40 × 40 miles, with no prospects, no high mountains, far away. To rot, ambitionless, neither seen nor heard?'

Where did he stand? What was he left with? What was he for, and what might he turn out to be against? Where did his loyalties lie: in

Trinidad, in Britain, in India, or nowhere? 'Have I any right to be in the Free World? Have I any obligation to cast my lot in with the Free World? Should I be against the Free World?' These were spacious questions for him to be asking, an early analysis of the critical global phenomenon of the next half-century: mass migration and the cultural collisions that would come in its wake. Did Vidia have any right to live in the 'Free World'?

> I want you to answer . . . for me, and for my poor father & family – growing up with no horizon save that of Port of Spain Harbour and unemployment? If you can manage it, put yourself in my place for a minute & let me know. Forget that we are attached to each other. If my father had 1/20 of the opportunity laid before the good people of British stock, he would not have died a broken, frustrated man without any achievement. But, like me, he had the opportunity – to starve. He was ghettoed – in a sense more cruel than that in which Hitler ghettoed the Jews. But there was an element of rude honesty in the Nazi approach; and they at any rate killed swiftly. The approach of the Free World is infinitely subtler and more refined. You cannot say to a foreign country: I suffer from political persecution. That wouldn't be true and wouldn't it be melodramatic & absurd to say: But I suffer from something worse, an insidious spiritual persecution. These people want to break my spirit. They want me to forget my dignity as a human being. They want me to know my place. You have the result in me, as I sit in a French café (not drinking anything) to write this. No fire in my room for two days and only tea & toast in my stomach. That is what the whole policy of the Free World amounts to. Naipaul, poor wog, literally starving, and very cold.

Pat, the stronger of the two at this point in their relationship, thought he should be more practical and needed to act fast to save himself. 'Don't shout at me . . . There is no one in the whole world besides me who takes you really seriously.'

Through everything, she remained optimistic. 'I think we'll be alright by Christmas. Just concentrate on keeping going in health and morale for the time being – and on obtaining white shirts for interviews.' It was too late for him to return to Trinidad, for he would only go 'with a terrible sense of failure and compulsion. But unless & until you get a job I think you should come to me or go home for you are "dying slowly" as you are.' She consulted a Mr W.J. Davies, who was responsible for helping West Indian immigrants in Birmingham to find jobs. Mr Davies was happy to help, and wrote on Vidia's behalf to several large firms in Birmingham including ICI and GEC, as well as finding him a clerical position in the Tax Office. Vidia was full of rage, refusing to be helped by a man he described as 'Birmingham's Protector of the Poor'. He would not involve himself with Mr Davies, a latter-day protector of immigrants, nor would he be classified alongside people who climbed off banana boats wearing zoot-suits and wanted jobs in factories. He was V.S. Naipaul, the writer. Pat was 'literally sick with worry & misery' and no less angry in response. 'By God your letter got me mad. I was half glad in a way for I'm a bit fed up with being eternally understanding and patient . . . I took the course I did because of the desperate letter you sent me on Friday, which incidentally accused me of doing nothing but sit still & preach. So I went straight out & did something . . . I shall have to go and see Mr Davies, thank him for his offer, apologise for wasting his time behaving all the while as if your behaviour is justified and absolutely nothing is wrong. I've had to do this before several times and presumably I shall do it again.' Vidia's lasting emotional incapacity meant that Pat would have to do it again, many, many times.

Henry Swanzy stepped in, making enquiries and arranging a meeting with the Jewish businessman and philanthropist Victor Sassoon (who had notoriously been insulted in a wartime broadcast by the poet Ezra Pound). Swanzy went to extraordinary lengths to help contributors to *Caribbean Voices*. Earlier in the year, he had lobbied Oxford University for funds from the Carnegie Foundation, saying that his BBC budget was insufficient to back promising talent such as Sam Selvon who had a wife and young child to support, Derek Walcott from Saint Lucia who was looking to travel to England and Vidia Naipaul, a Trinidadian student at Oxford.[27] 'Sassoon is interested in India & has lots of money,' Vidia reported to Pat. 'He thinks that in colonies like those in the Caribbean – where all the peoples speak English & have British institutions, and are educated in the Brit way, there should be a policy designed to incorporate these people into Britain.' In retrospect, once he had received a knighthood, become a millionaire and won the Nobel Prize, Vidia thought Sassoon had been insufficiently helpful: 'He was not interested in me at all. I think it's a mark against him.'[28]

Meanwhile, Vidia remained dependent on Pat's practical and financial assistance. 'I do not wish to alarm you but it will be an act of great charity if you can send me a small amount of money: this will enable me to eat a bit for two or three days ... I am literally starving these days, & have lost nearly 12 pounds since I left the Portrait Gallery. I have never sunk so low in all my life.' He even expected Pat – despite the formal ambiguities in their relationship – to act as his representative and calm the fears of his family, despite his own inability or refusal to involve himself with hers. 'What I would like you very much to do is to write home for me ... Stress the fact that I am not unhappy, but that breaking into a first job is always difficult. Don't mention a word about race or anything like that.' His lust for Jill continued, a distraction from despair. 'Jill has taken to putting on her stockings in front of me. Should I look away? Advise on this point of etiquette, please. Ha!' he wrote to Pat in late November. Whenever he spent time with Jill, he avoided showing her his distress and his poverty. He believed he was revisiting the collapse of two years earlier. 'I felt all my old nervous breakdown insensibly overpowering me & making the world dark & unreal. I know that you don't believe in breakdowns; but take my word – What happens is this: one's life is so unsatisfactory, so terribly insecure, so haunted by fear & doubt & sense of failure – that the mind in a clever beastly way removes attention from these truths so hard to swallow, and fixes it on an alien dread. It seems to be a different spirit within that says: Little boy finds these things so frightening; here, little boy, exercise your mind on this. Oh God, I wish, I do deeply wish that I don't lose my balance again.'

At the start of December 1954, as Pat had predicted, he had the crucial, inevitable breakthrough without which he would have gone on sinking. Swanzy was leaving England after being seconded by the BBC to run the Gold Coast broadcasting service. He offered Vidia a renewable three-month contract presenting *Caribbean Voices*. In a conversation recorded for a television documentary twenty-five years later, Swanzy asked whether the job had been helpful, coming when it did. Naipaul had no doubts: 'That saved my life, really. I was living more or less at the limit of despair.'[29] At last Vido had good news for Ma: 'I am doing the Caribbean Voices ... I only need to go out on the days of recording; for the rest I can stay at home, and do my own writing. They are paying me eight guineas a week as a start; and Kenneth Ablack, who is producing the programme, tells me that they will pay

me extra for any work I do ... I shall be saving up from twenty to
twenty five shillings every week to send home; because I know that
you are in difficulties ... Will you all love me, and live good lives, and
love each other? That is what a family is made for. All my love Vido.'[30]

CHAPTER NINE

'SOMETHING RICH
LIKE CHOCOLATE'

FOR THE NEXT FOUR YEARS, Vidia Naipaul had an insecure billet as a
stalwart of the BBC Colonial Service. It gave him an opportunity to
find his feet as a writer, to widen and extend his talents and to feel an
integral part of a circle of intelligent men, and a few women, of roughly
his own age and background. Gone was the white world of Oxford
University; he was again among people who reminded him of Port of
Spain and QRC. Henry Swanzy left Vidia and his colleagues in no
doubt that their material was real material. In their spare time, the
Caribbean Voices 'boys' would go to the George pub near the BBC, or
chat in the freelances' room in the old Langham Hotel opposite
Broadcasting House, a grand Victorian edifice with a literary heritage
(Mark Twain stayed there, Oscar Wilde drank there, Sherlock Holmes
sleuthed there). Vidia ate lunch in the BBC canteen, finishing with
heavy English puddings topped with custard. A decade later he wrote
in an Indian newspaper, 'I worked mainly for various overseas services
of the BBC, contributing to magazine programmes, doing tiny features
about books, doing interviews and taking part in discussions. To hear
oneself being introduced by an announcer with a well-known voice was
to feel honoured, and also nervous.' He believed the experience taught
him how to interview successfully, by 'lightly drawing out information'.[1]
In Frank Collymore's journal *Bim*, Vidia marvelled in retrospect at his
own audacity in taking the job as a literary presenter: 'For now I see I
fitted into none of the accepted categories of critics. I was not a
gentleman, to whom criticism meant a display of sensibility and polished
prose: an accomplishment, like a knowledge of pictures and wines,
which might grace one in society.'[2]

The contributors, actors and presenters who worked on *Caribbean
Voices* and other BBC shows came and went, month by month. They
were older than the precocious Vidia Naipaul, and with the exception

of the acculturated Sam Selvon, none was an East Indian West Indian. To Vidia, they seemed more experienced, adept and socially confident. George Lamming was born in Barbados, and had travelled to Britain in 1950 with Selvon and stayed in the same hostel. His influential book *In the Castle of My Skin* examined colonialism in the West Indies through the eyes of a growing child; Henry Swanzy thought Lamming had 'one fatal lack, a sense of humour'.[3] Errol John, brother of Pa's colleague George John, was an actor who wrote the play *Moon On a Rainbow Shawl*. Edgar Mittelholzer was a Guianese novelist who produced books at speed ('It pleased him,' Vidia wrote in *A Writer's People*, 'that he was not too much darker than his publisher Fred Warburg; it was an unexpected way of judging a publisher.').[4] Andrew Salkey, born in Panama and educated in Jamaica (he bears some resemblance to Percy in *Half a Life*), wrote folk stories in patois and was a lively and influential member of the group; he regarded literature as sacred, and with his wife Pat gave long Sunday parties at their home in Holland Park. Gordon Woolford was from British Guiana; he planned to write a novel but had never progressed beyond the first chapter. The resident reviewer was British, Arthur Calder Marshall, born in 1908, an early Marxist and friend of poets like Auden and MacNeice, who had written a travel book on Trinidad and been heralded in his youth as a coming writer – one of his novels used no fewer than sixty-seven first-person narrators. John Stockbridge was an English journalist, and 'a friend and encourager' to Vidia: 'He told me I dressed badly and would be a great writer.' Edward Brathwaite was a Cambridge graduate and poet from Barbados: 'He's become very black; when I met him then he wasn't so black.'[5] Sylvia Wynter, a Cuban-born Jamaican who 'used words like comprador bourgeoisie', would marry Jan Carew, 'a mulatto from Guiana, a tall and handsome man with pretensions to be a writer; he published a couple of books, but they've disappeared.'[6] As for Willy Edmett, he was 'a small, thin man who later started a shop in the countryside. He thought he was going nowhere.'

Despite his subsequent barbs and snubs, Vidia was a wholehearted member of this group. Jan Carew remembered: 'We would do broadcasts at the BBC and then go to a pub nearby. Vidia was a very good companion, very witty. Cruel wit. Some West Indians used to work at the back of the kitchen at the BBC cafeteria. He called them "the blackroom boys". He had an underlying sense of compassion for the less well-off West Indians in London, which later he was accused of not having. People of my generation spoke about race in a way that was full of jokes; there was no animus, we would joke about each other's background – race and class. Vidia didn't hold himself apart. There was certainly a sense of community. Before the independence movement developed, our group in London was much more integrated.' Carew thought the relationship between Gordon Woolford and Vidia had been 'very close and intense. We went to a party given at the house of Peter Abrahams, the black South African writer. I remember going back on the tube late at night, Vidia and Gordon Woolford were hugging and kissing. It could have been simply alcohol. Big drinking was more the rule than the exception at that time.'[7] Vidia remembered, 'Gordon Woolford was very important to me. He was thirty-five in 1954. He was an alcoholic, married a shop assistant, a very handsome man. He was a good reader, distinct. He had a sister who was a beauty queen. His father was Sir Eustace Woolford, a mulatto who became a speaker of the legislative assembly in Guiana. Now the joke they tell about him in Trinidad, a wicked racial joke, is that Eustace was sitting in his club in Georgetown playing cards with his back to the door. A white American comes up the stairs and says, "Hey, there's a nigger in here." And Eustace says, "Hmm, throw him out." '[8]

At the BBC, Vidia reviewed new novels, interviewed writers and chaired discussions on West Indian literature with scripted informality. He contributed to a series on 'Contemporary Negro Poetry', looked at the 'uncompromisingly worthy' Japanese novel *The Makioka Sisters* by Junichiro Tanizaki. He reviewed the film *Sea Wife*, making sure he was reimbursed eight shillings and sixpence for 'cost of a seat at the cinema'. With his reporter's notebook filling easily, he wrote and broadcast scripts about a model engineer's exhibition, the International PEN congress, literary teas at Harrods and the National Portrait Gallery.[9] He exchanged staged banter about trends in writing with Kenneth Ablack (who was not 'a black', but an Indian, or half-Indian; his father, Mr Ramprasad, had changed his name to something less classifiable): 'ABLACK: "Thank you Vidia Naipaul – now that you have given news of Samuel Selvon, ought I to mention that you are in the course of writing your own first novel?" '[10] Like Willie in *Half a Life*, involvement with the BBC gave Vidia 'a sense of the power and wealth of London' that he did not find elsewhere; like Willie he went to interview a rising African carver, a man named Felix Idubor, a sculptor and seducer from Nigeria: 'He walked Willie round the exhibition, the heavy African gown bouncing off his thighs, and told him with great precision how much he had paid for every piece of wood. Willie built his script around that.' Like Willie, he 'loved the drama of the studio, the red light and the green light, the producer and the studio manager in their soundproof cubicle.'[11] Working as a BBC presenter enabled Vidia to learn theatrical skills that never deserted him. 'They taught me I was never to let my voice drop at the end of a sentence. They taught me to speak from the back of my throat, which I still do – easy for an asthmatic – and never to talk from the mouth. I learned how to throw my voice. They taught you to have a picture in your head when you are speaking.'[12]

His friend Willy Edmett at the Colonial Schools Unit gave him plenty of work, and better still arranged swift payment. V.S. Naipaul wrote about 'Dr Livingstone the Geographer' for Edmett, and prepared a sequence of ten scripts on Shakespeare's *Henry V* to help children study for exams. He gave talks on George Eliot's *The Mill on the Floss* and H.G. Wells's *The History of Mr Polly* (a favourite book of Pa's, which was to influence *A House for Mr Biswas*) for a Colonial Schools Unit series titled 'Reading for your Delight', designed to generate another crop of culturally British colonials even as the Suez Canal prepared to flow through Lady Eden's drawing room. Collecting a guinea here and there, he read the part of Hounakin in a performance of Derek Walcott's one-act play *The Sea at Dauphin*, narrated short stories by John Figueroa and the Tobagonian poet E.M. Roach ('I liked his poetry: "Seven splendid cedars break the trades." A tender man') and earned two guineas reading a poem on a sister programme, *Calling West Africa*.[13] Alternating between BBC studios in Maida Vale and the West End, Vidia praised Edward Brathwaite's poetic fluency, narrated *The Strange Flower*, a short story by his newly discovered Trinidadian contemporary Michael Anthony, and called Edgar Mittelholzer 'the most professional and the most successful' of his fellow West Indian writers.[14] Later, having reinvented himself as a different kind of person, he forgot all these thespian performances: 'I am not an actor. I have no memory of reading other people's work, except my father's story [*Ramdas and the Cow*].'[15] Vidia's subsequent claim to have had no literary influences bar his father was a deliberate blanking of the role of his colleagues at *Caribbean Voices*, who were crucial in forming his idea of what did and did not work on the page. After the 1950s, now securely in print, he rarely found it necessary to test his literary thinking against the opinions or techniques of others.

Vidia interviewed Francis Wyndham, the writer and critic, Stuart Hall, his exact contemporary from Jamaica, who was emerging as a left-wing political theorist in Britain, and Sam Selvon, whose reputation as a novelist was still rising. Despite an excellent rehearsal, the recording with Selvon went badly. 'Woolford, who was listening in the studio cubicle, said I sounded as though I were a bored and blasé seventy year old don,' he wrote to Pat in Birmingham. It may have been an instinctive, emotional response to Pa's old literary rival and Kamla's former lover. 'At the end of that ordeal I was sweating, literally . . . Talking about Woolford, he came home last night and drank every drop of the wine I had there, and he begged me not to begrudge it him. What could I do? Incidentally, we were fooled with that sauterne. Some sugar remained at the bottom of the bottle and Woolford said it is an old trick of the wine merchants: sweetening cheap two and six wine with sugar and selling it for six shillings. One learns. Don't get angry about the wine. Woolford is an alcoholic and, poor man, he cannot get by without liquor.'[16]

*

In the new year of 1955, Vidia began to use a tiny pocket notebook. 'For writing overheard conversation & sharpening observation,' he noted on an envelope when he sealed it away for posterity.[17] It is the only notebook of its kind to survive. Later, he stopped collecting scraps of material or making notes, preferring to let ideas or memories rest in his mind before letting them come out in an accumulated, indirect form in his writing. For the same reason, he rarely kept a personal diary except when travelling to research an article. The notebook gives an evocative picture of his preoccupations during this seminal year. Pat is not mentioned once. It shows his direct experience of post-war London, a world of Lyons Corner Houses, down-at-heel bars, lodgings, poverty, friendship, alcohol, prostitutes, racial mingling and the sexual fascination and dissatisfaction that he would later depict in fiction. Vidia was usually an observer rather than a participant, a solitary figure watching and listening intently, jotting down what he saw and heard. He showed a London that would soon disappear, and there are moments in his writing when he seems to be describing a city from the nineteenth century, after Charles Dickens, Fyodor Dostoyevsky or Emile Zola.

At a late-night bar, he wrote: 'Pervading colour: cream. Cheese rolls. Fat, tarty woman, with a face like a man's, wearing a soiled overall. Fat, plump, white man, rimless glasses. Whores. Pimps ... Types of whores. Thin. Low forehead & villainous features. Half baked look ... The woman 2 seats away inquiring about the quality of what I was eating – through the man between.' He would record snatches of conversation from a bus ride, a cafe or the street: 'You Greek ponce ... Snappy Joey's must have been a terrific dive, eh. One girl had a large ? tattooed on her behind ... So I meets him and I says to him "'Ello!" and 'e says, "'Ello!" ... I might have a woman for you this week ... Kill time you know. Hardest thing to kill.' He recorded what he saw, simple images designed to create a possible spark for later stories. 'Girl bending back to straighten stocking ... The Nigger-Lovers. Drawings of blacks on wall. Couples no conversation ... Victoria on a hot afternoon. Cat & 3 pigeons ... Cloakroom. Single black hat on hook.' He noted a line from his loquacious landlady, Mrs Lloyd, about a coal delivery man: 'He asked for the lady with the Indian gentleman – but he didn't finish it because he was too embarrassed to say it. You don't mind, do you? He is a nice man.' He made observations, which at times implied a larger knowledge than he had: 'Sisters are invariably proud of brothers' sexual success ... The Decline of the Society Writer ... At one time I used to think my salvation would be a wife. Well, I got a wife. No what I need is a woman ... Man at Bow St. [Magistrates'] Court seeing pro[stitute]s come in. "They've come to pay their income-tax" ... A man who didn't believe all he read in the papers ... Woman who runs a paper on improving race relations but doesn't want black people in her house.' Race and sex were never far from his thoughts. One night aboard a double-decker London bus, he noted, '2 low-class Englishwomen with two flashily-dressed Indians. All drunk & singing at the top of their voices. Old, round Jewess & wizened husband come on top. Woman: Oh, let's go back downstairs. But they remain & foursome notice distaste. So: sitting behind old couple: Hey, Pop, can't you sing? Can't you sing? Woman: They're just angry because you're coloured. Man: Shut up.'

His relationship with friends and colleagues at the BBC such as Jan Carew, John Stockbridge, Gordon Woolford and Willy Edmett were central to his life at this time. He discovered something of London and the world beyond through their stories and romances, and the experiences which he himself did not dare to have. Stockbridge told how he felt unfaithful to his mistress whenever he slept with his wife, and Vidia recorded his conjugal woes: 'Going to beat him up, beat her up, & tell her I'll kill her if she does it again. It wasn't honour. It was self-pity. But I am glad it didn't get me down. I have come out on top. Must get a hat. – Why? – Feel like it. For the new tough male role I am filling. So we walk along a crazy, crowded Oxford Street to Dunn's & his face falls as he sees the prices, £2 etc.' Willy Edmett's quirky phrases were recorded, as was his response to a remark from Stockbridge. 'J.S. Met a practitioner of black magic yesterday. W. It is white magic when we practise it . . . Typical Willyisms: It's like dust. You didn't see it falling, but you suddenly say, hello, the table's covered with dust . . . Willy is a dark horse. Willy with black woman.' Jan Carew's attitudes and adventures impressed him: 'Another of J.C.'s stories: Court-martialled & dishonourably discharged. All terribly hush-hush. Wrote a seven-page memorandum to my commanding officer telling him how the army ought to be run. He is a married man, of course. But: You should see the Italian girl I have coming over here in a few days. 5' 10", built in the Roman way, with sex crawling all over her skin . . . Used to go out hunting in the jungle, when I was a boy, two weeks at a time. Butted a S. African last night. I was hungry & when I am hungry all my intellectual poses drop off.'[18]

Nights out with Gordon Woolford yielded notes like 'Gordon owes me 8/6'. One evening as they walked through Piccadilly Circus with its streams of people and electric billboards and the Eros statue,

> G[ordon] pointed at a woman in a doorway & said, 'I know you!'
> The woman looked G over & said, 'Let me see, I know you too. You are G.'
> 'How did you remember?'
> 'Meet Gordon,' she said, turning to her fellow-tart. 'He was in the RAF when I was in the WAAF [Women's Auxiliary Air Force].'
> Her eyelids and forehead & her hair were sprinkled with twinkle dust. Likewise her companion's.
> Woman grew definitely sad. Kind face. Glistening eyes.
> 'Well, G. I never thought I would see you in Picc[adilly]. Never thought I would see myself here either.'
> Chat about careers.
> 'Come and have a coffee.'
> No interest.

'Where?' she asked finally.

'Snack-bar in Dean St.'

Then, out of nowhere, a man: 'Snack-bar! Snack-bar! Don't want to break up your little what not –.'

Without a word both girls walk away, after ceremoniously shaking hands.

Vidia's encounters with prostitutes in 1955 remained theoretical, or chaste. His interest in women who would do imaginable sexual things for money dated back to his teenage days in Port of Spain. Seduction would not be involved; nor was the woman required to dissemble. A woman who sold herself to a man for sex embodied his internal collision between repulsion and desire. Speaking years later he saw his fascination with the bars of Soho and Shepherd's Market as youthful bravado: 'I used to go actually for the sex in the head, that kind of excitement. I was taken by it almost like a nineteenth-century French writer – although that didn't enter my head, about being like a French writer. I was lured by the idea of their bodies. It was just the idea of the bodies. I found them very attractive. One was young and inexperienced and . . . thank God I didn't have money. I would have probably done a lot of foolish things.'

He saw such voyeuristic contact as an imagined idea rather than a practicality, as a prolonged, intangible form of arousal, 'sex in the head' that did not involve the intimacy and risk of sex with another person's body. 'It is very much an innocent approach really, and all my time in London there was that innocence. I felt unhappy that I didn't have the money to be debauched. I loved the idea of debauchery.' His relationship with Pat did not, or could not, move beyond the shy, virginal form in which it had begun. They were both trapped by the formal taboos they had been raised with at a time of unspoken ignorance in Port of Spain and Kingstanding. Sex itself was 'an embarrassment, and I think it had to do with my own background. I was born in 1932, so I am very much a child of another age: the shyness, the embarrassment – and the absurd idea that the main thing was for me to have my ejaculation. That was very foolish. Nobody told me anything else. I've written about it some-where, and I think in the old days certainly – I don't know what it is like now – it's true of most Indian men, this very private idea of sex being something for you alone and not related to the person in front of you. The idea of sex as one of the talents of life doesn't enter into it at all. It's just something dark at the corner . . . I think Pat could never get rid of her inhibitions, her shame and everything else. And in the cinema, any scene of intimacy on the screen, I couldn't bear to look at it. It was just the way I was made. So I would look down. I would tell her, "When they have stopped kissing let me know." It went on and to this day it goes on. It seemed to me such an intimate thing, two people kissing, why should I be asked to look at it?'[19]

*

At the end of 1954 when he got the job at the BBC, Vidia had used his newfound financial security to move out of Owad's house. Getting accommodation was not easy, and the literary editor Karl Miller had a story about Vidia from this period: 'Asked on the telephone if he was coloured, by an English landlady to whom he was applying in his youth for a room, he was said to have replied: "Hopelessly." '[20] One of his cousins finally arranged for him to rent rooms from a Barbadian doctor in Notting Hill. The warmth of his sexual and emotional relationship with Pat revived; he could see a way ahead. He became affectionate. 'Write & tell little boy immediately what train you are coming down by. Have found flat – ideal as far as your visits are concerned. Moving Saturday. Do come, darling. It will be so depressing moving without you. Last week-end was a miracle of joy & love.' Pat came to London for the weekend and helped him move in to the house in Oxford Gardens. 'So,' he remembered in old age, tears running down his face, 'for the first time in my life, there was semblance of a household of my own.' Pat cooked a meal. 'It was a very, very moving moment for me, a sacramental moment. It was very beautiful. I have probably written about this in other ways in my work. For the first time I felt a little bit in control.'[21] It reminded him of his short story 'This Is Home', when a young couple move to a new house, and as the man leaves, the woman reminds him, 'This is home.' Within weeks, Vidia was 'thinking of moving to a better place, where one can type, where the ceilings are thicker, where there are carpets on the stairs, and where the doors lock properly.' With the help of a BBC doorman he found a sitting room cum bedroom with a little kitchen attached in St Julian's Road in Kilburn. Different people lived on each floor of this new house and shared a communal bathroom. Vidia would remain at St Julian's Road for two and a half productive years.

He knew that Pat held him together emotionally, and decided without enthusiasm to marry her, despite feeling that he would be going against his family's wishes. In retrospect he thought they might have done better to live together: 'It was the social pressures of those days ... She wanted to get married.' Vidia wanted a respectable witness and approached a fellow Trinidadian, Frank Singuineau, 'a mulatto fellow, a nice educated man, married to an Irish girl' who worked as an actor at the BBC and would later appear in films such as *Carry On Again Doctor* and *An American Werewolf in London*. But Frank Singuineau, the chosen witness, would not cooperate. Vidia and Pat were isolated. 'He said he couldn't do it because he was Catholic and didn't approve. I had to get somebody else.'[22] Gordon Woolford was the less-respectable substitute, accompanied by Vidia's cousin Deo Ramnarine.

The marriage took place on 10 January 1955. The groom was identified as 'Vidiadhar Surajparashad Naipaul formerly known as Vidiadhar Swraj-parashad Naipal, son of Supersal Naipal deceased Journalist', a 'Radio Script Writer (B.B.C.)'. The bride was Patricia Ann Hale, 'University Post Graduate,' daughter of a 'solicitor's managing clerk'.[23] They were both twenty-two years old. Neither family was informed of the marriage. Vidia produced no wedding ring, an oversight which Pat did her tentative English best to put right some months later. 'I do feel the lack of a ring very acutely. You did promise & I will think you don't quite realise how "odd" it seems to people. Don't be irritable about it – it isn't just a fancy, whim or extravagance & I don't think I am mistaken in regarding it as rather important.' A wedding ring represented all that Vidia wanted to avoid: expense, the trap of marriage, social expectation. He had chosen to marry Pat, but did not want to accept the consequences of doing so. Rather than address the chasmic inconsistency in what he was doing, he tried to turn his back on himself, and offered these bizarre subsequent justifications for his behaviour: 'I had no interest in jewellery. I didn't think it was important. I simply had no money.'[24] Pat finally bought herself a wedding ring, a plain gold band, which she rarely wore.

Initially she remained living with Miss Gilson in Birmingham while she completed her studies in history and philosophy, and only came down to St Julian's Road at weekends. Before arrival, she would send Vidia a shopping list and basic instructions in housewifery: 'bed made with one clean sheet (put top to bottom) & clean pillow cases'. Vidia kept her in touch with London by post, watching the other lodgers in the house with a writer's eye. 'Mrs. Cariddi has left for Italy, and she left very quietly, without telling anyone. The little wop boy is left alone, so very alone. But he is doing the illegal thing, with the assistance of the Rex Lloyds: he is working. Last Sunday, he asked me in, and offered me loads of macaroni and spaghetti (uncooked). I was really touched by this generosity and the effort to gain friendship. But alas, I don't like spaghetti or macaroni, and I had to refuse. This is when these people cease to be stupid, and become very, very sad.' He was re-reading D.H. Lawrence's *Sons and Lovers*. 'It is a very great book: the greatest writers can write only one book of that standard.' Pat lent him money to send to his family in Trinidad, which he was careful to repay. Ma made repeated requests for money to support herself, Sewan and Nella. 'Although Kamla is giving me every cent of her salary to spend in the house which I <u>must</u> be grateful for she also gives me the same amount of torture.'[25] Kamla added that 'even a single pound' from him would help to pull them through these difficult months. Vidia felt he was trapped in a vacuum. 'I have written a message of hope on that piece of cardboard the Thornhill laundry sends with its shirts: It is Foolish to Fear Failure. I did this last night, and the effect has really been wonderful, though the nagging, aching feeling of unease continues constantly, like a nail in the shoe ... At the moment I just can do nothing; the terror and the unease and the deep deep sense of futility seem to float just in a cloud above my head.'

Pat wished to tell her parents about their marriage, but did not. She visited them, and said nothing. She knew that Vidia was not being supportive, and reacted by nagging him rather than demanding he take responsibility for their situation: 'I just can't do it when I feel all alone ... I am seized by little fears that you resent my asking you, that you want to live in a vacuum writing your novel, that you want to hide from all those things.' She suggested that Vidia might write a letter to Mrs Hale telling her the truth. His reaction to this demand was not to confront Pat's parents, but to ignore their very existence: 'I wasn't interested in them at all. I was not interested in them.'[26] Soon after the wedding, in another doom-laden symbolic gesture, Vidia lost the marriage certificate. Pat urged him to obtain a copy, or better still 'look for the original. I can't help feeling a little miserable that you've mislaid something like that.' The secret of the marriage remained with them, and grew with each passing month, as rumours reached Trinidad. Vidia's mind was still as much on Pa as it was on Pat. A fortnight after his marriage, he wrote home, 'Two or three nights a week though I still dream about Pa – always nice things; and I see him as clearly as I did at home ... I am not lying when I say that I am trying to be a writer more for his sake than my own. I am at the moment tidying up his stories before sending them to an agent, but I burst into tears whenever I see his handwriting.'[27] Soon afterwards, Mira wrote mentioning a relation who had married a woman in England and kept it secret from his parents for more than a year: 'The poor souls are shocked, hurt and disappointed.' Three months later, Kamla dropped a heavier hint, 'Oh by the way, if in case you ever get married, please don't make yourself equal to these Indians in T'dad by not telling us.'[28]

Vidia did nothing, nor did he tell his friends about his marriage. Jill discovered about it in a way that caused her great embarrassment. 'I gathered subsequently that I was not the only one person he did this to – Brenda [her flatmate] and I had a party and we invited him. We invited twenty people and he was one of them. After the party I had his telephone number and I telephoned, I got the landlady and she said, Mr Naipaul isn't here but Mrs Naipaul is. I thought his mother must have come to visit. Pat got on the phone and I was absolutely appalled. How could he have done that? He never told me he got married, and I would never invite a married man to the party without inviting his wife. I had met Pat before, only I didn't know her well. I was extremely distressed and upset by this. It made me feel that she would think that I was carrying on with him.'[29] Vidia put a different construction on Jill's outrage, at least in retrospect, claiming it was because she was jealous: 'Brenda thought Jill would marry me.'[30] According to Jill: 'He reads it wrong. Vidia put me in a socially impossible position because he made me look rude by not inviting Pat.'[31] Jill's version of these events is more plausible, given Vidia's reticence in expressing his feelings to her at the time, and because she was engaged to another man. Her own happiness soon turned to tragedy when, six weeks after her wedding the following summer, her husband died. Not long after this, Vidia made his attraction more explicit. 'He once made a pass at me, but only once, in the flat in Chelsea after [my husband] died. I remember him making some sort of gesture. I think I was still mourning . . . Don't get me wrong. I have been laughed at over the years for my preference for what some people refer to as dark little ethnics. Indeed I married one, and have been happily married to him for more than forty years. So if I was brushing Vidia off, it was not because I was being standoffish about him being Indian.'[32]

When Vidia looked at his early correspondence with Pat many years later, with a view to writing a book called *In My Twenty-Fifth Year* – which he failed to complete because it was too emotionally disturbing – he made these notes:

I feel it would have been better for me if I had married >or made love to< Jill. Reading these letters I see (for the first time) that she was interested. Pat really had too many hang-ups. Too many complaints. Too many demons ... I had been in too deep with Pat, who did not attract me sexually at all ... I should have steered clear of that damaged family ... [Pat's letters] contain much of herself. Her virtue, her humanity ... And in spite of my feeling of two days or so ago, that I should not have married Pat, I find myself in tears again on reading her letters of 1952. Her love was beautiful. And is beautiful ... The relationship – on VSN's side – was more than half a lie. Based really on need. The letters are shallow & disingenuous. Trivial letters for the most part.[33]

*

In May, he sent $30 (£6.25) each to Ma and Kamla, and reported that the manuscript of the novel he had begun in 70 Bravington Road was 'being considered this moment by Arthur Calder-Marshall'.[34] He had taken his cue from George Lamming, whose *In the Castle of My Skin* was having a success. Calder Marshall had recommended Lamming to the publisher Michael Joseph, and on the strength of merely three chapters, the head of the firm had invited him to a meeting where Lamming was given a contract and a cheque on the spot.[35] (Willie Chandran has a similar experience in *Half a Life*.) While Vidia waited hopefully for a response, and prepared his scripts for the BBC, Pat sent him instructions: 'Now, it's Whit weekend. Therefore you must do the shopping on Saturday – now you must. That means you'll have to get the money today (Friday).' He went to the shops with his new wife's letter in his pocket:

1lb coffee (Jamaica medium ground) from Beverley's
Butter
Sugar
1 tin Tomato Soup!
1 tin Baked Beans
2 tins Garden peas
6 eggs Large
6 oranges
2 lbs New Potatoes
1 lb Carrots
Bread – 1 small brown, 1 Snow's small white
Sainsbury's lg chicken
or
2 chops (large) & Lambs Liver – ask for 1/4 worth

All my love dear. I pray that this Calder Marshall man likes the novel all the time.[36]

Vidia was still eating meat, although he claimed to be revolted by it. A couple of years later when Pat served him lamb's liver, 'I just broke down. Liver was intolerable. This was in the late 1950s. I felt I was a vegetarian who had been violated.'[37] As for the novel, Arthur Calder Marshall 'read it promptly, and wrote a long letter back with single spacing on two sides of a big sheet of paper. He began by saying, you must abandon this book at once. Then he said a few kind things. When that happens, and people tell you things which in your heart you know are true, you are at once relieved and full of anger. And it was out of that, that some despairing weeks later I began to write in the BBC, the first story of *Miguel Street*.'[38]

In early June 1955, in the freelances' room at the Langham Hotel with its ochre walls and pea-green dado, Vidia wound a piece of 'non-rustle' BBC studio paper into a standard typewriter and adopted a singular posture, his shoulders thrown back, his knees drawn up, his shoes resting on the struts on either side of the chair in a 'monkey crouch'.[39] Setting the typewriter to single space, he wrote: 'Every morning when he got up Hat would sit on the banister of his back verandah and shout across, "What happening there, Bogart?"' He had a sentence, a start. He tried to go on. 'The man addressed in this way would turn in his bed . . .' He crossed it out and began again. 'Bogart would turn in his bed and mumble softly, so that no one heard, "What happening there, Hat?"'[40] And Vidia had the opening of his first publishable book. Some figures in *Miguel Street* were simplified versions of people from Luis Street: Bogart was Poker, Hat was a man called Topi (the Hindi word for hat), Uncle Bhakcu was Power Mausa. For Vidia's family and other inhabitants of Woodbrook, the characters would be familiar. Kamla remembered meeting a fellow teacher when she went to work at a school in Pointe-à-Pierre in the 1970s: 'Her name was Lorna Lange and she said to me, "Kamla, I know you, so don't come with any style to me, I lived all my life in Luis Street until I got married and came south, I know Hat, Hat is Topi, you can't fool me, and Man-man is Thakrine's son, I know Bogart, and the drunken chap who started running a whorehouse." She knew every single character in *Miguel Street*.'[41]

The book is a lambent collection of linked stories, written with artful simplicity, depicting life in a Port of Spain street in the 1940s through the eyes of a fatherless boy. Although ethnicity is rarely made explicit in the book, most of the characters are the equivalent of St James or Woodbrook Indians, people with a slim chance of moving out of the ghetto and destitution. The men drink rum, and dream. To escape, they live little fantasies and concoct plans which come to nothing; humour and tragedy are laced together, and the cruelty is absurd. Man-man, for instance, has no luck getting elected to office and so arranges his own crucifixion. When people stone him, at his own instigation, he shouts, ' "Cut it out, I tell you. I finish with this arseness, you hear." ... The authorities kept him for observation. Then for good.'[42] Popo, a carpenter, is making 'the thing without a name'. B. Wordsworth is writing the greatest poem in the world. George turns his pink house into a brothel for American sailors. Eddoes, who drives a scavenging cart, has shiny shoes and boasts he knows 'everybody important in Port of Spain, from the Governor down'.[43] Elias studies hard and fails exams. ' "Is the English and litritcher that does beat me," ' he says. The narrator adds: 'In Elias's mouth litritcher was the most beautiful word I heard. It sounded like something to eat, something rich like chocolate. Hat said, "You mean you have to read a lot of poultry and thing?" Elias nodded.'[44]

For all its simplicity, Vidia had written an ambitious and remarkable book, sparked in part by the Spanish picaresque romance *Lazarillo de Tormes*, which he had studied and translated at university. To appeal to a British readership, Vidia might have attempted a Mittelholzer-like jungle romance, a clever Oxford novel or something set in Trinidad with English characters; he might even have written of Mr Teughnsend, cultivator of hallotments. Instead, he wrote about an alien world and used strange dialogue. Bar a woman with straw-like hair ('I hated that woman,' notes the narrator) there is scarcely a white character in *Miguel Street*.[45] V.S. Naipaul had turned a slum in Port of Spain into a setting for a universal fable. Pa's legacy, the critical success of Sam Selvon, the high standard set by Henry Swanzy and the encouragement and example of other writers on *Caribbean Voices* convinced Vidia that good literature could be written about his own country. He was a long way from Oxford now, far from the literary canon he had been taught by the dons. His chosen subject was the powerless: those who, although in the majority in the world, had appeared in European literature only as peripheral characters, or at best as Man Friday.

Despite some acts of kindness, the relationships in the book are bleak and survivalist. Men chase women, women try to trap men and 'make baby'; men beat women and women beat children. Hat says of Toni, ' "Is a good thing for a man to beat his woman every now and then, but this man does do it like exercise, man." '[46] If a character on the street tries to sound authoritative, another cuts him down to size. The larger world is unknowable, a place so far away it can only be guessed at, and ignorance makes people invent and falsify. When war breaks out, a pavement commentator says, ' "If they just make Lord Anthony Eden Prime Minister, we go beat up the Germans and them bad bad." '[47] The only character to move beyond this setting is the narrator, who by the end of the book is like a more sophisticated version of Vidia who 'takes rum and women to Maracas Bay for all-night sessions', to his mother's consternation.[48] Ganesh Pundit, 'mystic masseur from Fuente Grove', helps him to obtain an overseas scholarship and leave the island. The narrator walks briskly to the aeroplane, looking only at his shadow before him, a dancing dwarf on the tarmac.

This, then, was the book: but would anyone publish it? Stockbridge liked it, Salkey liked it and Gordon Woolford liked it a great deal. Vidia was loath to ask Calder Marshall for help again. Salkey had a suggestion. At the Piccadilly nightclub where he worked, a louche establishment called the Golden Slipper, he had met an editor from the publishing firm André Deutsch. She was named Diana Athill, moved in bohemian circles and had a weakness for West Indian men. Salkey made contact, and Vidia handed Miss Athill the manuscript in a coffee bar near her office. She remembered him at their first meeting seeming 'very young, just down from Oxford. He appeared absolutely confident in himself, and he was very clever and well read, that was obvious. I was impressed by him.'[49] She read and liked *Miguel Street*, but the eponymous André Deutsch, the Hungarian-born impresario behind the company, thought a book of short stories about Trinidad by an unpublished author was unlikely to sell. The manuscript was passed to the firm's reader, Francis Wyndham, who was as enthusiastic about it as Athill. After some months, she wrote saying they would like to see a novel if he had one, and might publish the stories later. It was the start of a crucial professional relationship for both of them. 'If there hadn't been someone like Diana Athill at the publisher,' Vidia said later, 'my work would never have got going. She was the best editor in the world at that time. I have the utmost regard for her.'[50]

His retrospective view of his fellow immigrant, André Deutsch, was less happy. 'Deutsch was a foolish man, really an illiterate, and he caused me a lot of anguish. He said stories don't sell, and of course *Miguel Street* has not been out of print since it was published. It has not been out of print. He tormented me in that way. So I had to write a novel, and I did *The Mystic Masseur* with great unhappiness.'[51] Quickly, he wrote this new book. It had a similar tone to *Miguel Street*, but was set mainly among rural Indians in Trinidad. It told the story of Ganesh, a character who owes much to Pa's *Gurudeva*. Like Gurudeva, he is a chancer, and progresses from failed teacher to masseur to entrepreneur, ending up as an author and politician. The narrator, who appears at the beginning and end of the book, is like the boy in *Miguel Street*. On the first page he visits Ganesh, the healer. ' "I know the sort of doctors it have in Trinidad," my mother used to say. "They think nothing of killing two three people before breakfast." This wasn't as bad as it sounds: in Trinidad the midday meal is called breakfast.'[52] The atmosphere and humour were set. Ganesh is cannier than Gurudeva, extorting money from his father-in-law by saying he is establishing a cultural institute in Fuente Grove, a hot, remote village with a single mango tree. He writes and publishes *101 Questions and Answers on the Hindu Religion*; American soldiers visit him for advice. In a narratorial intrusion, the larger implications of the book are suggested: 'I myself believe that the history of Ganesh is, in a way, the history of our times; and there may be people who will welcome this imperfect account of the man Ganesh Ramsumair, masseur, mystic, and, since 1953, M.B.E.'[53] By the end, Ganesh is an aspiring statesman named G. Ramsay Muir.

Although most of Vidia's 1955 notebook is buoyant, and revolves around his social activity with his BBC colleagues, towards the end there are the beginnings of a withdrawal. Vidia hated the idea of being rejected by people that he liked. 'The impact made by the discovery that someone, who has kept silent about it, really hates you & has been trying to do you down,' he noted. He saw people less and closed in on himself once Pat moved to London full-time in July. 'My circle of acquaintances grows smaller & smaller,' he wrote. 'I have even dropped out of it.' By the end of the year he had removed himself from his old social circle, established a permanent day-by-day relationship with Pat and begun writing properly. As a writer he was all set; but as a person his interaction and opportunities began to reduce. For Vidia, friendship could never be wholehearted. He could not extend trust to another person: neither at this point, nor later in his life, would he ever reveal or unburden himself in full. 'Never. I wouldn't do it. It's just not my nature. There is no moral quality in it, it's just the way I am. And I have never examined it before.'[54]

On 8 December, less than six months after he began writing *Miguel Street*, Vidia had good news for Ma. His telegram home said simply, 'NOVEL ACCEPTED LOVE. VIDO'.[55] Graham Watson of the literary agency Curtis Brown agreed to take him on as a client, if in a half-hearted way. By now Pat was working as a supply teacher for the London County Council. Vidia received a cheque in the post from Deutsch for £25, with a promise of another £100 to come. 'If it is of any use to you,' he wrote to Miss Athill, 'my telephone number is MAIda Vale 1054.'[56] When finally he deposited the £100 cheque at Barclay's Bank the cashier stood up, leaned over the counter and shook his hand.

News of his marriage to Pat was gushing across the Atlantic. Vidia confirmed the truth to Kamla, but asked her not to tell Ma; only in October did he write the dreaded letter, and his mother's response, written in her curling, spiralling hand, was forceful but magnanimous. 'Congratulation's on your wedding . . . I told Kamla a month before receiving your letter that your not writing home is that you are married . . . Well I am very disappointed that you really don't know your mother . . . In future always remember that I am a very good mother to all my children. I have given all of you freedom to marry who they like, but choose wisely. No secret from now.'[57] For Ma, Kamla, Sati, Savi, Mira, Sewan and Nella, it was not easy to hear of Vido's marriage: it meant that the first son of the family would not be coming home to support them. Pat told her parents, and they responded remarkably warmly by inviting the married couple to spend Christmas with them in Kingstanding. Told of Deutsch's cheque, her father wrote, 'I am very glad to learn that at long last Vidia is getting satisfaction from his publishers. He has been very patient.' In an effort to show acceptance to his son-in-law, Mr Hale tried to get him a ticket to a cricket Test match at Edgbaston. 'Now for news from home. I am sorry to say Uncle Reg died last Saturday . . . Now to more cheerful things. I bought Mummy another budgerigar. Same colour as old Bill.'[58]

Christmas 1955 at 593 Kingstanding Road proved an ordeal. The tiny family flat was owned by Mr Hale's employer, and

BURRELL-DAVIS & GOODE

was painted across the three sash windows in the front room, which had to double as an office for meeting clients. Kingstanding embodied Midlands dreariness, a poor suburb caught between the city and the countryside that was being developed fast and badly in a slum clearance programme. Vidia drank too much in an effort to cope with the unfamiliarity, and Pat made conversation. He remembered: 'It was a terrible experience when I went there for the first time. They were living in a flat, and it had been dreadfully neglected. Everybody was trying to be friendly, but it was painful. I was bored in an hour and I drank a lot of gin.' Going up the wooden steps from the back garden, Pat's sister Eleanor asked Vidia to put on her mother's wartime ARP helmet. 'She got a bat and she hit me on the head. She was about ten or eleven and she thought because of the helmet I would feel nothing. I remember that very well. It was stunning more than painful.'[59] Eleanor, a sporty child with piercing blue-grey eyes who did not share her sister's academic bent and had spent her early life convinced she was a boy, found Vidia to be unexpectedly good company. 'My mother told me Pat was secretly married and I told my best friend and that's how it got back to my father. It was a big disgrace marrying a coloured man. Immigrants were only in Handsworth in Birmingham then ... Vidia wasn't as I imagined, he was much darker than I thought he would be, and small. I thought he was going to be tall. I remember when we went to a stately home and the guide told us William the Conqueror gave a herd of goats to the original owner, Vidia said, "You get my goat." I thought that was very funny. He was jolly to me, I liked him. When he was young, he was snobbish but he was always joking; later he was just snobbish. My sister always said the Naipauls thought they were better than everyone else.'

Edward and Margaret Hale, Ted and Marg, had almost no point of contact with their new son-in-law. Pat's success at school, a result of the widening of opportunities that had stemmed from the 1944 Education Act, had introduced her to a world far from her origins. Soon after their wedding in Gloucester, Ted had got badly into debt and run off with another woman, but under pressure from her father the marriage was resurrected. Ted sold their house without Marg's knowledge, and they had to move north in disgrace to Birmingham. 'My mother was never a confrontational person,' Eleanor thought. 'If she didn't like something she would moan about it, but not do anything. My mother's family disliked my father, said he came from a family of ne'er-do-wells and his mother had ended up in the workhouse.'[60] During the Second World War, Pat was evacuated to Gloucester to live with Auntie Lu and her maternal grandparents, who manufactured confectionery. She attended a local girls' school, Denmark Road, where she remained through her education, returning the fifty miles to Birmingham only for the holidays. Both her parents supported her intellectual ambitions; her mother was a keen borrower of books from the local public library. In 1943 Pat was awarded a 'special place', which meant her fees were reduced to £6 a year. Intellectual self-improvement was impressed upon the pupils of Denmark Road; Pat took elocution classes at LAMDA and won a distinction.[61] In Eleanor's words: 'Pat was a swot. They taught you the Queen's English, how to say "round" and not "ree-ownd", and not to talk in a Brummie accent.'[62] In her last year, Pat wrote a Chekhovian play called *The School* about progress, sentiment and good Communists, with characters such as 'Ivan Sergeyevich Chubukov . . . a respected and intelligent worker on a collective farm.'[63] She was the only girl in her year at Denmark Road to win a state scholarship to Oxford.[64]

In an autobiographical note written during the days of women's lib and bra-burning in the late 1960s, Pat wrote that she had been liberated from the depressing influence of her mother by her Auntie Lu and cousin Jose: 'I accepted the received doctrine in my immediate family that being a woman was a dreary, dangerous business . . . I remember the red sweater Jo[se] gave me when I was a student. It was figure enhancing . . . She was six years older than me and I worshipped her as a child. "You need a bra." "Mummy, Jose says I need a bra." Words like bra stupefied my mother, let alone more serious matters . . . My tenuous breasts ached under my first bra. I come from a small-breasted family but mine are the smallest . . . I end as I began in the smallest size. But I will not be burning mine. Instead I celebrate the wearing of the bra . . . My happiness was suddenly cut short by the onset of menstruation for which I was totally unprepared. My poor father eventually realised the cause of my distress . . . My aunt, my mother's unmarried sister, was my constant companion as a child. I think she would have liked to be a man. She spoke sadly then of the motorbike she had owned but family pressure had forced her to sell.'[65] In 1975, examining her own behaviour in a diary during a time of trouble, Pat wrote of her mother: 'I think pride entered into her care for me . . . She sacrificed life to self-sacrifice. But the loneliness of life in the flat at Kingstanding must have reinforced her obsessions with her own fate, and with my future.'[66] Like many people, Pat could see the mistakes her parents had made with their lives, but was unable to avoid making different, though related, mistakes in her own. She too would, finally, sacrifice life to self-sacrifice.

CHAPTER TEN

BACK TO THE NEW WORLD

BY THE SUMMER OF 1956, Ma was in a desperate and unhappy state. 'Well as a mother to be so wretched and depending on a daughter for a loaf of bread is a disgrace to the human race,' she wrote in frustration to Vido, hoping he would come home to Trinidad.[1] Despite the pressure to support the family, Kamla was later adamant that she had not minded the obligation: 'Ma felt that she was a burden on me. I never felt that Ma was a burden on me, or that the children were. I never had that feeling. It didn't prevent me from having dates. I had a good life.'[2] Sewan, who was now known more formally as Shiva, wrote to Vidia that their mother had 'not the slightest idea, if and when you are coming'.[3] Before this letter reached him, Vidia wrote to Ma: 'It's all fixed now. I am . . . travelling down by the Cavina, an Elders & Fyffes' banana boat.'[4] The journey aboard the 7,000-ton cargo ship, sailing on one of its last voyages before being scrapped, would take nearly three weeks. Pat would stay in England. Her father wrote in July, 'I do not like the idea of your remaining in London on your own during the absence of Vidia and I suggest you come home for the Vacation . . . Remember me to Vidia. What does he think of this flipping weather.'[5]

At the end of August, Pat and Vidia took the train to Avonmouth on the edge of Bristol, the city where ships had been fitted in the eighteenth century for the Atlantic slave trade. Vidia wrote to her that night on Fyffes Line writing paper. 'I feel more emotion than I showed. As always with these things, the pain comes not with the cut but seconds later. When I came aboard the ship I felt very lonely and afraid and I loved you very much. I know what you feel: I will go away and never come back. It is the same fear that is over me. Am I seeing all this England around me – still around me – for the last time? But I know that I must come back; I want that more than anything else. I want it much more than you do. These people sitting around me at dinner and here as I write in the old-fashioned cosy lounge with chairs upholstered in flowered covers – these people are precisely the people I fled from, the people who make life in any colony hell. An emptiness and a horrible egocentricity, a callousness – all these irritations come out from them. A bit of the Naipaul travelling luck still clings to me. One man hasn't turned up so – instead of 3, there are only 2 of us sharing a cabin. And – remember my fears about having my valuables stolen? – my cabinmate is a Police Sergeant from Trinidad who is going back after a 6-month course in CID work!' Vidia even apologized for his anger before departure. 'I don't think I can forgive myself for my stupid and thoughtless behaviour on Tuesday. Looking back it seems more and more outrageous and I really am very sorry for it.'[6]

The other passengers were familiar and unfamiliar, part of the West Indian world that Vidia had escaped and was now recovering. 'I keep on saying "in this country", "here", "home", when I mean England; and the W. I.'s aboard look upon me, I imagine, as one of those affected scholarship chaps. Well, it doesn't matter. I don't think I could bear the thought of a permanent exile from England.' He sought to remain aloof, even as he relished their company. He reported shipboard gossip and manoeuvring. 'What is greatly offending the black people on this ship – 10 or 12 out of 60 passengers – is the rather ridiculous adoption of a baby by a Trinidad half-white woman. This gross old woman made a journey to England especially to get this baby and anyone who has been to England can see at a glance – saving your humanitarian sentiments – that the wretched baby has the stupidest and lowest of English faces; and don't tell me that you can't judge babies. She paid £25 for this child! And she got it from a Catholic orphanage! As you can tell, I am a little disgusted by this woman. There are hundreds of wretched things in Trinidad itself who need care.'

George, the black detective, offered constant entertainment. Vidia recorded his dialogue in the back of a notebook. 'The ship is going to rock like a whore', and, 'Man, it was cold and I was feeling for some "romance". Two months pass and I ain't see nothing coming my way. I say, George boy, you gotta do something man, I was hurting. Pick up this Jamaican – ugly like arse – but still, it was cold, you know. Eat'in, man. Had to have something.' He told Pat 'the Negro detective is now the most unpopular passenger aboard. He treats the stewards the way people treat servants in Trinidad and I just sit in my bunk and watch him . . . I never met a T'dad policeman before and this is a good opportunity. He is 33, married, the father of five; yet constantly unfaithful . . . He has told me of all his sexual experiences in London and he is worried that he might be 'breeding' a girl ... I like hearing him talk. His language is so vigorous. For example, speaking of two women: "one old, one half-old". Me: "What about the Trinidad prisons now?" He: "Getting better. But the fellers getting away, man." Again: (to me) "What about you, man? You breeding your wife yet?" ' George told Vidia he had a love for 'sweet' words 'like "reminiscent" (he read it in a cricket book about the 1939 MCC tour of the West Indies: some bowler was described as being "reminiscent of the great Larwood") ... Just as I was writing that, he came up and said, "Well, Nawab, what you doing? Writing shorthand?" '

On 2 September Vidia wrote, 'We are in the tropics now. Unmistakably. Coming down to breakfast this morning I saw everybody, many officers & stewards in white ... Last night was so warm we slept above blankets with the port[hole]s open and the fan going ... The swimming pool – a rectangular thing constructed from wooden planks and lined with canvas – was put up yesterday and filled with sea water this morning. So far I have not had a swim in it ... I had forgotten so many things about the hot weather: the intolerable brightness of the light; the sweatiness of the salt at table: it no longer runs; butter melts; ice cream melts; cold water becomes lukewarm in a few minutes; and I have had to have ice in my Guinness.' He visited the ship's radio room to listen to *Caribbean Voices*. 'My voice comes over much better on short wave; but my faults show up badly: particularly my inability to run words together.'

Within days though, his old worries were coming back; he was terrified by the idea of return. 'Frankly, Pat,' he wrote, 'this is one of the most horrible journeys I ever will undertake in my life. I don't mean it purely from the physical point of view. All my conscious life I wanted and strove to get away from the Trinidad atmosphere: to use a horrible word, it is far too "philistine" and I never was at ease in it. And now I find myself right back again in it – and time has done nothing to lessen my discomfort in it. I wonder if you can imagine the fear and the constriction I feel.' The idea of Pat offered him a respite; he could tell her his fears. 'I am missing you and loving you so much I can't know how to say it. I am so worried and a bit of my old nervous problem came over me this afternoon. It is this physical sense of being lost, of being between two worlds and respected in neither that afflicts me. I can't write any more. My eyes are hurting too much.' The next day his eyes were a little better, 'but my nervous depression is so strong. I am beginning to fear that the whole trip might be wasted if the depression doesn't clear up ... I have been thinking all sorts of things. And I have been wondering whether when I come back we shouldn't try to have a baby.' After they reached Barbados, Vidia admitted, 'I shouldn't write this, but I must. Knowing the state of mind better than you do, I did bring the "anxiety" pills with me. I took two yesterday; and using a skin ointment which the Negro detective kindly lent me, there have been no ill effects, and I feel better today. I assure you I thought twenty times before taking those pills. So you can imagine how bad I was!' During their last days at sea, George the detective gave up visiting the dining room and insisted on being served meals in the cabin, to the annoyance of the ship's stewards. After an argument with one of them over a cup of tea, George said to Vidia, ' "Hear what he say? Is only because I black and thing, you know. But he frighten now ... I hurt one report on the captain – no, the chief steward – and he loss his job long time, you know." '

*

On 12 September, the *Cavina* reached Trinidad. 'If you ask for my first impressions it will be of the wealth of the place,' Vidia wrote to Pat. 'It seems to be one of the few places left where people can make money. Kamla showed me the new districts that have been built in the last two years: modern architecture has come to Trinidad.' What future did post-war England offer? 'Do you know, if we both work here we will be able to pull in about £2000 a year right away? We must talk about this seriously when I get back.' He was impressed by his family, by his mother and sisters and brother, and by what they had achieved. 'I left a family poor and rather depressed,' he told Pat, 'now, thanks to Kamla, I find our family not so poor and highly respected. All sorts of local worthies who would never have come home, say four or five years ago, keep coming in ... We were like your family when I left – no friends, no callers. That's changed. And I think it's a good thing. Apparently the Chinese are very loyal friends.' Returning to Nepaul Street 'would have been worth it if only to see the happiness on my mother's face. She was getting so worried; and they tell me that if I had disappointed her this time, she might have gone mad. Her hair is now almost grey ... Everyone at home regrets that you didn't come up with me; but they have a shrewd suspicion that we are even poorer than we make out and they understand.'

On his first afternoon, Vidia went upstairs to lie down on his bed and his little brother came to the room bearing a piece of writing he had done. In a radio tribute to Shiva after his death, Vidia remembered the gesture: 'This moment with Shiva, then eleven, this welcome and affection from someone who was like a new person to me, remains one of the sweetest and purest moments of my life.'[7] He told Pat: 'I am really proud of all my family. The girls, Mira & Savi, rallied round magnificently after my father's death. Savi began to sew clothes: she made about £4 a week for that. The amazing quality about these girls is their great <u>strength</u>. It is a quality that strikes me all the time. Part of it is my father's character; part comes from the years of hardship. Going through the old books in my father's bookcase was a harrowing experience. Poor man, he knew he was going to die many months before he actually did.' He had tragic memories of his father and his kindness. 'Yesterday I actually broke down and wept. I remembered so many things. I remembered the time when money was so scarce. One day I badgered him to take me to the pictures. It was a Sunday & on Sundays the prices are higher. But we had overlooked this. When we got to the cinema we couldn't buy the two seats in the cheapest part in the cinema. I was hurt; but I said to him that he must go in: we were in a queue. So he went in and I returned home crying. Half an hour later, my father came back, very upset and saying nothing. He couldn't stay.' As for Shiva, 'My brother is going to be the Naipaul who will become the writer. At the age of eleven he has already started: he spends much time just writing. And it is good, I tell you.' Shiva would stand in the doorway of Vido's room, watching him as he lay on the bed, smoking cigarettes from a green tin. The sight reminded him of his fading image of Pa.[8] Savi remembered Shiva's fascination with Vidia, whom he saw less as a brother than as a missing father figure. 'Vidia couldn't be that. He wasn't cold to him . . . but I don't remember seeing him putting an arm around somebody. I saw him being very sympathetic to people with problems later on, but at that age I don't think my brother ever hugged me, or anyone.'[9]

After a few days, Vidia began to see Trinidad in a more splintered light. 'My accent, darlin, is killing people over here and I am frightened to open my mouth. People take me for a foreigner and therefore do their best to overcharge me.' His uncle Simbhoo was now a major figure in the People's Democratic Party or PDP. With Bhadase Sagan Maraj, Simbhoo had visited India and secured money from the Birla business family to build schools for Hindus and improve literacy, although the Birlas later withdrew funding when Maraj refused to keep accounts.[10] Indians were feeling a new sense of entitlement. As freedom loomed for Trinidad and Tobago, ethnic tensions grew and Vidia became frightened, far from England, 'People talk more loudly; they shout easily; windows and doors are open and every sound can enter your house ... In Trinidad nature is a fertile, swift and violent thing. Even the ordinary grass looks as though it might grow overnight into some mighty man-eating plant. Coconut trees, mango-trees, trees whose name I have forgotten: they all grow in Port of Spain. The trees are higher and the branches low; and it looks just as if the jungle is merely suffering Port of Spain to exist, and might at any time change its mind. The other impression is of the surliness of the Negro lounging at the street corners. They are crude and nasty; and there has been a recent mob-movement which has made things a little ugly ... Yesterday I went with my uncle's election motor parade through Caroni and – of course – we ran into a lot of trouble. There was a riot. People were beaten up. Forty were arrested. Bottles, stones, & knives were used.' Later Vidia said, 'My uncle was taking part in the election campaign. He was a kind of joke figure for me, [but] he thought I would appreciate the humour of the whole thing, so he took me around.'[11]

As the weeks ran by, Vidia's instinctive Indian, or Hindu, exclusivity, which had in the past been expressed more through comedy than enmity, changed gear. It was an irreversible shift; like Trinidad itself, V.S. Naipaul went through a hardening of racial attitudes in 1956. Old relationships died as old certainties unravelled. Even when he saw a friend like WAGS, something seemed different. 'He was a very generous boy, generous at heart,' Vidia remembered years later, 'he actually came to the house to see me. I was moved by that. But even then, there was the racial politics that had occurred in Trinidad. He was on the side of the Negro party, so an odd thing had happened. Something had fractured.'[12] A powerful new political force had emerged under the leadership of Dr Eric Williams: the People's National Movement or PNM. The broadly Hindu and loose-knit PDP was losing ground to this tightly controlled new party. Although Indians such as Dr Winston Mahabir, a Presbyterian island scholar, and the broadcaster Kamaluddin Mohammed, a Muslim, joined Williams and became PNM candidates, most Indians were unnerved by what they saw as a monolithic black movement, and some even planned to emigrate to the UK, Canada or elsewhere. The Hindu proclivities of Simbhoo's movement pushed Indian Muslims into the arms of the PNM. Vidia said later, 'There was a divide in Trinidad which came about with Eric Williams. He co-opted the Muslims into his Negro party.'[13] For Vidia at this time, Williams was one among several aspiring politicians, an island scholar who had been to St Catherine's Society, an undistinguished off-shoot of Oxford University. 'The Negro leader is a dictator-like fellow (St. Cath's man) and if he says he is not racialist – ie <u>anti</u> non-Negro – his canvassers say it for him. The Negroes don't want to discuss. You cannot say anything about their leader. Their bullies heckle and break up other speakers' meetings and preserve order at their own. The police and the civil service are all Negro. So one has no defence at all.'

Born in 1911, the eldest of twelve children in a mixed black and French creole family, Eric Williams had attended Tranquillity and Queen's Royal College before winning an island scholarship. He took a First in history at Oxford, became a professor at Howard, the black university in Washington DC, and published books including *Capitalism and Slavery* (1944), which proposed the revolutionary thesis that the rise of industrial capitalism in Britain had depended on the West Indian slave trade, and that slavery had been abolished primarily for economic reasons. The latter point is arguable, but Williams was the first indigenous, qualified Caribbean historian to contradict and rewrite accepted British versions of history. Returning to Trinidad, he held public seminars and wrote didactic articles about the virtues of national development for the *Trinidad Guardian*. In 1955 he engineered his own dismissal from an official body, the Caribbean Commission, and the following year founded the PNM, the first political party in Trinidad able to project itself as a disciplined, progressive national grouping capable of taking the country to independence.

Clever, small, touchy, deaf and opaque, wearing dark glasses and with a cigarette stuck to his lower lip, 'The Doc' rapidly became a national figure. He produced a party newspaper which was endorsed by George Lamming, and later edited by his friend and mentor C.L.R. James. He attracted prominent candidates such as the famous cricketer Learie Constantine. In a radical move, Williams gave bombastic talks about subjects such as Caribbean agriculture, slavery or economic history to crowds of semi-literate supporters across the country, telling them 'the only university in which I shall lecture in future is the University of Woodford Square and its several branches throughout the length and breadth of Trinidad and Tobago.'[14] Crucially he drew in both the respectable creole middle class and poor black voters, many of whom took to his cause with fervour. After centuries of oppression, it was a potent combination: here was a local black man, Oxford-returned, who had beaten the colonizers at their own intellectual game and could also appeal to the street. One follower described him as 'a modern-day Christ'.[15] Back in London, the civil servants at the Colonial Office, as so often in such situations, missed the point: an official described his lectures on constitutional reform as 'almost a case for a psychiatrist ... it surprises me that an audience can be collected for this kind of thing.'[16] But the audience did collect, and Dr Williams narrowly won the election of 1956, with the PNM forming the first party government in Trinidad.[17] In *A Way in the World*, V.S. Naipaul would write of the electoral campaign: 'The meetings were billed as educational; the square was described as a university. People hadn't of course gone to learn anything; they had gone to take part in a kind of racial sacrament.'[18]

On 29 September, Vidia told Pat: 'My uncle won a seat in the General Election on Tuesday; but the opposition Party won 13 out of the 24 seats & they are going to form the government. This winning party is a Negro party and their victory has not only made it embarrassing for any non-Negro to walk P.O.S. streets, but has got every other community very worried. In this election the Negroes were united and they won their majority largely because the opposition vote was hopelessly split. Strange alliances are being formed now – Hindus, Big Business, and Roman Catholics, Whites, Chinese, Syrians and Indians. After the victory Jean was accosted by a Negro in the market, "Aye, you Indian women got to make yourself nice now for nigger man." That is one example of (perhaps insignificant) offensiveness. But if this becomes the official policy, Trinidad will be hell to live in.' Offensiveness begat offensiveness: 'the noble nigger is really a damned nasty nigger. You should be here to see it for yourself. The galling thing is that these very people who are so offensive over here go to England and whine for tolerance! Even children hurl abuse at you in the streets. You should see it. You will find it very revealing.' He might have added that Simbhoo's colleagues spent almost as much time accusing each other of fraud, and denouncing each other for embezzlement, as they did fighting Dr Williams.

A week later, Vidia wrote to Pat again. In contrast to his letters of 1954, in which he excoriated the side effects of the British empire, here he expressed a rare nostalgia for colonial rule: 'I am not staying here much longer. If the election results were different, there might have been some point. But with the present government of noble niggers, all sorts of racialist laws might be passed; and life for minority communities could become tricky. Indians are talking of leaving; so are the Chinese. Because of its very smallness and unimportance in the world, the grossest injustices can be perpetrated here without people in England getting to know. And injustices – against individuals – are being done all the time. The police force is of course made up of the dregs of the noble nigger nation. And their crudity and bullying has to be seen. I don't want anybody to talk to me of S. Africa and the Southern States again. I would prefer a hundred times to be ruled from London, as in the old days, then to be ruled by the present people. Because, in this place, the Englishman's sense of justice and fair play shines like a jewel. If my uncle's party had got into power, they were going to staff the Police Force with English officers; the Civil Service with English heads of department – just to have fair play.' Vidia said later: 'I was extremely shocked when I went back by the racial conditions in Trinidad. I was outraged. My relations with Negroes have not been the same ever since, and there is nothing I can do about it. I was writing to Pat and I was delighting in shocking her.'[19]

Aged just twenty-four, he believed that his future as a Trinidadian was now fatally circumscribed, and that he would need to look to a new, wider identity. 'I don't know what's going to happen to me with the BBC when I get back. But I am not really worried. But I would really prefer not to have anything to do with the W. Indies in that way, since we Indians really have no stake at all here and we are rapidly being pushed into the position where we will have to become the Jews of the area: in business, etc., since other fields are closed to us.' Mr Sohun, the schoolmaster in Seepersad Naipaul's *Gurudeva and other Indian Tales*, had identified the invidious position of the island's Indians some years before: 'The difficulty lies in the fact that you are too much of a majority to assimilate, too much of a minority to dominate.'[20]

*

Vidia's younger sisters Savi, Sati, Mira and Nalini (or Nella) found their returning elder brother hard to handle. Savi remembered him being 'very critical about everything, never encouraging, never positive. As I grew older I began to understand this attitude of his a little bit more, but when I was that age, I don't think we appreciated the constant criticism. We were teenagers. We seemed to have nothing in common with him. So I would tell you honestly my sister and I used to hide, to keep away from him. I was considered very difficult because too many boys would call. If you were attractive it meant you were not concentrating on your lessons.' Ma was 'overjoyed to see Vidia but I think Vidia also became very difficult with her. He wanted her to be what she was not, what she was never educated to be. She was also menopausal which he wouldn't have understood. I think she would have become like a weepy, wimpering, complaining woman to him.'[21] Savi felt Vidia's attitude to his mother and siblings persisted over the decades. 'He harboured some kind of desire for us to do well, to do things. He still has it. As far as he is concerned none of our children has done anything even though ninety per cent of them have a university degree.'[22]

As the politics of the West Indies altered, the family politics of the Capildeos and the Naipauls remained as fraught as ever. Vidia saw few of his cousins except Owad and Jean. Meeting one of the Mausis during a visit to Chaguanas, he blanked her in the street, only realizing later the rudeness of what he had done. He advised Pat to stop seeing and helping his relations in London. 'Heaven know, what your friends must think of me when they see those cousins of mine. I really can't tell you how much I dislike this do-gooding. It isn't wise. In fact, it can lead to a lot of trouble.' The effect of being back in a family atmosphere with his sisters and brother softened Vidia, and made him think again of having children of his own. He wrote to Pat, 'I love you so completely that I am half lost without you, and I do believe that we should see about having a baby when I get back to London. Something very strange is happening to me. I am beginning to like other people's children and I actually talk to strange children in the street. I love you and I miss every part of you – physically and in every other way.' In later years, when it became clear that he and Pat were unable to have children, he would assert that he had never wanted them in the first place: 'I remember in that wretched house in Petit Valley making a decision never to have children of my own. I made a decision at the age of ten which I have adhered to, and not for a moment regretted.' A fact decided by human biology would be presented as a triumph of the will: 'It would have been impossible with my work. I just hated the idea of children. I made that decision in Petit Valley, very consciously.'[23]

He told Pat about everyday life in Trinidad. Savi was making dresses for her, and wanted precise measurements. Was her waist really 24 inches? He had visited the beach, hurt his toe, had asthma attacks and been on a happy trip to Cedros with Owad and Jean. 'Cedros is at the S.E. tip of Trinidad – an 80 mile drive from Port of Spain. Owad was making the run because he is Chief Labour Inspector. Last Friday we went. It was a beautiful drive. Jean kept on saying how she wished you were with us.'

Vidia even made an effort to learn to drive, and in early November passed a test which gave him a licence 'and an international driving permit; so I will be able to drive your father's car when I get back ... I don't believe I really deserved the licence.' Pat, who was spending most weekends in Kingstanding, replied to his letters briefly. Her father hoped they would come for Christmas. 'He wants to go out to lunch on Boxing Day as we did last year. He said he enjoyed it very much. Doesn't time fly? It seems such a short while since you were trying to warm that bottle of wine in front of the fire.'

Pat was required to represent Vidia in his dealings with the BBC over *B. Wordsworth*, a radio play he had adapted from a chapter in *Miguel Street*. It told the story of a chancer and poet, Black Wordsworth ('White Wordsworth was my brother. We share one heart') and his relationship with a young boy and his mother. 'My name is to be V.S. Naipaul (not Vidia N). I am <u>not</u> to be described as a West Indian; but as a "Trinidadian of Hindu descent". I insist on these things ... 6666!' Pat offered counsel. 'You've got to be able to get along comfortably with people ... "A Trinidadian of Hindu Descent." Forgive us darling but it is rather funny & quite incomprehensible to a <u>listener</u>.'[24]

Vidia was not feeling optimistic about his future as a writer. He even thought the Suez Crisis might undermine it. 'What about this Egypt thing? It has me a little worried. People here criticise the British & French; but I don't see what other steps they could have taken ... all I hope is that it doesn't spread. If it does my literary career will be nipped in the very smallest of buds. I am not coming back to London with any great love in my breast for *Caribbean Voices*. Because of my association with the programme I have had to mix with the literary boys over here and those things, as you know, really sicken me. The men are bad enough; but the drooling women are even worse. And one rather ghastly feature of the thing in Trinidad is the expatriate Englishmen & women going "native". They seem to become so stupid and despicable as soon as they start seeing vigour in all that is black and "primitive". They have been satirised for so long you would have thought that they would have died out – but, no, they carry on exactly as one imagines, larger than life. People here drink scotch. These people insist on rum. They are a sad, degenerate lot.'

Vidia felt sad and elated and sad, in emotional turmoil as he visited the home that was no longer his home. 'My depression is largely due to worry about my own future. Over here one is surrounded so obviously by people who are better off – people who have no more to offer than myself and people who started like myself.' Trinidad had supplied him with a stock of new material. 'From the writing point of view, this land is pure gold. I know it so well, you see. Pure, pure gold . . . Trinidad is a funny place. It has a population less than Nottingham's yet, while Churchill calls England an island, they call T'dad a country. And really it is hard to feel while you are here that Trinidad really is small. Jamaica is even worse. Jamaica is the world for Jamaicans.'

Throughout his two months in Trinidad, consciously and subconsciously, he was collecting ideas. 'I met the original of "Hat" shortly after getting here. He really is a surly man and the years are making him surlier. Of course we never were really friends. He only knew me as the bright boy in the street. Yet he gave me a choice mango the other day. He told my mother, "I have a mango for Vido." And when he saw me he just gave me the mango with a "Here, I have this for you," and walked off without another word. And would you believe it, I met a real-life Ramlogan! He keeps a dingy little shop in one of the remote villages of my uncle's constituency. Physically he fits the role to perfection. Only, he doesn't wear a striped blue shirt – only a dingy vest. He behaves like my Ramlogan too. He vowed eternal support to my uncle, assured him that the election was won; yet all along he was for the other candidate, as we discovered only on election day! And his name is of course Ramlogan. M. Ramlogan, licensed to SEEL SPRITUOUS LIQERS BY RETAIL. If we come to Trinidad I will make a point of taking you to see the man and his shop.' He had plans for a new novel. As *Miguel Street* captured life in Port of Spain, so he would describe a rural Caribbean election. 'I have an idea for a light novelette. In the country villages here elections are great excitements; election day is a day of fête. The poor candidate pours out money and rum and food. Into such a village – presided over by our good friend Ramlogan (of course he is in league with both candidates: he supplies rum to both) – into such a village comes "party politics". Politicians refuse to bribe. No rum. No food. In fact, there is talk that the local committees should fête their candidates and not vice versa. Imagine the upheaval in the village. The helplessness of the electors. The helplessness of those important gentlemen who "control" fifty or sixty votes. The anger of the village. The boycott of the election. The declaration against both parties, etc. What do you think, Mrs Naipaul?' The book would be the short and entertaining comic novel *The Suffrage of Elvira*.

*

In the second week of November 1956, Vidia said goodbye to his family in Port of Spain and sailed for Kingston, Jamaica. There he would board the *Golfito*, a small turbine steamer which plied the route to Southampton on the south coast of England. He was unhappy to be leaving, but confident he would soon be back. In Jamaica he stayed with old family friends, the Tewaris. Norman Rae, an Oxford friend who had joined the Banana Board of Jamaica, took him around and was 'really extremely kind and helpful.' Vidia was carrying home-made dresses for Pat, and was even trying to find a present for her father. He made a partial and failed attempt to retain a ring for her; like his wedding certificate, it soon vanished: 'My eldest aunt gave me a ring for you. She has had it for years and years. A simple, well-wrought, gold ring. I put the ring in the fob of my trousers; forget it there, take everything out from the trousers but the ring, and send the trousers to be pressed. Of course the ring disappears.' On arrival at Waterloo on the boat train, he wanted her to meet him, but none of his cousins. 'I don't want to see anyone but you,' he wrote, and Pat obliged.

Travelling back to the mother country, missing his mother, he wrote fondly to her on Fyffes Line writing paper. 'I do feel so sad leaving home. When I left in 1950 I was all eagerness and anxiety, ready to get away as quickly as possible. It was different yesterday.' He felt guilty that he had been cruel on his last day. 'Poor Ma, I did give you a rough time, didn't I? But you mustn't mind; and you mustn't worry.' The ship had sailed late, watched by a big crowd who 'had come to see off a red nigger woman who now sits opposite me in the dining room. Poor thing, she was so frightened at the thought of travelling alone for the first time out of Trinidad at the age of thirty-five. She palled up with me and begged me in case of any alarm or trouble to come and look after her.' Vidia amused himself by teasing her. 'The red nigger woman is really delightfully simple. You know, in ships, the chairs and tables are all chained to the floor to prevent them rolling about the place when the sea gets rough. I told the woman that the tables and chairs were chained to prevent people stealing them. And, she believed it. "Eh, eh," she said, "But look at that, eh." And again: passengers in different parts of the ship are assigned to different lifeboats (there are 6 on the Golfito). I told her that she had to find out which lifeboat was hers because, in case of any trouble, they were not going to let her get into any old lifeboat. In fact, if they found her in the wrong boat they were going to throw her into the sea. It was, I told her, the origin of the phrase "to be in the wrong boat."'

Back in St Julian's Road, it was Vido who wondered whether he was in the wrong boat, or an alien land. 'Well here I am back in London. It is rather cold and it is so strange to slip into bed between ice cold sheets,' he told Ma. His letter was a rare and honest statement of his deeper feelings about Britain; he felt caught between islands, between cultures. 'My publisher tells me that the book will not be coming out in March but in August next year. That is, 20 months after it was written. I can't tell you how horribly disappointed I am. I am really feeling pretty low and desperate. I can't even do any writing because I am feeling I am such a failure and such a fool. I just feel my present life has got to change or I will just break up under the strain . . . I feel that I am dreaming now in London. I felt much more at home with you than I do here in London. It all does seem strange to me – as though I have never been here before.'

He wondered whether Deutsch's verbal assurances were worth anything, and wrote to him in anguish: 'My other book, *Miguel Street*, you have now had sixteen months; no agreement has been made or is likely to be made soon.'[25] The anger he felt against his non-publisher was abruptly converted into creative energy, and he wrote *The Suffrage of Elvira* at great speed, alternating with work at the BBC. The process of writing distracted him from his fear about his future, his money worries and his anger against Deutsch. 'I raged,' he said later, 'impotent rage. I had no power, and out of that rage I wrote the third book, about an election in Trinidad. This is where the comic attitude conceals much pain and much difficulty.'[26] He told his mother he still hoped to pay for Mira's education, feeling it was his duty: 'I have begun a new novel and have written 10,000 words since last week Wednesday. I believe it is going to come out all right; but with novels you never know. This one is about the elections; but there is a crazy twist to the whole story. I think of home all the time. I always look at the clock and wonder what time it is in Trinidad and wonder what you are doing.'[27]

Early in the new year, he described his daily routine to Ma. Pat woke him 'at about 7.40 – usually in a panic because she fears she is going to be late at school. I pour out the coffee; go downstairs in my pyjamas and bathrobe for the newspaper and read it over coffee. Pat leaves about eight. I read and smoke until 8.30. Then I wash up and make up the bed and set to work. For lunch (in the weekdays) I have a tin of soup – Heinz Vegetable, Crosse & Blackwell Cream of Chicken and Cream of Mushroom – and this is quite simple and more than enough.' Writing to Kamla, he said he was seeking a post in the new Federation of the West Indies, an attempt to unify the islands of the region in a political bloc. 'I have already told old Willy Richardson that if there are any good jobs going in the Federal set-up, I am ready, provided the money is enough ... I am so glad I came home. I cannot tell you what it has done for me. I no longer feel separated from you. It seems that you are all within my reach and I have no fears at all that we will ever lose touch. Give my love to Ma; tell her that I think of her a lot, with much love and gratitude for her patience and her love which never seems to grow weary, despite all that we, thoughtless children, say or do. I struck Shivan once or twice. I cannot say how bitterly I regret that now; at times I almost wish the hand that struck would drop off.'[28]

At the start of June 1957, nearly two years to the day since he started *Miguel Street*, Vidia was able to tell Ma about the reaction of the critics to *The Mystic Masseur*. 'They are really rather good reviews for a first novel by a completely unknown writer ... And I believe I will be able to send some sums of money home.' He had watched a Test match in Birmingham: 'It was perfect weather for cricket; the result is: I am as black as anything now.' A month later, he and Pat shifted to a new flat in Muswell Hill in the further reaches of north London. 'We had to spend a lot of money on the move,' he told Ma. 'Moving itself cost us about $10. Then we had to buy a carpet sweeper ($7.40); a mop ($6); a draining board for the sink ($6.60) ... The people before us left it in a filthy state ... Dirt doesn't matter in Trinidad, with all doors and windows open all the time; but in England where rooms are kept enclosed most of the time, dirt matters. If I did no more than pull a window open, my hands smelled afterwards. The kitchen was the foulest place of all.'[29] Like a tiger-cub bringing home his first kill, he copied out extracts for his mother from the reviews.

The *Sunday Express* critic called *The Mystic Masseur* 'The deftest and gayest satire I have read in years.' The *Sunday Times* decided he was 'a sophisticated and witty young Trinidad novelist who immediately takes a front-line place in the growing West Indian school.' Vidia wrote out the entire *Daily Telegraph* review for his mother, including the lines: 'V.S. Naipaul is a young writer who contrives to blend Oxford wit with home-grown rumbustiousness and not do harm to either. He is a kind of West Indian Gwyn Thomas [a Welsh novelist and radio personality of the moment] – pungent, charitable, Rabelaisian, who deals with the small change of human experience as though it were minted gold.'[30] Ma reported that 200 copies of the book had been sold in Trinidad, and that she now needed a regular income to relieve Kamla. 'I bought gas, paid for light, paid for Meera glasses, and I kept $5 to do a puja for the success of your book.' When Mira read the book, she wrote: 'Boy, I really enjoyed it, and laughed like mad. Ma's family sure got their share.'[31]

The notices were mainly enthusiastic, but patronizing. Diana Athill thought its reception was helped by a passing British interest in new writing from the colonies, and particularly the West Indies; at the time, 'it was easier to get reviews for a writer seen by the British as black than it was for a young white writer, and reviews influenced readers a good deal more then than they do now.'[32] In the *New Statesman*, Anthony Quinton described *The Mystic Masseur* as 'yet another piece of intuitive or slap-happy West Indian fiction as pleasant, muddled and inconsequent as the Trinidadian Hindus it describes . . . This is an agreeable book but I wonder if it really deserves a Book Society recommendation.' V.S. Naipaul's writing was 'as sharp as a mango'; he was one of the 'calypso novelists' who were putting 'colour and punch into British writing'. In the West Indies, reaction was subtler. Writing in *Bim*, Frank Collymore commended Naipaul's willingness to satirize his own community with 'ironic detach-ment' at a time when 'the propaganda and clichés of emergent nationhood are so apt to occasion all the ill-effects of self-complacency.' The *Trinidad Chronicle* was even more enthusiastic, calling it 'the cleverest satire yet on Trinidad life . . . One has to know Trinidad to know that it could only happen here.'[33]

Looking back, Vidia remembered only the worst aspects – or his own version – of the reviews: 'Anthony Quinton actually said it's a bad book. Imagine not understanding the originality of the writing, the clarity and the humour . . . but these were the days when my kind of writing, my kind of person, was not taken seriously. John Bayley in *The Spectator* was very patronizing and said it was a "little savoury". There was an extraordinary review in the *Telegraph* by an academic called Peter Green. To my utter amazement he said I was looking down my Oxford nose at my people. This is the left-wing attitude – that if you are Indian, you cannot write humour; humour is for the bigger, the more secure cultures.'[34] Bayley's rankling words would be reworked years later. Looking for reviews of his first book, Willie Chandran finds the sentence: 'Where, after the racy Anglo-Indian fare of John Masters, one might have expected an authentic hot curry, one gets only a nondescript savoury, of uncertain origin . . .'[35]

In April of the following year, *The Suffrage of Elvira* was published. Penelope Mortimer in the *Sunday Times* commended it as 'a beautifully contained and balanced book . . . extremely funny and accurately cruel' filled with 'such remarkably rich and curious dialogue, that Mr Naipaul easily earns the title of a new Damon Runyon.'³⁶ Writing in *Punch*, Anthony Powell thought V.S. Naipaul showed 'unusual elegance and sense of style, though his characters need possibly a little more depth.'³⁷ The most astute assessment came from the novelist Kingsley Amis, who had recently risen to prominence with *Lucky Jim*. After giving Jan Carew and Edgar Mittelholzer some compliments and swipes, he noted that Naipaul's narrative was 'concerned with small-scale stratagems between neighbours, in-laws or rivals. It gradually dawns upon one that this humour, conducted throughout with the utmost stylistic quietude, is completely original.'³⁸ On *Caribbean Voices*, Arthur Calder Marshall praised the scope of the book; he thought it 'the more effective as satire because it is so free from ill-temper' and compared it to Dickens's writing on elections in rotten boroughs in *The Pickwick Papers*: 'Naipaul's gentle pillory may have an influence on West Indian politics for many years to come.'³⁹ Calder Marshall was perceptive; politicians would often refer to *The Suffrage of Elvira*, and half a century on the political theorist Lloyd Best, Vidia's contemporary at QRC, was recommending it to his students. Best called *The Suffrage of Elvira* the most important of Naipaul's novels 'in terms of political and social impact. He really founded a whole new school of empirical political science, in that he saw how the society worked, as distinct from how people thought it ought to work. In those days, that was almost impossible, with the colonial film on your eyes. People couldn't tell perception from reality, and he was absolutely lucid as to how the political system really worked, and how people actually behaved.'⁴⁰

In 1959, the year in which Vidia won an entry in *Who's Who*, André Deutsch Limited published *Miguel Street*. Vidia had written to Francis Wyndham, 'I don't believe a word A.D. says but if they are sending off *Miguel Street* to the printers, I hope you prepare it for press and I hope you write the blurb.'⁴¹ The *Times Literary Supplement* thought Naipaul had a 'fresh and original talent' and an ability to show the humanity of the very poor.⁴² Reviewing him beside Anthony Burgess, the *Sunday Times* reviewer called him 'another exotic gentleman . . . an intellectual in a zoot-suit . . . But even at half throttle he's good enough to make most of the professional Caribbean boys look a bit silly.'⁴³ The *News Chronicle* concluded that 'the time has come for Mr Naipaul to move on to something bigger.'⁴⁴ In the *West Indian Gazette*, Arthur Drayton was full of praise for the dialogue and the mix of tragedy and farce, but thought the author showed 'diffidence in facing up to the sociological implications of his material', an ideological complaint that was to be repeated by critics and readers from the Caribbean and elsewhere in years to come.[45] V.S. Naipaul was making his name. The *Observer* had given him 'a rave review', he told Kamla. Despite his rapid success, he wanted more, and faster: 'I seem destined to make my way very slowly.'[46]

CHAPTER ELEVEN

'HE ASKED FOR 10 GNS!!'

AS HIS LITERARY REPUTATION DEVELOPED, Vidia's relationship with the BBC frayed; *Caribbean Voices* was a place of opportunity, but it was also a racial ghetto. When he tried to get work on the General Overseas Service in 1958, a producer, the children's writer Mary Treadgold, told him it was impossible: 'The lady said, "We can't employ you, you are not a European." I think she was representing [official BBC] policy. I was furious. But that was how it was ... I cannot express to you sufficiently, this determination to be a writer, to write.'[1] The late 1950s were a time of change for Vidia and for England; race riots broke out in Notting Hill; social deference was in decline; the Suez debacle had induced a new mood of national insecurity; tall concrete buildings were sprouting across the nation's cities; teenagers were noticed and given voice by Colin MacInnes in his novel *Absolute Beginners*. Post-war hardship had been replaced by expectation, but much of this cultural shift was apparent only in retrospect, and Vidia still struggled to make his way. He applied to become a BBC general trainee, and the novelist Anthony Powell was persuaded to put up a letter of support stating that V.S. Naipaul had 'literary gifts and a general intelligence of a lively and uncommon order'.[2] Vidia's memory of the interview panel was vivid: 'They were sniggering as I entered; all of them were sniggering. There was a man there called Laurence Gilliam, famous as a so-called features writer, producer. He asked what I wanted to do. I said I wanted to do some features and they roared with laughter, as though I had said I wanted to write the Bible ... It was the historical moment. You couldn't be a [racial] victim in the 1950s. There wasn't the market. And these men have vanished and I have survived. But even at the time I knew they were fools.'[3]

Even with published novels under his belt, he was not able to break through and have his work read on a mainstream BBC service. The manuscript of *Miguel Street* was sent to the head of the Third Programme, the novelist P.H. Newby (who in 1969 would win the first

Booker Prize). Newby noted in an internal memo that he was disappointed by V.S. Naipaul's stories. 'He lacks the discipline you need to
write concisely and he hasn't even been able to set his material in
perspective ... It surprises me that he has succeeded in persuading a
publisher to bring it out.'⁴ The year saw further squabbles. Vidia left
the building when Leonie Cohn, a producer on the Third Programme,
told him to wait for five minutes, which provoked a flurry of internal
memos. In July 1958 he was asked to produce a piece on Thackeray's
Vanity Fair for the Colonial Schools Unit. On the booking form,
someone has scrawled, 'He asked for 10 gns!! Rang him cancelling the
project.'⁵ By August, it had been decided that with so many West
Indian writers now in England, *Caribbean Voices* had served its purpose
and a literary discussion programme would replace it. Vidia wrote a
script for the penultimate broadcast, praising the legacy of Henry
Swanzy and saying how much he had learned from the show. He took
a swipe at bad literature, and introduced a story by an undergraduate,
Frank Birbalsingh, adding that he would hate it if, 'on the strength of
this acceptance, he decides to make writing his profession.'⁶

The broadcast led to a permanent rupture, made worse for Vidia by
the knowledge that he was in the wrong. When he turned up late to
record his script, the BBC cut his fee. He wrote to them in fury that
they were being 'insolent and ungracious ... I grant that I made an
error and arrived late at the studio. But I arrived in time to hear the
first words of my script being read. The producer, following the
traditions of this secret service, told me nothing even at that time. It
was left for me to ask whether my script was being read for me. I got
a mere nod in reply. This colonial insolence is in itself intolerable.' The
producer in question was the competent Billy Pilgrim; aside from
sharing a name with the hero of Kurt Vonnegut's yet-to-be-published
Slaughterhouse-Five, Pilgrim was a Guianese musician and wartime
RAF veteran. An internal file – 'THE NAIPAUL CASE' – was created
to investigate the matter. It reveals that Pilgrim had expressed surprise
'that Vidia Naipaul, himself a former editor of "Caribbean Voices" and
a frequent broadcaster, should be so haphazard about matters of timing.'
The upshot was that Vidia was sent a letter of reprimand: 'You arrived
in the studio about 12.25 p.m. *when the recording had been completed* and
when one paragraph of the first page was being repeated for editing
purposes. As you spoke to [Billy Pilgrim] just after the ten second cue
was given, he held his hand up as he wanted silence.' Vidia, in shamed

fury, did not reply.[7] His retrospective comment was, 'I broke with the BBC. It was my misfortune to be thrown among second-rate people while I was trying to make a living.'[8] So it goes.

Only in 1960 did his star begin to rise again. Vidia gave talks on women's magazines, literary counties, bohemian novels, the working class in books and the shortcomings of authors such as Anthony Trollope and Patrick Leigh Fermor when they wrote about the Caribbean. Soon, he was back in dispute. The BBC Home Service – he was out of the ghetto now – wanted him to give a talk, but he demanded double the standard rate. 'If he could be shown to have a stature above that of the general run of literary contributors to the quality press and journals, we would certainly consider putting his rate up,' the talks booking manager noted in a memo. What was his status now? Did V.S. Naipaul deserve more than the oenophile Cyril Ray, who was paid thirty guineas for 1,000 words?[9] In August 1960, hearing that he was planning to make his first visit to his ancestral land, the Third Programme tried to sign up 'Mr V.S. Naipaul, the novelist and critic' to write a script 'about his first sight of India'. They offered the sum of eighty guineas, ten times what he had been paid for his early short stories. A letter came back from a representative of his agent, Curtis Brown, stating that Mr Naipaul 'has asked me to inform you that he considers this offer an insult', with a PS: 'Sorry about this!' A BBC memo concluded that 'in view of his outside reputation' the price should be raised to 120 guineas. He accepted, and with his renown both as a writer and as a tricky customer well established, V.S. Naipaul was on his way.[10]

*

While Vidia waited for royalties to arrive from André Deutsch, he made a temporary excursion into the world of conventional employment. After the death of her husband, Jill Brain had decided to make a fresh start by taking a teaching job in Rome. Her job as an editorial assistant at the Cement & Concrete Association in Grosvenor Gardens was going begging, and she suggested Vidia might like it. Although he turned up forty minutes late for the interview in the summer of 1957, Vidia was offered a position on their magazine at a salary of £1,000 a year. It enabled him to send money home to Ma. Jill described the C&CA as 'a truly weird outfit, and I well remember my dismay when I found out that being a dogsbody for them was all that my nice new degree seemed to qualify me to do. It was an association of British cement manufacturers, but for some reason they were determined to prove they had an aesthetic side, and published a magazine called *Concrete Quarterly* which was all about the architectural beauties of prestressed concrete buildings.'[11] Vidia was not cut out for office work: 'I lasted about ten weeks. It was awful. Nothing is as bad as working for people who are your inferiors. I was living in a flat in Muswell Hill, the top flat, in one of those red brick houses, so I would take the bus from Victoria to Muswell Hill. It was a long journey. I was exhausted because, young as I was, the fumes even then always took away my energy.' He produced articles 'praising the concrete. You were required to spin it out.' One day he went to have his hair cut, and when he returned, 'the lady who was running my department made a scene about it. I literally left that minute; I left so precipitately that my books, a few Penguin books and paperbacks that I had in my drawer, I had to go back and collect.'[12]

Vidia would use the office environment of the C&CA in *Mr Stone and the Knights Companion*. He met and made a good friend there, Ralph Ironman, a technical writer who had served in the war and now worked in the same office. 'That was one of the nicest things to come out of the Cement & Concrete Association, that friendship with Ironman.'[13] Together with Pat, he spent time with Ralph and his wife, Mary, and with their daughters Anne and Lotta. Ralph Ironman liked Vidia at once. 'I think we got on so well because both of us enjoy a good sense of humour ... Pat was a very sweet girl. She, of course, supported him by her teaching job while he strived to become a writer ... I do remember that our lady boss said that Vidia "couldn't write"! I spotted immediately that his command of English was superb.'[14] They would go for lunch together at a girls' cookery school where food was served at cost price, and Ironman noticed that although Vidia was 'very tightfisted', he had extravagant ambitions: 'He once used a month's worth of luncheon vouchers in a fancy restaurant, I think it was the Dorchester.' Around this time, Vidia managed to avoid being called up for National Service. Ironman remembered: 'He went for a medical examination, they took one look at him, a small Indian man, and said, "Run along, son, that's it." '[15]

The C&CA sent Vidia on a course in Wexham Springs in Slough to learn more about construction and architecture, a time he would use later in his novel *Magic Seeds*. On the course he met Jagdish Sondhi, a stocky engineer with a Sikh father and Hindu mother who had grown up in Kenya and been to school in India. Similarly displaced, they got talking and Vidia asked Sondhi to lend him £10. 'I felt that was the last I'll see of that,' said Sondhi, 'but sure enough a £10 note arrived at my sister's apartment. I thought, holy mackerel! It's rare to be touched for money and get it back.' Sondhi noticed Vidia's fascination with India, and the way he drank in information. 'He didn't talk much, but what he said was thoughtful. I noticed later, in his writing, that he is quite knowledgeable about houses and how they are constructed.'[16]

Vidia liked the library at the C&CA, and took out books on the Finnish architect and designer Alvar Aalto, and the Brazilian architects Lúcio Costa and Oscar Niemeyer. He thought it was 'the start of a slight education, the friendship with Ironman making me look, introducing me to the idea of modern architecture, about which I knew nothing.' In retrospect, he felt he had been duped into believing the modern lines of the 1950s were necessarily beautiful. 'Many years later, in 1994, I went to Brazil and saw the awful architecture of Niemeyer which we were so admiring of – we were required to admire him, the concrete fellow – and I actually entered one of his buildings in São Paulo. It roared with the sound of people walking. It roared. It was unbearable. He had just drawn it on a sheet of paper and they had built it in concrete: you could build anything out of concrete. Later, you see how mad it was to praise those people, and that it would be a gift to the Brazilian people to pull it down.'[17]

Although Jill was leaving for Italy, and would soon move to New York to start a new life on a different continent, Vidia's desire for her was unquenched. They spent a day together in Oxford and went for a walk by the river. Even then, despite some passing intimacy, Vidia did not declare himself and nothing came of it. Later, he gave her a copy of W.H. Auden's poetry, *A Selection by the Author*, and inscribed it 'Oxford, September 16 1958'. Jill remained unaware of the extent of his feeling, which arose above all from his deep sexual frustration, linked to an impractical idea of romance. She wondered later whether Vidia's attraction to her had arisen in part from her social status as a white, upper-middle-class Englishwoman. 'A lot had to do with the fact I was blonde and had a certain kind of accent. I think it was a race and class kind of fantasy. He implied to me that his family hoped Pat would have been more top-drawer than she was. I felt at the time that if she was good enough to support him, she was good enough to marry.'[18]

Vidia's physical attraction to Pat had never been certain, and after they married it declined further. He felt too embarrassed to talk with her about this situation. In the summer of 1958, turning imagination into reality, he started to have sex with prostitutes. He would find their telephone numbers in local newspapers and visit them in the afternoon in secret while Pat was at work. 'I couldn't go very often. I didn't have the money to do that. It was unsatisfactory. I was grateful sometimes for the release, the relief, but it was profoundly unsatisfactory. It was a stirring in the head.' He believed Pat had no inkling of what was happening. 'I didn't have the time to conduct an affair. I didn't have the talent. I didn't know how you conducted an affair because there was nobody to tell me what to do or to guide me.'[19] When he sought advice from other men, he misjudged, asking a Jamaican actor friend, Lloyd Reckord, 'Do you know any *fast* women?'[20] Diana Athill, who later lived with Lloyd's brother, the playwright Barry Reckord, remembered, 'They met in the street one day. Lloyd is as gay as they come and Vidia had absolutely no notion. He was very naive altogether.'[21] An attempt to plant a kiss on Diana one evening while she was carrying a tray of glasses was not a success. Vidia knew that paying for sex with women was not a solution to his dissatisfaction. Ideally, he would have had a relationship. 'I was always wanting something to happen. In a way, the people I met who were interested in me never really stirred me, I wasn't interested in them.' His one attempt at a more normal encounter was a humiliating failure. He met a middle-aged Canadian writer at the BBC. 'I actually went to her flat and she had arranged it and everything. But my sexual performance was pathetic. That is so upsetting to me. I never saw her again, and I was quite ashamed to discover a few weeks later that she'd told a friend. It was awful. I remember it so clearly. She was an experienced woman.'[22]

Through the late 1950s and 1960s, Vidia would go to brothels and to prostitutes, although not regularly. Convinced of his inabilities as a seducer, bought sex offered him a form of comfort and release. 'I was very glad they were there. I mustn't run them down. I was very glad. So there were some occasions when I felt almost grateful to these people for giving me this help. I mustn't forget that ... although I have stopped using their services for so long. I kept it separate from Pat. I always practised safe sex. Safe sex is rather joyless sex. I was always aware what I was missing; all the time I was with Pat I knew there was something wrong. I knew it was wrong, and it might be because of Pat that I have not pursued any English woman ... I didn't know how you seduced a woman, how you excited her and thought of her pleasure. I hadn't got that from my upbringing. There was no one telling me about it or talking about it. I realised all this later, much later ... A young taxi driver was driving me back from the [railway] station one day. He said his father had told him,

"Always please the woman first." A marvellous thing to tell the son, don't you think? I wish someone had told me that. But we grew up with this furtive incestuous idea.'[23]

In 1958, Pat was offered a job at Rosa Bassett School in Streatham, at the opposite end of London from Muswell Hill, which involved a long journey for her on the bus and Underground each day. Vidia remembered: 'She began to suffer travel fatigue. She was teaching history, and she was taking it extremely seriously. I pleaded with her that these children were not worth it.'[24] Kamla was living with them, having taken a year's leave from her teaching post in Trinidad to work at a girl's school in East Finchley. She had friends in London, and discreetly rekindled her relationship with Sam Selvon, without telling Vidia. Pat took Kamla to Cornwall, and to stay with Auntie Lu in Gloucester, where she showed her the cathedral, 'all these knights who had died and she would explain what each pose meant. I got along very well with Pat. Sometimes Vidia and I would have a little row. I'd pack my bags and I'd say, "OK, I'm off, I am not staying." Vidia's relationship with Pat seemed all right at that time. She was basically a very shy person, but you couldn't put her down.'[25] The following autumn Pat and Vidia moved south to 81B Wyatt Park Road, a furnished upper-floor flat with two bedrooms in a quiet street in Streatham Hill, overlooking a front and back garden, at a cost of £20 per month. Their landlady was a reader of the *New Statesman*, and knew Vidia's name; it was the first home in which they felt at ease.

*

Although Vidia's dealings with André Deutsch were often difficult, he found the man himself entertaining. Born in Budapest in 1917, Deutsch had been interned as an enemy alien on the Isle of Man before founding the publishing house Allan Wingate in 1945, aided by his friend and former lover Diana Athill. They had a success with Norman Mailer's *The Naked and the Dead*, in which the word 'fuck' – famously and ludicrously – had to be rendered as 'fug', but still attracted the attention of the Attorney General. When the firm collapsed, he started André Deutsch Limited, and would over time publish writers including John Updike, Jack Kerouac, Mavis Gallant, Jean Rhys, Philip Roth and Simone de Beauvoir. Deutsch was small, energetic, determined and perfectionist, with an ability to grab ideas from around the world and turn any contemporary happening into a book. He ran the company like a dictatorship, and paid his authors and staff poorly, including Athill, whose literary and editorial talent underpinned his success. *Private Eye* once reported that her salary was so small that she banked it annually. Much of Deutsch's time was spent seeking discounts, turning off lights, raising capital and cutting costs, with the result that the company lasted longer than it might have done, but was an eccentric place at which to work.[26] Vidia, who shared some of Deutsch's traits, was quick to spot his tricks, and many of his letters were of complaint: '80 per cent of monies accruing from an arrangement with an American publisher is 80 per cent. Not 70, which would be absurd,' he wrote in a dispute over *The Mystic Masseur*.[27] Why were his enquiries being ignored? 'I haven't received any royalty statements for this quarter,' he wrote to Athill in 1958. 'These things, amusingly enough, interest me.'[28] Jeremy Lewis, who later worked at the company, believed, 'Diana supplied the patience and the sympathy and the literacy and the attention to detail of the ideal old-fashioned editor' while André had 'the entrepreneurial energy, the single-minded dedication and the zest for wheeling-and-dealing and striking a bargain without which a firm like his would expire in a haze of lofty thoughts and fine intentions.'[29]

For all this, Vidia's early books enjoyed a good critical reception with the help of his publisher, and won important prizes aimed at encouraging younger writers. He received the John Llewellyn Rhys Prize for *The Mystic Masseur* and the Somerset Maugham Award for *Miguel Street*, with Willie Somerset Maugham personally sanctioning the award of the prize to an author who was not British-born. Deutsch managed to get the books published in America by Ballantine Books of New York, although they made little impact, and Lord David Cecil, an Oxford literary critic and scion of the eminent political family, was persuaded to write an introduction to the American edition of *The Mystic Masseur*: 'This is a delightful book [which] bubbles and sparkles with life and gaiety . . . Mr Naipaul is a humorist who likes the animal called man. This does not mean he thinks highly of him.'[30] Conscious of Vidia's ability, tetchiness and determination, Diana Athill tried hard to promote his work: 'I felt admiration for him and impressed by him, and very sorry that we couldn't pay him more money because he obviously was very short of money.'[31] Asked for information about him by an American publisher, she responded, 'Naipaul is really the hardest person to be gossipy about. He is by nature extremely reticent about his private life and somewhat anti-publicity of a juicy and titillating-to-the-reader kind.'[32]

Vidia's reputation was growing steadily, and commissions started to come his way. He picked up £21 for a short story in *Punch*, £25 for a piece in *Vogue*. His earnings and expenses were noted scrupulously in a cashbook: 6/4 for drinks with Willy Edmett in Maida Vale, 7/6 for lunch with Francis Wyndham, 3/1 for coffee with Colin MacInnes, to whom Wyndham had introduced him.[33] Unusually for a middle-aged white novelist of this period, MacInnes was interested in youth culture and in black culture, an interest that was linked to his attraction to young black men. In *City of Spades*, he did something other writers of the moment such as Kingsley Amis or John Braine never did: he included black characters, and portrayed the bohemian London found in Sam Selvon's work, a world that was being altered profoundly by immigration, particularly from the West Indies. Vidia was surprised that MacInnes, then at the height of his fame, took an interest in him. 'He had total enthusiasm for my work, and wrote to me about the books. Later, I think he became jealous, and he was insulting to me at a publisher's party. He was very romantic about black people.'[34]

Francis Wyndham, who was shortly to leave Deutsch and join the ground-breaking magazine *Queen*, was instrumental in the development of V.S. Naipaul's career at this point. He found the young Vidia to be 'attractive, very funny, dynamic, wonderfully subtle, very much alive. Later, he lived up to his reputation for irascibility, but he was much less touchy in the 1950s.'[35] Popular, gentle, solitary and eccentric, Wyndham lived with his mother, wore heavy glasses and high-waisted trousers, gave off random murmurs and squeaks and moved with an amphibian gait. Born to a well-connected literary family in 1924 and educated at Eton and Oxford, he was seen by his contemporaries as a literary talent, but his greater skill turned out to be for editing and encouraging others. He published fewer books than expected, but was the dedicatee of many. He would meet Vidia several times a month. Francis accompanied him to an Ibsen play, and introduced him to numerous people, including Dom Moraes, an Indian poet who had won the Hawthornden Prize at the age of nineteen. Moraes was reluctant to meet Vidia but Francis insisted, saying they had a lot in common. An awkward lunch took place at the French pub in Soho. Moraes mentioned this to a friend who laughed: ' "Don't you know what Vidia and you have in common? Francis may have been too polite to say so, but you both have brown skins." '[36]

Francis Wyndham advertised his protégé's talent to his friends, and persuaded Anthony Powell to read *The Mystic Masseur*. Powell, another product of Eton and Oxford, married to the daughter of an Irish peer, had started as a publisher and reviewer and by the late 1950s was the author of the early novels of a twelve-volume sequence, *A Dance to the Music of*

Time. Filled with minutely observed encounters, astute social commentary and self-congratulatory English humour, his books drew a devoted following. A perceptive, gossipy man with a large head, Tony Powell was a friend or contemporary of writers such as Evelyn Waugh, Henry Green and Cyril Connolly. Born in 1905, he was the fag – in the sense of servant – of Lord David Cecil when they were at Eton together, and according to the Anthony Powell Society, had 'such exquisite manners that he would ask the ladies before eating an apple, "Do you mind if I bite?" '[37] Powell (he liked his name to rhyme with 'prole' rather than 'prowl') sought out Vidia, a habit he had with upcoming writers. They met at El Vino, a famous journalist's bar in Fleet Street. He wanted to help this new prodigy, to whom he gave the pet name 'Viddy', and asked the *New Statesman* to try him as a reviewer.

A few weeks later, Viddy wrote a trial book review. 'It was a calamity. You know, one tried too hard. And they did it again after a suitable gap. I don't know why, but they did it again.'[38] Founded by Sidney and Beatrice Webb as a Fabian journal, the *New Statesman* had a circulation of nearly 100,000 under its long-time editor Kingsley Martin. From 1957 to 1961, the paper gave V.S. Naipaul a contract to review a book, or clump of books, each month. Although it was not his natural political home, the *New Statesman* had a reputation as a paper of quality, and attracted good writers. Vidia found his name on the review pages alongside the other V.S., the writer and critic V.S. Pritchett, the journalist Paul Johnson, the poet Charles Causley, the lutraphile Gavin Maxwell, the colonial administrator and literary spouse Leonard Woolf, the Labour politicians Richard Crossman and Barbara Castle, the Sinologist Joseph Needham, the archaeologist Jacquetta Hawkes and the Bloomsbury appendage Ralph Partridge. Like many bright young reviewers, Vidia tried to make his mark by being clever and spiky. It was hard work to read, assess and find something interesting to say about several novels at a time, all in the space of 1,000 words. Usually he would be sent about eight books, and ignore several. For four years, he would devote a week of each month to the *New Statesman* review, for which he earned ten guineas. Writing in 1964, he thought that too much reviewing had diminished his appetite for literature. 'I found that I was becoming badly read, that I had neither the time nor the inclination to read the books I really wanted to read.'[39]

His reviews give a snapshot of the post-war lull in British literature. The first, about the Elizabethan romance *Euphues*, began with the line 'This book easily qualifies for inclusion among what Graham Greene calls "the iron rations of the learned man"' – an uncharacteristic allusion, displaying knowledge while deferring to another writer.[40] Next he reviewed a shipboard memoir by the bisexual diplomatist Harold Nicolson, *Journey to Java*: 'A second-class passenger falls overboard and is lost; the matter is dismissed in a paragraph . . . And while Lady Nicolson, in a nearby cabin, sorted out the letters Virginia Woolf wrote her and composed 40,000 words of her biography of La Grande Mademoiselle, Sir Harold . . .'[41] He found his voice reviewing three books on Jamaica. One, commissioned by the Colonial Office, 'bears all the marks of forced labour'. Vidia used the style he favoured at home and at the BBC, saying mischievous things in an entertaining way. He had no interest in the Jamaica of 'Lord Beaverbrook and Noël Coward, the winter cruise and the £14-a-day hotel' – his concern was with 'immigrants who arrive at London's chilly railway stations in vivid tropical clothing and distinctive broad-brimmed hats'. A study by the 'colonial specialist' Mona Macmillan provoked his scorn. He ridiculed her suggestion that electricity might 'put an end to "the long dark evenings in which . . . the only possible recreation is sex."' He could see no economic future for the island except the export of agricultural produce: 'It is hard to see what anyone can do, except eat more Jamaican bananas without complaining. And perhaps – who knows? – a banana a day will keep the Jamaican away.'[42] He represented this subsequently as humour with a purpose: 'The review was a laugh from beginning to end, and it's a serious subject. We made those kind of jokes [at *Caribbean Voices*]. It was partly a joke, but dead serious. All jokes are serious. I wasn't aware that an English reader might worry about where I was positioning myself.'[43]

A Marxist novel by an Oxford-educated Jamaican, a near contemporary, provoked Vidia, despite its author having 'an occasional brilliant turn of phrase'. *The Last Enchantment* by Neville Dawes was 'a suffocating, depressing book about the burden of being very black in Jamaica.' Vidia believed that race alone was not a subject for a novel, and tried to mark out his own difference from a writer like Dawes, whom he saw as being excessively concerned with his own ethnicity: 'No writer can produce any body of work on this subject, since blackness, like whiteness, is no longer enough. And over and over we find Negro writers who make a personal statement and then have nothing to say. A writer cannot be blamed for reflecting his society, but it seems to me that these exhibitionist Negro books do little for the Negro cause.'[44]

Mostly he reviewed forgettable, parochial period novels turned out by hopeful London publishers. He waded through books on adolescent friendship in Llandudno, the minutiae of a Second World War tank battle and 'an epileptic red Indian whose sister is an atomic scientist'. *Cocktail Time* by P.G. Wodehouse was 'all very gay, but not one of Mr Wodehouse's best.'[45] He liked *Face to Face*, a memoir by a blind twenty-three-year-old Indian student at Oxford, Ved Mehta, told with 'passion, modesty and a good deal of humour'.[46] Gustie Herrigel's *Zen in the Art of Flower Arrangement* was written off: 'Her giddy burblings will help no one interested in the East or in flowers.'[47] *The Darling Buds of May* by H.E. Bates was 'a bucolic frolic'.[48] Eventually, he dared to be complimentary, calling Veronica Hull's pseudonymous first novel *The Monkey Puzzle* 'shrewd, barbed, lit up with delicious perceptions', even if 'Miss Hull has declared war on the comma'.[49] Sometimes he would be facetious in the manner of the time, revealing an immaturity behind his critical acuity. Of *Daddy's Gone A-Hunting* by Penelope Mortimer, he wrote: 'Mrs Mortimer is such a feminine writer that I wonder whether her new novel can be recommended to women.'[50] He tried witty and would-be sophisticated lines, referring to 'sex, of both sorts' and to 'the coy, "French" treatment of sex, obscene, sexless and irritating'. One author 'never smiles, and his characters smile only once, during copulation'.[51]

In December 1958 Vidia reviewed new novels by Sam Selvon, George Lamming and Jan Carew. Carew was labelled 'always readable' while Selvon 'who has won a reputation for his stories of West Indians in London' was given lukewarm praise. His novel *Turn Again Tiger* 'has, I feel, been "angled" in the light of the current vogue for Race, Sex and Caribbean writing.' George Lamming meanwhile, four years older than Vidia, was endorsed as 'one of the finest prose-writers of his generation'.[52] In later years, he amended his view of Lamming downwards, with a view to provocation: 'George did some Negro writing and that was that . . . Negro writing is something that can be described in this way: the books must come with a hassock, so you kneel and read them with piety. Every book comes with a hassock. It is a good spiritual exercise for everybody.'[53] He added, 'George Lamming's best things were his little jokes in radio scripts. He did something for the television on prejudice about immigrants, which was very witty, I thought. A picture of West Indian hands doing the laundry – "there are many black hands at work, keeping Britain white." Isn't that nice?'[54] Lamming was to remain an intermittent foe: in *The Pleasures of Exile* in 1960, he complained that Naipaul's books were unable to 'move beyond a castrated satire'.[55]

The Humbler Creation by Pamela Hansford Johnson was 'an engrossing novel' about a childless couple whose marriage has become sexually dead: 'as a study of a strange and sterile marriage, it is subtle and illuminating,' Vidia wrote empathetically.[56] He read extensively among women writers, and often gave them better reviews than the men. He enjoyed the first novel by the Irish writer Edna O'Brien: 'Miss O'Brien may write profounder books, but I doubt whether she will write another like *The Country Girls*, which is as fresh and lyrical and bursting with energy as only a first novel can be.'[57] He recognized the importance of Attia Hosain's novel *Sunlight on a Broken Column*, about the collapse of a noble Muslim family in Oudh before the partition of India, believing it put the author 'among the most accomplished Indian novelists writing in English'.[58] His most enthusiastic review of all was for *Memento Mori*, Muriel Spark's slim, cruel comedy about old age. 'There is a Waugh-like brilliance to this novel . . . Muriel Spark has written a brilliant, startling and original book.'[59]

For the first time, Vidia found himself inside a specifically British literary world. *Stories from the New Yorker: 1950–1960*, with writing by J.D. Salinger and Johns Cheever and Updike, was 'a frightening book. It isn't only that so many of its American stories are indistinguishable in style, sensibility and mood; it is that these stories, when read in bulk, seem to have issued from a civilization so joyless that it must be judged to have failed.'[60] His own literary world was a virtual community; as a reviewer, he might meet other *New Statesman* contributors on the page, and his contact with the publication was limited to the arrival of the postman with a brown paper parcel. But to readers, publishers, editors and agents, V.S. Naipaul became a name in literary London, as distinct from a colonial offshoot at the BBC. His reviews could be found amid disquisitions on 'the Channel Tunnel question', reports on new gramophone records, advertisements for *Mad* magazine and even a 'Labour Party Youth Rally and Sports Day with Jimmy Hill, Fulham's Inside Right'.

It was in most ways a lonely life. As he wrote later: 'I became my flat, my desk, my name.'[61] Although the *New Statesman* prided itself on its international flavour, assessing the policies of Jawaharlal Nehru and offerings such as *Eighteen Poems by Mao Tse-Tung*, V.S. Naipaul was nearly the only non-European name on its pages. Even then, it was an ambiguous and unrevealing name: 'V.S.' could stand for anything apart from the sesquipedelian 'Vidiadhar Surajprasad' with its seven complex syllables, while 'Paul' looked familiar, even Christian. 'Have I changed?' he asked in a review in July 1961. 'Or are bad novels getting worse?'[62] He stopped writing for the *New Statesman* later that year. 'I have been unfortunate as a reviewer,' he claimed later, 'I have seldom received good books. But I take my responsibilities as a reviewer seriously.'[63] His taste in literature had not altered substantially since his opinionated letters to Kamla at Benares Hindu University in 1950. In a whimsical, camp article in *The Times* in 1961, he wrote that the novel remained his 'main delight'. His instinct was to return to the classics. 'I like reading in Aksakoff of the Volga in flood, the Volga frozen, Aksakoff and Gogol make me feel the vastness of Russia; so do Turgenev's *Sportsman's Sketches*. And how important the weather is in the Brontës and in Dickens! . . . It would be easier to say what I don't like: Jane Austen, Hardy, Henry James, Conrad, and nearly every contemporary French novelist.'[64]

CHAPTER TWELVE

'THERE WASN'T ANY
KIND REMARK'

IN THE AUTUMN OF 1958, Vidia began work on a fourth novel, *A House for Mr Biswas*. It took three years to complete, ran to over 200,000 words and was, in all senses, a huge achievement. 'Believe me,' he told Kamla as he wrote it, 'this book is like the scholarship exam all over again.'[1] It was an imagined version of Pa's life. 'It really is dealing with the child's memories, so that gives it its special quality: it is fantasy working on a childhood memory.' The starting point was some pieces of furniture his father had collected over the years and taken with him to each house or bit of a house he occupied: a meat safe covered with a screen to keep out flies, some chairs that he had varnished, a bookcase, a bureau. 'Was there a hat rack? Or did I invent that? The book has destroyed memory in a way for me.'[2] He realized soon that it was a progression from his earlier work. 'As I was writing it, everything developed. The day came when I found myself doing subordinate clauses, because I needed to, and it was a great step forward.' Although Vidia would never write easily, rarely producing more than 500 words a day through his career, each sentence was designed to carry the narrative forward. 'I write in a very fast way. I don't delay. I don't dawdle. It looks as though I'm dawdling, but I don't dawdle. I fix every little moment with a picture.'[3] He allowed *A House for Mr Biswas* to be taken over by its characters as he moved for the first time into what V.S. Pritchett termed the 'determined stupor' out of which great books are written, as the writer becomes consumed by the writing.

When the manuscript was done, he noticed that one side of the gold nib of his Parker pen had been worn away. Vidia went to Italy with Pat for a holiday. 'I left the pile of papers on the dresser, a big dresser in the flat, and magical as Italy was, I was tormented by the thought of the papers. I had no other copy, and when I went back I was so relieved to see it there ... I broke down towards the end because I had

laboured so long. I began to do a revision. I did everything I could to
cure the pain in my fingers, put tape on them, so painful, the typing.
By the end I felt I had grown up; I felt I had become a writer.'[4] Like
many authors, he was careful about the mechanics of writing, believing
the making of a book was a kind of luck. 'I've become very superstitious
about the titles you give your books. If you write a book about a man
looking for a house, you might find yourself in the same predicament.
Be careful.'[5] For many years, Vidia would avoid speaking the titles of
his books out loud.

A House for Mr Biswas tells the story of one man's life: Mohun
Biswas. He tries his hand as a pundit, a sign-painter, a shopkeeper, an
estate overseer, a welfare officer and a journalist on the Trinidad
Sentinel: 'WHITE BABY FOUND ON RUBBISH DUMP – In Brown
Paper Parcel – Did Not Win Bonny Baby Competition' is one of his
stories.[6] At all stages, Mr Biswas's intentions are dislocated by circumstance, his dependent position and the restrictions of a colonial society.
When he takes a correspondence course in journalism from London, he
is advised to write pieces on 'Guy Fawkes Night' and 'Characters at the
Local'. Mr Biswas is a failure, but a picaresque hero. The novel, told
slowly, is universal in the way that the work of Dickens or Tolstoy is
universal; the book makes no apologies for itself, and does not
contextualize or exoticize its characters. It reveals a complete world.
The humour is gentler than in the first three books, and there is greater
sympathy for the characters, although it is not applied equally: the
Tulsis, representing the Capildeos, are viewed almost exclusively from
a negative angle. Moments and ideas are drawn from Pa's *Gurudeva*,
and from Vidia's own stories like 'Potatoes'; he takes a swipe at
Mittelholzer and Selvon by giving their attributes to a pair of black
labourers, Edgar and Sam.

Trapped early into marriage by the Tulsi family, governed by a
powerful matriarch, Mr Biswas spends the rest of his days trying to
escape their influence even while he depends on them for survival.
Much of his time is spent getting things wrong: even when he tries to
whistle, 'all he did was to expel air almost soundlessly through the
lecherous gap in his top teeth.'[7] He works hard to offend the Tulsis,
insulting the favoured sons, calling his mother-in-law a 'Roman cat'
behind her back and saying to Shama, his wife, ' "It look to me that
your whole family is just one big low-caste bunch." '[8] When he throws
food out of a window and spits water on his brother-in-law, he is

beaten and asserts himself by ordering Shama to buy him some peppersauce and a tin of salmon. She answers him: ' "You have a craving? You making baby?" '[9] Anger and comedy of this sort are threaded through the book, though the anger, and anguish, draws as much on Vidia's own temperament as on Pa's depressive outbursts. It was as if Vidia was imagining how he himself might have lived Pa's life. There is no suggestion that Mr Biswas was a literary achiever, or a man of sartorial style, as Pa was; for fictional purposes, it was easier to present Mr Biswas as obstinate and inept. In this way, Vidia sought to memorialize his late father and to distinguish himself from his legacy. The taut relationships within the extended family at 'Hanuman House' are brilliantly depicted: between sisters, between children and aunts, between old Mrs Tulsi and Mr Biswas. The critic Harish Trivedi, who had the advantage of reading both Hindi and English, believed 'a more detailed and authentic description of a Hindu joint family would be hard to find even in all of Hindi literature.'[10] In the final pages of *A House for Mr Biswas*, the old system breaks down as Trinidad changes and the two elder children go abroad on scholarships. Mr Biswas buys a house in Sikkim Street, borrowing money from a relation. His last thoughts, Vidia's thoughts, were: 'How terrible it would have been, at this time, to be without it: to have died among the Tulsis . . . to have lived without even attempting to lay claim to one's portion of the earth; to have lived and died as one had been born, unnecessary and unaccommodated.'[11] The house, finally achieved, carries a freight of symbolism.

Attempts by Diana Athill to cut parts of *A House for Mr Biswas*, apparently at the instigation of a putative New York publisher, were resisted. 'I worked very hard on that book and I worked with great judgement,' Vidia wrote. 'If the book is any good it will make its way . . . You must support me on this.'[12] Athill agreed, but when she told him that Deutsch intended to postpone publication, he was furious, writing to Francis Wyndham, 'At times like this I feel I should never speak a civil word to Diana or André again: they treat me so contemptuously.'[13] Looking back, Francis felt that Vidia's chronic complaints about Deutsch were not unreasonable. 'He paid his authors scandalously little. He didn't advertise Vidia, even when *Biswas* came out. I almost felt Diana and André didn't want it to be too much of a *succès d'estime* because they knew it wouldn't sell. They never promoted him as a star author.'[14]

Six months after publication, the book had sold an unremarkable 3,200 copies in hardback. No American publisher was forthcoming, and Vidia was reduced to depositing the book at the hotel of the New York publishing legend Blanche Knopf, who with her husband, Alfred, had founded one of America's most prestigious imprints. Vidia's agent Graham Watson made the suggestion: 'He couldn't place the book, and he said to me this humiliating thing, "Blanche Knopf is at Claridge's, why don't you just take the book to her and leave it for her?" He should have done that himself, of course. But I took it. It came back almost the next day. She didn't read it. She just knew it wasn't for her.'[15] Vidia's self-belief was not enough to carry him through; postcolonial literature had yet to be invented as a genre or as a profitable business, and his work remained an anomaly. Later, set against novels such as *Things Fall Apart* by Chinua Achebe or *Midnight's Children* by Salman Rushdie, *A House for Mr Biswas* would be seen as a seminal postcolonial text. Knowing he was being patronized, even while his patrons did their best to promote him, Vidia's reactions to the world at this time became ever less conciliatory. When he appeared on the television show *Bookstand* in October 1961, he had an off-air row with the BBC stalwart Grace Wyndham Goldie. 'I felt that his nerves must have been jangling,' Diana Athill wrote to the interviewer, Colin MacInnes. 'I wish he didn't *mind* everything so much (but then he wouldn't be the writer he is if he didn't).'[16] In the same year, he had a fleeting meeting with the novelist R.K. Narayan, who made a remark to him that would often be quoted later: 'India will go on.'[17]

Hearing that her son was publishing another novel, Ma wrote hopefully: 'I am very worried about your last book you are writing I hope that you will not mentioned anything about your Mamoos and Mousies in it to cause any unpleasant feeling.'[18] The response of the Capildeo family would be noisy. Rudranath telephoned André Deutsch in a fury on publication to demand the book's suppression. Diana fielded his call, and, knowing nothing of the family background, reported to Vidia: 'He says he is your uncle, back here for 6 months lecturing in Maths at London University, also that he is a barrister and an "important" member of the opposition . . . Now, is this gentleman a nut, or could he be a serious threat? (He could be both at once of course.)'[19] Lawyers were consulted, and Capo R. did nothing. Rampersad Ragbir of Chaguanas arrived at the offices of André Deutsch claiming to be a cousin, Diana informed Vidia. 'He spent quite a long time willing the Peace of God into me' and left an important note 'which he'd rather give you than the *News of the World.*' She forwarded the note to Vidia, which turned out to read, in full: 'I got a story about myself and Jesus Christ the Saviour.'[20] For Simbhoo, Rudranath and their families, *A House for Mr Biswas* would be viewed in perpetuity as an act of betrayal and misrepresentation. Simbhoo's granddaughter Vahni Capildeo has described how she was discouraged from reading books with the name 'Naipaul' on the spine: 'I kept away from all these armoured books. They were impenetrable. They were a source of contention, not of pride. For our paternal grandfather hated the Naipauls. Who were they, after all? Ungrateful lesser members of his extended family who had got away with spreading lies and wicked stories about him and his family and Indian people and everyone on the island whose independence he, Mr Capildeo, had worked for. Worse yet, these ingrates had made money from their treachery.'[21]

Reaction in the British press was substantial. Beneath the headline 'Caribbean Masterpiece' and a photograph of Vidia, Colin MacInnes wrote in the *Observer*: '*A House for Mr Biswas* has the unforced pace of a master-work: it is relaxed, yet on every page alert.'[22] The novelist Angus Wilson wrote that V.S. Naipaul had now joined 'the small group of unquestionably first-class novelists'.[23] Dan Jacobson in the *New Statesman* praised it as 'the most interesting novel to have been published in England in 1961.'[24] In the *London Magazine*, Francis Wyndham called the book 'one of the clearest and subtlest illustrations ever shown of the effects of colonialism . . . he has succeeded in filling an unusually large frame without sacrificing the finesse of the miniaturist's technique.'[25] Elsewhere, the poet Derek Walcott produced a full-page report for the *Trinidad Guardian* under the headline 'A Great New Novel of the West Indies'. Walcott thought Naipaul had established himself as 'one of the most mature of West Indian writers'. In an accompanying piece, he commented on the seeming gap between the compassionate author and the haughty man. 'Naipaul seems, on first acquaintance, to have alienated himself from all the problems of our society and particularly those of his race. But the books are almost contradictions of the man.'[26] Later, Edward Brathwaite would write, 'The novels of Vidia Naipaul . . . have come, almost overnight, to topple the whole hierarchy of our literary values and set up new critical standards of form and order in the West Indian novel.'[27] A letter arrived out of the blue from Gault MacGowan, who after giving up the editorship of the *Trinidad Guardian* had survived the Dieppe Raid. 'He thought that I was Pa, that I had become a great success after being a reporter,' Vidia wrote to Ma. 'It was a very kind letter, and I believe that you will be pleased to hear about it.'[28]

*

During the writing of *A House for Mr Biswas*, Vidia kept in close touch with his family, their letters feeding the book and Vidia's own attitudes feeding the letters his siblings sent him. Life in Trinidad, the alternative world in his head, was a constant presence. Ma was worried about Kamla, thought she was too flighty and should settle down, ideally with Dada Tewari, the son of family friends in Jamaica. Kamla was bored by Trinidad: 'I don't think it's doing me any good and mentally speaking I doubt if I can last the year.' She was worried about Shiva, who was now at QRC but had failed to win an exhibition. 'Do you know, the boy is always in the moon — the most absent-minded being you ever came across — the very image of Pa. He is intelligent but he does need guidance.' Vidia was not impressed when a letter arrived for Pat from Shiva: 'I have found myself greatly attracted to Communism or what might be more accurate Anarchic Communism ... I foresee a society as the Anarchists did based on co-operatives run directly by the people with no interference by the State.'[29] Sati was married to Crisen, and Savi had won a scholarship to study dental medicine abroad. Her plans changed when she met Melvyn Akal, a doctor. Melvyn had originally come to Nepaul Street to take out Kamla, until Savi caught his eye. She wrote to Vidia: 'Melo has already asked Ma's consent to marry me and she has agreed ... I will continue to teach and give every single penny of my earnings to Ma.' A couple of months later, she wrote with news that 'Your uncle Rood has announced to the public that he is the third greatest scientist ever to be and is having a good reception in Trinidad. Last night hundreds went to the Himalaya Club to hear him speak on "The Crisis Facing the West".'[30] Stories of this kind, which might have come straight from Vidia's fiction, were not rare (although Capo R. may have been parodying the PNM propaganda which described The Doc as the third most intelligent man in the world; the first two were never specified). The local press reported that a Mr Dookinan Naipaul had been fined $72 for giving injections and pretending to be a doctor. Shiva, aged fourteen, wrote: 'Kamla told me that the said Dookinan Naipaul claimed to be the brother of W.I. novelist V.S. Naipaul and you could imagine how we all laughed. When I went to school that day the boys all chided me about it.'[31]

In the autumn of 1958, Mira came to live in Streatham Hill to prepare for a degree in French and Spanish at the University of Leeds. Her education was to be funded by Savi and Mel, although Vidia would make some contribution. England was a new world for her. She had brought home-sewn clothes from Trinidad and a heavy grey military coat which a friend had given her to guard against the English winter. Pat disposed of it, and gave her money for a tweed coat. 'She was gentle and kind. Pat was not a huggable person, but she was nice to me in so many other ways and I felt welcome. Very shy, very modest, very sweet. A good heart. She was a good cook. Very small portions, and they would allocate small portions to me and I was ravenous. I was only about ninety pounds. Pat would go off to teach and I remember she began cutting a slice of bread for me in the morning and I would have liked to have two slices of bread. They got on very well. Vido would tell Pat at the end of the day how many pages he had written and what he had written. He would read things to me and if I chuckled he would get very happy.' Sometimes they fought. 'I went out to the shops and bought one egg here, one egg there. Vido accused me of "shopping like a nigger". I said you're horrible. He said get out. I went to a friend and he called and apologized.' Mira typed much of the final manuscript of *A House for Mr Biswas*.

That Christmas, Mira went with her brother and sister-in-law to stay with Ted and Marg Hale. 'I thought the mother was like a zombie and the father was polite, upright and correct. The mother was a strange, lonely looking, unhappy woman – as if she had no connection with the husband. She could have been his maid.' Eleanor seemed 'a nice friendly soul, very male, very different from Pat. Total chalk and cheese.' Mira was surprised at the flat in Kingstanding. 'I couldn't understand why they stored coal in the bathtub. Maybe they just washed with a little cloth.' It was the first time Mira had eaten at someone else's house in England. The party addressed a Christmas turkey in a tense atmosphere while Vidia ate a tin of salmon, which he had brought just for himself. Mira remembered: 'I am having my first bite and it is total silence around the table and Vido just out of the blue snaps at me, "Can't you say something? Can't you just say if you like it, or don't like it?" I was so shocked. I suppose he wanted me to say once I had tasted the food that it was really wonderful ... It was some sort of pressure or stress he was feeling and he was taking it out on me, he just jumped on me and I began to cry because I was in shock, and embarrassed.'³²

After she got her degree, Mira went to live in Edinburgh with Savi and Mel, who was doing a doctorate in dermatology at the university. For Savi, life in Britain made her comprehend Vidia and Pat better. 'It took me just six months in Edinburgh to understand class and people and behaviour. You had done Jane Austen and you had read literature but you had not lived in the country.' It no longer surprised her that Pat was so reticent, or that she kept her family hidden – things that had previously baffled her. Like Mira, she was dismayed by the minuscule portions of food Pat offered, and presumed her frugality arose from Vidia's objection to anyone who was fat. 'My children remember being taken on a picnic and having risotto. Pat was always very sweet and caring to them, but they felt that they got a tablespoon of rice.'³³ Nor could she understand why Pat 'never learned to cook anything of Vidia's home food, never tried. I always remember being shocked, my God, he's sending out to buy dhal and rice? It just seemed absurd.'³⁴ When Mira gained a diploma in education from Edinburgh, she returned to Trinidad to teach, and in 1963 married Amar Inalsingh, an ambitious doctor from a prosperous Indian Christian family.

Vidia was conscious that despite his critical success, his sisters were doing better than he was in worldly terms. He disliked that fact that Pat still had to work in order to support them. She was a conscientious teacher. In a testimonial from Rosa Bassett School, the headmistress Miss Jewell Hill praised her intellectual attainments, her devotion to girls of differing ability and her willingness to arrange trips to museums, historical sites and films in her spare time.³⁵ Veronica Matthew, a pupil at Rosa Bassett, remembered 'Pat Naipaul was small and slim, quiet and mousy. She was played up by some of her classes. She always wore black: black blouses with little Peter Pan collars, straight black skirts and flat pumps – all quite fashionable at the time.' The school must have been 'rather a dispiriting place to work' since most of the girls pitched their aspirations so low . . . 'Higher education was generally regarded as a waste of time, as the number of earning years would be reduced . . . We were completely unaware at school that Mrs Naipaul was married to a well-known writer. At dinner once a girl on my table remarked, while Mrs Naipaul was on dinner duty (but out of earshot), that she was married to "a darkie". When I was in the upper sixth Mrs Naipaul left school to accompany her husband on a trip to the Caribbean. Later I read the book he wrote of that experience

[and] was amazed that there was absolutely no reference to her whatsoever in the book. He made it appear that he had travelled to the Caribbean alone.'[36] Pat was to remain a silent witness until after her death.

Shiva liked reporting Trinidad gossip to his elder brother. The hot news in 1958 was that Capo R. had left Ruth and come to live 'with a young English thing in a new flat opposite the Dairies'. The aunts were outraged, but when Dool Mausi berated him, he shouted at her. Shiva wrote: 'The press compares him to Einstein and Newton, yet recently a student wrote the longest letter I have ever seen saying his science is naive and elementary.' Early the following year Shiva reported that Kamla was seeing a married Danish man who ran a paper factory, and 'went out almost every night with him, until two or three in the morning . . . Savi and Melo came down from San Fernando and told her that it was all looking very bad . . . Ma decided to talk to her. Then the fireworks really began . . . So Kamla left the house, after throwing a glass at Ma, swearing that she was going up to San Fernando to kill Melo.' Kamla was able to stir up her brother afterwards by reporting that 'Savi & Melo . . . didn't like "Miguel Street" . . . By the way, thanks for the dedication – but why?'[37] Vidia, nearing the end of *A House for Mr Biswas*, was thrown when he heard this suggestion: 'if I had not been so worried by the news that Melo and Savi didn't like Miguel Street I might have finished it last week . . . I dedicated Miguel Street to you and Ma because it is the first book I wrote, a small recompense for not being at home.'[38]

Later that year Kamla agreed to marry Harrinandan 'Harry' Tewari, the brother of Dada, who was now in disgrace owing to the discovery that he had two children by different Chinese women. It was a pragmatic choice by a woman nearing thirty who realized that her life was not working out in the way she had hoped. She told Vidia: 'I must confess that I am not at all in love with Harry but he is just about willing to lay the world at my feet. By the way he has bought me a £287 diamond ring. (What wouldn't you have done with the money? Or me or Ma?)' To Pat, she wrote, 'I'm being married Hindu-style in a sari and what not . . . I have no dreams, no hopes, no plans. I will just meet the future as it comes and I do have a lot of confidence in Harry.' They got married in Jamaica, and the press ran a photograph of Kamla looking glamorous, saying she was the sister of 'noted West Indian writer Vidia Naipaul of Trinidad'. In a letter in November she described her new life to Vidia. She would make breakfast of saltfish fritters and boiled green bananas, and spend the day doing little. Harry owned a cinema and a cocktail lounge in Kingston, where they would go most evenings: 'Harry keeps his prices high to encourage only the highest class.'[39] Kamla thought later: 'Maybe it was just a form of escape. I imagine so. I can't say that Harry treated me badly. That would be a lie. His only problem was that he drank a bit, but he never came home and behaved badly – he came home and just fell fast asleep.'[40] Later, Kamla began teaching again and they had three children.

*

In 1959, as Trinidad moved towards independence, the chief minister Dr Eric Williams made a move to attract former scholars back to their home country. He had previously described V.S. Naipaul to the *Trinidad Guardian* as 'obviously in the front rank of West Indian novelists'.[41] Mel Akal wrote: 'Eric Williams is contemplating sending for you and George Lamming to spend 3 months in Trinidad early next year . . . It is expected that you, in return, will give a few lectures . . . there is a drive to attract West Indians of benefit to the new federation back home. Good jobs are being offered – and with your qualifications – you may be in line for a job as a Consul, much as Solomon Lutchman [last spotted wearing the blazer of a Caroni Cricket Club in Oxford] now is in Venezuela – with prospects later of being an Ambassador.'[42]

A letter duly arrived from Dr Winston Mahabir, a family friend who was Trinidad's minister for education and culture, offering a scholarship. 'Dear Vidya, Greetings! . . . 1. First-class return passage by boat for yourself and your wife. 2. The salary of a Queen's Royal College Master while you are here in Trinidad. (I believe this will be in the vicinity of £100 per month.) . . . There will be no political strings attached to the award, but you will be expected to fulfil certain general obligations, for example, radio talks, public lectures, meetings with literary groups, etc. However, I have emphasized in representations to Cabinet that you should be free to saturate yourself once more in the atmosphere that is congenial to art. I am hoping that you will find it possible to be here by the middle of September this year, and that these proposals inter-digitate with your fellowship to India . . . P.S. It is a pity that there is as yet no offspring because the scholarship involves full return passage for at least one child!'[43] Being co-opted in this way did not appeal to Vidia, but he decided to accept as a break after the exertions of *A House for Mr Biswas* and the stress it had imposed on Pat. He wrote later to Ralph Ironman, who had moved with his wife Mary to Denmark, 'Children grow so much in four years; if we leave it much longer Anne and Lotta . . . will be new and

Vidia's maternal grandparents

Above
The Capildeo clan

Left
Pa with his car

Opposite page
Top, left Pa, Ma, Kamla and Vidyadhar
Top, right Pa's self-portrait, done while unwell
Bottom, left Kamla and Vido
Bottom, right Ma, Shiva and Nella after Pa's death

Above
Pat and Vidia at Oxford

Left
Vidia in the Front Quad
at 'Univ'

Above Dorrit Hinze in Paris

Right Jill Brain

Henry Swanzy, George Lamming, Andrew Salkey,
Jan Carew and Sam Selvon in the *Caribbean Voices* studio

Top, left
Vidia with Sati,
Mira and Kamla in
Trinidad, 1956

Top, right
Ma in heels with an
Oxford-returned
Vidia, 1956

Above, left
Researching *The
Middle Passage*,
1961

Below, left
Up the Rupununi
by boat with
Amerindians,
1961

Above Kamla gets married, 1958

Above, right Shiva marries Jenny

Right Pat in London, 1965

Below Pat and Vidia in
Streatham, 1961

V.S. Naipaul and Derek Walcott square up, 1965

Aged
nineteen

Aged
twenty-
seven

Aged
thirty-four

Aged
forty-five

complete persons with whom we shall have to establish a relation from scratch. What news can I give you of Pat? I can only say that by August 1960, when Mr Biswas was finished, we were both physical wrecks. Pat, in particular, was in dreadful shape.'[44] Pat secured a place as a teacher at Bishop Anstey High School in Port of Spain, and they agreed to spend several months in the West Indies.

'When I was in Trinidad,' said Vidia later, 'Eric Williams called me, gave me lunch and asked me to do a book which turned out to be *The Middle Passage*. So my life took another turn, which was a fortunate thing.'[45] In some respects it was not a fortunate thing, since Vidia's caustic presentation of the Caribbean would mark him as a writer at odds with his society and the conventional nationalism of the 1960s. The Trinidad government would finance his travels and purchase 2,000 copies of the resultant book. He travelled alone by ship, with Pat following later. *The Middle Passage* began with quotations from the Victorian writer James Anthony Froude, a man denounced in his day as a 'negrophobic political hobgoblin', and Vidia's opening sentence ran: 'There was such a crowd of immigrant-type West Indians on the boat-train platform at Waterloo that I was glad I was travelling first class to the West Indies' – which itself may have been inspired by a letter written by Kamla after her year in London: 'From the moment we left Euston it was as though I had said goodbye to England. The tone of the coach was strictly West Indian. There were little black babies screaming all around me. The chaps were all dressed in hot shirts and hats and they were talking [in loud] voices about the English being the "wus eatin people in the world" and about the "cold pressing straight thru your bones". . . . I feel no kinship with any of them – even the Indians & I feel absolutely lost.'[46] Quickly in the book, Vidia was describing 'a very tall and ill-made Negro' with a grotesque face, huge nose and thick lips.[47] The writer was set apart as someone who travels first class – if on the immigrant ship *Francisco Bobadilla* – and disparages the appearance of the first ill-made Negro man he sees. As Diana Athill pointed out, 'Vidia could not resist placing him right at the start of the book and *describing him in greater physical detail than anyone else in all its 232 pages*.'[48] To Pat, he wrote: 'The company is small but pleasant: one Portuguese of 55, perpetually ill: his toe has a corn, his head has an ache, and his tummy hurts . . . I wanted to tell you how much I loved you on that terrible Friday [the day he left] . . . and how much I have been loving you ever since.'[49]

Vidia said later of the opening of *The Middle Passage*, 'It's true, all

that's true. I'm not setting myself up; I'm being very mischievous . . . I'd
be allowed to say things like that among the West Indians who were doing
that Caribbean programme. We made those kind of jokes. I wasn't aware
that an English reader might worry about where I was positioning myself.
I was positioning myself always as writer, and if I wasn't, I wouldn't have
made all those lovely jokes in the first chapter – the steamer crossing –
some of the dialogue, those things are in my head to this day: the
Portuguese whom I called Correia, a kind of mulatto fellow who was at
our table, talking about a football team from Trinidad and the man whom
I called Philip asking him about Skippy. And Correia says, "Well, you not
going to see him again. Son of a bitch catch a pleurisy and dead. Frankie
and Bertie and Roy Williams. All of them dead like hell." '[50]

He presented the West Indies now as barely redeemable, a region
colonized only for the cruelties of slavery: 'The history of the islands can
never be satisfactorily told. Brutality is not the only difficulty. History is
built around achievement and creation; and nothing was created in the
West Indies.'[51] Through the force of his tirade, or detonation, V.S. Naipaul
was seeking a response. As the book continues, his desire to shock subsides
and he makes many perceptive observations about colonialism. 'To be
modern is to ignore local products and to use those advertised in American
magazines. The excellent coffee which is grown in Trinidad is used only
by the very poor and a few middle-class English expatriates.'[52] He observes
that almost no African names survive in the New World, and that, 'Until
the other day African tribesmen on the [cinema] screen excited derisive
West Indian laughter . . . This was the greatest damage done to the Negro
by slavery. It taught him self-contempt. It set him the ideals of white
civilization and made him despise every other.'[53] The corruption of identity
had led to competitive racial hostility: 'Like monkeys pleading for evolu-
tion, each claiming to be whiter than the other, Indians and Negroes appeal
to the unacknowledged white audience to see how much they despise each
other.'[54] The partial advent of democracy had brought new dilemmas:
'Nationalism was impossible in Trinidad . . . There were no parties, only
individuals. Corruption, not unexpected, aroused only amusement and even
mild approval: Trinidad has always admired the "sharp character" who,
like the sixteenth-century picaroon of Spanish literature, survives and
triumphs by his wits in a place where it is felt that all eminence is arrived
at by crookedness.'[55] Vidia does not plead, at any point in this book, for a
reassertion of imperial control, but makes it plain that independence will
provoke an avalanche of fresh problems. At the time, to a country

preparing for freedom, these words seemed above all to be an insult; today, they seem prophetic.

As soon as he reached Nepaul Street, Vidia was unhappy to be back. 'I behaved very badly for the first few days,' he told Kamla in Jamaica, 'I was bitterly depressed.'[56] He had no one to look after him as she had in 1956, or to arrange his trips around the island. The little family house, home to Ma and Shiva and Nella, now aged seven, was too hot and noisy. Nella was terrified of her big brother. 'He would ring my ears, hold them and twist them, if I got my sums wrong. It was crude behaviour from such a fastidious man. I remember him shouting – screaming – at my mother.'[57] In Port of Spain, Vidia claimed helplessness; writing would be impossible. Soon he was writing to Francis, 'The government have loaned me a car, a huge red thing . . . I am having a rough time with the intellectuals here . . . They invited me to parties and have apparently been hurt because I just was without the energy to drink through the night with them. So now I believe I have a reputation for stand-offishness, and perhaps worse.'[58] Lloyd Best and his wife arranged a dinner for Vidia and C.L.R. James. 'They got on splendidly. You'll be surprised how they loved each other.'[59]

The West Indian Federation (which would fall apart in 1962) had created a sense of anticipation in Trinidad, which made Vidia suspicious. He told the *Jamaica Gleaner* that Caribbean novels had made little impact on the English reading public, and even the critics had now lost interest in them. A group of writers and artists from different backgrounds had collected around Derek Walcott, who was writing and staging plays as well as working for the *Guardian*. Walcott, two years older than Vidia, born on the small island of Saint Lucia, had moved to Trinidad in 1953. He wrote strong, physical poetry and led a rowdy, vigorous life. His wife, Margaret, recalled the creative party atmosphere of the time: 'We had all been away, our scene. Derek referred to us lot as "anchored in the mid-Atlantic." Vidia came to our house, and Pat. She was not a very social person. He said he was a vegetarian, and I learned how to make a quiche real fast. He came across as a snob, in that he wouldn't dance and drink rum. But Vidia liked me . . . When I got a divorce he was concerned about me, very gentle . . . There was a party at the country club for Norman Manley, the Jamaican premier. Vidia says to Derek in his stupid affected accent, "Are you here as a guest, or as a reporter?" Derek said to me later, "What a little shit." '[60] Walcott himself was dynamic and turbulent; Pat wrote later to Mira: 'He's very peculiar but a very good poet.'[61] Vidia was conscious of his own early achievement, and determined to separate himself from the other West Indian writers he met now. Like Ralph Ellison after the publication of *Invisible Man*, he maintained that he was in a category all of his own, and that he had special insights denied to others. The mask of the master remained intact.

Early in 1961, Vidia and Pat flew to British Guiana, a territory on the South American mainland that historically had formed part of the Caribbean. Like Trinidad, it had a large Indian population, and Amerindians too. Much of the country had been owned by the Booker group of companies. 'The capital, Georgetown, is one of the most elegant cities I have seen. The buildings are wooden and white and the local builders can do marvellous things with wood,' Vidia told Francis. He had met the premier, Cheddi Jagan, the son of an Indian cane-cutter, and his American wife, Janet. They were a controversial pair, reviled by Britain and America as communists, but Vidia did not judge them in this way. 'I see much of the Jagans, and am altogether taken with them ... How sad these first leaders of colonial countries are!'[62] With Pat he flew to the Rupununi, the savannah on the Brazilian border, and travelled to the interior by boat. His instinctive affinity for Amerindians was tested by their living and eating conditions. 'I felt then that reverence for food – rules for its handling, interdictions – was one of the essentials of civilization.'[63] His dislike of colonial conditioning extended to Christian conversion of indigenous people: 'The missionary must first teach self-contempt. It is the basis of the faith of the heathen convert.'[64] They travelled next to Surinam where slavery had ended late, and Vidia became conscious of its constant legacy across the Caribbean: 'There is slavery in the food, in the saltfish still beloved by the islanders ... nowhere in the world are children beaten as savagely as in the West Indies.'[65] In Martinique, a department of France, Vidia was repelled by the sanctimonious pretence of equality: it made him 'long for the good humour, tolerance, amorality and general social chaos of Trinidad.'[66]

They travelled finally to Jamaica, where he lambasted Rastafarianism as nonsensical and wrote pleadingly to Francis Wyndham: 'Could you find out from Deutsch or Graham Watson (neither of whom has replied to my letters) exactly what they are doing about the novel?'[67] A sojourn with Kamla and her new husband, Harry, ended in argument, and Vidia went off to stay with Lloyd Best, who was starting an institute of economic and social research at the university. They talked and played poker late into the night. Best arranged for Vidia to give a lecture to the students. 'Everybody was looking forward to this evening because Naipaul was a big drawing card. But of course the local culture was that if something was announced for seven o'clock, you got there at eight and you were comfortable. Vidia Naipaul would put up with none of that.' At one minute past seven, Vidia walked out and insisted on being driven back to Lloyd's house. The audience followed the speaker. 'By ten o'clock the house was full to overflowing. He was holding court to all the students, he was in his element.'[68] Vidia was conscious of the poor conditions that the urban Jamaicans who were migrating to Britain at this time were escaping. 'The slums of Kingston are beyond description. Even the camera glamorizes them, except in shots taken from the air.'[69]

By May, he was in Streatham Hill writing *The Middle Passage* at speed in order to ensure it was completed by the end of the year, after which he planned a new journey – to India. The political situation in Trinidad was becoming more tense. Simbhoo's party had merged with other groupings to join the Democratic Labour Party or DLP, which was now the principal opposition to Eric Williams's PNM. Racial resentment was fiercer even than it had been in 1956. Williams called the Indians of Trinidad a 'hostile and recalcitrant minority' and proclaimed 'Massa Day Done' – meaning it was time for independence, and absentee European planters had no future. His chief opponent in the 1961 election was Capo R., who had come back from London University in triumph to snatch the leadership of the DLP. This created a lasting rupture with his brother Simbhoo, who believed he had a deeper understanding of Trinidad and its problems, and the family dispute was exacerbated by a fraternal battle over ownership of the Petit Valley estate. Rudranath was presented to the electorate as a brilliant figure, cleverer even than Dr Williams. A song of the time ran,

> The PNM say, boy we will have a hard time,
> Because that man more educated than The Doctor . . .
> Dr Rudranath returned to Trinidad,
> Like Raja Rama to Ayodhya.[70]

In November 1961, Ma wrote to Pat, 'This man Williams is doing everything in his power to cause a civil war, but I can tell you I have never before seeing our Indian people so tolerant they are determine that Williams cannot form the New Govt.'[71]

The election campaign was marked by bitterness and violence, with DLP meetings being broken up by PNM supporters while the black-dominated police force looked on and did nothing. The crisis was fuelled by provocative and slightly deranged speeches from Rudranath

Capildeo, who announced that his knowledge of Einstein's theory of relativity would enable him to compress time and effect political change faster than his rivals. Williams and the PNM took two-thirds of the seats in the election, and the British government called a conference at Marlborough House in London to discuss independence. After Prime Minister Harold Macmillan's 'wind of change' speech in South Africa in 1960, Britain was seeking rapidly to divest itself of its colonies. Under the chairmanship of a minister from the Colonial Office, Hugh Fraser, the delegates argued. Williams and Capildeo finally reached an accommodation during a tea break, enabling Trinidad and Tobago to become an independent country within the British Commonwealth. Demands for constitutional protection for the Indian minority were effectively ignored by the British government, and the new constitution gave exceptional legal latitude to the office of the prime minister.[72] With the DLP stranded, Rudranath Capildeo returned to academic life in London while for a time managing simultaneously to remain leader of the opposition. Eric Williams was left in a commanding position in Trinidad until his death in 1981.[73]

As the only begetter of *The Middle Passage*, Williams never reacted openly to the book, although his own conception of colonialism as a provoker of 'inward hunger' was not far from Vidia's thinking. Andrew Salkey described *The Middle Passage* in the *New Commonwealth* as 'the severest jolt to West Indian smugness since beet sugar ... Mr V.S. Naipaul is a truly remarkable writer [who] has trampled on nearly everybody's cosy myths of West Indian quaintness.'[74] The response of the Jamaican novelist John Hearne was more representative of critical reaction in the Caribbean: it was 'flawed, unattractive, often superficial ... he is a surgeon who has surrendered to despair.'[75] For Evelyn Waugh in the *Month*, the book was evidence of the dangers of decolonization: 'Mr Naipaul is an "East" Indian Trinidadian with an exquisite mastery of the English language which should put to shame his British contemporaries. He has shown in his stories ... that he is free of delusion about independence and representative government for his native land.'[76] Waugh was the first of a parade of reactionaries who would seek to appropriate Naipaul's writings, stripping them of their ambiguities in order to make a political point. Waugh's private thoughts were more insulting. In a letter to his friend Nancy Mitford in January 1963, he wrote, 'That clever little nigger Naipaul has won *another* literary prize. Oh for a black face.'[77] For all the critical acclaim, Vidia's position in Britain remained tenuous. To Waugh, who embodied an outlook that was still common in Britain, the white, fusty, musty, dusty, tea, coffee, cocoa, black, dark black, racial distinctions of the Caribbean were irrelevant. Vidia's reaction when he learned what Waugh had written to Nancy Mitford failed to address the underlying hostility: 'Bron Waugh [Evelyn's son] never mentioned it to me. I think it is a bit of showing off. I think he's acting.'[78]

In a BBC retrospective with Gordon Woolford and Henry Swanzy in 1978, by which time Gordon was a declining alcoholic and Vidia was irritable and famous, the subject of *The Middle Passage* came up. Gordon Woolford observed that George Lamming, Sam Selvon and Edgar Mittelholzer had all come to London in search of a publisher, and asked: 'Is that one reason that brought you, Vidia?'

NAIPAUL: No, I came to join civilization.
WOOLFORD: In *The Middle Passage* you savaged Trinidad.
NAIPAUL: Gordon, why 'savaged', why use that word?
WOOLFORD: Well, it was so, you know. [Laughs] There wasn't any kind remark.
NAIPAUL: [Ferociously] Was it untrue? Anything false? Anything proved wrong in sixteen years? Or everything proved right?
WOOLFORD: You had gone down there on money given by the Trinidad government.
NAIPAUL: They asked me to go back . . . I wrote as I found.
WOOLFORD: Does your heart lie very much in the West Indies, in Trinidad?
NAIPAUL: I don't know the West Indies. I only come from Trinidad, and I left it when I was eighteen and have more or less washed my hands of it, as I have washed my hands of India. I have shed all these colonial political concerns.[79]

The contrast between Naipaul's rich, grand tones, dripping with certainty, and Woolford's unsure, wheedling voice, with its slight London accent, is dramatic.

At the start of 1962, as Vidia prepared to travel to India for the first time, he was aware that his identity had been compromised by external events. Trinidad faced black majority rule, with the unstable Capo R. claiming to represent the interests of the island's many Indians. Britain was closing the door to immigrants. Under a new law, Commonwealth citizens would be denied the automatic right to move to the UK, and could be deported more easily. Vidia regarded the Commonwealth Immigrants Act as a betrayal. In a copy of *A House for Mr Biswas*, he wrote his signature and, 'For Andrew Salkey, in London, from which one may in future be banned.'[80] The mother country had abandoned a generation of orphaned children. Because of the haphazard way in which immigration had been handled during the 1950s, racial tension in Britain was rising as the white working class in areas like Brixton and Notting Hill felt themselves outnumbered by a boisterous, alien culture. The army put a quota on the number of non-white personnel, and almost the only black faces on British television were in the popular *Black and White Minstrel Show*. As a regular on shows like *Bookstand*, Vidia was an oddity. 'Six appearances in 8 weeks; the work so good that two programmes were telerecorded,' he told a friend.[81] His fame caused him consternation when he was recognized in bed: 'A prostitute said to me, you've been on television. I said, how can you recognize my face? How can you say that? She said something very flattering to me, she said your face is unforgettable.'[82]

Ambitious, protean, made of smart material, deracinated by the accelerated politics of the end of empire, Vidia made a conscious choice to refashion himself. The vogue for West Indian writing was over and, uniquely among his contemporaries, he saw the implications of this early enough to do something about it. Jan Carew remembered a conversation: 'The last time we met was in a café in the Tottenham Court Road. By then, there were rumours that Vidia was living in some part of London where West Indians were not welcome, and was taking up with different people. He told me he was going to become English, and I thought he was pulling my leg. The English are very strict about letting you in, particularly if you are a different colour. I thought it was one of his jokes, but he was quite serious about it. He meant he was giving up his West Indian imprimatur and taking on an English one.'[83] Vidia wrote to Ralph Ironman in Aarhus, distance making him intimate, 'We had planned to drive to India; we had ordered the Volkswagen van-conversion (splendid job, and so cheap, without purchase tax); we had paid the deposit; and then we found no one willing to give us the comprehensive insurance required for the journey. So now we are going to India, securely if prosaically, by sea; and as we intend to be away for at least a year, and as I shall have to work like the black that I am when we get back, it seems unlikely, unless something unexpected occurs, that we shall meet before 1964 or thereabouts.'[84]

During his years in and out of England, Vidia Naipaul had been awarded a degree by Oxford University, got married, become a radio presenter and a television pundit, produced journalism and book reviews, written short stories, comic novels and a coruscating study of the West Indies. Above all, he was the author of what would come to be seen as the epic of postcolonial literature, *A House for Mr Biswas*. Now he was heading for the land of his ancestors, to see what he might find. He was twenty-nine years old.

PART TWO

CHAPTER THIRTEEN

THE HOMECOMING

'AMERICANS EVERYWHERE; they are a very strange race,' Vidia wrote to Diana Athill from Athens on St Valentine's Day 1962. 'We leave tomorrow for Alexandria to take the ship for India.'[1] Vidia and Pat made the two-day crossing to Egypt on a cramped steamer, a journey which would provide the opening for *In a Free State*. He reported to Ma, with her concern about miscegenation: 'The Egyptians are not a pure people; they have a considerable amount of negro blood, and many of them look like West Indian negroes. The Arabians are purer.'[2] Aboard a slow cargo ship, the *Hellenic Hero*, they sailed down the nationalized Suez Canal, were detained at Cairo to argue with officials, and proceeded through the heat of the Red Sea with a day excursion to a 'Fuzzy Wuzzy village' in Sudan, according to Pat's diary.[3] Vidia took no notes, kept no journal; he drank in the experiences, letting them settle inside him. After three weeks at sea they approached Karachi in Pakistan, and on 18 March arrived in Bombay, the great port and teeming commercial hub on the west coast of India. 'We have no plans for India,' Vido wrote to Ma. 'We don't know what hotel we will be staying at in Bombay; how much time we will be spending there; or anything. Our plans, vaguely, are to settle down in some reasonably pleasant small town for a few months. I shall try to do a little work, and Pat shall try to get a teaching job.'[4]

India had been independent for nearly fifteen years now. Gandhi's mass campaign of non-violent protest had stirred the subcontinent and inspired nationalist struggles by colonial peoples across the world. British rule ended in 1947 when the country was partitioned into India and Pakistan in response to Muslim demands for a separate homeland; under a new constitution, the Republic of India became the largest democracy in the world; the British-educated prime minister, Jawaharlal Nehru, proclaimed a socialist dawn and a fresh era in international relations. By 1962, though, Nehru was old and ailing, and the glitter of the Congress Party's revolution was fading. For all his five-year-plans,

India was still painfully poor, and commerce was ruled by the 'Permit Raj'. The national mood of fatigue coincided with the arrival on India's shores of its doubly displaced son Vidia Naipaul, whose approach to his ancestral land had been decided many years before. While other Trinidad Indians of the 1940s drew inspiration from the struggles of Mahatma Gandhi, and Simbhoo Capildeo sent letters of supplication to Congress, Vido was wary. Aged barely seventeen, he had written to Kamla at Benares Hindu University: 'I am glad you told off those damned inefficient, scheming Indians. I am planning to write a book about these damned people and the wretched country of theirs, exposing their detestable traits. Grill them on everything.'[5] Now it was time for Vidia to write that book, and to grill them on everything: *An Area of Darkness* was the result, the most influential study of India published since independence, offering a passionate analysis of what was wrong and right with the country. 'Indians will never cease to require the arbitration of a conqueror,' he announced; and over the next five decades, Indians were certainly to show a remarkable willingness to be lectured about their failings by a Trinidadian.

From the first paragraph in his 'Traveller's Prelude', V.S. Naipaul's status as an insider–outsider was set. A man from a travel agency comes aboard the ship as soon as the quarantine flag is lowered in Bombay, and whispers, ' "You have any cheej?" ... He was tall and thin and shabby and nervous, and I imagined he was speaking of some type of contraband. He was. He required cheese. It was a delicacy in India. Imports were restricted, and the Indians had not yet learned how to make cheese, just as they had not yet learned how to bleach newsprint.'[6]

What could be more ridiculous than a people who wanted cheese but were unable to make it? It was a harsh and perceptive observation, but was Vidia understanding the man correctly? While Pat had troubled to learn a little Hindi before setting out on the voyage, dutifully mouthing the words and practising the Devanagari script in her notebook, Vidia's left-over childhood knowledge of the language was cursory. It is likely the tout was asking in rough Hindi whether the young traveller had 'cheej' or 'cheez' – meaning 'stuff'.[7] Understandably, he thought Vidia would comprehend him. But was this 'Trinidadian of Hindu Descent' Indian, West Indian, neither, or both, here in this alien setting? Or was he nothing? Take the moment of first contact: 'Now in Bombay I entered a shop or a restaurant and awaited a special quality of response. And there was nothing. It was like being denied part of my reality. Again and again I was caught. I was faceless. I might sink without a trace into that Indian crowd.'⁸

How was Vidia to establish himself? He was staying at Green's Hotel on Marine Drive with his 'companion' (Pat appears momentarily, fainting, in *An Area of Darkness* under this designation; only in the American edition does she become 'my wife'; had he used her as a character, he said later, the book would have been 'another kind of family expedition. The best way of judging it, why it is difficult to do, is when you read women writing about "my husband" – or you have a figure called, "Bill". It becomes another kind of book').⁹ Anxious, faceless, nervous of sinking into the crowd of 450 million, he sought out those who might help to lift him above the herd. His alma mater saved him: the ever-helpful Peter Bayley had given Vidia an introduction to a pair of Univ men, Adil Jussawalla and Ravi Dayal, and in their hospitable, Indian way, they looked after him; Dayal even came to their first meeting wearing a Univ tie. Jussawalla, a twenty-one-year-old Parsi who was shortly to publish his first volume of poetry, invited Pat and Vidia to dinner with his family and showed them the sights of Bombay. 'Bazaar with Adhil Joosewala,' Pat wrote in her diary, the repository of many of the experiences that would find their way into *An Area of Darkness*. 'Piles of fruit, spice in pyramids and other shapes. Incense. Bangles. Prostitutes in crowded boxes or pens. Some beautiful, some old and grotesque. Some with faces powdered white.'¹⁰ To Jussawalla, who was at the time 'in a swadeshi [patriotically self-sufficient] sort of phase' wondering for instance whether it was ethical for an Indian to write in the English language, Vidia appeared 'charming, but sharp. He seemed always to be thinking about something. He said things which to me were shocking at that time – he used the phrase "slave society" of the West Indies. Pat was always on the sidelines when he said such things, saying "Oh, Vidia", trying to stop him.'¹¹

Ravi Dayal worked for Oxford University Press. He had read and admired *A House for Mr Biswas*. Slight, witty and laconic, five years younger than Vidia, he came from a successful family and had won a Tata scholarship to read history at Oxford after graduating from St Stephen's, the top college at Delhi University. Peter Bayley had taken him under his wing, a position of shelter from which he sought to escape: 'I used to dodge Bayley a bit. I felt he was sort of befriending former subject peoples.'¹² When he met Vidia, Dayal noticed his denim shirt and tight trousers, enjoyed his sense of humour and doubted his claimed caste inheritance: 'I couldn't see a pukka Brahmin becoming an indentured labourer.'[13] Vidia joked to him about having a bottle of whisky impounded by customs officers. 'He was extremely funny, a very good mimic, doing accents and tones. He was a wonderful storyteller in those days. It didn't have the acid of *An Area of Darkness* at that stage . . . I think when he got [the whisky] we all celebrated and finished it off.' Dayal noticed that Vidia was in a state of high nervous tension, 'upset by the dirt' and 'endlessly looking for clean food'. The Naipauls' room at Green's Hotel was 'back-facing, while the more expensive rooms were sea-facing – cockroach infested, people going around in shorts swabbing floors and so on, dirty toenails, liable to be picking their ears and then serving you some food. We gave him some medicine to soothe his stomach.'

Pat was 'a bit of a school ma'am, but very kind, at the receiving end of Naipaul's irritability. They were equals at that point. It was as though he was leaning on her a lot, and she was soothing his disappointments and frustrations . . . I think he was fashioning himself a bit, and India was slowly becoming a character for him. His idea was very amorphous when I first met him in Bombay. He looked like everyone else and felt totally different, and people didn't realize he wasn't Indian. He tried behaving as though he was, but he didn't speak the language. To begin with, I think he probably wanted to feel much more at home in India.' Through Jussawalla and Dayal, Vidia was introduced to the burgeoning cultural world of Bombay: he met the founder of the *Economic Weekly* Sachin Choudhury, who reminded him of his father, the theatre director Ebrahim Alkazi, the poet Nissim Ezekiel, and the editor of the influential policy journal *Seminar*, Romesh Thapar, and his wife and colleague Raj. He narrowly missed a poetry reading by Allen Ginsberg and Peter Orlovsky, who were at the start of a subcontinental journey in search of sex and spiritual enlightenment. Pat wrote a letter to Ma saying she liked Bombay, but that 'Vidia was very gloomy for the first few days, partly because it is very expensive, and talked about going straight back to England. But people have been very kind and he is now feeling more settled.'[14]

In early April, Pat and Vidia made the long train journey to Delhi. Accommodation in the capital was a problem. 'Installed in exp[ensive] flat,' Pat wrote in her diary. 'The landlady – craze for imported things.'[15] They spent ten days trailing around trying to see places and get things done, exhausted by the heat and the bureaucracy. They met Ravi Dayal's future father-in-law, the lawyer, novelist, columnist, politician, editor, diplomat, voyeur and literary gadfly Khushwant Singh, who found Vidia 'reserved, pleasant and I think a little disappointed that he hadn't been given the kind of reception he expected as a son of the country who had done well.' Singh made up for it by taking them on an excursion to the Qutb Minar and Tughlakabad Fort. He remembered Pat looking 'distinctly unhappy'. They ate bacon and egg sandwiches and drank coffee in the shadow of the fort, overlooking ancient ruins and a valley of blooming red flame-of-the-forest. 'I saw him look at it for a long time,' Khushwant Singh said, 'because it was really a spectacular scene, and thought, now I'll read a lyrical account of this.' But Vidia was more interested in the urchins who swarmed around him, 'grubby little fellows in loin cloths with flies all over their faces – not a pleasant sight. I realized that he went for the squalor and dirt much more than the beauty. He was quite allergic to being touched. He almost recoiled when anyone greeted him with an embrace. The only feeling I got was that he had a chip on his shoulders. I attributed it to his being a coloured man in England.'[16] Later Singh took Vidia to a couple of parties, and to meet his father Sir Sobha, a Sikh contractor who had built parts of New Delhi, and to lunch with the German Jewish novelist Ruth Prawer Jhabvala, who was, Pat noted, 'thin, highly sensitive, nervous yet assured'.[17]

Writing to Francis Wyndham, Vidia was struck above all by Indian indifference to suffering. 'Porters are called coolies; they have no barrows, which would simplify their labour; they carry incredible loads on their heads and people who are no doubt friendly and hospitable and charitable walk behind them, concerned only that their luggage should not be stolen.' He had been asked to write some articles for the *Observer*, but was unsure what to write about, and was infuriated by a piece in the paper by George Patterson: 'So much of this talk about the Christian Nagas strikes me as being revivalist and mischievous. An independent Nagaland is an impossible absurdity: the injection of religion into politics is the curse of this country, and it is sad to find the Observer's correspondent encouraging this sort of thing, which will throw India more and more into the hands of the Hindu reaction, as distasteful as any other type of fanaticism.'[18] At this stage, then, he saw no virtue in the reassertion of Hindu identity, or in those who sought to use it to mobilize dormant political energy.

*

In one month, Vidia had noticed much about India. He retired to a lakeside hotel in Kashmir to think and write. Central to his conception was the idea that people failed to notice what was happening around them. Press reports were no use; destitution and begging had religious sanction. 'Indians defecate everywhere,' he wrote in *An Area of Darkness*, in Churchillian cadences, 'They defecate, mostly, beside the railway tracks. But they also defecate on the beaches; they defecate on the hills; they defecate on the river banks; they defecate on the streets; they never look for cover ... the truth is that *Indians do not see these squatters* and might even, with complete sincerity, deny that they exist.'[19] In fact, 'It is well that Indians are unable to look at their country directly, for the distress they would see would drive them mad.'[20] In an era of nation-building, these observations about defecation were not well received. Vidia's lines attracted much hostility, and he observed laconically: 'I begin to feel that I coined the word and devised the act.'[21] The son of Kashmir's last maharajah, Karan Singh, sent an unsolicited article about *An Area of Darkness* to *Encounter* magazine, asserting that the building of toilets would bankrupt the country: 'While it can at once be admitted that our standards of public sanitation leave much to be desired, it should also be pointed out that the construction of flush latrines for five hundred million people would mean that all our other development schemes will have to be wound up.'[22]

Vidia's ambition was to stay in the Kashmir valley and write a short novel – it turned out to be *Mr Stone and the Knights Companion* – but his experiences at Mr Butt's Liward Hotel on the edge of Dal Lake in Srinagar provided plenty of material for *An Area of Darkness*: visiting pilgrims who tore up the lawn to get mud to scour their dishes, a battle over the tuning of the dining-room radio, the ceaseless demand for references which Vidia dutifully typed out on his portable typewriter, his concern over his helper Aziz's clothing, and his touching fury at himself for being driven so often to anger.[23] The Kashmir section of *An Area of Darkness* reads like a novel, with perfect characters and minute social interchange at the lakeside hotel; unusually, the narrator himself emerges as a likeable personality. The language was beautifully economical: 'The police *shikara* passed often, the sergeant paddled by constables.'[24] Or, 'Being an unorthodox hotel, we attracted the orthodox.'[25] Or, setting out on an expedition to the mountains,

'I decided, too, that the coolie was unnecessary; and the sweeper was to be replaced by a small spade. Aziz, defeated, suffered.'[26]

He was conscious as he wrote *Mr Stone and the Knights Companion* that it was a departure from what had come before. 'I had used up my Trinidad material, my childhood material. Then I had gone and done without premeditation *The Middle Passage*, which was a wonderful experience for me, going to South America and seeing these places, understanding, having a sense of those colonies.' Trying to find his way was not easy: 'Between August 1960 and December 1965, five years, *Mr Stone* was the only fiction I did. It was a big gap.'[27] Much of the book drew on his relationship with Pat and on his days at the Cement & Concrete Association, although he assured Ralph Ironman in a letter, 'I don't believe I have used any material you might want to use.'[28] His greatest worry was that he did not know enough about his adopted country to make a success of the novel. He wrote to Francis in June, 'I will certainly need your judgement and help with this one, for it is set in England, and has only English characters, the sort of thing that makes one very shy of submitting it. Angus Wilson promised to check the dialogue of any English novel I wrote; and it really is difficult to write dialogue which does not speak itself naturally in one's head.'[29] Francis responded favourably to the manuscript when he read it later that year.

Mr Stone and the Knights Companion is a short novel about an old man with regular habits and a dull life, and is notable now as a curiosity: Vidia had managed to pull off a plausible book using exclusively English characters. As Ronald Bryden wrote in a review, it was a 'feat of acculturisation' by a 'superb writer of world stature'.[30] There is a certain Hindu fatalism about Mr Stone, a librarian at a firm called Excal, but the dialogue and the social interchange convince. He marries Margaret Springer, a widow; they sleep in separate beds, and are embarrassed to be sharing a bathroom. Stone sets up the 'Knights Companion', a scheme to enable retired Excal employees to stay in touch. The book is a study of Vidia's loneliness in post-war London and a portrait of a marriage, drawing on solitary days at his desk and the stasis of sexually unsatisfactory married life. When Whymper, a public relations man with hints of John Stockbridge about him, says he enjoys spending hours with his head between his girlfriend's legs, this news seems 'unexpected, frightening, joyless' to Mr Stone.[31] In a broadly complimentary review in the *New Statesman*, V.S. Pritchett noted, 'Naipaul is not interested in the passions. Like Beckett, the master of old age, he is absorbed by "tedium". He is a minute watcher of habits and changes of mind.'[32] Vidia was profoundly interested in the passions, but had not yet found a way to translate or enact them in either his books or his life, except through purchased sex. The restrictions he felt as a man were mirrored in his fiction. *Mr Stone and the Knights Companion* was a feat, but it did not offer a way forward as a writer. He could not write further novels about dull life in London, nor could he return to the world of *Miguel Street*; his knowledge and his patois were out of date. In the same review, Bryden wrote: 'Isn't it time we killed off V. Selvon Mittelholzer?' The 'composite Caribbean author writing sunnily of quaint brown lives in the sugar-fields' was certainly finished.[33]

Pat's diary records many activities in Kashmir, such as Vidia taking photographs, adopting a stray puppy ('rescued from horrible boys who were treating him very cruelly,' she told Auntie Lu) and arriving by horse-drawn tonga for dinner at Karan Singh's smaller palace.[34] In retrospect, these were years of comparative ease and peace for Kashmir; Nehru had made Singh a figurehead ruler with the title Sadr-e-Riyasat. A man of 'heavyish build but face etc of a reader', Karan 'Tiger' Singh showed the visiting novelist and his wife family portraits and religious books, and commended his own philosophical writings. In June he gave a dinner with a dance band for the heads of the local women's colleges, the diplomat (and Nehru's sister) Vijayalakshmi Pandit and her daughter the novelist Nayantara Sahgal. Pat noted afterwards: 'Singing of Kashmiri, Dogri, Urdu, Arabic (Egyptian) songs. Also Am[erican] songs – "That is how much I love you, baby", etc. "Tiger, sing the isle of Capri, that's my vintage".'[35] When Vidia met Nayantara Sahgal many years later and she reminded him of his own role in the after-dinner singing, he angrily denied that his song had been Trinidadian. Karan Singh remembered the dinner: 'I like Indian classical, ghazals, western pop – but I might have been singing Presley's *Wooden Heart*, "Can't you see I love you, Please don't break my heart in two".'[36] Most of Pat's diary entries were happy; only occasionally did she record distress: 'Vidia's distaste for me combined with the grudge he bears (no housework, eating) reaches a head.'[37] In a letter to Ma, she reported that she had celebrated her thirtieth birthday with hotel staff and the vendors from Dal Lake, one of whom had brought her lotus flowers. Her life matched a prediction she had made in a letter to Vidia in 1953 when they were both at Oxford, although it differed in a crucial respect: childlessness. She wrote then with touching dedication and aspiration: 'At the age of thirty – this is my clear picture – we shall be just emerging from a very hard life. You will be working all the hours of the day. We shall have two children at the crawling (noisiest) stage – one very fretful the other good-tempered – and you will have just published a novel – not a best seller but a good one. Darling I do adore you honest.'[38]

In July they travelled to the beautiful mountain setting of Gulmarg, carpeted in wild flowers, to stay with a couple they had met, Zul Vellani and his wife, Nimmo. The four spent some intense, hard-drinking days together. Pat's diary degenerated into a haphazard jumble, as Vidia began to behave in an unstructured way. 'We find Zul & Nimmo playing Scrabble. Drink, lunch at 4 . . . drink, midnight dinner. Zul's life story. July 12: Read Blitz, etc. Evening walk. Sunshine mountain. Calypsoes. July 13: Frozen lake . . . Bottle of whiskey & talk until 12.' A month later, after going on a pilgrimage to the ice cave at Amarnath on the advice of Karan Singh, they visited Zul and Nimmo again. Zul was a scriptwriter and actor of Indian Muslim origin from East Africa, Nimmo was a singer and political activist, and both were fiery, attractive and opinionated.

Pat's diary went on to record a 'seizure' she had at their bungalow, brought on by the frenetic, drunken atmosphere: 'Aug 21: Pouring rain . . . Drink & talk.' Another guest was there, a communist poet named Masoud. 'V[idia] fills M[asoud]'s glass repeatedly. Outburst about Hyderabad. V shouts. M sits with eyes lowered and lower lip thrust out. I pull V into other room where "lunch" is ready . . . M – "He said something very offensive to me." "A rabid communalist." Z had shouted to V to stop from other room.' Another pair of visitors had been there recently, a sitar player named Maboob and his attractive but unstable American girlfriend, Mickey. 'Aug 22: Kashmiri singers. Zul's stories about Maboob. My seizure. Aug 23: Walk down to Tangmarg . . . Mickey & Maboob come for tea at Liward. Aug 25: M & M married to tune of 100 R. by Mufti.'[39] These characters would all be reworked accurately into *An Area of Darkness*: Zul as Ishmael, Maboob as Rafiq, Mickey as Laraine, 'a new type of American whose privilege it was to go slumming about the world and sometimes scrounging, exacting a personal repayment for a national generosity.'[40] For Zul Vellani, it was in retrospect a wild time of drink-fuelled conversation and argument. 'We had a bungalow at the top of the golf course in Gulmarg . . . My wife didn't like Vidia Naipaul. I don't know why I liked the bugger. He had a remarkable talent for observation, but he was disastrously prejudiced. One night, at two in the morning [Nimmo] woke me up [and said] that girl is screaming, I think something's wrong, so I went there and I found that Vidia Naipaul was slapping his wife. I said, what you are doing? He says, Zul, you don't understand, she suffers from hysteria, a sort of fit. My wife said there is no excuse for slapping the woman.'[41] In Vidia's recollection, Pat had suffered from a nosebleed in Gulmarg. 'I never hit Pat. Never.'[42]

During calmer times, Vidia wrote to his family from Hotel Liward. He told Mira and Savi that the Kashmiris, 'barring the Tibetans, are possibly the dirtiest people in the world. They very seldom wash . . . They associate – like the Indians of Trinidad and our family – cleanliness with godliness; only on religious days, therefore, they wear clean clothes . . . They have nevertheless a tremendous charm; perhaps they have this charm because of all their faults. Certainly there are few things more attractive than the friendliness and broad smiles of the Kashmiri children.'[43] He told Shiva, who was applying for a place at Oxford University, that he should not worry about the noise from the local rum shop. Why, last year he had bought a desk for £12, but was so happy writing at a cramped kitchen table that it was there 'this book about the West Indies, *The Middle Passage*, which is being published at the end of July, and will cause quite a furore, was written . . . I am glad you say you have no intention of writing fiction. Because I can now, without fear of depriving you of material, ask for your help.' He had written four stories about Trinidad in a week, one about a Negro baker who makes money only when he employs Chinese, another called 'The Night Watchman's Occurrence Book', a small masterpiece told through entries in a logbook at a rowdy hotel. Could Shiva think of odd incidents for him, for 'though I am in lovely Kashmir, I long to be back in Trinidad.'[44] He made a similar request to Mira in Edinburgh: 'Now you mustn't think this is a form of cheating. Gogol wrote to his mother for stories when he was writing those stories of Russian rural life.'[45] His book would be called *Trinidadians*. Writing to C.L.R. James in Tunapuna, Vidia did not mention his desire to return to Trinidad, but did admit: 'I feel quite differently to England since the Immigration Bill; and though I will have to go back there, I think it unlikely that I will stay there for any length of time.' India had produced 'fewer writers than we have with less talk . . . I wonder what you will make of my book about the West Indies. Attack I wouldn't mind; but if the book fails to arouse among West Indians some discussion about their situation, then I will have to think it a failure.'[46] To Ironman, he presented himself as fatally detached from England. 'Bluntly, we are looking for a country to live in. Perhaps Denmark might take us in.'[47]

*

A fortnight after his thirtieth birthday and a day after Trinidad became independent, Vidia and Pat Naipaul left the Kashmir valley after almost five months. It had been an extraordinarily productive time. Their days and nights were full of adventure; they had met people, been on journeys and a pilgrimage, Vidia had written a novel and a crop of short stories. Their first stop was Jammu 'as the guests of the Maharaja of Jammu and Kashmir (nothing to pay!)' he told Ironman. 'This Indian trip is proving hideously expensive. The average Indian can sleep in the open. To want a room is to be demanding; to want a bed is to be luxurious; to want proper sanitation is to be almost wanton.'[48] They travelled by train and by bus to Agra to see the Taj Mahal by moonlight, to Delhi to stay with a rich cousin of Nimmo's named Jiti, and on to Muradabad to meet Ravi Dayal's brother, Virendra. In retrospect, Ravi Dayal wondered whether he had been too free with his introductions. 'I liked Naipaul and honoured his work. I wanted him to be reasonably happy, to look around, to feel at home in India. I think that we may have actually been just too warm and helpful. Friendships were given to him too easily. It's conceivable. He had access to a lot of special people whom he may not have had easy access to at that stage.'[49]

Virendra Dayal had been Rhodes scholar, and was now an Indian Administrative Service (IAS) officer in a volatile, mixed Hindu–Muslim area in north India. He installed Mr and Mrs Naipaul at government lodgings and took Vidia around the district as he sorted out disputes and dispensed justice. According to Dayal, his generation was 'full of hope and imbued with the nationalist ethos. We never felt marginalized from the world . . . India was a great civilization, however fractured, and we had to assume responsibility for the future of our country.' As an accidental, occidental Indian from 'the most amusing island that ever dotted a sea', Vidia felt included and excluded; a contemporary like Dayal was both like and unlike himself. 'Vidia's need to be in the mainstream of history was completely understandable,' said Dayal.[50]

After Muradabad and Lucknow, the Naipauls took the sleeper train south to Hyderabad to visit the ruins of the great Hindu city of Vijayanagar. For Vidia, it was a moving and melancholic experience, a reminder of distant historic grandeur. Lurking inside the remaining buildings were 'the inheritors of this greatness: men and women and children, thin as crickets, like lizards among the stones.'[51] In Bangalore, he became entangled with a man known as Visky. In *An Area of Darkness* he appears as 'the Sikh', and insults everyone he meets. Like Vidia, who seemed to identify with him in a horrified sort of way, 'the Sikh' is enraged by the inadequacies around him. Pat's diary records these encounters: 'At 3 Aces Visky seizes upon barely perceptible turn of head to pick quarrel with man next door who turns out to be a Punjabi ("No, a Sindhi"). Visky grasps him and strikes him gently; he leans back amazed and frightened . . . Vidia starts quarrelling . . . Visky begs us to go and have a drink. We refuse and Visky sulks. Pulls out a reefer.'[52] Life on the move in India was more dramatic than the news from Kingstanding. 'Your Uncle Roy has had to have an operation to take away his appendix,' Pat's father informed her. 'He is going on nicely now, of course he will have to take things quietly for a bit.' Eleanor, who was planning to become a physical education instructor, reported on a rock climbing expedition to Wales. The food at the hostel had been poor: 'The main course was a large plate containing, neatly placed in the middle, <u>one</u> pilchard. Second course was a thin slice of jam roll and to finish off we had doorsteps of bread and marge.'[53]

Passing among the sound of the 'excessively vowelled' languages of the south, they reached Madras in mid-October, where Ravi Dayal had been sent on a posting by the Oxford University Press. He introduced them to yet another lively, creative set: David Horsburgh, an Englishman who spoke Tamil, wrote children's books and played the *mridang*, his serene wife, Doreen, and Jacques Sassoon, a Bengali-speaker who was studying Carnatic music. 'Vidia relaxes and expands,' Pat noted.[54] He pondered how to write about India, his caustic views encouraged by a developing border conflict with China. India's diplomatic and military incompetence would lead finally to a Chinese victory, and as Khushwant Singh put it: 'The sense of euphoria went out of the country and the sense of disillusionment began. 1962 was when the Chinese gave us a drumming on the battlefield. We were a beaten nation – and all the big talk that Nehru had been indulging in as a great world leader came to nothing.'[55]

Writing home, Vidia told Mira that Madras was his favourite city in the subcontinent. 'What is worrying me is this India book. I really don't know how I am going to set about it; and if I don't write it, I will have to pay back Deutsch £500. Heigho!'[56] Glossing his insecurities, he told Shiva: 'I have kept no journal, and the Indians are such elusive, odd people (they puzzle you even more when they pretend to be people like you or me) that the time I have been here has not been enough for me to understand them.'[57] After leaving Madras, Vidia and Pat visited Pondicherry before

travelling to Nagpur, Calcutta, Benares and Delhi. November found them
in the district of Faizabad near Ayodhya with Manmohan 'Moni' Malhoutra
(St Stephen's, Rhodes scholar, IAS), an urbane colleague of Virendra
Dayal. 'I welcomed his company,' Malhoutra recalled. 'Life in the districts can be lonely and he was a very entertaining companion, intensely
curious. He asked a lot of questions, he was a wonderful listener, and so it
went extremely well. Pat was always trying to pacify him, calm him,
prevent him from getting into an unnecessary rage. She was a gentle,
sweet woman.' Moni Malhoutra was still under training and persuaded
his boss, a cigar-smoking, sun-helmet-wearing commissioner, to let Vidia
accompany them. 'I think that gave Vidia a real insight into the function-
ing of the administration, or the non-functioning of the administration, in
this country. We went to a village where some communal lavatories had
been constructed. Vidia wanted to know whether they were being used and
all these young people said, no, we don't use them. He said, why not?
And they said, in a very matter of fact way, the air is fresher outside.'[58]

A journey to Nilokheri in Punjab to visit Zul and Nimmo was not a
success, and by December they were back in Bombay, visiting the caves at
Ajanta and Ellora. Vidia and Pat had made a huge, detailed sweep of the
subcontinent over nine months. On Christmas Eve, Pat sailed to England
to find a new place for them to live in London. 'The idiotic appearance of
white passengers,' she noted as she went on board.[59] Vidia stayed in
Bombay, and was interviewed by the *Times of India*. With engaging vanity,
he wrote to Pat, 'I was photographed more than I have been in my life;
and really some were the best things that have been done of me. So in
last Sunday's paper (yesterday's) there was a piece (alas, illiterate) about
me, with a photograph of me with cap tilted back!'[60] He visited Rupa,
the Indian publisher that distributed his books, and was unimpressed by
their lack of interest. He told Diana Athill: 'You know I did not care
for the typographical design of *The Middle Passage*, but allow me to say
that the book is otherwise beautifully produced; it was a pleasure to handle
it in Rupa's office; the jacket was marvellous.'[61] He took the chance to
harry André Deutsch: 'You seldom reply to my letters, but I would be glad
if you could take note of this one.' He complained of missing royalties,
altered percentages and a failure to tell him that the paperback rights for
A House for Mr Biswas had been sold to Collins. He objected that 'four of
my books were sent in March to a Mrs Brown of Trinidad. I don't know
any Mrs Brown. I never authorised anyone to send off books, to be debited

to my account, to any Mrs Brown. AND I HAVE NO INTENTION OF PAYING FOR SUCH BOOKS . . . please give me my £2.7.11 back.'[62]

*

Vidia's plan was to spend a few more months in India gathering material. Raj Thapar arranged for him to rent a flat in New Delhi belonging to the composer Vanraj Bhatia. According to Bhatia's account, Vidia was rude about the flat and insulted his servant. 'He was snobbish, nothing nice to say – a thoroughly nasty human being.'[63] Pat was told another version: 'The place that Raj arranged was disastrous. No sheets! The Garhwali servant boy squatting on the lavatory seat, with disastrous results! No cups, nothing.'[64] Instead, he stayed with Ruth Prawer Jhabvala and her husband, Cyrus, known as Jhab. 'She comes from Golders Green,' he told Francis, 'a refugee since the age of 9 from Germany; she is married to a Parsi architect. They live quietly, almost in seclusion.'[65] The end of January found Vidia on the move again, this time on the border between India and Nepal on a tiger shoot in the company of Moni Malhoutra and a senior IAS colleague. Moni shared a tent with Vidia, and noticed his agility. 'He was very athletic and he used to do a particular movement with his leg, he used to pick it up and bring it up towards his head from the back. It's the kind of posture which you'll see in some sculptures in the Tanjore temples, a very, very difficult thing to do. He loved to do that.'[66] By the light of a Petromax lamp, Vidia wrote to Pat of the awfulness of seeing a tiger skinned: it had been 'so whole, so beautiful, so noble'. The sight of the dismembered hind legs, 'all muscle, like those of a male ballet dancer in skin-tight white rubber tights' had made him 'a great opponent of big-game shooting; for, to be blunt, the so-called hunter faces almost no risk. The knowledge is provided by the locals; they undergo such risks as are involved.'[67]

Three days later, Vidia took the train to Gorakhpur for the conceptual climax of his homecoming tour of India: it was his intention to visit the village of his maternal grandfather, Pundit Capildeo. In *An Area of Darkness*, his trip ends in self-reproach and flight; in the version sent to Pat immediately after his first visit to the village, his reactions were happier. His guide was another IAS officer, Dr J.P. Singh, who remembered: 'I was a Joint Magistrate in Gorakhpur. Moni said there is a friend of mine, a writer from the West Indies, can you take him around and show him whatever he wants to see? Naipaul was short with the hotel chaps. For example, he wanted to have hot water for his bath. It had to be carried to him in his room but it used to take time, so he used to say they are very, very lazy chaps ... I thought he was having all this anger and contempt primarily because he wanted the country to develop. The account he wrote of our trip in *An Area of Darkness*, it was accurate.'[68] Vidia told Pat: 'Gorakhpur is hell. It has reduced me to the early-Indian stage of my hysteria. Imagine ... hotels which literally stink of the sewer; imagine waiters in the filthiest clothes and with the filthiest hands, serving tea in cups which they arrange in their usual finger-dunking way.' The village was 'one of the neatest and cleanest I have seen in India; it is shaded by trees; the people were dressed in white and, this being a village of Brahmins, they were all wearing the sacred thread.' Feeling 'ridiculously afraid and shy', he explained his connection to Capildeo to the villagers, using Singh as his interpreter. When someone mentioned Jussodra, the woman with whom his grandfather had eloped from Trinidad in 1926, Vidia felt 'deeply ashamed'.[69] At this moment, in Dr Singh's words, 'An old woman, toothless, bent, wearing a not very clean sari, came out.' Jussodra! 'V. S. Naipaul didn't know she was alive, and she started speaking English in a West Indian accent and she started weeping. This fellow was dumbfounded.'[70] Jussodra explained the family story: she was his grandfather's third wife, as he already had one in India before he married the formidable Soogee.

'All this while the crowd was gathering,' Vidia told Pat, 'And they are good-looking people; slender, some tall, many well-built, with beautiful brown complexions ... This is where Ma's family & my sisters get their looks from, without a doubt.' Jussodra took him to a hut, held his feet and wept. He was left feeling that Capildeo had been 'a man of exceptional force of character ... I admire him for his three wives, for his decision to abandon all (however temporarily) for love much more than I have ever done ... As you can imagine, I fell in love with these beautiful people, their so beautiful women who have all the boldness and independence (no coyness) of Brahmin women (according to my IAS interpreter), and their enchanting fairy-tale village.' This, though, was not all: he met a cousin he never knew he had. The letter to Pat concluded: 'And what of the young man who, himself Capildeo's grandson by his Indian marriage, embraced me like Michael Redgrave embracing Margaret Rutherford in The Importance of Being Earnest?'[71] This young man's father was the source of Vidia's change of mood, evidenced in *An Area of Darkness*, where he is referred to as a 'beggar' and a 'monk' called Ramachandra Dube (Dube, pronounced doo-bay, being a Brahmin caste name). He appeared at Vidia's hotel in

Gorakhpur, and was later to be found on his bedroom verandah: 'I was towelling myself when I heard a scratching on the barred window.'[72] Vidia sent him away, and when he visited the village again, avoided Ramachandra and his requests for assistance. Thus his first-born maternal uncle, the senior to Capo S. and Capo R., was dismissed. 'So it ended, in futility and impatience, a gratuitous act of cruelty, self-reproach and flight.'[73]

Back in Delhi he stayed with the Jhabvalas, with whom he felt at ease. He wrote to Pat, 'I think of you, like a foolish young boy in love, every night, I touch myself and imagine that you are touching me. I long for your smooth breasts and all of you. Alas, alas: will performance match expectation? We've really been married too long and have been sleeping together too long for me to feel so sharply.' Pat responded that she had found a less than perfect place for them to live at 5 Waldenshaw Road on the fringes of south-east London, helped by a 'To Whom It May Concern' letter from Diana Athill recommending Vidia as an ideal tenant and 'one of England's leading young writers'.[74] Pat decided to take a teaching post at Haberdashers' Aske's Hatcham Girls' school. Staying in Delhi, Vidia enjoyed the company of Jhab, whom he commends on the final page of *An Area of Darkness*. Less happily, he had a chance encounter with his former host Jiti, who asked him to smuggle a cheque out of the country: 'Now this is highly dangerous; and . . . if one is offended by corruption, one can hardly indulge in corrupt practices oneself. Jiti is therefore, I believe, greatly annoyed.'[75]

It was with relief then that Vidia took a flight to Madrid, pausing only to purchase a photograph of himself taken as he walked from the aeroplane clutching his typewriter and an untied parcel of cloth. As he had promised, he wrote letters at once to J.P. Singh and to Moni Malhoutra, telling them of his reactions on leaving India. The letter to Malhoutra anticipated the book that would follow:

> The point that one feels inescapable is the fact of India's poverty; and how deep is one's contempt for those Indians who, finding no difficulty in accepting one standard in India and another outside it, fail to realise this, and are failing to work night and day for the removal of this dreadful insult and humiliation . . . The lavatories at Palam [airport] were literally covered with shit and the aerodrome officer could only speak of the shortage of staff (i.e. sweepers). I wonder, wonder if the shitting habits of Indians are not the key to all their attitudes. I wonder if the country will not be spiritually and morally

regenerated if people were only made to adopt the standards of other nations in this business of shitting; if only they could be made to see that they owe some responsibility . . .

So goodbye to shit and sweepers; goodbye to people who tolerate everything; goodbye to all the refusal to act; goodbye to the absence of dignity; goodbye to the poverty; goodbye to caste and that curious pettiness which permeates that vast country; goodbye to people who, though consulting astrologers, have no sense of their destiny as men. From here it is an unbelievable, frightening, sad country. Probably it all has to change. Not only must caste go, but all those sloppy Indian garments; all those saris and lungis; all that squatting on the floor to eat, to write, to serve in a shop, to piss. Probably the physical act of standing upright (think of the sweeper prowling about like a dog below your cafe table) might regenerate the people. Probably I am mad. But it seems to me that everything conspires to keep India down.

These ideas would mature in *An Area of Darkness*, and in his later books on India.

The return to London left Vidia depressed, and it took him a couple of months to get started on the writing. He told Moni Malhoutra in May: 'I suppose I miss India more than I imagined; and, I say this without flattering you, I miss Lucknow and Fyzabad [he unconsciously used the spelling of the Trinidad town, named for the Indian Faizabad] more than anything else. I wonder whether I shouldn't buy some acres in Ranikhet or some part too cold for Indians and run a little farm.'[76]

Soon, once the book was under way, his Tolstoyan vision was put aside. Pat tried to persuade him to be more generous and forgiving in his treatment of India: 'She loved India. She saw dignity and beauty and things like that; I saw the calamity.' Pat's political or social views, at this time and subsequently, did not have the effect of softening Vidia's position. His instinctive response to another person's line of argument was to harden his own views, and to be made more certain that his particular insight was rare and correct, and needed to be expressed. 'She was a profoundly liberal person. This wasn't just an attitude. It was so nice . . . I provoked her constantly. I was very, very provocative. She was speaking quite genuinely, and I would play the fool; I would often play the fool.'[77]

CHAPTER FOURTEEN

'LOVELY *VOGUE*, JUST BOUGHT'

AFTER NEARLY A YEAR of travel and enquiry, India remained for V.S. Naipaul 'the land of my childhood, an area of darkness ... I had learned my separateness from India, and was content to be a colonial, without a past, without ancestors.'[1] This was a premature and inaccurate conclusion: he was not content to be a colonial, and would continue to seek an Indian ancestral past. When *An Area of Darkness: An Experience of India* was published in autumn 1964, Francis Wyndham, to whom it was dedicated, wrote: 'Your book is really an important book. I suppose it will make some people very angry.'[2] John Wain in the *Observer* judged it 'tender, lyrical, explosive and cruel'. The *Times Literary Supplement* praised it as 'beautiful, sensitive and sad'. The *Daily Telegraph* thought it a 'sour recital'. V.S. Pritchett called it 'the most compelling and vivid book about India to appear for a long time.'[3] BBC television put Vidia on a chat show with some furious Indian students from the London School of Economics. One remembered: 'Naipaul unperturbed and smiling, held his ground: "India is on its death bed, there is no point in wasting life-saving drugs on a terminally ill patient" ... He advised us students not to return to India but to seek jobs in England.'[4] Deutsch's distributor in India refused to handle the book, and copies had to be smuggled in. The publisher Sir Allen Lane complained about the de facto ban in 1968 to Morarji Desai, the deputy prime minister, who responded that the decision by Indian Customs had arisen 'because of some misapprehension on the part of the dealing officer', and would be lifted.[5] Nissim Ezekiel wrote a spirited and much discussed attack, 'Naipaul's India and Mine'. Rudranath Capildeo, in a speech in parliament in Port of Spain, apologized through Mr Speaker to the people of India for this 'notorious book ... Pope Paul VI went to India and he left his heart in India, but one of our countrymen went there but left his excrement.'[6]

An Area of Darkness was to provoke and fascinate readers in and out of India for decades; Naipaul's willingness to try to judge a nation and assess, as his father's son, the moral and cultural affect of Hinduism on human behaviour made the book both a target and a talisman. At a time when relativism was starting to become the accepted theoretical response to any postcolonial nation's failings, the strength of Naipaul's views looked like a shocking return to the days of absolute, imperial judgements. Significantly, his book would influence the outlook of two generations of Indian writers, particularly men: Amitav Ghosh, Farrukh Dhondy, Amit Chaudhuri, Tarun Tejpal, Amitava Kumar and Nirpal Dhaliwal have all written of its impact. Naipaul's pessimistic intensity, his self-laceration and his refusal to engage in wishful thinking made the book influential as an approach to be either rejected or embraced. Pankaj Mishra said that he was left 'shocked and bewildered' when he read *An Area of Darkness* aged sixteen: 'I didn't know that you could write like that about India. I think it was the first book I read in English that contained the world I lived in.'[7]

Before he left Bombay, Vidia had given an interview to the *Illustrated Weekly of India*, a long-established and influential English-language newspaper. It was an intense, passionate performance, containing much of the thinking and sentiment that would be played out in *An Area of Darkness*. The interviewer initially found him 'playboyish . . . still in his dressing gown though it was nearer midday', making facetious remarks about England: 'It is such a boring place that one can do nothing else but work.' When he spoke of India, though, there was a shift. He talked with angry passion: 'I suppose you don't want me to enlarge upon the dreadful sanitation, backward villages, and the dishonesty prevailing everywhere . . . I never thought that Indians were such consummate hypocrites, preaching austerity, preaching godliness and indulging in the grossest type of materialism in any society. I never thought that the Indians would be so callous to human suffering. I never thought that one would find oneself in a slave society – and this is what it is – with so many politicians . . . Equally, I never thought I would enjoy the company of Indians as I have done . . . the Indians one meets and talks to are the most interesting people I have ever met.'

It had been a homecoming; Vidia was a child of the Indian diaspora who wanted to understand the civilization of his forebears. The interviewer felt he had 'a love-hate relationship towards India'. In turn, he thought the country was suffering from a surfeit of mediocre writers who spent their time 'in dreadful little conferences' complaining about problems of translation. 'The word "writer" like the word "minister" is much abused in India. Perhaps there will also be "deputy writers" soon.' Nor was he optimistic about the capacity of the state to recognize that the last years of the Nehruvian era were marked by self-satisfaction. 'India, as it is, has no future . . . And the reason is that India has not adjusted itself to the modern world.' The interviewer's response was surprisingly benign. 'I did not attempt to contradict Naipaul because he was speaking out of a real concern . . . The severe strictures were valid, for it is time we, in this country, stirred ourselves from the moral complacency of assumed righteousness and looked into the mirror.'[8]

The editor of the *Illustrated Weekly of India*, an impressive man named A.S. Raman who was seen as a father-figure by many of his journalists, asked Vidia if he would write a monthly 'Letter from London'.[9] He could write about whatever he liked. Vidia took up the offer at £30 a letter, and for the first time was forced to assess his adopted home country directly. He had the advantage of comparative anonymity: writing for a foreign audience in the days before the internet, he knew he could express himself freely, even experimentally, and that it was unlikely anyone in London would read his words. He started frankly in the spring of 1963, making it clear he saw himself as a visitor in England, just as he felt a stranger in every country. 'To me, departure is always more welcome than arrival.' He expressed the loneliness of the city, stuck in 'one's private cell' or on twisting Underground trains or buses, 'Everywhere one feels enclosed.' Characteristically, he gave no signal that he shared his 'cell' with another person in a land where 'home-making is the aim and almost the point of this culture'. His detachment made him look at his adopted country with an encompassing eye. He tried, not altogether successfully, to see Britain with the same analytical detachment he saw India or the West Indies. 'Satire is now all the rage . . . With the destruction of a century-old order in England, nothing is settled, and the pace of disturbance increases.' He was conscious that the satire was parochial: 'No novelist has chronicled the astonishing changes in England in the 50 imperial years after the Indian Mutiny' and British playwrights and novelists preferred material such as 'jokes about the Foreign Office and about Eton and Harrow . . . And London, so far as literature goes, remains

Dickens's city ... on the modern mechanised city, its pressures and frustration and sterility, English writers have remained silent.'[10]

For the next two years, Vidia's life and opinions can be read through the themes he explored in his letters for the *Illustrated Weekly*. It was the only time he would ever write regularly on contemporary culture. He discussed cricket, the Beatles, television satire (*That Was The Week That Was*), the plight of the 'colonial' in British society, Angry Young Men, *Queen* magazine and the Queen herself. 'The Royal Family has ceased to be esteemed ... The newspapers now openly say that the Queen's tour of Australia was a failure, and a *Guardian* columnist went so far as to do a debunking piece on the Poet Laureate.'[11] He discussed the growth of advertising. 'The London Underground would be grim indeed without those advertisements for women's underwear that flash by one after the other as we go up or down the escalators.' Now even political parties were advertising themselves, 'just like Rinso or Ovaltine'. Naipaul remained party apolitical, turned off by the simplicities of Labour and the Conservatives. At the next election, 'I will go down to the polling station, vote for the man who is almost certain to lose, and do what I can to cheer up his agent.'[12]

In the summer of 1963 he covered an unfurling scandal. Jack Profumo, the minister for war, had resigned after lying to the House of Commons over his relationship with a part-time prostitute who was also sleeping with a Soviet naval attaché. Vidia thought the publicity and furore was overdone, since it 'might suggest to the researcher of the future that in the 1960s the English were given to Roman-scale orgies ... It seems to me foolish to raise the cry of hypocrisy and to deduce from this scandal that England is on the verge of moral collapse.'[13] When one of the figures in the Profumo case, Stephen Ward, killed himself a few weeks later, Vidia wrote a more introspective piece about sex and prostitution, which was also an oblique, naive, partial confession of what he saw as his own sexual failings, mixing truth with lies. Rebecca West had written in a newspaper that the problem was one of 'animal training', and that society needed 'to get the goats and monkeys under control'. Vidia, writing under the headline 'Of Goats and Monkeys', thought the problem was one of sexual desire. He said he had been told by an 'elderly retired prostitute' (covering himself by stressing the woman's age and undesirability) that there was too much bad language on radio and television. 'Prostitutes do exist;

they have clients; and they make money. But I have never met a man who has been with a prostitute. I have met few who have not professed horror at the thought ... Prostitutes are outlaws, necessary to some and denied by all. They are little known and greatly feared.'

Here was the difficulty: Vidia felt powerful sexual desire which he thought he could satisfy only by buying sex, but was ashamed of his lust, an essential aspect of himself. 'A denial of opportunity is not a suppression of passion ... From this self-disgust the younger generation is free. For them, more sexually permissive than their elders, prostitution is an old-fashioned, unnecessary custom.' Writing days after his thirty-first birthday, he was caught somewhere between the older and younger generations, trapped in a circle of sexual frustration which spilt out in his troubled interaction with other people, and in his disapproval of himself for living a double life. 'Mightn't the problem raised by the Ward affair be simply that of a society still in certain quarters too much "under control"? ... Sex is an appetite. Seduction is a faculty like sprinting or pole-vaulting. We are not equally endowed, either with appetite or faculty.'[14]

Cricket was also on his mind in the summer of 1963. In a rare exercise in nostalgia, he wrote about the importance of the game in his early life. 'Cricket was one of the delights of my childhood in Trinidad in the 1940s.' He described a cricketer he admired, Lance Pierre, 'a tall, lean man with long hands attached to wrists that worked as if on hinges. Simply to see him flick a ball to a fielder, with a slight underhand movement, was enough.' In those days, he had resented the cricketers from Barbados who came each season to play at the Queen's Park Oval. 'No one who spoke with such an accent could be taken seriously, and it was hard to credit that men who looked so much like our own should suddenly, by their speech, betray their immeasurable difference. It was my especial xenophobia, and it was restricted to Barbadians.' In Britain, though, a new solidarity had emerged. He found himself on the same side as fellow West Indians, like the legendary Clyde Walcott. 'It never occurred to me then that one day I might find myself willing Walcott C. to a century.' Recently, though, hearing the fast bowler Wes Hall chatting outside a cricket ground, his old prejudice had returned. 'It was pure Barbadian ... I had imagined him like a Trinidadian, like one of *us*.'[15] To an East Indian audience at least, V.S. Naipaul was still positioning himself as a West Indian in 1963.

At the start of 1964, ethnic prejudice against immigrants from the

Indian subcontinent was in the news. In the London suburb of Southall, which had a growing Punjabi community, indigenous white residents were trying to stop the newcomers from buying properties, and in the Midlands town of Smethwick, a senior Labour politician looked set to lose an election over a racial issue. Smethwick was home to many subcontinental immigrants, and the local Conservatives were reported to be using the slogan, 'If you want a nigger for a neighbour, vote Liberal or Labour.' Unusually, Vidia made an explicit public statement of his own attitude towards race relations, developing the exclusivist Hindu thinking he had been brought up on by his parents and grandmother, and assuming his view would be shared by many in India.

'The whole world knows why there must be prejudice against Negroes. Negroes want to be integrated with whites; they want to sleep with white women; and they have immense sexual energy. Now here are the reasons why the Conservatives of Smethwick are pressing for discrimination against Indians and Pakistanis. Indians and Pakistanis do not want to be integrated; they do not want to marry white women . . . they do not even want to learn English.' He contrasted left-wing interest in overseas poverty with the reality of British prejudice. The charity Oxfam had held a public meeting in Trafalgar Square at which idealists lunched on bread and water, and a 'rescued' African baby was displayed to the media. 'Which is more important?' Naipaul asked. 'The Oxfam campaign, rescuing starving black babies, or the report in *The Times* that it is virtually impossible to "place" a child with African blood in an English adoptive home?' Much press coverage, he felt, was created by prurient reporters who thought 'race is as spicy as sex . . . And it is not surprising to find that as the volume of "correct" writing on race grows so does the number of "Europeans Only" and "No Coloured" notices in the "To Let" column of suburban newspapers.' A solution would come not from 'a magical change of heart' by the English, or 'the display of more fattened little Africans in Trafalgar Square', but from conspicuous success by immigrants. Failure was not an option: 'Prejudices are made meaningless by achievement, and racial prejudice is no exception.' He swept aside the pieties of the colonial freedom movements of the 1960s in favour of a muscular nationalism, and rejected the Nehruvian piety that India had a moral duty to give public guidance to other nations: 'The dignity of Indians everywhere depends on the power of India. The speeches of even the most respected politician will have less effect than the achievements of a scientist or an industrialist, for he is the man who produces a country's wealth, which is its power.'[16] It was a way of thinking that was to find favour in India at the end of the century, with V.S. Naipaul's encouragement.

By the time he wrote his final piece for the *Illustrated Weekly* at the end of 1964, Vidia was depressed about his own future in Britain. Since finishing *An Area of Darkness*, he had got stuck, and was not sure how best to proceed. 'A sad song's best for winter. It is a gloomy season anyway, in spite of all the lights in Regent Street. The newspapers and some politicians are screaming for black blood, and not only in the Congo.' He wrote of the optimism he had found in Nirad Chaudhuri's *A Passage to England*: 'It was an enthusiasm some of us who grew up in the days of Empire had; it overrode whatever we might have felt about Empire; it lay at the base of the old concept of the Common-wealth. If the Commonwealth has turned out to be fraudulent, too grand an idea for the country which sought to be its head, it is because this idea of England was, in truth, insubstantial.' There was a 'blinkered cosiness' among British novelists and playwrights. 'People like myself, unwilling or unable to enter these private cultural sports, have no business here.' Vidia had achieved some social success, but it gave him no sense of security. 'My acquaintance steadily widens, but I feel more and more like a visitor, no longer at ease.' London, in the aftermath of empire and of the Second World War, was parochial. 'The city has been generous to me. It has permitted me, an unknown and unprotected outsider, to acquire a niche of sorts.' Writers like himself who had migrated within the Commonwealth 'might be said to have become refugees, victims of the idea of London and England, of self-delusion and sentimentality, which are always dangerous, even at Christmas.'[17]

*

Around this time, Vidia began to see C.L.R. James, thirty years his senior and his father's former rival. Besides publishing *Minty Alley*, 'Nello' James had led an extraordinarily varied itinerant life after leaving Trinidad in 1932. He became a Marxist and political activist in England, wrote about cricket for the *Manchester Guardian*, promoted self-government for the West Indies, published a seminal study of the 1791 slave revolution in Haiti, *The Black Jacobins*, which influenced Eric Williams's thinking, encouraged civil disobedience against segregation in the USA until he was deported, visited Trotsky in Mexico to discuss racial politics, developed early theories of pan-Africanism and provided intellectual ballast back in

Trinidad to Eric Williams and the PNM in the late 1950s, although by now he had quarrelled with Williams. 'We had a little joke about C.L.R. James,' Vidia recalled. 'James said to Trotsky, "What can the Communist revolution do for the Negro?" and Trotsky answered, "You are asking the wrong question. You should ask, what can the Negro do for the Communist revolution?"'[18] Self-taught, well-read, a lover of Verdi and calypso, James was in some ways a typical Caribbean intellectual of his time: eclectic, spontaneous and a devotee of Western rationalism. By the 1980s, lionized internationally as an elderly pioneer of black studies even as he was attacked for his perceived Eurocentrism, James would baffle interviewers and researchers who failed to see the Queen's Royal College colonial tradition out of which he had emerged, or its distance from modern African and African-American experience.[19]

With Vidia, he had a friendly but sparring relationship, believing that as West Indian writers of different generations they served a common cause. Writing from Kashmir in early 1963, Vidia thanked 'Nello' for sending him a review of Derek Walcott's poems, *In a Green Night*, and added: 'I was glad to find in your quotations some of the Walcott poems I have always liked: As John to Patmos, Letter to a Painter. I have always felt about Walcott that here, in the most unexpected, purest way, we had a poet, someone of startling vision and muscular expression; some of his poems have never left me.' This was a substantial compliment, since the poems in question had been self-published by Walcott when he was eighteen. 'I am glad that Walcott has at last been published; it is the barest reward for a long devotion to his craft.' Vidia's occasional personal antagonism towards Walcott did not affect his critical judgement, at least as far as these early poems was concerned. Before slighting Walcott's later work in his memoir *A Writer's People*, Vidia wrote: 'Reading these poems in London in 1955, I thought I could understand how important Pushkin was to the Russians, doing for them what hadn't been done before. I put the Walcott as high as that.'[20]

James and Naipaul met, corresponded and went to watch cricket. In the *Illustrated Weekly of India* in the summer of 1963, Vidia described a journey to Birmingham with an unnamed man to watch a match. 'He has a background of Marxism and African nationalism; but cricket, the subject of his last book, remains his passion.' Vidia thought West Indians were reviving English cricket, since they had given 'in more ways than one, a new complexion to the game ... When a West Indian batsman gets his century cushions and mackintoshes will be thrown into the air; men will spontaneously dance.'[21] In *Encounter* magazine, he praised the originality of James's study of the culture of cricket in the West Indies, *Beyond a Boundary*, comparing himself to the author: 'we have both charmed ourselves away from Trinidad'.[22] In response, James wrote commending Vidia's plan to write on India. 'I can imagine no one doing it better and it will come very well from one who is himself one of the breeds without the law.'[23] This was the sort of racial coupling that Vidia disliked – James was alluding to Rudyard Kipling's poem 'Recessional', with its line about 'lesser breeds without the law'. In a follow-up letter, after debating various points in the review of *Beyond a Boundary*, James stressed the obligations of the Caribbean writer. Although he felt 'profoundly sympathetic' to the way Vidia wrote 'in human and subjective terms' about the countries he visited, he wondered whether it was right to do so 'unless we at the same time or within its context are penetrating into and showing our awareness of the terrible crises of Western civilization . . . I believe that effective as we are in stripping the wrappings from the underdeveloped countries, we will be more effective if, maybe not directly, but certainly we indicate that we are ready to strip or have already stripped the wrappings from Western civilization itself.'

James was hedging in this long letter, but he appeared to be saying that as a Marxist who knew that any country's problems were based on 'economic, social and political foundations', he did not think it wise for a writer to be too harsh on a developing country. It was an argument that would be put to Vidia many times over subsequent years: was it right for him, a former colonial subject, to write so unsentimentally and even cruelly about the failings of countries that were struggling to come to terms with independence? Why did he not turn a comparable searchlight on the more stable and prosperous countries of the West? 'Believe me, my dear Vidia, it is with no idea of propagandizing you . . .' James continued, although this was precisely what he was trying to do, and concluded, 'I wish I saw you more often. I am sure I would benefit by it and I don't think that I would either bore or annoy you.'[24] This was an odd tone for a man of James's seniority to be using, and may have reflected his reverence for Vidia's literary success in London. His correspondent, temperamentally averse to being steered by anyone, did not reply to the letter. Vidia's attitude to the questions James was raising had been settled in his own mind many years before. As he wrote to Pat when they were both twenty, he was the spectator, free of the emancipatory fire, who had no wish to reform the human race. He was the man without loyalties, whether to India, the West Indies or to anywhere else, who would write the truth as he saw it. Contrary to the depredations that would be launched against Vidia with increasing force over the coming decades, his moral axis was not white European culture, or pre-Islamic Hindu culture, or any other passing culture: it was internal, it was himself. When *An Area of Darkness* was published James remarked: 'Naipaul is saying what the whites want to say but dare not. They have put him up to it.'[25] C.L.R. James, as a person and as a type, remained on Vidia's mind, though it would be thirty years before he settled his score with him, and this time in fiction.

*

Looking outwards was one thing; looking inwards was another. Vidia's problem was that he had reached a climax of thought and creativity with the writing of *An Area of Darkness*, and was now stranded, despite the literary prestige he had amassed. 'I have been concentrating on occasional, money-making work since I came back – articles, broadcasting, book-reviews, etc,' he wrote to his mother in June 1963, 'and so far I have not been able to settle down to any book. I would like to do so though. To earn money Pat has gone back to teaching.'[26] He reviewed a book on Kipling for the *New Statesman*, and later a biography of James Bond's creator, Ian Fleming: 'I recognise in myself something of Fleming's own romantic attitude to the very successful and very rich.'[27] In a negative assessment of *The Burnt Ones* by the Australian writer Patrick White, he noted that there were now 'as many emergent literatures as there are emergent countries.' This had left him with an 'uncertainty about the function of the novel, and a conviction that the novel as we know it has done all that it can do and that new forms must be found.'[28] It was a theme that V.S. Naipaul would develop and return to over the next four decades, particularly when he was having trouble with his own writing, as he put together a thesis that the novel had become a worn-out form, unsuitable for capturing the complexity of modern, patchwork societies. His thinking would reach its apogee when he wrote in 1999, 'Literature is the sum of its discoveries . . . what is good is always what is new, in both form and content . . . The new novel gave nineteenth-century Europe a certain kind of news. The late twentieth century, surfeited with news, culturally far more confused, threatening again to be as full of tribal or folk movement as during the centuries of the Roman Empire, needs another kind of interpretation . . . It is a vanity of the age (and of commercial promotion) that the novel continues to be literature's final and highest expression.'[29]

Creatively blocked in 1963, he took out his anger on Britain: 'I don't know why people stay in this country.'[30] Two years earlier he had written to Francis, 'I would regard banishment from England as a death sentence.'[31] The price of housing was ridiculous, he told Ma, and 'the lower classes of this country are an absolute menace, animals eating far more than they deserve.' In the long term, he and Pat would need to buy a property of their own, but where would they get the money to pay a mortgage? 'Can you imagine buying a flat for [TT]$23,000 [£4,800]?' he asked. 'And that's cheap!' Ma was now supporting herself by managing the workers in her brother Simbhoo's quarry. Vidia asked her to tell him the exact time of his birth, so he could have his horoscope told by a man in India. He had some reasons for optimism. Deutsch was taking him more seriously, and had personally visited Nepaul Street. He even told Vidia that Ma was 'one of the three most distinguished people he had met in the West Indies. Eric Williams and Frank Collymore of Barbados were the others.'[32] The following year, the producer of the BBC arts show *Monitor*, Christopher Burstall, wrote to Vidia, 'I was delighted to see that Deutsch are bringing out a uniform edition – big deal! It only remains now for you to choose your own official biographer.'[33]

In July 1963 Vidia made a pair of programmes for the Third Programme about the calypsonian 'Sparrow', with extracts of music and vigorous commentary. Pa too had liked calypso, writing in praise of 'the Negro troubadour' in the *Trinidadian* magazine in 1934, tracing its origin back to the French settlers whose songs were incorporated into 'the carousals of the liberated slaves or bongo dancers'.[34] The audio recording of the programme is revealing. Vidia speaks in a clipped, dated BBC accent, saying 'clessical' for 'classical' and rounding his sentences with the voice of authority. When quoting Sparrow, Lord Invader or The Caresser on Edward VIII ('It's love, love alone, that force King Edward to leave the throne') he reverts to a Trinidadian accent. Most striking, is his infectious enthusiasm for the art of calypso.[35] The cover of the album *Spicy Sparrow* was later printed with the line: 'But where Naipaul can observe, from afar, without getting a speck of dust on his impeccable person, Sparrow, more tactile, sees life as one long boisterous contact sport.'[36]

By now, Vidia was consciously cutting away from West Indian circles in London, and many of the people he had known at *Caribbean Voices* were going home, or pursuing a future in Canada or the USA. Andrew Salkey's wife, Pat, thought 'Vidia wanted to disassociate himself. Gradually he lost all his friends, they all drifted away from him. Andrew and Vidia fell out – I don't want to say how, but Andrew was fed up with the way Vidia spoke to people. He could be quite insulting. We still did see a lot of Sam [Selvon], but Sam was a very loveable character. You couldn't say that of Vidia.'[37] But if he rejected his West Indian friends, who or what was to take their place? Pat was reticent, and hesitant to form friendships. She had no family or professional connections to help them. Vidia was more socially competent, but this was partly a performance, a man acting a necessary role. Might a section of British society accommodate them, and his interests and ambitions? Might there be space perhaps amongst the effortless upper classes, who had a tradition of lionizing bright young visitors from the colonies? Could Vidia go the same way as the Lucknow-born Mirza Abu Taleb Khan, who visited London in 1800 and wrote that 'the Nobility vied with each other in their attention to me'?[38] Rudranath Capildeo might meet Hugh Fraser at Marlborough House, but his nephew Vido would meet Fraser in his drawing room.

Francis Wyndham unlocked the door, introducing Vidia to Antonia Fraser, previously encountered as leader of the college haughties in the pages of the Oxford *Isis*, now the comely young wife of the prominent Conservative politician Hugh Fraser. 'I liked Antonia's wit,' Vidia said later, 'the way she talked, the way she made the world an interesting place.'[39] Through Antonia, Francis and Anthony Powell (his wife, Violet, was Antonia's aunt), Vidia gained access to a new group of privately educated, well-connected British people who were willing to accept him as a curiosity, particularly once he gained the imprimatur of literary success. In 1962, realizing the extent of his talent, Powell wrote in the *Daily Telegraph* that it was time for V.S. Naipaul to be recognized simply as 'this country's most talented and promising younger writer'.[40] Vidia seemed to become a member of this extended, interlocking group, but remained an inquiline. He met Lord and Lady Glenconner (who were wealthy from powdered bleach and Trinidad estates, connected to royalty and related to Francis Wyndham), their daughter Emma Tennant (a novelist and reluctant socialite, her world brilliantly evoked in the memoir *Girlitude*), Julian Jebb (a talker and book reviewer who dressed in garish clothes), Teresa ('Tizzie') and Peter Gatacre (who owned a castle in Holland), Hugh

Thomas (a rising historian) and his wife, Vanessa (the daughter of an eminent diplomat, Lord Gladwyn), and Edna O'Brien (a seductive Irish novelist).

Ten days younger than Vidia, Antonia came from a large and loquacious family, her father being an Oxford don turned Labour minister, and her mother a political activist. Many family members wrote books, although her brother Thomas Pakenham made the point, ' "We are not writers at all. We are talkers disguised as writers." '[41] Fragrant and resolute, Antonia led a vigorous life after leaving Oxford, worked in publishing, engaged in humanitarian activism, wrote a history of toys and produced six children. Her husband, Hugh, nearly fifteen years her senior, came from a prominent Scottish family and had fought in the Second World War with the Lovat Scouts, a regiment founded by his father. Antonia's first book told how to give a children's party, and gave no hint of greater things to come; she advised readers to play Hunt the Slipper, combine Bite Food and Bright Food and always obey the hostess: 'If she does not mention little Cuthbert on the invitation, do not jump to the conclusion that she just didn't know Charles had a younger brother.'[42] When her father inherited an obscure Irish peerage on the death of his brother in 1961, she gained the nominal right to put the word 'lady' in front of her name, a right she pursued with vigour. Vidia admired Lady Antonia's social ease, and her ability to bring together discrete social, political and literary spheres; her interest in politics and in people was not partisan.

At Hugh and Antonia's large, late Georgian house in Campden Hill Square, Vidia, and occasionally Pat, would soon meet politicians, writers, actors, socialites: Jackie Kennedy, Iain Macleod, Anna Massey, Rebecca West, Michael Holroyd, Enoch Powell, Germaine Greer. His first invitation was to dine with Dr Eric Williams. 'We had to have Williams to dinner, my husband being at the Colonial Office,' Antonia recalled. 'Hugh and Vanessa Thomas came, and Williams and Pat and Vidia. We were really friendly from that moment onwards.' V.S. Naipaul and The Doc, both of Queen's Royal College and the University of Oxford via a colonial scholarship, failed smartly to discuss *The Middle Passage* or anything of consequence when they met in this setting. Antonia could see no social distinction between herself, Vidia and Pat: 'After all, we had all been at Oxford together [and] the Sixties wasn't a time of social gaps ... The house was full of colonial people.' Her only worry was when on another occasion 'a terribly rude woman insisted on coming for a drink, to get a book signed, and she wouldn't speak to him. It was really awful. I think it was colour prejudice. I was appalled, and Vidia was just so cool. When she went I said, "I'm frightfully sorry, it's awful." He said, "The only upsetting thing is if you were upset, Antonia." Very elegant.'[43] Vidia pocketed the insult. And kept it in his pocket.

From 1963 until the early 1970s, Lady Antonia gave Vidia significant hospitality and friendship. Her house in Campden Hill Square provided him with a remote idea of security and familiarity. Adopting a manner last encountered in his correspondence with his pen pal, 'my dear Beverly', he sent her occasional letters from diverse and distant locations: India, New York, Kenya, Wiltshire, even a residential hotel on the edge of London. His tone was new, social, chatty, politely flirtatious; 'Vidia N.' commended a 'relaxing and delightful party' Antonia had given, and seeing her picture in the glossies wrote: 'Lovely Vogue, just bought. This issue also tells of a new fish restaurant at 73, Baker Street called Hook, Line & Sinker. Shall we try this before Ravi Shankar?'[44] They listened to the sitarist in concert, Antonia heavily pregnant with her son Damian. In April 1967, Vidia posted her a green silk sari and a note from Delhi: 'it worried me whether the colour was the colour you said you didn't want . . . I chose it with the advice of an Indian actress whose knowledge of these things one must defer to.'[45] Sensing no competition, he even gave her literary encouragement. In early 1969 Antonia published her first biography, of Mary, Queen of Scots. She told Vidia of editorial battles, of being 'put into the ring with a girl . . . aged 22, like bull and matador, to argue out each individual correction.'[46] He responded jauntily, 'Still, what a lovely letter you made . . . all good things in writing do come out of suffering; but remember at least that you have here an appreciative audience. And, really, knowing the young, and knowing the "editor"-figure, I imagine that [she] was probably just plain infuriating.' When a finished copy reached him, he even sent a telegram: 'YOUR BEAUTIFUL ENVIABLE BOOK THANKS CONGRATULATIONS VIDIA.'[47] Antonia thanked him for 'one of the nicest letters I have ever had in my life', adding that her husband Hugh was taken up with the Biafra crisis, and she had been 'terribly terribly pleased, and often extraordinarily touched by the reception of MARY'.[48] With *Mary, Queen of Scots*, Antonia found her feet: she went on to write big, popular, well-researched narrative histories and biographies, often focusing on monarchs or women in history.

For Vidia, this was a new style of friendship. A role was being shown to him, as friend, as swain, as object of intellectual admiration, and he enjoyed it, despite a degree of uncertainty about what was expected from him. Once the relationship had been formed in this way, it stuck, and when in later years he failed signally to return Antonia's hospitality, she ignored the signs of rejection. Like the colonial governor's wife in *The Mystic Masseur*, 'The more disconcerting the man or woman, the more she was interested, the more she was charming.'[49] Swiftly, then, Vidia was taken up by a whole new world. When he was awarded the Hawthornden Prize, Tony Powell wrote 'Dear Viddy' a letter which ended, 'Violet, of course, joins me in these congratulations and sends her love to you both.'[50] Lord Glenconner ('Glenc' to his friends) became Vidia's patron, impressed by his performance at the dinner table. Francis Wyndham was the conduit: he informed Vidia that the peer, through one of his companies, was willing to give him an unsecured loan to buy a house. 'I don't know why he did it,' Vidia said later. 'I was very moved, and I remained very attached to his memory. It was a very grand thing to do. Mark you — a very wealthy man and a wealthy company.'[51] According to Francis, Lady Glenconner was the impetus behind the patronage: 'She admired his books. She was a great friend of Cyril Connolly, Anthony Powell and other writers. Glenc arranged good terms. I saw it as a friend doing a favour.'[52] Using an Oxford contemporary, Michael Carey, as his solicitor, Vidia bought a flat in Sydenham Hill in south London at a cost of £3,500, repayable to Tennants Estates at 5½ per cent over fifteen years. The flat overlooked Sydenham woods, and appeared to be the answer to all his and Pat's problems. When the purchase went through in late 1963, Carey told Vidia, 'This would be the appropriate time to write to Lord Glenconner, if you haven't done so.'[53]

Soon, though, there were difficulties. On their first night together in the flat, he and Pat noticed the main road outside was busy. With both of them sensitive to external disturbance, the noise of the traffic became an obsession and a terminal complaint. The sound of the noise and the prospect of the noise became, somehow, the reason why a book would not come to Vidia. He tried everything he could think of to quell the disturbance: complaining to the council, writing to the builder of the flat, George Wimpey & Co., installing a soundproof window that turned out not to be soundproof. After a few tormented months, they decided to move again. The chosen destination, after much searching and toing and froing, was a house on three floors in Stockwell Park Crescent, to the north of Brixton. It was a mixed-up area, a white working-class part of south London that had become mildly West Indian and was now enjoying the beginnings of an influx of bohemians and middle-class professionals; an actor lived next door, and next door to the actor lived a Jamaican family. The Sydenham Hill flat was sold for its purchase price and, using a fresh soft loan from Tennants Estates, Vidia paid £7,200 for the house in Stockwell and sent in builders to renovate and decorate the property. In the meantime, he and Pat moved to a prim residential hotel in Blackheath. 'We were there for four or five months. It was terrible. Terrible. I felt virtually homeless. We could do up only a part of the house. There was no money.'[54] Dom Moraes took him out to lunch for an interview with the *Illustrated Weekly*. When Vidia moved to the new property in early 1965, he drew a picture in a letter to Ma depicting the two bedrooms, the dining room, 'library' and 'drawing room'. An Irish cleaner, Mrs Bannon, was engaged to look after the house when they were away.

Shiva arrived in England, having won a place at Univ. It was another phenomenal achievement for the Naipaul and Capildeo clan. The *Trinidad Daily Mirror* reported that he 'speaks fluently of Shakespeare and Plato, but is tongue-tied and shy when talking about practical things like the birds and the bees. The 1964 Island Scholarship Winner is – you guessed it – the younger brother of internationally famous author Vidia . . . Can Trinidad ever hope to produce another family as brilliant as the Naipauls? Shiva is only the latest in a long string of scholarship winners. Vidia was the first, in 1949 . . . Then came sister Kamla . . . Another sister, Savi, won an Island Scholarship in 1955 – and turned it down to get married. Not to mention Dr Capildeo himself (uncle of the clan), who won the Island Scholarship of 1938!'[55]

Shiva wrote later that his childhood had been 'dominated and darkened' by the need to get the scholarship: it 'was less an educational process . . . than a prolonged struggle, ruthlessly prosecuted, for survival.' Like his elder brother, he saw Trinidad as a dead end: 'I was escaping from the island whose narrow confines and tropical sameness had always seemed like a prison.'[56] Psychologically, Shiva was in the same fragile position Vidia had been in when he went to Oxford, although without the reassuring epistolary presence of a loving father. Standing above him was the banyan tree, in whose shade nothing could grow: Vido. From his earliest days, Shiva had been made aware that he had to match his elder brother's achievement, and wrote later, 'No one ever quite lives up to the demands of an Absolute.'[57] After a few tense days at the residential hotel in Blackheath, where he was instructed in table manners and treated with paternal concern and irritation by Vidia, Shiva moved on. Francis saw him at the hotel: 'I remember Shiva there, very young, saying he wanted to be a writer. Vidia adored Shiva, but was very heavy-handed with him.'[58] Seeking a room in a boarding house in Earls Court, Shiva was depressed to discover that he was regarded as 'coloured', and accommodation was hard to find in London. He wrote home to Ma that Vido was 'living a very disorganised and financially wasteful life. He has bought this house, which has been standing unoccupied for over three months. While he stays in a hotel grumbling and waiting for the architect to put in an appearance. Money is his main topic of conversation. He is always complaining how poor he is and at the same time living extravagantly. He has gone and bought himself an electric toothbrush, and now insists that I do the same. Most amusing!'[59]

Although Vidia's financial position had improved when he secured a post at the BBC back in 1955, he and Pat remained steeped in poverty. By the late 1950s, he was earning on average £373 gross a year, or around £5,800 in today's terms. In the 1960s, even while his literary reputation rose, his income stalled; he was climbing a long ladder, and was still on the lower rungs. It never occurred to him to be anything other than a writer. Between 1960 and 1969, his gross income after expenses (which he claimed frugally and scrupulously for things such as postage, stationery, typing fees and publications) averaged £1,963 a year, or around £25,400 in today's terms. The levels of personal taxation in the 1960s meant that much of this money never reached him. In 1969 he was saved by an Arts Council bursary of £3,500 secured by Francis Wyndham and Angus Wilson. In 1970, his income sank as low as £773, and he was forced to draw on money he had made by selling the Stockwell house.[60] Vidia thought in retrospect: 'It was a bad time. Tears lay just below the surface. You would not meet a more diligent tiller or harvester in the field of literature than me. I don't know how I did it. There was no market in America for colonial writing until after Vietnam. One was in a bind. If Christopher Glenconner hadn't helped me I don't know what would have happened.'[61] In the summer of 1964, he and Pat were invited to stay with Glenc and his family at their house 'Glen', a castellated Victorian mansion in Scotland.

Vidia blamed his financial failure in part on his literary agent, Graham Watson, who was a less than ideal representative for him. Nineteen years his senior, the son of a rich sardine shipper from Newcastle, Watson had taken part in the D-Day landings before joining the literary agency Curtis Brown. A shrewd and respected agent with connections in New York, he represented authors including Harold Macmillan, Gore Vidal and Bernard Levin.[62] Watson admired Vidia's talent but never realized his wider

potential, considering him a well-reviewed ethnic writer with dim commercial prospects. Vidia particularly resented the way in which Watson's other
authors were serialized in the Sunday papers while he was not. Looking
back, he called him 'a very bad agent' who 'kept me in poverty for at least
ten years . . . He did me down as a job of work. He was more concerned
with pushing authors like Hammond Innes.'⁶³ Watson's colleague at the
agency who dealt with film and television, Dick Odgers, regarded this as a
misrepresentation: 'Vidia was a difficult bugger, there's no doubt about
that, but Graham had a very high regard for him. He thought he was a
great writer.'⁶⁴

Over Christmas 1964, stuck in the genteel confines of the Blackheath
hotel, Vidia had a break: 'The waitress comes to the dining room and says
there is a telephone call for you. Before I lifted the phone, I felt there was
some element of rescue. It was a man involved with a filmmaker, asking if
I would come to New York and do a script. They wanted an original
story, something related to *Miguel Street*. They liked the outline I did, and
paid some more money for me to expand it. I went down to Trinidad and
stayed with my sister Savi and wrote what became *A Flag on the Island* . . .
I got about £5,000 in the end from that deal.'⁶⁵ He was put up in the St
Regis Hotel in New York and, a little overwhelmed by the hospitality,
produced an outline. The director Lionel Rogosin, maker of the quasi-
documentary *On the Bowery*, told Vidia that the film was to include
American stars, and possibly Frank Sinatra. Vidia wrote to Pat that 'the
only idea I have been able to come up with is that of having a character
who, because of his resemblance to Sinatra, begins to ape his mannerisms
and is known as Sinatra. They are delighted with the idea.' The film
people took him to a nightclub in Harlem, where he was astonished by the
music and the dancing. Outside, the whites were insulted and 'Even I,
hoping to pass, came in for a little abuse when, looking for a taxi, I
momentarily was alone.' He flew to Trinidad to develop the script. When
it was finished, he told Pat: 'It is a hideous thing, not really destined to
appear in my complete works, but the stenographer helped. I only feel that
if I do this in the future I should ask for five times the money, to make up
for the sense of violation.'⁶⁶

A Flag on the Island never became a film, and was not successful as a
story, but it enabled Vidia to make a creative breakthrough. Visitors arrive
on a ship at a Caribbean island; the dialogue is staccato and baffling; it is
not clear what is going on; there are brothels and drunkenness; Mr
Blackwhite is H.J.B. White, a writer whose most successful work with the

tourists and foreign foundations is *I Hate You*. Vidia's move forward came
not from the setting or the content, but from the discovery that he might
write elliptically, and communicate more through a story that is not
perfectly comprehended by the reader. The early drafts of *A Flag on the
Island* are in fact more powerful than the published version. A list of
characters, typed by the stenographer given the spelling, gives a sense of
the story: 'THE NARRATOR: An American now a salesman in South
America who first knew the island during the war where he was stationed
at one of the bases. From time to time he come back for his own big
purging debouch. SELMA: His occasional partner. Portuguese-Chinese-
African. She was born in Arima, came to Port of Spain during the war,
and there she remained steadily rising in respectability. Mr HENRY. African.
Butcher in 1939; a Broffle keeper in 1942; and night club owner in 1946;
and impresario in 1956; a legislature in 1960.'[67]

Soon after he finished *A Flag on the Island*, Vidia wrote the opening
pages of what would become *The Mimic Men*, a novel about a postcolonial
politician, Ralph Singh, told through flashbacks as he stays in exile in a
residential hotel in England. Much of the material is tangential: how Singh
made a fortune speculating in land, how his father became a kind of holy
man after leading a failed uprising. Singh's upbringing on the Caribbean
island of Isabella and his experience of trying to govern a people
shipwrecked by slavery or indenture opens up a barrage of enquiry into
the way in which the world was developing after the Second World War.
Does a postcolonial government rule its people, or does real power still
reside overseas? 'Industrialization, in territories like ours, seems to be a
process of filling imported tubes and tins with various imported substances,'
he says.[68] In its form and in its concerns, *The Mimic Men* was new work
for V.S. Naipaul. He used moments from his schooldays, from his
marriage, from brothels (and the resultant self-loathing), from his social
encounters in Trinidad in the 1960s and from his new experiences of the
English upper class, but the novel was a subtle, circuitous, imaginative
departure, in which even the racial insults are oblique: 'The Niger is a
tributary of that Seine.'[69] The risk of this approach, Graham Greene
commented in the *Observer*, was 'a new obscurity, a style which falls more
and more like a net curtain between author and reader.'[70]

Working on the film script at Savi and Mel's house in Trinidad in 1965,
Vidia was surprised by 'the tremendous adulation that one receives from
ordinary people – waiters recognise me and have read one's books! – this
sort of fame is poisonous ... The more personal sadness is the state of

Sati's children. The boy and girl are grotesquely fat because their father feeds them ceaselessly from morning till night.' He was worried by Nepaul Street. 'It is a sad, almost derelict house. My mother is out all day at the quarry and apart from her there is only Nelly and a deaf old servant,' he told Pat in an affectionate letter.[71] He gave a provocative interview to Derek Walcott at the *Guardian*, illustrated with a photograph of the two men seated across a low table, squaring up to each other. Vidia denounced Trinidad as a 'very sinister place' inhabited by 'insecure and unfulfilled' people. 'Also, manners here are not very good.' Would he ever support a political cause? His answer was revealing, linking Nazism to apartheid: 'I think there have really been only two good causes within recent times: against Hitler and possibly in South Africa, which represents the absolute triumph of a European proletarian culture.' A long question about local pride in his achievement and the respective position of writers and cricketers yielded the tart response: 'I am not a cricketer.'[72] His combative stance would develop into a standard interview mode. He wrote to Pat, 'Derek Walcott has been extremely charming this trip. He is more relaxed and while I think this is because he has at last been published, he tells me that I was insecure and aggressive in 1960. Hard to believe . . . CLR James [who was then under surveillance and house arrest by Eric Williams for encouraging trade union activism] wrote a long attack on me in the Guardian; he referred to me throughout by my first name! . . . Ronald Bryden, a fellow Trinidadian, was here for Carnival and Derek Walcott gave a little party for the two of us.'[73] He arranged to meet Pat in Lisbon after the end of the school term for a holiday.

Back in London, Vidia was stuck. The idea that would become *The Mimic Men* was half-formed. He went on *Writer's World*, produced by a young Melvyn Bragg, being interviewed about 'The Writer in Exile' in Stockwell Park Crescent. Appearing on radio and television shows or writing film scripts and reviews was not what Vidia wanted to be doing. He pondered his future; news reached him that his old colleague Edgar Mittelholzer had burned himself to death, on purpose, supposedly because his career as a writer was on the slide. At the back of Vidia's mind was a strong desire to see Africa. Having visited India, the land of his forefathers, he felt a need to observe and understand the ancestral home of his fellow Trinidadians. When an invitation came from the Farfield Foundation to be writer-in-residence at Makerere University in Uganda, he accepted. 'I wanted to be on the move again . . . It was a very fruitful visit. It gave me *In a Free State* and the background for *A Bend in the River*.'[74] Lady Antonia

Fraser invited him to Campden Hill Square to meet the former governor of Uganda, Sir Andrew Cohen, and Francis Wyndham supplied an introduction to the local ruler, the Kabaka of Buganda. Pat gave up her teaching job to accompany him to Africa. Vidia said years later in an interview: 'Just as I have a feeling for Indian peasant movements or Indian working movements, so I have some kind of feeling for Africa. I wasn't going to Africa cold – or with any sexual intent.'[75]

Stockwell Park Crescent was let out to Mira and Amar, who was studying radiation oncology in London. Mira was still on good terms with her brother, but found him increasingly short-tempered. He seemed to have a growing sense of entitlement, borrowed perhaps from his peer group. One evening at dinner Pat served an undercooked roast chicken, and 'Vido jumped up and shouted, "My God Pat, the chicken is bleeding. It is not cooked. The chicken is raw", and so on. And Pat began to weep.'[76] Vidia was still eating chicken, eggs and fish when they took his fancy; more a Pork Brahmin than a pukka vegetarian, his concern was that he should be served food which in some way distinguished him. Francis noticed rising tension: 'Pat was scrupulous, reserved, she always told the truth. Over the years Vidia would say something reactionary and she never got used to it. That would irritate him, and it made them rather a nightmare couple, but it was one of the things I liked about her.'[77] When Mira expressed a wish to give Ma a holiday in England, Vidia forbade it as a piece of pointless extravagance: 'Vido said, "I don't want my mother to step foot in this house. I do not want her presence in this house." He had a book of rules for us. Basically what we had to do and what we mustn't do, to do with cleaning and scrubbing. We were not to touch the walls, and make sure that our little daughter who was only fourteen months didn't touch anything ... Then he called us up a couple of days before the move saying he would like to ask us for a little more money and we were really appalled. We were a young couple, counting the pounds.'[78] Embarrassed to tell Ma about Vido's ban, Mira kept her visit a secret, until Ma let the cat out of the bag in a letter to Pat: 'I must thank you and Vido for staying in your home ... and the rest of the children on the financial side to make my holiday a big success in my life the first one in fifty-three years.' She was glad to have helped Shiva, who had already run up capacious debts at Oxford: 'I see that he had shoes, socks, underpants and all clothes that he needed for summer before I left.'[79]

CHAPTER FIFTEEN

THE SCHINTSKY METHOD

VIDIA'S FIRST IMPRESSION on arrival in Kampala in early 1966 was that he had made a dreadful mistake. There was no house waiting for him and Pat, and he was expected to join the teaching staff at Makerere. Their first fortnight was spent saving money by staying in the spare room of a senior lecturer in the English department, David Cook. According to a colleague, 'David was the classic gay white liberal – "African writing is so wonderful" – that kind of thing. He wore silly shirts in African cloth ... a little too tight [and] had an African boyfriend.'[1] The Farfield Foundation was rumoured to be a CIA front organization fighting Cold War cultural battles against communist influence in Africa. Vidia made it clear to Makerere University and to the Farfield Foundation that being a writer-in-residence meant just that to him: he would sit in his residence and write. He adopted an almost Gandhian policy of non-cooperation: 'I never went to my office. I couldn't be disturbed too much. I was writing in my bungalow, and if they asked me to teach, or to talk, I paid no attention.'[2] This stubbornness was not mere provocation. After two years of false starts, he had begun writing the moment he reached Uganda. *The Mimic Men* would turn out to be an intricate, inventive, many-layered book, written unexpectedly fast. In earlier drafts, Vidia had tried to shift the characters back and forth across the Atlantic.[3] Now, as often happens to a writer, he saw a simple solution to what had seemed an insurmountable problem: he would use a first-person narrator, who could carry the direction of the story with him. In his attitudes and ironic perception, in his awkward confessions and the conviction he has been wounded by history, Ralph Singh contained much of Vidia. Singh's own tone was directly inspired by the letter sent by Dr Winston Mahabir, Trinidad's minister for education, inviting Vidia to return to the island on a scholarship in 1960.[4]

In a hot, noisy, freshly built campus bungalow on a slope, he incorporated the atmosphere of dislocation into the developing narrative, and by June was able to send a manuscript to Diana Athill. Her reply sounded more impressed than delighted: 'I only finished reading THE MIMIC MEN three minutes ago, so it hasn't simmered down enough for comment, really – but I must quickly say: brilliant.' It was 'horribly disturbing. It gave me an almost physical sense of vertigo, as though I were going to start a migraine.' Vidia replied, 'It is a horrible book' and might 'alienate some people who liked my earlier work ... Many thanks for reading and writing so promptly. Very considerate, very generous, very Diana.' While *The Mimic Men* awaited publication, André Deutsch brought out a version of *A Flag on the Island* as a novella, abetted by some short stories Vidia had written in Kashmir and for *Caribbean Voices*. It was dedicated to Diana. Vidia berated her boss: 'André: couldn't you, in your address book, put a little note on the page which carries all my various addresses, saying that they are not to be divulged? I have begged and pleaded so often.' Deutsch swiftly responded, 'I swear we are not guilty. I have given a rule here that if the closest member of your family were to ask, we would not yield.'⁵ Vidia fired off an angry letter to Graham Watson of Curtis Brown, complaining he was failing to secure foreign translation rights for his books. Watson responded that Vidia was lucky to be published at all overseas. 'An author doesn't basically get paid for his reputation, he gets paid according to the amount of money which he can earn for himself and his publisher.'⁶ This – the idea that authors should receive performance-related pay based on sales rather than status – was not something he wanted to hear, now or later.

At Makerere, conscious he had put on weight, Vidia took up running. 'At four-thirty every afternoon,' he informed Antonia Fraser, 'a young American and myself, each giving moral support to the other, run once around the sports ground, walk round it twice, run once, and so on, until we drop. It was a system we worked out when we began: a system of weakness. But sports experts have noticed us and informed us now that we are following the Schintsky method, devised quite recently by some trainer in Scandinavia. So we no longer feel embarrassed.'⁷ The young American, a teacher at the university named Paul Theroux, remembered the running. Vidia had 'a manual called The Canadian 5BX Plan, which was a handbook of exercises for the Canadian military. He called the (mainly English) expats "infies" (for inferiors) ... and he decided that they were not only morally and intellectually and socially inferior, but physical wrecks. I can't remember whose idea it was, but we began running around the track at Makerere – an awful torture in the equatorial heat. He also practised bowling on the cricket pitch. He had no stamina for running and wasn't much of a bowler, but he had a lot of enthusiasm for punishing himself to prove he wasn't an "infy". He loved the fact that only Africans and Indians were practising on the sports field (soccer, cricket, running), no expats. Afterwards we always went for tea. He refused the biscuits and cakes while I dived in. The exercise gave me a tremendous craving for sugar. I always tried to resist, but Vidia would say, "No, eat them. The body knows what it wants. Obey the body," as I tucked into another.'[8]

Uganda was newly independent, with King Freddie, the Kabaka of Buganda, as a figurehead monarch and Milton Obote as prime minister. Optimism among Europeans and Americans about Africa as the emerging continent was high, and Makerere University seemed like a beacon of progress in the region, staffed largely by white expatriates who felt proud to be building a new nation while atoning for the wrongs of the colonial era. Vidia was an anomaly. Fascinated by Africa – its scale, its landscape, its art, its traditions, its people – he saw it through Trinidadian eyes as the mystical homeland of his compatriots who had been undone by the middle passage. Above all, it frightened him. As Ralph Singh wrote in *The Mimic Men*: 'Hate oppression; fear the oppressed.'[9] Vidia believed that many of his white colleagues at Makerere were playing out private fantasies of their own, and would be undone. He lacked their instant status among black Africans, and was at once aware of the antipathy towards the Indian traders and shopkeepers who controlled parts of the East African economy. Despite wearing sturdy shoes and a bush hat, Vidia looked like one of them.

With Pat, he travelled widely, to Nairobi and Eldoret in Kenya, to rural Uganda and Kigezi on the Congo and Rwandan border. He took an interest in the various clans of the Baganda people, the followers of the Kabaka. Later he flew to Dar es Salaam in Tanzania to give a lecture at the university, and the students walked out en masse; the combative intellectual style he had learned at QRC did not go down well. In Nairobi, crossing the street, he ran into Jagdish Sondhi (from the C&CA course in Slough) and he and Pat spent a month staying with his parents on the coast at Mombasa, an experience that would provide material for *A Bend in the River*. The Sondhis' house overlooked a creek and had a squash court built by Jagdish, since he was not allowed into the British club. 'We both grew up in colonies', said

Jagdish Sondhi, 'where the Englishman was the master, so it was natural we should have a love-hate relationship. When my brother asked Vidia who the best writer in the English language was, he said, "I am, of course."' In Jagdish's copy of *An Area of Darkness*, Vidia wrote: 'This, the book which I consider my best: a book written out of pain and concern; less about India than about people like yourselves and myself.' He recalled Vidia's anxiety about the fate of local Indians with the rise of African nationalism: 'He sent a ten-page dossier to the Indian High Commission, but nothing came of it.'[10]

In the debate over Africa's future, as the wind of change blew ever harder, Vidia found himself, as always, on nobody's side. 'It greatly helps in an understanding of the place', he wrote to Antonia, 'if one starts from the premiss that Africans are a primitive people – it is the one thing Andrew Cohen left out that day at your place – and then moves on to the obscenity of their dispossession in the Twentieth Century by a truly second-rate crowd, who after fifty years have no artist or writer to show, no culture or civilisation, who talk endlessly about their "characters" and who constantly compare themselves, to their own advantage, with primitive people. Side-taking is impossible; the situation is obscene.'[11] While he was completing *The Mimic Men* at the Kaptagat Arms, a hotel on the edge of the Rift Valley in Kenya, Milton Obote staged a bloody coup (which would in time lead to the rule of Idi Amin) and made himself president of Uganda. Vidia was infuriated by the 'castrated' response of the British press towards this 'absolute savage massacre ... People use too many big words about Africa: the problems of this continent – I am serious – are semantic. To give you an example. The young tribesmen are alleged to be "interested in writing". Do you know what this means? It means that they are literally interested in taking up a pen and making marks on paper ... words like "feudal", "democratic", "modern", "reactionary" are utterly without meaning, but continue to be misleadingly used. When the [*New*] *Statesman* talks about a Ugandan politician being "modern & forward-looking" it is talking absolute nonsense. The place is overrun by anthropologists & sociologists who ... interpret in a series of alien concepts.'[12] To Diana he wrote, 'We were here in Kenya when the trouble started. I believe they have slaughtered 1,000–2,000 people. African armies are frightfully good against civilians.'[13]

The scale of East Africa's political upheaval reminded him of what he had seen in the West Indies. He knew that the fragility of state institutions and the comparative lack of an indigenous trained and educated elite in most of Africa meant that the capacity for destruction and lawlessness was much greater. To Francis, who was making a reputation for himself as an editor at the *Sunday Times* colour magazine, with his contacts ranging from Jean Rhys and Bruce Chatwin to David Bailey and the Kray twins, Vidia wrote: 'It is unbearable to see once again – in spite of the lessons of so many African countries – African politicians fashioning the very instruments by which they and their countries are in the end destroyed.'[14] Pat, contemplating a career as a journalist rather than as a teacher, attended parliament in Kampala and wrote a protracted article about the situation in Uganda. Francis thought it 'full of interesting observations' but 'a bit inconclusive' and suggested, 'Why don't you send it to the Guardian?' The features editor there responded in automatic language: 'Dear Miss Hale, Thank you very much, but we have a man visiting Uganda at the moment.'[15]

The places and people Vidia encountered during his nine months in Africa gave him a plethora of literary material. David Cook would be cruelly rendered as Bobby in *In a Free State*. Murray Carlin, a white-haired lecturer at Makerere who had written the play *Not Now, Sweet Desdemona*, provided the spark for Roche in *Guerrillas*, a man who appears to stand for something but has betrayed himself. When Vidia began the book in 1973, Pat wrote in her diary: 'He recalls Murray Carlin and his poor wife >she killed herself< sitting on the step of their dreadful bungalow and their rather common daughters, expelled from South Africa for his liberal stance, discovering where Vidia stood and showing him his (anti-African, anti-negro) cartoons. "Secretively?" I say. Yes.'[16] Jim de Vere Allen, a bright, rugged history lecturer, became a friend and was later used in another book; as Vidia noted on some archive papers: 'Jim Allen (Kenya-born and bred, but of simplish Australian background) is the original of De Groot in *A Way in the World*.'[17] The owner of the Kaptagat Arms, Major Bobby Tyers, would appear as the colonel in *In a Free State*. The displaced international characters and restricted campus setting of Makerere would be used in both *In a Free State* and *A Bend in the River*. With its uncomprehending, colliding inhabitants, all following their own cultural ideas, this became Naipauland.

In July, Pat returned to England. During his last weeks in Africa, Vidia travelled to Rwanda for several days with Paul Theroux, and went to Dar es Salaam to lecture. Theroux was twenty-five years old, an enthusiastic former Peace Corps volunteer with a Nigerian girlfriend named Comfort Iruoje and ambitions to become a writer himself. Vidia liked his application, his love of books and his brash self-confidence. Theroux was at once in awe of Vidia, happy to play the part of bag-carrier and disciple, and Vidia responded to the admiration by playing up to his own caricature as someone who would do and say outrageous things. They shared a willingness to upset the academic and social conventions of Makerere. Theroux noted the way that Vidia would be funny and provocative, teasing and twitting people for his own enjoyment, or to obtain information, and using archaic place names such as 'the Gold Coast' in order to outrage liberal sentiment; asked to judge a literary competition, he awarded only a third prize. Vidia gave Paul Theroux advice about writing, offered to help him find a publisher and invited him to stay when he came to London.

In Tanzania, in a Proustian moment, Vidia developed asthma for the first time in years. Feeling low, he was distracted by entertainment arranged by Hugh Fraser (who had stepped down as 'secretary of state for air' with the arrival of Harold Wilson's Labour government). Hugh had cabled a diplomat friend in Dar es Salaam to tell him of Vidia's presence. 'The sequel,' Vidia wrote to Antonia:

> a Sunday morning in my USAID house, a morning as blank as only mornings in Dar es Salaam can be, a man in shorts bursting through my kitchen, whipping off his dark glasses, smiling broadly, extending a hand and saying, 'I'm Skinner.' I later had dinner with him. An American negro homosexual, his middle-aged English mate; a ferociously liberal couple; and the Skinners. Delicious caviar, and then the negro, to my astonishment, without any provocation from anyone, decides to do his James Baldwin act.
> 'I'm sitting here with you people, but I think I should let you know that I really hate you.'
> Mrs Liberal drops her fork with pleasure; her eyes widen. 'But you have so many white friends.' Playing the game, being in the now slightly passé intellectual swim. Coaxing, dying to hear more.
> 'Darling, I have hundreds of white friends.'
> And the delight that this arouses is the delight of people thinking: how lucky we are, participating, even in Dar es Salaam.

I ask: 'Why do you say this, here?'

And of course I nearly spoil the party. You don't need to come to Africa to know what it is like. You can sit in London and make it all up.[18]

*

When *The Mimic Men* was published, V.S. Naipaul's critical reputation moved up a notch. In the *Financial Times*, his friend Julian Jebb declared it 'one of the four or five best novels in English since the war.'[19] Angus Wilson noticed the book's ambiguities: 'A Conradian irony suffuses all the events, speeches and the thoughts of this book – and suffuses them to great effect – but the final viewpoint remains obscure.'[20] In the *New York Review of Books*, V.S. Pritchett wrote: 'Among the younger English novelists Mr V.S. Naipaul is a virtuoso. A brilliant chameleon from the Caribbean, the descendant of Hindu immigrants, he has grown into the English novel with more lasting assurance than almost all contemporaries in the West Indies or Africa who are in the same case. This has not been achieved by intelligence and education alone ... His advantage is that he shares with many English novelists natural and serious feeling for the fantasy life of his characters.'[21] Karl Miller wrote in the *Kenyon Review* that Naipaul was 'someone with conservative leanings who nonetheless writes movingly about the poor and aspiring, a compassionate man who is also fastidious and severe.'[22] Despite the book's pessimism, Eric Williams, blooded now by office, wrote in his 1970 study of Caribbean history *From Columbus to Castro*: 'V.S. Naipaul's description of West Indians as "mimic men" is harsh, but true ... psychological dependence leads to an ever-growing economic and cultural dependence on the outside world. Fragmentation is intensified in the process.'[23]

A remarkable letter was sent to Vidia by Michael Manley, the son of the Jamaican premier, who would himself become prime minister. Known as a trades union activist and a vociferous anti-imperialist, Manley thought *The Mimic Men* 'a masterpiece in itself. I wanted you to know that I found it both beautiful and exciting, if a little terrifying. The handling of the theme of disorder set off echoes of recognition even as it sounded warning bells ... I wish there was a greater tradition of reading in the Caribbean society and among the politicians who are its corollary ... If you are ever passing through Jamaica and have a moment, let me know.'[24] Michael's mother, the sculptor Edna Manley, had written previously to Vidia: 'I am very impressed. I have lived through some of what you write about.' She commented that her husband had made pencil notes all over the book. 'So you see some people do love you.'[25] Vidia consistently resisted invitations and blandishments from West Indian government ministers during these years, anxious not to go the same way as C.L.R. James. His distance from any political movement was part of his presentation of himself as a displaced, unaffiliated, unCaribbean writer. It would not be until the 1990s, and this time in India, that he would tentatively allow himself to be co-opted by politicians.

The British literary establishment, conscious of the implosion of the British empire and anxious to appease the unpredictable meteor that was flying in its wake, awarded Vidia another significant prize: the W.H. Smith Award, presented by the chairman of the Arts Council, Lord Goodman. Vidia had become a fixture on the London literary scene, but somehow at an angle to it, the object of discomfited reverence rather than love; as he later remarked to an interviewer, 'I'm the kind of writer that people think other people are reading.'[26] Michael Frayn, later a playwright of distinction but at this point a budding novelist, wrote to him: 'I'm still digesting The Mimic Men. I think it's a great triumph – a most extraordinary book, quite unique, and totally <u>itself</u> in every page ... I'm appalled by the great freight of disgust it bears.'[27] Aware of the rising tide of praise, Graham Watson decided that André Deutsch was not doing enough to promote Vidia, and pressed him to improve distribution to bookshops and to put advertisements 'in the "intellectual" papers like Encounter ... Vidia is now firmly in the class where there will be a continuing interest in anything he writes.'[28] Although Diana Athill disagreed, Francis Wyndham took the view in retrospect that Vidia was failed by his publisher: 'Vidia was absolutely right about Deutsch treating him badly.'[29]

Back in Stockwell Park Crescent in October 1966, Vidia apologized to Ralph Ironman for being out of touch. 'I find I have fallen into a new type of itinerant life. It works like this: a few months in London, a few months abroad ... Next March I go off to Trinidad and the United States to write a book for an American publisher.'[30] The book was to be a study of Port of Spain, but when it was completed, the editors at Little, Brown were disappointed not to receive something like a guidebook. Bob Gottlieb of Knopf picked up the manuscript in the USA, and André Deutsch was happy to have a narrative history of Trinidad based on primary research. For many months, Pat had sat in the archives of the British Library and Vidia had attempted to give shape to an unknown story. Francis thought it 'the most devastating <u>and</u> illuminating study of colonialism ever written –

such an unbelievably squalid muddle of a story.'[31] Diana proposed possible titles: *Dusty El Dorado*, *Empires in their Brains*, *The Mountain of Diamond*. Vidia thought of *The Port of the Spaniards: An Adventure*. It was not a history book or a travel book: 'The adventure is, basically, the discovery and desecration of one part of the New World,' he wrote to Diana.[32]

The Loss of El Dorado anticipated the sort of history that would become popular thirty years later. Vidia took an obscure dot on the map and reconstructed its past from scarce sources. In the British Library, he found a document in Spanish which revealed the origin of the name 'Chaguanas': a letter from the Spanish king ordering the extermination of an Amerindian tribe, the Chaguanes. In his Nobel lecture, Naipaul said: 'The thought came to me in the Museum that I was the first person since 1625 to whom that letter of the king of Spain had a real meaning.'[33] Unlike British historians, depending securely on their predecessors, he was flying blind, trying to establish the history of the defeated, the disappeared, the unrecorded. The result was a complex account of adventurers like Francisco de Miranda and Walter Raleigh, and more than this a revelation of the terrible, degraded cruelty of Trinidad's early past: Amerindian rulers burned and chained by Spaniards, Negroes castrated and kept alive by Caribs for food, a young girl tortured, slaves eating dirt to kill themselves, ears clipped as a punishment; poisoning, witchcraft, flogging, revolt. Bob Gottlieb told Vidia that although it had sold only 3,000 copies in the USA, he was 'convinced that *The Loss of El Dorado* is a very important as well as very beautiful book, and that it will endure.'[34] In a review in the *Guardian*, Richard Gott commented that it was 'nothing less than a description of the formation of an entire culture'.[35] Vidia's preoccupation with the void at the heart of Trinidad, the idea that it was a remote island where each person was an interloper come to experiment in human cruelty, came true now: he was producing evidence for his prejudice. Small wonder that his final line referred to the erection of a metal sign over the gates of Port of Spain jail in 1812: 'PRO REGE ET LEGE: For King and Law'.[36] He loved order, hated lawlessness. This was too narrow an approach for the time or for John Updike. 'Never ask an artist to do the ordinary,' he wrote in the *New Yorker*. 'But in viewing an entire hemisphere as a corrupted dream, Naipaul dissolves what realities there were. *The Loss of El Dorado* rests upon an unexamined assumption, of metropolitan superiority.'[37]

The Loss of El Dorado was a prodigious piece of research and recreation, but it was not the sort of book that marked a way forward for Vidia, any more than *Mr Stone and the Knights Companion* had been. Although his literary reputation remained high and his upper-class patrons continued to encourage him, the four years that followed his return from Africa in 1966 were to be the worst of his career. They were a time of floundering, professional exhaustion and fear about money. Nearing forty, Vidia had intimations that his best work might be behind him. He was profoundly frustrated by his lack of sexual fulfilment, despising himself for resorting to brothel sex; he did not know how to convert his singular background and recent experience into new fiction; he mistrusted the social and political movements of the time: the creative avant-garde seemed to him an irrelevant indulgence, and he detested hippies, yippies, beatniks, free schools, flower power, Black Power, flag burning, hair growing, sit-ins, be-ins, teach-ins and love-ins. The sharp Naipauline vision that had arisen from his family background and sound colonial education now appeared to be at odds with current thinking, particularly about what was coming to be called the Third World. In 1969 in *Literature and Ideology*, H.B. Synge started what was to become a critical trend by calling V.S. Naipaul 'a despicable lackey of neo-colonialism and imperialism'.[38]

Angered by the prevailing mood, Vidia wrote an article for the dying *Saturday Evening Post* which would later cause him embarassment, called 'What's Wrong With Being a Snob?'

> It is too late, of course. The cause is all but lost . . . I write from a country where, in the midst of a decay that is social as well as economic, the romance of the 'classless' new society is ceaselessly offered as compensation. There are classless sports nowadays, classless clothes, classless youths. When groups of these classless youths, products of a welfare state, stage a riot in a seaside town, it is said that society is failing them. There is dishonesty in this . . . Entertainers from the slums replaced the Queen as a cause for national pride. In the hysteria of self-congratulation, the new greed expressed itself most hideously in the persecution of immigrants from the former Empire. Yesterday's slogan on the wall – SEND NIGGERS HOME – was embodied in today's White Paper on limiting immigration. Pop entertainment, pop politics: politicians were no longer in a position to lead; they could only follow.[39]

He wondered whether he was in the right place, or whether he and Pat might do better abroad. The fresh vegetables, open skies and sense of wonder in Africa were often on his mind. Jim Allen wrote from Makerere to say he had 'engaged a Mututsi version of Jeeves to take the place of Zozima (who has suddenly dipped into a drunken and rather dirty old age) early next year. Didas looks like a black Oberammergau Christ, cooks superb French food and will drive me around when I feel weak.'[40]

Much of Vidia's best work during this time turned out to be journalism, writing for Francis Wyndham at the *Sunday Times Magazine*, and for John Anstey, the famously unmanageable editor of its rival, the *Telegraph Magazine*. Both publications were stretching public expectations of taste and design, using colour photographs in a way that had not been done before in the mainstream press. When Vidia wrote a *Sunday Times* feature on 'Mauritius: The Overcrowded Barracoon', the cover showed a nearly naked white woman kneeling on a beach, and the pictures accompanying the text were taken by the photojournalist Don McCullin. Ideas for stories were similarly imaginative. Anstey would fire off random suggestions to Vidia for articles: 'What, in fact, is the Brazilian idea of "freedom" – political or otherwise?' was one question that needed to be answered, but never was. 'Would you be interested in writing an article about Norman Mailer and his current plan to run for Mayor?' he asked in 1969, and Vidia said yes.[41] Journalists on both magazines were notorious for their extravagance, and some other freelances were baffled that V.S. Naipaul's expenses claims would come in below rather than above the limit; they thought he was setting a bad example. He filed from India, France, the Caribbean, New York, Honduras, and was paid around £400 a time, a reasonable fee, negotiated by his agent, but the scale of his travel and research meant his annual earnings remained low. In 1968, at Graham Greene's request, he went to Antibes and wrote a bored, passively aggressive interview with the sixty-three-year-old author, whose recent work he had disliked.

Early in 1967 he flew to India to write 'A Second Visit', a pessimistic and limited article for the *Telegraph Magazine*, before going on to Japan to interview a businessman who had nonsensical plans to end the Vietnam War. From the Imperial Hotel in New Delhi, he had written to Diana: 'I really like living in hotels. I like the temporariness, the mercenary services, the absence of responsibility, the anonymity, the scope for complaint. And even a noisy hotel is such a good place for working.'[42] Later, worrying about money, he had moved to stay with the Jhabvalas. Pat was in urgent need of £100 to pay a tax bill: would he send a cheque? She told him she needed clothes. 'I do not have anything respectable to wear during the day that covers me up entirely. There is still some wear in my blue and white summer coat (two years old) but it is not good enough if one wants to look good . . . if there is such a thing as sex appeal, dreadful phrase . . . I suppose ordinary vanity might lead me to believe I possessed it in some small measure . . . Please do not think that my letters are exactly what I plan to write. I have long conversations with you on buses or in queues that never get reproduced.' Vidia had written back from Bombay: 'There must be something wrong with the long mirror in this hotel room. It throws back an awful, unbelievable dwarf-like reflection, which I do not recognize but which I fear might even be true.' Ruth Jhabvala told Pat in a letter how much she, Jhab and their children had enjoyed having Vidia to stay. 'Even the most nervous of our dogs, who that week were biting people's ankles right and left, showed him nothing but affection.'[43] A meeting with Zul Vellani was a failure: 'He was icy. He was very cold with me.'[44]

Judging the Duff Cooper Prize that year, Vidia fixed its award to Nirad C. Chaudhuri, the Bengali anglophile whose *Autobiography of an Unknown Indian* had earlier impressed him. Ruth thought Chaudhuri clever and imaginative, 'but alas, alas, often, alas especially in success, a particularly silly old man.'[45] She had a point; before coming to England to collect the award, Chaudhuri had instructed Vidia: 'My special purpose in writing is to make you my "security man" against certain undesirable attentions.' No Indian writers 'unless they are respectable' should be permitted to approach him. He was nervous of being insulted. 'Most especially I am thinking of that little half-caste rat Dom Moraes, who if he comes near me will get a whipping as sure as anything.'[46] In the event, all Nirad Babu had to contend with was dinner with Pat alone in Stockwell, since Vidia was away in India. 'Mr C. is a very methodical man,' she reported, 'but had talked so much that although we started eating at 7 had not finished his second course and did not want to leave at all.'[47] When Chaudhuri died in 1999, Vidia was asked to write his obituary by the Royal Society of Literature, and produced a slanderous and malign text, daring its commissioners to reject it:

> Nirad Chaudhuri was an old fool . . . In 1966 I worked very hard to persuade my fellow judges to give Chaudhuri the Duff Cooper prize – not, of course, for *The Continent of Circe*, but for the *Autobiography*.

John Julius Norwich [Cooper's son] told me later that Chaudhuri
... spent some part of his prize on 'male toiletries'. This was
unexpected enough. I had no idea then that the prize was going to
lead to the man settling in England and setting himself up as a
clown in Oxford for his last thirty years.[48]

The chairman of the society, Michael Holroyd, had to write a diplomatic
letter to V. S. Naipaul declining to publish.

Pat gave an unlikely supper party over Easter 1967 for Shiva, his
girlfriend Jenny, Anthony Powell's son John and Eleanor, fresh from 'a
hockey festival in Ramsgate'. (The previous year Eleanor had hitch-
hiked to the soccer World Cup at Wembley to see the England victory,
paying a tout £4 for a 10 shilling ticket.) Shiva drank keenly through
the evening. 'He is going to pay for one of the three bottles of wine
consumed,' Pat told Vidia. She took Eleanor to see Antonioni's *Blow-
Up*, which she described in uncool terms as a 'semi-documentary on the
swinging London scene with breathtaking shots of Dulwich Park ...
Catherine Tennant, the centrepiece of a smart drugtaking party (looking
very pretty) rolling a marijuana cigarette and giving the famous
Catherine giggle. Catherine Pakenham was there too.'[49] Later in the
year they went to Holland to stay in Peter and Teresa Gatacre's moated
castle, and to Denmark to visit the Ironmans. 'We are looking forward
very much to seeing Mary & yourself and the children after 8 years!!'
Vidia told Ralph.[50] After the trip, he wrote to Paul Theroux, 'Every
little village has its Porno shop; there are advertisements in the
newspapers for Porno models – they prefer "pairs", in whatever
permutations. To me now the very word "Scandinavian" is a horror
word, full of ice and death and sullen coitus. I prefer vice myself, and
like it to remain a little vicious.'[51]

Ruth Jhabvala corresponded occasionally with Vidia. 'Why Holland?' she enquired, when told of the holiday. 'My aunt, who lived in
Amsterdam (till the Germans took her away to Auschwitz), always used
to say that Dutch isn't a language, it's a disease of the throat.'[52] Five
years his senior, slight and shy but with a strong personality, Ruth
shared Vidia's asthma, incisive literary perception, need for privacy and
sense of displacement. Her novels such as *The Householder*, with their
phoney gurus and deluded Westerners, led many readers at the time to
assume she herself was Indian. Ruth had moved to Delhi in the 1950s
after marrying Jhab, a witty architect and lecturer who would later be

immortalized as the acerbic Yamdoot, messenger of the god of death, in Arundhati Roy and Pradip Krishen's cult movie *In Which Annie Gives it Those Ones*. She had begun the collaboration with Ismail Merchant and James Ivory that would lead to many films and her winning an Academy Award for the screenplay of *A Room with a View*.

With the Indian economy in a poor state and the Congress party imploding, she felt glum, writing to Vidia, 'I cannot tell you what a difference it makes, how encouraging it is in the midst of one's own loneliness and isolation, to have someone talk such brilliant sense about this place, after all the lies, all the jargon mouthed by people either too naive or too stupid or too crafty to look and talk straight . . . you are the only other person I know who becomes physically affected by being in uncongenial company: as when we came home from the intellectual evening at Khushwant Singh's.' She wrote of her frustrations with 20th Century Fox and the world of film, and advised Vidia to make sure he secured his position in advance if he ever wrote a script. 'I have long ago come to the conclusion that the world owes us first-class hotel accommodation and such things – that it's our natural right, to be provided for us without question. Not that I've ever got it, but that doesn't alter my case.' In August she wrote a pointed description of a party given 'for David Frost who was passing through Delhi to do something for Oxfam.' The guests, 'the usual younger-married-set bores from Defence Colony', had under 'an easy flow of wine and very good food' given the impression that they were 'young and bright and gay' despite not having 'a spontaneous thought or feeling between them'.[53]

Through this period, Shiva was a constant worry to Vidia. Rather than take a holiday job, he had spent the summer vacation of 1966 in Turkey and been relieved of his possessions on a train in Yugoslavia on the way home. 'It was not really my fault though,' Shiva wrote to Ma. 'I need a hundred pounds! Could you possibly get it for me?'[54] In November the Dean of Univ wrote to Vidia saying he had run up debts of nearly £300; his annual grant from the Trinidad government was £850. A bookshop had served a court order against him for taking books on credit; his landlady had thrown him out; he had started to study Chinese, for no apparent reason; his family needed to find £200 at once. Vidia wrote to Savi, racially humiliated on their brother's behalf, 'You must realise that Shiva has grown so dirty that he stinks, quite literally. He launders nothing; he changes nothing; he never wears a tie or a collar but that pullover which gives off the ripest of sweat-

and-dirt smells. His face, with the long, very long hair falling over both cheeks, is perpetually oily. He is known to everyone in the College, students, dons and college servants, as an Indian who stinks.'[55] Vidia went to Oxford to negotiate with the college authorities. Shiva failed to meet him, and when they ran into each other in the street, Vidia exploded. Peter Bayley witnessed the scene: 'My god, Vidia behaved like a burra saheb, he tore strips off him, he said, "What the devil do you mean, you were supposed to meet me at two o'clock in the [porter's] lodge!" I was staggered. I didn't realize that he had that kind of power in him ... Shiva wasn't good news really. He was very tall and was a smoker, cannabis and stuff. He fancied himself with girls, and was very much thronged by them.'[56]

The following week, Shiva bounced a cheque and Vidia returned to Oxford and asked his brother to come back to London with him. He understood that Shiva was going through an emotional breakdown, and it reminded him of his own collapse at Oxford, and of Pa's mental torment. 'We are not going to expect much if he comes here,' Pat wrote to Ma. 'I'll make the meals as nice as I can and try to give him a regular life. Vidia will continue the hard work of persuading him to keep accounts.'[57] Two days before Christmas, Shiva wrote to their mother from Stockwell Park Crescent, 'Vido has been excessively kind to me, as well as Pat. Please be reassured that everything is under control. I would like to think the year of depression and disaster is finished ... I have also cut my hair.'[58] Vidia felt a mixture of love, rage and worry in dealing with Shiva. He hoped each crisis would be the last, but knew it would not be. In June 1967, Shiva fell on his feet; he married Jenny Stuart, who gave up her university degree to take a job as a secretary and support them. Francis Wyndham remembered: 'Vidia was furious when Shiva got engaged to an English girl, and didn't want to go to the wedding.'[59] Vidia did not want to be maritally emulated, least of all by his brother.

*

Over Christmas 1966, Stockwell paid host not only to Shiva, but to Paul Theroux. Vidia tried to introduce him to figures in literary London, taking him to dinner with Edna O'Brien and tea with David Pryce-Jones. Pryce-Jones remembered, 'I had never met Paul Theroux at that point and Vidia suddenly whispered in my year, "He's from the CIA, you know." And I was very impressed by that.' (Vidia was joking.) During tea, the host made the mistake of playing a record that he had obtained free with a copy of *Private Eye*. 'It was a spoof Betjeman parody in which somebody was sitting on the lavatory with their trousers down and it was very funny. I could see Vidia's face twisted with dismay at this scatological joke . . . He minded very much. He didn't like it. That's a side of human life that doesn't appear in Vidia's writing at all. The fastidious side of Vidia would never accept that kind of coarseness. I greatly regretted playing this little record.'[60] The atmosphere became awkward and the two guests left abruptly. Paul recalled, 'Vidia was conflicted about David Pryce-Jones, sometimes calling him "that epicene young man" but much admiring his marrying a rich woman.'[61]

From Makerere, Paul had been writing often to Vidia: 'You were "typically English" to some people and "typically Trinidadian" to others; while to still others you were a "settler-type". None of the people who expressed these opinions knew you, or had met you.'[62] He told tales he thought would go down well, echoing Vidia's prejudices. Last weekend, 'I was staying with an infy headmaster . . . He lives in the two-storey house of the former provincial commissioner, has a huge garden (very much like Kaptagat), drives a Mercedes, says bloody, drinks a lot and has nothing to say.'[63] A colleague was depicted 'doodling in his office with the shades drawn while his sable breth'ren sat with their feet up . . . sipping and complaining.'[64] Paul was energetic, flattering, eager to please, seeking advice, offering racist jokes and tidbits of praise. 'This is a compliment on your fine review in the most recent *New Statesman*.'[65] When he read that Vidia had won the W.H. Smith Award, he wrote: 'The whole picture is of a fiercely intelligent Mandarin Hindu of anywhere from 35 to 42 years of age . . . I don't mean to burden you with a letter. I was pleased to see that you had such a good press over the award, and wanted to tell you that I don't think it could have happened to a nicer guy.'[66] As for himself, 'I would be very happy to meet a decent, tolerant, intelligent girl that isn't fat.'[67] Soon he found one, Anne Castle, an Oxford graduate and his future wife: 'I am also in love with a very pretty girl; she is English and is one of the best typists I've ever laid eyes on.'[68] Later, Theroux came to regret the tone of his letters: 'I was writing to Vidia in his language, because he has a special language and the closer you are to him, the more you see how funny this language is . . . I conceded more than I should have to his vision because I knew more than he did about Africa but he knew more about the colonial process and he knew more about Indians. I began to see it through his eyes a lot, I think somewhat to my detriment.'[69]

In his first letter from England, Vidia wrote of money and agents. 'East Africa seems very far away and shabby and unimportant, dangerous in some ways for the thinking person. But I don't wish to go over old ground.'[70] Later, he confirmed the invitation to visit for Christmas. 'I haven't had a real winter for some little time and I am thinking of spending a week or so in some bleak part of Scotland. Bathing in the fresh frosty air. Would you like that when you are here?'[71] In the end they remained in London, but when Paul overstayed his welcome at Stockwell Park Crescent, Vidia withdrew. Throughout his stay, Paul had found him troubled, melancholic and moody. A holiday friendship, freely given in the atmosphere of Makerere, was altering. Pat stepped in two months later to explain Vidia's failure to answer letters: 'We have both been very busy but the truth is we are both abominable correspondents.'[72]

In February 1967, while on his way to India, Vidia sent Paul a sarcastic letter of dismissal on the crested writing paper of the Bristol Hotel in Beirut, a missive designed to brush off a more sensitive man. He attacked his use of language as inaccurate, claimed his classical knowledge was imperfect and said Diana Athill's decision to turn down his novel was right. He wrote a cruelly dismissive line to a would-be novelist: 'I am happy that your journalistic ventures thrive; in this and in your other endeavours I wish you the best.'[73] If Vidia had been sent a similar letter, with his colonial alertness to social slights, he would have backed off. For Paul, a more open and abrasive personality who had grown up in Medford, Massachusetts and been roughened by four years in Africa, it was no more than a bad-tempered letter, characteristic in its peculiar way of Vidia. Vidia claimed to be surprised that Paul did not comprehend the insult: 'After he left in 1966, he was an absolute bore. I wrote a very ironical letter to him thinking this would put an end to those letters . . . But it never did. It was not important, I think. Probably these things helped to give one a reputation . . . Theroux didn't know what he thought about anything. He had no views. It's as though he didn't know he was in Africa. But he pestered me with letters, long letters being written to me every two or three weeks at a certain time.'[74] At the start, the relationship had hints of symbiosis. Each man provided information to the other, and Vidia enjoyed having a willing follower, a young aspiring writer who at times amused him and would do his bidding. Soon, though, Vidia became bored. Up to 1972, Paul wrote him fifty-four letters and received thirty-two in response; from 1973 to 1980, Paul wrote Vidia twenty-two letters and received no replies, except by telephone, but this seems not to have dented his faith in the friendship. He saw Vidia's behaviour as a mark of his eccentric talent, rather than as rudeness, indifference or rejection.

Letter after letter came from Makerere. 'How can one make any lasting comment on a place so valueless?' Paul asked. He was using precisely the phrases – and worse – for which he would later reprimand Vidia in his 1998 memoir *Sir Vidia's Shadow*. 'I don't see how one can write about this race; you succeeded ... because they were people to you, not Negroes.' Paul had been promoted: 'Until the post is Africanized I am Principal of the Adult Studies Centre ... There are reliable people under me ordering bananas etc ... I am doing exercises now (push-ups, sit-ups etc). If you have a moment would you describe what exercises you do?'[75] Paul complained of 'the infy crowd' and tried to out-Vidia Vidia, repeating stale jokes: 'A banker from Tanzania tells me that there is a new joke there among the out-going managers. When they see an Af. they say, "There goes our new branch manager." '[76] In the autumn of 1967, despite being in Uganda, he pleaded to be allowed to find his would-be mentor a place to stay in America. 'Please do drop me a note – just one line – telling me what your departure dates are, and if there is anything (I repeat) I can do to make your stay in the US comfortable please let me know. I could find out prices of cars, hotels etc.'[77] He despatched 'a gift I bought you in Nigeria, a briefcase which I thought might be useful to either your or Pat.'[78] Vidia was entertained by the adulation, and responded smartly with a request for an ivory cigarette holder, or 'a bulky smooth yellow' meerschaum pipe, and apologized for forgetting to thank for the briefcase. 'How awful it must have been for you to hear nothing...'[79] As Paul observed when he came to London, Vidia was happy to go out for meals when they met, but made no attempt to pay the bill.

Despite some irritation, Vidia gave succour, telling Paul there were 'few writers whose letters are as good as yours. I find them as nice as those of Scott Fitzgerald.'[80] Anne Theroux, now married to Paul, realized how important Vidia was to her husband. She found Vidia 'rather frightening and shocking at first, but he was never unpleasant to me: on the contrary, he could be charming.' Pat was 'by no means a drudge ... I admired her ability to engage intellectually with Vidia.'[81] Later that year the Theroux family moved to Singapore, where Paul had a teaching post at the university. He continued to send letters, no longer signed 'Love, Paul' but 'Best wishes, Paul'. Each time he was snubbed or ignored, he came back a little keener, a little more anxious to please, creating expectations that were liable to be dashed. He reported on life in Singapore:

'The brothels are quick, cold places staffed by teenagers from Indonesia and managed by secret societies.'[82] He was writing a stream of stories and novels while working full-time: *Girls at Play*, *Sinning With Annie*, *Jungle Lovers*, his fecundity impressing Vidia. Again and again, he offered his services: 'I wonder if there is any item of furniture you would like made here and sent ... If there is something you'd like, please send a little sketch, with measurements, and we will take care of the rest.'[83] Vidia's responses were cursory, and when he complained of being tired from work, Paul responded: 'that feeling of exhaustion you get from finishing a book is a sure sign of your genius, a feeling only a real writer can experience.'[84]

In his spare time, Paul went to the library and read Vidia's old book reviews from the *New Statesman*. He had decided to write a book about him. 'Would it gripe you terribly? ... I am just running this idea up the flag-pole, I suppose, and waiting for a salute.'[85] Vidia agreed, and signposted a specific vision of himself which Paul endorsed and ran with. In a shrewd piece of self-representation, which would be repeated by others, V.S. Naipaul presented himself as unprecedented, underprivileged, alienated. 'Think of it like this: imagine the despair to which the barefoot colonial is reduced when, wanting to write, and reading the pattern books of Tolstoy, Balzac et al, he looks at his own world and discovers that it almost doesn't exist.' Unlike an American, he had been born with 'no prospects in journalism, State Department, General Motors. No, one is a colonial as well, with all the spiritual and economic limitations and all the spiritual blight.' His privacy should be respected: 'I opened myself to you at various times without reserve, and sometimes with flippancy, which may not always be understood.'[86] Paul continued to write letters. He knew he was being intrusive, and ended, though it was only the second day of May 1970, 'Don't, please, answer this letter until July, or later if you wish.'[87] Ceaselessly prolific, he typed out extracts from books he thought might interest Vidia, reported the birth of 'another son, Louis', described hiking in North Borneo and sent some stories he had written for *Playboy*. He had sent a letter to the magazine too: 'The claim is that they have the best writers in the world and I wrote to the editor saying if this was true why had nothing by VSN been printed so far?'[88] The more enthusiastic he became, the further Vidia stepped back, while at the same time offering little prods of encouragement.

CHAPTER SIXTEEN

THE WORLD

BY 1968, VIDIA WAS falling apart. His finances were in a mess. *The Loss of El Dorado* was unwieldy and unfinished. He was sick of England, and feeling unwell. Then he twisted his ankle. New restrictions on immigration had left Pat wondering whether they might not do better to start over, in Canada. In April, Enoch Powell declared that like the Roman he saw the River Tiber foaming with much blood. Writing to Ironman in faraway Denmark in the same month, Vidia could be frank. He was 'staggered' by the British attitude to the effective expulsion of Kenya's Asians: 'I thought the Lord Chancellor's speech in the Lords one of the most shocking things I had ever read. And I felt . . . that a very special chaos was coming to England; I also felt that I could no longer stay here. We decided to leave. We have virtually sold our house; and as soon as my book is finished, will be on our way. A very distressing decision – all my adult life has been spent here, all my intellectual life and all my friends are here . . . I have been totally impoverished by the Inland Revenue.'[1] They had friends to abandon now, and none of them was West Indian: Antonia, Francis, Tony and other literary sorts, Julian Jebb, working at the new television channel BBC2 and recovering from a tight upper-class Roman Catholic upbringing, David Pryce-Jones, formerly of Eton and Oxford and now an upcoming novelist and literary editor, Tizzie Gatacre, thin and beautiful and well connected, Tony's son Tristram Powell, directing a television quiz show *Take It or Leave It*, and his wife, Virginia, a painter. Tristram and Virginia, who were shortly to have their first baby, agreed to purchase Stockwell Park Crescent.

Vidia and Pat needed somewhere to go. They moved from place to place, cadging weeks here and there, staying with acquaintances like Michael Astor at his house in Sandwich. A few years earlier, Vidia had been sitting at dinner beside an exuberant Italian, the daughter of an opera impresario from Bari. She was Marisa Masters, and when she began to praise *A House for Mr Biswas* and he said he was the author, she was ecstatic. 'For me he was a little kind of God. He was very badly dressed, and didn't have much money, and I gave him a lift home.'[2] Marisa was married to Lindsay Masters, who with Michael Heseltine had built the magazine publishing company Haymarket. She gave Vidia and Pat the run of her house in Kensington while she and Lindsay were on holiday in Spain. The Naipauls were scrupulous guests. Vidia wrote, 'We used the telephone a lot. <u>Ten</u> local calls & one long-distance to Yeovil. To cover laundry and telephone we are leaving 16/3. The whisky is to welcome you back & to thank you for your splendid, trusting generosity.'[3]

Knowing that Vidia wanted to finish writing *The Loss of El Dorado*, Hugh and Antonia Fraser lent him their country house on a private island in the middle of the River Beauly in the north of Scotland, Eilean Aigas. 'I have been working for the last six weeks or so in a rather fine Scottish house, in a library in which the taste of the 30's and 40's is, as it were, deep frozen,' Vidia reported grandly to Paul Theroux.[4] 'I rented a house in Scotland (for the peace & absolute quiet),' he told Ralph Ironman.[5] Fraser family retainers looked after him; he paid ten shillings a day towards the cost of the central heating. Pat found the house gloomy, and was glad when they left. At first, Antonia's relationship had been primarily with Vidia, but a friendship had grown with Pat, who responded to her warmth and admired her ability to manage such a full life: researching books, running lovers, giving parties, having children. Despite their mismatch, Antonia never made Pat feel awkward about lacking such things herself. Pat would write admiringly of her friend's appearance on television quiz shows, and praise her books; Antonia had 'multiple talents,' and *Mary, Queen of Scots* was 'the sort of visual history we have been thirsting for: court ceremonial and dress (wonderful wardrobe detail), the sense of place and the long rides on horseback.' Pat's presentation of herself in their correspondence was invariably self-deprecating. Lying in the summer sun, while Vidia sought to avoid it, was described as, 'trying to bring about the annual miracle, the transformation of my skin from slug to putty.' She would apologize for not writing sooner, or more fully. Her life with Vidia was presented in an endearing, conspiratorial way: he was 'growing that beard again'.

Shortly after staying at Eilean Aigas in 1968, Pat dared to raise an unmentionable subject with Antonia: her childlessness. Might her worldly, fecund friend be able to recommend a gynaecologist? This was at a time before medical advances in fertility treatment; IVF had yet to be invented, and a woman who had trouble getting pregnant was viewed as barren and abnormal. Pat took the blame, and felt the failure; it was a subject she could not discuss freely with anyone, including Vidia. Until they had this conversation, Antonia had assumed, like all their other friends, that the Naipauls had made a choice never to have children. She suggested that Pat might see her own gynaecologist, Mr John Blaikley of Guy's Hospital. 'He was very kind,' Pat reported in a letter from Edna O'Brien's house, where they were now staying. 'It cheered me up enormously that, as far as he could tell, I was normal. Other tests take 2–3 months at clinics which would not be convenient in our present itinerant state.' Pat was thirty-six years old and had never conceived a child, yet she allowed itinerance to provide her with an excuse not to take tests. She made a passive choice to leave her future to fate, or to nature, and focused her maternal instincts on her increasingly cranky and infantilized husband. The letter to Antonia concluded: 'As Vidia said, he is in hiding until he finishes the book. I leave Edna's when there is someone to look after him.'[6]

By November, the book was complete and Vidia and Pat were ready to depart. He intended to go to the Caribbean, then Central America, then the USA, then Canada. Most unusually, he decided to appear on *The World at One* on BBC radio and make an explicitly political complaint about the plight of immigrants and ethnic minorities. He spoke of a 'deepening resentment' around the world about the way in which people were treated in Britain. 'It has been really rather astonishing that in the past year immigrants have been subjected to an unparalleled vilification from Members of Parliament and the press . . . Another aspect of the last year which has been so distressing is that there has not been a single spokesman for these immigrants from among themselves. Immigrants are just discussed as though they don't exist, as though they are objects outside in the street . . . It is extremely foolish and extremely short-sighted.'[7]

Vidia had some commissions from the *Telegraph Magazine*, and reserve money from the sale of the house. In a farewell interview to the *Times*, he dismissed Britain's politicians as 'shabby, sharp dealers', said its historians were 'indulging in these self-laudatory exercises' and denied any connection to Lamming, Selvon or Barry Reckord. The interviewer noted that V.S. Naipaul was living in a hotel in central London. 'It is a transit camp, murkily entered by a moving escalator, carrying numberless foreign nationals getting their first experience of Britain, wanly lit by inset pictures of limbo hotels around the world.'[8] Statelessness was a condition imposed on Vidia when he left Trinidad in 1950. Now it was something he sought, from a position of experience. Creatively and personally, he needed something fresh.

The dislocation of the following years would lead to a new perspective and to extraordinary books such as *In a Free State*. Displacement gave Vidia a distinct view of the world. At this time, there was no other writer of stature who was analysing societies in this detached, global way. V.S. Naipaul was of everywhere and of nowhere, rooted in an English literary tradition, but outside it. His attitudes and outlook had been formed by his family background, his colonial education and his experiences of Britain and beyond in the 1950s and 1960s: his instincts and prejudices were intact, but his eyes were wide open, missing nothing. 'It looks easy,' he said later, 'the writer coming and finishing his childhood material and then naturally moving on to England. It was very hard to do, and you will find that many people from far-away countries insist on writing about the far-away country. Their view never amplifies to take in the new experiences that they have actually been living ... People are at their most creative when things are very disturbed.'[9]

*

In December he wrote to Diana Athill from Kamla's house in Jamaica. 'I came here two days ago after about 10 days in St Kitts − Anguilla, a situation that looks funny from the outside but is deadly serious. Interesting, though, because it catches the Negro-colonial tragedy in a most manageable, Lilliputian way. Now the job of reducing it to two 3000-word articles. I find that I enjoy this job of foreign correspondent and have a way of finding out − not cunning: it is just the same as in ordinary conversation: genuine interest always brings out the best in people.'[10] As violence unfolded in Jamaica, he wrote, 'A little note about the black power nonsense and the shootings here. Protest after protest, enemy after enemy: this is what passes for political thought in these primitive societies ... It is a stupid and vicious movement here, Black Power, besides of course being imitative and totally irrelevant in a black country with a black government ... Jamaican Black Power, like all other types of racialism, which appear to be brave and defiant, operates of course in a situation of security.'[11] The articles that followed were merciless and brilliant: 'Papa and the Power Set', about two political rivals fighting over the tiny island of St Kitts, and 'The Shipwrecked Six Thousand', about Anguilla in the days before tourism: 'The island has its own prophet, Judge Gumbs, Brother George Gumbs (Prophet), as he signs his messages to the new local weekly. He is not without honour; he is consulted by high and low. When the spirit moves him he cycles around with a fife and drum . . . The Anguilla problem remains: the problem of a tiny colony set adrift, part of the jetsam of an empire, a near-primitive people suddenly returned to a free state, their renewed or continuing exploitation.'[12] Asked by an interviewer from the *Trinidad Guardian* whether he was in touch with other West Indian writers, he answered, 'The contact is most intermittent. Some I have not seen for years. We don't have anything in common, you see . . . I have no fixed base at the moment.'[13]

Next he went to British Honduras or Belize, London's last colony on the American mainland, where he was looked after by the premier, George Price. The result was an unremarkable article, much of it using clipped reported speech to give a portrait of Sir John Paul, the governor. Afterwards, Price sent photographs and a letter: 'We were honoured by your visit and enjoyed your company on our trip to the mountains.'[14] In February 1969, Vidia travelled with Pat to the United States. The American consulate in Trinidad had given him a four-year journalist's visa. Desmond Dekker's 'Israelites' was about to hit the Top Ten, paving the way for the rise of other Caribbean musicians such as Jimmy Cliff and Bob Marley.[15] Flying in to JFK airport, Vidia and Pat found New York carpeted in thick snow. 'Intellectually I feel an intruder,' he reported to Francis Wyndham. Listening to Norman Mailer and Leslie Fiedler debate whether rationalism was dead at a 'Theatre of Ideas session' left him baffled. 'I felt it – surprisingly – to be very like India, only much, much richer. And of course one realises how simple one's vision of Americans is. They are really now a group of immigrants who have picked up English, but whose mental disciplines are diluted-European. Quaint mixture, not easy to interpret. Irony is absent . . . I miss London and the people I know very much.'[16] Keen to save dollars, he jumped at the opportunity when the manic poet Robert Lowell ('the only American who has read my work') and his wife the critic Elizabeth Hardwick offered to lend him their book-lined studio apartment on West 67th Street while they were away on a trip to Israel and Europe.

The Naipauls' social and intellectual way in New York was smoothed by Robert B. Silvers, to whom Francis had provided an introduction. 'Silvers has been very good and charming to us; he is an extremely important figure in the literary-political world here at the centre, one feels, of all sorts of king-making intrigues.'[17] He agreed to publish Vidia's articles on St Kitts and Anguilla in his magazine, the *New York Review of Books*. Founded during a newspaper strike in 1963, with Lowell, Hardwick, William Styron and Mary McCarthy writing for the inaugural issue, the *New York Review* had quickly turned into the house journal of America's liberal intelligentsia, though with an anglophilic slant. The editors were Bob Silvers, formerly of *Harper's*, and Barbara Epstein, who had edited and promoted Anne Frank's diary. Both were ferociously dedicated to the magazine, which was to prove much more than a review of books, carrying long articles on the cultural and political issues of the day. It was an incestuous but remarkable publication, reviewers and reviewed rotating cheerfully fortnight by fortnight. The *New York Review* took off during the civil rights movement and the Vietnam War, and although it was often radical in content, it was not doctrinaire. Over the subsequent decades, Vidia was to become an important contributor to the magazine; his political distance from many other contributors in no way diminished Bob Silvers's belief in the singularity and importance of his writing.

V.S. Naipaul was not alone in his attempt to storm America in 1969. In a letter which reveals the extent of his connections in two great cities, he wrote to Antonia Fraser:

> I got the impression the first few days here that all London was
> surreptitiously over here in dollar-gathering missions. A glimpse
> – or rather a hearing – of Isaiah Berlin in a hotel lobby;
> Stephen Spender everywhere; John Gross coming shyly out
> from behind some books in somebody's flat; [Anthony] Sampson
> around somewhere (J. Gross giving a party for him tomorrow);
> Penelope Gilliat turning up for dinner at Ivan Morris's. Almost
> as soon as Conor Cruise O'Brien saw me he behaved like a man
> who understood what it was all about: he offered me some
> dollars to be a visiting professor in his 'program' at New York
> University. Silvers (a great fan of yours) had fixed it, I believe;
> I believe they are all a little angry with me for saying no. I
> don't believe they understand how much I am afraid of
> organisations, intrigue, jobs, regular duties, and this writer
> destroying American-universities railroad.[18]

Aware that he was not a name in America as he was in Britain and the Caribbean, Vidia emphasized his disconnect from the writers of the day. 'News:' he wrote to Paul Theroux, 'Podhoretz is dead (of course in the literary sense) after his febrile butterfly life of the autumn. They are killing Trilling; Baldwin has lost; Bellow's lungs have collapsed; and Malamud is eating the sour grapes of Roth . . . I don't understand half the time what they are writing about; I don't like their Teutonic wordiness; and I prefer the other thing, where a man slowly becomes a writer and stays.' He became lyrical, identifying with those who had been driven out or destroyed: 'I alternate between great happiness and great rage at the violence done to the American Indians: I feel the land very much as theirs at dusk, the sky high above Central Park.'[19] To Diana, he explained his quandary: he felt like a provincial. His agent John Cushman, who represented Curtis Brown in America, was little help. 'I now dread meeting Americans, especially their alleged intellectuals. Because here the intellect, too, is only a form of display; these people are really egomaniacs in the most Asiatic way; so that, in spite of all the chatter about problems (very, very remote if you live in an "apartment" in Manhattan: something that appears to be got up by the press) you feel that there is really no concern, that there is only a competition in concern . . . The level of thought is so low that only extreme positions can be identified: Mary McCarthy, Mailer, Eldridge Cleaver and so on. Ideas have to be simple . . . The quandary is this. This country is the most powerful in the world; what happens here will affect the restructuring of the world. It is therefore of interest and should be studied. But how can one overcome one's distaste? Why shouldn't one just go away and ignore it?'[20]

He felt more sympathy and affiliation when he saw three Nigerian writers, undone by war and famine in the Biafran blockade: Gabriel Okara, Cyprian Ekwensi and Chinua Achebe. Vidia had met Achebe the previous year at the house of Peter and Teresa Gatacre. He went for a 'most distressing lunch' with them, he told Diana, 'Distressing because they are so brave and full of good humour still and because they are now so thin and clearly not having enough to eat at home. Cyprian said they had sought me out so that, when I saw the name Biafra in a newspaper, I might think of them as people . . . The blacks here (that is the correct word here) are very hostile to Biafra; they have got it slightly wrong, of course; they see Nigeria as the free black country and Biafra as the "strife" . . . It was especially painful for me because 14 years ago I used to run into Cyprian a lot in the BBC; in those days he used to carry a novel in a briefcase and had no other problem than that of finding a title and a publisher.'[21]

When Robert Lowell came back and Vidia and Pat had to move to the Excelsior Hotel on the Upper West Side, New York seemed even less alluring. They made a visit to Washington DC, where at a diplomatic party an Indian representative told Vidia he had been forgiven for *An Area of Darkness*. In practice, he could see no future for himself in America. Did Vidia really want to be interviewing writers such as Mailer and Lowell? He would go to Canada after California, where he intended to write a cover story for the *Telegraph Magazine* on the legacy of the recently deceased John Steinbeck, 'Cannery Row Revisited'. It contained an important opening line, a lesson to himself: 'A writer is in the end not his books, but his myth. And that myth is in the keeping of others.'[22] He and Pat spent some days with John Gross and his wife, Miriam, both literary journalists from London, and stayed for a couple of nights with Jill Brain and her Japanese husband in their Greenwich Village apartment. Jill had reinvented herself when she moved to New York in 1959, changed her name and become an academic. She was not impressed by the new Vidia: 'I thought he had gotten a bit pleased with himself. I felt very sorry for Pat. At dinner he got to talk and she got to lean across the table and say, "Vidia has written a brilliant book." '[23]

In July they moved to a sparsely furnished flat in Victoria, British Columbia, which had been arranged by acquaintances, and Vidia began work on a sequence of stories. This was to be their new home. Pat wrote fondly to Antonia Fraser of her husband's demands and foibles: 'He particularly likes the carrots, sold here with the fresh furry leaves attached. I have of course, teased him about the components of his diet (you'll be relieved to hear that there is an acceptable brand of oats for his porridge) but the last straw came when he asked me whether he could not have a plate of washed carrots at his side while he worked. For his teeth you know.'[24] Canada, new, open, the home of many Indians and many West Indian East Indians, appeared to represent the future, but by September Vidia had changed his mind. Anguished, angry and feeling lost, he returned to England. They moved to a serviced flat in faceless Dolphin Square in London. Later, and without justification, Vidia blamed Pat for the decision to go to Canada, implying that he had been too feeble to resist her blandishments over the benefits of migration. 'Pat wanted to leave England. It was a very foolish thing because she put an end to one of the first periods in my life when there was a kind of stability . . . Something about immigration had upset her and she thought she could use me to make a statement. She had no idea where to go. She never told me. I think she had some foolish idea about Canada – she was thinking of a liberal country.'[25]

*

At the start of the next decade, the 1970s, Pat and Vidia were homeless. After an unspecified crisis at Dolphin Square, they returned to the days of Miss Gilson and Bravington Road: they were lodging at 23 Armscroft Place, the little home of Auntie Lu near the railway station in Gloucester. It was a far cry from Cal and Lizzie's studio apartment in New York. 'The only cure is work, to finish something, if only for oneself,' Vidia wrote apologetically to Francis. 'I will never be so weak or so proud again . . . if it is possible, we will stay on in England for three or four months, until I finish my work, or get it reasonably advanced. Does Emma [Tennant] still have a vacant cottage?' Once more, Francis swung into action, and fixed something. 'I've just spoken to Emma, who has taken a house on Elba . . . and is anxious to let her own cottage in Wiltshire at a small rent to "reliable tenants" and would love you and Pat to have it more than anyone!'[26] Meanwhile, Vidia sought the hospitality of Marisa and Lindsay Masters, who had a top-floor flat in their five-storey house in Elsham Road. 'I wonder now whether you could take me in for a couple of days next week,' he wrote humbly from Gloucester in January 1970. 'The BBC TV programme Review has asked me to judge a film competition and I have to look at the entries.'[27] Marisa responded that he could have his own key. 'Lindsay and I would "welcome" you any day and for any length of time. This of course applies to Pat also.'[28] Marisa was consistently generous and enthusiastic, writing often to Vidia. She took up Shiva too, as an additional Naipaul protégé. In her own words: 'Shiva and I got on like fire-engines together.'[29] When her daughters Georgia and Camilla were baptized the next year, Vidia was persuaded to be their godfather, the godmother being the purported inventor of the miniskirt, Mary Quant.[30]

In response to several demands, Vidia reluctantly arranged a meeting between his sisters and Hugh and Antonia while they were staying with the governor of Trinidad. Antonia looked back on this visit as 'tremendous fun. What I think we hadn't expected was to find these extremely lively, jolly young women . . . They were sort of middle-class, short-skirted, very glamorous.'[31] To Savi, the former parliamentary under-secretary of state for the colonies and his lady seemed 'very relaxed, very at ease. They came for tea and they landed up having rum punch and wine.'[32] Nella took them out on the streets to 'jump up' during Carnival, presenting a different version of Trinidad to the one Vidia had proposed to Antonia in an earlier letter of guidance: 'After Fort George . . . you go on to MARACAS BAY . . . now a marine slum. It used to be breathtakingly beautiful, until they cut down the trees on the hillside, quite recently, to provide allotments for people who had votes. Something was destroyed; nobody's problems were solved.'[33] Pat was pleased that Antonia was meeting Vidia's family, and praised each of her sisters-in-law in turn: 'Savi and Mira are both married to doctors and have university degrees. Sati hasn't a degree but Vidia thinks she reads the most books. Nalini has just done very well in her O levels, eager to taste the world . . . I may be prejudiced but I find them all beautiful, kind and clever.'[34]

Each sister kept Vido updated. Sati's son Neil Bissoondath, who wanted to become a writer, was going to study in Canada. 'We have been staying at Nepaul Street for the last five months awaiting the completion of work on our house,' wrote Mira. 'The contractor, MOHAMMED, TURNED OUT TO BE A CROOK. I should have listened to Ma when she said never trust a Musulman.' Kamla told him that Shiva and Jenny had been staying with her. 'Sewan has put on a great deal of weight but I have never seen anyone whose features have undergone such a drastic change. I had difficulty recognising him . . . I guess you know by now that Rudranath died. There was great grief and shock in the family . . . I am almost sure it was his dying wish that no one be told – which is as he lived, selfish and vindictive.' Aged fifty, Capo R. had died from terminal renal failure, a malign and disappointed man, leaving scattered children: his son Rudy, a daughter by one of his students and a son by one of his own nieces.

In September 1971 Mira reported that André Deutsch had been on a trip to Trinidad to visit his authors such as the black activist Michael X. The Naipaul family's willingness to indulge Deutsch's constant expectation of hospitality had worn thin. 'As you know he always likes to bum a meal. Well this time he did not succeed in being fed by the Naipauls, but Savi and Melo did open some splendid champagne.' Nella wrote her brother a touching, sincere letter: 'I never seem to know what I should say to you, or how I should say it. I suppose it must be because of all the people I know best, I know you least. Do you understand? . . . I was 18 a few weeks ago.'[35]

A suggestion by Paul Theroux that he and his family might move to England did not appeal to Vidia. 'I would like to say first of all that it may be damaging for you to withdraw from the world and set up as a writer in the country, without a job, without links with the society where you live, at your age . . . I am concerned, too, about your choice of England.' Paul would have to be sure what he was doing. 'To have nothing on hand and to live in Gloucester or Salisbury (where I am about to go, to a house on somebody's grand estate) would, I think, be quite insupportable.'[36] Vidia told Paul he had been depressed and 'ill with bronchitis and pneumonia . . . I have earned <u>nothing</u>. A terrible intimation of age, failing powers, mortality.'[37] When the Theroux family moved to a house in Dorset, Vidia resisted issuing an invitation to visit. 'If you are in London, let's meet; if not, when will you be free?' Paul asked hopefully. 'I light a joss-stick every night for your Booker.'[38] Vidia was happy for Paul to fete him with a magazine profile: 'His marriage is a confident, supportive influence, and intensely private, based on the respect which comes of deep love . . . He is a reasonable vegetarian, out of preference rather than any Hindu stricture. I once asked him about it . . . He made a face and said, "Biting through sinew. I couldn't do it." '[39]

In a semi-detached house in Gloucester under the care of Auntie Lu, far from glamour and competition, Vidia unexpectedly flourished. He took up where he had left off in British Columbia, writing connected pieces on a theme of displacement. The main story, which he thought might become a novel, was *In a Free State*. Pat was able to talk to Auntie Lu about family matters she felt embarrassed to share with Vidia. Her father had gone off with Vera, the barmaid from the Kingstanding pub, referred to by Marg Hale as 'his fancy woman'. Calling themselves Mr and Mrs Hale, the pair had now moved to Lichfield; Pat refused to see her father. Eleanor remembered paying a visit and Vidia teasing her aunt gently. 'He would encourage her to put the world to rights, and say something quite outrageous to make her rail.'[40] The sheer normality of Gloucester life forced Vidia to calm down, and to work. He and Pat would go for long walks in the Gloucestershire countryside, which she loved from her childhood. 'We'd take a bus outside Gloucester to some parts we knew, and walk in that area. These wonderful walks. It's always nice to begin a walk with a nice steep hill – clears the lungs – and there was a Roman villa in the woods. During one of those walks we saw a fox, and we walked behind the fox for a while. The fox was quite unconcerned, its bushy tail swinging delicately from side to side. Was it Cleeve Hill? Was it Cranham Woods?'[41] Writing another story, 'Tell Me Who to Kill', about two Trinidad brothers in London, returned him to the idiom of his childhood. 'Vidia has been thinking about his family a lot recently,' Pat wrote to Kamla. 'I guessed this because he has been falling back into using T'dad locutions and when I asked him he agreed and said he found himself using a T'dad expression in an interview he gave recently.'[42]

While he was writing *In a Free State*, Vidia interviewed the artist David Hockney for the *Telegraph Magazine*. He chose never to have the profile reprinted in his collections of journalism. Written in the continuous present, it described Hockney's flat and his world and his techniques of working. Afterwards, Vidia purchased a drawing of his studio assistant Mo slumped post-coitally naked in a deckchair – the start of an art collection. He avoided saying much about Hockney's painting, although he admired it, and concentrated on reporting the man. 'He is a tall, chunky man. He is sensitive to beauty in others, but does not think he is himself beautiful. His hair is flawlessly blond; he wears big, round, black-rimmed glasses.' He quoted Hockney at length, giving a sense of his personality and the way in which he operated: 'When I was in Bradford I was so sexually naive. Now in London the way I live sex is much more important.' A sensual undercurrent runs through the article; although homosexual acts between consenting males had been legalized in England and Wales three years earlier, Vidia used allusion, implying an ambience. 'Young men are turning up in pairs. Most of them are small, fine-limbed, with fine, tremulous features; some look fatigued . . . The young men sit on the big tan leather settee in the drawing-room; the record player goes; conversation becomes general. The working day is over. When he is in London Hockney goes out every evening,' the article concludes.[43]

In his writing, Vidia would almost always describe men in greater physical detail than women. He was ever captivated by the beauty of the male body, but the idea of sex between men, and in particular anal sex, frightened and fascinated him. His reaction to Hockney's visitors appears to have been less a direct sexual attraction than a sense of excitement at the proximity of sex, and an awareness that he was himself attractive to gay men. In *Magic Seeds*, published in 2004, Vidia tried for the first time to address or explain his own impulses through the character of Roger: 'The idea of sex with a woman, exposing myself to that kind of intimacy, was distasteful to me. Some people insist that if you're not one thing you're the other. They believe that I'm interested in men. The opposite is true. The fact is all sexual intimacy is distasteful to me. I've always considered my low sexual energy as a kind of freedom.'[44]

*

Out came the book, starting from actual moments and real people, but ripped from his imagination. It started with a prologue, about crossing from Piraeus to Alexandria on a steamer full of all nationalities and refugees, and watching a tramp be mistreated; an epilogue has desert children being whipped, and a Chinese circus visiting Luxor. The first story is 'One Out of Many'. Santosh is a servant from Bombay who sleeps on the pavement until his employer is posted to Washington DC. The aeroplane journey unnerves him. He climbs on the toilet and squats. At immigration, he is made to empty his pockets. 'I pulled out the little packets of pepper and salt, the sweets, the envelopes with scented napkins, the toy tubes of mustard. Airline trinkets. I had been collecting them throughout the journey, seizing a handful, whatever my condition, every time I passed the galley.'[45] Santosh has Vidia's sensibility; everything he sees in America is alien. White Hare Krishnas, with their robes and cymbals, baffle him. He sleeps in a cupboard. Black people are 'hubshi', the Hindi equivalent of nigger: 'A lot of the *hubshi* were about, very wild-looking some of them, with dark glasses and their hair frizzed out, but it seemed that if you didn't trouble them they didn't attack you.'[46] Santosh abandons his employer when he meets an Indian restaurateur, and ends up marrying a black woman: 'I am now an American citizen and I live in Washington, capital of the world.'[47] The second story is 'Tell Me Who to Kill', written partially in dialect in a deliberately opaque style, a return to an earlier technique. 'He get back his confidence and it looks as though what he say is true, that he really like studies, because as fast as he finish one diploma he start another.'[48] It has moments of breakdown and madness, and as in 'One Out of Many' the narrator sees an alien world afresh, from the inside out, the effect coming from a complex naivety of perception. *In a Free State* tells of a white man and woman, Bobby and Linda, making a journey by car through an erupting African country. In its cruelty and precision, it anticipates *Guerrillas*. Diana Athill called it 'the first entirely unsentimental novel about Africa' and suggested it be published alone, without the accompanying stories and material.[49]

In a Free State is a disconcerting piece of writing, so taut and ambiguous that the author's point of view is never apparent. This was deliberate. Vidia said later of the book: 'I was not responsible for the world I was discovering. I was recording what I had discovered. I had no point of view. I think I just laid out the material, the evidence, and left people to make up their mind.'[50] It works by implication. Sympathy, like power, shifts back and forth. Take Bobby in the bar of the New Shropshire, wearing a shirt designed and woven in Holland, with a 'bold "native" pattern in black and red'. Well-dressed African civil servants and politicians sit in the bar. 'They hadn't paid for the suits they wore; in some cases they had had the drapers deported.' Bobby alights on a small Zulu man who holds a plaid cloth cap, 'now putting it on and pulling it over his eyes, now using it as a fan, now holding it against his chest and kneading it with his small hands, as though performing an isometric exercise.' Everything about the encounter unsettles. 'The cap made the Zulu appear now as a dandy, now as an exploited labourer from the South African mines, now as an American minstrel, and sometimes even as the revolutionary he had told Bobby he was.' The interaction is unstable. He appears to be a prostitute, and they seem to reach an agreement. 'There was silence between the two men. Then, without moving his hand or changing his expression, the Zulu spat in Bobby's face.'[51] Later in the story, Bobby is beaten by soldiers, and although the author's treatment and depiction of him remains mean throughout, he is in some ways a morally exemplary character. Linda too, and the colonel at the failing hotel, contain aspects of Vidia, aspects that are inevitably undone as the narrative shifts. 'I had the exhilarating sensation that I was one of the first to read a manuscript that would be analysed and argued over for years to come,' Francis told Vidia. 'It is magnificent . . . quite amazingly original . . . the most extraordinary and disturbing story, a tour de force of subtlety and ambiguity.'[52] Michael Astor disliked the book so much that their friendship came to an end. Paul Theroux wrote: 'The book amazed me, it was a great surprise, an unexpected form, a beautifully light touch . . . Anne had some reservations about the Africans who "left their stink behind" or "left turbulences of stink", but it is a true observation.'[53]

Graham Watson realized Vidia had written something exceptional. 'How on earth do you go on doing it!' He extracted an advance on royalties of £2,250 (£23,300 in today's terms) out of André Deutsch, a significant leap from earlier payments, and more than he had earned in royalties on any book, but still low by comparison with his commercial contemporaries.[54] Like Diana, and Bob Gottlieb at Knopf, Watson thought the additional material was a distraction from *In a Free State*. 'From the point of view of your gifts, my dear, I don't think you have ever done people better,' Diana wrote in October. 'The novel is so brilliant that it ought to come out alone.'[55] Vidia refused, and it was published as a thematically connected narrative in the autumn of 1971. To be sure that nobody at André Deutsch became confused over its form or its worth, Vidia drafted 'a guide as to how the blurb can be written . . . "Sequence" is the key word: it is the word that I had in my mind during the writing . . . This may be V.S. Naipaul's best book. It is certainly his most original and complete,' he suggested.[56]

The critics enthused. Naomi Mitchison gave Vidia 'an alpha plus on style', and Francis King thought it his best piece of writing yet.[57] In the *New York Review*, Alfred Kazin wrote: 'After seven books of fiction and three works of nonfiction . . . Naipaul has become one of the few living writers of fiction in English wholly incommensurable with anybody else.'[58] Nadine Gordimer noted that V.S. Naipaul was 'past master of the difficult art of making you laugh and then feel shame at your laughter'.[59] In the *Times*, Dennis Potter took a sideswipe at Anthony Powell: 'Some years ago a distinguished Old Etonian pontificating in an extremely conservative journal described Vidiadhar Surajprasad Naipaul as one of our most promising young writers. I wondered at the time if the brown man born in Trinidad of an Indian Hindu family was at all troubled or amused by the ambiguities helplessly inherent in that once so virulently acquisitive "our". V.S. Naipaul, after all, is brilliantly and satirically alert to every nuance of identity, of place, of inheritance . . . *In a Free State* is a book of such lucid complexity and such genuine insight, so deft and deep, that it somehow manages to agitate, charm, amuse and excuse all at the same pitch of experience. Do not miss the exhilaration of catching one of our most accomplished writers reaching towards the full stretch of his talent. Our? Well, yes, no.'[60]

*

During the course of 1970, living frugally with Auntie Lu, this success was some distance away. Over the Easter weekend, Vidia went alone to Amsterdam, and ended up spraining his ankle when he fell down some steps. At the end of the year, they left Gloucester and moved to Teasel Cottage in Wiltshire, a bungalow in the extensive grounds of Wilsford Manor. 'Emma's cottage is beautifully situated close to the river but on a bank above it. It is close to the road but below it so that the thatched roof is almost level with the road,' Pat reported to Marisa.[61] Wilsford was owned by Glenc's brother Stephen Tennant, a rouged and perfumed eccentric with dyed red hair and a fondness for jewels, fans and seashells, who pretended to be a writer and artist and considered himself 'a legend'. In his youth he had been exceedingly thin and a lover of the poet Siegfried Sassoon, but now he was grossly fat and liked to spend the winters in bed, alone, looked after by his retainers Mr and Mrs Skull. As Paul Theroux observed in *Sir Vidia's Shadow*, 'An idle, silly queen, Stephen Tennant was upper class and rich, so people laughed at his jokes and called him marvellous.'[62] For over a decade, Vidia and Pat were to be Stephen's tenants, paying a nominal rent of a little over £3 per week, which included the cost of electricity and local council rates. The surrounding landscape of woods, barrows, chalk streams and downland was relentlessly rural, and the nearest non-white face was to be found not in the adjacent village of Wilsford cum Lake, but at The Golden Curry in Salisbury. 'It sounds like a terribly classy address,' Ralph Ironman observed, 'have you joined the landed gentry?'[63] After a visit in 1971, Savi's husband, Mel, wrote, 'I told everyone that all you needed was David Lean to arrive with his cameramen and shoot the scene around your cottage cum Lake. Writer and wife at peace with the world. No phone, occasional taxi and wild ducks.'[64]

Needing money, Vidia wrote intermittent journalism but was adamant, as a matter of pride, that despite any shortage Pat should not return to school teaching. An article on the illogicality of Black Power in black-majority countries was rejected by *Life*, and Bob Silvers suggested it might be tempered; Vidia refused, and Silvers still ran it. Sati had told him of 'fires, shooting, looting and rape', of curfew and house arrests as Eric Williams sought to defuse the movement in Trinidad by embracing its precepts. 'Right now we do not know if it is really "Black Power" dignity or Communism.'[65] A crowd of 10,000 had marched through Port of Spain demanding an end to racism and the foreign ownership of banks and oil companies. Vidia was unimpressed when he read a pamphlet published by Lloyd Best's Tapia House movement praising 'the assertion of blackness by the men from below' and condemning 'whiteness' as 'the enemy'.[66] Vidia's 'Power to the Caribbean People' was a polemic, equating a radical cause that was gathering pace in the West Indies with the fantasies of Carnival. In Jamaica, 'There was a middle-class rumour, which was like a rumour from the days of slavery, that a white tourist was to be killed, but only sacrificially, without malice.' He saw this as 'rage, drama and style', a protest movement that would lead to destruction, a 'sentimental trap' of racially based identity, borrowing foolishly from the dissimilar situation of African Americans. 'In the United States Black Power may have its victories. But they will be American victories.'[67] When the piece was published in Trinidad's *Express*, Nella wrote to Vidia that his opinions were 'strongly disapproved by the public and furious replies are being sent into the paper . . . The family is rather enjoying some of the inane letters opposing your article.'[68]

Underlying Vidia's reaction was a personal antipathy to figures such as the 'honorary prime minister' of the Black Panthers in the United States, Stokely Carmichael, alias Kwame Ture, a former Tranquillity pupil. More irritating still was Michael de Freitas, alias Michael X, who had displaced Vidia as the most famous Trinidadian in England. A pimp, thief and hustler who had founded the Black House in Islington and the Racial Adjustment Action Society, 'Michael X' was being inflated in the press as a poet and Black Power leader by figures such as John Lennon, William Burroughs, Alexander Trocchi, Colin MacInnes and Richard Alpert (who liked to call himself Baba Ram Dass). In reality he was the son of a black Trinidadian woman and a Portuguese shopkeeper, who had come to London to seek his fortune through crime. 'He wasn't even black; he was a "a fair-skin man", half white. That, in the Trinidad phrase, was the sweetest part of the joke,' Vidia wrote later.[69] Michael X served time in prison for inciting racial hatred, suggested Queen Elizabeth should have a black baby and briefly became 'minister of defence' for the Black Eagles, an outfit run by Radford Leighton 'Darcus' Howe, himself formerly of Queen's Royal College.

Aided by wealthy white patrons, Michael X claimed to have tens of thousands of followers and to be the most famous black man in the world. Like Vidia and Eric Williams, he was published by André Deutsch: *From Michael de Freitas to Michael X* was his ghostwritten guide to revolution.[70] Joining him in the catalogue was Hakim Jamal, formerly Al Donaldson, a handsome African American criminal turned social activist, who while having an affair with the movie star Jean Seberg had been invited to London by Vanessa Redgrave, in the spirit of Sixties radicalism, to start a school. Jamal was a relation by marriage of Malcolm X, of whom Michael de Freitas was a pale imitation. Farrukh Dhondy, who managed to be one of London's leading Black Panthers although he was the son of a Parsi army officer from Pune, described the Black House as a 'fantasy outfit' and remembered Jamal as 'wily and alluring. His manner was to show supreme contempt for people. Both Jamal and Michael were full of horrible rhetoric about whites, and then they would go off and screw white girls.'[71]

Jeremy Lewis, an editor at André Deutsch, believed that as publishers they suffered from 'a guilty feeling that more should be done for black writers.' As a result, 'Every now and then Jamal or one of his cronies would come into the office and behave in a way which, had he been a middle-class Englishman, would have led to his being seen off the premises.'[72] Diana Athill later wrote a painfully honest account of this period in *Make Believe*. When Hakim Jamal arrived at the Deutsch offices for the first time, 'I sat down near him . . . and within two minutes he had put his hand on my shoulder and was watching to see if I would flinch at being touched by this impertinent nigger.' She did not react: 'He must see that I was "different": the classic reaction of the white liberal on meeting a prickly black.'[73] Diana became friends with Jamal, but believed Michael X was a conman; he was prone to turn up at her office 'ranting that he had secret information about concentration camps for blacks being built in Wales.'[74] All of these people provoked wrath and contempt in Vidia, who was determined he should not in any way be publicly linked or identified with them. In his published work, presenting himself as an outsider with special inside knowledge, he was careful to shield the importance of his continuing personal and family links to the Caribbean.

His predicament was complicated further by the arrival at André Deutsch of another author called Naipaul: Shiva, who had written a novel. He had planned to study Chinese history at Harvard on a scholarship after Oxford, but when he got a third-class degree the plan had to be discontinued. His early attempts at fiction were unsuccessful. 'I can't seem to summon the necessary patience and constancy,' he told his elder brother, 'flying into recurring fits of impatience and destroying everything I have already written.'[75] Once he got writing, he showed great talent. If Pa's *Gurudeva* was the prequel to *A House for Mr Biswas*, Shiva's *Fireflies* was the sequel. It told the story of the Lutchmans, who live in the shadow of their extended family; the father buys a house and dies young, his sons study and travel abroad, the mother is left to struggle on. Jenny wrote to Ma that there had been 'another tremendous review . . . the first reappearance of Auberon Waugh in the Spectator for years, & all on Shiva's book!'[76]

While Shiva was completing *Fireflies*, Diana wrote to Vidia: 'He lacks an edge you always had, but I believe he may blossom in the more relaxed form of the novel – I suspect that his strength may turn out to be in his warmth. He is getting rather fat – lazy boy, he says he never goes out – but was delightful and I enjoyed his company. Looking ahead, I wonder if he ought to use a pen-name? He says he's thought of it but feels disinclined to do so; André feels that there'll be great muddles if he doesn't.'[77] The name on the spine was Shiva Naipaul, and before long there were muddles. Excited by a new talent, editors wanted to hear his opinions. While Vidia toiled over *In a Free State*, Shiva appeared on *The Arts This Week* sounding like his clone: 'The true world was the world which existed outside the West Indies . . . the metropolitan country . . . make your way in the world . . . if you fail, you are nothing, the foreign city pays you no attention.'[78] To many listeners, and to any commissioning editors who thought of Vidia as old talent, this was new stuff. In 1971, Michael Robson of Curtis Brown wrote to the BBC: 'Our client, the novelist V.S. (Vidian) [sic] Naipaul tells us that there has been some confusion within BBC Copyright or Contracts with his younger brother, Shiva Naipaul . . . Vidian is now worried lest the BBC is attempting to base his fees upon fees already offered to Shiva.'[79] Mira thought Shiva's obesity stemmed from anxiety about his status, and that things might now improve for him. Vidia wrote back to her, 'I suppose we underestimated his distress at being my "shadow". It isn't something I understand myself, but then I have never felt oppressed by any presence, as he felt by mine. I wish I had understood earlier.'[80]

Vidia's status fluctuated. He was penniless; he was staying with Pat at the house of his patron Lord Glenconner in Corfu. Academics began to write books on his books, and he was asked to address conferences on world literature. In 1970 the government of Guyana invited him to attend its celebrations at becoming a republic. Vidia did not go. He was awarded the Hummingbird Gold Medal 'for loyal and devoted service to Trinidad and Tobago' (Sam Selvon, William Demas and Derek Walcott had been given it the previous year) but did not visit the High Commission to collect the medal.[81] In 1972 he was asked to open the book fair at the Commonwealth Institute, since the Duke of Edinburgh was unavailable. He became famous enough to attract crankish fans. A Mr E.M. Rimmer began to correspond: 'I once met a young man who said you were his father, and who was so fortunate – or deluded – as to be able to reckon only 4 or 5 acts of pure cruelty performed in his whole life.'[82] William Demas's sister-in-law wrote from Market Drayton asking how to get Naipaul's novels included on a college syllabus. An importuning man wrote from Sweden: 'I am an Indian from New Delhi, and I have written a book of about 130 typed-pages: *Silence with the Storm*. It is a sort of philosophical autobiography. I shall be very, very thankful if you or your brother will agree to go through it and suggest me a suitable publisher.'[83]

This was the age of arts television, and rather than being ghettoed at literary festivals as they would be later in the century, authors were invited to speak to the nation. Vidia was a frequent guest on *Take It or Leave It* at forty guineas a time, appearing alongside Cyril Connolly, Hilary Spurling and Angus Wilson. Descending in a lift after a show with John Betjeman, Auberon Waugh and Margaret Drabble, Waugh said, 'Everyone calls you "V.S." But what is your name?' 'Vidia,' was the reply. 'May I call you Vidia?' 'No, as we've just met, I would rather you called me Mr Naipaul.' There was silence as they waited for the lift doors to open.[84] Vidia used the same trick on the journalist Prem Shankar Jha. The actress and cookery writer Madhur Jaffrey wrote to Pat later, 'Three of us went out for lunch – Prem Jha, Vidia & myself. Somewhere, midway through the lunch, Prem said, "I say ... I can't go on calling you Mr Naipaul – dashed formal and all that........?" There was a L O N G pause. Everyone stopped chewing. Finally Vidia said, "You are embarrassing me" – and that's all he said. Nothing chummy like, Do call me Eddie or Herbie or whatever!!'[85]

Julian Jebb included Vidia in a documentary film on BBC2, *An Imaginary Friend*, in fact a spoof about a non-existent character, John Woodby; contributors to the programme included Elizabeth Bowen, Betjeman and Peter Cook. Vidia refused to let *Play for Today* have the rights for *In a Free State*; according to his agent, 'he thinks it would be badly done on television.'[86] Jonathan Miller attempted to turn *A House for Mr Biswas* into a film. The playwright Julian Mitchell failed to produce a stage adaptation of *The Loss of El Dorado*. 'We tried every likely place, but the size of the black cast defeated us,' he wrote to Vidia in 1972.[87] The director Peter Brook had faced a similar problem when he commissioned a musical of *A House for Mr Biswas* in 1961. The composer Monty Norman subsequently took the song 'Bad Sign, Good Sign', written for sitar and tabla ('I–I was born with this unlu-ucky sneeze and what is wo-orse I came into the wo-orld the wrong way round, pundits all agree that I-I'm the reason why my father fell into the vi-illage pond and drowned'), and adjusted it into one of the best-known tunes of all time – the theme for the James Bond films.[88]

Vidia was happy to appear on television or radio shows and interact with other panellists or the interviewer in a way that he would refuse to do in later years. On *A Word in Edgeways* with Brian Redhead in October 1971, he chatted happily with the composer Peter Maxwell Davies and the sculptor Mitzi Cunliffe about the role of the artist in society. It was 'the sheer wish not to sink personally' that made him write. 'I don't see my role as educating . . . I have never had this missionary thing.' His ambition, which he admitted showed 'a kind of arrogance', was to perceive the world in a different way to others. 'I am altering ways of looking and [altering] a set of values that have come down to us.'[89] A couple of months later he re-established contact with Andrew Salkey, agreeing to do a long interview with him on *The Arts and Africa* on the BBC. 'You left Trinidad. I left Jamaica. Have we really escaped?' Salkey asked. 'Yes. It's more than 21 years. My concerns are now more global . . . I have lost the innocence of the man from the small island who doesn't understand what power is, and [understand] the weakness of one's present position . . . it is a kind of day-to-day truth.' By writing *In a Free State* in the form he had chosen, Vidia was refusing to adjust information in order to make a conventional novel. 'I was no longer going to manufacture an artificial, contrived story.' Africa terrified him for its transformative effect. 'It is a place where anyone from outside is automatically in command. You can be the man with the whip, or you can be the man with the healing touch . . . it is so exploitable.'[90] In a later discussion with Margaret Drabble, he came back to the theme of Africa as a place that encourages the breakdown of moral values: 'I was much more concerned about the English people who were in Africa. I am much more concerned with people who find liberation among their inferiors.'[91]

*

After *In a Free State*, Vidia travelled as a journalist, writing an incisive two-part account of an election in Ajmer in India for the *Sunday Times Magazine*. His local guide and interpreter was Bharat Bhushan, a schoolboy from the prestigious Mayo College, lent by the headmaster. Bhushan wrote an account of the experience, describing the author at work: 'At another time we found ourselves at a tea-shop in Nasirabad, outside Ajmer, late at night. Naipaul insisted that the shopkeeper wash his cup and saucer with soap. The shopkeeper asked his young son — about seven or eight years old — to wash the cup. Naipaul wanted to know why the child was not in bed. Did he not have to go to school the next day? How did he expect him to pay attention in class if he was forced to work till eleven at night?

The shopkeeper heard out Naipaul with a resigned smile. One night our car ran out of fuel. We found a petrol pump but as there was no electricity, the petrol had to be pumped out by hand. Naipaul pushed the attendant aside and started working the crank himself explaining, "I need some exercise."' After the article had been published, another pupil blamed Bhushan for some insulting references to his father, a murdered maharajah. 'I was upset enough to write to Naipaul about putting such hurtful stuff in print. He wrote back that sometimes truth had this effect on people but it had to be told.'[92]

Vidia's finances were still unruly. In February 1971, the month in which Britain adopted a decimal currency, he ordered a bespoke coat from Simpsons of Piccadilly at a cost of £99, but a few weeks later Pat was writing to him that she could hardly get by on £25 a week: 'I find I can only afford to go up to London once in ten days. I drink a half bottle of wine every two days and keep sherry in the house but find I have to avoid meals out and the record department in Smiths.'[93] He went to Jamaica to see Kamla, and to Trinidad to see Ma and his sisters. Savi was now a tutor in sociology at the university, and Mira was soon to emigrate to America, where Amar had been given a position as a radiation oncologist at Johns Hopkins Hospital. At the end of March, Kamla wrote to Pat, 'Vido was very tired and very thin when he got here ... For the first few days he complimented us on the garden and how much we had achieved. Of course, this was too good to last. He then demanded instantly a tree "filtering the sunlight" to be planted on the front lawn ... Harry was under the ivy covered front porch. Vido, with green hat, from the cool bedroom, was peeping through the louvres with such occasional outbursts as "Drop that fork into the hole so that I can see if it is deep enough." "Dig some more." "Sprinkle a bit of bone flour. It does wonders." And there, around the hole were Pooloo & Dada & myself – three twits in the blazing sun.' A touring Indian cricketer had fallen in love with Nella. 'He would give to it his most serious consideration ... Then one morning he would emerge from his bedroom, talking loudly to himself – "No! No! No! Penniless cricketer! Indian crook!" ... [P.S.] What a massacre in East Pakistan! Those bloody Muslims!' Diana Athill had also paid Kamla a visit in Jamaica: 'Diana surprised me. I was expecting someone older looking, very bookish and rather stodgy.'[94] Diana's reaction to Trinidad echoed Vidia's: 'Rueful remark of elderly man who is in charge of the "public" beach at Mt. Irvine Bay (the dottiest piece of mimicry, that beach): that it was a funny thing, but here it still seemed unnatural to give orders to, or take them from, someone of your own colour,' she wrote to him.[95]

Vidia had come to attend a meeting of Caribbean writers at the Jamaican campus of the University of the West Indies. With Black Power in its heyday, there was 'a strong undercurrent of resentment against Vidia – against his ethnicity, against his writing, against his very presence,' thought Kamla.[96] Sharing a stage with other authors and some rivals from his days at *Caribbean Voices*, Vidia had barely begun to read his paper when a black Jamaican librarian, Cliff Lashley, jumped up from the audience and said that he ought to be killed, preferably shot.[97] The conference organizers made no attempt to reprimand Lashley, or to apologize to Vidia, who left the conference and returned to Kamla's house. A Trinidadian academic, Kenneth Ramchand, thought the situation was handled very badly. 'There was total silence, no reaction to Cliff Lashley. The proper thing would have been to eject him.'[98] Vidia blamed the outburst, for no obvious reason, on his former BBC colleague Edward (now called Kamau) Brathwaite: 'He organized a racial ambush of me in Jamaica in 1971 . . . He ran me down and became a great enemy of mine, but I didn't reply, I didn't reply.'[99]

Vidia travelled to the island of Mauritius to write 'The Overcrowded Barracoon', which would give him the title of his next book, a compilation of journalism and essays. Mauritius was not 'a lost paradise' as travel writers were then suggesting, but a big plantation 'far from anywhere, colonized, like those West Indian islands on the other side of the world, only for sugar, part of the great human engineering of recent empires, the shifting about of leaderless groups of conquered peoples.' His eye was drawn to the helpless and the hopeless, the malnourished boys who came to a political meeting 'in over-size jackets that belong to fathers or elder brothers' to listen to empty slogans. 'The rain, the bush, the cheap houses, the poor clothes, the mixture of races, the umbrellaed groups who have come out to watch: the hysterical scene is yet so intimate: adults fighting in front of the children, the squalor of the overcrowded barracoon: the politics of the powerless.'[100] Mauritius would go on to become one of the most prosperous countries in Africa, helped by tourism and a stable political system; a rare instance of Vidia misreading an atmosphere at this time. He said later, 'I was always thinking when I was travelling, will this make sense in twenty years. I allowed my depression and rage to take me too far in the thing I wrote about Mauritius. My analysis of the place was correct but I had no idea that they were going to find ways of dealing with it. I thought they were going to drift into starvation . . . I didn't know they were going to alight on this idea of the export zone, which has been a great saviour for them, and I had no idea the world was so heartless, that people would want to go and have a holiday where everyone was starving.'[101]

On return to Britain, Vidia was laid low with bronchial pneumonia, a complaint induced in part by a continuing feeling of being unfulfilled and in the wrong place. 'I have been getting a whole series of minor illnesses,' he told Kamla, 'stomach, lumbago, influenza, headaches etc.'[102] He thought again about quitting England to live elsewhere. But where? For the rest of the year, he kept up a busy correspondence with Kamla, analysing his own past and wondering about his future. 'You were hurt that we never recognised you as a writer. What a false impression. We are absolute bores, the way we talk about you constantly,' Kamla wrote back. In October 1971, she wrote: 'You claim you were starved. Erase it from your mind. It's not true . . . I am not so sure that the dahl, roti and daily fresh vegetables were such bad fare after all.'[103]

That month he had a postcard from Carmen Callil, who was shortly to leave André Deutsch to found the Virago Press: 'For the Booker prize, you and your wife will be asked to a dinner, Thursday November 25. I have been asked to tell no-one but you and André that you have one.'[104] One what? He had one? Had won? Had he won the Booker Prize? Despite the cost, he made a daytime telephone call: he had won! Outside the ceremony at the Café Royal in London, a BBC *Bookcase* microphone was waved beneath his nose, and he was asked if he minded that the Booker group had interests in sugar and mining, and if he was pleased to have won the prize. For once Vidia had no words, and when he did respond, he sounded like a member of the royal family: 'Well I tell you one's overwhelmed, I think one is so overwhelmed by a thing like this that one can't quite react.'[105] The following year, the Booker went to John Berger for *G*, who railed against the prize and said he would share his winnings with the Black Panthers. He travelled straight from the award ceremony to a north London pub, where he met Farrukh Dhondy and Darcus Howe. Dhondy was the only Black Panther with a bank account, and Berger cheerfully wrote him a cheque for £2,500 to purchase a house in Finsbury Park. It served as a base for the movement for some years, until Dhondy received a visit from four men with machetes who persuaded him to give up the property. An article in the *New Statesman* observed that most

Booker employees in the Caribbean were of Indian origin, and quoted Vidia saying that John Berger's statement was 'ignorant, absurd, not just rubbish but damaging ... Most of the Black Power writers are only speaking to white people ... It's a nightclub turn, it's television ... None of these black writers has been to Guyana to study the role of the CIA there – in fact very few black writers have written about black regimes at all.'[106]

Letters came for Vidia from around the world, amazed he had won yet another prize. Ruth Jhabvala wrote: 'Do accept our congratulations, all of us very thrilled, especially me who always sees in your success hopes for my own future too. I don't know why – perhaps because we're both so far-out and alone? Out on a limb?'[107] (She would win in 1975 with *Heat and Dust*.) 'You certainly continue to write brilliantly. For this, I am sure you realise, some of your dear West Indian colleagues will never forgive you,' wrote John Figueroa from Puerto Rico.[108] 'I wish there were a gesture of homage which one could put on paper,' Michael Frayn told him. 'There are very few writers (even among those I enjoy and admire) to whom I feel inclined to make this act of submission. Your writing has some kind of "otherness" which detaches it from you, and gives it an absolute life free of the efforts and compromises one can sense in most things. I gather the Booker committee took counsel's advice on what constitutes a novel; good that they should be forced to do so.'[109] Peter Bayley sent a letter from Univ, after many years: 'I thought A House for Mr Biswas was wonderful – in a wild marvellous Dickensy imaginative way; In a Free State seems astonishingly far beyond that. But as a result I found it profoundly disturbing ... perhaps I was wrong to see personal unhappiness, alienation, loneliness, humiliation so clearly behind it all.'[110]

Although Vidia did not want to hear this, and resented his former tutor's willingness to speak to the press about his Oxford days, Peter Bayley was right. A month after the Booker dinner, Vidia again uprooted himself and Pat, and travelled back to the West Indies. He might stay there, or he might visit Nigeria, or the new state of Bangladesh, or what he liked to call 'Spanish America'; in particular, he might visit Argentina.

CHAPTER SEVENTEEN

'WITH THE AID OF A
CUTLASS BLADE'

PAT AND VIDIA FLEW to Trinidad two days after Christmas 1971. Pat was writing a new diary, and began by setting their life in a literary context. Vidia was doing an article on Jean Rhys for the *New York Review* and reading Thomas de Quincey's *Confessions of an English Opium Eater* and the plays of Oscar Wilde, which he liked to do while lying unshaven in a hammock wearing winceyette pyjamas from Marks & Spencer. She was reading Joseph Conrad's *Under Western Eyes*, Vladimir Nabokov's *Pnin* and John Updike's *Pigeon Feathers* and *The Centaur*, a book which left her feeling regretful: 'I relate to Vidia's seeking out his roots. Feel my own vulnerability.'[1] She wrote about the renovation of the Lion House, a visit to Owad and another cousin, Seromany, a party with Savi and Mel where she drank too much rum punch, and a conversation with Derek and Margaret Walcott at Sally Stollmeyer's house: 'Walcott tells Savi how violent he gets when drunk and people annoy him.' Ma was depicted treating Pat like one of her own children, talking about 'temple politics' and going to the quarry she managed for her brother Simbhoo: 'Ma greets various Indians, some in Hindi. One old man driving a truck: she strides up to the cab and says, "I was wondering who could know me, who was smiling at me from a lorry."' Vidia was shown in glimpses, playing cricket on the beach, watching the 'delicate and glistening' tazias paraded at the Hosay festival: 'Vidia allows himself to be carried away as this is Indian drums and drumming. I dart out into the road and grab him as he is following happily.' Elsewhere, there are references to tension: after a telephone call to Kamla in Jamaica, Vidia 'came up and there was an outburst about homelessness and anger with me.'

'No adventure, no journeys yet. I am just queen-beeing it here at my sister's, resting and trying to get better,' Vidia wrote to Paul Theroux in February 1972. The *New York Review* wanted a travel article

from him. 'I am very keen on Bob Silvers; and they will print anything
I want to write about S. America. But they just can't afford to pay.' In
the meantime, Vidia was left contemplating the failings of women from
a position of ignorance: 'I am getting very bored with the drama and
self-dramatising of the female soul – really just the pleasuring of the
body – and I am beginning to feel more and more that women are
trivial-minded, incapable of analysing or even seeing their motives; that
they long for witnesses to their pleasure or their distress.'[2] He went to
visit elderly relations in Trinidad and contemplated writing an autobiography, or another novel. Pat made a note in March: 'Yesterday Vidia
went off to San Fernando early in the morning with Melo. Expecting to
be the Rotary Club's guest of honour. They had another guest, a
speaker, to whom Vidia was introduced. Whereupon he walked out.'
Mel Akal's recollection of the trip to the Rotary Club was more florid:
'The secretary came and said, "Vidia, we have an American businessman passing through Trinidad and he will be the main speaker today."
He exploded, he cursed the man and called him a shit. We just walked
out. I think he was quite right to do that.'[3]

Some weeks after Vidia and Pat reached Trinidad, graves were
discovered in Arima containing the bodies of a black man and a white
woman. The previous year, Michael X had moved back to Trinidad to
start a commune, fleeing the courts in London, and now calling himself
by the Muslim name Michael Abdul Malik. Local Black Power activists
were doubtful, but he began to display wealth and received John
Lennon and Yoko Ono as well-publicized house-guests. Soon Malik
was visited by Hakim Jamal and his English girlfriend cum slave Gale
Benson, alias Halé Kimga (an anagram of 'Hakim' and 'Gale'), who
was the daughter of a Tory MP (Captain Leonard Plugge, who claimed
to have invented the two-way car radio). In London, Jamal had been
given keen coverage in the press as an educator. 'Everyone in this story
was at some time or another at least a little mad,' Diana Athill wrote
later, and her act of lunacy was to offer him a 'loan' of £200. He
accepted on the condition he might give her a weekend of loving,
adding tactlessly that she should not think of herself as 'an old woman
who is reduced to buying sex'.[4] Diana was outraged, but invited him to
stay all the same, accompanied by Benson, who promptly stole the
money from a dressing-table drawer. Permissive to the point of
aberration, Diana let the pair remain. Jamal took over her house, told
her she had vacated her body and taken possession of Benson's, and

inveigled another £200 out of her. They moved to Trinidad at the end of the year, where Jamal accepted Michael Abdul Malik's demand that a human sacrifice was needed: Gale Benson was hacked to death with a cutlass by Malik's followers and buried in a shallow grave. A month later, a local man named Joe Skerritt was murdered there too. It would be many months before these and other details would become clear, many of them pieced together meticulously by Vidia.

V. S. Naipaul was never wholly aware of the nature of Diana Athill's alternative life, for they saw little of each other outside the offices of André Deutsch, apart from occasional lunches at the cheap restaurants where Deutsch permitted his editors to entertain. Born in 1917, Diana had enjoyed a 'middling English gentry' childhood of ponies, lawns and housemaids, and at Oxford had become engaged to a bomber pilot. Then the Second World War started and her fiancé's letters stopped. 'I never heard from him again until I received a formal note, two years later, asking me to release him from our engagement because he was about to marry someone else.' Soon afterwards, he was killed. Needing to earn her living, Diana teamed up with Deutsch as a publisher and had 'foolish and always short affairs . . . Lack of energy prevented me from ranging about in pursuit of men, but if they turned up, I slept with them.'[5] Now in her mid-fifties, Diana wore her grey hair in a bun and spoke with a cut-glass accent. She was profoundly unconventional, extending hospitality to random visitors and having a particular susceptibility to foreigners who had fallen on hard times. Unlike many of those she befriended during the 1960s and 1970s, Diana was not deceived: she was able to look at the element of fantasy behind the social idealism of the era with an amoral eye; she was interested in watching how people behaved.

When news of the killings broke, Pat was disturbed and Vidia felt a resonance with a story that had already formed in his head: 'Vidia said that the idea he was playing with ended in a stabbing.' His mental image was of a murder at a commune, and the murderer looking through the slats of a Venetian blind at a commune member coming up the road in the sun.[6] A letter arrived from Diana which, Pat noted, 'talks about an inevitability that these three mad people should meet in this mad place . . . Vidia asked me whether he should write a book about Malik. Interview him. Follow the trial.' Diana wrote of Gale Benson, 'It was impossible ever to imagine anything but a disastrous end for her (I would have betted on suicide), but what appears to have been the extreme horror of the actual killing is worse than anything I foresaw . . . She was . . . an astonishingly talented linguist, deft and neat about the house, a great deal of charm, rather beautiful to look at, very brave (really astonishingly brave) – yet absolutely not alive except in terms of the man's fantasy.'[7] Vidia suggested to André that 'quite a book could be made of the affair, which lights up so many things in our world: race, perverted sex, boredom, communes, communal lunacy, conscience, fraudulent politics (black & white), liberalism etc.'[8] In addition he wrote to Diana (unaware at this point of the nature of her involvement with Hakim Jamal): 'The atmosphere here is perhaps like the atmosphere in the old days when some lunatic Negro "plot" was uncovered: the threat of punishment makes everybody sober straight away – until the next lunatic abscess ripens. Lunacy and servility: they remain the ingredients of the Negro character. I wonder why this isn't written about, why the Negro writers continue to be sentimental about themselves.'[9] While the investigation proceeded, Jamal fled back to Boston where he was murdered by De Mau Mau, a militant organization that had been established by black US soldiers in Vietnam.

Vidia made a trip to the 'Memphis' Black Power settlement with a local architect, a visit that would provide the impetus and detail for the chilling scenes at the commune in *Guerrillas*. The architect, Bernard Broadbridge, was 'nervous of Vidia & nervous of what he will find', Pat wrote in her diary. 'The Black Panther leader, Aldwyn Primus . . . is small and quiet . . . We have been told that Primus is transformed on the orator's platform. Cannings supply them with food and other things. They are sponsored by Rotary, Chamber of Commerce etc. That is how the nervous, but nice, Bernard has got involved. They have a large piece of land, 93 acres. Their cultivation seems to consist of a couple of small patches of tomatoes. Laughable in view of extent of their kingdom . . . We go down to see the tomato seedlings being planted out, with the aid of a cutlass blade in very muddy soil.' Vidia made precise notes: 'The concrete floor, the beds; at the other end the store (ducted) and in one corner, below seating, supplies & stores. Open at both ends. Mr Primus was said to be having a bath. A small slender-hipped man, really very attractive, with blue-coloured glasses & a very large shiny knob for a nose, with the acne pits enlarged & prominent, miniature moon craters.'[10] In *Guerrillas*, he would merge Primus with Malik, since Malik's involvement with the Black Power movement in Trinidad was in practice tangential.

The same day, they went to the murder scene. Pat wrote: 'The side turning to Malik's burnt-out house is blocked by a police barrier . . . We see the upturned earth of Skerritt's grave and are taken to see the small square where Gail [sic] Benson was found in a sitting position.' A BBC reporter 'walks up and takes a still photograph of Vidia by the grave. He then asks whether he is going to write a book about Malik. Vidia says he might but has not made up his mind.' Days later, Pat was still upset: 'Was that very clean neat square hole it? The two old seedling boxes, the lettuce boxes?' Black Power was exacerbating Trinidad's ethnic divisions; Savi's Indian driver Ralph Roopchand told Vidia and Pat, 'Although we are poor, my father is still a very racial man.'[11] Francis Wyndham suggested that Vidia might write about the Michael Abdul Malik case for the *Sunday Times Magazine*, and offered to pay 'extra well' given his connection to the subject, and its hold over the popular imagination in Britain.

*

Leaving the murder trial to one side for a moment, Vidia agreed with Bob Silvers to write about Argentina's political unrest for the *New York Review*. After the fall of Juan Perón in 1955, Argentina had veered between civilian and military government, and violence had grown as more than a dozen armed groups competed to overthrow the state, and the state repressed them brutally. Peronism, with its mixture of populism and authoritarianism, was still potent, as was Perón's late wife Eva, or Evita, the orator and propagandist who had a mystical hold running far beyond Argentina's borders. Vidia had long been interested in her: 'I had wanted to write about Evita since 1952, when I saw a newsreel at Oxford.'[12] Some Argentinians were now calling for the return of Juan Perón, who was exiled in Spain.

Bob Silvers borrowed money to fund the trip from his girlfriend Grace, Countess of Dudley. 'We heard that there was something going on in Argentina and I just said we were very frustrated, it would be so great if we could send someone like Naipaul, and Grace said, "I'll be glad to help." She was a great admirer of his work . . . That was the last time any outsider contributed anything to the paper.'[13] Silvers arranged contacts in Buenos Aires too, in particular Norman Thomas di Giovanni, an Italian-American who was the amanuensis and 'walking-stick' of the celebrated blind poet and fabulist Jorge Luis Borges. In a reminiscence of Silvers, Vidia described the background to the article: 'I telephoned Bob; within two days he had sent expenses money to a Trinidad bank. This sounds easy to do now ... Seven or eight years later Bob told me that money was scarce at the *Review* in 1972, and he had personally borrowed the expenses money he had sent to the Trinidad bank with such swiftness and style. Such faith in a writer, too: it was humbling.'[14] On 12 April 1972, newly bearded, his head still full of 'race, perverted sex, boredom, communes, communal lunacy, conscience, fraudulent politics (black & white), liberalism etc', Vidia flew due south from Trinidad to Argentina. Grace Dudley's impetuous generosity, Bob Silvers's faith in a writer and Vidia's own Oxford interest in the person of Eva Perón had conspired to make the trip to Buenos Aires happen: it was to be the start of a revolution in his life.

Lying in bed on the night of her husband's departure, a few months short of her fortieth birthday, Pat wrote, 'Two sleeping pills, but perhaps perversity prevents me sleeping. And mosquitoes? I think of the last three years. I think of the racial inturning. Seeking false ancestors, nostalgia, attenuated, poetical talk about horsemen & snow at the end of the world.' This was a reference both to Vidia and to Ralph Singh's Aryan fantasies in *The Mimic Men*, 'I have visions of Central Asian horsemen, among whom I am one, riding below a sky threatening snow to the very end of an empty world.'[15] Pat was alone, lonely and childless, her hair was lank and grey, her clothes were wrong and she was underweight. Her husband was having sex with prostitutes and wanted another life, yet he still depended on her. Like Thomas Hardy and his wife Emma, childlessness exacerbated their estrangement; it was an area of silent and secret guilt, which they both rationalized in public by saying they did not want to have children, since it would interfere with Vidia's writing. Pat felt unable to speak to anyone about the unease of her situation, and took refuge in her diary. A few days earlier, she had written: 'Exchange of awareness between Savi and I when talk turns to the old Indians who had wives and families in their different situations as emigrants and immigrants ... Also discussed with Savi the Naipaul propensity thru' three generations to give mother and wife a hard time.' Even with her sister-in-law, Pat felt unable to communicate fully, and Savi in turn found her 'extremely private. Pat remained so – cool, distant ... She was essentially passive.'[16]

Pat had written a journal in India in 1962, and a daily narrative, which has since been lost, while they were staying with Auntie Lu in Gloucester. In Trinidad, she noted, 'A diary should not be a confessional or a repository for grudges?' quickly undermining herself with a question mark. Her diary would be a record of her life with Vidia, and of his work. A little later she asked, 'Should I write about him? Began out of sense of obligation and duty while he was writing *In a Free State*. Now unwarrantable.' Warrantable or not, she continued with the diary until 1995, writing hundreds of thousands of words in twenty-four large notebooks. Pat would almost always be the passive observer, the diarist who witnesses events from the sidelines. She never sought to inflate her own role, and often tried to reduce it. Her diary was snatched, scrappy and intermittent, lacking the mental agility of her letters, let alone the fire of her Oxford correspondence with Vidia in the 1950s. It was a collection of thoughts rather than a clear narrative, and is not easily quotable; it was not inventive, and it feels reliable. Pat would write the same thing in different forms, sometimes illegibly, or jot it on a piece of paper and insert it between the pages of the diary; she would use different pens and pencils, different coloured inks, different types of notebook; she would make insertions, using an asterisk and a scribbled note to amend an entry; she would pick up the diary or put it down for months at a time. Despite its inconsistency, Pat's diary is an essential, unparalleled record of V.S. Naipaul's later life and work, and reveals more about the creation of his subsequent books, and her role in their creation, than any other source. It puts Patricia Naipaul on a par with other great, tragic, literary spouses such as Sonia Tolstoy, Jane Carlyle and Leonard Woolf.

*

Argentina was familiar and unfamiliar for Vidia, another part of the New World that had been conquered by force by the Spanish, its indigenous people driven or wiped out, its social and political structures borrowed from abroad, a large, long country with a small population, stretching from the Bolivian border to Tierra del Fuego, bounded on either side by the Andes and the Atlantic, a land of rivers and fertile plains or pampas. In the sixteenth century the conquistadors had come to Tierra Argentina, the land of silver, finding a wonderland on the edge of nowhere inhabited by Amerindians who ate corn and sweet potatoes.[17] Soon the plains were turned into giant ranches or estancias to raise cattle; there were so many cows that the meat would be cut and the carcass left to rot on the grassland. Slaves came too, and lawless cruelty as the Spanish fought off the Portuguese. By the early nineteenth century, when the region declared independence from Spain, there was a thriving trade from Argentina, soon to be boosted by the invention of refrigeration ships for beef. Blood was everything; women of Spanish descent would be depicted in paintings with a slight moustache to show they had no Indian heritage. By the time of the First World War, the new country was wealthy and immigrants were pouring in from Spain and Italy. Argentina had railways and industry and a capital, Buenos Aires, with a subway, boulevards and skyscrapers. BA considered itself the southern hemisphere's answer to Paris, and was home to a beautiful opera house, the tango, innumerable servants, psychoanalysts, grand Catholic churches and white prostitutes from eastern Europe. Its citizens believed they spoke Castilian Spanish. It was the sort of place that might have been designed to impress, stimulate and irritate V.S. Naipaul.

He stayed at the Hotel Nogaró and moved fast, reading books and magazines and making telephone calls. Journalists helped him, including Robert Cox, the British-born editor of the English-language newspaper the *Buenos Aires Herald*, and the prominent cartoonist Hermenegildo 'Menchi' Sábat, who found Naipaul 'a very peculiar fellow, unbelievably intelligent. He thinks only in words, while I think in images. He has the illumination in advance as to what is going to be important.' Vidia asked to watch a football match, and Menchi made the arrangements: 'I bought the tickets. During the first half he just said, "Let's go." He was bored to death. I couldn't believe it.'[18] Vidia was soon jotting down notes and conversations, including several in Spanish, the language coming back to him from his days at QRC and Oxford: 'Un prejuicio racial integral contra todos [A built-in racial prejudice against everyone] . . . Dios es argentino [God is Argentinian] . . . The teenagers now who didn't know Perón think that Perón is a genius. They study peronismo more anxiously than Marx . . . The Clark Kent attitude.' Of a lunch, he wrote: 'All men, including elegant Argentines – very handsome, aristocratic. Peronist. The talk of curanderos [folk healers].' He noted a line from another guest at a dinner in Barrio Norte: 'Once this city was a great port. But now it's fucked up, baby. I want out. I am dying, I am dying, I am dying.'[19] The material slid easily into his article for the *New York Review*. In the final version, a witness describes guerrillas like the Montoneros: 'They're anti-American. But one of them held a high job in an American company. They have split personalities; some of them really don't know who they are. They see themselves as a kind of comic-book hero. Clark Kent in the office by day, Superman at night, with a gun.'[20]

As ever Vidia needed a pilot, and Norman Thomas di Giovanni fitted the part. Stocky, cocky and gabby, di Giovanni might have been a character from a Saul Bellow novel. Born a year after Vidia, he had been named for the American socialist leader Norman Thomas and raised in a disputatious immigrant suburb of Boston. He had edited an anthology of Latin American poetry, but retained something of the street hustler about him. After hearing a lecture by Borges, he had moved to Buenos Aires to collaborate with the 'living monument' in putting his work into English. Each day they would go to the National Library, where Borges was nominally the director, and di Giovanni would read sentences to the blind old man which they would translate together.[21] Norman di Giovanni had heard of Naipaul, and liked the idea of him. 'V.S. rang me right off the bat. He wasn't happy in his hotel. He never let on whether he spoke Spanish, but he wanted me to speak to the manager and arrange things for him, as if he couldn't do it himself.' Vidia opened out to Norman, giving the impression of friendship. 'At our first meetings I found him depressed and depressing, but I knew he was a literary genius and was happy to help him. We hit it off. I saw him each night for dinner and opened the door to Borges. Vidia has a way of flattering people by noticing a detail, like the texture of your shirt. I told him the score and made fun of the class system in Argentina. We used to laugh like hell. I arranged for him to stay at the house of a journalist who was away – for free, so he was very pleased.'[22]

As well as Borges, Vidia met the elderly doyenne of Argentine literature Victoria Ocampo, and was invited with Norman to her house in San Isidro, following in the steps of André Malraux, Rabindranath Tagore, Igor Stravinsky and Graham Greene. Borges told Vidia he had met Tagore at Victoria Ocampo's and found him 'a rather pompous old gentleman, very vain and rather pompous'.[23] Vidia was interested in Borges, and thought in retrospect he had failed to notice his grandeur. At the time, he noted, 'He asked where I came from. When he heard I was an Indian he said, "How do you pronounce sahib?" I said, "sahb."'[24] Later, Vidia wrote a piece for the *New York Review* on Borges: his global reputation 'as a blind and elderly Argentine, the writer of a very few, very short, and very mysterious stories, is so inflated and bogus that it obscures his greatness. It has possibly cost him the Nobel Prize; and it may well happen that when the bogus reputation declines, as it must, the good work may also disappear.'[25] Norman, with hindsight, found the article to have been remarkable. 'He really had Borges absolutely perfectly. The piece is more solid than I thought at the time.'

Vidia was frank with Norman about his own situation, telling him he was 'written out' after *In a Free State*: 'He said his marriage was in trouble, and that when he finished a book he would hang out with whores, and that he might have to leave England because of the racial tension there. He told me he and his wife had single beds, but sometimes she would come into his room at night. I knew by now he had an eye for the girls – and Buenos Aires was a feast for the eyes: well-groomed, slim, tanned healthy young women . . . So I rang him one day and said, "Come to tea in my apartment at 5.00." '[26] There was only one other guest that day, 28 April 1972. Vidia was standing on the balcony of the tenth-floor apartment in the Rio Bamba looking at passers-by and hooting cars and the fringes of a street demonstration when a woman came into the room. His response was instantaneous:

> I wished to possess her as soon as I saw her. She was wearing a kind of furry pullover because it was the beginning of the Argentine winter and it was slightly dirty, the way these things can get dirty, and that was very affecting to me . . . So she came in and I was completely dazzled. I loved her eyes. I loved her mouth. I loved everything about her and I have never stopped loving her, actually. What a panic it was for me to win her because I had no seducing talent at all. And somehow the need was so great that I did do it.[27]

By the end of the day Vidia had a new entry written in his notebook: a telephone number, and above it a name, 'Margaret Murray', and above the name the word 'Gooding'.[28]

CHAPTER EIGHTEEN

MARGARITA

TO SOME SHE WAS MARGARITA, to others Margaret; some knew her as Murray, others by her husband's surname, Gooding, and a few thought she was called Smith. Norman had met her a few months earlier at a lunch given by her stepfather, Lawrence Smith, an Irish Catholic literary agent who ran a successful office in BA selling rights for plays and novels in South America. Margaret had three children, claimed to be twenty-nine years old but was thirty. Her English was husky and sexy, with elongated Spanish vowels. Norman found her 'vivacious, attractive, dressed like all members of that class in high style – behind the times by American standards, but very classy – with matching shoes and handbag etc.' At their first meeting, she had asked Norman whether he would like to translate Argentine writers, and he was flattered; he was excited too, but introduced her to his American wife, Heather, 'to put a wet blanket on it'. They became friends. He could see her marriage to Roy Gooding was stranded: 'Margaret had an oppressive Catholic boarding school upbringing, and she just wanted to fly.'[1]

Margaret came from a small but significant social group: the Anglo-Argentines, families of English, or often Scottish, Welsh or Irish descent, who liked to follow their own customs and marry within their own community. They took pride in their fair skin and supposedly British accents, and in some cases made a point of failing to learn Spanish properly. As informal members of the British empire, they had contributed to the Allied war effort in the Second World War and, like West Indians, spoke of the 'mother country' and joined the wartime RAF and Royal Canadian Air Force. In the 1970s, Anglo-Argentine men often had jobs in commerce or the professions, and held vigorous sports such as rugby, tennis, and polo in high esteem. Anglo-Argentine social activity in BA centred on the Hurlingham Club, named after the country club in west London but pronounced in the Spanish fashion: 'Ooor-ling-ham'.

Margaret was born in Buenos Aires on 15 February 1942.[2] Her father, Bruce Murray, was a Scottish architect who had been brought up in India; her mother, Nancy, was part English, part Hungarian and part Dutch, the daughter of a successful grain broker in Argentina. When Margaret was two years old, her father died from a heart attack and her mother moved to her parents' house in Belgrano, and in 1946 married Lawrence Smith, who treated Margaret and her younger sisters Rosemary and Diana as if they were his own children, although they retained their father's surname. Two more children were born, Lawrie and Susie. Aged only six, Margaret was despatched to a boarding school in the hills in Córdoba in central Argentina, 400 miles from BA. Apart from a week's break in July, this meant she only saw her family during the summer holidays – December, January and February, a dislocation that was considered normal in their culture. She was later sent with her sisters to a Catholic girls' boarding school in BA run by Irish nuns, where she was elected head girl and voted the most popular pupil in the school. It was a narrow, restricted education. She was impressed neither by the Roman Catholicism of the nuns and her stepfather, nor by the formal social strictures of the Anglo-Argentine community. Aged just nineteen, Margaret married Roy Gooding, an executive with Shell, and they soon had three children: Karin, Alexander and Cecilia. By the time she stood in the apartment in the Rio Bamba eleven years later, she had run through several lovers and was bored.

Vidia persuaded Margaret to see him: it was what he called 'a calamity'. They slept together, he had a quick orgasm and she called him a creep. He paced the streets of Buenos Aires, trying to concentrate on his article and wondering how to pursue the woman he now desired most in the world. Weeks went by. Norman was the intermediary: 'I had a call from Vidia. I had to persuade Margaret to see him again. I was the pimp. Margaret was not at all interested in Vidia. She was interested in bestselling writers. For a start, Vidia is very dark in colour, which is anathema in BA. I had to tell her he was a famous writer and something interesting might come out of it. She said, "He's so awful, all he wants to do is get me into bed."'[3] Norman's plan was to invite Margaret to join his wife and baby son Tom in Bariloche, a picturesque, snow-covered resort in the foothills of the Andes. Vidia would be there, waiting in the wings like a character in a Broadway farce. The conifer forests and alpine lakes might work their charm. Vidia remembered: 'He thought he should encourage Margaret's [step]father to allow her to go away and I would be there and try to seduce her. It was all really humiliating.'[4] Norman persuaded Lawrence Smith, a stern and respectable man who employed Margaret in his office, to agree to the trip. 'I had a pretty young wife, so he thought I was safe. Everyone knew we were going – but not that this dark-skinned man from Trinidad was coming too.' Margaret arrived on a later plane on 31 May, and came to the hotel. Vidia was, in Norman's words, 'scared shitless. He appeared out of the shadows. Margaret was a bit horrified, and insisted they had separate rooms. But I tell you, one of those rooms never needed to be dusted.'[5]

Through this time, Pat was staying with Ma in Nepaul Street, getting up each morning at six to attend the Malik inquiry and make notes for Vidia in case he decided to write about it. Her letters to Argentina were filled with advice, queries and devotion. Antonia's father, Lord Longford, was holding an inquiry into the baleful influence of pornography, and his assistant Marigold Johnson, wife of the former *New Statesman* editor Paul Johnson, wanted Vidia's views: 'She thought writers were underrepresented and suggested your comments would be "immensely valuable".' On the very day he met Margaret, Pat wrote: 'Look after yourself and dress sensibly but don't pile on the clothes indoors with central heating and try not to get too obsessed about your chest . . . Set aside a little time for relaxing every day – really switch off and do something light and frivolous . . . I hope Spanish America is exciting you – or feeding you somehow . . . I am trying to imagine what you are doing. But I can't. Argentina seems terribly far away. Must go to bed altho' the Carnival rumpus is beginning to build up. I suppose you would be impossible if you were here but I would not mind.'[6] Argentina was feeding Vidia in a way that Pat could not imagine.

When it was time to leave the snow slopes and warm bedrooms of Bariloche, he was in an ecstatic state; he even forgot his passport at the hotel and Norman, ever the fixer, had to take a taxi from the airport to race back and collect it. Vidia found the experience 'staggering. But there was lots of ineptitude. And thereafter I thought if that thing hadn't occurred in my life I probably would have shrivelled and died as a writer.'[7] Descending through the clouds to BA, his mood altered; according to Norman, Vidia had terrified visions of the husband Mr Gooding or the stepfather Mr Smith waiting at the municipal airport with a shotgun. 'The plane lands. The plane taxies. Vidia runs to the building and jumps over a fence. This little Indian guy is just running out of the airport. He bolted – he was terrified that someone from Margaret's family would be there.'⁸ A day later, Vidia flew back to Trinidad. He knew at once that his life had changed. Oh my Spanish America, my new found land! 'I felt good for the first time. I believe that a sexual relationship between two people has to take time, for each to get used to one another, even the bodies have to get used to one another. Probably I am wrong but my experience is quite limited. And the thing is I never really believed that I could be the recipient of love . . . I don't know why, probably a deep diffidence . . . I was passionately looking for sensual fulfilment, but passionately, and when it came it was wonderful, and I will never run it down. All the later books in a way to some extent depend on her. They stopped being dry. *The Mimic Men* is an important book for the cultural emptiness in colonial people. But it is very dry. The books stopped being dry after Margaret, and it was a great liberation . . . Nothing was missing. The world was complete for me. I have often thought how strange it is that I lived for so long in England and I really had no English affair.'⁹

*

Early on 4 June, Pat went loyally to the airport at Piarco to greet her husband: 'Vidia returned from Buenos Aires this morning at 1.15 a.m. Ralph Roopchand peered through the doorway of the customs hall. "He looks well." And so he did. Tho' the face looked thinner and ferociously intellectual. Yet gay. The change – if he really is thinner – is from January when he started to grow the beard . . . And he looks youthful.'¹⁰ They spent ten days in a guest house at Mount Saint Benedict, a monastery of celibate Benedictine monks on the north of the island, before moving to Savi and Mel's house at Valsayn Park. Vidia set to work correcting the proofs of *The Overcrowded Barracoon* and writing his article about Argentina. He did not tell Pat about Margaret, although she noted in her diary that he hoped 'the Spanish American interlude would act as a sort of release' and added that his 'American friend, di Giovanni, concurs in urging Vidia to start a new life.' Vidia did tell Savi about his attraction to Margaret, coming to her bedroom door early one morning while Pat was elsewhere. 'He knocked and said, "I must talk to you, something has happened, I must talk to you." I had to arrange for someone else to take my children to school. We had never spoken about anything evenly remotely related to sex. It is not the kind of conversation Vidia ever would have had, so I was absolutely shocked.' Savi listened sympathetically as her brother spoke about 'the complication of the husband, children'. She presumed the affair would soon blow over. 'Argentina was a long way off from England, and Vidia was always so tight complaining about never having enough money. So who was going to finance this big romance?'[11] A telegram arrived: 'ARE YOU STILL INTERESTED IN WRITING ABOUT MICHAEL X CASE QUERY MAGAZINE WILDLY ENTHUSIASTIC IF SO STOP LOVED YOUR EVITA PERON AND LONGING TO SEE YOU BOTH STOP WYNDHAM.'[12]

Vidia unburdened himself obliquely to Paul Theroux, writing with emotion to the only correspondent he could think of who would offer him unconditional support. He began with instructions: 'I would be most grateful to you if you could spare the time to look through the proof and let me know whether there are certain things that dismay you. A very dirty proof, though: full of errors . . . I met a girl in Argentina. One day she copied out two pages from The Return of the Native to give to me. In those pages the heroine reflects on the melancholy of her life and her situation. "The meanest kisses were at famine prices." How that chills: the shock of "famine" & "prices" after "kisses". And the heroine cries out, send me some great love, or I shall die . . . See how this jolly letter has turned out. Strange things happen when a writer sits down on an off day to write to a friend.'[13] When Paul's painstaking critical study of Vidia arrived in the post, it was Pat who thanked him for his 'insights and the love for Vidia combined'. She reflected on the writer's life: 'I remember thinking how marvellous Sonia [Tolstoy]'s diary was – the extracts read to me – and feeling I ought to be able to do something like that.' But 'such writing would be unsuitable in this age no, I don't mean that . . . I am trying to write this amongst family noise (Vidia is upstairs in the quiet room) – Top Cat on T.V. and a lovely thing called dahlpuri being made in the kitchen which I feel I ought to try and make myself some time.'[14]

In early July, Vidia flew to New Zealand and Pat went to Jamaica to see Kamla, Harry and their children. She wondered whether she should return to teaching or try to become a journalist. Before breaking off her diary for several months, she wrote: 'Under the influence of sleeping pills I make resolutions yet again: abstinence, determination.' In a later piece of autobiographical writing, she described her feelings at this time: 'In 1972 I was in Trinidad, at the time of the Michael X murders. There I had to cope not only with the Genius but with the Genius' family, kind and loving but every bit as determined as he was; they knew what they thought about everything. Sometimes, late in the discussion – too late – they would take pity on me. "What do you think," they would say. Of course I could not tell them ... I was in any case beginning to play with the idea of myself as a sort of free-ranging, freelance journalist. I was unemployed at the time and playing with the idea of myself in a number of roles. I realised that if I was to write about anything knowledgeably it ought to be about Britain.'[15] She thought she would write about politics when she returned, in the manner of Bernard Levin, but was unsure how best to begin.

Despite the emotional turmoil he was going through, Vidia wrote an acute and careful article about Argentina. In his first draft, he opened with the image of the seventy-six-year-old Juan Domingo Perón in exile in Madrid. Then he altered the opening to make, unusually, a homage to another writer: 'Outline it like a story by Borges. The dictator is overthrown and more than half the people rejoice. The dictator had filled the jails and emptied the treasury. Like many dictators, he hadn't begun badly. He had wanted to make his country great. But he wasn't himself a great man; and perhaps the country couldn't be made great. Seventeen years pass. The country is still without great men; the treasury is still empty; and the people are on the verge of despair.' After six, turbulent weeks in Argentina, he summed up: he wrote of inflation, kidnappings and 'jack-booted soldiers in black leather jackets' – and deduced that 'Argentina is in a state of crisis that no Argentine can fully explain.' He set a global and historical context, seeing a colonial, artificial society obsessed with its European links which had imposed itself on stolen Amerindian land and was now being destroyed by killers who lacked a discernible programme. The Argentine press seemed 'incapable of detecting a pattern in the events it reports'.[16] It was to become a familiar Naipauline theme, and in this case his pessimism was prescient: within a year, Perón had returned to a cheering crowd of more than 2 million people.

Bob Silvers wrote to him delightedly, 'As I cabled, the piece is a marvel, really one of the best observations and reflections about this part of the world I've ever read. We hardly touched it. It is perfectly written.'[17] When it was published in the *New York Review* and the *Sunday Times*, angry letters arrived, one from the Royal Institute of International Affairs calling Naipaul a 'fairy tale writer', another from the University of Sussex saying Argentina had 'produced at least one great man in this century, Che Guevara, and probably a great woman, Eva Perón.'[18] Some BA journalists were angered by the article, and attacked it as the work of an outsider, though Menchi Sábat, a thoughtful man with a big, expressive face, felt it contained fundamental truths: 'His article was absolutely right. This is a hypocritical society. The trouble here is that Argentinians think "we are the best" and nobody wants to discuss what makes us the way we are. Naipaul thinks he has the power to judge a country, to make a signal to the country.'[19]

The most extreme form of literary criticism came from the leadership of the Montoneros guerrillas. Bob Cox, a brave editor, had paid $100 to run the article in the *Buenos Aires Herald* at a time when other newspapers were self-censoring and journalists were being murdered. The Montoneros – and many others in this socially conservative, Roman Catholic country – took particular exception to some lines written by the now sexually initiated Vidia Naipaul about Evita: 'Her commonness, her beauty, her success: they contribute to her sainthood. And her sexiness. "Todos me acosan sexualmente," she once said with irritation, in her actress days. "Everybody makes a pass at me." She was the macho's ideal victim-woman – don't those red lips still speak to the Argentine macho of her reputed skill in fellatio?'[20] Andrew Graham-Yooll, the paper's young news editor, was blamed for the article; it was decided he would be killed with a desk bomb at the *Herald* office near the Plaza de Mayo. The Montoneros had used this method before: opening a drawer would pull a wire which released the pin from a hand grenade taped inside the desk. A former Peronist MP, Diego Muñiz Barreto, arrived at the underground meeting after the order for the assassination had already been given and the killer had left the building. Luckily for the target, Muñiz Barreto said, 'You can't do that to Andrew. We trust him. Let's investigate further.' After a discussion, the order was countermanded and Andrew Graham-Yooll survived. He had met Vidia briefly during the trip, and found him uninterested in his own views about the country. 'He had bought a pair of expensive leather gloves. Naipaul said, "These are really *good gloves*. Argentines make *good gloves*." I think he preferred being with important people like Borges.'[21]

*

On 13 June, Margaret wrote to Vidia saying she wanted to meet him in Morocco – a plan they had been discussing – and thought he might try to get the Moroccan government to invite him, suggesting the financial saving would appeal to his thrifty soul; she was also significantly overestimating his influence. Then she got down to more serious things: she was practically sure that she carried his child, and told him she would probably have no choice but to get rid of it. Margaret felt she ought to refuse to sign the letter, joking that she might be the famous one in ten years, while he would be forgotten.[22] This was big, potent news for Vidia: not only was he good at sex, but he was fertile, able to father a child. He wrote back wondering whether she should go ahead and have the baby, and also accusing her of blackmail, in a letter which Margaret told him she considered nasty, and in character.

He had previously been invited on a cultural and literary tour of New Zealand by UNESCO. It was the last thing he wanted to do, but he accepted in order to see Margaret again: to get to New Zealand, he would fly via Panama, Los Angeles and Tahiti, but return via Buenos Aires. He wrote to Menchi Sábat asking him to get in touch with Margaret and warn her he was coming back to Argentina. 'He used me as a pigeon,' said Sábat.[23] In New Zealand, Vidia was looked after by Michael Neill, a young lecturer in the English Department at the University of Auckland. Neill had spent his early life in Britain and Ireland, and remembered Naipaul as an interesting but complicated guest: 'He said the British Council had entrapped him into travelling to this benighted place, and that it was taking weeks out of his life.' Neill felt some sympathy for Vidia: 'He had to address an audience of weekend women writers in Nelson. I took him to a restaurant and he ordered scallops, not crumbed. They came crumbed. He was very annoyed. He told me then that he had once hurled a glass paperweight at a person in a travel agent in Trinidad. I think at that point a chanteur in the restaurant struck up "Do you know the way to San José?" for the second time.'[24] Beneath a large photograph of V.S. Naipaul looking troubled in a roll-neck sweater, the Wellington *Dominion* reported: 'Mr Naipaul has been speaking at universities and teachers' colleges and meeting with local authors and literary societies.'[25]

As soon as he arrived in New Zealand, Vidia had begun to feel remorseful, and wrote to Pat with the guilt of the adulterer on 11 July: 'I think that our homelessness has damaged you more than me, and is perhaps responsible for a good deal of the strains we have both been experiencing. You in your way give such great love – for which I am and have always been so grateful, and feel so undeserving – you have concentrated more on my distress . . . A woman needs a house, a fortress of her own, which she creates & governs; I wonder now that we never thought of that. I think that we must . . . find some kind of house which will be yours and, because it will be yours, will also be mine.' It was a loving letter: they

would, like Mr Biswas, make a new start in their own house. He knew Pat
had been under stress, and that she often caught coughs and colds. 'One
of the other things I wanted to say,' he wrote, truthfully, 'was that much
of the strength I now have has been given me by you; and I recognise it
as the most horrible kind of exchange, because I can see that it has depleted
you. What a melancholy thing. I do want you to eat well & rest and sleep
and recover your health; you must understand that it will be better for
both of us if you become well again.'[26] Many years later, he acknowleged
that his relationship with Margaret effectively undid Pat's life: 'I was
liberated. She was destroyed. It was inevitable.'[27]

He did not deliver on his fine intentions and sentiments about the need
for a fortress; he wanted to resurrect his marriage to Pat, just as he wanted
to be with Margaret, and hoped she might have his child. Might he manage
all of it, somehow, if Margaret had the baby and he and Pat brought it up
as their own? For the first time in his life, he went to a jeweller and bought
a ring – for Margaret. One night he was invited to dinner by Michael Neill
and his Chinese Malaysian girlfriend Pek Koon Heng, a politics student.
Neill shared a house with two colleagues from the university, a big wooden
building that had once been the Tongan royal family's residence. A dozen
people came to dinner, with V.S. Naipaul as guest of honour. 'We were
younger than him,' said Neill, 'and he vented the most provocative views
on all kinds of things. Various people took offence. I remember feeling
more and more tense during the meal and saw a drop of sweat fall into my
soup.' Pek Koon Heng found him to be 'pretty mellow, very curious,
meticulously turned out, discussing Borges. I remember he was extraordinarily struck by the lettering on signposts in New Zealand.'[28]

Later in the evening, in what Neill took to be an 'emotionally generous'
gesture, Vidia turned to the table for guidance. 'He exposed his own
vulnerability. He said, "I have this problem which I would like you to
advise me on. I have a woman in Argentina who I would like to have my
child. I thought I could take the child back to England and perhaps my
wife and I can raise it. Do you think I could do it? Do you think it would
be a good idea?" '[29] Lulled by the comfort of strangers, Vidia had asked a
question he would never have raised in a more familiar setting. The guests
were astonished. Within days, though, the question of the child became
theoretical when news from Margaret reached him. She did not know
whether he would be pleased or not, but she had gone ahead and dealt
with the problem on her own. The experience had been harrowing, and
expensive, but she regarded it as a consequence of the curse of being a

woman. She was glad to have received a photograph from Vidia showing him with Pat, who she thought looked remarkably serene given the attitude and personality of her husband.[30] Vidia sent her a cheque to pay for the abortion, and a copy of his article on Argentina, 'The Corpse at the Iron Gate'. Many of Margaret's own sentiments about her country were contained in the article, which she told him was beautifully written.

Looking back on these events, Vidia linked the idea of the unborn child, which he imagined to be a boy, with his own creativity in the years that followed: 'Margaret was going to have a child. I was quite happy for it to be aborted. Wicked people have said it was someone else's, but I think it was mine. I still play with the idea though that the child, born in 1973, would have been a man of nearly thirty now. I would have had to give up so much. These were very creative years for me: *Guerrillas*, the Congo, *India: A Wounded Civilization*, *A Bend in the River* ... My friendship with Margaret released all of that ... It was part of my father's irresponsibility to have all these children. It was a decision to end the line with me, with myself: let it end with me.'[31] Margaret's abortion was linked in his mind to primogeniture, and with an idea of himself as the summation of the male line of the Naipauls. In December 1973, Shiva and Jenny had their first and only child, a son: Tarun Shivaprasad. In May of the same year, Pat paid a quiet visit to a Harley Street fertility specialist, Mr J.M. Brudenell. On the back of a doctor's letter, she noted, 'Laproscopy £95 ... slit pencil light tube ... see ovaries & tubes ... Also tests menstruation.'[32] Pat did not proceed; long gone were the days when she dreamed of having their little baby, Humphrey Naipaul.

*

Margaret was Vidia's ideal woman, a woman of a kind who had existed previously only in his fantasy life: he could string her along and mistreat her, with her abject consent. Margaret was unlike Pat in almost all respects: tempestuous, cynical and sexy. Their relationship, battered and disturbed, would endure for almost a quarter of a century; a kink in his personality met a kink in hers, and snagged. The affair was to be intense, and intensely sexual, and sexually aggressive, to their mutual pleasure. When a man is violent towards a woman, particularly out of sexual jealousy, she either leaves him or becomes possessed by him; Margaret did the latter. She would love Vidia and hate Vidia, abase herself and worship him, degrade herself and degrade him. She was in thrall and addicted to him, sexually and emotionally. She liked to be his slave and his victim, and he was snared by her; although he appeared to be in control of how things unfolded, he was mentally hooked. Margaret gave him the power, much of which was generated out of a new self-belief and physical confidence, to push ahead with his literary ambitions. Many of the gruesome sexual depictions in his subsequent novels were not the work of the imagination, but drawn from his life with Margaret. Like F. Scott Fitzgerald with Sam Goldwyn, she always knew where she stood with Vidia: nowhere. Years later, when asked how their relationship began he liked to say, to irritate her, 'It was not a meeting of minds.'

Norman di Giovanni was encouraging, playing the role of *homme de confiance*. Travelling to England in June 1972 he wrote, 'Margaret loves you madly & you must return to see her . . . I've helped make the break with her lover. Your letters and my insistence did it. I'm afraid it will cost you a loan of $350, however.'[33] Later, Norman and his wife, Heather, came to Wiltshire for the day by train and taxi. He remembered: 'I told Vidia I was writing a novel. He had no interest in that. Pat gave us trout and almonds, and we went for a walk to look at Salisbury Plain. She was colourless, mousy.' The contrast between the wife and the lover was apparent. 'Vidia found Margaret alluring as an Argentine woman of her class. Pat didn't have any of that. I saw, in time, that he didn't like the way his passion for Margaret took him over.' In a letter to Savi, Pat described the di Giovannis' lunch, and the stroppiness that preceded it. She and Vidia had returned from Trinidad after a stopover in Luxembourg:

> We flew back to London to the tune of 'I hate Europeans', 'Bloody sub-Kraut Krauts' (Luxemburgers) until he was rendered speechless by a really nauseating snack . . . I raced into Salisbury and shopped on Friday, started preparing before breakfast on Saturday and had lunch ready in time . . . When they were 5 minutes late your brother decided they were not coming and demanded his lunch. I watched him eat it stunned. He had almost finished when they arrived. I leaped up, welcoming, repairing the damage done to the food by extracting one helping and catching things (including squashable items) thrown down by their one-year-old baby. We then went for a two hour tramp up and down the downs, taking it in turns to carry little Tommy who, they said, weighed two stone.[34]

In London, Vidia introduced Norman to Diana Athill, Francis Wyndham at the *Sunday Times* and the critic Derwent May at the *Listener*.

At Wilsford, drawing from life, Vidia made notes for a novel that would eventually turn into *Guerrillas*. Glimpses of a story had been shown to him, but he could not see how to bring it together. 'The white panther becomes involved with the black panther. Moral black-mail. The farm. The commune . . . Someone like Carlin who carries his private hurt. Where does he come from? I can't make it South Africa . . . What is wrong with this woman? Why is she so dissatisfied? . . . I see my Asiatic being involved with this woman. I see their tortured relationship. The triviality, the spoilt woman. I blow hot and cold . . . The Asiatic's tormented vision of this woman's degradation & her husband . . . Why is the airport about to close? Why is the currency crashing?' He put the idea aside, and made notes for another novel, *The Mystery of Arrival*. Vidia was to start and restart this book many times, stripping out elements from it for his later work. The initial draft began: 'In his last year at Oxford Anil's thoughts turned to getting a job; and it grieved him that he should have sunk so low.' He wrote more worried notes later, troubled about his literary future. 'The process of writing is a mysterious business – how do the ideas come and how does one execute them? And today I am desperate, feeling myself full of talent and will, but also feeling that I may have already said, in twelve books, all that I have to say.'[35]

In September, Vidia confirmed that the Morocco trip was happening. Margaret booked herself a flight and arranged a double room at a hotel costing $25 a night. She teased him that since he was not Aristotle Onassis, she would pay half the cost. Her mother had given her some money to have a holiday. She also promised that her mood would be much better than it had been in Buenos Aires, where she had been obliged to put up with tiresome social conventions and the people at the Nogaró hotel. She sent him a photograph of herself, and promised to arrive in Casablanca shortly after lunch on 10 October. Before leaving, Vidia wrote grandly to Paul Theroux: 'I passed back through Argentina; spent ten days in Trinidad; and now have been here, back at the manor, for the last four days, slowly thawing out.' He raged briefly against Africa; Idi Amin was expelling Asians from Uganda: 'It is an obscene continent, fit only for second-rate people. Second-rate whites with second-rate ambitions, who are prepared, as in South Africa, to indulge in the obscenity of disciplining Africans . . . you either stay away from the continent, or you go there and discipline the savages.'[36] A few days later, after looking through *V.S. Naipaul: An Introduction to his Work*, he complimented Paul on a 'marvellously responsive and humane' study, and hoped it would bring reward for his 'great sensitivity, labour and love'.[37] His follower responded keenly, 'If you saw love in that little book, believe me it was there – you weren't mistaken.'[38]

Vidia flew to meet Margaret in Casablanca. They spent two nights there, and another two in Marrakech at the Hotel Mamounia, where their bill listed little but 'étage' (room service), suggesting they were too busy to leave the room.[39] After Bariloche, Morocco was a further revelation for Vidia. Might he spend the rest of his days and nights with Margaret? On return to England, he felt his life slipping and sliding beneath him; everything might now be changing. He wrote Paul Theroux a request, scripted in an uncharacteristic, angled hand, full of insertions – the last letter he would write to him for nearly nine years: 'Here is something I would like you to do for me, assuming that it is in your power to do so. I need a <u>lot</u> of money very badly (or at least it seems to me that I need a lot of money). The only asset I have is my manuscripts >(drafts etc.)< & my other papers (correspondence etc). A pretty complete documentation of my writing life from 18 to 40.' He had told the British Museum that 'the minimum price I would like – for <u>all</u> that I have, >which is all that exists< – is £40,000 ... I would therefore like you to pass the word around that I am thinking of disposing of <u>all</u> my papers; perhaps someone >in the US< may be interested.'[40] Paul Theroux diligently sounded out contacts at universities and institutions, but did not get far: V.S. Naipaul was not yet a big enough name in America.

Margaret arrived in London, and Vidia found reasons not to be in Wilsford. To save money, he borrowed John Powell's flat as a place for them to go, but when he asked another friend for a similar favour, it was refused. They ended up in hotels with names like the Ivanhoe, Vidia haemorrhaging money he did not have. Norman di Giovanni had moved to a house in Wheatley in Oxfordshire, and Vidia and Margaret went to stay with him at the end of October. Norman remembered: 'They would disappear for days on end into the bedroom. He was fucking crazy about her, and crazy about fucking her. He couldn't wait to get his trousers off. She said living with him would be impossible: she would be watching television in the other room, and he would want her to turn it off because it was disturbing him.' Norman remained friendly with Margaret but Vidia soon turned against him, resenting his garrulous generosity and his role in bringing them together. When

Vidia denounced Norman, Margaret defended him, reminding her lover of the masterful bit of salesmanship that had made their relationship possible; without Norman, he might have remained the grim, ghastly man she had first met. A little later, after a bad argument, Norman telephoned Vidia on Margaret's behalf to press her case. 'He was furious. He thought I was badgering him. I didn't see Vidia after that until the 1980s.'[41] Despite the rupture, Norman was in April 1974 one of the first people to nominate Vidia for the Nobel Prize, in response to an enquiry from American PEN.[42]

Margaret spent some of November in London, going out one evening with a man who was staying at the Dorchester. Vidia invited Diana Athill to meet her at a restaurant in Soho, but otherwise kept her hidden from his friends, embarrassed by the relationship. Diana was immediately conscious of the contrast with Pat. 'I liked her. I thought she was a nice woman. I remember she had a kind of Latin American look, and was so professionally feminine and sexy in a charming way, and he was loving that. It was obviously absolutely fascinating for him. She seemed very cheerful, that she had got him just where she wanted him.' When Vidia next saw Diana, he told her he was thinking of ending his marriage. 'I was horrified. I said, "Vidia, you can't." He made a wonderful remark, "I am having carnal pleasure for the first time in my life, are you saying I must give it up?"' Diana suggested he should have an affair. Now it was Vidia's turn to appear horrified. Looking back, Diana Athill thought, 'It would have been better for Pat if he had [left her] because she was stronger then, and would have probably made more of her life. But I thought it would kill her. Everybody felt that she was completely dependent on him.'[43] Vidia also told Marisa Masters he was thinking of leaving Pat. Standing in front of the window in the huge kitchen at Elsham Road, she berated him in her rolling Italian accent: 'I say: "How dare you? Now you are famous and people are around you? You have a wife who has been working for years to make you write your books. It's disgusting. She has taken care of you." He is silent. He say: "I was a virgin when I married Pat." I tell him I understand a writer needs to get a bit of knowledge. I say, "*Go with the woman*, but don't leave Pat." '[44]

*

Margaret returned to Argentina in early December, and thought of him constantly, in all the finest ways and also the most degenerate. She had visited her brother in Madrid, and he had not let her mope. Back in BA, her mother realized something was wrong, so she told her about Vidia and had a sympathetic response. Margaret posted him four photographs, including one with her children and her husband Roy from 1969, and another of her upper body, wearing only a bra. Ten days later she informed him that she carried his child once again, and expressed worry that he might think it was someone else's. She made plans for a termination. Margaret was full of blind rage now against her lover, although she blamed herself, not Vidia, for the pregnancy. Her friend Silvina had pointed out that Vidia had never made a single sacrifice for her, and doubted he ever would. Margaret replied simply that she was helpless, because she loved him. She knew what she wanted, but understood that her position was hopelessly precarious. 'I want you to come and live with me, think about that,' Vidia had told her over the telephone while she was in Madrid. And now, penning her thoughts on the writing paper of the Lawrence Smith Literary Agency in Avenida de los Incas, she wondered whether he meant it. Living with him would be such a massive shift, but she could not seem to live without him.

Did Vidia mean it? He meant it and he did not mean it. Indecisive, frightened, excited by the situation he had got himself into while unable emotionally to cope with it, worried about money and Pat and his literary future, he sent Margaret some books and took refuge in the putative journey to Stockholm. As his father had once said, he was impulsive and unpredictable. He followed his compulsion to write, but rarely wrote to Margaret. His failure to be with her arose in part from the intellectual gulf between them. Looking back, he said, 'I believe if she had any literary judgement or feeling for my work, I think I would have gone away with her. It was as simple as that. But it wasn't there. In a strange way, I got to like that too – that we had another kind of relationship . . . I could take the passionate side of life, which I was very nervous of before.'[45] Margaret gave him sensual fulfilment, Pat the cerebral equivalent. Like Graham Greene and Catherine Walston, they would meet in unlikely locations around the world for sex and excitement while the travelling writer went about his business.

Over the following weeks Margaret wrote page after page of letter after letter, some eight or ten sides long. She wrote lying on the grass in Palermo Park watching the children feed the ducks, and lying by the pool at the Hurlingham Club, soaking up the sun and using one of Paul Theroux's books as a prop on which to rest her paper. She had decided to go to an analyst, against his advice. He asked her to write and telephone, but never wrote himself, which she complained about continually. She said he should not think she would be willing to hop over to England every few months to satisfy his carnal desires, although she rued the fact that only he seemed to be capable of satisfying hers. Vidia should dismiss his fear that she might turn up one day out of the blue in Wiltshire, baggage in tow. She laid down the law: she would not always be the one who wrote letters, and did all the talking on the telephone. Margaret's letters to him were long and frequent, her shaky grammar and random use of apostrophes causing Vidia more amusement than distress. Sometimes she was erotic and teasing. She complained he had never taken her to Mirabelles or to the Savoy, and said that recently she had been out for an ice-cream, moulded to a point on the cone in the Argentinian way, and observed what a lovely phallic symbol it made, adding that she had deliberately chosen chocolate in order to be reminded of him. She sent a Ravi Shankar concert programme for her lover, and teased him that he was black and ugly. She ridiculed his happy boast that Miriam Gross and Antonia Fraser had told him women found him attractive. Perhaps Vidia had misheard, or alternatively his friends might be blind? Nobody could possibly be under the impression that he was the most attractive man in London. Margaret was reading *The Sensuous Woman* by 'J', and suggested he might produce a companion volume about the sensuous man, instead of writing all that stuff about displaced persons.

It was unsubtle writing, but it aroused Vidia. Margaret was pressing the most obvious buttons of sex and aggression. She tried to make him jealous by telling him of a trip to a nightclub called Mau Mau, where she had worn a sexy top with a bare midriff and no bra. Had Vidia been present, she taunted him, he might have been tempted to rape her. She typed out a Sanskrit poem for him, and a line of Robert Graves: 'Love is the disease most worth having, for its opposite is the doleful serenity of death in life.' She praised Vidia, saying that being together was like living on champagne, and that she knew she would receive an awful lot of punishment when they were back together, and might release what she termed his horrible streak of sadism. She berated him for not writing a word about her abortion, apart from saying that she had got pregnant to blackmail him. It was a form of behaviour that did not seem to fit his character, although on second thoughts Margaret wondered whether he might in fact do just about anything to save himself from taking responsibility or decisions. He seemed to think he could steamroller anybody and sacrifice anyone in the name of his work. But at the same time, she declared that she was still doing exercises to make sure she looked smashing when they next saw each other. Even by January 1973, she had not heard a word from him about the abortion. Not one word – and now she was sick that he refused to mention it. He should go to hell: she hoped that he would not become a black eminence hovering in the background for the rest of her life. Vidia admitted later that his conduct at the time had been 'rough and crude . . . I took no interest.'[46]

Every few weeks they had short, snatched telephone conversations, cut short if Pat or Roy or Margaret's children appeared. In the early 1970s, international calls were expensive rarities and a telephone was a single, fixed, bulky contraption kept in one place such as a hall or a sitting room, attached to the wall by a wire; it was not easy to have a private conversation. She wanted US$450 for an air ticket so she could come and see him in April. Finally Vidia sent her a letter at the end of January. She responded that she was interested to hear about his weekend staying with Anthony and Violet Powell. Were all his friends oldies? She felt he was already an old man in spirit, and that as far as she could tell, when he was not writing he was busy having dinner with grand people and rich lords and ladies. She told him he was a hypocrite. The Curtis Brown representative in BA had informed her that Vidia's work stood little chance of being published in Argentina. His books had already been sent to the major publishing houses, but they had decided there was no market for them. Well, he would just have to win the Nobel. Why did neither of them have any money? She said Vidia could not even afford to buy her, much though she would love to be bought by him.

Margaret flirted and flattered him, believing his tenuous, half-hearted promises. The one thing that pleased her greatly was the fact that he had told her they were now going to live together. She got delirious just thinking about it. She wanted him, but he should learn to be more trusting of her. Why, he had asked over the telephone whether she was up to her old tricks again, to which her answer was a resounding no and a declaration that she hated him. Trying to start a college of one, he sent her books: Marlowe's translations of Ovid, Restoration comedies, *Sir Gawain and the Green Knight*. She thanked him, and said she had never loved another man in the way she loved him, and never would again. A few days later, sending a photo of herself looking sexy lying on a lawn, she told him she could hardly wait for April, when they would begin living together. She reminded him that it was her birthday on the fifteenth, and she would be thirty years old. (In fact, it was her thirty-first birthday; not an easy slip to make.) Margaret was still angry over his silence on the termination and the question of who would pay for her ticket to England. Still, she hoped that some day she might become what she termed his beloved wife and super whore. Vidia had been invited to lunch at Buckingham Palace. He was instructed by Margaret to have fun with the Queen and remember to speak only when spoken to. She believed that despite his pretence that money, titles and luxury were of no interest to him, he was bound to enjoy himself; secretly, it might be what he liked most. She would expect to hear full details of his lunch with the Queen and her boorish husband.

Vidia sat between Sir Martin Charteris and Alistair Cooke, who was to the Queen's right, eating a vegetarian preparation while the others had Selle d'Agneau Sarladaise followed by Rocher de Glace Dalmation.[47] Pat wrote to Ma afterwards: 'It is a great honour and as you would expect he responded to the occasion honestly and sweetly. He was overwhelmed at the moment when the Queen entered the room ... He liked the Queen, found her sensitive and intelligent, thinks she has suffered in her life. She is 47.'[48] Ma wrote back, 'Congrats to Vido ... Your father only brother Persad Chadra [Ramparsad] died on the 7th June and was cremated on the 11th June Whit Monday, the Guardian had a little writing Vidia's Uncle for Cremation.'[49]

As for Margaret, she still did not know what was happening. It occurred to her that although they had been apart for over four months, Vidia had only bothered to send her two letters. She understood his enthralment at the idea of the Queen and Stockholm — everything paled before what she described as the deity on the one hand and the glory on the other. If Vidia wanted to end their affair, why not say so? At least he could write her a letter. But he did not. She told him she had been out with a man, and a telephone call came at once in response, Vidia's voice full of jealousy. It reminded her of the times when she had flirted mildly with other men, although the difference was that Vidia was not able to hit her over the telephone. She had to distract herself: after all, she was not the one seeking to write Nobel prize-winning novels. No other man could give her the sensations he gave her. She said she had done things to Vido that would have made her sick with anybody else, and yet she still longed for the time when she could do them again. It was agreed: they would meet in Trinidad in April, where Vidia was going to write about the Michael X case.

CHAPTER NINETEEN

ENGLAND AND ARGENTINA

THROUGH THIS YEAR of emotional turmoil, Vidia had remained focused on two things: himself and his writing. He produced careful articles on Argentina for the *New York Review*, made preparations for an autobiography and tried to start two novels. Publication of *The Overcrowded Barracoon* led to publicity and interviews. Vidia linked up with Yves Leclerc, his old friend from Earls Court days, who was working for the French service of the BBC, and they had an interesting dialogue about political causes. In the summer he made a fleeting visit to Scandinavia. At the Academy Bookshop in Helsinki, a woman told him they had met previously – in Paris. She was Dorrit Hinze, last encountered in a shapeless dress outside Notre-Dame cathedral in 1951. They talked. She remembered the box of chocolates he had bought her, and how she had lived on it for days. Dorrit was now married to a successful surgeon. Vidia was aroused by the meeting, and thought later he would have liked to have had an affair with her. Passing through Denmark for a television interview, he apologized to Ralph Ironman for not calling: 'No time for anything . . . I am not built to cope with it. I feel myself becoming an actor and very bogus. It is better to say what you think, but if you do a lot of these interviews the secret, they tell me, is to say the <u>same</u> thing over and over. Which is a kind of degradation of the word and the self.'[1]

The trip to Helsinki was followed by a writers' symposium in Sweden, attended by the likes of Wole Soyinka, Philip Roth, Gabriel García Márquez, Michael Frayn and Heinrich Böll. Neither Vidia nor Michael Frayn had ever taken a sauna before, but seeing a notice that one was available for men from 6–8 each evening, they thought they would try their luck. 'We went through a room with benches at the side,' Frayn remembered, 'and found an exercise room beyond it. So we turned round and went back to the first room, stripped off and sat on the benches, waiting for them to switch on the heat. After a few minutes we agreed that it seemed to be getting hotter. "It's quite hot now. It's really very hot." Then Kurt Vonnegut came in and asked why we were sitting in there with no clothes on. I said this was the sauna. He laughed until he couldn't breathe, and pointed to a small door in the corner. The sauna.' Frayn noted Vidia's reluctance to make his own bed. 'He is a Brahmin, so he wouldn't do any physical work. We were asked to make our own beds, just to pull back the duvet, but Vidia refused. "I can't do that." He paid the housekeeper's son each day to do it for him. Vidia was a very grand figure even then, an immensely commanding figure, though charming.' At a dinner in London, Frayn introduced him to his colleague John Silverlight, an *Observer* journalist: 'He was a true liberal, and Vidia cottoned on and became more and more outrageous, saying immigrants should be deported, people should be hanged for stealing bicycles, that kind of thing. John Silverlight was jumping up and down, having another glass of whisky, trying to calm himself. Pat was there saying, "Oh Vidia, you don't really mean it." They all went home happily.'[2]

Far from proving a distraction, the emotional and intermittent physical presence of Margaret in Vidia's life focused his work. Arriving in Trinidad, he concentrated on his research and hid her away in the Queens Park Hotel in Port of Spain. 'She had to just sit in the hotel and wait till I got back from seeing Skerritt's mother and all these other people, all these strange people,' he said later.[3] The sadistic element of their relationship was kindled by the heat of the island and the macabre material Vidia was collecting. Margaret praised twelve magical and unbelievable days together, and ordered him to cherish the wounds on his arms as marks of great passion.[4] He introduced her to Savi and Mel, but they felt awkward because of their loyalty to Pat. Savi found her brother a changed man. 'Oh my goodness, then there was a spring in his step . . . freer, more open, happier. Pat and Vidia were never affectionate, never ever. With Margaret, there was open affection.'[5] Afterwards, Savi wrote to Pat, 'He has worked at a furious pace and seemed to have revelled in working and travelling at the most difficult and energy sapping hours in the early afternoons.'[6]

Pat, still unaware of her husband's relationship with Margaret, stayed at home in Wilsford affectionately rereading *A House for Mr Biswas*. 'You've written some big books, man,' she wrote to him. 'Biswas had the impact of a classic on me. And I was struck by that little passage (Proustian) at the end of Biswas about memories >(the children's)< of the period before the house giving back the past.'[7] Vidia responded to her no less warmly, giving news of the investigation, knowing how interested she was in the Malik case. 'Absolute, fantastic luck. I went to see Choko and the first thing he did was to offer me two boxes of M[alik]'s papers, rescued by him the night of the fire. It is possible to plot M's career from this, because he kept everything, even dry-goods bills, even solicitors' threatening letters. Lots of autobiographical writings; crazy schemes by his English associates for a "university of the alternative" under his "government" & so on ... Also, I fear, among Hakim's papers are 3 letters from Diana Athill which are like business-love letters which give me a creepy feeling that D had found herself another negro lover. I would like to think otherwise, but here we have Diana offering H[akim] the fare to get to California from her savings. I wish I hadn't found these letters; it gives me a terrible sensation, to intrude into the private correspondence of someone I know.'[8] When he returned to Wilsford, Vidia made a note to himself: 'My life, physically – I mean as far as my surroundings are concerned – is ideal. It is the writer's dream. But it is, without the work, a kind of death.'[9]

The long report on Michael Abdul Malik was to be one of Vidia's most remarkable and disturbing pieces of non-fiction, written at full throttle. It united many of his personal fears and obsessions. Joan Didion thought it was 'for Naipaul one of those dense situations in which a writer finds his every concern refracted'.[10] The new editor of the *Sunday Times Magazine*, Magnus Linklater, later described the article as 'the finest that we ran during my tenure'.[11] In the late 1960s, Michael X had been the best-known Trinidadian in Britain, an underground anti-hero who was taken up by the mainstream press and made a spokesman for black people, despite being a manifest crook. His fame was based not on achievement but on deception: he was the black to Naipaul's white, the negative to his positive: his doppelgänger. Yet interestingly, Vidia's greatest venom would be reserved not for Malik – whom he treated with a collusive sympathy, seeing him as a 'dummy Judas' playing an assigned role, having understood that in England 'race was, to Right and Left, a topic of entertainment' – but for the British patrons who let him flourish, 'the revolutionaries who visit centres of revolution with return air tickets, the hippies, the people who wish themselves on societies more fragile than their own, all those people who in the end do no more than celebrate their own security.' When Malik was finally convicted and hanged in the Royal Gaol in Port of Spain, his overseas promoters maintained that he was innocent ('a plea of insanity would have made nonsense of a whole school of theatre') despite the strong evidence against him. The countercultural ambassador John Michell even produced a *Souvenir Programme for the Official Lynching of Michael Abdul Malik*, describing him as a 'gentle mystic' and 'architect of the Holy City'. Beneath a drawing of a white woman trying to have sex with the hanging corpse of a black man, the American feminist Kate Millett was quoted: 'It's the hideous combination of racism and sexism that permits these kinds of trials to happen.'[12]

Vidia began his article with a line pregnant with anticipation, fear, and some humour: 'A corner file is a three-sided file, triangular in section, and it is used in Trinidad for sharpening cutlasses.' He placed Malik within a West Indian context, and used his private papers, including an attempt at a novel, to expose him: 'An autobiography can distort; facts can be realigned. But fiction never lies: it reveals the writer totally. And Malik's primitive novel is like a pattern book, a guide to later events.' In a postscript to the article, published when the legal process and appeals were complete, Vidia closes not with one of the stars but with a local petty criminal who got caught up in the action, Stanley Abbott: 'His was the true agony: he rotted for nearly six years in a death cell, and was hanged only in April 1979. He never became known outside Trinidad, this small muscular man with the straight back, the soldierly demeanour, the very pale skin, and the underslept tormented eyes. He was not the X; he became nobody's cause; and by the time he was hanged that caravan had gone by.' The most chilling aspect of Vidia's text is the way he takes no explicit moral position on Gale Benson's murder. The phrasing he uses to describe the moment of her killing is peculiarly unnerving: 'She was held by the neck and stabbed and stabbed. At that moment all the lunacy and play fell from her; she knew who she was then, and wanted to live ... It was an especially deep wound at the base of the neck that stilled her; and then she was buried in her African-style clothes. She was not yet completely dead: dirt from her burial hole would work its way into her intestines.'[13]

In July, after reading the piece, Diana wrote with news of one of the suspected killers, Kidogo. 'He has been living with [Hakim] Jamal in Boston, and is now somewhere in Mass[achusetts] living <u>under the protection of the district attorney</u>, with the other witnesses to Jamal's murder.' Diana explained in detail to Vidia why she thought he had misunderstood the sort of person Gale Benson was, pointing out that she had seen Jamal as her 'possessor' rather than as a racial guide.

'She'd have gone for anyone sexy who offered her a cult, even if he'd been as white as milk (cf Charles Manson and his girls).' Diana also observed that far from wearing expensive clothes, as Vidia had reported, Benson was the possessor of a blue cotton dress, some home-made 'dashikis' and a scrounged sweater. In short, Benson smelt dirty, ate almost nothing and was mentally unwell. Diana concluded that Vidia had used her inaccurately in order to make a point about middle-class white girls: 'you are cutting your cloth to fit your pattern, and that's unlike you.'[14] Full of a new sexual aggression, a disdain for everything he believed the murdered Gale Benson represented and disapproval of Diana's involvement in the events he had been describing, Vidia ignored her representations. Understanding an aspect of his character that no one else had seen before, Margaret told Vidia that she could feel her own presence in the article.

*

Back in Argentina with her husband, still full of sex and passion, Margaret called out for her lover. She told Vidia that she had been talking in her sleep, asking in English if he would buy her a Coca-Cola. She and Roy had again discussed separation, and she had made it clear that the only way she could remain married was if he agreed to turn a blind eye to Vidia. Roy was not willing to be complaisant, at least as far as V.S. Naipaul was concerned. She wondered whether she should leave, and asked for guidance, telling Vidia that her future was in his hands. It had taken him forty years to find love, desire, passion and intimacy, and yet she felt he would throw it all away if he thought it might disturb his life. Within weeks she was angry after a telephone call, seeing the relationship for what it was and realizing Vidia was offering her nothing. She summarized what he had said on the telephone, pointing out that great literary minds do not make mistakes when they talk. He wanted her to be his mistress, six thousand miles away, behave like a nun and sometimes come to England – or wherever in the world he happened to be travelling – for eight or ten days at a time to be the object of what she called his cruel sexual desires. She discussed the situation with a friend, who told her she must be mad to even contemplate such an arrangement. She did not have the courage to admit that Vidia even expected her to pay for it.

Margaret was addicted to Vidia: she loved him, was caught by him, amused by him and liked to be dominated by him. The cruelty was part of the attraction, which had the effect of stepping up the cruelty. She had received no letters from him because he said that writing to her would take up what he deemed to be Malik's time. Was there no part of his day that belonged to Margaret? She sent him what she called a whorish photo to keep him going. As for that Kate Millett woman, she had no time for her: she was a women's lib leader with a cause – probably her own; women like that always had causes. Contemplating what to do, while doing nothing, Vidia told Margaret over the telephone that her letters were irritating him, and that he was worried what would happen to Pat if he left her. What was Margaret to do? She responded crossly that he probably expected her to be lying on her tummy receiving just punishment for ruffling the feathers of his lordship the high priest. Later, Vidia wrote what she thought was a beautiful letter, which made her sick with longing. He was worried about Shiva, and sad she had aborted his child. His assertion that they must be together for a good long time delighted her. She sent him a photograph of herself wearing flower-power trousers, riding a bicycle on a friend's lawn. In reply, Vidia told her he hoped they would be together soon, related his lung trouble and called her his 'dear and lovely girl'. Margaret asked whether she might join one of those high-flying British vice squads so popular with the English aristocracy. She had a feeling that he knew Lord Lambton. Did he? Before their next meeting she promised to let her armpit hair grow thick and bushy in the way he liked, although while she was in BA she really could not be expected to go around looking like what she laughingly called an Italian cook cum whore. By June, his silence was making her feel hate and rage. There were temptations. What woman would care about selling herself to a rich man, if she did not give him her soul? She said the only difference between now and the past was that Vidia had found a woman more willing to accept the hurting and the violence. The arrangement gave him what he wanted: Mama at home, a whore in South America.

Though she was full of complaint, Margaret made her submission clear. She felt like putty in his hands; she had decided he was a horrible black man with hideous powers over her. For Vidia, the combination of lust and control could hardly be more potent. Margaret could tap in to his deepest anxieties, and say things to him that no one else was permitted to say, prodding and stimulating his secret fears and insecurities. By July, he had finished the Malik article, and was telling her to be calm. She replied that he sounded like Perón telling Argentina to keep calm. There was only one reason for being told to keep calm, and that was because there was a good reason for not being.

The Lion House

Anguilla, 1968

India, 1962

Left Pat and Khushwant Singh in Mehrauli

Above Pat and Vidia take tea by the pool at the Ashoka Hotel, New Delhi

Right Vidia in Kashmir

Far right V.S. Naipaul quits India

Eleanor Hale

Diana Athill

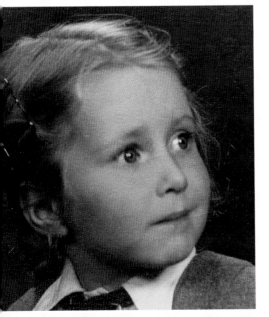

Vinod Mehta   Moni Malhoutra at Wilsford

Pat, Antonia Fraser
and Vidia
photographed
by Hugh Fraser
at Wilsford,
October 1971

Vidia photographs
Antonia, Hugh and
Pat on the same
afternoon

Margaret

Vidia and Margaret

'He was only playing bad; he was half-respectable, working a little family plot
up in the hills, and suffering with other farmers from low nutmeg prices . . .'
from 'Heavy Manners in Grenada', 1983

Polaroid of Vidia and Paul Theroux, 1986

Tony Powell at Wilsford, 1971

Gillon Aitken and Andrew Wylie

Selby Wooding

Francis Wyndham, 1990

Banning Eyre

Margaret in Indonesia, 1995

Vido and a proud Ma after the award of the Trinity Cross

Pat at Dairy Cottage

Vidia and Shiva at Queen's Royal College

Vidia photographed by Margaret

V.S. Naipaul in Oklahoma

Vidia and Nadira on the day of their engagement

Why was he still stuck in that infernal bungalow in Wiltshire? She went sailing with friends, and sunbathing, and in August looked for a flat to live in, feeling calm and strong, she told dearest Vido. It would cost £100 to £130 a month. She felt good about his plan for a book on Malik, and sure that it would sell very well. After all, it had a popular theme: murder. She thought it would be more appealing to the uneducated than his book about Indians in cupboards – a reference to Santosh in *In a Free State*. They planned a trip to Caracas together, where they would stay with Sir Lees Mayall, an impeccably connected Wiltshire landowner who Vidia had met at Tony Powell's house, and who was now serving as Her Britannic Majesty's Ambassador to Venezuela.

In September, Margaret left her husband and children. Vidia recanted at that precise moment: he would have nothing further to do with her. As he said later, 'What was extraordinary about our relationship was that I gave her very little, almost nothing. People give the people they are attracted to – they load them with gifts, don't they? Well of course I couldn't do that.'[15] Her letters sat unopened on his desk. He did not read the letter in which she said he was a nasty horrid black man but that she still wanted to show him her parents' crumbling estate before it was sold to the Peronistas, or that she had bought nice candy-striped lingerie and was glad he loved her letters. He did not read the letter in which she said he was vain to call his penis a god, but that she hoped to make a pilgrimage to the shrine. Then Vidia changed his mind and contacted her. They would meet in Montevideo, in Uruguay. Delighted, Margarita promised to kiss him on the weak spot she had discovered in Trinidad. Would he bring a copy of *The Honorary Consul* by her pet author Graham Greene – a novel set in the same morally compromised South American territory that Vidia was considering writing about? Or perhaps Greene was her second pet author, she conceded.

In Uruguay, Margaret felt disturbed and upset as she wondered what to do with her life. Was she right to leave Roy? Did Vidia want her? What did she want? The subsequent article, 'A Country Dying on Its Feet', reprinted as 'Kamikaze in Montevideo', was highly pessimistic: inflation was out of control, the bureaucracy had failed and Uruguay was suffering a vicious war between the government and the Tupamaros, a popular guerrilla group that had earlier kidnapped the British ambassador. Menchi Sábat, who was born in Montevideo, was quoted in the text: 'They were parricides, engaged in a kind of kamikaze.' Vidia's conclusion was escapist: 'Those who can, get out.' His equal dislike for revolutionaries and state torturers was clear; the most emotional line in the piece refers to the prelapsarian past: 'A monument in the Prado park commemorates Uruguay's last four Charrua Indians, who were sent as exhibits to the Musée de l'Homme in Paris, where they died.'[16] When Menchi read the piece, he wrote, 'The article is simply superb. When I'm in front of an orange, I would like to have the ability to say, "This is an orange." And you have that ability ... Excuse my non shakespearean English.'[17] Professor E. Bradford Burns of the University of California was less wholehearted: 'I am discouraged to find the *New York Review* printing such uninformative and misleading essays.'[18]

As Vidia and Margaret's relationship continued and she confided in her friends, rumours spread in social circles in Buenos Aires that the affair was more than tempestuous, and that the glamour of being V.S. Naipaul's mistress came at a very high price. Andrew Graham-Yooll thought Margaret 'liked the idea of getting laid by the well-known novelist. There were stories that he was violent towards her. The view of her friends was, "Poor Margaret, she fell in love with V.S. Naipaul and now he beats her." '[19]

*

In October 1973, Vidia returned from Uruguay and had the inspiration for a novel. 'I came back and made a bonfire at Wilsford Manor,' he said later, 'and as the leaves blazed I wrote down the structure of *Guerrillas*, the whole thing, and stuck to it. I remember raking the leaves and burning them.'[20] He told Pat about his other life with Margaret – and, characteristically, recalled the disclosure of infidelity in terms of his own suffering: 'I was full of grief. I went back to the bungalow and I told Pat, as I might have told my own mother. I was lying down in my little bed in my own little room and she wondered what was wrong with me and I told her. A very strange relationship I had with Pat. She was so good: she tried to comfort me ... I was so full of grief myself that in a way I expected her to respond to my grief, and she did.'[21]

Once the truth was out, he shared his anxieties with her as if she were a confidante rather than his wife, and she tolerated his conduct. Savi regarded Vidia's claim that Pat accepted the situation as 'absolute rubbish, such profound vanity'. Pat escaped to a tiny flat they had recently bought in Queen's Gate Terrace in Kensington, aided by an Arts Council grant of £1,000. On holiday in London around this time, Savi and Mel found themselves turned out of the flat because Pat needed somewhere to go.

'We were the first people to actually sleep in that property. It wasn't even furnished. Pat left us on the doorstep. I think she'd left Vidia, I'm not sure. Vidia said to me Pat doesn't want you to stay there.'[22] Savi felt that once Pat realized she would not have children, and that Vidia was set to be permanently unfaithful, her confidence in herself as a woman disappeared. 'I think from then on she was crushed, and there was a distinct change in her attitude to everybody. She withdrew, as if into a shell. Every time we said to Pat, let's do something, she couldn't do it. Always her excuse was that she had no clothes. She would say, "I have no clothes, I would not be able to go." '[23]

Distraught about the way in which her life was unravelling, Pat restarted her diary. At the same time, emulating Brecht, who had begun a journal at the age of forty, Vidia himself began to make occasional notes: 'I have at last distilled (or decided on) my characters – Jane, Roche, Jimmy. All people over the hill as it were, in an island like Trinidad-Jamaica. All fantasts, to some extent; but Jane, who is trivial, is to be killed. She needs men who appear to be active but are in fact toys. What delays me . . . is my inability to plot the two events that must lead to the murder. The two crises which the narrative needs. I have always been bad at plotting. It's a miracle I have written so much. I asked Pat for help. She said she couldn't write my books for me. I said I couldn't write them either. A joke. Work will absorb my sexual torment; but the torment rises higher with my non-writing. I toy with the idea of <u>running away</u>, becoming again the boy of 1954–55, starting afresh, going to Spain say; and contracting to do a review a month for the Observer or something like that.'[24]

At the end of November, Pat wrote: 'Tonight, by the fire, Vidia told me he was very excited about his two books but did not know about the other half of his life. That he was now two people. He showed me the photographs that she had sent. One of her alone, on a beach . . . one with Vidia ("Look how sad I'm looking, much sadder than she is" – I can't say I had noticed. Neither looked particularly sad).'[25] It seems not to have occurred to Pat to leave him, or to ask Vidia to leave. 'And me?' she wrote. 'Some feeling of sexual excitement but not as much as when Vidia was away. I think of talking – momentarily – to Antonia or to Sheila [Rogers] and dismiss it. Think of being silent. For the rest of my life?' Silence, or complicity, was to be her response. It enabled Vidia to break her confidence, while at the same time incorporating her into the process of literary creation. He relied on her guidance and support, even while he harried her; he said he could not imagine working without her. So Pat

stayed, cooking and washing for him, nominally still writing her own
article about Michael X and the killings in Trinidad, fetching the coal from
the outhouse, overhearing his telephone calls from Argentina, observing
the gardener Mr Elford working in the garden, reading books and watching
the television. (Trevor McDonald, educated at Naparima College in San
Fernando, had recently became ITN's first black reporter.)

Vidia's unconscious hope may have been that if he were sufficiently
horrible to Pat, she might disappear. Alone in her room at the cottage, she
dutifully recorded his insults: 'On Saturday night Vidia told me to put the
Malik thing aside. "It's not your talent" . . . He has not enjoyed making
love to me since 1967 . . . "You know you are the only woman I know
who has no skill. Vanessa paints, Tristram's wife paints, Antonia, Marigold
Johnson" . . . To Lindsay and Marisa for dinner . . . He said this evening
before Sheila arrived that we were two people who had destroyed one
another.' Even when she was alone, Pat felt she had failed her husband.
After going up to London to watch a play with Antonia, Francis and Julian
Jebb, she concluded that while she was there she had 'lived up to Vidia's
dictum: "You don't behave like a writer's wife. You behave like the wife
of a clerk who has risen above her station."' Witnessing Vidia's work
became a substitute for living. Now that Pat urgently needed the support
of friends, it became ever more difficult to confide in them.

Worried by the situation, Marisa Masters took it upon herself to
intervene. In early December, she wrote to Pat that Vidia had telephoned
her. 'His words were direct, he interrupted my nonsense and said: "Marisa
listen, I have got to tell you something that will please you; I have told
Margaret that all is finished." Vidia of course knew I was pleased. He
added that he liked his life as it was and that he had confessed everything
to you: That was beautiful.'²⁶ Marisa spoke of her own earlier marital
problems, and told Pat that she was lucky to now know the truth. The
reply was written in a weak hand: 'The love & the regard you have shown
me in writing as you did has given me strength & comfort . . . I have not
quite found my bearings.'²⁷ Although she did not say so, Pat knew that the
affair was far from finished. Writing to Antonia Fraser during this period,
the same shift in tone was evident. Her letters became apologetic and
cursory, and her handwriting poorly formed: 'I know you are very busy
. . . I would love to see you. Come and lunch, or something . . . We did
not talk much. My fault.'²⁸ Although Antonia tried to maintain the
friendship, she had to accept that Pat had become an extremely reserved
person. Her own life was increasingly complicated at this time, even as she

achieved professional success. The magazine *Private Eye* renamed her 'Lady Magnesia Freelove' and published a cartoon after the manner of H.M. Bateman showing a group of surprised men above the caption, 'The man who admitted he hadn't been to bed with Lady Antonia Fraser.' She lived stylishly; an attempt at seduction by the ill-favoured Australian humorist Clive James was said to have been rejected with the line, 'I only sleep with the First Eleven.'[29]

Pat's state of mind was worsened by the fact she was now dosing herself regularly with Mandrax, an addictive sleeping tablet also known as Quaalude which was a popular recreational drug in the 1960s, and was widely prescribed as a sedative before being banned for its unpredictable side effects, which include euphoria, emotional disturbance, sexual arousal and depression. A doctor in north London, Dr Toszeghi, would prescribe her 100 pills at a time, together with 100 doses of Valium. 'Use them sparingly,' he advised.[30] Pat became intimately involved with the creation of the new novel during the long, cold winter of 1973–74, while OPEC sent oil prices soaring and Britain lurched towards economic disaster and a three-day working week. Each night she would record the book's progress and the way in which its powerful, destructive force was wrapping itself around the two of them:

> He has been typing the story out ('Guerrillas') ... Emma and Teresa 'essentially bogus'. I connect that out of them he has created a tragic figure ... I say that [Jane] has become rather imaginative, too imaginative for an *Express* reader. 'I know. I can't write about stupid people. They all have to have something of myself in them' ... He says he has always written like that, Mr Stone was him ... She will have affair with [Jimmy] Ahmed out of self-disgust. Nihilist, not out to hurt the man. But he is appalled and sets out (subconsciously?) to destroy both of them ... Do I think Emma will recognise herself. I say she probably won't read it. But Teresa will ... Vidia says as if the story exists, read it already. He wants to get the people acting on an empty Robinson Crusoe stage.

As the night closed in, she wrote:

> The longest day, wet and dark ... A telephone call from Argentina ... I say I am conscious of [Jane] being the victim – he says she is becoming the victim >Roche is depriving her of will, ability to take decisions< without knowing it. The sexual excitement is still there but situated in the cunt not overmastering, my mind is free ... I

have never experienced anything like this before. Listening and learning. His face dark and exhausted ... He talks about how he has arrived at his understanding of this type of woman. Sexually I am very excited ... He got the vision of her appearance from a French, or American, girl waiting on the breezy runway of Easter Island (Chile), her trousers tremulous in the wind.

On Christmas Eve 1973, caught like a fly in Vidia's web, Pat wrote: 'Vidia takes the opportunity to say that we have had good times together ... and maybe I should live alone ... And then he read the *Nibelungenlied*. I said "Don't bother" and he said "Don't be silly, Pat." The killing of Siegfried. I felt I was Siegfried with the cross on my clothing, vestment. And now I am trying to get the strength of mind to put his pillows in his room.'

At other moments, he would explain his literary techniques to her, such as his use of the reveal, when he shows a character physically before confirming his identity.

Going over how to get Jane out of the hut ... into the sunlight, the silence behind her, the bare concrete ... His people move: first figure, then face, the expression on the face. He first did this in *An Area of Darkness* in describing the pilgrims (going towards the cave) ... Only a very few critics will appreciate everything that goes into such writing ... He has to do very difficult, complicated things very simply. That is what writing, 'style', experimental writing is: to write in a thoroughly modern way.

So in the opening chapter Jimmy appears first as a frightening but absurd figure in a conversation between Jane and Roche, next as a name painted on a board outside Thrushcross Grange People's Commune: 'JAMES AHMED (Haji)', then as the answer to a question, ' "Mr Ahmed bathing"', until finally Jane and the reader see Jimmy for the first time as 'a man in the doorway at the far end of the hut. The man was at first in silhouette against the white light outside. When he came into the hut he could be seen to be naked from the waist up, with a towel over one shoulder.'[31]

*

When Margaret got home from Uruguay in early November, Roy prevented her from seeing their children while at the same time trying to persuade her to return. She made plans to publish a local edition of *Mr*

Stone. Vidia had to ask Penguin to agree. She loved being with him, lying beside him and listening to him talk. He should ask the bookseller who was valuing his work what he would pay for love letters. She had read *Mr Stone*: the temptation to find out about Vidia's marriage was too great to resist. He was having trouble writing and she tried to encourage him. She said she liked living alone, and sent him some photographs to brighten his day and take his mind off the nasty British economy, including one of herself pregnant, ten days off having a baby. Would they ever have a baby together, she wondered? She had seen a picture of Paul Theroux in *Time*, and was not surprised to hear he was successful with women.

Margaret wanted to know whether Vidia had told Pat about their affair: he would be defrauding all three of them if he continued with things as they were. He mentioned practical details to her, but she did not know what he meant in practice – was he seriously asking whether she would work to support his two houses and his harem? The answer was that she had worked for most of her married life, and he should stop distrusting her. Why – when he telephoned, his first question was usually to ask who she was in bed with. Now Margaret felt sad living alone in Buenos Aires, and had allowed herself to be taken out to dinner. She had a temporary job as a secretary in a telephone company, GTE International, which Vidia disliked, but as she informed him, she was unable to live off the air. She felt that he was treating her badly, and she would always be denied a leading role in his life. She said she had no doubt that he would come back to her to be serviced, and then would expect to be sent back looking lovely to his good and understanding wife and all his constant friends. She complained that his letters to her were always conditional, with lines like 'we will and we should have' rather than a straight commitment.

In December she wrote that she had been getting things in order, and making preparations to change her life. It was such a big step she was taking: the greatest burden had been telling her children and her family that she was leaving, and she was glad that part was over, although it had been amazing how well they had taken it. Roy was pressing her hard to go back, but she believed that to do so would be like stepping into a coffin alive. She was slowly developing a tan, and had become the laughing stock of the swimming pool with all the black hair under her arms. Since Vidia was so keen on statistics, she told him what she had recorded: they had made love thirty-one times in twenty days, although on three of those days they had made no love at all – only hate. Surely the answer was to have a child? Vidia's family might think he was a eunuch, but she knew very well he was not. Maybe she should have had the child when she got pregnant? She adored the pin-up poses she had been given showing him in his underpants, but thought he was disgustingly vain. She asked him for the third time to send her the Malik article. She even clicked out a message of love to Vido on adhesive plastic tape and stuck it schoolgirlishly to the letter.

Christmas and New Year were impossible, spent in discussions with lawyers, with Margaret's parents refusing to talk to her. It was so depressing to be arguing over who would have the children, but she had been given an ultimatum that she either had to go back or give them up. Roy said he would even ignore her having affairs – as long as she did not have one with V.S. Naipaul. The writer was in a torment of indecision, obsessively working on *Guerrillas* to keep his mind off making a choice. In a telephone conversation just before Christmas, he left Margaret fairly assured that they would soon live together, but then a month went by without any confirmation. He spoke of the shattered futures he and Pat now faced, which provoked Margaret to anger. In her view, his marital relationship had always been shattered, and he had not changed a damn thing in his life. If anyone had given him a new lease of life with his writing, she had. He would certainly have shrivelled up otherwise. She was beginning to think that he regarded her as just a woman to be slept with and enjoyed. She was now in a soul-destroying job at the Division Industrial of the Singer Sewing Machine Company. Roy wanted her back. Life was lonely, eating solo while he had the companionship of a wife with whom he could eat and sleep at his leisure, a situation that made Margaret see red. All of this would be worth it, though, all this sacrifice would be worth it if in the end they could be together. But for the moment she was left with absolutely nothing. She had lost her children and she hardly spoke to her parents. She wanted an end to the uncertainty, to all the ifs and the buts and the living in the past and hoping for the future. She had not had a letter from him for over a month, and even the porter at her apartment block realized there was a problem as she was always asking for the post. He had said to her, 'Vamo a tener que retailo a ere morochito (darkie!)'. 'I am going to have to scold this swarthy little fellow.' And then the porter asked whether Vidia was coming back. Margaret was humiliated, having to answer sheepishly that she did not know.

Finally Vidia telephoned at the end of January to say that since people were rebuking him, their relationship was over. 'Feel yourself free,' he said graciously. Margaret was irate. A relationship of such importance could not be finished in this way, she wrote. What had become of all his talk about integrity, and of his promise that she would only be his? What else was there left to believe in now? She posted the letter unsigned, crying bitter tears, and wrote again from a friend's country house, a ten-side letter on GTE International writing paper, pleading, raging that her eyes were red rimmed from crying. Her recollection of their telephone call at the end of December was that he had said they would shortly be living together, and she would always have him. She could not live without him. His telephone call had left her like a lunatic with grief. She loved only him. Could it be because of her father's childhood in India? And she knew that only she could give Vidia the joy he sorely needed: he had been like a shrivelled-up prune when they first met. She was left with empty assurances. He could have promised her Versailles, for all it meant. She dreamed about their sexual games together, and said she would never agree to abandon the feeding of the lollipop, or the country of the Baganda, or visiting the very special place of love. She would not abandon the magic genie or playing doctors.

What was Margaret going to do? Everything in her life was directed at eventually living with him. She did not specify whether this meant in England, in Argentina or elsewhere. Now she felt as if she had been thrown off a cliff and was floating in space. Her friends had warned her, warned her and warned her. So perhaps Menchi had been right, Silvina had been right and her stepfather had been right. It made her flesh crawl just to think of it. She had been betrayed. Now Vidia responded by flinging every smart excuse at her, even, absurdly, the plight of another Margaret, his mother-in-law Marg Hale, as an excuse not to act. What was Vidia saying? She understood about his book, his uncertainty, his problems over money, his wife, his wife's mother, the situation in England. She understood all of that. But what she did not understand were the broken promises. Was her love in vain? She swore at him, in Spanish. After their conversation in December, she had been to her lawyer to make the separation from Roy final. Although she supposed that it did not now make much difference, she said she certainly had the guts to see it through. She described a dream from the previous night of a visit to Vidia's cottage in Wiltshire. Thomas Hardy was sitting in the garden, and Margaret had asked him about the meaning of sorrow, but he did not answer. Vidia took her for a walk and they kissed and kissed and he licked her face and licked away all her salty tears. Finally, a response came. Vidia recanted partially, and said the relationship might continue.

Margaret went to the resort of Necochea, and sent him a postcard of skyscrapers and women in swimsuits, reverting to talk of desire and their Lawrentian religion of sex. She said she had seen lots of Negroes on the beach, but none looked as nice as Vido. She hoped that the god was shrunken and unexercised. Next she went to stay on a friend's estate with her children. She had a low view of the local Argentines, who stood outside bars with moronic looks, the women with curlers in their hair and the men wearing pyjama bottoms and string vests. The telephone operator in the nearby village had a mad son who was prone to peep at her through the door, and sometimes he would come into the phone booth and mutter obscenities under his breath. For the first time in her correspondence with Vidia, nearly two years into their relationship, she mentioned one of her children by name. They had all been asking her whether she felt sad, and she replied that she was. Her daughter Karin thought she knew why: it was because of 'Naipaul'. If her mother loved him and he made her happy, what was the problem? Margaret said she had been to the local nightclub with some polo players: Vidia knew that she loved dancing and fooling around, and that usually she would come to life whenever she heard blaring music. But that evening she had felt like a lifeless thing and had wanted nothing except to have his arms around her and his head on her shoulder and his hard body leaning in against hers.

Margaret was soon employed by Massey-Ferguson, manufacturer of tractors, working for a lunatic who was prone to kick his desk. She told Vidia that all she wanted was to be fucked and fucked and fucked and fucked. She was exercising religiously and had bought herself some new clothes. She admitted to him that she would try to distract herself every now and again with a classy fella – though none was as classy as him. A letter came from Vido. She would give considerable thought to his suggestion that she should have his love child. Might they even have a little girl? She wanted to pour champagne on the god and get drunk on love. She had sent him a shirt and a Frank Sinatra record via her sister; he did not bother to thank her. His latest plan, as he sat in Wiltshire tormenting himself with *Guerrillas*, was that they might meet in Argentina at the start of May and go to Córdoba on a sleeper train. Margaret passed on some gossip that had reached South America: Vidia's friend Antonia was rumoured to be having an affair with the actor Robert Stephens, who was married to Maggie Smith. Nobody but Vidia had made her feel the freedom of the world and the pleasures of the flesh, but nobody had made her suffer so much. As he had told her, pain was part of the passion. On writing paper engraved with a bull's head above the legend 'SHORTHORN DE DRABBLE', Margaret told him once more how much she adored him, illustrating the point with a 1:1 scale drawing of his erect penis, done in dark-brown felt-tip; the penis wore sunglasses and a lime-green cowboy hat.

*

In the new year of 1974, Mr and Mrs Naipaul took the train from Salisbury to London to attend one of Sonia Orwell's carefully crafted dinners. 'Vidia did not want to come out of his solitude and his obsession. We spent a long time on Salisbury station – the 10.53 only runs on Saturdays and the 11.24 was cancelled,' Pat wrote in her diary. 'Vidia grew hysterical in the buffet waiting-room.' Francis and Miriam Gross were there, as was the painter Francis Bacon. Vidia's new beard caused comment; he told the party 'that it makes women take notice of him, they react in the shops in Salisbury.' Afterwards, Vidia and Pat hurried home. The next night found them watching *Othello* on television, with Laurence Olivier in the title role. 'He thinks the play is written out of experience and suffering,' Pat wrote, and recorded this exchange:

> 'An old man's passion.'
> 'A distinguished man,' I say.
> 'All distinguished men have their Iagos.'

She worked up the courage to ask whether he was still involved with Margaret. 'He told me that he was still in love with her. "It's my life. I'm sorry, Pat." ' They planned to go to Holland for Easter with Teresa and Peter, but Vidia pulled out at the last minute and they went to see the Powells for the day instead, driven there by Tristram. 'After lunch Virginia went to paint and Tristram took the children down to the lake. I joined Violet in the kitchen . . . I spoke about Vidia's work and she immediately about Tony's. She always counters like this.' Back home, they discussed John Powell's recent breakdown. 'Vidia spoke about his [own] illness at Oxford . . . how you hate the man who tells you the truth about yourself, you never want to see him again; how he did not have enough shillings for the gas when he planned suicide.' Kamla's thirteen-year-old son Ved came to stay with them for a couple of weeks, 'a sweet boy', which gave Pat some respite from the intensity of the creation of *Guerrillas*. She walked with Ved to Stonehenge. 'Larks were rising and we saw a hare.'

As the months passed, the telephone calls from Argentina kept coming. 'Am quaking. Try to return to the Malik. Thinking of my revoltingness and folly. Think it would be nice to win the respect of Savi, Vidia. And others whom I have repelled. Nearly midnight. Seized by self-disgust and anger. And today Sati's letter came saying how badly Vidia must feel because he was unable to pay Nella's fees.' Their relationship went on, its fractures being incorporated into Vidia's writing. 'Yesterday afternoon the sex went bad and Vidia lost his temper . . . On Saturday afternoon I read the next, short section, where Jane returns to Port of Spain in the car and am a little bemused to find that Vidia has utilised recent events and words between us so that this whole experience is becoming intricately interwoven.' Vidia was working at a constant, nearly mad pitch of intensity, writing the book with a fine red biro in a miniature hand, sometimes cramming two lines to each line of a narrow-ruled notebook, sometimes squeezing up to thirty words to a single line: the word 'cigarette', for example, is less than a centimetre long and less than a millimetre high.[32] The more dramatic or frightening the story, the more cramped his handwriting became.

Pat recorded her husband's thoughts and assertions, and her own hallucinatory responses to them.

While I was in London he had a dream. This small woman (slightly malformed?) was fixing this medical apparatus to his arm . . . Then she attacked him, bit his genitals . . . He is the book and lives the book . . . As he sat in the yellow chair last night and spoke of Roche – his smugness and cruelty, his mouth, he became Roche . . . He thinks the book is sympathetic to Negroes . . . 'There will be no Indians in this book.' This afternoon he will cut out the reference to Indian prayer flags near the airport . . . He has told me that nothing unfinished is to be published . . . 'If I die, edit with Diana' . . . He values my judgement, my approval as high as that of Francis . . . 'Somerset Maugham was very wise when he said that the powers of invention grow as you become older, young men don't have the powers contrary to belief' . . . He feels that this novel will unleash a great period of productivity . . . Calm now. Have taken one Mandrax . . . I suppose it is the greatest book of the century.

In the thousands of pages of Pat's diary, Margaret is never mentioned by name. She is rendered as 'this woman', 'his friend', 'her', 'the person'. The closest Pat comes is in the sentence: 'I could write her name.' Vidia continued to confide in his wife, and their own sexual relationship revived. In February she wrote, 'Vidia told me he was "grieving for that girl" ... Says he has no one to talk to about it so must talk to me. So we talk till one in the morning.' Later, he 'emerged to say he was too sleepy and to ask me to come and make love. I put the Japanese kimono on.' He told her that couples sometimes took pornographic photographs of each other, her naivety making him seem worldly: 'I would not know about this if I did not have Vidia to tell me about it ... Call it vicarious experience? But without him I sometimes feel there would be no experience, no knowledge.' He said he wanted to write about sex in the book, but was nervous. He talked around the subject before beginning the scene of Jane's anal rape: 'Vidia still did not describe the sex act. It would horrify us but it does not horrify her and it will not horrify others.' Weeks went by, and he continued to circle. 'He is about to write the sex between them which he still will not talk about.' Finally he wrote it and 'read it to me. It was terrifying and I began to feel slightly faint and asked for us to leave the small stuffy room. "But not offensive. I've tried to avoid offensive words." Not erotic. Anti-erotic.' Days later, Pat wrote that Vidia was returning to Margaret: 'Had made up his mind to go to this girl ... We spoke late into the evening. We made love more experimentally, more lovingly. Dusk fell. We were cold in the room.' She wrote an initialism in her diary, 'H h n d t w h,' which may stand for, 'He has never done this with her.'

Pat felt powerless to act. She compared herself in her diary to Jimmy's assistant Bryant, his catamite and executioner, and years later wrote that she was 'ashamed that anyone should know – of course they know – ashamed that I saw something of myself in Bryant. But it is no good just trying to hide it – the only hope is not to be it, not to be servile.' Sometimes, she felt more terrified than ashamed; after all, *Guerrillas* is a story of violence and betrayal that ends with Roche packing his suitcase and telling Jimmy over the telephone that Jane is in her room packing, although he knows that Jimmy has murdered her. His final words are: ' "Jane and I are leaving tomorrow ... Are you hearing me? Jimmy?" ' and Jimmy Ahmed replies with a single word, the last word in the book: ' "Massa." '[33] Pat wrote: 'This picking up of life as he is living it in the novel is now at a very serious level – not small things as earlier. Leaving, things packed, a drawer pulled out is serious for me.'

One day, Pat was inspecting a rathole in a wall of the cottage. 'Vidia comes out of his room and I say, "No one asked you to come out of your hole, Mr Rat." "How extraordinary you should say that. I was just about to write that. Bryant. Rat is the Trinidad word for prostitute.' And there, in tiny handwriting, using the red biro, Vidia wrote the death scene: killing Jane, killing Gale, killing Margaret, killing Pat, Diana, Emma and Teresa, killing what he hated and loved and embraced and rejected:

> He ran back into the lean-to, and when he turned to face them he had a cutlass in his hand and he was in tears.
> He cried, 'Jimmy! Jimmy!'
> Jimmy locked his right arm about Jane's neck and almost lifted her in front of him, pulling back the corners of his mouth with the effort, and slightly puffing out his shaved cheeks, so that he seemed to smile.
> He said, '*Bryant, the rat! Kill the rat!*'
> Bryant, running, faltered.
> '*Your rat, Bryant! Your rat!*'
> Her right hand was on the arm swelling around her neck, and it was on her right arm that Bryant made the first cut.
> The first cut: the rest would follow.[34]

These were, Pat wrote solemnly in her diary, 'Good words. Given to him "by God" a month ago. He will not change them. When he reaches the words "Bryant, the rat! Kill the rat!" he shouts . . . He is aware of the symbolism. Afraid that the girl he is killing is "my friend". (I had thought of this. Men are terrible.)'

CHAPTER TWENTY

THE MARRIAGE OF
MANDRAX AND VALIUM

VIDIA FINISHED THE FIRST DRAFT of *Guerrillas* in May 1974 and promptly took off for Argentina. Pat was humiliated. 'All of London knows he is going back to her ... He rages that he won't be made to feel guilty ... I began to plead and protest in a rather sickening way.'[1] Vidia and Margaret spent two months together, staying in Buenos Aires and travelling to Córdoba to stay in a house in the hills. Using a Rolleiflex camera, Menchi Sábat photographed him against a street kiosk scrawled with the graffito: EVITA VIVE. Menchi had got to know Vidia, and concluded, 'He was terribly competitive. I found in general when he measured himself it was against British people, or white people like Harold Pinter. He has an aura. When you are with Vidia, you are convinced you are in front of a very important person. But I don't think he's come to a solution about his own origin. He wanted to be born white.'[2]

Soon after Vidia returned to England, Juan Perón died and was replaced by his wife Isabel, or Isabelita, which provoked further unrest. The king was dead, Margaret told Vidia: she had watched the funeral procession, and had observed people filing past the coffin, some of them hysterical, some kissing Perón's face or wiping their handkerchiefs across the forehead of his rotting corpse. She thought that although the experience was macabre, the Argentines had loved it.[3] Vidia's first letter to Margaret when he got home was warm and hopeful: 'Here I am, on a Monday morning, thinking about you. When really, as I told you on the telephone on Saturday, I should be worrying about the damned Conrad lecture, which the Sunday Times want for August.' He was glad she might soon be coming to London. 'So we'll either leave England together and go away and write the book somewhere; or will decide the other, sad thing. But for the last time: no more hesitations. I cannot tell you how <u>new</u> the weeks with you were for me. A little lifetime they seem to me now: you must understand that I have not been used to that kind of intimacy; that I have never known such a period of passion. I wish I had been freer in my mind.' He told Margaret she must be patient while he made arrangements for their future together. 'There are so many practical things that have to be settled before one can make a move. The lease for the cottage; the furnishing of the London flat; the matter of contracts for the autobiography. And, of course, the key thing: the revision of the book, for which I need <u>calm</u> and no emotional upheavals.'[4]

Vidia was thinking hard about Joseph Conrad, to whom critics often compared him, for a conference at the University of Kent at Canterbury. As he said in the opening line: 'It has taken me a long time to come round to Conrad.'[5] When he was picked up by an academic for a minor factual discrepancy, he was distraught: 'The error is unforgivable.'[6] Margaret considered Conrad a dull subject, telling Vidia he should lecture on passion instead of on fuddy duddies. Meanwhile in Wilsford, Pat noted in her diary: 'His manner towards me is cool with a hint of patronage. He is very cheerful.' Vidia spent the summer correcting the manuscript of *Guerrillas*, reading Balzac's *Eugenie Grandet* and going shooting near the cottage with his air rifle. By September, the book was complete. 'I feel slightly stunned. It's a novel of amazing intensity,' Diana wrote. 'I didn't feel, finally, that the woman you had set up was a woman to whom this would have happened. There were times when her graceless awfulness seemed to be her raison d'être . . . It's a terribly depressing and frightening book: such hopelessness!'[7] Later, Diana felt she had been too blunt with Vidia about *Guerrillas*: 'I thought I had handled it badly, so I was rather ashamed . . . I thought it is a very offensive thing to be told that the actual characters weren't working. It was a sort of build up of being irritated by him, it was coming out.'[8] In her memoir *Stet*, Diana described how her complaints over *Guerrillas* led to Vidia deciding to leave Deutsch: she was in fact confusing this stand-off with an event that occurred two years later.

Publication came the following autumn. 'Couldn't you have found an honest job slinging coal, or washing dishes?' asked a Christian correspondent from Kathmandu. 'I feel as betrayed as if the great Jeeves himself had suddenly begun writing four letter words on the walls of Brinkley Manor. And it is perhaps instructive to note that P.G. Wodehouse, the greatest humorist of this century, managed to turn out more than 90 books without dipping his pen into the toilet.'[9] An

American reader wrote: 'I have just finished reading your novel *Guerrillas* and I am very angry ... Sure, women like Jane exist, but women are changing and leaving behind the qualities they are supposed to have: the passivity, the masochism, the mindlessness.'[10] Proud of the masochism, Margaret told Vidia that her sister's husband Kiffy had added to his royalties by buying a copy of *Guerrillas*. Her brother-in-law had made the perceptive observation that Jane was the most important character in the novel, a deduction, Margaret noted, that had been overlooked by almost everyone else. But only she and Vidia knew quite why.[11] Paul Theroux told Francis Wyndham, 'I found myself almost gagging on this book – gagging with admiration and a kind of horror.'[12] It was a fair response.

'Naipaul is a scourge. He never relents,' wrote Joe Klein in *Mother Jones*. His work 'can best be described as a literature of buggery: his main purpose seems to be the desecration of his audience.' All the same, Klein admitted, 'I, as a devoted reader, cannot resist the temptation to be ravaged.'[13] An old opponent, Raoul Pantin, wrote in *Caribbean Contact* that the book was 'shattering evidence of the deepening sense of personal distress, of private desolation, that Naipaul feels after a remarkable creative career that has spanned nearly 20 years.'[14] Some reviews were positive. Peter Ackroyd thought *Guerrillas* 'a powerful and thoughtful novel' and Anthony Thwaite commended 'a brilliant artist's anatomy of emptiness, and of despair'.[15] In the *Listener* John Vaizey wrote, '*Guerrillas* has the fashionable sexual explicitness, which succeeds in being vulgar without being forthright – coy, in fact – and adds to the impression that the novel is not a story, but a vehicle around which a series of magazine articles, on sex, on women, on delinquency, are hung like placards.'[16] Tony Powell wrote unconvincingly to Vidia, 'It is a splendid book. How absurd of some reviewers to compare it with Graham Greene. If his name is to be mentioned at all, that should be only because your novel is a contrast to the sentimentality, phoniness, and falseness of feeling with which his works almost always abound.'[17]

In the autumn of 1974 Vidia told Pat, 'we were at the end of our relationship and that it would be worse (for me) in eight years when I am fifty ... I was stupid, talked too much about Proust, myself, my early attitudes and stupidity.' He had decided finally to be with Margaret: ' "I want her with all her follies." ' Pat had slim, desolate consolations. 'We took the 6.32 bus into Salisbury and had dinner in The Golden Curry. This was a big treat although the food was not very good.' With reluctance, she moved to the flat in London to begin a new life. After more than two years of work on the Malik article, she decided she might show it to Antonia. 'Ridiculously,' she noted, 'I am making these moves to write, work, rehabilitate myself at the moment of break-up.' At a party given by George Weidenfeld, John Gross 'asked me what books I would like to review. Francis came over and I told him and his eyes were amused, ironical.' She visited her mother in Birmingham, and travelled to its suburbs to follow 1974's second general election campaign, after the collapse of Harold Wilson's minority government. Soon, Vidia was telephoning in anguish to say he was having a recurring dream of a human head exploding. 'I hurried back to him.' He was convinced that by applying his mind he would solve his emotional worry, although it was his mind that was causing him torment. After a few days cosseting her husband in Wilsford, Pat went back to London alone. Always, she protected and cared for Vidia, treating him like the child she did not have. She might leave behind a note: 'Mon. Dinner: soup (1/2) (sardines?) quiche grapes. Tues. Lunch: Baked fish & 2 veg. apple crumble. Dinner: soup (1/2) eggs, remains of apple crumble?'[18]

At the end of July, Margaret had sent Vidia a bitter letter, typing it because she did not want him to read her mood from the handwriting. Her nihilism begat his nihilism; they brought out the negative in each other, and fed off it. For the preliminaries, she told him of local gossip and the daily reminders of his presence: the remnants of his beard in the basin, and bits of tobacco under her bed. Her children had been sent to La Cumbre, a mountain resort in Córdoba province, for the winter holidays. After considerable thought, she had taken her lover's point of view that Argentina was a mediocre country, where mediocrity triumphed. Then came the news: she was pregnant by him for a third time, she said, either out of love or out of hate, and was taking the appropriate measures. She knew that Vidia would not be willing to take any responsibility for what had happened. He did not understand living things, she asserted, because he had spent his life protecting himself from life. He was the product of a dead marriage and a dead childhood. She quoted his words back to himself: 'Aridity, I write out of aridity.' She wondered what he might have written out of fulfilment? She was left with reminders of his presence: a thickened waist, which she knew he would dislike, and a bruise on her body. But that was what happened, she informed him, if you were brutal to someone and threw shoes at them. For all this, though, for all her resentment and her pain, she felt betrayed by an agony of longing. At night, she was with Vido in her dreams, and in those dreams their love was tender and perhaps greater than it had ever been. Although she acknowledged that it might be foolish on her part, she could give herself to no other man. Nobody else would be able to offer her such ecstasy. Must she remain his whore, she asked?

In character, Vidia did not answer Margaret directly. Instead he internalized his reaction in a strange, murderous piece for the *New York Review*, 'The Brothels Behind the Graveyard'. It has no clear narrative, avoids setting a context and assumes much background knowledge about Perón and Argentina. Again, he identifies only with the Amerindians. The country had 'as yet no idea of itself'. Those who attempted to place it historically were ignoring the reality of a place where 'people are still being killed and kidnapped in the streets'. It was a 'brutish land of estancias and polo and brothels and very cheap servants ... full of military names, the names of generals who took the land away from the Indians and, with a rapacity that still outrages the imagination, awarded themselves great portions of the earth's surface, estates, estancias, as large as counties.' By imposing Evita and then Isabelita on Argentina, Perón had wrought 'the roughest kind of justice on a society still ruled by degenerate machismo, which decrees that a woman's place is essentially in the brothel.' Women had few rights or opportunities: 'They are meant to be victims; and they accept their victim role.' He worked himself into a frenzy of loathing: this was 'a society spewing on itself'. His concluding image of BA, intended to sum up the nation, was of the garish brothels near the funerary monuments at Recoleta. He made the absurd claim that, 'Every schoolgirl knows the brothels; from an early age she understands that she might have to go there one day to find love, among the coloured lights and mirrors.' And there was more: Naipaul deduced that Argentine men were 'diminished' by their apparent preference for anal sex. 'The act of straight sex, easily bought, is of no great moment to the macho. His conquest of a woman is complete only when he has buggered her.'[19] The Argentine embassy in Washington DC sent the *New York Review* what Bob Silvers termed an 'oddly threatening' letter, suggesting 'some personal problem' on the part of the author, and stating that 'perhaps in the long run it will cause more problems to your publication than to the Argentine Republic.'[20] Andrew Graham-Yooll recalled the outrage among the Anglo-Argentine community: 'People said, "We invited him to our house and – look – he says we go about buggering women." '[21]

At the start of August, with Vidia still silent, Margaret let him know that she was recovering physically and mentally from what she termed her little murder. He had said or done precisely nothing to sustain her, and she wondered whether these days people simply did not bother to acknowledge such trifling matters. Yet for all his indifference, she still wanted him. She planned to visit Spain and France for two weeks, and would meet him in London in the middle of September. The tone of her letter was cool, different – and Vidia was suspicious. They met, and he took her down to Wilsford to the cottage. Something was wrong; Vidia found a letter from a scion of a prominent banking family in Argentina. Margaret had entered into an arrangement with him in order to visit the man she loved. Vidia recalled: 'She came to Europe with an Argentine banker. It was terrible when I found out. She was having a relationship with the banker for the means to get to me. She said she would have slept with him a hundred times to get to me, and I believed her actually . . . I was extremely upset. I was very violent with her for two days; I was very violent with her for two days with my hand; my hand began to hurt . . . She didn't mind it at all. She thought of it in terms of my passion for her. Her face was bad. She couldn't appear really in public. My hand was swollen. I was utterly helpless. I have enormous sympathy for people who do strange things out of passion.'[22]

When Margaret left Wilsford, evacuated by her sister Diana, Pat received a telephone call. 'He told me he was in a terrible state and asked me to return. "There is nothing in it for you." When I got back I would not let him ask me to look after him for the sake of the book . . . He told me of the violent scenes here between the Friday and the Sunday morning when the sister came for her, trembling . . . I love him – at last.' Vidia abandoned his decision to end their marriage. Looking back, he claimed: 'If Pat were a stronger person or more at ease in the world, I might have left her to look after herself. I couldn't do that. That's when I discovered the strength of the weak . . . I should have left. I didn't have the brutality. Isn't it strange? People would say that what I was doing was quite brutal.'[23] He had a mental dependence on both women: the 'master' in a masochistic relationship can have less psychological control than the 'victim'. Vidia found himself unable, despite repeated efforts, to break away from either Margaret or Pat: the only way he could have escaped the situation was if one or both of them had left him. The intensity and violence of this episode marked a culmination in his relationship with Margaret; after the events of

September 1974, they reached a kind of stasis. 'So that was when I stopped writing [to her]. Just one of these odd decisions one makes. But we were together after that for around twenty years. I went and met her family, a family lunch in a restaurant with her brother from Spain. So I was very much part of the family, and it was all very nice for me really. It was so much nicer for me than Pat's family. I liked Margaret's sister very much indeed. But there was one thing – I couldn't just shed Pat you see. Many times I thought I could but I couldn't. Pat was rather alone in the world.'[24]

A few months later, back in Argentina, Margaret wrote to Vidia that England seemed like paradise compared to the squalor of Argentina. She felt she had been stimulated intellectually by being with him, and was at a loss now she was home. Her memories of being together were all delightful, and remarkably enough she even spoke happily of their time in Wiltshire, with what she called all its upheavals. She said to Vidia that without him she felt numb, and missed his arms and his thighs and the god. Taking the hit, she apologized for offering him unrest and anxiety rather than peace and quiet. She had not given him happiness, but she had offered him love.

Later in the year, angered by the way Vidia continually presented himself as incapable, Pat wrote, 'I thought just now as I was undressing and washing my face that I have, obediently, taken responsibility for his suffering, but that he has always assumed a pathetic pose and something of that has become habitual . . . Before he slept he spoke disturbingly about Diana and her attitude to the book. I confirmed that I spoke to her about Vidia possibly needing the help of a psychiatrist. She spoke to him about my family being "common".' In a volatile state of mind, Vidia went to London for a party given by Hugh Thomas: the star turn was Gabriel García Márquez, a writer whose response to the Caribbean was the antithesis of Vidia's. He shaved off his beard and returned to Wilsford. Vidia wanted everything: Pat, Margaret, both, neither, Wiltshire, London, Argentina and Spain. He was nothing if not indecisive. He told Pat he would pursue Margaret, 'do what she wants and live with her for six months – in Madrid. He just told me he is living through a nightmare: he gives his decision and then spends two or three hours reversing it.' Pat felt 'outraged to be left here'.

*

On the last Sunday in October, Pat and Vidia Naipaul put on a show of marital solidarity for some visitors. She was still taking Mandrax in an effort to stabilize herself. Her sole record of the lunch party is a list of the guests and the sentence, 'I let myself be deflected when Vidia raged the night before and did not prepare the dishes I had intended when my life depended on being accomplished and prepared.' One guest, Paul Theroux, had more elaborate memories. In *Sir Vidia's Shadow*, he devoted a chapter to the lunch. It is entertaining and revealing, giving an intimate glimpse of V.S. Naipaul in his home setting, among his friends. As in other sections of the book, he has perfect recall of people, atmosphere, even of the dialogue in conversations.

Theroux takes the train from London to Salisbury alone, since his wife Anne does not wish to come. Vidia has sent a car to meet him at the station, driven by 'Walters', but Walters turns out to be a taxi driver who charges Theroux £4. On arrival at the cottage he is met by Vidia and Julian Jebb, 'a small elfin-faced man wearing tight velvet trousers and a red and gold waistcoat . . . the sort of Englishman who could express his humorous side only by speaking in an exaggerated American accent.' Soon they are joined by Hugh and Antonia Fraser, Antonia 'dressed like a shepherdess, her soft skin set off by a frilly lavender blouse and a velvet peasant skirt.' Hugh is tall, slow and lopsided, bearing an 'aura of helpless authority'. The other guests are a young couple, Malcolm and Robin; Malcolm is red-faced and socially inept, 'a beaky Kiwi in the throes of pedantry, proving his point to the Poms', while Robin is 'sweet and square-shouldered, wearing a soft, unnecessary hat, as New Zealanders seemed habitually to do.' Theroux writes with a novelist's eye: each character has a stereotypical narrative function. Hugh is an upper-class MP. Antonia is seductive, the object of an extended sexual fantasy. Pat remains in the background, serving food. Julian is camp, vociferous and irritating. Malcolm and Robin are class-conscious Kiwis, prone to say things like, ' "Beaut book, Paul." ' During lunch, Vidia is given smoked salmon while the others have oxtail soup, and Malcolm, an expert on the Augustan writers, tries and fails to shock Lady Antonia by quoting bawdy poetry. Afterwards, they all go for a walk by the river and shoot at a paper target with an air rifle; 'Robin scored the highest.' The guests leave separately and Theroux takes a train to London, despite the unexpressed desire to be conveyed in Hugh and Antonia's purring Jaguar.[25]

It is a vivid and plausible account of a day in the country with the tetchy, pompous V.S. Naipaul and his guests, with Paul Theroux as the perceptive observer. It is, though, some distance from the truth. Julian Jebb was not at the lunch. Malcolm and Robin were Michael Neill and Pek Koon Heng; neither had a New Zealand accent. In Neill's words, 'The account of my conversation with Antonia Fraser is false . . . Pek Koon was a stylish woman from Kuala Lumpur, studying at SOAS. It is bizarre that Theroux described her as a vulgar Kiwi. I recall him being pleasant company; we gave him a lift back to London in my car, a disreputable Morris 1100.'[26] Pek Koon Heng added: 'I don't wear hats. Period . . . Theroux was very much the acolyte, giving Naipaul a lot of face, a lot of deference.'[27] Antonia Fraser's reaction to Theroux's account was, 'Well, a guy can dream, but it wasn't at all how I remember it.'[28] Her recollection is confirmed by a diary entry for 27 October 1974: 'Visit to Pat and Vidia Naipaul in Wiltshire.' Antonia and Hugh had arrived first to find Vidia looking 'fairly high . . . despite being on valium to overcome depression and nerves of finishing the new book . . . Paul Theroux, a nice earnest American novelist who has written rather a dull but honest book about him, was coming.' She described a conversation with Vidia about writers and the imagination, and a shooting competition: 'Vidia a bit too high to win, in fact Theroux and I tied first.' Walking in the autumn sedge by the river, she asked Vidia the colour of the sky. ' "Mauve not amethyst." He says he plays a game noting colours precisely in his mind . . . "But I don't need to write it down. I have a perfect memory you see." He is other worldly springing about in the darkening reeds with his perfect memory and his genius and his valium . . . and he has the bungalow for another 9 years thanks to Glenc.' Her diary entry concludes, 'On the way home, sleepily, Hugh and I reflect that it is Pat who is thin and pale and perhaps doesn't have a perfect memory. V is thoroughly OK.'[29]

Michael Neill, Pek Koon Heng and Antonia Fraser – the three surviving members of the lunch party apart from Naipaul and Theroux – have matching accounts of what happened that day. Theroux's account appears to be significantly inaccurate, even deliberately fictive. What then of *Sir Vidia's Shadow*, with its queasy subtitle *A Friendship Across Five Continents*? Reviewers almost without exception treated it on publication as a reliable memoir rather than as a fictionalized account of a real relationship. It has been presented as a reliable, even essential account of the life and opinions of V.S. Naipaul, quoted not only in countless press articles but in academic studies of his work. Theroux insisted later on the honesty of *Sir Vidia's Shadow*. 'When I wrote the book I wanted to make it as deliberately truthful and accurate as possible,' he told the *Telegraph Magazine*.[30] 'I

knew I had to be scrupulously truthful – a far cry from fictionalizing,' he
assured the *Atlantic Monthly*.[31] This claim was taken at face value, despite
his having recently written two autobiographical novels which blurred the
line between truth and fiction, both of them featuring V.S. Naipaul in
disguised form. *My Secret History* devotes a couple of chapters to 'My
friend, S. Prasad, the writer' and uses material that is repeated in *Sir
Vidia's Shadow*.[32] In *My Other Life*, Theroux gives lines of Naipaul's
conversation to a passing character, Walter Van Bellamy.[33] Both novels are
fluent and emotionally disengaged, imagining events in Theroux's life had
it turned out a little differently.

The material in *Sir Vidia's Shadow* combines the accurate, the fictional
and the appropriated, and they merge to the point where they cannot be
disentangled. The early part of the book, set in Africa, feels authentic
although the dialogue is invented and characters such as Haji Hallsmith
did not exist. The portrait of Pat and Vidia's life at Makerere is believable:
Vidia enraged by the expatriate teachers in the Senior Common Room, or
walking through a market with 'an inspector's gait, hands clasped behind
his back, moving fast yet looking at everything.'[34] Many of the phrases
Naipaul uses are convincing, such as, to a hotel manager: '"Don't you
have a rule saying that all staff uniforms must be dirty?"'[35] Other lines are
less plausible, and sound closer to Theroux's idea of what Naipaul should
have been thinking: '"This is turning me into a racialist, for God's
sake."'[36] Later, as their symbiotic relationship at Makerere is replaced by
Theroux's more distant and servile attempt to maintain a friendship, the
encounters become rarer and the portrayal more speculative; Naipaul ends
up as a caricature and a crank. Some details still come from close
knowledge: Vidia's distress at a builder sitting on his bed, or his pessimistic
appraisal of Hugh Fraser's handwriting, or his reaction to a graffito, KEEP
BRITAIN WHITE: '"I would put a comma after 'Britain'."'[37] Other material
is invented, for example the details of the Wilsford lunch, Theroux meeting
Vidia's future wife, Nadira, as a child in Nairobi, or the claim that he
prevented him from winning the Booker Prize for *A Bend in the River*.[38]
Pat's small breasts are inflated lasciviously, 'her cheeks and lips wet, her
large breasts tremulous with grief'.[39] Some sections are taken from
Naipaul's letters to Theroux, which are summarized (for copyright reasons)
or rendered as dialogue. Further material is borrowed from *Conversations
with V.S. Naipaul*, a compilation of interviews used by Theroux while
preparing *Sir Vidia's Shadow*.[40] For instance the comment, 'I have never
had to work for hire; I made a vow at an early age never to work, never

to become involved with people in that way. That has given me a freedom from people, from entanglements, from rivalries, from competition. I have no enemies, no rivals, no masters; I fear no one,' is taken from an interview with Naipaul published in *Transition*, a magazine founded by a Makerere colleague, Rajat Neogy.[41]

Despite the fictionalizing and the misconstruction, *Sir Vidia's Shadow* remains an entertaining study both of literary friendship gone wrong and of aspects of V.S. Naipaul's character. Theroux's unreliability as a narrator makes his tale no less compelling; like the brothers Goncourt, his oddity of perception is no disadvantage. The book is an act of vengeance, but also an act of homage. He is consistently harsh on himself: for his literary envy, for failing to challenge his mentor, for tolerating his meanness. The book reveals as much about Theroux as it does about Naipaul – his incomprehension of the English, his sexual vanity, his eagerness to be snubbed, the relentlessness of his pursuit. Theroux rationalizes his mistreatment, since 'in friendship, time is meaningless and silences insignificant, because you are sure of each other.'[42] Underlying the memoir is a sense that Theroux did not fully understand the nature of his encounter with Naipaul, or the extent to which he was goaded for years. Generous, shameless, inquisitive, friendly, but lacking a gift for friendship, he failed to see that Naipaul had no loyalty to him, and regarded him primarily as an aide and entertainer, and that his final rejection was inevitable. Paul was baffled when he received his fax of dismissal, orchestrated by Vidia but written by Nadira: 'The more I reflected on her letter, the louder I laughed. Its obsessional style and bad grammar and clumsy handwriting were proof that Vidia had not seen it before she sent it ... The woman was a highly visible person who would have been denounced or ridiculed on sight as "colored" or a "Paki" in most of Britain.'[43] Theroux missed the signals, accepting the popular idea that his hero's arrogant behaviour must arise from a Hindu sense of caste: 'Until I met Vidia, I had never known a person who recognized no one as his equal. He's a Brahmin, the local Indians said: all Brahmins are fussy like that.'[44] Vidia's old schoolfriend Lloyd Best made a more perceptive observation: 'Theroux's book exposes Naipaul as a real Trinidadian in every sense – including the way he would not pay for the wine. All these little Trinidadian smart-man things: the way he would sing calypso and whistle, the way he would take the mickey out of people, provoking them. Naipaul expects the responses that he's going to get; I'd say that it's second nature to him, performing in that way.'[45]

The understandable response to the merging of truth and fiction in *Sir*

Vidia's Shadow would be to see it as a form of postmodern experimentation, Theroux undercutting the autobiographical form in his next literary step after *My Other Life*. The book, though, is more peculiar than this. Theroux saw *Sir Vidia's Shadow* as veracious. Asked about the inaccuracies in the version of the Wilsford lunch, he said he did not remember Pek Koon Heng being Malaysian Chinese, and that he did not receive a lift back to London with her and Michael Neill. On Julian Jebb's absence, he said, 'He used to come all the time and I was conflating two visits. He said all the things that he said. I put him in there because Vidia used him in *The Enigma of Arrival* and he was his friend, and I thought he belittled him terribly.' As to pretending he had met Nadira in Nairobi in 1966, he said, 'It could have been Nadira because the age is exactly right [he was wrong by six years, and Nadira was living in Dar es Salaam at the time]. It wasn't fictionalizing because in my opinion it has poetic truth in it. I am not saying that was Nadira. Of course it wasn't Nadira. But it could have been her . . . to me it was true.' Regarding his own attitude to Naipaul, Theroux suggested, 'I couldn't talk about my books because he really wasn't interested in them, so we always talked about his books. We couldn't talk about money because I had more than him. We couldn't talk about children because he didn't have any. He complained about England: that was his subject . . . But it was as near to a friendship that I have ever had with anyone, really, and certainly with any other writer . . . My kids used to say that I really didn't have any friends. I lived in London for seventeen years. I go back and I don't see anyone.'[46]

V.S. Naipaul's response to *Sir Vidia's Shadow* was to ignore it. He did not read the book, and his subsequent remarks about Theroux were consciously theatrical and Olympian, reconstructing the friendship: 'He spread this idea that I was his great mentor and adviser, but since Africa, since 1966, we've hardly met. He came here twice. He was infinitely amusing to me in that jungle, this rather common fellow who was in Africa teaching the Negroes, he pestered me and pestered me, wrote me letters all the time . . . In the nineteenth century there were serious travellers who went to unknown places and did reports on it. Travelling was hard for them; now, travel has changed. Travel has become a plebeian, everyday matter, it has become a lower-class adventure, and there are books now written for lower-class travellers. I think Theroux belonged to that category: he wrote tourist books for the lower classes.'[47]

*

1975 started unhappily, and got worse. Marg Hale telephoned on New Year's Day to say that stones had been thrown through her bedroom window. Pat and Vidia listened to Melvyn Bragg interviewing Antonia on the wireless. Pat wrote: 'I asked him whether it altered his judgement, modified his opinions about the state of the nation and he said no.' Vidia was off to Zaire, following obliquely in the footsteps of Joseph Conrad, seeking his own heart of darkness; Pat learned by default that he would not be alone: 'The Lunn Poly girl rang to say that the double rooms at the Intercontinental Kinshasa were all booked . . . Vidia is abstracted. He collected his valium ("I don't want to fly off the handle at anyone in the Congo") and malaria tablets . . . He spoke of his fear, and foreboding: that the person was wrong. That he was ashamed of his marriage but not now.' He mentioned an old cartoon from the *Illustrated Weekly of India*, which showed a boy found by his father looking at pictures of naked women, with the caption 'What is the point of being a Brahmin if you can't control your passions?' He stated, less than accurately, 'I have always controlled my passions.' On the night before he flew, he told Pat they had 'a fellowship, that he was very lucky to find me, that we were very lucky to find one another.' With pathetic gratitude, she noted: 'He gave me the blue, lighter and the red biro with which he wrote *Guerrillas*' – the same blue lighter and red biro that are used in the plot to signify Jane's death.

While Vidia was in Zaire, Pat went to London, but was too nervous to confide in her friends. She spent a day at the Haberdashers' Aske's School for Girls, wondering if she might return to teaching, and shared her professional worries with her childhood friend Sheila Rogers, herself a schoolteacher. In Sheila's words: 'Pat's experience was in selective schools, but those had been closed down by the time she wanted to get back into teaching. We all agreed that Pat must be an absolute saint to cope with Vidia. She had a very sensitive mind.'[48] As Pat wrote three years later, 'My job, as housemaid and helpmeet, had run out. I was casting around for another career.' She told Teresa a little about her situation, and regretted it at once. 'I forgot that she is deceitful. In case anybody reads this I don't mean anything really bad . . . I have behaved like a treacherous, repulsive ass. Teresa. Miriam. Antonia. I have seen the light of affection and sympathy die in Antonia's and Miriam's eyes. Antonia has offered me the job of researching her book of love letters.' Pat spent days alone in the flat in Queen's Gate, depressed and introspective, seeing no one, scarcely eating, and sent a letter to Francis Wyndham alluding to her sense of shame and failure. Before Vidia left for Zaire, she had written in her diary after a visit to the Powells, 'I was clumsier than ever, in spite of my resolutions . . . Julian [Jebb] looked tired and as when he left us that weekend, smelt rather sweaty. Both he and Tristram spoke a lot of wisdom . . . Of course I omitted to speak of the contempt I felt from Tristram and John. And of my stupidity and clumsiness.' Julian Jebb was himself in a bad state. A successful maker of documentaries on the likes of Christopher Isherwood, Virginia Woolf and the Mitford sisters, he was tormented by his own demons. A little younger than Vidia, Jebb was a puckish, talented, flamboyant man, addicted to Gauloises and vodka, and uneasy about his homosexuality. Above all, he was troubled that he had not lived up to early ambitions to be a writer and creator.[49] In Michael Holroyd's memory, 'He was a depressed man who came alive in the heat of the television studio.'[50]

Things were falling apart for Pat. When Vidia returned to England in the middle of March, the round of conflict began again: 'He wanted to know what I was doing. I think I said I was trying to earn some money. "What have you done?" I would not talk. "You've done nothing?"' Margaret was staying in Wilsford. Stuck in London, a broken woman, Pat brooded as a wife and a homemaker on 'the awfulness of them handling my things, my kitchen things.' The next month, she took a tentative step forward, having lunch with the poet and critic Ian Hamilton, who was editing the *New Review*, a monthly magazine funded by the Arts Council. Francis had suggested that Hamilton might publish her article on Michael Abdul Malik. They went to a pub next door to his office and discussed it. Pat was thrilled to be treated like a fellow writer and a normal human being. 'It was a working lunch – the first I've ever had . . . I have never felt so good after wine at lunch . . . He asked me what I had written before, what I had published before. So what name would I use. His face is quite beautiful, his eyes darkish, compelling.' Francis thought, 'When Pat wrote, she over-researched. She wasn't a good journalist. I think Vidia was extremely irritated by it. I got the feeling that he was the opposite of supportive.'[51] The proofs came. It was an observant article, concentrating on the intricacies of the trial. 'I sobbed over the phone to Miriam and changed the name. On Thursday I changed it back again.' The author was to be – Patricia Naipaul. She went to lunch with the art dealer Kasmin, who had first editions of all Vidia's books, and dinner with Paul and Anne Theroux, finding 'Paul, with his success, has acquired gravitas, pipe smoking.' Pek Koon Heng and Michael Neill invited her out; despite their inauspicious meeting, they both liked Pat: 'She was quiet, self-effacing but with a sharp intelligence, one of those wives who quite deliberately puts herself to one side to look after her husband.'⁵²

Pat tried hard to develop her professional ambitions, going to literary parties and meeting Sonia, Antonia, Teresa, Francis and Edna. Antonia was being paraded mercilessly through the gossip columns, having recently begun a relationship with the playwright Harold Pinter, fulfilling a lifelong ambition to become the handmaiden to a genius. Pinter's wife, the actress Vivien Merchant, cited Antonia in their divorce case and denounced her to the press for having big feet – size 9½, reportedly. *Time* reported that, 'Lady Antonia, a lithe blonde, has been married since 1956 to Tory MP Hugh Fraser . . . She is an avid collector – of white dresses (she has 100), and of personages literary, theatrical and political. Her companions have included Author Norman Mailer, Actor Robert Stephens and Lord Lambton, the Tory MP who quit Parliament last year after being photographed in bed with a call girl. Pinter, by contrast, is the only son of a Jewish tailor from London's rugged East End. Darkly handsome with thinning hair, he spent almost a decade as a stage actor, turned to writing in the 1950s, and soon developed into an acclaimed, though sometimes confounding chronicler of English subsociety.'⁵³ Hugh Fraser, meanwhile, was attempting to become leader of the Conservative Party; he came a poor third to Margaret Thatcher in the first ballot, who to widespread surprise went on to defeat the incumbent, Ted Heath.

Pat attended an extremist political rally with a view to writing a second article for the *New Review*. 'The National Front held their "Anti-Mugging March" in Hackney,' she wrote in her diary. On the Underground on the way home, after watching windows being smashed in Hoxton Market, 'I got into the same carriage as the tall attacker and heard him say that he had kicked the young man in the face. He said that it made it all "worth it".' The piece used her own background in Kingstanding as a window onto Britain's rising racial tension: '"Our Dora's National Front." That had been a surprise too . . . I had known Dora and her father, a Birmingham shopkeeper, for most of my life.'⁵⁴ She wrote an article on the referendum over whether Britain should join the European Common Market, and a piece on the writer Aleksandr Solzhenitsyn, who had recently been exiled from the Soviet Union. When it was turned down by Miriam Gross at the *Observer*, her ambitions retreated. This coincided with a shift in her relationship with Vidia. 'He thinks he has come back to me. That there is no feeling left – but affection and concern. He has been living at the dentist's. On Friday he went and she was waiting for him. He believes she loves him ... I feel the crisis of hysteria ebbing away and doubt the value and safety of writing this as a form of therapy ... My distress is real.' The tone of her diary changed now, the entries become briefer and more impersonal, concerned with public events: 'Yesterday the Concorde took off on its inaugural flight ... The new plan for British Leyland has been announced ... Robert Lowell is dead ... Hugh Fraser's car was blown to pieces.' This referred to an IRA bomb placed beneath his car that exploded prematurely, killing a neighbour and narrowly missing Fraser and a house guest, Caroline Kennedy, the teenage daughter of Jackie and the late JFK.

Pat lacked the necessary confidence and resilience to make a success of freelance journalism; Antonia's invitation to research an anthology of love letters suited her academic temperament better. The division of labour worked perfectly: Antonia was happier making love than researching it, and Pat needed something to do. She went by bus to the London Library in Piccadilly for three days each week, dutifully saving her 40-pence return bus tickets as receipts. David Pryce-Jones would invite her out for coffee. 'I would see her sitting in the London Library doing research and trying to write in Vidia's own style and it was very pitiful ... She seemed tortured, absolutely tormented. There was something obsessive about Pat. She would have done anything for Vidia. There is a human phenomenon called "a great man's wife" and she was such a thing. Mrs Nabokov was another. [They] are absolutely convinced of their husband's genius and will do anything that the husband asks to promote that genius ... She wanted more of Vidia than he was prepared to concede.'[55] In a later letter to Pat, Pryce-Jones wrote, 'I hold firmly to the view that talented people like Vidia, of whom there are few, are their own justification. I think we hold this view in common; I hope so anyhow.'[56]

Antonia wrote Pat a note saying she required 'A Treasury of Great Love Letters' and made a grand total of three suggestions for inclusion: Sarah Bernhardt, Victorien Sardou and Jean Cocteau. Pat assembled and copied letters by Mozart, Chekhov, Keats, Hugo, Byron, Heloise, Balzac and Napoleon. As Antonia put it later, 'Pat really did most of the work, and when I made lavish acknowledgements she kept crossing them out. In the end she wanted to be Patricia Hale, so no one knew who she was. That was very typical ... My own marriage was breaking up ... Pat was so reticent, so apologetic. She would arrive apologising for being late, or early, or for bothering you. She had a permanent cold. And I was madly in love with Harold. She was a very sweet person, but certainly gave the impression of being a very unhappy woman at that time. We never talked about Margaret. She was very, very reticent.'⁵⁷ Pat was paid £300 for the work by Antonia and the publisher, and £100 for expenses, much of which she insisted on returning. 'I repeat, and will keep on repeating, my enormous gratitude to you for your arduous and imaginative work,' Antonia wrote as she tried to persuade Pat to keep the money she was due for expenses. 'Do keep writing yourself!'⁵⁸ *Love Letters* sold well, and has been through many reprints.

The leisure of research gave Pat an opportunity to ponder. She spent days reading other people's thoughts and sentiments, way beyond the call of obligation. F. Scott Fitzgerald's talented and manic wife interested her: 'I have just been reading Zelda Fitzgerald and recognise myself and an eternal predicament . . . she told him in her letters that her writing was for him, the opinions of others did not exist. And yet she kept her writings secret from him.' Above all, she was fascinated by Jane Carlyle, the wife of the Victorian social thinker Thomas Carlyle, seeing her as the epitome of the clever woman who sacrificed all for her awkward husband's greatness: 'It was her nature to suffer . . . She voluntarily yielded her emotions and her talents to their relationship, to an ideal of married love . . . Whatever the stress and suffering, it seems to me a perfect marriage, in the sense of two people becoming one and indispensable to one another, part of one another, almost exchanging personalities . . . After her death Carlyle reproached himself with her unhappiness . . . She was brilliant. I think [she was] his equal but her genius went into their life together. To try to make that genius fit the strait jacket of latter-day Women's Lib is to misunderstand her nature.' The domineering side of Jane Carlyle – witty, gossipy and intrusive – was left to one side in this interpretation. Here, Jane became a version of Pat, or Patricia Naipaul as she might have been: the respected and loyal wife of a great man who thrives in a marriage of equals, the exact arrangement she had dreamed of in 1953 when she wrote to Vidia, 'The union of two real people is nobler than one-sided submission.'

Her husband would not entertain equality. Vidia's conception of himself was too fragile and narcissistic for his personality to be merged with another. He depended on the idea of his own singularity: without it, he might crack. Pat could support and enable him, but she could not share in creating. Although she was intelligent and well read, she was not by this stage his intellectual equal, and was clever enough to realize her limitations. Pat's social or political ideas, in particular her innate liberalism, had no influence on Vidia except as an attitude for him to reject. Her soft-left orthodoxies gave something for him to fix on and oppose, and made him define his own position more clearly. He had no wish to synthesize opinions. Vidia had a view of the world that he would do anything to maintain, just as he would sacrifice anything or anybody that stood in the way of his central purpose, to be 'the writer'.

CHAPTER TWENTY-ONE

'I WANT TO WIN AND
WIN AND WIN'

FOR THE NEXT TWO DECADES, the triangle between Vidia, Pat and Margaret persisted, shifting from an equilateral to a scalene depending on his work, mood and location, and the emotional pull exerted by each woman. When Vidia travelled to research a book, it would often be with Margaret, and then he would go home. Again and again, he thought he would leave Pat for Margaret, or give up Margaret for Pat. In Vidia's peer group in England, running two women in this way was considered unusual. His reaction to the awkwardness of the situation was not to introduce Margaret to his friends, but to avoid mentioning her existence, although they knew about her, and he knew they knew. As Antonia Fraser put it, 'I never met her . . . If Vidia had asked me to meet her, I would have done so, because it would be his judgement, not mine. But he never did.'[1] Sometimes, things happened differently. Vidia brought Margaret to Elsham Road to see Marisa Masters. 'She said, "Marisa, will you tell Vidia he cannot have his cake and eat it too?" I thought, how can she use that phrase in respect of a writer? What a pedestrian way of expressing it.'[2] Paul Theroux was permitted a momentary conversation in a cafe. Kasmin, who advised Vidia on buying art and was expected to take him out to lunch from time to time, met both Margaret and Pat: 'I sensed that Margaret was able to defend herself in any situation. Pat didn't open up in his presence. She was diminished by Vidia.'[3] David Pryce-Jones remembered, 'He was coming to dinner one evening, and he rang up and said he'd be coming with Margaret. So I said fine, and I then felt that I had better ring up the other guests and I rang up and said, Vidia is not coming with Pat but with a lady called Margaret. But when he arrived, he arrived with Pat, and I got a very funny letter from Hugh Thomas who was present at this dinner, and he said, "I am glad you warned me that he was coming with Margaret because I might very well have mistaken her for Pat." '[4]

In Mobutu's Zaire in early 1975 for the *Sunday Times* and the *New York Review of Books*, Vidia was accompanied by his mistress. 'I took her to places she had never been. I took her to the Congo, and she turned up there in jeans with a nice, lovely straw basket – you could hold the handles together – as if for a Brighton excursion. It was as though she thought the Congo was a beach resort.'[5] Vidia was disturbed by the condition of the country. As he wrote in the finished article, 'The Congo, which used to be a Belgian colony, is now an African kingdom and is called Zaire. It appears to be a nonsense name, a sixteenth-century Portuguese corruption, some Zairois will tell you, of a local word for "river". So it is as if Taiwan, reasserting its Chinese identity, were again to give itself the Portuguese name of Formosa. The Congo River is now called the Zaire, as is the local currency, which is almost worthless.'[6] He wrote to Francis from Kinshasa, 'There has been a "radicalization of the revolution"; and everybody is very nervous, especially the local citizens (a technical word of the revolution) . . . the visitor is required <u>by law</u> to spend 20 Zaires a day (i.e. $40) . . . Nothing really works, without the expatriates; so that, although I plan to go to Stanleyville (now Kisangani) & take the steamer back to Kinshasa, I am no longer sure whether anything as elaborate as that is possible. It is absurd, but one is a little like an old-fashioned African traveller, i.e., a hostage of a sort.'[7]

In his notebook, he mentioned many ideas that would find their way into *A Bend in the River*, and wrote prophetically of Zaire's likely future under the charismatic kleptocrat Joseph Mobutu, who was now calling himself Mobutu Sese Seko Kuku Ngbendu Wa Za Banga. 'The curious kingship. The distortions & bogusness & despair of authenticity cf W Indians and Obeah. African art. Confusion, especially of the évolué [a term used in colonial Congo, similar to 'babu' in British India] . . . The difficulty of Africa: one reaction multiplied by another. Irritation multiplied by concern for individuals who must feel, with their new sense of pride etc, unsupported by their society . . . Like Leopold II of the Belgians, in the time of the Congo Free State – much of whose despotic legislation >(ownership of the mines in 1888, all vacant lands in 1890, the fruits of the earth in 1891)< has passed down through the Belgian colonial administration to the present regime, >and is now presented as a kind of ancestral African socialism – like Leopold II,< Mobutu owns Zaire.'[8]

In a smaller, fliptop notebook, he recorded the names of the Belgian diplomats and academics and Zairois journalists whose knowledge he was seeking. 'Mr Van Krombrugghe (offer him Mr G's greetings) . . . Omer Marchal (works for Spécial dedicated to Mobutu) . . . Professor Benoit Verhaeghen.' A separate notebook recorded daily activities, avoiding any mention of Margaret. 'I find that it helps to help the officials. They are probably self-conscious about their lack of skill and are likely to resent being laughed at. The Belgians, who appear to know the country, push their way forward . . . The feeling one has that one is asking stupid questions . . . The Greeks & Portuguese and Indians have been asked to leave . . . The great surprise is the magnificence of the women . . . Rusty corrugated-iron roofs. Bumpy roads, great dips, the piles of garbage on the road. The little boys playing in the dust, springing off a tire & doing somersaults in the air. The prison: concrete barracks behind a whitewashed wall.'[9] This fluent daily diary was transcribed and published as a limited edition by Sylvester & Orphanos in 1980, and dedicated to 'MM'. Overlying Vidia's response to Zaire was a sense of fear about the way in which rival or tribal groups were ready to take whatever opportunities reached them. He saw, in Africa, 'a dream of a past – the vacancy of river and forest, the hut in the brown yard, the dugout – when the dead ancestors watched and protected, and the enemies were only men.'[10]

Back in Europe, he lived for five weeks with Margaret in a parador in Javea in Spain, working hard on the article. Pat spent her time in Wilsford and in the flat in London, wondering what to do next. Through this period, with a new, partial stability in his relationship with Margaret, Vidia was intent on his work. He wanted to go to India, to South America, or to the Caribbean. Bob Silvers understood the vitality of Vidia's ambition at this time, and decided to make the most of him. Might he like to write a series of articles about India, which was lurching towards economic and constitutional chaos, with Prime Minister Indira Gandhi on the verge of declaring a State of Emergency? He would, and Margaret would accompany him for much of the trip.

*

'The monsoon rain was blown over the concrete by the aeroplane as it landed,' Vidia wrote in his journal on 20 August. 'I had never been in Bombay during the monsoon and began to grieve for the plastic mackintosh I had left behind at London airport . . . With each successive arrival in

India my dismay and apprehension lessen. It may be that I have learned a new way of seeing or know better now what to expect, it may also be that one's sense of dissolution has now spread: that there are no longer places where one can retreat; that I am now aware of a more general insecurity and am, perhaps importantly, less of a colonial.' During this journey through India, Vidia would hone the technique he was to use in his subsequent non-fiction writing: he found experienced local journalists to guide him, took whatever assistance or hospitality was available, interviewed people in great detail, linked what he had discovered to his exisiting ideas about the country, and wrote up the results fast. Using his literary prestige, the mad strength of his new personality and a rare ability to project himself as if in mortal need of assistance, he was superb at persuading people to help him.

In his India journal, kept over months and written in a neat and careful hand, Vidia recorded his conversations and experiences, and gave no indication that he was travelling with another person. Sometimes Margaret was allowed to take dictation, or to glue newspaper cuttings into a book. His tempestuous interaction with her throughout the trip was sectioned off in his mind and kept separate from his work. Her presence leaks out in other ways, in his focused anger and his increasingly misanthropic view of the world. Intimate passion came out as cold passion on the page. It also affected his dealings with others: antagonism was becoming a default position, a way of attaining what appeared to be an advantage in any encounter.

Sometimes Vidia's conclusions were perceptive, at other times merely bitter. He was good at picking up new pieces of information, and seeing how they might become important. Talking to a consultant engineer in Bombay, Shirish Patel, to whom he had been introduced by his old friend from his 1963 trip Moni Malhoutra, he learned about the Shiv Sena, a chauvinist local political group that was later to assume national relevance. Vidia noted 'its organisation & growth; the theatricality of its leader, Bal Thackeray, a failed cartoonist . . . Again, I have the feeling of a country only just discovering what it has committed itself to – independence, industrialization, democracy; a process achieving a dynamic that is now beyond the control of any leader.' He milked his hosts for information, often causing a scene when he set off an argument, and was happy to dismiss many of his helpers afterwards as fools and idlers. Khushwant Singh's son Rahul, a journalist, took him to dinner in Bombay with Charles Correa, an architect, and Prem Shankar Jha, a *Times of India* columnist.

'The narcissism of "Who am I" – the questions raised by Prem Jha. The simplistic view of identity . . . One felt the irrelevance of this middle-class element, so parasitic, these advertising men, offering nothing of value really, speaking only to their own group. Jha assaulted me. He allowed no conversation to develop. No idea was explored. He was the Indian journalist – making simple patterns of simple facts. Such shoddy ideas adrift in this society. Like Adil Jussawalla's New Left idea. Adil has apparently, poor Parsi boy, married a rich Frenchwoman, whom he keeps in hiding.'[11] Prem Shankar Jha remembered, 'He was always looking for offence, looking for the hidden barb . . . I felt misrepresented – he had already decided what he wanted to say, and was looking for evidence. Margaret was very nervy, and showing all the signs of wear and tear you would expect from living with him.'[12] The antipathy was returned by Vidia, with interest: 'I thought Jha was a windbag. A windbag. He always had a view about everything, and there was little selectivity in what he said . . . Everything was a crisis. But if you write a column, that's what happens to you.'[13]

In Delhi in September, Vidia found the Emergency was making people reluctant to speak to him openly. Indira Gandhi had suspended elections, censored newspapers, imprisoned political opponents and banned strikes. Middle-class society in the capital was split between those who were delighted that the buses were running on time, and others who were frightened, believing democracy in India was finished. Uniquely, Vidia thought the Emergency was inconsequential. He told Vinod Mehta, a magazine editor, 'Don't worry, this will pass.' Mehta thought at the time it was a 'quite extraordinary' thing to say, but Vidia was right.[14] In retrospect Vidia said: 'People so much clammed up on that journey that after Shirish Patel's introduction to the Maratha landscape and the houses in Bombay which I wrote about, I didn't go on. People were frightened. So then the book became an analytical book. I loved that.'[15]

At a dinner, Vidia saw Ravi Dayal, who had left OUP and formed his own publishing company.

Naipaul had been defeated by the numbering of the houses in Defence Colony. 'You shouldn't worry about India, once you accept the fact that it is a third-rate place. You can't even number your houses logically.' And there were lots of people who took offence to that – 'What do you mean? What about our great religious inheritance and our ancient mathematicians.' Naipaul was quietly

purring away, he was very pleased to take a rise out of people . . .
He had a little group and he was enjoying himself, you know,
whipping India a bit. Some very nice earnest fellow who had been
at Harvard, actually confessed, 'That is interesting. I have lived in
America. I am good at my books. But now that you mention it,
there is something lacking in me. I think I wasn't quite a complete
person, a bit like India' – or something like that. Naipaul looked
very triumphant and called me over. 'Here is this very honest
statement,' and the poor man had to confess it again. And that
irritated me. I thought Naipaul was being a bit merciless.

Dayal noticed that Vidia became awkward when he met old friends
such as himself and Ruth Jhabvala. 'He got slightly embarrassed with
us, he said, "Pat couldn't come." And he casually started to distance
himself. I think he was dodging the prospect of meeting people who
remembered Pat with affection.' Dayal was not impressed by Margaret.
'I remember finding her rather distasteful. She seemed so clueless. Quite
frankly I didn't know what their relationship was. He was extremely
off-hand with her, and it seemed to me that she had no business to be
with him, somehow. I didn't really know what she was doing in India.'
Vidia was seeking a distinct interpretation of India, and was dismissive
of the theories his earlier friends and acquaintances were offering. 'By
then he had perhaps outgrown everyone. People like myself, or Ruth. I
was publishing lots of books. He seemed unfamiliar with my world by
then. He wasn't aware of the ideas that India was generating, a lot of
which I had a hand in publishing: the heavy economists, Amartya Sen,
K.N. Raj, the historians, M.N. Srinivas with his sociology. So much
original work was coming out. Vidia's historical reading of India is a
very old one.'[16]

   Vidia made a note of an encounter at another dinner, an example of
his willingness to make huge deductions from casual conversations: 'At
Ashok Khosla's on Tuesday, in the suburb of Delhi known as Vasant
Vihar,' he wrote. 'A woman in yellow on the sofa next to me . . . She
came to India from time to time; but she 'related' only to her family.
Such security. Consider all that that statement implies. India will go on.
My family will go on . . . We talked about the people of Bombay. I
asked whether she saw them. She said of course she did. What was the
most noticeable thing about them? She said, "They were having their
being."' Another guest piped up and said the inhabitants of Bombay
wore a certain kind of sari. 'How remarkable that neither of the Indians

should have mentioned that the people of industrial Bombay are very small, the men about 5 feet high, considerably smaller than the middle class.' These observations would be played out in his final text, with few alterations. The end of the month found Vidia escaping the city for the countryside, travelling through Jodhpur and Jaisalmer in Rajasthan. '9 p.m. bus for Kota, where arrived this morning 29th at 7.30 & welcomed by official. Now in Circuit House ... Regular halts at tea-stalls.'[17] Next came Haryana – where he had a stormy falling-out with Margaret. 'I had to send her back,' Vidia said later, as if she were an unwanted parcel, 'I had to send her home.'[18] This was to be a pattern on their foreign tours: passion, dispute, dismissal.

Vidia's helpers found him both stimulating and difficult. 'I think he was very much the anthropologist who needed the native informant,' suggested the psychoanalyst Sudhir Kakar, whose theories on Indians and sex were taken up by Vidia in his articles. 'We met several times, and we went for a walk on Janpath. I remember him talking of his early years, saying he had suffered from depression, he was quite open. There was intensity.'[19] Rahul Singh, who acted as a gofer on subsequent trips, said, 'I devoted time and energy because I liked the man and I admired his writing. He was often at a loose end. I brought him to a friend's house who said, "You're a good writer, but Dom Moraes is a better one." Vidia turned his back but laughed about it later ... I noticed that when people spoke to him in Hindi on the street, he would get uncomfortable ... He never paid bills. There were a couple of occasions with others when I expected the bill to be split, but he would make no gesture. He likes to put people on the back foot. Margaret would usually stay in the hotel when we went out. Vidia would lose his cool and get impatient with her. She was a nice person.'[20]

Shirish Patel and his wife Rajani liked Margaret too, and invited her and Vidia to dinner. They admired his books, although not *An Area of Darkness*. 'We thought he was obsessed with excrement. We would tell our children, mind you don't put your foot into a Naipaul ... We suggested that he meet a couple that we knew, and I asked, what did you think of them? And he said, "I met them at a party, I didn't have too much time with them, just a few minutes, but I'll give you a face reading." He then described the personality of each of them, and the relationship, with a precision which was uncanny. I'd known them for fifteen years and this reading – in a few minutes he had come to this assessment of each individual and their relationship. I was completely

awestruck.' Shirish Patel took Vidia to the Bombay slums and to a rural
development scheme he was running near Pune, and found his report
of the trips acute. The four of them arranged to meet in Jaisalmer.
Margaret showed Rajani photographs of her children, quietly, afraid it
might anger Vidia. She came to the Patels' room saying he had refused
repeatedly to take a telephone call from the local bigwig, the Collector,
because he did not like the travel arrangements that were being laid on
for him. 'The Collector said at the border, at the rest house, an official
from the other district will meet you. You take a break, change cars,
wash or anything and the other car will take you around. Vidia said,
no, if you can't give me a car to go to Kota, I don't want your car.
The Collector said, I'm bound by the rules. I cannot take the car out
of the district . . . Vidia is not happy, he says, "I'll take the bus." So at
night we go to this bus stand and he and Margaret are put on the state
transport bus, full of goats, sheep, farmers. It's jam-packed. We had got
them front row seats, but . . . Naipaul just took Margaret on that bus.
She didn't say anything. We saw Vidia again, but she wasn't there. And
we never asked him. I was too intimidated.'[21] Patel and Kakar found
that subsequent attempts to contact Vidia over the years were ignored.

Through 1976, spending much of his time alone in Wilsford, Vidia
wrote up his conclusions about India. Feeling like Charles Dickens, he
worked against the clock, and the articles were published in seven
instalments in the *New York Review of Books* over the course of the
year. Amalgamated, and with slight alterations, they became a book,
India: A Wounded Civilization. Vidia focused less on the effects of the
Emergency than on an analysis of what made India the way it was. He
wrote of the chawls of Bombay, the rise of the Shiv Sena, of bonded
labour, caste, rural stagnation and the Naxalite movement, which sought
to overthrow the state, of well-intentioned but futile attempts at
progress, like the designer who had invented a pair of 'reaping shoes'
for peasants. Using public figures who interested him such as the
novelist R.K. Narayan, Mahatma Gandhi and Gandhi's imitator Vinoba
Bhave, he sought to explain and understand the psyche of India, a
formidable task for any writer. At the back of his mind, using the
ruined Hindu city of Vijayanagar as his template, was a certainty that
India had been incapacitated by the Muslim invasions of earlier centuries. 'I wrote the whole of *A Wounded Civilization* with an idea of the
invasion in my mind, in a broad way, the way Indians talk about it as

though it's an act of God. I am enraged by the way Indians don't wish to understand their history, I am enraged. I think unless you begin to understand your history, you can't have a new writing.'[22]

When the book was published in 1977, India hands were wheeled out to examine it. Louis Heren in the *Times* deduced that 'a novelist of Mr Naipaul's stature can often define problems quicker and more effectively than a team of economists and other experts from the World Bank.' It was a 'brilliant but emotionally charged polemic', wrote John Grigg in the *Spectator*; and wrong. Grigg thought Gandhianism, far from being the solace of conquered peoples, still represented 'the spirit of liberation from foreign and domestic chains'. Martin Amis in the *New Statesman* judged *India: A Wounded Civilization* a work of accurate pessimism, 'chasteningly right ... a book as compelling as it is distressing to read. Although always measured and elegant, there is nothing writerly in these pages; there is no relish.'[23] A common response came from John Keay in the *Sunday Telegraph*: 'There is a perversity about Mr Naipaul. He travels during the monsoon; he stays in air-conditioned boxes. Wherever he goes ... he finds nothing but squalor, inefficiency, disillusionment, violence, triviality. And perhaps because he is himself of distant Indian extraction, he is scandalized. Another observer, only slightly more compassionate, might find as much to respect, envy and – dare one say it? – enjoy.'[24] Vidia had a marked aversion to foreign Indophiles. In an interview with Elizabeth Hardwick in the *New York Times*, he declared, 'How tired I am of the India-lovers, those who go on about "beautiful India" – the last gasp of a hideous, imperialistic vanity. And the mark of a second-rate mind.'[25]

*

Although Stephen Tennant was too busy being a recluse in the confines of Wilsford Manor to come out and meet Mr and Mrs Naipaul, he would send them occasional letters, written in a florid hand with many underlin-ings, or perhaps chocolates in a perfumed package, to be delivered by Mrs Skull. Fancying himself as an artist (he did proficient pen and ink drawings, generally of lascivious sailors), Tennant enjoyed having a famous writer living in his grounds, like a Victorian hermit. He would send forth reports on his own important work. 'I am very busy – working on a long Novel & Essays on Theology & Religion also 368 Poems – for a new Volume – called Pagan Earth; these poems are very terse, & dry, only for those who

care for truth; and sincere thought.' On another day, he might be working
on 'a thrilling Play' or busy revising one of his poems such as the as yet
unpublished 'A Plea for the Highbrow':

> Sophists, and Pedants, I deeply love:
> I revere the patient Sage,
> Who, – wingèd as the skies above:
> Exalts Earth's Pilgrimage.

At other times, Stephen Tennant would offer more practical local
advice. 'Do go to Hellier's Garden Centre, in Winchester – it is
pleasant ... & the Cathedral is most attractive & unique. What a vile
world it is – lazy thinking everywhere: cheap, sordid values. – Bad
books. – But I like the Autumn Beauty.'[26] In response, Pat would send
flowers and polite notes to their landlord: 'Thank you for the pleasure
and the encouragement your poems have given both of us. But me
especially.'[27]

At home in England, Vidia received a letter from Margaret wondering whether they inhabited different worlds. She thought he lived in the
world of his intellect and his writing, which she longed to share, while
she subsisted in a bourgeois nightmare. For all she knew, he might
never even get to read her letter, because when she went to the post
office she was told they had no stamps. It sounded like one of Vidia's
jokes.[28] Moving swiftly, he skittered off to Buenos Aires with the
assistance of the *New York Review* to write an article, and to be with his
lover. Argentina was more brutalized than ever: Isabelita Perón had
been overthrown and thousands of people were being 'disappeared' by
the military dictatorship, or junta. Andrew Graham-Yooll had gone into
exile, soon to be followed by Bob Cox when a death threat was sent to
his eleven-year-old son. During this and later trips to Argentina, Vidia's
relations with Margaret's family were satisfactory. He met her children
and her former husband, Roy Gooding, and even interviewed him
about the state of the nation: 'Roy was a very intelligent man, with fine
views. He had thought-out views about Argentina.' Only Margaret's
stepfather, Lawrence Smith, remained consistently hostile to Vidia,
believing with good reason that he was treating his daughter badly, and
could not be relied upon to protect her. 'He said I should be shot. I was
very amused. "Shoot the fellow." I think he was using language beyond
his means. I took all of that without any anxiety.' Once when Vidia
visited the family flat with Margaret, her daughter Karin was asleep in

bed. 'She sat up and said, "Naipaul, I love you." I think she was about twelve or thirteen. All that was very nice for me, nice family life.'[29]

Vidia's article opened with a memorably bathetic line: 'In Argentina the killer cars – the cars in which the official gunmen go about their business – are Ford Falcons.' Silence had come, and a 'private war' between the guerrillas and the police and army had turned to a 'public terror'. He compared Argentina to Haiti, a society 'similarly parasitic on a removed civilization'. The walls in BA were whitewashed, the old political slogans removed, and the city that had considered itself European could now only look across the ocean at 'something far away, magically kept going by others ... an attitude not far removed from that of the politician of a new country who, while fouling his own nest, feathers another abroad, in a land of law.'[30] It was an acidic judgement, but few in Argentina at this time felt anything other than despair about the direction in which the country was heading.

While he was with Margaret in March 1977, Vidia was arrested, an experience he would use in *A Bend in the River*. He described what happened in a later article, removing his lover from the picture:

> One morning I took a bus for the town of Jujuy, in the province to the north, on the border with Bolivia. Just outside Salta the bus stopped, perhaps at the provincial boundary. Indian [Amerindian] policemen in dark-blue uniforms came in and asked for identity papers. Argentines are trained from childhood to carry their papers. I had none; I had left my passport in the hotel in Salta. So – with my gangster's face momentarily of interest to the other passengers, who were mainly Indian – I was taken off the bus, which then went on again.

Vidia was taken to a 'small white concrete shed' then driven to a police post. The men who had brought him there went away. 'Salta began to feel far away. My idea of time changed; I learned to wait. I gave my details once again.' They were far from BA, and telephone calls would not go through. 'I sat on a bench against a smooth plastered wall. I looked at the bush and the light outside. I smoked the pipe I had brought with me. After some time I wanted to use a lavatory. I was told there were no facilities in the little building. The policeman with the smiling eyes pointed to a spot in the bush some distance away: I was to go there. He said, "If you try to run away, I'll shoot you." With the smile, it sounded like a joke; but I knew that it wasn't.' Finally,

V.S. Naipaul was told that he was on no list of suspected guerrillas, and could go.

> The senior policeman said, with something like friendliness, 'It was your pipe that saved you. Did you know that? That pipe made me feel that you really were a foreigner.' It was an African pipe, a small black Tanganyika meerschaum I had bought in Uganda eleven years before: I had noticed that it had interested them. But all the time I had been trusting to my appearance, my broken Spanish, my Spanish accent. It was only now that I understood that to these Indian policemen of the far north Argentina would have been full of foreigners. So it was only at the moment of release, coming out of the slight shock, my disturbed sense of time, that I began to understand how serious my position had been. In the city of Tucumán, just a few days before, I had stood with a small group of townspeople watching policemen with machine guns below their raincoats getting into their unmarked cars. Like a kind of country-house shooting party; but in Tucumán the dirty war was especially dirty, and Tucumán was just to the south of Salta.[31]

Reviewing *The Return of Eva Perón*, a compilation of Vidia's South American essays and pieces on Malik, Zaire and Conrad, Martin Amis wrote in the *New Statesman*: 'In his peripatetic journalism, V.S. Naipaul is turning into the prose-poet of the earth's destitute; he is also becoming world-weary – or Third World-weary, anyway.' Amis saw a formula: 'He begins with a passionately tendentious run-through of a country's recent history, in a style that could be regarded as the demonic opposite of a *Look at Life* documentary (in which, for example, a clotted refugee camp might be described as a hardy workforce crying out to be tapped),' follows it with 'a gloomy cacophony of local voices' and 'settles the hash of whatever indigenous culture happens to be on offer'.[32] Amis wrote later, 'V.S. Naipaul, in his travel books, puts nation states on the psychiatrist's couch and then takes a reading of their mental health.'[33] *The Return of Eva Perón* was introduced by an odd 'author's note', feigning helplessness, as if fiction was obliged to 'offer' itself to the creative writer: 'These pieces ... bridged a creative gap: from the end of 1970 to the end of 1973 no novel offered itself to me. That perhaps explains the intensity of some of the pieces, and their obsessional nature.'[34] Neal Ascherson in the *Observer* called the essays on South America 'the most brutal and brilliant in this volume', a view shared by Nicholas Shakespeare, who had lived in Argentina during the 1970s: '*The Return of Eva Perón* is possibly the best piece of non-fiction he has written.'[35] Naipaul himself regarded his essays on Argentina as 'among the most important things I've done'.[36] According to David Pryce-Jones, Vidia had fatally undermined postcolonial pieties: 'Challenging guilt in the name of truth-telling, Naipaul has changed the recent climate of opinion as no other English-language writer has done.'[37] In the *New York Review*, Joan Didion commented on his changing reputation: 'It is hard not to note a certain turning in the air when V.S. Naipaul is mentioned, a hint of taint, a suggestion of favor about to go moot ... One catches the construction "brilliant but": brilliant but obsessive, brilliant but reductive ... Increasingly now he is consigned to this role of the special case, the victim of a unique cultural warp, the outsider obsessed (notice the vogue for "obsessive" as a dismissive adjective) by disgust for his colonial origins, the reductive (ditto "reductive") wog with a taste for the high table.'[38]

With his lover, he travelled to Caracas for the summer, and to the island of Margarita between the South American mainland and Trinidad, where they were joined by Kamla. Vidia located Poker or 'Bogart' ('What happening there, Bogart?') who kept a little shop, an encounter he would describe in 'Prologue to an Autobiography'. One day in Venezuela, Margaret turned to Vidia and said a sentence which stuck in his mind, an explanation for infatuation: 'Being with you is like always being in a film.'[39]

They visited Trinidad (which had recently became a republic under a new constitution arising from a report produced by, among others, the eminent lawyer Solomon Lutchman: a president would be elected by parliament, the voting age lowered to eighteen and structural political changes introduced). The trip was not a success. When Vidia and Margaret arrived at the airport in Port of Spain, they were greeted by Kamla, who told them that nobody in the family wanted to have them in their house, and they would have to stay at her own rented property. She had recently separated from Harry and left Jamaica, and was building a house on a plot of land given to her by Ma in Charlieville. Kamla said later that her fifteen-year-old-son Ved had advised her on protocol. 'He said, put them to sleep in one room because they must be sleeping together anyway. So they stayed with us.' Kamla took an elder sisterly dislike to Margaret, not helped by her brother's attitude to his mistress. 'Vidia told me that Margaret had a vocabulary of only fifty

words . . . I didn't see anything in Margaret to be quite honest. I didn't
see anything that Vidia would fall for. I never really took to Margaret.
She complained about Pat too much. My loyalty was to Pat. And then
Margaret had left all her children – she had three children – and I
couldn't personally understand that. Leave your husband, that's fine
enough, that doesn't bother me. But leave your three children? Oh, no.
I couldn't do that.'[40] Mira, living in America with her husband the
cancer specialist, blamed Margaret for Vidia's growing hostility to his
family. 'I personally feel that the change came about when he began
having an affair with the Argentinian woman, because his life took a
new turn. There was the wife whom we all knew and got on well with,
then there was the woman, and there was something to hide. Nobody
told me about this Margaret – her name was Margaret? – for years and
years. I was totally shocked when I discovered it.'[41]

Savi remembered coming to Kamla's house to see Margaret and
Vidia. 'Margaret said to me, "Why did you not want us to stay with
you?" And I said, "Because it would be wrong in my children's eyes.
Their only aunt is Auntie Pat." Vidia didn't speak at all.' According to
Savi, she had in fact never made a prohibition on Margaret entering her
house, only on staying there, and Kamla made the situation worse by
saying there was a ban. Ma refused to meet Margaret, and an altercation
followed. The upshot was a lasting family rupture: except for Kamla,
Vidia barely spoke to his sisters or to his mother for the next decade.
Kamla's relationship with Savi was affected too. 'It was the year my
mother went to England, and I think Vidia had my mother to tea in the
apartment alone. He did not invite me, or my son, and I know my
mother never had an invitation from Vidia after that. Never to England.
She went there to visit Nella. My mother was always deeply hurt by
this, and one of the good things about my mother is I don't think she
ever put the blame on Pat. I guess she realized her son was different
[from other people]. I don't think she wanted to be abused by him.'[42]
According to Droapatie's nephew Suren, who gave her occasional
financial support, 'She never spoke about Vidia, but was hurt that her
son had abandoned her.'[43] Vidia interpreted this debacle in his own
distinctive way: 'I was letting them meet Margaret as a kind of special
favour, because of her importance to me . . . I took Margaret to Nepaul
Street. My mother was with Ma'am, a black woman who told her
fortune every few days. My mother refused to look at Margaret. We

went away. Sati wouldn't meet her either. I broke completely with all of them, to my great relief.'⁴⁴

While he was in Trinidad, Vidia spoke to the pupils of Fatima College, a boys' secondary school. An amateur film of the seminar shows V.S. Naipaul wearing a roll-neck sweater, sitting with tightly crossed legs before an old-style microphone, puffing on his pipe, looking camp and uneasy, listening to inept questions from teachers and students. He was determinedly confrontational, a style he would repeat in his occasional public appearances in the West Indies over coming years. Was *The Middle Passage* out of date? No. He had looked at it a few days earlier, and been 'quite frightened by my own percipience'. Did he like Trinidad's steel bands? 'I don't like noise.' Was his novel based on guerrilla activity in Trinidad? 'No, no, no, no, no, no, no, no, no, no, no, no: the word is used ironically.' Dripping with sarcasm, he said, 'When I was a child, the word "black" was an insult. I think people liked to be called "coloured". The word "African" was an insult. Now of course, "black" is a very popular word, it is the accepted word. It has been a great revolution.' Exasperated, Vidia turns to a boy in the audience and asks whether *A House for Mr Biswas* had chimed with his own experiences of school. There is no reply. A teacher intervenes: 'The problem is that he is Venezuelan.' Vidia tries again: 'I would like people to try to come to grips with the emptiness of this society, try to understand the kind of bastard culture we inhabit, how we are all cut off from our ancestral roots. We've had a kind of colonial melange here, which deprives people of a past . . . Don't give way to despair, or find political slogans. Try to face that.' The more forceful and fervent V.S. Naipaul becomes, the more baffled his multi-ethnic young audience look.⁴⁵

Margaret left Trinidad to stay with her sister, Diana, in London and complained to Vidia afterwards that during the flight she had received the attentions of what she termed an obnoxious coon, handsome and of mixed blood, who had failed to persuade her to sit beside him. By November, after another series of angry exchanges, she decided finally to bring their relationship to a close. She had enjoyed it while it lasted, and she wanted Vidia to remember it as an experience of great passion and love. She looked presciently into the future: Margaret predicted that he would become more famous, while she would finish up in a bed-sit. People had often told her that Vidia was offering her no security at all for the future, and she could find no good reason to think otherwise. She felt she had no alternative but to move on, since she was unable to please him in so many ways. Everybody, all his family including Savi, Kamla and most of all 'P' wanted her to get out of his life, and she knew that in practice she was unlikely ever to spend more than a few months with him. He might complain that she had given him an ultimatum, but in fact he was the one who had given her an ultimatum – to tolerate whatever he commanded. She told him calmly that if she was forced to depend on him for anything at all, she might be left naked and starving.[46]

*

In the early autumn of 1977, Vidia had an 'illumination' for a new book – 'his theme, the paradox of civilisation' – and needed Pat's help in order to write it.[47] Over the previous two years, they had seen little of each other. He might telephone his wife occasionally to say he had 'dreams he is being hanged' or that he was having trouble with his work. This time, Vidia said he would only be able to proceed if he had her physical presence, and Pat was flattered to be wanted. Bored by life and obsessed by her husband's writing, she returned to Wilsford; it was her sacrifice, her destiny, the life of her choice. Vidia worked at odd hours, often into the night, sleeping until midday. He might leave her a little note, scribbled on an envelope: 'Patsy Please let me sleep Still awake at 2.15.'[48] He had put aside a plan to write an autobiography, finding the idea too difficult to face. Pat recorded disparate phrases he was now throwing out: 'Scattered people looking for somewhere to go ... Africa ... Men as prey – the Indians in London, lost, living at the end of a civilisation, blind ... He said that he was feeling very fertile. He wants to write the draft quickly ... Told me he can only write with me around. I create an aura. I feel it is so undeserved.'

'Full of admiration,' Vidia read Tolstoy's *Haji Murad* and *The Cossacks*, finding that reading was becoming a form of thinking, a way of shaping his unwritten, Conradian novel. One night shortly after his forty-fifth birthday, the idea was hatched. He had been watching the Last Night of the Proms on television, and said to Pat, 'I want to be alone with my thoughts.' Half an hour later she went into his room. He told her that the book would open with the lines: 'My family come from the east coast. Africa was at our backs. We are Indian ocean people.' Then he outlined to his wife the plot and principal characters of the story that would become *A Bend in the River*. 'I wondered and asked him, "You mean you can come in here for half an hour and think all that out?" He is sitting so quiet writing it down.' This would be V.S. Naipaul's greatest novel, with the conceivable exception of *A House for Mr Biswas*, a book which brought together all his experience and the uniqueness of his perspective, a late twentieth-century global narrative that could have been written by no one else.

It was softer in tone than the books which preceded it. Narrated in the first person by Salim, who has come from the coast to a French-speaking state in the centre of Africa to purchase a shop, it traces his relations with a network of characters: his servant Metty, descended from slaves, Indar, his childhood friend, Zabeth, a river trader and sorceress, and her son Ferdinand, who has high status in the new dispensation, Father Huismans, a priest with a deep respect for Africa who gets beheaded, Raymond, a white academic and promoter of the ruler's tyranny, and his wife Yvette, with whom Salim has a violent love affair. The physical setting of the book is evoked beautifully, whether at the river docks in Africa ('damp-haired young monkeys, full of misery, tethered tightly around their narrow waists and nibbling at peanuts and banana skin and mango skin, but nibbling without relish, as though they knew that they themselves were soon to be eaten'), or in London, or in the foreigners' campus, the Domain, where people listen to Joan Baez records: 'It was make-believe – I never doubted that. You couldn't listen to sweet songs about injustice unless you expected justice and received it much of the time.'[49] Vidia's spark for the novel originated in a chance encounter in Kisangani. His plane had been taken out of service, and he found himself at the airport talking to a young Indian man. 'The hotels were closed because Mobutu was in town, and he said come and sleep at my flat. Everything that happened over the next two days, I used in *A Bend in the River*. He was a businessman running a shop, and his "Jeeves" talked a lot of rubbish about going to Canada. He told me about his private life, that there was a woman, and took me to look at her house. She was a Vietnamese woman; that disappears in my narrative. We can call him Salim. The essence of the book is: what is this man doing here?'[50] Some personalities – Zabeth, for instance – owe something to the Trinidadians of Vidia's childhood. 'I combined my 1975 trip to the Congo with my knowledge of black people from Trinidad. I could think myself into an understanding of who they are.'[51]

By October, Pat and Vidia's sexual relationship had rekindled, and she relished the opportunity to show her care and devotion. They would go for walks along the banks of the River Avon, parts of which were choked with weeds, the chalk streams of Wiltshire provoking ideas for a novel set near a wide expanse of water in the heart of Africa. One afternoon, Vidia raced back from the river to continue working, but when he got home he felt tired and lay down. 'At 5.00 I took his shoes off (protest – he likes the weight) and wrapped his feet up. He has started typing again.' Later, 'He wrote like an angel: the arrival of Methi [later Metty, named for Metti, the Petit Valley overseer], after the revolution on the coast.' Within days, the rediscovery of tranquillity was upset when Pat copied out his business accounts in black ink rather than red: 'so more abuse and humiliation.' Even the arrival of Shiva, Jenny and their young son Tarun for the day could not dent his mood of literary optimism. Vidia sat down to read the manuscript of Shiva's new book *North of South*, and made 'correction after correction, big and small . . . In the evening Vidia told me how much he loved Sewan, always had, but Sewan rejected him when he first came to England.' His brother remained on his mind. Vidia telephoned him to give instructions on the craft of the writer: 'It is not the writer's business to complain but to explore. Urges him to read *Master and Man*, by Tolstoy, and the early English writers.'

Vidia found he was writing with greater fluency than he had for many years. By Christmas he had completed 40,000 words, and was holding the whole book in his head. *A Bend in the River* was a mature work of the imagination rather than disguised autobiography; it was the product of assimilated experience. Although it contained much that was observed or personal – Africa, Margaret – his travels and memories were a starting point for invention. The book was the work of a middle-aged novelist marked by experience but in full command of his creative powers. It lacked the anger of *Guerrillas* or *India: A Wounded Civilization*: as one character says, 'It isn't that there's no right and wrong here. There's no right.'[52] As Vidia continued, his mood swung back and forth, with Pat taking the strain. Despite being thin, she worried she was greedy, lazy, clumsy, incompetent. 'Whatever the truth, I am not much good to anyone and Vidia is probably, almost certainly, right when he says I have nothing to offer him.' But without her, he insisted he could not continue. Savi noticed that Pat and Vidia had become obsessed by food. 'She got thinner and thinner and it was as though both of them decided that carbohydrates were not to be eaten at all. They got this compulsive behaviour, and even at lunch, Vido would say to me, "You may leave the potato." It wasn't up to him whether I had it or not. It was there on my plate. Vidia was obsessed that his thighs were too fat. "These Capildeo thighs" he called them.'[53]

Through the months it took to write *A Bend in the River*, Pat recorded each step of her husband's progress. Paul Theroux telephoned to say he was going to South America, which made Vidia angry, although 'the situation was saved by Paul's sweetness. He said something to Paul about [Menachem] Begin, and I am sure Paul must have been comforting, but he did not go the whole hog about the Jews destroying the West, or Western culture.' This was a rare instance of anti-Semitism in Vidia's conversation.

When he reached the middle of the book, Indar (who was called Indrajit in the first draft) was reintroduced to the plot. '"Indrajit will be me." . . . Every character . . . has a narrative function.' A British-educated Indian from the east coast of Africa, Indar was able to say and see things that are hidden from the other characters. He tells a story. Turned down for a job at India House, he meets an American man at a lunch party who 'spoke of Africa as though Africa was a sick child and he was the parent.' He gives Indar a job with a foundation, 'using the surplus wealth of the western world to protect that world'. In a crucial passage, speaking to his friend Salim, Indar outlines his – or Vidia's – philosophy. As he comes from a community of deracinated Indians, overlooked by history, he has a rare opportunity to make his own way in the world:

> I'm a lucky man. I carry the world within me. You see, Salim, in this world beggars are the only people who can be choosers. Everyone else has his side chosen for him. I can choose. The world is a rich place. It all depends on what you choose in it. You can be sentimental and embrace the idea of your own defeat. You can be an Indian diplomat and always be on the losing side. It's like banking . . . The Rothschilds are what they are because they chose Europe at the right time. The other Jews, just as talented, who went to bank for the Ottoman Empire, in Turkey or Egypt or wherever, didn't do so well. Nobody knows their names. And that's what we've been doing for centuries. We've been clinging to the idea of defeat and forgetting that we are men like everybody else. We've been choosing the wrong side. I'm tired of being on the losing side. I don't want to pass. I know exactly who I am and where I stand in the world. But now I want to win and win and win.[54]

Immediately after writing this paragraph, Vidia felt exhausted, but knew there was more to come. He sat hunched in a chair 'taking the odd pinch of snuff' and dictated to Pat. 'I was also, with my hurrying pen, conscious of the mounting excitement towards the end,' she recorded,

'and I wanted to show this and my understanding by reading dramati-
cally.' A few days later, she helped him again. 'Cary Welch [an expert
on Indian art] and his wife Edith came with Tony and Violet Powell.
Vidia was very helpful and attentive at table. Quite soon after they had
gone, with wine headache and everything, Vidia began dictating to me
and made the transition from Indrajit's story back to the bend in the
river ... The imaginative flight, the reintroduction of the water
hyacinth came to him as he was dictating ... His expression, while he
was thinking and dictating, most of the time with eyes closed, changed
about three times, like weather. To begin with, he was concentrating,
intent, brow knitted. Then half-way through, his face looked very
serene. Finally fairly firm and powerful ... It was a terrible life writers
lead, he said, quite comfortably, afterwards.'

Next he wanted to write about Yvette and Salim. 'Last night, in the
kitchen while I was cooking, he outlined the next stage: the beginning
of the affair. He said he was "nervous" of the sex. I said perhaps he did
not need to write sex scenes but he said "I want to." He told me he
must be "left to myself", be very private, as he will be "embarrassed".'
Avoiding any hint of pornography, he wrote truthfully about sex for
the first time, drawing on what he had learned with Margaret: '[L]ike
many men who use brothels alone, I had grown to think of myself as
feeble, critically disadvantaged.' With Yvette, 'the sexual act became
for me an extraordinary novelty, a new kind of fulfilment, continuously
new ... I was full of the wonder of what had befallen me. And
awakening from minute to minute to the depth of my satisfactions, I
began to be aware of my immense previous deprivation. It was like
discovering a great, unappeasable hunger in myself.'[55]

The weather was turning cold; for two days the house was snowed
in and the milkman could not reach them to deliver milk. Wearing
coats and gumboots, Pat and Vidia walked down to the river. 'He
waded to the bank and walked along it a little way in his Kenya
sheepskin coat, warm, pinkish in colour. He came back, wading, looking
down as he put each foot forward, an expression of pure, quiet happiness
on his face.' This version of pastoral could not last long. The writing
got stuck. Vidia took up a book on the mystical sage Swami Vivekan-
anda, and 'broke off to make hostile comments about his own mother –
"I always hated her" (which is absolutely untrue).' Events from outside
intruded. 'Vidia is very excited about the Israeli invasion of Lebanon.'
Pat was starting to irritate him, and his temper erupted even as he

returned to writing. A summons to see local friends was accepted, which was a mistake. 'On Saturday evening we had drinks with the Mitchells . . . the next day he began making a lot of fuss: shouldn't have got to know them, etc. Horrified by present-day gentry, the gentry of our valley. "England is dead." He has been talking a lot about parasitism – "I'm waiting to meet someone who makes something."' Incorporating himself into the person of Mobutu, the 'Big Man' in the book, he sent Pat away. 'He has been writing the President's speech,' she noted. 'I have behaved foolishly all day and have ruined every last relationship I have. I have agreed to go back to London after the weekend. Vidia says he can't stand my eccentricity any more and I will destroy him.' Alone in Wilsford, Vidia was excited and distracted by the arrival of occasional letters from Margaret in Buenos Aires, saying she was bored. She had met a man whose estate adjoined the police station where they had been arrested near Salta, and what was more he turned out to be a friend of the local superintendent. If only she had known him at the time! She had been having dreams about Vido, including one where she was taking a shower and he came in feeling enraged and handled her suitably roughly.[56]

In the spring of 1978, Vidia and Pat went together to watch Luis Buñuel's film *That Obscure Object of Desire* in London. Afterwards he returned to Wiltshire alone and telephoned her. 'He has written the violent scene with Yvette. "Doesn't it speak of passion," he said, when he had read it, "of Salim's pain." I had found it shocking. Did not have anything to say . . . He laughed afterwards and said that seeing the Buñuel had helped really. "But it is better than the Buñuel." Discussing the shocking character of the scene he said that he had worked carefully – using the passive tense – "she was hit" – "I hit her" would be to make Salim just a tough man.' The scene drew directly on his violence towards Margaret in Wilsford in the fall of 1974.

Pat's diary is a chronicle, but it is also an abdication, a means of avoidance. It is, like the voice, passive. Nowhere does Pat ask herself to what extent Vidia's writing is drawn from life, and specifically from his life with Margaret. Her diary is a record of a kind of blankness. The nature of their relationship meant that she would never ask Vidia anything of this kind directly, and preferred not to consider it, even if at some level she 'knew' what he was drawing on. If she ever looked for or looked at his love letters and erotic photographs, there is no record of it in her diary. She appears to have been convinced by the explanations he offered, for instance by his assertion that Salim's violence towards Yvette was a symptom of love, or that his use of the passive prevented Salim from seeming 'a tough man'. In fact, it arose from Vidia's opinion that he, as much as Margaret, was the victim of his violence: he had been helpless in the face of his own justified anger at his lover's infidelity with an Argentine banker. Despite this attempt to shift the blame, Vidia hated the way in which he had behaved, seeing it as a personal failing and a cultural stigma: 'I despise it passionately, despise it because it is very much an Indian failing. When I say Indian, I mean our community. And it's always a sign of defeated people, isn't it? I think this thing about beating your wife is more Indian than Negro . . . My father's stories deal with wife-beating and as it were, he gives it an Indian ancestry, a village ancestry.'[57]

Returning to Wiltshire from London, Pat found 'Vidia's door was shut and he was very silent. A large, red fire was burning in the sitting-room. Shortly afterwards he drew me into his room to read the rest of the violent scene with Yvette. Looking back, I recognise the artistry. >Vidia had to point out some of this, the folds in the sheet, the magazine falling; he also helped me by saying that Salim obviously loved her (Vidia is so proud of never using the word love) enabling me to understand this passion, this love.< At the end I did not register, or exhibit, excitement or approval. I expressed some concern at the violence. (I did not say so, but the reiteration of the blows and, to a lesser extent, the spittle was foremost in my mind.) . . . I was a spectator of the writing, of his exhilaration, looking back now, of his look of triumph.' Pat believed or accepted Vidia's analysis of these scenes. Later, when a reviewer suggested the treatment of sex in *A Bend in the River* was unbalanced and peculiar, Pat wrote but did not send a letter in response: 'Sex and race are very difficult. They are the topics of our age. Each of us has to wrestle with them.' She defended her husband's depictions of sexual violence. 'You were wrong I think to compare the two scenes in *Bend* with the two similar scenes in *Guerrillas*. They are not identical. I would like to point out one thing. Jane threw down the challenge. She humiliated Jimmy at the start, women have this urge sometimes – it can be a dangerous thing to do . . . But perhaps I have been too close to this book, too familiar with it to read it objectively.'[58]

As winter turned to spring, she continued to record Vidia's remarks and the progress of the book. 'He spoke of his life lacking savour and grieved that he had never treated that woman well. Had never been

with her more than three weeks, had sent her away, had rejected a very
"pure affection".' Sometimes he needed Pat to help him with his work,
a job she relished, regardless of the time of night: 'He called me into
his room at about 1.0 (I was falling asleep, without Mandrax) to take it
down. I made him porridge. Then there was further quarrelling; then
he looked at it again and spoke some of the versions again ... We
finally separated fairly calmly at 3.0 or after.' Finally, in May 1978, 'At
about 12.30 last night he called me in and spoke the end of the book. It
took an hour to an hour and a half.' Once he had said the words out
loud, he was ready to write them, nearly verbatim. The material seemed
to be given to him from nowhere. 'He made the remark, which he had
made before, that when "the work is good I am not responsible."' This
was how *A Bend in the River* closed:

> The sky hazed over, and the sinking sun showed orange and was
> reflected in a broken golden line in the muddy water. Then we
> sailed into a golden glow ... Water hyacinths pushed up in the
> narrow space between the steamer and the barge. We went on.
> Darkness fell. It was in this darkness that abruptly, with many loud
> noises, we stopped ... The searchlight lit up the barge passengers
> who, behind bars and wire-guards, as yet scarcely seemed to
> understand that they were adrift. Then there were gunshots. The
> searchlight was turned off; the barge was no longer to be seen. The
> steamer started up again and moved without lights down the river,
> away from the area of battle. The air would have been full of moths
> and flying insects. The searchlight, while it was on, had shown
> thousands, white in the white light.[59]

Now Vidia decided to go and live in the USA, with Margaret.

CHAPTER TWENTY-TWO

A HOUSE FOR MR NAIPAUL

VIDIA WAS RISING. As people and ideas shifted between countries in a way they had not done at previous points in human history, an author who took the world as his subject was no longer impossible. He could carve out a space for himself as a new sort of writer, claiming to come from a place without history, a mere dot on the map. *Guerrillas* had proved an unexpected success in America, and Francis Ford Coppola wanted to turn it into a film. Within academia, non-white voices were sought, even if V.S. Naipaul fell into no standard postcolonial category. Letters and invitations came. Would he like the Neustadt International Prize for Literature, for which he had been nominated by Derek Walcott? Might he speak to the Cambridge Union? Did he wish to become a Regents' Professor at Berkeley? Would he deign to open a conference at the University of the West Indies? Was he ready to become a Knight of Mark Twain? Would he be a writer-in-residence at the University of Western Australia?

Wishing to spend time in a different place and to attempt living with Margaret for the first time, Vidia took up an invitation from Phyllis Rose of Wesleyan University's English Department. Rose flew to London to meet him: starting in September 1978, he would spend an academic year teaching courses in creative writing and literature and 'alien cultures' at the small, private liberal arts college in Middletown, Connecticut, in exchange for $30,000. The university arranged for him to rent a house of glass and weathered cedar from a philosophy professor, Victor Gourevitch. 'They are very good to me here, leaving me absolutely alone,' he wrote in a letter in October.[1]

'He said as soon as he got off the bus in Middletown, he knew he'd made a mistake,' Rose recalled. 'It's an old New England mill town, semi-derelict in parts. I do think it was only his sense of honour that kept him there to the end of the year. The courses he taught were brilliantly inventive. He started out tremendously popular – until the first paper was due. When the work was not on time, he got furious in a way which American students are not accustomed to: "You are like officials in the Congo. You are corrupt." He was killing sacred cows left and right in those courses, saying Isak Dinesen – she had just been discovered, and this was in the first wave of feminist criticism – didn't know anything about Africa, and *Out of Africa* was trash. The English Department wanted him as a representative of the Third World, and Vidia couldn't be anything less like that.'[2] Students who thought they might approach him for Third Worldly advice were mistaken. The mother of one Alvin Lee Peters wrote to complain: young Alvin was preparing to go to India to stay with a family 'as a part of the program sponsored by the Experiment in International Living ... With that background I hope that you can understand my astonishment, my bewilderment and my growing anger when I learned that you refused to talk to my son even though he is a Wesleyan student, had just read your book, and is on his way to India. Perhaps there is a rational explanation for the brush-off you gave a student interested in your work and your country. If so, I would be interested in knowing what it is.'[3] Phyllis Rose thought 'the students were mainly liberal or left, from middle-class professional families, proud of their slovenly dress and progressive ideas' and ill-equipped to cope with Vidia's acerbic responses to their conventional statements. The *Sunday Telegraph Magazine* reported him saying: 'I would take poison rather than do this for a living ... I thought I'd meet lots of people who passionately wanted to write. I was shocked to find some take the course in the same way as basketwork or karate.'[4]

The anonymous teaching evaluations at the end of the year show that students tended to either love or hate V.S. Naipaul. 'This is nothing short of a brilliant, witty man,' wrote one. 'I can think of almost no praise too strong for Mr Naipaul,' wrote another. 'He stimulated more interest in me and more honest appreciation of literature than anyone else I have worked with ... I will remember this course and this year with very fond and brilliant memories because of Vidia's presence and his constantly percolating imagination,' wrote a third. From another direction, a graduate wrote: 'He had no office hours and tended to say things such as, "Well, I only have to spend 2 hours a week with students, so goodbye." He was detrimental even to the enthusiasm of some of my classmates and myself ... He was, simply, the worst, most close-minded, inconsiderate, uninteresting and incompetent professor I have ever met.' Another said he favoured only a chosen few. 'Mr

Naipaul, lacking the professional objectivity of a teacher, neglected most of us – and considering how important our writing is to us – hurt us.' Five people who failed the course wrote a joint letter demanding a re-mark: 'In the context of this university, and of academe in general, these grades reflect work and performance of extremely low caliber.' The students who liked him were more than content: 'Mr Naipaul is not a usual teacher, and cannot be evaluated in the usual ways . . . It has been an outstanding honor and experience, both to see a great mind at work and to learn how to see in a different way.'[5]

Living with Margaret in this alien setting did not go smoothly. She became bored, and he became irritable. Vidia taught classes, wrote about Indian art for the *New York Review* and edited the proofs of *A Bend in the River*. When Kamla read the novel, she wrote to him, 'It must be your best book. In fact, it must be one of the best books I have ever read.' She kept him in touch with news from home: 'More of Frederick Street has been burnt down. Fires are in fact, a weekly occurrence. Anti-Indian slogans are also very much in evidence. Walls in Valsayn are now scrawled with suggestions about starting the dougla [African-Indian] race.'[6] Once a week Vidia took horse-riding lessons, convinced they would be good for him. 'I wonder how you're finding the college crowd,' wrote Paul Theroux from London. 'Am I alone in finding American students unteachable – sweet, yes, but unteachable. You ought to do your Makerere thing: examine handwriting, urge creative writing students to get into cash crops . . . if there is anything I can do for you here or there, please let me know.'[7]

Vidia could not see his way to another novel. 'I only have ten years left,' he told Phyllis Rose, convinced his writing life was coming to an end. She gave a party, attended by Vidia and Margaret: 'I had a buffet dinner, made beef stroganoff and a special kind of fish for him. He says, "I think the fish was not prepared with as much care as the beef" . . . I was quite fond of Margaret. I thought she lived on a grand scale and was smart and funny. She didn't talk about books; we had household, gossipy talks.'[8] Vidia and Margaret got to know two of the more talented Wesleyan students, Jeff Hush and Banning Eyre. In a reminiscence, Eyre described Vidia as a dandyish figure, consciously at odds with the university. At his first class, 'He wore grey flannels, a dark blue blazer, and heavy black-rimmed sunglasses for which he quickly substituted reading glasses once he was seated. He spoke in a resonant British accent, and I thought his manner elegant and refined. From time to time, he paused and delicately inhaled some Fribourg & Treyer snuff off a little silver spoon. And then his whole face would smile. Controlled delight.'[9] After Vidia had gone, Phyllis Rose wrote:

> Did you see the write-up about you in TIME, the one that ended with a marvellous statement from you about "caste arrogance" and people in preppy clothes with empty heads being more dangerous to America than oil embargoes? Well, the radical students had it reproduced in a very elegant little folder and passed them out at commencement as though they were programs . . . And everywhere I went on the east coast around that time, people were quoting you.[10]

Middletown was close enough to New York for Vidia and Margaret to spend weekends at the Algonquin Hotel. For a longer period, with the assistance of the ubiquitous Bob Silvers, they borrowed the East 75th Street brownstone apartment of John Richardson, a homosexual art critic who ran Christie's in America. 'Vidia's life in New York revolved very much around Bob, who admired him and was tremendously generous to his writers,' Richardson recalled. 'Margaret seemed to be having a rough time of it. I slightly had the feeling she enjoyed that, this rather broken-down Argentinian lady. I was fascinated by Vidia, but I didn't take to him. He was so discontented within himself, and he seemed to think he was doing me an honour by occupying my apartment . . . I felt he enjoyed the unorthodoxy of gay men; he was at ease with them because he was self-invented. He had some identification with the gay man as an outsider.'[11] Vidia found Richardson to be part of a wilder scene than he was used to in Middletown or Wilsford. One night as he and Margaret lay in bed at the apartment, the telephone rang. A voice said, 'John? John! Master! I am coming over now.' 'No, no,' replied V.S. Naipaul. 'I think there has been a misunderstanding.'

When *A Bend in the River* was published, journalists attempted to fathom the author, 'an elusive man' who had 'somehow managed to remain an enigma'.[12] His income was still not keeping pace with his status, although at $25,000 his advance on royalties from Knopf was higher than it had been before. When a *New York Times* columnist tried to contact Vidia, Diana Athill wrote back, 'I'm afraid we have the strictest instructions from Mr Naipaul not to divulge his address to anyone under any circumstances.'[13] No longer was he a calypso writer or a curiosity from London: he was a world-class novelist. There was no going back. Saul Bellow sought to meet him. Letters arrived from around the globe. 'I love you because you are so mean . . . You are better than Elvis. (Meaner, too),' wrote Eve Babitz, a fellow Knopf author.[14] A telegram came from Deutsch: 'YOURE 99 PERCENT CERTAIN TO WIN BOOKER PRIZE AND THINK YOU SHOULD MAKE YOURSELF AVAILABLE FOR SOME TELE-PHONED COMMENT TO BBC.'[15] But Vidia did not win the Booker; it was awarded by compromise to Penelope Fitzgerald's *Offshore*, and when he was offered the James Tait Black Memorial Prize and the Royal Society of Literature's Winifred Holtby Award, he turned them both down.[16]

'For sheer abundance of talent, there can hardly be a writer alive who surpasses V.S. Naipaul,' wrote Irving Howe in the *New York Times Book Review*. 'Naipaul is considered in Europe to be one of the living masters of English prose. Deservedly,' concluded Nelson Algren in the *Chicago Tribune*. 'There are not many writers today who see so steadily and so far,' said Bernard Levin in the *Sunday Times*. The *Evening Standard* located Arthur Calder Marshall, now in his seventies, who praised *A Bend in the River* as 'an astonishing double achievement' that revealed more about Africa than 'any ponderous work of non-fiction . . . I can think of no other novelist who could have written this book.' In the *Spectator*, Richard West made a claim that would be shared by many reviewers: Naipaul had written 'one of those books that make you question many assumptions about the world today.' In 2004, the author Alexandra Fuller wrote: 'I am not of the limited and limiting school that supposes only black Africans can write about Africa . . . But you have to be willing to be fresh and above all honest about the places which exist on this continent in order not to sound like a stuffed Victorian. V.S. Naipaul did it with chilling accuracy in *A Bend in the River*.'[17]

Assumptions were being questioned. A rising disillusion with the postcolonial project in many countries led to Vidia being projected as the voice of truth, the scourge who by virtue of his ethnicity and his intellect could see things that others were seeking to disguise. Why were so many African countries ruled by thieves? Why was Iran having an Islamist revolution? What had become of the gracious optimism of the 1960s and 1970s? Where was Black Power now? Perhaps V.S. Naipaul was right when he wrote the terrifying opening sentence of *A Bend in the River*: 'The world is what it is; men who are nothing, who allow themselves to become nothing, have no place in it.'[18] As corrected liberals began to praise Vidia's vision, others tried to strike him down. Derek Walcott took a bite out of him in a lecture, which started a running antagonism, and Edward Said, whose recent book *Orientalism* had crystallized a prevailing intellectual trend which held that Western perceptions of the Orient were based on prejudice and misconception, complained he was dismissing all 'national liberation movements' as 'fraudulent public relations gimmicks' and 'half native impotence . . . He prefers to indict guerrillas for their pretensions rather than indict the imperialism that drove them to insurrection.'[19] In academic circles in particular, Vidia began to be presented as indefensible, even while his books were put on college reading lists. Banning Eyre remembered how at Wesleyan, 'V.S. Naipaul became widely known as a terrible ogre: a sexist, a racist, a snob – people knew him as these without even knowing he was a famous novelist.'[20] Vidia's response to the growth in his reputation as a villain was to stoke it. Whenever he got the chance in an interview, he would denounce something or somebody; in a Caribbean symbiosis, the subtler and more intense his writing grew over the years, the more throwaway his public remarks would become. In a much-quoted comment, when asked to explain the symbolism of the bindi (the coloured dot worn on the forehead of Indian women) he said, 'The dot means: my head is empty.'[21]

In 1980, *Newsweek* put him on the cover with the headline 'The Master of the Novel'. Sitting in the middle of a field holding a stick, a jacket slung over his shoulder, V.S. Naipaul glared out at the world. 'Such is the screen that Naipaul erects around his life that few people know that he is married – to a former fellow Oxford student, Patricia Hale.' He was an 'East Indian Brahmin raised in Trinidad . . . a creative craftsman of such surpassing talent that Britain's leading literary critic, V.S. Pritchett, calls him "the greatest living writer in the English language".' In the opinion of *Newsweek*, 'He is a strong contender for this year's Nobel Prize in Literature.' The tone of the profile and accompanying material was indicative of the uncertainty in the press response to Vidia, and his own willingness to shift between profundity and picong. Interviewed back in Wiltshire, he played the fool: 'In England people are very proud of being very stupid. A great price is being paid here now for the cult of stupidity and idleness . . . Living here has been a kind of castration, really.' Then he changed gear, dismissing the notion of 'the Third World' as a cliché. 'What disheartens me is that there are certain cultures where people are saying, "Cut yourselves off. Go back to what you were." There is nothing to replace the universal civilization they are rejecting. The Arabs, the Muslims, some Africans are doing this. I think it's a disaster. The great Arab civilization of the seventh to twelfth centuries was the world's most eclectic civilization. It wasn't closed to outside influences. It was endlessly incorporating the art of Persia, the mathematics of India, what remained of the philosophy of Greece. The mistake of Western vanity is to think that the universal civilization that exists now is a purer racial one. It's not the preserve of one race, one country, but has been fed by many.'[22] As in other profiles of Vidia at this time, Paul Theroux was quoted in *Newsweek* as an admiring defender and long-time friend. On the BBC in the same year, Theroux declared, 'He's proud, dignified, very funny . . . The embodiment of all those things is being a Brahmin. You must never forget that he's a Brahmin.'[23]

*

While he was at Wesleyan, drumming his heels in Professor Gourevitch's house, Vidia had spent time watching television. He was fascinated by the stirrings of the Iranian revolution, and in particular by speeches given by exiled clerics calling for the overthrow of the Shah. He believed they were lying, and that what they really wanted was not a revolution, but to kill their opponents and establish a theocratic state. 'What with all the back to Islam movement and the Ayatollah, I have gone back to the old thinking of my family,' Kamla wrote. 'You know, I had got rid of that deeply ingrained distrust of the Muslim but now it's all come back.'[24] The development of Islamic radicalism, and the idea that it might be a serious threat to the world, became a growing obsession for Vidia. He decided to write a book about it, to be called *Among the Believers*. His thesis was based on the assumption that Islam, with its emphasis on a text written in Arabic and on pilgrimage to holy places in Saudi Arabia, was innately imperialist, requiring its followers to diminish their native culture. He would travel, therefore, to four non-Arab Muslim countries: Iran, Pakistan, Malaysia and Indonesia, breaking away from his previous territory. Wanting money, he sold the book in advance. Vidia went through at least seven drafts before he got the proposal right for the publishers. 'What I have in mind is travel reportage, light in tone, even humorous, on an entirely serious subject – Islamic revivalism or fundamentalism, as it has developed in the postcolonial era . . . Each country has a quarrel with the modern world; and my own feeling is that Islam, in these countries, is as much a looking away as a looking back. Is it despair, a recognition of intellectual and scientific incapacity? Is it nihilism? Doesn't this kind of anti-intellectual movement . . . commit these countries to a continuing dependence on the technology and science of the West? Independence, then, leads back to dependence . . . In tone and form I will be aiming at something like my Middle Passage of 1960–62.'[25]

His latest ambition coincided with a professional shift. In 1977, the year in which he parted company with his accountant and found a replacement, Vidia had switched publishers. He felt that Deutsch was not promoting his talent with sufficient vigour, and that Diana Athill had been unflattering about Guerrillas. Graham Watson delivered the coup de grâce, and Diana was distraught. 'I am more upset than I can tell you at Graham's message that you want to leave us – and as for André, he can hardly talk about it, he's so miserable . . . I think we ought to be able to talk about it face to face.'[26] André wrote to Graham, 'I did not try to persuade him to change his mind; I merely said goodbye. He sounded sad and talked about our on-going relations with all his books, etc. I told him that we will continue to look after him as well as I think we have done in the last twenty years.'[27] Soon, though, there was trouble. The new bride, Secker & Warburg, described V.S. Naipaul in their catalogue as a Caribbean author; he took offence, and resolved to return to Deutsch. Watson told him this was a bad decision, since Secker & Warburg had made an 'innocently contrived mistake' but Vidia insisted on returning to his old publisher. Had he known that Deutsch was still putting out publicity material like – 'He is not a practising Hindu, although he retains the habit of vegetarianism instilled by a Hindu upbringing. Like ninety-nine West Indians out of a hundred, he has a passion for cricket' – he might have been less sure.[28] Once Vidia had reversed his decision, it remained reversed, and by February 1979 he was writing to André to praise his dealings with European publishers: 'Thanks for everything. You have been marvellous in so many things; I want you to be around forever.'[29]

In the same month, he decided that his problem was not Deutsch, but Watson. When he read the manuscript of A Bend in the River, Graham Watson had been content, but not rapturous, and Vidia made his resentment clear. 'Sometimes you are rather hard to please!!' came the response: it was 'a majestic and important novel . . . and if you have deliberately pitched the theme on a cerebral level, that was clearly what the subject demanded.'[30] Vidia chafed. Paul Theroux had enjoyed commercial success with *The Great Railway Bazaar*, a travel book about a rail journey across Asia published by Gillon Aitken of Hamish Hamilton, whom he described to Vidia as 'one of your very tall Englishmen'.[31] When Aitken set up as a literary agent in 1976, Paul had joined him, followed by Shiva. Vidia was quietly and painfully aware that both Paul Theroux and his brother were making more money from their new books than he was. Shiva received a good advance for *Black and White*, a book on the Jonestown massacre in Guyana. When Vidia met Aitken at a party given by the art dealer Michael Goedhuis, they discussed Pushkin; Aitken had translated his work, and sent Vidia a copy of the book afterwards, as he had promised. They met in New York, and Vidia decided to defect. His letter of departure to Graham Watson was short: 'I feel the time has come for me to leave Curtis Brown. The organization doesn't give me the overseas representation I should be getting. I am reserving all rights that are unsold, lapsed, or in negotiation.'[32] Watson answered that he would not end a relationship of twenty years by post, and requested a meeting. Gillon Aitken flew back to London with a bound proof copy of *A Bend in the River*: 'I read it on the plane and I think it was possibly the best novel I had ever read. It was a masterpiece, an extraordinary book, and it was very nice to read it in that captive position, being on the aeroplane.'[33]

At his final meeting with Watson, Vidia was in no mood to take prisoners: 'I settled that account. I settle all my accounts. He cried when I left him. He came out with me to the corridors [of the Curtis Brown office]. He was saying, go and get a new agent, but let us collect the money for you. Would you believe this? And I saw then that I had given twenty years of my work to scoundrels. I outlined *Among the Believers* to Gillon, and immediately we did very well. We got a big deal from the *Observer*. From making £10,000 a year I jumped to making about £60,000. It was a bad, bad story.'[34] This was no mere boast. Gillon Aitken saw Vidia's financial potential in a way that Graham Watson never had, and realized that literary status could be converted into cash in a new commercial climate in British and American publishing. His West Indian origins need no longer trap him in a lesser category. Aided by his colleague Andrew Wylie in New York, known to journalists as 'The Jackal', Aitken used his own mercantile nous and faith in Vidia's writing to parley talent into money. Journalistic assignments began to generate serious sums, and the advances for his books headed towards six figures. Vidia earned $75,000 from *Vanity Fair* and another £10,000 from the *Sunday Times* for a long article, 'Prologue to an Autobiography'.[35] Even a token piece for American

House & Garden in 1985 produced $5,000. In the 1970s, Vidia earned an average of £7,600 a year after agent's commission but before expenses and tax. During the 1980s, using an equivalent analysis, his annual income would jump to £143,600. This was a sevenfold rise, allowing for inflation.[36] Feeling more optimistic, he wrote to Paul Theroux of *The Mosquito Coast*: 'The idea is at once simple and appetising: the way good ideas should be. Another Theroux blockbuster! . . . I run across your name and your books everywhere and I always feel slightly proprietorial.'[37]

What was Vidia to do with his relative wealth? He would buy a dilapidated house, a dairyman's cottage in Salterton, up the valley from Wilsford Manor, and have it converted in just the way he wanted. It would take some time. Meanwhile, tiring of Margaret, he had left America to spend the summer of 1979 with Pat. They entertained visitors, went on a short trip to France (Vidia thought the Pompidou Centre should be pulled down) and discussed the possibility that she might accompany him to east Asia. He was profiled reverently by *Vogue*: 'He has never wanted children. His life is distinguished and shaped by extreme fastidiousness. It manifests itself physically as a brahminical fear of contamination. He didn't want to borrow a shirt to be photographed in . . . He keeps fit by flipping over backwards until the palms of his hands touch the ground behind him and whipping upright again 200 times a day.'[38]

Margaret told him everything was over, and spoke of posting things back and splitting costs. She had been waiting to present him with a bill left over from their time together, but had avoided doing so because she could not bear the thought of all his insults. She hoped he might agree to pay half. As for the future, she wished him well, and said his success had at least in a small way been down to her.[39] By the autumn, when Vidia departed for Iran and Pakistan, they were back together, but by the time they reached Kuala Lumpur, the relationship was collapsing. As Vidia intoned, 'In Malaysia, with a very heavy heart, I asked Margaret to leave me, and let me do the travelling alone.'[40] She returned to London to be with her sister Diana, went to the ballet, jogged in Hyde Park and watched a programme about Vidia on television. Her house in Argentina had been sold by Roy, although he had not yet told her the price, and she would have a little more money. Things were changing. She admitted sadly that she was no longer thirty, and Vidia's ties were in England. But her feelings for him had never changed, and her desire for him had never wavered. Her excitement at seeing him had always felt the same. It was a matter of great sorrow that they had never had a child together. Vidia was offering her nothing but fleeting moments, wherever in the world he happened to be travelling; somehow she converted this parsimony into her own failure. She would like to want what he was offering, but could not cope with it any longer. She was sorry — it was not his fault, it was hers. In times to come, he knew he could rely on her love, her passion and her support.[41]

With no distractions, Vidia caught up on correspondence. Antonia had just read *A Bend in the River* twice ('it's such an extraordinary book that I will not presume to say more than just that').[42] Vidia thought it 'extraordinarily nice' of her to say so. 'Your handwriting has subtly changed. Has anyone told you? The same personality, but rejuvenated, even girlish — and I don't mean this in any unkind way ... I hope it will be possible to see Harold and you when I get back and start living a more ordered life.'[43] Distracted from his own problems, he was able to think about how others might cope with theirs. He advised a troubled Banning Eyre how to deal with his family. Banning was wondering what to do now that he was finishing at Wesleyan: whether to pursue a musical or a literary career, and how to resolve the myriad emotional complications that were thrown up by the daily life of a young man in a free society. Should he keep his personal thoughts to himself, or share them with his parents? 'Honesty simplifies, but it also wounds and destroys,' Vidia wrote from experience. Banning responded that he was 'touched by your thoughtfulness and concern'.[44] He was writing a novel, and a thesis on Vidia's work.

In the interim, Pat had been summoned in imperative terms to take Margaret's place: it was her turn to be harassed, even as Vidia's global aspirations spread. 'You will get your Indonesian visa. You will say you are travelling to Java and Bali when they ask for your itinerary. You will also get a leather strap for your suitcase ... Open my bank statement. Make a note of the balance of my current account and the date & bring the information with you ... Yes, I think it would be better for you to bring out a woollen shirt for me (Brooks Brothers green) and a pullover and a light tweed jacket.'[45] Pat did as she was told. 'Your little house sits unconverted on the side of the hill,' she told Vidia, enclosing a cutting from *Private Eye*: 'There were some red faces at *Vogue* last week when highly-regarded author V.S. Naipaul yelled angrily down the telephone to a box-wallah about a piece which they were about to print. "What is more," V.S. shouted, his slim frame trembling with irritation, "I do not like the photographs taken by that jumped-up little photographer of the Sixties." He was referring, of course, to Lord Snowdon.'[46]

Pat was conscious, even before she left Heathrow for Jakarta, that she had been getting everything wrong. What had she been doing, apart from eating too much, listening to the radio and drifting around the London Library? While Vidia was living with Margaret in America, she had half-confided her unhappiness to Teresa, and had cried to Francis when she saw him.[47] An article about the Notting Hill Carnival, which she had reworked to death, had been rejected by the *Spectator*. She knew that Vidia, whom she had begun to refer to in her diary as 'the Genius', might be 'rough' towards her. She comprehended his ambition. A few months earlier during a train journey down from London, while speaking about the world of books and writers, Vidia had 'leant forward and said that he intended to hold the dominant position in the 1980s. Was I pleased with his decision? I said I was.'[48]

Now, she stepped into his world. Vidia was a scrupulous traveller, going only where he needed, collecting only the material he required for the book, protecting himself from sickness and time-wasters. He was full of praise for the way he had persuaded young Indonesian men to act as his guides. An early trip to Bandung was a success. Back in the hotel, 'I have a drink (gin with lime), he does his exercises, looks very pretty when he jogs (on the spot) . . . then – typically – he has to force himself, raising his legs higher, forcing his strength.' As for Pat herself, what should she be doing? 'Thought of writing to Teresa. What to say? To be dishonest? To tell her that all is not roses? That would be foolish . . . How to act? Really write, create something.' So Pat made desultory notes about Margaret Thatcher and trades union legislation.

By the middle of January 1980, they were in India taking a break, and the initial calm of Jakarta was swept aside as Vidia was consumed by exhaustion and randomly directed anger. 'He has been increasingly frenzied and sadly, from my point of view, hating and abusing me. He loved the walk but darkness fell. I was wrong to make us go beyond the Gandhi statue on the way back. The walk up the unlit road upset him more and more. A car swerved at us, he stepped and pushed me back. He stepped on my bare, big toe. I said "Oh God" not so much out of pain as out of general concern. He abused me – cunt etc. – didn't I realise that he was trying to push me out of the path of the car . . . There are in the M[ahabharat] and the Ramayan a number of ugly and wicked women and I go in, of course, for a certain degree of self-identification.' Pat was not his only enemy that week. In Madras, Vidia 'told me that he had thought out his relationship with André and Diana to a "sad" conclusion. André is a small timer. He has outgrown Diana.' In Bombay, wearing the mask of the master and raging like a Britisher from a previous century, her husband was 'wavering between hatred of tourists and hatred of India. Difficulties with taxi-drivers and resentment at effect of package tours on his beloved Taj hotels are bringing out, as he says, his racist and fascist instincts . . . He is angered by the ugliness of the poor package tour people. He upsets me talking about wogs and whips. And wanting the Emergency back.' Soon, it was the turn of the manager of the Taj to quake. 'Dear Mr Naipaul, Thank you for filling in the Guest Comments form and bringing to my notice the flaw in the design of the Tea-pots.'⁴⁹ Pat returned home while Vidia went on to Pakistan alone. All was not well, as he recalled: 'A waiter in a dirty jacket served me "fish mexique" in Rawalpindi; I was left with sickness and a migraine. My health was damaged.'⁵⁰

By the spring, Vidia was back in England, trying to lead a regular married life. Soon, he collapsed. 'I began to choke, and what you do when you begin to choke, you lean forward on the table to make it easier and in the end you are sitting in your chair and spread across the table. I was putting off the moment of telephoning the doctor. I had to do it late at night, and Dr Smith came and he gave me the adrenaline injection and there was a great reaction. I had been drinking a late-bottled port to comfort myself. No food or anything, and I spewed it all out. They sent an ambulance and equipment for the oxygen tent and so I went in like that, I went to hospital in Salisbury. I liked it very much, I liked the ritual, but very quickly they sent me away. They gave me a wheelchair that carried me to the taxi. When I came back I immediately began to write, in spite of everything, I just sat on my table and began to write.'⁵¹

Normal life resumed. Mr and Mrs Skull were invited over to look at a pair of Indonesian puppets. Eleanor came on a visit. Miriam Gross invited Pat and Vidia to her new house, and Teresa, now divorced from Peter Gatacre and shortly to marry the actor John Wells, held a dinner party where they saw the art historian David Carritt and the playwright Tom Stoppard. 'Vidia made very happy by meeting again and conversation with Carritt, a charming, handsome, fair-haired man. Stoppard pretty, a little like Mick Jagger.' Clarissa, Countess of Avon, the widow of Anthony Eden ('we go beat up the Germans and them bad bad') who lived on the other side of Salisbury, took up the Naipauls. They saw Selby Wooding, Vidia's schoolfriend from QRC, who was now a lawyer in Port of Spain.

In Wilsford they entertained Antonia and her new husband, Harold Pinter. Vidia admired few of his British literary contemporaries, but rated Pinter, and had examined the way in which his dialogue was thought out and put together; being a playwright, he was not a direct rival. Pat wrote of Pinter, 'Vidia made a very interesting remark about his talent. It is adolescent: about childish fears and sexual longings. He arrived at this conclusion through recalling early stories he wrote at the age of 16–17, when he began writing.' Moments before their arrival, as was apt to happen when guests were eminent and imminent, Vidia became enraged. 'Stretches of calm and happiness in the cottage. This was ended, shattered prior to Antonia and Harold's arrival by hysteria about shirts and it wasn't funny; it was very alarming.' At the lunch, Pat served a vegetarian speciality of the era: nut-loaf. Harold failed to eat it, Vidia was silently offended ('Pat had made it with her own hand') and the invitation to visit Wiltshire was never repeated. Antonia wrote cheerfully afterwards: 'Thank you very much indeed for entertaining us with such panache – nut-cake is a new discovery for me and if white wine not exactly <u>new</u>, that was particularly delicious! I had often described Wilsford to Harold and was thus so pleased to be able to show it to him, looking as it ever did like a house in a fairy story ... We are both looking forward to reading Vidia's book on Islam, and we pondered, and discussed, his wise words all the way to London.'[52]

Among the Believers: An Islamic Journey came fast, intensely, taking ten months to write. Vidia passed through swings of emotion. In the autumn, Pat noted, 'He is very depressed, does not want to write another El Dorado, another "dud".' Sometimes she took dictation, at other times she listened while Vidia read long chunks of the text aloud. It was almost 200,000 words long. She helped to check and copy-edit the final manuscript, and was obliged to answer all his letters. 'Vidia is very angry with me for not writing straight away on his behalf,' she informed Ralph and Mary Ironman. 'I still try to write but most of the time I fiddle about ... Vidia's high-powered, new, agent called yesterday ... I try not to let the cottage get too untidy and depressing ... I have to read his reviews in secret ... He spoke to Roy Plomley on Desert Island Discs. Yes, he has received this accolade.'[53] Vidia had written earlier in a private notebook of 'my detestation of music – the lowest art form, too accessible, capable of stirring people who think little', and in exchanges with Mr Plomley on the BBC sounded disconcerted, his voice thin and clipped.[54] 'Your father was a journalist?' 'Yes.' 'On a daily pepper?' 'Yes, the local paper' ... 'Of course, you married a fellow graduate at Oxford, an English gel.' 'Yes, 1955' ... 'Are there many Indians in Trinidad?' At the end, Vidia says, 'I hope music lovers will forgive the illiteracy.' His chosen book was a study of mathematics for 'intellectual excitement' and his luxury was a statue of

the enlightened Buddha.[55] Swiftly, he returned to *Among the Believers*.
Extracts from the book ran in the *Atlantic Monthly*, and the US Air Force
wrote to Gillon Aitken requesting permission to reproduce them for the
benefit of USAF technical teams in the Middle East.

Vidia was reviewed as a writer at the height of his powers, investigating
mysterious lands with a ruthless, encircling eye. Unlike novelists who
wrote about Islam after 11 September 2001 and took refuge in jargon,
pretending they knew what 'hadith' or 'tajwid' meant despite having
minimal or no experience of life in Muslim countries, he concentrated on
his own observation, and avoided reading too many books. Vidia's interest
was less in Islam than in Muslims, in what they thought and did in the
countries he visited. John Carey wrote in the *Sunday Times* that V.S.
Naipaul was 'beguilingly casual. He wanders around, chatting with students
and taxi drivers, munching dried fruit and nuts, asking mild but pointed
questions ... even when his conclusions are hostile, he never lacks
sympathy.'[56] That paper's literary editor, Claire Tomalin, wrote to him,
'You are the best reporter as well as novelist now at work. Your book has
made so many things comprehensible to me for the first time.'[57] Paul
Theroux told Vidia it was 'deliberate, purposeful travel – a kind of seeking,
a setting-out to discover ... It is a profoundly human book, with a
masterful use of dialogue.'[58] In the *Washington Post*, Edward Hoagland
thought he had 'a naked, contentious bias against Islam' arising from his
Hindu background, 'which unfortunately may only win him additional
disingenous praise.' Some liked this approach: 'Let me be candid,' wrote
Anthony Quinton (who had once doubted whether *The Mystic Masseur*
deserved a Book Society recommendation), 'I got a profound, Khomeini-
hating delight from V.S. Naipaul's *Among the Believers*.' Devoting pages to
Vidia, *Newsweek* called the book 'a brilliant report of social illness' and
prodded him in an interview to say things he would not have said in print:
'If Arabs piss on my doorstep in South Kensington, I can't *not* notice.'[59]

The sharpest criticism came from Edward Said, who with his variegated
life might himself have been a character from a Naipaul novel. He
dismissed Vidia jealously and zealously as an Uncle Tom figure, 'a kind of
belated Kipling [who] carries with him a kind of half-stated but finally
unexamined reverence for the colonial order ... Naipaul the writer now
flows directly into Naipaul the social phenomenon, the celebrated sensibility
on tour, abhorring the postcolonial world for its lies, its mediocrity,
cruelty, violence, and maudlin self-indulgence.' Said's reaction drew the
academic battle-lines for years to come: against him stood Bernard Lewis,

for whom *Among the Believers* was 'not a work of scholarship, and makes no pretense of being such. It is the result of close observation by a professional observer of the human predicament. It is occasionally mistaken, often devastatingly accurate, and above all compassionate. Mr Naipaul has a keen eye for the absurdities of human behavior, in Muslim lands as elsewhere . . . Mr Naipaul will not toe the line; he will not join in the praise of Islamic radical leaders and the abuse of those whom they oppose. Therefore he is an Orientalist – a term applied to him even by brainwashed university students who ought to know better.'

In a piece now redolent with irony, Marvin Mudrick wrote in the *Hudson Review* that V.S. Naipaul was being 'monotonously alarmist' about the dangers of political Islam. What did he fear, seriously – Bedouins 'sweeping like the simoom out of the desert descending on Bloomingdale's with fire and sword and no-limit credit cards?' His counsel amounted to '*Grand Guignol* with Dracula make-up and howls from the wind-machines in the wings as Islamic fanaticism threatens the very foundations of civilization: the sky is falling! the sky is falling!'[60] On September 11, when admonitory pessimism proved justified, the sky did fall.

Bernard Lewis, a scholar of Islamic history who would later be vilified for stimulating George W. Bush's chaotic military adventure in Iraq, was correct when he said that *Among the Believers* was a work of close observation. Although Vidia began his travels with a notion about antimodern nihilism in certain Muslim countries, little of the book is devoted to theory, except at the end of chapters in a sometimes redundant way. His text was closely based on his notes, written up neatly with barely a correction in the confines of his hotel room each evening, heedless of the presence of Margaret or Pat. He might focus on Mr Jaffrey, a Shia from Lucknow who worked on the *Tehran Times* and discoursed on the failings of Khomeini while eating a dish of fried eggs, or describe bear-baiting in a dusty field in Sind, the bear crushing two yelping dogs to death: 'It was village entertainment and, like the faith, part of the complete, old life of the desert.'[61] In his private notes, Vidia empathizes. 'I liked Mr Ishaq immediately (But I like them all) . . . His explanation of his Islamic passion was simple. "Our people emotionally reject the West" – in spite of our dependence on it.' Of Ali Ahmed Brohi, an official in Pakistan, he recorded, 'Swift friendship, swift treachery.'[62] After publication, a letter of explanation came from Mr Brohi: with his Indian name, Vidiadhar Surajprasad Naipaul had been thought to be a spy and 'passed on to me by my federal counterpart as "an unwanted baby" . . . You must be having a colossal memory – and a very fertile and retentive one too, because, I never found you taking any notes . . . it will long remain a striking example of a book which, by sheer honesty of purpose and brilliancy of execution, has beautifully succeeded in depicting the facts as they are.'[63] Similar letters came from others whose stories had been told in the book, praising the fidelity of Vidia's accounts, done from memory.

*

Although some of its deductions are partial, *Among the Believers* lacked the cruelty of *India: A Wounded Civilization*. His malice was reserved for those close to him, and in particular for Pat. She irritated him; he was cruel to her; she became more feeble and pathetic; his irritation increased. Her diary becomes progressively more desperate during the 1980s, and entries start to tail off. 'My destructiveness – not deliberate, just stupidity. I wanted to get into bed with him . . . If only I had kept to the right and noble decisions I made when a girl. But would I have developed? I should have been more continuously courageous. Less of a baby . . . I feel that perhaps what I might have written, might yet write, could be more important than Vidia's book on Islam. I am foolish to feel this, more foolish to say it . . . Unemployment going up by thousands. Break-away MPs forming group, of 11, for Social Democracy . . . He went to Norway on Tuesday. I foolishly summoned Stanley [a taxi driver] and met the plane yesterday, a day early.' In their fiftieth year, Vidia told Pat he intended to move to the new house, Dairy Cottage, alone. 'I went on forlornly, going on about being treated as an equal . . . He looked for a clean vest, I produced his present favourite sleeveless style from the airing cupboard and looked out, at his request, another thermal top, asking whether he has a washing machine in Dairy Cottage. Yes it's all waiting there ready. My stomach turned over . . . Sexual yearning, quite deep. Will it ever stop? . . . Have not washed my hair for ages . . . But incapacity may be fundamental, in my genes, early conditioning and self-indulgence . . . We went into Salisbury on the bus shopping together yesterday morning. Vidia kept me waiting for ages in Snells [a coffee shop]. We then fortified ourselves with chocolate gateau and danish pastry. Shopping disorganised. Vidia waited for ten minutes outside Crouch [a greengrocer; now Costa Coffee] and felt he had chilled down . . . We went on from Beech [a bookshop; now an Italian restaurant] to look at the [Cathedral] Close under snow. The sun was shining through the windows of the nave.' Soon, he reversed his decision: 'Last night Vidia said he wanted to move to Dairy Cottage with me – with qualifications. The night before he declared affection twice. He doesn't dislike me, he doesn't dislike anything about me, I only irritate him.'

In Karnac's bookshop in Gloucester Road, they bumped into Bharat Bhushan, Vidia's schoolboy guide from more than a decade earlier when he had covered an election in Ajmer. 'The conversation built up, in volume apart from anything else, quickly. Vidia seizing upon his use of the word fascism and delivering strictures – the young man, Bharat, had been studying engineering . . . I did not listen to the conversation or interfere, only hovering a little after a bit, indicating, or trying to a little, that it would be better to be a little quieter, calmer.' Bharat Bhushan wrote his own account:

> 'Patsy,' he shouted out to his wife Patricia. 'Meet Bharat. I had met him when he was in school. He has become a Rejecter now.' 'That is his description,' I mumbled. His wife herded us out of the bookshop. Naipaul cooled down a bit and asked me to write to him about I how felt about life now . . . A fortnight later while walking down Gloucester Road I saw Naipaul again. His wife was a few steps behind him. 'Hello Mr Naipaul,' I said. 'Oh, hello, hello,' he replied in an off-hand way and walked past me. His wife stopped me and apologised for his behaviour at the bookshop . . . 'Vidia, give him our telephone number,' she told Naipaul . . . He looked at me in a manner which was at once condescending and arrogant. 'I will give you my telephone number only on the condition that you do not pass it on to any researcher, literary critic, journalist or other such pests,' he said. Something snapped in me and I told him, 'On second thoughts Mr Naipaul, forget about it. I don't think you have anything to say to me and I certainly don't have anything to say to you.' He threw the pen and paper angrily back at me and walked away.
>
> I still read Naipaul admiringly.[64]

Much of the time, Vidia and Pat kept apart, one in the city, one in the country. She went to a memorial service for Sonia Orwell without him, and sat between Antonia and Teresa; she attended hearings of the Scarman Inquiry into the recent Brixton riots. She preserved Vidia's notes, folding them into her diary: 'Gone to Wiltshire, hoping to calm down & behave better. Bring milk etc. See you later.' Pat in turn would leave advice when she departed: 'Cheese, Cheddar & Double Glos . . .

EAT THE SMALL AVOCADO ... Nuts – cashews.'[65] Occasionally, she went to visit her family. 'I went to Birmingham for my mother's birthday. Eleanor took us to The Bell at Coleshill, a pleasant pub buffet ... My father in the flat. Family gathering. Little to say.' By now, Pat had cut off almost all contact with Ted Hale, and had never met his common-law wife, Vera. In a shaking hand, her father might write a birthday or a Christmas card and enclose a £10 note; but Pat left the money in the envelope, rejecting him. 'I would see my father once a year at a pub to exchange Christmas presents,' Eleanor recalled. 'Pat asked me not to give him her address.' Eleanor was working at a comprehensive school near Birmingham, teaching physical education: football, netball, trampolining, cross-country. She lived with Rose Crockett. 'It was a gay relationship. I once took Pat and my mother to a gay club in Birmingham with Rose. It went off all right.' The sisters rarely spoke of personal matters, although Pat once said 'very matter-of-factly' out of the blue that she was intending to separate from Vidia. She avoided mentioning Eleanor's lesbianism, though she sometimes bought gay liberation magazines such as *Out* and *Sappho*, perhaps out of curiosity or solidarity. The two had almost nothing in common. A not uncharacteristic entry in Pat's diary ran: 'Spoke to Eleanor last night. She was fitting polystyrene covering on the lavatory wall.' Eleanor once started to read *The Mimic Men* and found, 'It wasn't to my taste. I can enjoy classics, though I prefer to watch them dramatized on the television.'[66]

Finally, in February 1982, it was time to leave Wilsford and move up the valley to the converted Dairy Cottage, a four-bedroom house down a private lane, shielded by trees, the only disturbance coming from the scream of military jets from a nearby training base and the odd passing rambler. The garden, which Vidia was determined should remain green rather than being filled with flowers, was criss-crossed overhead with power lines and stretched down to the banks of the River Avon. The previous month their London flat had been burgled; Pat's nebulous wedding ring had disappeared. Comparing herself to Bryant in *Guerrillas*, she recorded her tentative, shamed efforts to carve out a space for herself in Vidia's new house. He asked: 'Would I be moving out again soon? ... I made a bedroom for myself in the little pink room, Vidia settled himself in the red.' During the spring in a separate notebook, a silver hair dropping between the pages, she made jottings. For the first time, aware of the effort she had made to leave a

record of her life with Vidia for posterity, Pat addressed herself to me
– and to you:

> The Genius has gone to South America to check up on feeling
> there, amongst other things, giving me the chance to reflect ...
> 1982 Personal Crisis. In my case past? Just grindingly coping >or
> not, only partly<. I made a brief note about my relationship with
> the G., in the autumn, that it was not sufficient for life. And I
> address you, reader – you would not want me for life but then –
> what presumption – perhaps you would. But perhaps you would.
> Perhaps you are my destiny. After all.[67]

Where could she turn for guidance, with her husband away with his
mistress? She felt unable to ask anyone at all for help. Margaret had
stimulated Vidia's return easily, writing a vigorous and erotic response
to the rare appearance of a letter from him in Buenos Aires. Never in
her wildest dreams had she imagined that she would actually come
home and find his longed-for handwriting slipped beneath her door.
She could scarcely believe her eyes. She had even been tempted to kiss
the letter, and hold it to herself. As for the man behind the letter, she
could scarcely remember what he looked like. Was he still black, she
asked? Was he still muscular and strong? Was he still cross and
intolerant? She hoped so – otherwise she might not recognize him.
Excited, Vidia had gone to Brazil and Venezuela. In her diary, Pat
wrote, 'He has just left for Gatwick on his way to Brazil. We did not
touch or embrace – I just touched him on the side of his shoulder.'
Who would satisfy her yearning? When Selby Wooding came to stay,
she put on her kimono and made a tentative attempt at seduction. Selby,
gently, saying nothing, declined the invitation. It was an easy enough
mistake for an unconfident, unworldly woman like Pat to make:
alighting on friendly, cuddly, gay Selby.[68]

*

In the early 1980s, Vidia was at the peak of his fame, a presence and an
absence in the world of English letters, a writer who was there and not
there, globally itinerant, a prized name in America, his books available in
Greek, Serbo-Croat and Hebrew. Academic studies of his work were
published in many languages, each more speculative and hypothetical than
the last. He was an author who had fashioned himself into a special,
incomparable, unclassifiable case, who presented himself less as the product

of historical, social or geographical circumstance, than as a pristine talent, detached from his West Indian past. British fiction had been lacking in energy since the Second World War: with the conceivable exception of William Golding, it was hard to spot another novelist who matched the creative power of an American like Bellow or Roth. Writers born in the 1940s such as Angela Carter, Martin Amis and Ian McEwan were doing something fresh, but for the moment Vidia stood alone, separate, himself. In innumerable interviews, each of them billed as 'rare', he provided perfect copy to journalists seeking an original insight. Vidia made a spectacle of himself, alluding to his discovery of sensuality late in life, failing to elaborate, saying nothing of Pat, revealing bits of his daily life while remaining intensely private. His technique was to repeat things he had said before, but make them sound new, throwing out controversy like chaff to deflect attention from his real, inner, writerly self. Writing had become its own purpose, its own justification, the only way of life he knew. When academics berated him for his views, he responded in Trinidian street style, making it sound like British haughtiness: 'Africa is a land of bush, again, not a very literary land. I don't see why it should get mixed up with Asia . . . chaps in the universities . . . make investments in a political-academic stock market. Some are at present trading in African futures, creating a little calling.'[69]

When asked about Edward Said, he made a point of mispronouncing his name as the past participle of 'say': 'When the reporters from Belgium and other places come and quote something by a man called Said and other people, I have to tell them again and again, "I don't know these people, if you ask me that I'll have to send you away. You must go and talk to Mr Said about it. Ask Said. And you are a big enough man to judge him." '[70] Or, 'He is an Egyptian who got lost in the world and began to meddle in affairs he knew nothing about. He knew very little about literature, although he passed in America as a great, wise literary figure. He knew nothing about India, for example. He knew nothing about Indonesia. He had not travelled to Tehran or seen the revolution. I have never replied to any of those criticisms.'[71]

Vidia had become a phenomenon, a writer whom other writers were required to like or dislike, a cultural purgative and an applauded panto-mime villain. Apocryphal stories were told about him. Did you hear about V.S. Naipaul at the smart party in New York? A literary groupie is searching for Ved Mehta, disbelieving that a blind writer could produce

such vivid descriptive prose. Finding a distinguished Indian man sitting on
a sofa, she grins and waves her hands in front of his face while he looks
on unblinking and unperturbed. 'Well,' she admits to her friend. 'He really
is blind.' The friend corrects her: 'That wasn't Ved Mehta. That's V.S.
Naipaul.' This was a good fictional anecdote: in Vidia's words, 'It was an
American story, cooked up to amuse people.'[72] After meeting him in 1982,
Saul Bellow said that Naipaul had an 'eagle-on-the-crags' look, and
remarked: 'After one look from him, I could skip Yom Kippur.'[73] David
Hare, in his play *A Map of the World*, reproduced him as the outrageous
protagonist Victor Mehta, an Indian man in his early forties with thick
black hair, dressed in a light-brown suit and tie, the author of a novel
about journalists called *The Vermin Class*. He orders champagne, and
argues with other delegates at a UNESCO conference on poverty. 'The
work alone ought to be sufficient. But my publishers plead with me to
make myself seen ... Socialism, a luxury of the wealthy. To the poor, a
suicidal creed ... All old civilizations are superior to younger ones. That
is why I have been happiest in Shropshire.'[74] And in 'The Spoiler's Return'
in 1981, Derek Walcott wrote, 'I see these islands and I feel to bawl, /
"area of darkness" with V.S. Nightfall.'[75]

   Increasingly, Vidia paid the price. With the attention of his peers came
the curiosity of the reading public; people found out his telephone number
and called with strange requests. Obsessives wrote out of the blue. His
unbidden correspondents tended to be people who were in some way
deracinated, like Alan Kaul, whose father had moved from Kashmir to
Seattle in 1922 and never told him he was Indian, or Alain Lacoste,
'French, white, socialist, Catholic-educated but now without religion,
humble economic teacher of secondary school, living in Morocco since 8
years.' People made enquiries. Would he speak to a gang of reformed
young criminals in 'Brooklyn's impoverished Bedford-Stuyvesant ghetto'
asked John Norbutt, 'a Black of moderate education'? Why did he take
snuff? Would he donate autographed copies of his books to the Ealing
Community Relations Council? Did he want the free services of an
assistant ('I have a shorthand speed of 90 wpm')? Did he want to try LSD,
or 'the syllasybin [psilocybin] mushroom'? Might he like to appear on *In
the Psychiatrist's Chair* with Dr Anthony Clare? Would he agree to meet
Rudy Duyck, 'a first-licentiate student in Germanic Philology at the
Rijksuniversiteit Gent'?[76] The answer to these questions was usually no –
and it was Pat who had to pick up the telephone or write the letter of

rejection, assuming the query could not simply be ignored. Even to an old friend and encourager like Francis Wyndham, Vidia rarely wrote more than a few lines now.

His daily irritation was unstinting. At a dinner at Teresa's in 1983, he was put out not to be served a vegetarian dish all of his own, as usually happened; he had to make do with the common vegetables, tainted by the forks of others. So he left. 'Vidia rang John [Wells] the morning afterwards to ask him why he did it,' Pat noted in her diary. Versed in Vidia's tyrannical demands, Teresa took the blame: 'I am desolate about what happened last night . . . It was all gross mismanagement: a new, small, hot, stuffy kitchen; a temperamental & irritable cook' – but not 'deliberate provocation'.[77] Not long afterwards, Pat wrote with tragic anguish in her diary, 'Increasingly, these days, I regret the loss, the damage of Vidia's rages and quarrels. Simple losses – of the beautiful food I have cooked, happy days, days of one's life. It was my fault: I was anxious and told him not to "overdo it" when he proposed to go out and use the Flymo . . . he was resting, the weather, sunshine & breeze, so lovely and I was wishing he would come out. He cheered up; he was whistling. He dressed in his old khaki cotton trousers & the green polo checked cotton sweater and straw hat. At my words he struck his head and burst out, "the bitch" etc and went back up, removed the clothes & put indoor clothes on, heavy dressing gown & switched on the heat in his bedroom. "Don't speak to me" etc. "I shall only despise you more."'

In the same year, Vidia wrote a private note exploring his state of mind, something he almost never did. Success had not brought him contentment:

> What is the truth about my situation at the age of 51? After the life of the writer, the labour entailed by the vocation, I am still as dissatisfied, as [unclear], as empty as at the beginning, in those days in London, and later at Oxford, and later still, after Oxford, in London again. So many beginnings; so many zests; so many let downs afterwards. The solitude is the same, almost. I live in a small house in Wiltshire now. I have enough money to see me through for a couple of years . . . I have a wife. I have had a lover, a mistress, these last eleven years. We live a distorted, a disjointed triangular life.[78]

In a questionnaire in the *Frankfurter Allgemeine Zeitung Magazin* around the same time, he revealed aspects of himself. His vision of earthly bliss?' 'It lies in the past; the delirium of reciprocated sexual passion.' The characteristics he most valued in a man? 'Honour (where it is personal, rather than the code of a class or a group); reliability.' What did he value most in his friends? 'I have no friends. It has been hard to keep them through the twists and turns of a long creative career.' His favourite heroines? 'The women who have loved me.' His favourite writer? 'Balzac, I suppose.' His greatest fault? 'Gentleness.' His real-life heroes? 'I don't believe in the idea of the hero.' What political reform did V.S. Naipaul most admire? 'The abolition of slavery.'[79]

The business of being a famous writer took up time. Acceptance speeches had to be written. In 1980 Vidia went to New York to receive the $12,500 Bennett Award, was lauded for creating a fictional world out of the wreckage of empire and invited on *The Dick Cavett Show*. The University of Leicester offered him an Hon. D.Litt. and he turned it down, but accepted one from St Andrews, proffered by Professor Peter Bayley. When he spoke at the MIT Writing Program, the posters advertising him were defaced with the words 'Elitist Pig'.[80] He was invited to the American Academy and Institute of Arts and Letters to become an honorary member alongside R.K. Narayan and David Hockney, and to Columbia University to be given an honorary degree. Vidia was accompanied by a friend whose status was never explained to his hosts. 'Margaret came to New York for it, she came to that ceremony in Columbia, the honorary degree, and I gave her $1,000. I was feeling rich . . . and she promptly went and bought a kind of fur-collared coat. I was rather impressed. I liked the gesture.'[81]

A trip to Holland in 1982 was a debacle. A Dutch television programme recorded the tour: V.S. Naipaul is signing books and telling an Indian expatriate it will take centuries for India to advance. 'You're suffering from discovering you're an individual,' he tells the man sharply. 'What do you think about minority groups?' asks a dank Dutch boy. 'I think it's rather shameful, they seldom offer rights to people of another religion, but in England they claim rights under the other man's law. It's the slave's attitude.' Now, in Amsterdam at a PEN event, he is looking furious. The audience ask hostile, half-hearted questions and complain he is 'prejudiced'. He loses control, saying their questions are absurd. 'Probably we should call it off. It's a waste of my time. It's an insult.' Now he is with a television presenter. The presenter is accompanied by a female sex doll. The shot cuts to Naipaul talking to his publicist: 'I have too great a regard for what I do to expose myself to this sort of nonsense.' He leaves for the airport saying, 'It began badly with that shoddy ticket you sent me. I knew it was going to end badly.' And with that he strides off to board his plane, looking mortally insulted and dapper in expensive shoes and an overcoat.[82]

One prize or degree begat another. In 1983 it was the turn of Israel. André Deutsch warned Vidia his suitcases would be thoroughly searched at the airport to make sure he 'didn't have an Arab inside'.[83] Vidia surprised his audience by saying he had become a writer in order to be free, and to avoid being employed. 'It was our honour and privilege to have you here in Jerusalem, to spend time seeing the city together, and above all to present you with the Jerusalem Prize,' wrote Teddy Kollek, the mayor. In Cambridge he received a doctorate alongside Helmut Schmidt, wearing a gown and bonnet.[84] Kamla was concerned he had not got the Nobel: 'I wish they would cease punishing and give it to you ... If someday you do get it, will you invite me to see you receive your prize? That will be the happiest day of my life.'[85] He submitted to interviews in Germany, but refused to lecture at the University of Mysore. Next came the Ingersoll Foundation's T.S. Eliot Award, the previous winners being Borges, Powell and Ionesco. Through these years of enthronement, Vidia always remembered the lesson given him by William Demas at the cricket nets at QRC: never put things off until tomorrow. As a scholarship boy who had achieved his goal, he felt all the uncertainty of success; he had been brought up to aspire to an ideal invented in England, and the sense of being expected to do better than those he lived among would never go away. Basking in fame was not a possibility. Each award was assessed for its value and accepted or rejected. Being a writer, he had to write. Vidia travelled the world seeking ideas, then went home to Dairy Cottage and started working. At the back of his mind was the knowledge, or fear, that his creativity might be waning. How long could a writer go on producing fresh work, rather than reprising the old? The career of a great novelist rarely lasts more than twenty years; Dickens had managed twenty-four, and in Vidia's view, he died of self-parody. Much earlier, Vidia had written to Francis that 'to read a biography of Dickens is to get the impression of a man who drugged himself with work. So do many writers.'[86] It was true of himself.

In the summer of 1982 he tried again to write an autobiography, a project he had conceived in the late 1960s. The difficulty was that he was not willing or able to examine his own past behaviour, and had no wish to write a light book of anecdotes. Vidia was not introspective, or introspective only on favoured subjects, such as his relationship with his father or with India, which he linked to his vocation. He kept himself hidden and hardly ever spoke to anyone, for instance, about his marriage or his relationship with Margaret; his perception was turned outward and applied to others. His brooding was chanelled into his books. Over time, as he aged, the act of blocking out emotional contact made him more contrary and provocative, as he sought reactions and tried to recover the ability to have genuine, sharp feelings. When *Vanity Fair* magazine was revived and the new editor, Richard Locke, wanted an inaugural autobiographical piece by V.S. Naipaul, he tried again. 'The disorder of my childhood ... My father's nostalgia – and mine, derived from his – for this Indian world, of villages & pundits & work-in-the-fields ... Writing given me as my vocation, my caste.'[87] He thought of investigating his time at Oxford. Pat wrote in her diary: 'Last night I spoke of him letting me know the morning, nay the afternoon after our marriage, that he didn't really want to be married to me. Yes, he said, he wanted to ask my permission to write about that ... Would anyone, I asked, enjoy reading about that? I put in my usual plea: fiction & comedy ... I am very low. But then it is perhaps my own fault.' The finished article avoided any of this personal material, and was called 'Prologue to an Autobiography'. It was a beautifully evocative account of his own beginnings as a writer, and a tribute to his father. It opened: 'It is now nearly thirty years since, in a BBC room in London, on an old BBC typewriter, and on smooth, "non-rustle" BBC script paper, I wrote the first sentence of my first publishable book.'[88] ('American usage would be nonrustling,' noted a useful US sub-editor; Vidia stuck with non-rustle.[89]) Nothing in 'Prologue to an Autobiography' was untrue, but it was a partial account, processed through his own adjusted recollection, stripping the powerful presence of Ma and his sisters from his childhood, and more understandably removing Margaret and Kamla from his excursion to Margarita – 'the pearl' – in search of Poker, the original of Bogart.

Margaret wanted to be part of the process of creation. She complained about the way in which he would insist that his writing could only emerge out of a sterile, ordered daily life. Perhaps, she suggested, he only held that belief because things had never been any different. She wondered at times whether sterility just bred sterility.[90] After finishing *Among the Believers*, he had chosen to be with her. He avoided

taking sides publicly over the Falklands War, but wrote articles for the
Daily Mail (dictating them to Margaret in the São Paulo Hilton and
laughing at her handwriting) in which he decried the brutality of the
Argentine regime. 'In a remarkable analysis of this nation of strutting
machos, V.S. Naipaul, the distinguished writer, reveals the real Argentina behind the belligerence and the bluster' ran the subhead.[91]

In November 1982 he went to West Africa for the first time and was
guided by expatriates, travelling through Côte d'Ivoire and Senegal to
write 'The Crocodiles of Yamoussoukro', a solid, sardonic piece of
work that never catches fire. An anthropologist specializing in drum
communication was recommended to him: 'I found out fairly soon that
Mr Niangoran-Bouah was academically controversial, that if he was a
world expert on Drummologie it was because he had started the subject and had in fact invented the word.'[92] Vidia praised President
Houphouët-Boigny's administration, but saw Africa as a place of magic
and sorcery where the real life remains hidden. His way was smoothed
by his old Univ friend Lawrence O'Keefe, now the British ambassador
in Dakar and a pseudonymous novelist, who caused a chain reaction
among regional diplomats: the American ambassador in Abidjan sent a
member of staff to locate V.S. Naipaul, and the British ambassador said
he was the first distinguished man of letters to pass that way since
Barbara Cartland, 'who, come to think of it, doesn't qualify on either
count!'[93] Staying with the O'Keefes in Dakar, Vidia decided that he
would live with Margaret permanently, but by January they had argued
and she was put on a plane. He was furious with her at the airport;
everything was finished. Margaret was distraught over the way he was
behaving, and complained afterwards that she could hardly believe he
was angry about her sense of disappointment. Despite everything that
had happened between them in the past, she had still believed him when
he promised they might yet have a future together in Wiltshire. Now
he had turned silent on her again, and sent no word. She asked what
she could have done to become the recipient of such wrath? She was
wretched that a relationship that had sustained for nearly eleven years
should have ended in such horrible circumstances.[94]

It had not ended, of course. A year later they were back in Senegal
at a diplomatic dinner in honour of Mr V.S. Naipaul and Miss Margaret Murray. 'Vidia rang last night,' Pat recorded. 'He had been
"assaulted" by four twelve-year-old boys in Dakar, actually only
robbed of £80 in francs . . . while reading about himself in Le Point.'

When he returned to England in June, Lol O'Keefe sent a package and a letter, and offered to find out about selling his archive papers to an American institution: 'Herewith one pair of pyjamas which turned up after you left.'[95] Again, the trip had ended badly, with Margaret being blamed for her lover's frustration. She knew she could not make him content. She begged him to understand that she had not sought to do anything other than to please him. It was so difficult to be someone's mistress, it was such a flimsy position and she had realized by now that it was impossible for a man to be with two women at once: eventually one of them had to go. So she went, but was ready to return when the summons came. Margaret was now in her early forties, spending more time with Roy and their children, putting on three kilos, taking tennis lessons and playing mixed doubles every Sunday, staying in the apartment of her friend Margaret Gunningham, doing translation work and travelling to London from time to time to see her sister Diana and her family. As for Buenos Aires, not much ever seemed to happen there: life in the city was taken up by politics, money, tennis, the Hurlingham Club and the odd man who took her out to dinner. Margaret had always been pretty and sexy rather than terminally beautiful, and now she was ageing unhappily, conscious that she was no longer what she had been to Vidia. As a woman who had passed through life easily sparking the attraction and desire of many men, a woman whose sense of herself was predicated on the evocation of an instinctive response, it was a hard moment for Margaret to be facing. She might still inform Vidia from time to time that she wanted to suck the life from the living god, or that he was a black, monstrous, murderous emperor, or that she wanted him to lick her back and thighs and tear her apart – but the spark had left the relationship. It continued regardless, sadly and intermittently.[96]

Much of the time, Vidia travelled alone. 1983 found him in Grenada after the execution of the political leader Maurice Bishop and the US invasion. 'Heavy Manners in Grenada' was equally astute about 'American Psy-Ops people', visiting revolutionaries and the Grenadian politicians who were defeated by their own upheaval. In the end 'the revolution was a revolution of words. The words had appeared as an illumination, a short-cut to dignity, to newly educated men who had nothing in the community to measure themselves against.' Washington's use of military force, 'helicopters of a sinister black colour' hovering over the island, was contrasted momentarily with Whitehall's postcolonial attitude: 'In a glass case in the rough little museum in the centre of the town was Britain's gift to Grenada at the time of independence nine years before: a silver coffee service and twenty-four Wedgwood bone-china coffee cups, all laid out on undyed hessian.'[97]

Kamla recalled the effort her brother made to understand the thinking behind 'the revo', interviewing a member of the New Jewel Movement on her verandah in Charlieville while she brought out cold drinks, then coffee and cakes, then lunch. 'Vidia was not much given to patience. Yet with this young lady he had spent six long and tiring hours trying to get a little insight into what seemed to be the senseless slaying of Bishop and some of his comrades. And he got nothing.'[98] The next year he was at the Republican Party national convention in Dallas, aided by innumerable contacts of Bob Silvers, worrying how on earth to write about American politics. His solution was to treat the experience as wholly alien. In the perfectly titled 'Among the Republicans', he relied on peripheral events rather than political analysis to tell the story, and conveyed more about the alliance of money and religious righteousness that defined the Reagan administration than any number of more regular accounts: 'The scale and the mood, and the surreal setting, made me think of a Muslim missionary gathering I had seen five years before in a vast canopied settlement of bamboo and cotton in the Pakistan Punjab. And I felt it would not have been surprising, in Dallas, to see busy, pious helpers going around giving out sweets or some kind of symbolic sacramental food.'[99]

'Prologue to an Autobiography' and 'The Crocodiles of Yamoussoukro' were folded into a book and published in 1984 under the title *Finding the Centre*. In a collusive foreword which seduced the reviewers, Vidia said the articles were united between hard covers because 'both pieces are about the process of writing. Both pieces seek in different ways to admit the reader to that process.'[100] Admitted, then, Anthony Powell in the *Daily Telegraph* deduced, 'These two narratives are rich in good things, things to be found nowhere else.'[101] In the *Dublin Sunday Tribune*, John Banville felt 'the Prologue is moving in a restrained, stoic way that is admirable both in its intensity and in the skill with which it is brought off.'[102] An astute review by Martin Amis in the *Observer* noted: 'One sees, in the diffidence and difficulty of this essay, how little of the self is present in Naipaul's work. In the novels, a past is used, but a self is not used. In the travel writing, a controlling intelligence is present, but the self remains inscrutable and undisclosed (even during the frequent losses of self-command).'[103]

By the middle of the 1980s, Vidia had a partially acknowledged sense that his years of creation were behind him. The quickening impulse had gone from his work; in its place was a technical brilliance, and an uncanny ability to analyse the information he received through his eyes. Remarkable books were to come – *The Enigma of Arrival* and *India: A Million Mutinies Now* – but none would have the lyricism of *Miguel Street*, the originality of *A House for Mr Biswas* or the force of *A Bend in the River*. In his closing decades, Vidia would rely less on intuition and more on thought. Like Isaac Newton, he would deal with a problem by thinking on it continually. All his subsequent work would in some form be a reconsideration of what had come before, a reprise – or reprisal. V.S. Naipaul, the writing personality, was fully formed.

CHAPTER TWENTY-THREE

'UNDOING MY SEMI-COLONS'

WITH NO FAMILY OF HIS OWN, Vidia's thoughts were often on his mother and siblings, nephews and nieces. This did not mean he felt benevolent towards them, although he did commit acts of random kindness, like paying off Kamla's mortgage to the tune of US$32,550 and helping with the college fees of her son Ved.[1] Vidia worried about Ved, writing in a long letter to Kamla,

> He is in California, the land of drop-outs and 'cults' . . . He told me on the phone that he had shaved his head in the Mohawk style – a central tuft between shaved strips. He explained this by saying that 'you only live once' . . . Ved gets not only his words – but the ideas that come with the words – from the people he is with . . . He is being influenced by the people around him who are more secure than he is and who at the end of the day will have families and all the possibilities of the United States to fall back on . . . You know I love Ved. He is an honourable boy. At the moment he is 'hiding' from us; the freedom of California is too much for him.[2]

Later, to Ved, Vidia praised the application with which his sister Shani was studying nursing in England: 'She likes the work and is very keen and wins golden opinions all round. She has unfortunately been over indulging in sweet things and has lost some of her good looks because she has become so fat. Her face has especially fattened out. I gather she has decided to take herself in hand, but possibly it is now too late. She will be a fat thing, like your mother's aunts.'[3] Sati's son Neil was another long-distance protégé. He lived in Canada, taught in a language school and was determined not to return to Trinidad. He appreciated Uncle Vido's guidance: 'The advice you gave me about finding out about myself and my past . . . is really so important to me now. It's a little frightening, but at the same time, very exciting.' Vidia offered encouragement, and by 1985 Neil Bissoondath was the author of a book of short stories with an enthusiastic quote from V.S. Naipaul on the cover. When his novel *A Casual Brutality* was published three years later, he was heralded as 'the most widely praised young Canadian writer in years'. His uncle's books, he told a magazine, had been 'icons of possibility' which made him realize a world existed outside Sangre Grande.[4]

Sometimes, it was easier for Vidia to be generous or warmhearted to strangers, or to those he never saw. When Marg Hale was obliged to leave 593 Kingstanding Road, he purchased a two-bedroom terraced house in Asquith Road in Birmingham and let her live there without paying rent. A random fan might be treated with concern, like Jackie Michaud from Maine, a blueberry grower and aspiring writer with whom he had a long correspondence during the 1980s, encouraging her to tell him of her daily life and reading. A zoologist and yoga teacher, Stephanie Alexander, gave him remote advice on posture and breathing exercises. A visiting interviewer, the Angolan journalist Sousa Jamba, was surprised to have 'a congenial tête-à-tête' with this reputedly 'aggressive, irascible figure'. Then Jamba made the mistake of quoting C.L.R. James's observation that Naipaul was liked by white people because he said what they wanted to hear. 'Abruptly, Naipaul's West Indian accent stood out as he began shouting at me. Suddenly I became terrified of the great man before me. I would not relish the idea of meeting him again, yet I remain an ardent admirer of his craft, vision and dedication to the writer's life.'[5] An encounter with a pair of German documentary-makers shows the way Vidia could speedily switch modes. The two women had been to some trouble to research a film about him, and he was welcoming and cooperative. When their questions arrived in advance of an interview, he wrote back, 'I have looked at the material you have sent me, and I feel I do not wish to take part in your film. I do not like the questions. They ignore far too many aspects of my work over the last twenty-five years, and seek only to involve me in a simple, over-flat political debate ... Nothing that I have written here (I am writing about my own work, remember) lessens the personal regard I have for both of you and my gratitude for your courtesy in visiting me in Paris.'[6]

Since his ill-fated visit to Trinidad with Margaret in 1977, Vidia had had little contact with Ma or with his sisters, barring Kamla. Her daughter Shani found Uncle Vido and Auntie Pat hospitable and eccentric when she went to stay at Dairy Cottage. 'He would sit for hours in his dressing gown and think into space. You could say nothing.

You couldn't turn on the TV, and had to tiptoe around him. Then he would go and write in the evening, and read it to Pat and me. There was always a tension. I couldn't imagine him writing without Pat ... They were too protective of me when I was in London. When I said I was going to the Notting Hill Carnival, they rang Trinidad to complain ... Auntie Pat was an amazing gourmet cook: artichokes in butter, mussels and rice, goat's cheese soufflé.'[7] Shani persuaded Vidia to come to her twenty-first birthday party in London. He reported back to Kamla: 'Nalini [Nella] came along to that, with her two daughters; and so I saw Nalini for the first time for eleven years. Fatter than ever. Almost as fat as Shani. But nothing about that subject, now. Shani arranged her party with the utmost elegance ... Mira's two daughters came over and I saw them – for the first time since 1971. Absolutely American.'[8] One daughter, Nisha, came to stay in Wiltshire. 'Uncle Vido was unbelievably nice to me. Pat cooked salmon and potatoes and green beans, and he talked about wines. She was a bit like a servant, taking care of him ... He complained about London: "Little Negro children running up and down the street, causing me distress."' Another time, while she was living in San Francisco, Nisha accompanied her uncle on a visit to Francis Ford Coppola in Napa Valley to discuss the possible filming of *Guerrillas*. 'It was a nice house, and he cooked an Italian meal for us – pork. Uncle Vido didn't like that. George Lucas dropped by and started talking about the making of *Star Wars*. Uncle Vido was very quiet, and he did his calculated thing, saying he didn't know about the entertainment industry, "I don't know *Star Wars*, I am not interested in films."'[9]

Later that year, in November 1984, the family were united in a different way when Sati died. Before going to Trinidad to join his siblings, Vido observed her cremation by surrounding himself with photographs of his sister, and sitting alone in silent communication, a moment he would describe in *The Enigma of Arrival*. He was distraught as he flew out to join his family (the previous week Julian Jebb had killed himself with an overdose of heminevrin). Vidia's sorrow and guilt were exacerbated by his own earlier behaviour. At Kamla's house the previous year, he had been sitting in his room writing about the invasion of Grenada when Sati came to see him. 'Why are you hiding, boy?' she called. But Vidia kept the shutters shut, sitting irascibly with his thoughts and his typewriter, and did not greet her. He never saw Sati again.[10]

Nine months later, after this grief and the inevitable unity that follows death within a family, another disaster struck the Naipauls. Shiva, aged forty, died from a heart attack. He had been seriously overweight for years, and drinking hard, and now he had gone the same way as Pa, leaving Jenny a widow and eleven-year-old Tarun without a father. 'I don't want you to get a breakdown,' Ma told Vido, 'I want all my children to say that the Great Lord had given him to us for only forty years and Sati fifty years. I am trying to keep myself so that I don't get sick. The same apply to you and Pat.'[11] There was grief outside the family too, since Shiva had been popular and sociable in a way Vidia could never be. Gillon Aitken remembered him as 'immensely affable, comical, easily amused – charming boy . . . He was quite different to Vidia, metabolically very different. He was the big one, Vidia was the greyhound, and Shiva was sometimes recklessly drunk.'[12] In Mira's view, 'Shivan was actually the opposite of Vido. Shivan was like this kind, soft wonderful one. We all adored him and he loved my mother.'[13] Shiva's friends within the London literary world rallied around his memory, and a memorial prize was established in his honour by the *Spectator*, a magazine which took pride in kicking against political correctness and had seen Shiva as perfectly ethnically situated to man the barricades.[14] As Diana Athill wrote after reading his novel *The Chip-Chip Gatherers*, there had to be 'some very rare and awe-inspiring gene roaming about among the Naipauls'.[15]

His widow Jenny had been secretary to Alexander Chancellor, the former editor of the *Spectator*, who wrote: 'Working for an "island scholarship" is clearly a full-time occupation. So far as I could tell, Shiva had failed to master even the most elementary of practical skills. He couldn't boil an egg or mend a fuse. If a tap was dripping, so to speak, he would telephone Jenny at the office and she would rush home immediately to deal with it . . . If, in his literary persona, he tended to ignore her existence, his dependence on her was nevertheless absolute.' Chancellor made an interesting observation about Shiva's writing persona: he presented himself as 'a solitary, gloomy, self-obsessed person, lacking the gift of companionship. It is a portrait in this last respect so misleading that it fairly takes the breath away. What keeps coming back to me at the moment is his laugh: high, rasping and infectious.'[16]

Shiva's literary inheritance had given him an identity and a burden. Vidia's style had developed out of Pa's, and been appropriated by his younger brother at an early age when he learned chunks of *The Mystic Masseur* by heart. Shiva never broke free to find a style that was less dyspeptic and more suited to his own personality. He was a gifted writer, though he was often detained by distractions, but his books reverberate with the echo of his brother's voice. In *Black and White*, we encounter whores and 'tawdry' goods, learn that the Guyanese have 'behaved badly' and that Surinam displays 'incipient Third World frailties', all within the first two pages.[17] In *North of South*, an account of a journey through Africa, we have Andrew, who wants to escape via a foreign patron. 'He is defenceless ... Black and white meet and mingle at the point of fantasy, aggravating an already deformed vision. Fantasy is piled on fantasy.'[18] Away from this Naipauline philosophizing, Shiva's writing lifts off in *North of South*, for instance, through his skilful and funny use of dialogue.

In his private correspondence with his brother, there is a sense that Shiva was trying to impress, needle, emulate and implore him, all at the same time. A letter from Bombay in 1973 is characteristic. Vidia's friend and contact Rahul Singh had introduced Shiva to 'absurd' people such as '[Russi] Karanjia, the editor of Blitz'.

> I went to a little talk he gave at Rahul Singh's flat. He arrived with his fashionably dark, short-skirted mistress in tow while he himself was dressed in a weird boiler-suit type outfit. Karanjia believes that the salvation of the country lies in the creation of what he calls a 'land army' with Mrs Gandhi as its Commander-in-Chief. This land army will build dams, divert rivers and, occasionally, join them up ... I constantly have to cope with the backwash of your notoriety. The wounds inflicted by 'Area of Darkness' still seem to smart. On the other hand, your notoriety has not led people to read your other work ... I do my best to defend you but recently I have stopped listening ... Write soon – if you're not too angry with me.[19]

Vinod Mehta, who met Shiva in India, felt he was 'absolutely the opposite of Vidia. He drank a lot, he ate a lot, he made a general nuisance of himself and didn't hide his dislike for his brother at all ... This guy wanted to be taken to parties and he fell in love with an Indian woman, made an ass of himself, wanted to marry her ... but at every party invariably he would be mistaken for Vidia. "Oh, so you are the great writer V.S. Naipaul," and this guy was squirming, "That bugger never helped me, never lifted a finger for me, I've done it all on my own." '[20] Vidia would be casually derogatory about his brother in turn, telling Nikhil Lakshman, an Indian journalist who admired Shiva's work, 'He always tried to emulate me, but he was very mediocre.'[21] Vidia complained that Shiva had used his writing to settle personal complaints and grievances: 'I don't think anyone in my family apart from my brother was a gatherer of injustice. We were doers. While he drew breath, he whined.'[22] Or as he complained cruelly later: 'I was really hoping when my brother came along – before I was told about his alcoholic idleness – that he would, as it were, show me a new way. But he was just using me as a template. He was patterning himself on me.'[23]

In August 1985, reeling from the sudden disappearance of an absent presence, Vidia felt nothing but heartache. His irritation with Shiva when he was alive had always been bound up with love and a paternal, fraternal sense of unfulfilled responsibility. Now his only brother was gone, leaving a young boy to bear the Naipaul name. To Antonia, in response to a letter of condolence, Vidia wrote, 'It's a great grief; and it has brought, suddenly, a new feeling of loneliness (though we seldom met) . . . since my father's death in 1953, I have never really known grief as sharp as this.'[24] Not long before he passed away, their cousin Sita had sent Shiva a letter about a slighting remark he had made regarding her father Simbhoo in a *New Yorker* article. Now the letter was circulated through the family: Sita retailed the news that Simbhoo had funded this ingrate through school. Moreover, 'When you nor your brother could send a shilling to your mother in Trinidad [my father] supported your mother and Nalini . . . You and Vido have made a living writing about the family, but nowhere is there any indication that it was due to our grandmother & then to my father – "the uncle who was not the Leader of the Opposition" – that such is the case.'[25] The extended family was filled with what Kamla called 'hurt, rejection and selfishness'.[26]

Days after Shiva's death, Pat noted: 'Sewan's pictures on the mantelpiece. "I think about my brother all the time." Grief, tears overtake him often . . . "Every time I hold a pen I think of him." ' In December there was a memorial service, 'a grand assembly of London, Spectator-related, niceness & intellect . . . Vidia had to stop a number of times in the first part of his speech . . . Auberon Waugh, & others, arrived late & created about while Vidia speaking.' In the New Year, Vidia and Pat went to visit Tarun and Jenny at their flat in Belsize

Park. Afterwards, Pat wrote: 'Vidia is happy with & about Tarun. Saw his knife collection, table tennis table etc.' A reciprocal visit and Christmas cards ensued. 'Thank you for the money you sent me . . . I am in the Senior School now and it is much harder but more fun . . . Hope to see you soon, Lots of love Tarun.'[27] Over time, Vidia found it too painful to be reminded of Shiva, and withdrew: he did not see his nephew any more. Jenny was content with this decision. 'Vidia still sleeping, looking very thin last night, in the candlelight, grieving for Sewan,' wrote Pat in her diary. 'Discovered just now, on Vidia's scales, that I weigh 6½ stone [41 kg].'[28] It was a bad omen, this unexplained weight loss: Pat had undiagnosed breast cancer.

*

In 1973, a few years after moving to Wilsford, Vidia had begun to make notes about rural life, oriented around the estate workers who enabled Stephen Tennant's bucolic idyll to flourish, and the retainers who lived at the manor looking after him. After he moved to Dairy Cottage, he recorded information about Mr Wilkins, who helped to maintain the property whenever he and Pat were away. He would add memories of his upbringing, and thoughts about his own position in the world: 'I knew so many family quarrels when I was young that I made a promise to myself never to have any when I grew up. I thought I would live in peace with my sister . . . Mr Wilkins had been conscious all the time, so the "herdsman" had said . . . I see the seasons now; I wish I didn't. I am less stressed now than I was twenty-five years ago by the feeling of isolation and racial oddity . . . We gave some fruit from the garden to Mrs Wilkins.'[29] Would this material make a book? A year before Shiva's death, Pat had written, 'Vidia "made a breakthrough" in his writing. Going to begin The Valley with Jack.' Reading an early draft of what would become The Enigma of Arrival, she was 'surprised at the verisimilitude, fleetingly thought of libel'. Vidia wrote more. 'He told me last night that he deliberately lengthened out the narrative, Pitton walking up to the gate etc, so that we stay with the dismissal of Pitton, it is not over too soon. "You didn't know that?" Said he thinks all this out . . . He is also fortifying himself with white wine, e.g. towards the end of the morning, unusually, to quell "nerves" before setting to write . . . It occurs to me, for no exact reason, to record that he told me that if he died, Paul would be able to advise on editing . . . He is "good at that." ' But it was only in the months following Shiva's abrupt death that Vidia saw a clear way forward with this book. Unexpectedly, swiftly, living quietly and ascetically in Wiltshire with Pat, he was able to write *The Enigma of Arrival* in a little over a year, consumed by a sense of resignation over the inevitability of change and death; it ends with Sati's funerary ceremonies, and is dedicated to the memory of Shiva. As always, Pat helped with the writing. 'She never gave editorial advice ... She knew what was bad, what wouldn't work. She would just say, "I don't like that. This is all right. That's enough." You doubt everything when you are beginning [to write a book]. It all feels a little fraudulent, and you want somebody to say, there, you carry on.'[30]

The Enigma of Arrival was unlike any other book, a work of intermittent brilliance, a cross between a partially fictional autobiography and an essay and a slowly revealed study of the life of the mind, but billed as a novel. It was an unusable masterpiece. John Bayley observed in the *New York Review* that the vision of English rural life at the end of the twentieth century set around a crumbling house and realized through the perception of an outsider from Trinidad had 'a profound, tender, and disquieting originality, as if Eden was being seen for the first time by someone with much sharper eyes than Adam and Eve ... the unique quality of his discourse, in *The Enigma of Arrival*, is in the way it combines the sense of innocence and wonder with an eye and an understanding that are quietly and totally penetrating. It is a combination unlike any other, and no other writer today could produce anything like it.'[31]

To create this hypnotic atmosphere, Vidia stripped his life of its context. Some names were changed, Wilsford becoming Waldenshaw, Brian becoming Les, Mrs Skull becoming Mrs Phillips (Phillips Lane leads to Dairy Cottage; Pitton is a Wiltshire village). Salisbury remains Salisbury, 'Tony' is Anthony Powell and Stonehenge is Stonehenge. Alan, a literary man with 'no book to his name' is Julian Jebb, leavened with Simon Blow, another upper-class scion who would appear from time to time at Wilsford Manor, speaking of novels he intended to write. Vidia did not mention the social connections that had brought him to Wilsford, or the machinations of the class system in the valley. He did not allude to his alternative existence in London or Buenos Aires, although he wrote subtly of the circumstances that had led him to England from Trinidad. He did not say that the manor was owned by the flamboyant homosexual aesthete Stephen Tennant, but by 'my landlord' (the term borrowed from *Wuthering Heights*), a figure with 'accidia', whom he never met.

He did not mention Pat or Margaret, but appeared to inhabit his cottage alone, living off thin air; as in his fictional fiction, he found it difficult to deal frankly with women or his own emotions towards them. The closest reference to sex is a disapproving focus on the soon to be murdered Brenda, the wife of a farm worker, 'a short woman with heavy thighs' who 'sunbathed in the ruined garden, seemingly careless of showing her breasts'.[32] Even when recollecting the year of wandering after the sale of the Stockwell house and the long stay with her Auntie Lu, Pat remains absent from the text: 'In London I rented a serviced flat in Dolphin Square ... I went eventually to stay in a private house in the town of Gloucester ... a small, mean, common town. It was not a place I would have gone to out of choice. But now it offered a house, shelter, hospitality.'[33]

The Enigma of Arrival is achieved through a detective's power of observation: instead of speaking to people, as he would when travelling for his journalism, Vidia or the narrator watches for instance through a window and guesses the connection between Les, Brenda and Mr and Mrs Phillips: 'I couldn't tell who out of the four was benefiting most from the relationship ... They were servants, all four. Within that condition (which should have neutered them) all their passions were played out. But that might have been my own special prejudice, my own raw nerves. I came from a colony, once a plantation society, where servitude was a more desperate condition.'[34] This, and other realizations, arose directly from the distinctive, reclusive manner in which he and Pat lived in Wiltshire, noticing rather than participating. In her diary, there are anticipations of the material Vidia would use later, almost entirely from memory, in the book. 'John Skull has just confirmed that it was Mr Tennant in the car yesterday. He waved at Vidia and, Vidia said, "looked very benign" ... As a backdrop to all this the Skulls and their friends, Brian and his wife. Last night he passed naked to the hips with a bandolier >cartridge belt< round that line. There has been considerable toing and froing, the night before last hammering etc. to a chicken house behind the yew hedge ... There was a letter from his past, excited by the television programme about him and London, from Carmen. He said he must write to her.'

The most memorable thing about this mesmeric and oddly unclassifiable work is the incidental observation. It has no plot – it is a book more for writers than readers – but consists of an endless stream of perception. It is full of surprises. These might be small, like the observation that at this point in English history, hay is no longer collected in ricks or bales, but in 'great Swiss rolls ... too big to be lifted or unrolled by a man' or that the countryside is marked by 'padded passing-places' made by 'rolling blue plastic sacks around the barbed wire and tying them with spiral after spiral

of red-blond raffia or nylon.'[35] Or it might be a reflection on the speech of
Mr Pitton, a West Country gardener (so unlike the Trinidadian gardener,
'a weeder and a waterer, a barefoot man, trousers rolled up to mid-shin,
playing a hose on a flower-bed'):[36]

> It was Pitton who one year, talking of the pear trees on the
> 'farmhouse' wall, gave me a new determinative use of the preposi-
> tion 'in'. The pears were ripe. The birds were pecking at them. I
> mentioned it to Pitton, thinking that with all the things he had to
> do he mightn't have noticed. But he said he had noticed; the pears
> were very much on his mind; he intended any day now 'to pick
> them in'. To pick the pears *in* – I liked that *in*. I played with it,
> repeated it.[37]

The writer, with memories of the flimsiness of buildings in Petit Valley
and undeclared knowledge that the Tennant family wealth came in part
from Trinidad estates, might be struck by a ruined greenhouse, full of
weeds, in the grounds of the manor: 'It had been "over-specified": its
timbers, the depth of the concrete floor (on two levels on the sloping
site), its door, its hinges, its metal-work – everything was much sturdier
than was strictly necessary.'[38] Or he might deduce that Mr Pitton's neat
and stylish clothes were modelled on 'an army officer of twenty or
twenty-five years before whom Pitton had served or served under
(someone still alive in Pitton's memory: Pitton's imitation this officer's
chief memorial, perhaps).'[39] He might even establish why the better
women's dress shops in Salisbury tended to fail: people with important
shopping to do usually did it in London, and new owners rarely studied
in advance 'the location of the car-parks, the very roundabout one-way-
street system, or understood the way shoppers moved about the town
centre.'[40] (I would confirm, having spent more than a decade living in
an estate cottage in a valley on the other side of Salisbury, that the
observation about shops and the one-way system is wholly accurate;
and it was only after reading *The Enigma of Arrival* that I noticed
Bernard, who drove the van and did the deliveries for Shrewton Steam
Laundries, wore his 'laundry leather moneybag ... slung over his
shoulder and chest like a bandolier'.[41])

'My admiration for Naipaul keeps mounting,' wrote the celebrated
editor of the *New Yorker* William Shawn to Gillon Aitken. He extracted
early sections of the book, paying $78,000. Shawn told Vidia he was
'enchanted' by the title *The Enigma of Arrival*, taken from the name of

a Giorgio de Chirico painting used on the jacket.[42] The book sold satisfactorily in Britain and America, and in translation, but critical responses varied. Joseph Epstein in the *New Criterion* had no doubt Naipaul was 'the most talented, the most truthful, the most honorable writer of his generation.'[43] In the *Boston Review*, George Packer said *The Enigma of Arrival* would be read when other supposed master-pieces were forgotten.[44] 'Oh Gawd, man, you can write!' wrote John Figueroa.[45] David Pryce-Jones suggested the book was 'a celebration of le mot juste'.[46] Margaret Drabble wrote, 'I have been struggling for some time against the temptation to write you a fan letter about The Enigma of Arrival, but have decided at this dark dull end of the year to succumb . . . I admire all your work, but this novel in particular.'[47] In his diary, Anthony Powell wrote: 'What strikes one is the parade of rural characters observed from outside, without inherent awareness of the sort of persons they are, which someone brought up in England would possess, anyway up to a point.'[48] Susan Sontag wrote a baffling letter to the *Times Literary Supplement* complaining about a lukewarm review Vidia had been given.[49] Salman Rushdie, writing in the *Guardian*, admired the author's 'magisterial technical control' but wondered why *The Enigma of Arrival* was so sad, and why the word 'love' seemed to be absent from its pages. 'When the strength for fiction fails the writer, what remains is autobiography.'[50] On television, the *South Bank Show* devoted an edition called 'The Enigma of Writing' to V.S. Naipaul and his new book. It was a solemn, joyless production. Melvyn Bragg frowned and stroked his chin while Vidia walked around the Wiltshire fields looking smug and tormented. He spoke in a clipped voice, in circumlocutions: 'One still thinks one had many lucky escapes . . . About ten years ago one thought one . . . was making one's own life . . . but, no, one was a prisoner of the past.'[51] He said that in refusing to write an autobiography, he had created *The Enigma of Arrival*.

Americans liked the book, and it would later be singled out by the Nobel committee: 'In his masterpiece *The Enigma of Arrival* Naipaul visits the reality of England like an anthropologist studying some hitherto unexplored native tribe deep in the jungle. With apparently short-sighted and random observations he creates an unrelenting image of the placid collapse of the old colonial ruling culture.'[52] Derek Walcott did not see it in this way; the book was an affirmation of 'the squirearchy of club and manor'. His review bubbled into an assault, although he praised the tenderness of the early sections: 'The myth of

Naipaul as a phenomenon, as a singular, contradictory genius who survived the cane fields and the bush at great cost, has long been a farce.' What about Edgar Mittelholzer, C.L.R. James, Jamaica Kincaid and the legendary Bob Marley? And what of V.S. Naipaul's celebrated frankness? Would people still praise his 'nasty little sneers' against black people if they were turned on Jews? His rival's prose was 'scarred by scrofula, by passages from which one would like to avert one's eye; and these reveal, remorselessly, Naipaul's repulsion toward Negroes.'[53]

Walcott's declaration of war had enjoyed a long gestation, and was a reaction less to the contents of the book than to the public pronouncements that had preceded it. His own reputation existed in opposition to Vidia's. As Walcott wrote in the 1979 poem 'The Schooner "Flight"':

> I'm just a red nigger who love the sea,
> I had a sound colonial education,
> I have Dutch, nigger, and English in me,
> and either I'm nobody, or I'm a nation.[54]

His poetry was an epic celebration of Caribbean life; he presented the region as a place at the centre of world history, much more than a collection of scattered islands. Piloted by Cal Lowell and Lizzie Hardwick, he had sailed happily through America's more prestigious universities, teaching literature, wowing students and enjoying the admiration of East Coast intellectuals. Despite his exemplary public love for the Caribbean, Derek Walcott lived in Boston and New York.

*

Moving fast, wanting change, demanding reverence, and more unhappy than ever, Vidia thought he might travel abroad with Margaret. Before leaving, he wondered if purchasing a property for himself in London might ease his dissatisfaction. Gone were the days of a latchkey to Marisa and Lindsay's house: instead he commanded Marisa to find him a flat in Kensington, costing up to £250,000. It should have, he informed her, 'at least two bedrooms. Quiet is essential ... I spend all day in the place where I live. Therefore I am very sensitive to disturbance & nuisance.'[55] A Chicago Tribune interviewer noted in 1986 that V.S. Naipaul seemed 'poised to strike – a man whose mind moves with such daunting clarity and speed that in his presence the term "food for thought" can take on an uncomfortably literal meaning.'[56]

Seeking greater success in the USA, Vidia travelled to North Carolina to research a new book, *Slave States*. He planned to start with a string of articles about the South, and produced a hasty, indefinite book proposal for publishers. At the Republican Convention in Dallas in 1984, he had realized that the Caribbean was linked historically to 'the America of the South and plantations and slavery'. Now he would travel through the old states, and hear what people had to say. His model, once again, would be *The Middle Passage*. Seeing the connection between the West Indies and the slave states of America, 'made me wonder why the idea hadn't come to me before . . . I am interested in nuance, complexity, ambiguities, rather than in strong black-and-white issues.'[57] It was a notably weak proposal, but Gillon Aitken wrote to Bob Gottlieb at Knopf that 'if Vidia is going to write a big breakthrough book for the American market, this is it.' The implication was that since Vidia was a world-famous writer, the new work had to be accomplished. Gottlieb offered an advance of $125,000, against $175,000 from Harper & Row and $180,000 from Putnam's. Vidia was disheartened, and felt let down. At this point, Gottlieb replaced Shawn at the *New Yorker*, and was in turn replaced by Sonny Mehta, who had left India for England and made a stupendous reputation for himself at Picador by unleashing the power of trade paperback books, and by wearing sneakers and blue jeans to the office in the days before such behaviour was standard. Aitken remembered that Mehta was trembling with fear when he met Vidia for the first time, but was anxious to publish the book. More money became available, and a spectacular $500,000 joint deal was secured for *Slave States* and a yet-to-be-written novel. UK rights for *Slave States* were sold to Viking Penguin for £75,000. Penguin was still selling most of Vidia's titles in paperback, though in low numbers; only *A House for Mr Biswas* sold more than 10,000 copies in 1986, because it was on school and college syllabuses.[58]

Vidia spent the spring and summer of 1987 travelling through America, making notes, accompanied by a driver. In his words: 'Without knowing what I was doing I told Margaret, you'll drive me in the South, and at the time when I feel I can do the book or the book is there, I will pay you $40,000 – would you do it on that basis?' And she willingly agreed. So I remember in Georgia, I gave her the forty thousand . . . and she was quite crazy with delight.'[59] The money enabled Margaret to buy an apartment in Buenos Aires. Norman di Giovanni saw Vidia there after a break of more than a decade: 'I remember his pride, his chest was literally puffed up in pride that he had bought the flat. He was laughing. "I paid for this, and hasn't she done it up nicely." '[60] Vidia and Margaret's tour of the South cost him nearly £50,000, mainly in hotel bills, which he was able to offset against income tax as a business expense.[61]

Driving through America, Vidia and Margaret did not divert to see Mira and Amar and their children in Florida, where Amar was running a successful cancer hospital in Braverton. Instead they drove through Atlanta, Charleston, Tallahassee, Tuskegee, Jackson and Nashville, Vidia opening his notebook to the people he saw, and recording their observations at length. Armed with a stack of 'release' forms for his interviewees to sign, he made sure his interviews could not provide the basis for future legal action. He told the *Atlanta Constitution*, which caught up with him in a hotel lobby, that he had 'never read William Faulkner or any other Southern writer, not does he intend to' and had come to the region with no preconceptions.[62] His initial steps were helped by his allies in New York. Bob Silvers and Sonny Mehta sought out local contacts whose details were faxed or posted to Vidia as he travelled. Rea Hederman at the *New York Review* also smoothed the way; he came from Mississippi, and had made a name for himself by dragging his family's newspaper the Jackson *Clarion-Ledger* away from its racist past. Hederman made hotel reservations for Vidia and Margaret in Memphis and Nashville and organized meetings with friends.

Once Vidia was safely in the loop of Southern hospitality, many doors were opened to him. Richard A. Allison of Atlanta offered the use of his house in Alabama: 'If you can give me any sort of notice as to when you might arrive, I would be happy to have our cook (Emily Jones) be in attendance to cook your dinner.'[63] In practice, many of the meetings that were arranged remotely led to nothing. Vidia's most interesting encounters came almost at random as he travelled, staying in the best hotels he could find, and the strongest sympathy and interest in the finished book – called *A Turn in the South* – seemed to be reserved for the poor blacks and poor whites he met. 'In the hundred years after the end of slavery the black man was tormented in the South in ways that I never knew about until I began to travel in the region.'[64] Talking to a woman pastor in Tallahassee who described the campaign to end desegregation in Washington, DC in 1941 ('You can't imagine the things that were said to us. People would spit in our faces. If we drank out of a glass they would take it up and throw it away') left Vidia in tears.[65] In Alabama, grouchy and exhausted, he was admitted to hospital following an asthma attack ('Name of nearest relative, Margaret Gooding').[66]

When the travelling was done, he retired to the Hotel Sofitel in

Montpellier, a big and bland hotel in southern France, to write for four months. The atmosphere was suitably sterile for the rapid creation of a substantial book. It was dedicated to Seepersad Naipaul 'in ever renewed homage'. But when Vidia came to write, the first draft did not run easily. His notes were in a less even hand than usual; the narrative and theme were unclear. He switched direction between slavery, religion and the nature of rednecks, and his efforts to draw parallels with his own social background were unsuccessful. Vidia pushed on, not always pausing to sift or mediate his encounters, or to separate a story from extraneous material. Many interviews were too long, and the best lines came by chance. At Graceland, he noticed the obesity of redneck women: 'It was at times a pleasure and an excitement to see them, to see the individual way each human frame organized or arranged its excess poundage: a swag here, a bag there, a slab there, a roll there ... but I also began to wonder ... whether for these descendants of frontier people and pinelanders there wasn't, in their fatness, some simple element of self-assertion.'[67] The result was a book that lacked the rigour and analysis of his usual travel writing. In the *New York Review of Books*, Roger Shattuck wrote that 'Naipaul writes as if a modern oracle had chosen to speak through him. The individual sentences and paragraphs read easily enough. The mysterious oracular quality comes from Naipaul's willingness to follow random leads and his disinclination to pull everything together into a set of conclusions ... Despite its brilliant moments Naipaul has not worked this book up to his highest standard.'[68]

From the publisher's point of view, it could not be anything except a hit; they had hundreds of thousands of dollars to recoup. The copy-edited manuscript was sent to Vidia for inspection, but Sonny Mehta soon received a fax back from him in May 1988:

I thought it might have been known in the office that after 34 years and 20 books I knew certain things about writing and didn't want a copy-editor's help with punctuation ... I didn't want anyone undoing my semi-colons; with all their different shades of pause; or interfering with my 'ands', with all their different ways of linking.

It happens that English – the history of the language – was my subject at Oxford. It happens that I know very well that these so-called 'rules' have nothing to do with the language, and are really rules about French usage. The glory of English is that it is without these court rules: it is a language made by the people who write it.

My name goes on my book. I am responsible for the way the words are put together. It is one reason why I became a writer.

Every writer has his own voice ... An assiduous copy-editor can undo this very quickly, can make A write like B and Ms C. And what a waste of spirit it is for the writer, who is in effect re-doing bits of his manuscript all the time instead of giving it a truly creative, revising read. Consider how it has made me sit down this morning, not to my work, but to write this enraged letter.[69]

Mehta did his best; he was 'mortified', 'appalled', understood 'just how frustrating and dispiriting' the experience had been, and promised it would never happen again. He would do all he could to ensure *A Turn in the South* was a success. Yet at precisely this moment, Vidia was arranging to sell the rights to a big travel book on India, rather than write the unspecified novel he had already sold to Knopf. Andrew Wylie, who acted as Gillon Aitken's associate in New York, demanded $600,000 for the privilege of publishing this unwritten masterpiece; Mehta reluctantly offered $200,000. But Vidia had already plotted to move elsewhere, knowing that another publisher might produce more money for a book on India. In honeyed words, Aitken wrote to Mehta that 'Knopf have not really been successful in moving Vidia out of a somewhat conservative sales pattern ... Your own intimate knowledge of your own country, which I saw only as an advantage to Vidia, runs the risk, in our view, of operating as an inhibition.'[70] The defection was set in train, and Vidia prepared to travel to Bombay at the end of the year, accompanied by his ever biddable mistress.

A Turn in the South made a loss for Knopf, who were also left with an unwritten novel ticking in their accounts. Mehta was not the only man to be driven mercilessly in negotiation; when Vidia took on Gillon Aitken as his agent, he refused to accept the standard commission of 20 per cent on foreign contracts: 'Until I hear from you, all negotiations should be stayed ... I would like a monthly sheet from you recording all contracts or pieces of business pending, and their respective states.'[71] The cut dropped to 15 per cent. Over the coming decade, relishing the role of *homme de confiance*, Gillon would become increasingly bound to Vidia's life and work. Born in Calcutta in 1938 to a stern Scottish jute trader and his wife, he had been sent to a boarding school in Darjeeling at the age of three. His childhood was like something from the days of Kipling: going to the Tollygunge Club with his kind English nanny,

Cissie Bacon, and being attended by 'an eager Indian bearer'. Gillon retained few early memories of his mother and father. In 1945, the family sailed to Glasgow and he was installed at a prep school in Devon. It would be some three years before he saw his parents again. His vacations were spent at rough 'holiday farms' or with his grand-parents. After leaving Charterhouse early, Gillon taught at a boys' school in Surbiton, learned French, German and Russian, worked as an eavesdropper in military intelligence in Berlin and become Evelyn Waugh's publisher at Chapman & Hall.[72] Heightist, haughty and charming, commercially ruthless but apparently patrician, a lone wolf who relied only on himself, Gillon Aitken was the ideal agent for Vidia.

During the 1980s, he pushed his client's reputation forward, sharing Vidia's view that he deserved to be treated as a special case by publishers. Using the unique power of the successful artist to make unreasonable demands, Gillon harried André Deutsch over his ineffi-ciency, pursuing him like a prosecuting barrister over his Tippex-covered royalty statements, and finally arranged Vidia's defection to Viking Penguin with *The Enigma of Arrival*. Deutsch's firm was losing money, and he became ever more parsimonious, inviting Vidia only to the cheapest restaurants. In Francis Wyndham's memory, 'Lots of writers like Mailer and Updike had left Deutsch, but Vidia stayed loyal, and left when it was going down the plug. Vidia had good reason to dislike him. Why could he never take him to lunch at the Connaught?'[73] Aided by Anne-Louise Fisher and later by his colleague Sally Riley, Gillon expanded the sale of foreign-language rights in Vidia's backlist around the world. This was an arduous process: 'Vidia is being extremely difficult,' he told Riley in a 1989 memo, 'and wishes to withdraw from the deal with Kiepenheuer & Witsch if they do not pay the full £50,000 on signature.'[74] When André Deutsch Limited was bought out by the publisher Tom Rosenthal, Gillon discovered that the head contracts to Vidia's books (the contracts from which the right to publish paperback editions derived) had been sold to Penguin, and a legal battle ensued as he sought to recover them. Next came the news that the new management at André Deutsch had sold off the archives of the company, which included many letters from Vidia, to the University of Tulsa in Oklahoma. As Vidia's new books were written, Gillon shifted him between publishers, upping the money, selling *India: A Million Mutinies Now* to Heinemann in the UK for £175,000, and returning to the arms of Knopf after it was published in the USA by

Viking Penguin. Helen Fraser, his new British publisher, found Vidia to be 'an appreciative author. *A Million Mutinies* was one of the most successful books I published at Heinemann.'[75]

The working relationship between Vidia and Gillon was complex and symbiotic. A dispute with the *Sunday Telegraph* over some articles which had been paid for but not published gives an idea of its nature: 'I suppose we could have sued the newspaper, but I think we were right to pull away grandly,' wrote the agent to his author. 'I do not think there is anything that could constructively be done, except to remember and punish later.'[76] As Vidia's reputation for curmudgeonly behaviour grew, Gillon used it as a bludgeoning tool in negotiation, telling editors of his terrible anger over minor lapses, and working up a palaver. In a pincer movement with Andrew Wylie in 1990, he offered some book extracts to the *New York Review of Books* for $125,000, a figure way beyond the magazine's usual fees. When they offered $10,000 instead, he told Bob Silvers his client was fatally offended. Never one to forgive a past favour, the man without loyalties threatened to break his links with the *New York Review*. An anguished letter from Rea Hederman arrived at Dairy Cottage: 'Gillon said any damage could be repaired in part by our offering $20,000 ... Bob is sending Gillon his personal $10,000 check which represents the difference between the agreed figure with Viking and Gillon's estimate of damage reparations ... This is a simple, sincere gesture by Bob to put an end to an episode that has greatly troubled him.'[77]

When the director of the National Portrait Gallery, Charles Saumarez Smith, asked Vidia to sit for a portrait and mentioned that another writer was unavailable, it was Gillon who had to interpret the lack of a reply. He was 'hesitating to raise this matter' with V.S. Naipaul and 'extremely loath to attribute to him sensibilities he may not possess,' but suggested his silence might be because he did not relish 'standing in for the unreachable Derek Walcott!' On one occasion, Gillon caused Vidia undisguised joy. In 1991, the Inland Revenue ruled that he had no tax liability for the year in which he was out of the country writing *A Turn in the South*. In addition, aided by arguments from Vidia's accountant Barry Kernon, they accepted that he was non-domiciled for tax purposes in the UK – meaning that since he might one day return to his country of origin, he need pay no tax on money kept offshore in a bank account in Jersey. From São Paulo, where he was sojourning with Margaret, Vidia wrote Gillon the most enthusiastic letter of his life: 'I am <u>utterly delighted</u> by your fax with the news from Barry Kernon.'[78]

*

In his Wiltshire incarnation, lunching or dining occasionally with people in whom he took a marginal interest, Vidia never spoke of Margaret, and said little of his travels. He kept his own counsel. Once or twice a year the Naipauls had lunch with the Powells, who lived thirty miles away in Somerset in substantial bucolic style, with sheep, a lake and grottoes. In old age Anthony Powell published his private journals, which lurched further into self-parody with each successive volume. He would complain about social breaches, such as 'unsophisticated people' addressing his wife as Lady Powell rather than as Lady Violet, and liked to record pieces of random gossip, like the news that Lady Antonia Fraser had a black chauffeur who 'talks like Chokey in *Decline and Fall*', or that Harold Pinter was irate about the untidiness at his tennis club.[79] Publication did little to improve Powell's reputation as a novelist, but the volumes do provide observant glimpses of Vidia masquerading as a country squire. Tony Powell had a 'tradition' that whenever Pat and Vidia visited, they had to be served 'curry', which he took pride in cooking himself.[80] A friendly and sociable figure, he introduced them to other upper-class families in the extended neighbourhood. Vidia had little respect for his talents as a novelist, but liked him. After Powell's death, he wrote maliciously in *A Writer's People* that he had finally read an omnibus edition of his books, and been horrified by his vanity and lack of narrative skill: 'It may be that the friendship lasted all this time because I had not examined his work.'[81] Helen Fraser, who published both men, thought Powell had no great interest in Vidia's writing. 'He had a benign, amused novelist's curiosity about everyone, and he was most interested in Vidia as a personality, as an unusual type of person.'[82]

Tony Powell admired Vidia's quick intelligence, his ability to interpret handwriting and faces, and in particular his outspoken political and racial opinions, which in his eyes were made authentic by his alien background. In May 1982 during the Falklands War, he recorded: 'Vidia said we ought to have bombed Buenos Aires right away, now too late. Added that the Argentines . . . are vain, aggressive, not amenable to anything but force. I am sure he is right.'[83] He invited Vidia to a 'luncheon' at Claridge's in 1986 to celebrate the publication of his book *The Fisher King*, attended by the likes of Roy Fuller, Alan Ross, Hilary Spurling, Kingsley Amis and

Miriam Gross.[84] After being driven over to Dairy Cottage by his son John in 1988, Powell wrote, 'Vidia was as usual in great form, he delivered a terrific diatribe against rich Arabs, indeed Muslims in business anyway, their dishonesty in financial matters, conviction that it does not matter swindling "Unbelievers", in fact is a praiseworthy act. The food good, if rather oddly assorted, lobster soup, odds and ends of crab, almond crumble; excellent Pauillac (missed the Château) '76.'[85] Powell saw Vidia as an insider. After meeting the *New York Times* critic Mel Gussow and his wife Ann at lunch, he thought Ann Gussow had 'seemed a bit bewildered by it all, V[iolet] thought possibly on account of Vidia's being so essentially part of the British social and intellectual life. Americans are always so acutely conscious of racial tensions.'[86] Mel Gussow had been an early promoter of Vidia's work in the American press.

On a visit to Dairy Cottage in 1983, Violet and Tony Powell met Gillon Aitken, his wife Cari and Vidia's German translator Karin Graf. 'The Aitkens were perhaps in middle of a matrimonial row. He recently had his licence removed for drunk-in-charge, and there had been some car trouble on way down,' Powell noted. 'Vidia was in good form, funny in his best manner about the Pakistan [sic] writer Salman Rushdie (who won Booker Prize), and said something disobliging about Vidia in *Harpers & Queen*, or similar periodical: ". . . I'm sorry . . . I'm very sorry to hear that . . . No respect for his elders . . . He will learn that sort of thing is a mistake . . . People merely think . . ." All perfectly true. I haven't read any of Rushdie's books, but he sounds an ass from interviews. Vidia produced nice red Graves. Pat looked rather harassed, as indeed she probably is.'[87] Powell would record mundane but revealing aspects of his friend's life: 'Vidia has now bought a car (Saab), after years of existence in taxis. His great interest is now wine, which he buys at Marks & Spencer, where it is apparently very good.'[88] In his journals, he collected local gossip; lunching in Hampshire with Tanya and Anthony Hobson, to whom he had introduced Vidia, he discovered that, 'Pat Naipaul is apparently not allowed by Vidia to garden (quite why is not clear), if she does so clandestinely while he is resting in afternoon he will suddenly pull aside the curtains and denounce her from the window.'[89]

In a diary entry in March 1985, Tony Powell described a dinner held at 10 Downing Street, organized by Hugh Thomas, at which the other guests included Hugh Trevor-Roper, Anthony Quinton, Iris Murdoch, Noel Annan, Max Egremont, Theodore Zeldin and Vidia. After the meal, a staged intellectual discussion took place centring around the prime minister, Margaret Thatcher, and moderated by Hugh Thomas, to whom she had given a peerage. Vidia sat beside Thatcher, and another guest, David Pryce-Jones, recalled his conversation. 'Iris Murdoch said at a certain point that what was required was a caring and compassionate society. Vidia was like a knife. He said, "Iris, I first heard those words twenty years ago. They had no meaning then, and they have less meaning now." It was just devastating in front of Mrs Thatcher as a put-down to Iris, who then didn't speak again. Mrs Thatcher clearly enjoyed Vidia. He was – I would say – one of the stars of that particular evening.'[90]

Although Vidia was happy at times to accept invitations of this sort, he made little effort to seek social advancement. He and Pat never became part of a group of friends in Wiltshire, although they would accept the hospitality of well-connected people, and occasionally entertained guests for lunch or tea. During the late 1980s and early 1990s, when Vidia was not travelling, they spent most of their time alone. Gillon's office had to deal with administrative matters such as automatically turning down requests for permission to quote from Vidia's books, but the two occupants of Dairy Cottage received ceaseless enquiries. Some were a cause for concern or anger: reading a copy of *Departures* magazine (sent free to Vidia as an American Express gold card holder), Pat found an article by the photographer Mirella Ricciardi which copied sections of 'A New King for the Congo', published in the *New York Review* in 1975. Gillon sought and won an apology, and compensation. Ricciardi's excuse was an original one: she had copied the material from 'an old and dilapidated magazine article from which both title and signature were missing and there was no way that I could have known who the author was . . . I am not familiar with the laws covering plagiarism.'[91]

Pat still made occasional use of her diary, and was hoping to write an autobiography. It became an attempt to expiate her deep unhappiness. Like her other writings, it was disjointed and went through dozens of drafts before stopping, undone:

> I really began to feel this urge to write, about the world in which I found myself, in the late sixties. I had been lucky, I had been able to travel quite widely, mainly in the New Commonwealth . . . I was in daily contact with someone >– I will call him, for convenience sake, the Genius –< who could do the sort of writing I wanted to do, any sort of writing, superbly well. It wasn't his example which set me off, I was strangely dead to that, it was his character. He was

once supposed to have said to a woman, the wife of an important man, whom he had just met at a party, 'It doesn't matter what you think.'[92] He didn't need to say that to me. He made it painfully obvious ... He was no male chauvinist, not then. He was like it with everybody in a way. In company his conversation was prized for its directness and fun, and a certain outrageous quality. He was always capable of an exchange of wit that was quick and generous, >or of sympathy at a personal level< but of an exchange of views – never ... He held strong, not to say extreme views about many things. Some of them affected me. I can't say they clashed with mine because, I can admit it now, I didn't have any, only positions taken up long ago and never relinquished. I felt assaulted but I could not defend myself.[93]

Pat could not defend herself. She was not sure what she should be doing, or whether any other kind of life was possible. Her diary trailed off during the 1980s, though sometimes she would write a few paragraphs. 'I saw Margaret Thatcher as an image, a beautiful idol who could, through a change in circumstances, some dreadful magic, become ugly. I saw her as the goddess Kali, double imaged, turning to reveal the tusks, the blood. She promised "to heal the wounds of a divided nation" I thought she might tear it apart.' When Bernard Levin – whom Pat had long admired – came to lunch before interviewing Vidia, she noted, 'He has beautiful tiny feet, beautiful brown brogues ... Talked only about himself – as he has already written in his articles.' Interested in progressive politics, Pat liked the idea of a party that was neither Labour nor Conservative, but found it impossible to become a devotee: 'Do I believe in the Liberal Democrats, their policy? Probably not. Do I like them? If I were honest, not very much ... the odd grey-faced man who had come down to talk to us from "Cowley Street" in smoke-filled rooms filled me with dismay. And some of the bumph, leaflets etc. which emanate from the same source are simply ludicrous.'[94] Pat tried again to write autobiographically: 'I married out of my race and nation while I was still a student.' She became angry when she saw a television interview with Kingsley Amis. 'In it he had attacked American novelists, Updike particularly (I had enjoyed Couples) and had said, with deliberate frivolity, that he would rather read the work of a popular writer like Dick Francis any day.' Why did people put up with this? 'Why are they so tolerant of extremes, petulance, childishly reactionary views? We just believe that middle-aged writers are like that. We have this ridiculous faith, we believe it is a protective covering, the wizard's cloak, beneath which they preserve their real selves for serious work. It is the tribute we pay to their talent.'⁹⁵

In 1989, soon after Vidia returned from India, Pat learned that she had cancer. She had been for breast screening in the nearby town of Amesbury, and was told to go for further tests. Vidia went with her and Mr Keel, a local taxi driver, to a Southampton hospital for a biopsy. 'I was deep in writing *A Million Mutinies*. There was that dreadful drive and I was enraged at the hospital because it was such a messy place . . . and then I had to go back in the afternoon to pick up Pat, and we got lost . . . I just couldn't find out where Pat would be waiting. Eventually I found her. She was in a wheelchair, obviously terribly stressed, very unhappy and obviously in pain and waiting in solitude and I had been very angry all of that day. When I saw her, I became so ashamed. It was very upsetting for me. As long as Pat could look after me, it was all right. When I felt this [illness] had come to her, I was full of shame at my rage. I should have done more. It's the thing about the work. If you are travelling for material or to write a book, it isn't that you are self-centred, it is that you are with the work. You are obsessed with what you are doing. And when you start writing, it is such a delicate thing, writing, shaping a paragraph, a page, shaping a chapter, having a sense of the bigger structure of the book, you've got to be with it all the time. You are carrying it in your head, and things that upset you are very irritating.'⁹⁶

Pat told no one about the details of her illness, but when Mel Gussow visited for lunch in July he learned that an operation was planned, and that it appeared to be for cancer treatment. A theatre critic and friend of Harold Pinter, Gussow shared the news with Antonia Fraser, who wrote to Pat: 'I heard in a roundabout way – from Mel Gussow, who was <u>very</u> diffident about telling me but I'm glad he did – that you are having an operation on Friday. What rotten luck! Though I hope it may turn out to be in the end <u>good</u> luck. And a total cure.'⁹⁷ The surgery was severe: she suffered the indignity of a mastectomy, losing her right breast, making her feel less than a whole woman. The treatment appeared to have worked, and for the next two years there was no recurrence of the disease. Pat kept silent, even to herself, about the trauma of what had happened to her body, avoiding the subject altogether in her diary. Like the name of her husband's mistress, the word 'cancer' does not appear in her writing. She wore a 'tru-life breast prosthesis', the hospital providing her with a list of local underwear shops where she could go for specialist fitting: 'Mrs Haskell in Contessa at Shirley (Not Wednesdays)' and 'Wendy Miles in Vanity Fayre, Station Road, New Milton'.[98]

Meanwhile, letters kept coming to Dairy Cottage, requiring answers.[99] For the most part, they were simply ignored and filed away by Pat for posterity. Contrary as ever, Vidia took particular pleasure in turning down importuning interviewers. 'Dear Mr Bellacasa, Nothing in your questions suggests any knowledge of my work. An interview would be a considerable waste of my time and energy.' He gave passing attention to Selwyn R. Cudjoe of Wellesley College, who had spent ten years writing a book about his books and wished to talk of Barthes and Bakhtin; he rejected an appeal by *Vanity Fair*, and took no notice of Marina Salandy-Brown of the BBC, who tried to wrong-foot him by saying that since she was 'a fellow Trinidadian' he was sure to refuse her. Sometimes he responded warmly, for instance to a woman whose husband, an art teacher, had died of a brain haemorrhage the day after reading *The Enigma of Arrival*. Letters came from old acquaintances like Banning Eyre, who was busy writing software manuals and learning about African music, and Karan Singh, who was 'hoping that you would get the Nobel Prize this year, although Octavio is also an old friend.' Vidia gave unexpected hospitality to Hanif Kureishi, who had achieved fame with his script for *My Beautiful Laundrette* but was wondering where to go with his writing. Kureishi said his father too had been a journalist who had wanted success as a novelist, but never achieved it. Vidia invited him to Wiltshire for cake and Indian champagne, and gave advice on writing and how to look after his bad back – a common topic of conversation between working writers. In turn, Kureishi invited Vidia to meet him in London, and said, as others would: 'You have been a great inspiration and example to young writers like myself. When I was in my teens there were no other Indian writers living and working here that one could refer to.'

Each day, there were questions – intrusions – for Pat or Vidia to ponder. Would V.S. Naipaul open the Hounslow Book Mela? Would he give an interview to *Izvestia*? Would he like to acquire two gouache paintings inspired by *The Enigma of Arrival*? What did 'string bed' mean in *A House for Mr Biswas*, asked his Brazilian Portuguese translator? 'What kind of pipe is a "cheelum"?' Would he come to Conrad Black's 1992 election-night party at the Savoy for 'Champagne,

Crustaceans and Breakfast'? Would he give out the prizes at the Society
of Authors annual awards ceremony? Would he come for an 'informal
talk' with the Indian prime minister, Narasimha Rao, at London's
Nehru Centre? Would he have lunch with his MP, Robert Key, to meet
the environment secretary, Chris Patten? Would he sign a petition
supporting Salman Rushdie, who had been sentenced to death by
Ayatollah Khomeini and was now being defended by every right-
thinking littérateur in the world, with Harold and Antonia leading the
charge of the righteous in London? No, and for good measure he
added, 'I don't know his books, but I've been aware of his statements.
I found them usually left-wing and trivial and antiquated.' And what of
Khomeini's fatwa? 'It's an extreme form of literary criticism.'[100] Would
he sign a letter to *The Times* about the landscape around Stonehenge?
He would – in the company of a bishop, a solicitor and Richard Stilgoe
from *Countdown*, Vidia's name heading the list: 'The threatened land,
which forms habitat for larks, lapwings, stone curlews and English
partridges, would be destroyed for ever, and for the sake merely of
upgrading the existing A303.'[101]

CHAPTER TWENTY-FOUR

ARISE, SIR VIDIA

WHEN VIDIA'S RELATIONS and foreign acquaintances visited Britain, he did his best to avoid them. Ralph Ironman had been surprised while in London in the early 1980s to be asked to meet Shiva instead, who took him to an Indian restaurant and told him that he would have been able to tolerate hotter food if he had been to a good public school.[1] Moni Malhoutra was an exception. While visiting England on Indira Gandhi's staff, he was invited to stay the night in Wiltshire. 'Vidia pulled out a very expensive bottle of port which he wanted me to drink. I had my first sip and he jumped down my throat and said, "That's not the way to have port." So I said, "How am I supposed to have port?" "You are supposed to chew it." So he took it into his mouth and masticated noisily. "This is the way to enjoy port." So I did that. Pat treated him with great reverence. Always. It was almost like appreciating a deity. She was awed by him, and I think it made it difficult for her because she was aware that she had to do her bit to encourage the flowering of his talents: if that meant not creating a single creak when walking in the house, so be it. She was a very Indian wife in many respects – more Indian than most Indian wives – the way the woman sacrifices her own life for her husband. It was an unusual kind of relationship for an Englishwoman.'

Later, when Moni Malhoutra was working at the Commonwealth Secretariat in London, he would be invited with his wife, Leela, to view Vidia's Indian miniature paintings.

My wife thought that he was very self-centred and didn't observe the normal courtesies that people do. But Vidia is Vidia. It was a mutually enriching experience. He said to me one day, 'Why does the Indian Council for Cultural Relations, financed by the Government of India, send out Indian classical dancers to perform in Africa? What's the point of it? They have no eye for this kind of thing, you are wasting your money, you are wasting your time and

it reinforces the belief about Indians being a weak race.' So I asked,
'What do you think we should do?' He said, 'You should send
circuses.' I said, 'Vidia you are not serious.' He said, 'I am absolutely
serious. When I was in Nairobi an Indian circus came there. An
Indian opened the lion's mouth with his hands and put his head in
and there was pin-drop silence. The Africans were absolutely
stunned to see an Indian doing this. The next day the entire cabinet
came to witness this performance. That's what you should do.
Please tell your prime minister to stop sending high culture to
Africa. You should send circuses.' He also said – and I think he was
right – that this huge programme you have of bringing African
students to study in India is counter-productive. It doesn't win you
any friends; it only makes you enemies. They experience the full
weight of Indian colour prejudice. He was utterly serious. From his
own experiences . . . both in the Caribbean and in Africa, people of
Indian origin have been treated badly. That must have had an effect
on him.[2]

In December 1988, Vidia reactivated his contacts for his new book,
India: A Million Mutinies Now. Earlier in the year, he had been excited
to start using an IBM word processor. His old Blue Bird typewriter,
which he had bought to type out the final draft of *A House for Mr
Biswas,* was put away in the attic at Dairy Cottage. Lacking techno-
logical nostalgia, Vidia loved the idea of now being able to store his
work electronically. He wrote to Gillon Aitken: 'How lovely to compose
on the screen, to consume one's rage there. And then to print so
beautifully, in proportionally spaced letters, with right-hand justification.
And then, would you believe, to tell the instrument to save the letter in
its capacious memory. So I can call up the letter in a tick, make a
correction, and then print another copy.'[3] Aged fifty-six, he would
spend five months travelling in India, braving the heat and the noise
and the bureaucracy and the dust and the poverty, beginning in
Bombay, looping south through Goa, Bangalore, Mysore and Madras
before heading north to Calcutta and working his way west to Delhi,
interloping in Lucknow, the Punjab and Kashmir. Old helpers like Adil
Jussawalla and Rahul Singh were asked to provide introductions and
information.

Vidia began his research while staying in style in one of the country's
finest hotels, the Taj in Bombay, overlooking the Gateway of India.[4]
Vinod Mehta, the editor of the *Indian Post*, found himself overwhelmed

by the visitor's sense of entitlement; Mehta was expected, with the help of his reporters, to locate gangsters, poets, extremists, corporators, slum dwellers and feudal Muslims from the north:

> Vidia gets four or five people to help him, and makes life hell for those five people. He's a weird person. He doesn't understand the position of others. If someone turned up late for a meeting, I would get the blame . . . It became very difficult for me, because he wanted my car all the time. And so twice or thrice I would send him the car and I found that the driver would say, he's called me again tomorrow. I had to tell him that my car was going for servicing and it's somebody else's car. He is very tight-fisted, there is no question about that . . . I was an editor, so I had a secretary, and I had staff. I thought initially that maybe the great writer doesn't want to get involved in mundane things like booking an air ticket, or getting a taxi. But Vidia went a little further and suggested he just couldn't do this, that it was beyond him somehow: 'Oh, it is very complicated, you know.' When Margaret was there he just transferred everything on to her. Her devotion to Vidia was so total and complete, but I don't think she was a very intelligent person. He used her shamelessly.

Mehta was aware that Vidia's stimulating conversation and 'great sympathy' when he learned that he had been sacked from his previous job did not mean their relationship was on any normal footing. 'I never got the impression he was grateful. He expected it of me, as if I was privileged in the sense of aiding him in that great venture. I was a source, a handler, then I became a friend. After twenty years this didn't extend to him giving me his telephone number. I think overall he is one of the most complex human beings I've met: I've never met anyone as insightful, or as brilliant. But he is certainly not an easy person to know . . . He was not a person who was going to tell you a great deal about himself. His books will tell you about himself, but he won't tell you.'[5]

India: A Million Mutinies Now started well, and got better. 'Bombay is a crowd. But I began to feel, when I was some way into the city from the airport that morning, that the crowd on the pavement and the road was very great, and that something unusual might be happening.'[6] Something was happening: a celebration of the Dalit leader, Dr Ambedkar. India was at the beginning of a social, political and economic upheaval that would lead to the nation's triumphant rise at the end of the century, a million mutinies leading to a new phase of creativity and progress. 'Independence had come to India like a kind of revolution; now there were many revolutions within that revolution.'[7] Once again, Vidia sensed that something important was taking place in a country where others still saw only a continuation of old patterns. The book would be long – too long – but exceptional in its narrative perception. In the first section, set in Bombay, he wrote of Dalits, of local political leaders, of activism, of people who were raising themselves and their communities from difficult beginnings. The author is present in the text, enquiring on behalf of the reader. A Muslim tells of seeing a man murdered when he was a boy; Vidia wants details: the man was lying on a handcart with his head nearly severed. 'What clothes?' 'Underwear. Shorts and a singlet. And the body in the throes of death caused the handcart to capsize.'[8] So the reader has a picture of the murder scene. Nor did he hide the role of his guides or interpreters, such as 'Nikhil, a young magazine journalist I had got to know' or 'Charu, a young Maharashtrian brahmin'.[9] The result was a book in which discrete voices were heard, and stories were told that had never been told before. A chapter was devoted to 'The Secretary's Tale', recounting the twists and turns of the unremarkable but somehow representative life of 'Rajan', an assistant to a powerful Bombay politician.

In order to bring this off, Vidia exploited his contacts, driving them hard to deliver the interviewees he wanted in the settings he wanted. Through sheer force of will, using his fame, grandeur, necessity and a pretence of incapability, this least incapable of men found the living subjects he needed. Nikhil Lakshman, the young journalist, took him on an outing to the suburbs:

The trip to Thane and back was really exhausting, a whole day trip. We went by train, first class . . . He didn't pay for the train tickets, he was a 'kanjoos', thrifty, kind of an Uncle Scrooge. Mr Naipaul was an anachronism in his suit and I think he had his felt hat on. When we came back he wanted his shoes shined because obviously there was a lot of dust on the roads of Thane, and at V[ictoria] T[erminus] the shoeshine boy looked at him. He was talking to me about magical realism: he just hit it out of the park, dismissed Márquez with the contempt that he brings so eloquently, 'There's far too much reality in Colombia and writers must express it with realism rather than resort to all these gimmicks.' He was talking and this shoeshine boy who probably came from the same part of the world as Naipaul's ancestors looked at me and said, 'Hamare jaise dikhte hein, lekin angrezi to bolte hein saab jaise', which means, 'He looks like us, but look at his English, he speaks like an Englishman' ... I dropped him off at the Taj and I asked what he was going to do. He was surprised to hear the question. 'I'm going to write up today's notes.' That's what I keep telling [other journalists]: you may be the greatest writer in the world but at the end of the day, you have to go up and write your notes. I really learnt from him that you can't have a dream and not invest that kind of commitment in it. He was the master.

Later, Vidia told Nikhil Lakshman he was too fat. 'He said how are you going to lose weight? I said, I am going to walk. "That's not going to do anything. You've got to enrol in a gymnasium. Is there a gymnasium near your office?" ' He was shocked by Vidia's casual conversation, and the way he spoke of one of his own heroes: 'The *Illustrated Weekly* broke the story in 1988 about this Hindi film actress Neena Gupta having a baby by the West Indian cricketer Vivian Richards. Mr Naipaul said, "How could she have a child by that nigger?" I was appalled. For a lot of us, Viv Richards is God.'[10]

Charudatta Deshpande, the 'Maharashtrian brahmin', a thirty-two-year-old political journalist who had been asked by his editor Vinod Mehta to help Vidia, spent two or three weeks arranging interviews. He made it clear beforehand that he did not like Vidia's earlier books on India. 'I didn't think he had a desire to deliberately distort, but he had a preconceived notion. I believe that he worked from a larger picture and he knew basically what he wanted to see, and tried to fit everything into that conception. It's like creating your own world.' Deshpande was asked to fix a meeting with Vithal Chavan, a local Shiv Sena leader on the fringes of criminality. He asked Vidia if he could telephone him from the Taj: 'I found that he was hesitating. He said when you come up to my room, you'll meet a friend of mine. Then I walked in, and a lady was looking out of the window. I felt that the air was quite hostile, quite tense between them. I talked to Vithal and fixed up the appointment. It was very awkward to stand in that room and not to have any conversation with the lady. I said, so how are you finding India? The moment I broached the subject, she just came out and said, I feel completely bored ... She stayed in the Taj. She would never accompany him.'

At the chawl or slum where Vithal lived, Deshpande interpreted: 'Vithal Chavan couldn't speak in English, Naipaul couldn't understand Marathi. The funny part was Vithal wanted to talk about his political career, and Naipaul was interested in his personal life, how twelve people managed to live in a room. Naipaul would go into excruciating detail, asking what happened to his wife, what happened to his sister, how she ran away, all those details. Vithal got very edgy. I said, a time will come, this person may get a Nobel Prize and I said you'll be very happy that you figured in his book. Vithal told me, it doesn't make a damn difference to me what he writes in English, and look, in case he has some problem with admission for his children to school, let me know, I can fix it. So I told that to Mr Naipaul and he laughed and said, no, no, no, I haven't any admission problems, I don't have kids at all.'[11]

Over the following months, as he travelled through the south and then the north, Vidia collected cuttings, pamphlets and books: *Final Victory is Ours* by the Tamil Eelam Liberation Organization Propaganda Unit, *Rural Development (Village Reform)* by Periyar E.V. Ramasami, *The Anguish of Punjab* by the Council of Sikh Affairs. At each stage, he listened carefully and wrote up his notes in the evening in the hotel in tiny, precise handwriting. His helpers were amazed by his ability to recall detail. Sadanand Menon, a writer from Madras, told Vidia about the Dravidian movement: 'Just once in a while he would pull out a notebook from inside his coat pocket and say, "May I write that down?" Very neat handwriting. He would write down one sentence, then the notebook would go back. Whereas in *A Million Mutinies* he has quoted me for about ten or twelve pages. It is so accurate, every full stop and comma. I was amazed. Later I even asked him, did you carry a tape recorder? Just about every Indian writer in English today unhesitatingly mentions Naipaul as his style guru; his politics is a different matter.'[12] H.V. Nathan – 'Rajan' in 'The Secretary's Tale' – expressed similar feelings: 'I must say he has been absolutely faithful to what I told him. Not a single departure.'[13] Another interviewee, M.D. Riti – 'Kala' in the book – commended the accuracy of his redaction, as did Nasir Abid, a copywriter from Lucknow who was rendered as 'Rashid': 'It was verbatim; he hadn't paraphrased.'[14]

Problems arose however when Vidia was required to assess unreliable information. Sadanand Menon was disappointed by his reaction to 'Naxalite' revolutionaries: 'It so happened that during that time it was the high point of the Maoist movement. A lot of young people were being arrested or killed in "encounters" with the police ... Now to get close to that movement, he made the mistake of contacting the Inspector General of Police [in Madras], who had a huge handlebar moustache. This guy was bringing thirty, forty of these young boys and parading them for Naipaul at the Taj Coromandel Hotel. It was a tragic scene. They were just brought in, paraded as Naxalites and the interpreters were invariably police. It was a fix. I think he got taken for a nice ride there, whereas if he was genuinely interested he could have met more articulate elements of the movement who were writers and poets. It was a joke.'[15] Nor did Vidia like the hotel in Madras: 'This room (which was booked for me quite a while ago) has a filthy carpet,' he wrote to the manager. 'It has no chair, and must be one of the few hotels not to have a chair. It has a television set, but it hasn't been plugged in. I was promised a chair by someone who came to the room. The chair hasn't come.'[16]

Madras was a rare lapse; most of the time, Vidia relied on the background knowledge of unpaid local reporters to ensure the veracity of his interviews. Personal relations were another matter. His behaviour outraged Nasir Abid, twelve years his junior. On the day he was leaving Lucknow, Vidia asked Abid for a further interview.

> So we trooped back into the hotel room and I told him some stories. He was leaving for the airport. 'I know, Nazia – Naipaul could never pronounce my name properly, he cultivated a lot of idiosyncrasies in his mannerisms, in his speech – I know, Nazia, we'll talk on the way to the airport.' I am tired. I have been taking this guy around for five days. I used to miss lunch sometimes. So I made a wry face. 'I'm coming to the airport with you, am I?' Then I realized what a big blunder I had committed. He clammed up and said, 'I appreciate what you have done for me.' So he paid the hotel bill and he got into a taxi. I am now feeling miserable for having been so rude. He sits down in the taxi and I say, goodbye, Vidia. I don't get any reply from him. Vidia, goodbye. The car engine started. A third time I tried, Vidia, goodbye. He didn't reply. He turned his face and the taxi left. That really hurt ... He took advantage of the Indian tradition of hospitality.[17]

By now, Margaret was no longer travelling with Vidia, having been dismissed in New Delhi. The split came after a meeting with a cub reporter from the *Sunday Observer*: in Vidia's words, 'Somebody said to me, you must talk to Harinder Baweja about the guerrilla crisis in the Punjab, so I invited her to dinner. Harinder is a very small Sikh lady, very nice. So I talked to her. I was leaning across the table. Margaret was enraged. "You ignored me all evening." I couldn't deal with that. So I had to send her home.'[18] Harinder Baweja was unaware that her briefing had provoked a serious rupture: 'Naipaul was treating [Margaret] badly and she was taking it, pecking at her food, getting angrier and angrier, behaving worse than a submissive Indian wife.'[19]

Some people were entertained by Vidia's manner and style. In Calcutta he and Margaret had dinner with Malavika Sanghvi and her husband Vir, both upcoming journalists, who served Dom Perignon and black-market Russian caviar. Malavika found Vidia 'a charming gentleman, very interested, asking a lot of questions about our lives. Vir asked him why he hadn't gone out in Calcutta, and he said he feared going to an intellectual's house and at the end of the evening a lady presenting him with a slim volume of poetry. I had just published a volume of poetry, and it was lying on the table waiting to be presented to the great man. So I hid it under the sofa!'[20] Vir asked Vidia about the book he was writing: 'He said he had changed his mind about India, that when he first came it was a very different place . . . but now it was transformed. He said, "I find so much energy, I find so much happening." Then we discussed whether he would ever get the Nobel Prize and he said, "Of course I won't get it, they'll give it to some nigger or other." But everybody was drunk and it may have been said in a jokey sort of way.' Vir Sanghvi felt that Vidia's relationship with Margaret was friendly, and that she was 'his window to the world. She seemed to complement Naipaul. She made all his calls, all his arrangements. I said something about *The Return of Eva Perón*, and Margaret got extremely agitated and said the book just showed that he didn't understand Argentina at all, and he had got it completely wrong, he got the men wrong because this is not the way Argentinian men treat their women. "Vidia, you really shouldn't go to countries you know nothing about." And he took it with very good grace, he giggled and laughed. It was obvious they had had this conversation before.'[21] Later, when Vidia called Vir Sanghvi's office, the staffer who picked up the telephone failed to believe that he was speaking to V.S. Naipaul. 'He said, "Oh yes, I'm Salman Rushdie." So Naipaul said, "Well, ring me at the Oberoi." So the guy called up, and was put through to a pastry chef whose name was Nagpal.'[22]

During his months of travel for *India: A Million Mutinies Now*, Vidia opened himself to a new vision of the country. To the surprise of readers of his earlier books, he saw beyond the corruption and violence to something original and redemptive. It was a personal homecoming, as he continued to seek an ancestral past, trying to link himself to a nation that was, in his imagination, his own source. He travelled to Kashmir and met Mr Butt and Aziz from the Liward Hotel; he went to the south to find another memory of 1962, a pilgrim from Amarnath named V.C. Chakravarthy, whom he renamed 'Sugar' in the book. Often, Vidia was lionized. When he went to the Punjab to a site of recent, terrible slaughter, a police chief who was suppressing the separatist militancy was so delighted by his eminent visitor that he flew him back to Delhi by helicopter. Vidia's inclinations were becoming increasingly authoritarian, although he still upheld the dignity of the individual. As he told a visiting interviewer from *Time* who had caught up with him in Madras, ' "I'm for individual rights and for law." It's a long view that includes his fascination with ancient Rome ("I can barely express my admiration for it") and the imperial record of the English.'[23] To those he encountered during his long journey, though, V.S. Naipaul seemed in his operating methods and self-assertion and racial statements to come from a different, halfway world, as he sought to out-Indian the Indians: in his appearance and performance, he had emerged from an unfamiliar, faraway island. Nasir Abid noted how he dressed in Lucknow. 'He was wearing a tropical suit. His collar buttoned. It was very hot. Short white trousers with white socks showing. Loafers with a little bow. His skin was parched, like dried wood, walnut . . . If he kept his hat on he could pass off easily as a Negro. He looked more like a Chicago mobster with that hat, tight collar. He didn't look like your ordinary run-of-the-mill Indian. No Indian buttons his collar without a tie.'[24]

When the book was published in late 1990 the reviews were good, and importantly for Vidia, the sales were too. Large extracts ran in the London *Sunday Telegraph*; he journeyed through the United States, being paid to lecture; he won the Premio Nonino and the British Book Awards prize for the best travel book of the year. His publisher, Helen

Fraser at Heinemann, told him he was at number ten in the *Sunday Times* bestseller list. 'We are absolutely thrilled. The paperback has reprinted 3 times and copies in print are up to 60,000.'[25] For Paul Theroux, *India: A Million Mutinies Now* was 'literally the last word on India today, witness within witness, a chain of voices . . . from the so-called Untouchable, the Dalit, to the maharajah.'[26] *Tatler* praised Naipaul's 'dramatic change of tone'.[27] In the *Financial Times*, K. Natwar Singh deduced that he 'may well have written his own enduring monument'.[28] Janette Turner Hospital in the *New York Times* observed, 'No sensory detail, no sign or symbol, is too small for Mr Naipaul's attention,' but felt he had neglected to interview enough women.[29] Auberon Waugh found that the cruelty had disappeared from Naipaul's wit: 'He has become a gentler, kinder, infinitely more tolerant person. His sympathies extend to everyone, the religious and the anti-religious, even to the Muslims.'[30] Ian Buruma wrote in the *New York Review*: 'The extraordinary achievement of Naipaul's latest book is that we can see his characters; more than that, we can see how they see, and how they, in turn, are seen by the author . . . Whatever his literary form Naipaul is a master.'[31] From another perspective, the maverick polymath T.G. Vaidyanathan noticed that although the book was 'an ostensible paean to the triumph of subaltern India over the centuries-old might of Upanishadic India' it was in fact a respectful 'elegy to Brahminism'. T.G.V. had no doubt which community V.S. Naipaul admired most: 'The Brahmin, then, is the real hero of the book.'[32]

*

As the 1980s drew to a close and the manuscript of *India: A Million Mutinies Now* approached completion, Vidia received letters, the first from Lingston Cumberbatch, acting high commissioner, offering him Trinidad and Tobago's highest award, the Trinity Cross, and another proffering a knighthood from the Queen in the 1990 New Year's honours list. Although he had turned down the opportunity to become a Commander of the Order of the British Empire in 1977, this time Vidia succumbed to the blandishments of flummery. Like Sir Walter Raleigh before him, he went down on one knee before his monarch and arose a knight. Letters came: from John Fawcett of Univ days, from Jim Allen in Kenya, from Jan Carew's old flatmate, from Angus Wilson in a Suffolk nursing home, from his bank manager ('Dear Sir Videadhar'), from Lol O'Keefe in the British Embassy in Prague, from the Spanish ambassador, from his French publisher Ivan Nabokov, from Anthony and Violet Powell ('I had long felt that an honour was overdue'), from David Pryce-Jones ('England has been lucky to have you, and is saying so') and from Hugh Thomas ('I wish you wd come soon to the Lords too for it is a complacent place & needs your attention'). The most moving letter contained a single sentence – 'We are both glad that we were there at the beginning' – followed by two names: André, Diana.

'It was a very low-key affair. I went alone, wearing a charcoal grey Daks suit. I took an Underground train to St James's Park, and walked to the palace. People were snapping away; I had no photographer with me. We had lunch afterwards at the Bombay Brasserie with the Suttons [his old Univ friend James Sutton and his wife].'[33] A few days after attending the investiture at Buckingham Palace, Vidia flew home. At Piarco airport, in Kamla's words, 'A taxi driver recognized Vidia and welcomed him. "Come Mr Naipaul, let me take you, eh? These people don't like you, you know." '[34] One afternoon, while he was staying at Kamla's house, Vidia was greeted by an unexpected face. In his late sixties, his writing career over, living in Canada but on a visit to Trinidad to stay with a friend, Sam Selvon had come to say hello to his old flame Kamla. His friend Ken Ramchand described the encounter:

> Naipaul says, 'What are you doing here?' Sam says, 'How you axing me a thing like that? I ent locked in to the writing like you, I ent no proper writer. If I up in Canada and the cold bussin' my arse an' I decide to go by Ken and have a few drink and thing, I just go by he.' Naipaul didn't take it amiss. He was a bit patronizing. He says: 'I see your books are on the CXC [Caribbean Examinations Council] syllabus, you must be making some money.' It was a cordial meeting, with a little bit of needle introduced by Sam ... He says, 'Ken get a boat, we goin' fishin' in de mornin'. We passin' for you at 4 o'clock, you be ready and waiting.' Vidia says he will be. When we leave, I say to Sam, 'Why you say that, you want to impress your brother-in law?'

The next morning, Vidia was ready and waiting. As the three men drove through the dawn light to Cedros to pick up some food from Ken's mother's house – Ken taught at the University of the West Indies; his father had been a motor mechanic on a coconut estate – Vidia stuck his head between the two front seats to listen to a story that Sam was telling about a woman. 'And Vidia says, "What she say to that?" For the rest of the trip, he spoke dialect, he relaxed, became one of the boys.' In Cedros, they were each given a bag containing two rotis:

> Vidia says, 'I will have one now.' Sam says, 'Don't you go be axing me for one on de boat.' I had hired a boat, a pirogue. It was about twenty-foot long, pointed at the front, with an outboard at the back. We went to Soldado Rock [in the Gulf of Paria], looked at Venezuela in the distance. Sam said he wanted to swim. It was a real hot day. Vidia says, 'I would love to, but I don't have my bathing things.' Sam says, 'I swimmin' in my jockey shorts.' Vidia says, 'I can't do that.' We were in the sea, then kerplunk, V.S. Naipaul was in the water, swimming around the boat in his jockey shorts.[35]

With a high literacy rate and growing national wealth from the export of natural gas, Trinidad was some way ahead of the island Vidia had left behind in 1950. He received the Trinity Cross from the hand of Noor Hassanali, the country's first Indian president (there was yet to be an Indian prime minister). 'Happy Naipaul gets his Trinity' was the lead headline in the *Guardian*, with a photograph of the proud scholarship boy and his beaming mother. ' "I'm glad that this has happened," Sir Vidia said of the award ... Asked whether he still considered Trinidad and Tobago and the rest of the Caribbean as a backward place as he had stated in his earlier writings, Sir Vidia said he preferred not to answer. "These are immense questions, my life's work is about that" ... Sir Vidia's mother, Droapatie Naipaul, also attended the award ceremony. "I can't explain how happy I feel," Mrs Naipaul said tearfully, explaining that it was her son's first visit since 1984.'[36] Savi gave a party in Vidia's honour, at which he wore the Trinity Cross on a ribbon around his neck. 'Talk about country bookie, wearing the cross in that way,' said a guest, Margaret Walcott. 'It showed a side of him that was very human.'[37] Despite the photo in the *Guardian*, Vidia and his mother were not properly reconciled. Not long before she died, Nella went to visit her and said, 'So how is your son?' Ma replied, 'I have no son. The son I had died.'[38]

Only months later, in January 1991, at the age of seventy-eight, Ma passed away in her sleep. The prime minister, A.N.R. Robinson, wrote to Vidia expressing his deepest sympathy. 'Truly, she was the matriarch of one of this country's most distinguished families ever, and the nation is deeply indebted to her.'³⁹ Her surviving son did not go back to attend her funeral, though later that year he visited Guyana and wrote a sympathetic portrait of Cheddi and Janet Jagan, and in 1992 gave a lecture in Trinidad organized by Selby Wooding, at which he met his old QRC friend William Demas, now an eminent economist. Having read *The Loss of El Dorado*, Demas spoke of the cruelty of slavery in the days of the governor Thomas Picton, and suggested his name be removed from the Port of Spain street that bore it. 'It was strange to me (though perhaps it shouldn't have been) to find that in his sixties, and with his success, Demas should have developed racial nerves which I don't think he had had >(or shown)< when we were at school together fifty years before.'⁴⁰

Back in England, Vidia had more awards to face: an honorary degree from Oxford in the company of bedels, proctors, Dame Joan Sutherland and the Queen of Denmark; Trinidad's Humming Bird Medal, which had been given to him in 1970 but never delivered; an honorary degree from the universities of York and London; membership of the happening Harbour Club – one day he found himself exercising alongside Princess Diana, only realizing later that it was the princess herself, rather than a young woman trying to look like the princess. In 1993 he won the first ever David Cohen British Literature Prize, awarded for a lifetime's achievement. In his acceptance speech, he suggested it might have gone instead to Harold Pinter or to Anthony Powell. Pinter wrote in his giant, disjointed hand that he was 'very touched' by the reference, and invited Vidia and Pat to watch his play *No Man's Land* and have supper.⁴¹ 'I cannot remember sitting next to Vidia emanating approval and enjoyment to that degree for so long for years and years,' Pat wrote to Harold and Antonia afterwards.⁴² David Pryce-Jones, always slick with a compliment, told Vidia he deserved to win the prize every year: 'Nobody else has contributed to our literature as much as you. This old island has no right to be the recipient of your gifts, and you do it an honour by being here. I'm so glad that due notice is being taken.'⁴³

The year ended badly, when Vidia was banned from driving. Pat blamed herself in her diary: 'We went to have dinner with Barbara Neill & Andrew Christie Miller at Clarendon Park in order to meet Francis. I criminally discouraged him from summoning Michael [a taxi driver]. Following instructions to turn right twice finding our way home Vidia drove across the A36 dual carriageway, was stopped by police, breathalised and arrested.'[44] In his column in the London *Evening Standard*, A.N. Wilson wrote, 'We have many goodish writers in this country but few great ones, and V.S. Naipaul is a great writer. He should be cherished, not persecuted. If he happens to be found by the police rather the worse for wear on the public highway, they should have the courtesy to drive him home and tuck him up in bed instead of dragging him through the courts.'[45]

As Vidia's global status developed and stabilized around this time, he made a rare attempt to analyse his own philosophy in an address to the Manhattan Institute in New York. Speaking on the title 'Our Universal Civilization', he suggested in optimistic, even idealistic tones, that a universal civilization or modernity now existed in the world. It had been 'a long time in the making' and transcended any racial boundaries. As a child, 'worried about pain and cruelty' he had discovered 'the Christian precept, Do unto others as you would have others do unto you. There was no such human consolation in the Hinduism I grew up with, and – although I have never had any religious faith – the simple idea was, and is, dazzling to me, perfect as a guide to human behaviour.' Later, he had come to see 'the beauty of the idea of the pursuit of happiness. Familiar words, easy to take for granted; easy to misconstrue. This idea of the pursuit of happiness is at the heart of the attractiveness of the civilization to so many outside it or on its periphery. I find it marvellous to contemplate to what an extent, after two centuries, and after the terrible history of the earlier part of this century, the idea has come to a kind of fruition. It is an elastic idea; it fits all men. It implies a certain kind of society, a certain kind of awakened spirit. I don't imagine my father's parents would have been able to understand the idea. So much is contained in it: the idea of the individual, responsibility, choice, the life of the intellect, the idea of vocation and perfectibility and achievement. It is an immense human idea. It cannot be reduced to a fixed system. It cannot generate fanaticism. But it is known to exist; and because of that, other more rigid systems in the end blow away.'[46]

As the legend of V.S. Naipaul grew, would-be biographers sought him out. The first candidate was Jeffrey Meyers FRSL, a serial producer of books and articles, living in California. With verbal encouragement from Vidia, he began collecting material and planning a book of essays as an accompaniment to an authorized biography, and asked around American institutions to see if they wanted to buy his literary archives.

Meyers went to see Paul Theroux, now living in Cape Cod. 'This man is not a shrinking violet,' Vidia was informed by Paul, no viola himself. 'He and Mrs Meyers were in my library yanking books off the shelves even before we were introduced (Sheila [the second Mrs Theroux] let them into the house). Such nosiness is probably in the biographer's temperament but I found him intrusive – and also over-certain and dogmatic.'[47] Enquiries and closely typed letters from Meyers arrived at Dairy Cottage ('This month I had essays in the American Scholar, the New Criterion and the Virginia Quarterly Review') until, after more than a year of work, Gillon Aitken was told to put him out of his misery.[48] Caught between his sure-footed attackers, Meyers did not know what had happened. He believed he had been betrayed by Vidia and his 'hitman' Gillon. Naipaul was 'a great manipulator, a great manager of his own reputation and public image. He thought he could order a biography as one might a publicity release ... I broke off relations with him, and felt lucky to escape with my wits and integrity intact.'[49] Next came Ian Buruma, a highbrow journalist, who told Vidia in 1993 that he would be interested in writing about his life as a writer but that, 'To understand you as a man, other, more private friendships and relationships cannot be left unmentioned.'[50] Dealing obliquely with Buruma, using Gillon as his necessary foil, Vidia left the matter hanging while agreeing to a long-term biographical venture.

For all the lauding, Vidia knew he had to write the book he had contracted to Knopf and Heinemann. In March 1992 he sent an enigmatic letter to his agent, intended for onward transmission to his publishers, saying that he had started work on *A Way in the World*. 'The book is not in the standard novel form; it is a sequence of narrations and I believe its effect will be more concentrated than the standard form would have been.'[51] In another letter on the same day, he told Gillon he faced a major operation on his back to relieve compression caused by a narrowing of the lower spine. Bone spurs had developed, exacerbated by the rigour of his old exercise routine, and needed to be cut away. He feared permanent incapacity. The pain had been with him for months. 'For a year I couldn't walk. I could walk for about a hundred yards in total during the day. I was writing through all of that, doing hard writing.'[52] The operation took place at New Hall Hospital in Salisbury, paid for by his private health insurance.

Vidia spent the rest of the year convalescing, depressed, but still writing. When a mosque built by the Mughal emperor Babur in

Ayodhya was smashed by Hindu zealots in December, he felt a surge of excitement. In his pain and anger and contrariness, Vidia seized on an event that was being presented by the world's media as the end of Indian secularism, and decided it represented evidence of regeneration. He gave an interview to the *Times of India* which suggested in guarded terms that he approved of what had happened: 'One needs to understand the passion that took them on top of the domes. The jeans and the T-shirts are superficial. The passion alone is real. You can't dismiss it . . . The movement is now from below . . . Wise men should understand it and ensure that it does not remain in the hands of fanatics. Rather they should use it for the intellectual transformation of India.'[53] Letters of applause arrived from supporters of Hindu assertiveness, in India and abroad. Vidia defended his stand over the coming years, his opinions luring him to greater controversy. 'For the poor of India to identify something like this, pulling down the first Mughal emperor's tomb, is a marvellous idea. I think in years to come it will be seen as a great moment, and it will probably become a public holiday. It would be a historical statement of India striving to regain her soul.' Hindu nationalists planned to excavate beneath the mosque in order to find the birthplace of the deity Ram; but Ram was a mythological figure. It was a mystical view of history, lacking rigour, choosing pieces of evidence that supported the idea of undoing the past. 'What puzzled me and outraged me was the attitude that it was wrong, that one mustn't undo the [Muslim] conquest. I think it is the attitude of a slave population.' The political fragmentation and the hundreds of deaths in the rioting that followed the destruction of the Babri Masjid were not his concern: 'I didn't kill them myself. What was I doing in 1992? That was a very bad year. That was the year when I could barely walk. I had surgery on my spine.'[54]

Other problems had occurred during that year. Pat's breast cancer returned, and in May she followed Vidia to New Hall Hospital for treatment, using her health insurance. In January 1993, she had a further surgical procedure at Chalybeate, a private hospital in Southampton, and in April received radiotherapy and chemotherapy in an effort to bring the disease in her remaining left breast under control. Pat's mother had died the previous summer after a long stretch with Alzheimer's disease. Vidia found that the house he had bought her in Birmingham was hard to sell, and kept it. Eleanor dealt with the practicalities, writing to 'Dear Lady Pat!' about fixtures and fittings.

The sisters shared £7,000 from their mother's will. Pat spoke occasionally to her father on the telephone, but still refused to see him, despite cards and letters describing his decline. She kept in touch with Auntie Lu, who was ailing, in and out of hospital, and worried that 'Socialism & the Welfare State has ruined the character of most people.'[55] Pat's life was circumscribed, but she had glimpses of light: a kind letter from John Wells praising her delicious scallops, a contact from an old pupil at Rosa Bassett School whose life had been inspired by her teaching, a copy of a letter to Hugh and Vanessa Thomas from a man she had met at dinner: 'When I sat down next to Lady Naipaul, I thought it best to explain that I could not see her because I am blind in my left eye. She said: Well I am not much to look at at any rate . . . But she seemed to me to be a delightful person in every way . . . when you next see her – and using a subtle charm that I don't possess – can you tell her that she is very pretty.'[56] About once a year, Eleanor would visit Dairy Cottage. She had given up teaching, and was now working as a coach driver at a special needs school in Birmingham: 'I used to go down and pick a lot of their fruit. Vidia liked me to take the elderberries because the birds used to take them and crap all over the patio. Big purple blobs. About four years before she died, Pat told me she was in hospital, and then someone called Angela got the fruit. Pat wouldn't tell me what was wrong, so I guessed it was something below the waist. Then she said it was cancer, a few months before she died. We went out for a meal in Salisbury. Vidia was abroad.'[57]

Aged sixty, thinking of death and posterity, aware of his own mortality and Pat's illness, Vidia arranged for his archives to be valued for sale. They were sitting in numbered box files in the warehouse of Ely's of Wimbledon: the novel he had begun in Trinidad in 1949, the manuscript of *The Shadow'd Livery*, his translation of *Lazarillo de Tormes*, his scripts for BBC *Caribbean Voices*, his diaries from his years at Oxford, his journals for *The Middle Passage*, the manuscripts and typescripts of all the books he had written before moving to Wiltshire, notes and letters from his first trip to India in 1962, most of the letters he had received in the 1950s and sixties, his own 'Letters from London' for the *Illustrated Weekly of India*, his travel journals from Africa in 1966, and the notebooks and diaries of his early journalism. When Pat went to retrieve them, they were all gone. After investigation, it turned out that Ely's, instructed to destroy files marked NITRATE (belonging to the Nitrate Corporation of Chile) had taken those marked NAIPAUL as well. Having spent a lifetime meticulously recording himself, Vidia had lost around a third of his total archive.[58] Always conscious of his own projected destiny, he had preserved everything. 'I kept it for the record. I am a great believer in the record, that the truth is wonderful and that any doctored truth is awful. Doctored truth is not truth. I destroyed nothing. I think the completeness of a record is what matters. I have great trouble reading other people's autobiographies because I feel it is doctored. So the stuff that was destroyed in the warehouse, lots of embarrassing things, that was part of the record.'[59]

Two other things occurred on the day that he heard news of the loss, 8 October 1992. Gillon Aitken received a letter from Jeffrey Meyers observing, 'Vidia's work deserves the Nobel Prize. There are also very strong racial, geographical and linguistic qualifications in his favor. But candidates don't win the prize on merit alone.'[60] And the Swedish Academy made an announcement of the winner of that year's Nobel Prize in Literature: Derek Walcott. Under the convention of regional rotation, it meant that the chances of another writer of Caribbean origin writing in the English language winning the Nobel over the next decade were slim. Walcott compounded his offence by devoting his Nobel Lecture to a passionate defence of the glories of Caribbean ethnic diversity. His opening sentence ran:

> Felicity is a village in Trinidad on the edge of the Caroni plain, the wide central plain that still grows sugar and to which indentured cane cutters were brought after emancipation, so the small population of Felicity is East Indian, and on the afternoon that I visited it with friends from America, all the faces along its road were Indian, which, as I hope to show, was a moving, beautiful thing, because this Saturday afternoon *Ramleela*, the epic dramatization of the Hindu epic the *Ramayana*, was going to be performed, and the costumed actors from the village were assembling on a field strung with different-coloured flags, like a new gas station, and beautiful Indian boys in red and black were aiming arrows haphazardly into the afternoon light.[61]

Vidia returned to work on *A Way in the World*. Although the book had an odd and seemingly haphazard structure, he had thought out its pattern some years before. It was a 'sequence', using a literary technique he had first tried in *In a Free State*. It was also a return to the West Indies and to his own origins, a reworking of what he saw as his dud book, *The Loss of El Dorado*. The fate of the region's postcolonial political activists had been on his mind since he wrote *The Mimic Men*. In 1982, Pat had written in her diary: 'He has gone back to this thing, he says apologetically, the Eric Williams figure – he doesn't want to write about black people but he hasn't anything else to write about.' In May 1993, she wrote, 'Reflecting a little, about Vidia & his present writing. Phrase occurred to me, as it does now & again: he had "sold out". [A] *Way* [*in the World*]' is, in effect, answering the rather reflexive – and not reflective! – remarks and reactions of "black"/"negro" individuals and interest groups.' Despite this, Pat liked the book – a form of approval that was always of great importance to Vidia. That summer, she recorded this conversation: 'He then said that Gillon had sent the completed stories to Andrew Wylie (who liked them) and said he was "at the top of his form". He said later in the day that he was "excited" that I liked it.'[62]

Many of the ideas and themes in *A Way in the World* emerged from a little notebook that Vidia had been keeping since 1977: 'Hassanali, the artist from St James – "I went to see him at the funeral home. The girl at the desk said, "Go right in." He was there, neat and dapper, dressing a body" . . . Odette sells "wines" . . . Francisco Martinez . . . sat next to me on the LAV flight to Caracas. A small elderly man with the broad wrinkled brown face of a coastal mestizo . . . his curly hair tied up at the back in the manner of an 18th century wig.'[63] In another notebook, under the heading 'stories', he wrote: 'The Red House – Fish-glue, Arthur Calder-Marshall . . . CLR James – beginning with the dark copy of his book in the v dark bookcase in the 6th form at QRC, Eric Williams & his daughter, Deutsch . . . Andrew [Vidia's driver in Makerere], Walter Rodney [a black Marxist he had met in Tanzania], Jim Allen, Rajat, Paul.'[64] He also had press cuttings, located by Kamla, about the funeral of C.L.R. James in 1989 after his body was flown home from England at the expense of the Trinidad government. Kamla added her memories of the event, which she had watched on television: 'The wife a small, neat woman appeared mixed and her son was more white than anything else.' She kept her brother stocked with news from Trinidad, and ideas that would spark his writing. 'They fed some of the mad people at St Ann's some bad eggnog and so far, 13 of them have died. Some are wondering if the milk came from Chernobyl. The police were supposed to have produced some 128 pieces of crack to nab a pusher but they couldn't find the crack. The police said rats ate the crack.'[65]

A Way in the World contained some beautiful writing and immensely
subtle thinking, but like *The Enigma of Arrival* it held a marginal appeal
for the general reader. Marketed as 'A Sequence' in Britain and 'A
Novel' in America, it began with a 'Prelude' about a trip to Trinidad
where the author was told by a schoolteacher about 'Leonard Side, a
decorator of cakes and arranger of flowers' who dressed bodies at
Parry's Funeral Parlour, using his hairy fingers for each of the three
jobs.[66] (The teacher was Kamla, Leonard Side was Hassanali; like the
surname of Edward Said, Side was a corruption of the Muslim name
Sayed.) A slice of slightly fictional autobiography follows, about the
young narrator working as a clerk in the Red House. Indirectly,
Naipaul brings the narrative back to the present, describing the 'black
men and women dressed like Arabs' who had appeared in Port of
Spain.[67] In July 1990, calling themselves the Jamaat al Muslimeen, they
stormed the Red House, killed people and held the prime minister and
cabinet hostage. History loops again now, and the chapter ends with 'an
English marauder' putting the Spaniards to flight, and finding in the
island's gaol, 'the last aboriginal rulers of the land, held together on
one chain, scalded with hot bacon fat, and broken by other punishments.'[68] Returning to the material he had used in *The Loss of El
Dorado*, Naipaul deconstructs the next story even before he tells it. 'The
narrator is going up a highland river in an unnamed South American
country. Who is this narrator? What can he be made to be?'[69] Using
ideas that would be replicated in *Magic Seeds*, he is made to travel
through the forest on some revolutionary mission, following his guides.
One of them, a boy, he seduces; later he is presented with a perished
Tudor doublet, sent by an earlier foreign visitor, 'new clothes of three
hundred and fifty years before, relic of an old betrayal'.[70]

In 'Passenger: A Figure from the Thirties', Naipaul again merges
complex memory and imagination, examining a well-worn subject in a
wholly original way. He looks at Trinidad, the physical island, on a
trip to Point Galera and sees it through the eyes of Columbus, thinking
that the point was named not for a large 'galley shape' on land. Rather,
'black rocks and twisted trees off the point of the island would have
reminded him of a galley under sail: the rocks standing for the galley,
the twisted trees standing for the sails . . . I had never tried to do that
as a child: pretend I was looking at the aboriginal island. No teacher or
anyone else had suggested it as an imaginative exercise.'[71] As he was
growing up, representations of the West Indies could be found mainly

in books by white visitors. He thought 'the writers of these travel books were really acting, acting being writers, acting being travellers, and, especially, acting being travellers in the colonies.' They could say whatever they wanted about the people they saw, for there was nobody to contradict them. Indians might be ignored as 'a people apart', and Africans 'might be put into new and squeaky two-toned shoes; and the writer might go on to say that Africans were so fond of squeaky shoes that they took brand-new shoes to shoemakers and asked them to "put in a squeak".'[72]

'And then in 1937 a young English writer called Foster Morris came and wrote *The Shadowed Livery*, which was another kind of book.' He wrote of the oilfield workers' strike led by Tubal Uriah "Buzz" Butler, and treated Butler and the people around him 'as though they were English people – as though they had that kind of social depth and solidity and rootedness.' But Foster Morris, 'with all his wish to applaud us, didn't understand the nature of our deprivation.' He failed to see that though Butler was treated as a messiah, he was also viewed by the same people as 'a crazed and uneducated African preacher, a Grenadian, a small-islander, an eater of ground provisions boiled in a pitch oil tin.' Butler was interned during the war, and on release 'went away for long stretches to England, "to take the cold", as it was said; and he was supported by contributions from his old Grenadian supporters. Once, when he came back, he insisted on thanking the crew of the aeroplane.' Then, while working at the BBC in the 1950s, Vidia – or the narrator – meets Foster Morris, who is reviewing books for a Caribbean radio show because his literary career is failing. Vidia shows him the manuscript of his own first novel, and is told to abandon it. Foster Morris then explains that the views he expressed in *The Shadowed Livery* were not sincere: he thought Butler was a racial fanatic, but did not say so for fear of encouraging the reactionaries in the colonial government. And he had been sexually taunted by one of Butler's associates, a Trinidadian-Panamanian communist named Lebrun.[73]

Everything is turned on its head here. A book which appeared to give voice to a subject people was not what it seemed, and its author did not believe what he wrote. But that was not all: Foster Morris did not exist; *The Shadowed Livery* was, with an apostrophe, Vidia's first book; its rejector was Arthur Calder Marshall, the reviewer at BBC *Caribbean Voices* who had in 1939 published *Glory Dead*, a travel book about Trinidad which presented itself as being on the side of the oil workers, and praised "Buzz" Butler and Adrian Cola Rienzi as men of the future. 'A new spirit has arisen among the workers. They have tasted freedom; they begin to know their power.'[74] As for Lebrun, the subject of the next chapter of *A Way in the World*, he was clearly modelled on C.L.R. James (though his name may have been borrowed from Learie's father Lebrun Constantine, a famous Trinidad cricketer himself). He is the author of a book on early Spanish-American revolutionaries, such as Francisco de Miranda, which was kept unread in a glass bookcase at Queen's Royal College. In old age, Lebrun lands up in England, 'in a world greatly changed, where black men were an important subject' and ' "discovered" as one of the prophets of black revolution'.[75] In the pages that follow, the narrator alternates between admiration for Lebrun's critical perception and abilities as a talker, and distrust for his political ambitions. He sees him as one of 'the first generation of educated black men in the region' who 'talked big in one place – the United States, England, the West Indies, Panama, Belize – about the things they were doing somewhere else.'[76] Most of all, the narrator feels unease at an attempt by admirers of Lebrun to co-opt him; at a dinner in New York (this part is fiction) gefilte fish is prepared in his honour: 'The idea of something pounded to paste, then spiced or oiled, worked on by fingers, brought to mind thoughts of hand lotions and other things. I became fearful of smelling it. I couldn't eat it.'[77] Lebrun is caught by the Back-to-Africa movement and ends up promoting tyrannous regimes, but in the end Vidia – or the narrator – gives him a soft landing:

> The profile-writers and the television interviewers, who promoted him with self-conscious virtue, were serving a cause that had long ago been won. They risked nothing at all. They had no means of understanding or assessing a man who had been born early in the century into a very hard world, whose intellectual growth had at every stage been accompanied by a growing rawness of sensibility, and whose political resolutions, expressing the wish not to go mad, had been in the nature of spiritual struggles, occurring in the depth of his being.[78]

At this point, Naipaul goes back in time to earlier pirates of the Caribbean, and the book goes off the boil. Using his knowledge from *The Loss of El Dorado*, he imagines a conversation between Walter Raleigh and a ship's surgeon, much of which reads like didactic historical fiction. Another story concerns Lebrun's subject Miranda, and here too the historical learning is obscure and detailed, presupposing a knowledge of the region and its past. Only in the final section, 'Home Again', does the narrative lift. The narrator is in an unnamed East African country, living in a compound like the one at Makerere. 'The country was a tyranny. But in those days not many people minded. Africa had just begun to be independent, and the reputation of the president was that of a good man using his authority only to build socialism.'[79] The social interchange within the compound is brilliantly done, the competition between blacks and whites, and the hierarchy of houseboys. A visitor arrives, Blair, a tall man last encountered working as a civil servant in the Red House, and now an international figure come to advise the government. Blair crosses the president, and is murdered at a showpiece banana plantation. He is fictional, though inspired by Walter Rodney, the author of *How Europe Underdeveloped Africa*, a pan-Africanist and devotee of C.L.R. James who was assassinated by a car-bomb in Georgetown, Guyana, in 1980. The narrator imagines his death, 'a big man floundering about in silence in his big, shiny-soled leather shoes in the soft mulch, between his sure-footed attackers. There would have been a moment in that great silence when he would have known that he was being destroyed, that his attackers intended to go to the limit; and he would have known why. And I feel that if, as in some Edgar Allan Poe story, at the moment of death, while the brain still sparked, a question could have been lodged in that brain – "Does this betrayal mock your life?" – the answer immediately after death would have been, "No! No! No!" '[80] Again, it was an affirmation. In the last sentences of *A Way in the World*, the author considers the return of Blair's body to Trinidad, and its arrival at the airport: 'Would the embalmed body in its box then have been transferred to a hearse? The hearse didn't seem right. I made inquiries. I was told that the box would have been taken away in an ambulance to Port of Spain, and then the shell of the man would have been laid out in Parry's chapel of rest.'[81] We are back with Leonard Side.

Taking nearly two years, Vidia had written a work of many layers, a text of great depth and complexity which circled back and forth over itself and his own earlier writings. It dealt with historical subjects that were unfamiliar to most of his readers, and much of the book remained mysterious even to the Caribbean intelligentsia. In the *Trinidad Guardian*, Wayne Brown spent three successive Sundays attempting to decode

A Way in the World: V.S. Naipaul seemed to have 'mellowed' and was showing an 'inclusive comprehension' of human frailty, giving his characters a dignity that was lacking in earlier books.[82] American reviews were good. Michiko Kakutani thought it was 'less a conventional narrative than a free-form essay on Mr Naipaul's continuing efforts to come to terms with the history of Trinidad' and that its various characters were 'alter egos of sorts for Mr Naipaul'.[83] In Britain, coverage was less enthusiastic, and puzzled. As before, few European or American reviewers were fully able to understand his work. Peter Kemp in the *Sunday Times* thought V.S. Naipaul was endeavouring to overcome writer's block, and that the later material was 'torpid both as narrative and dramatisation'.[84] The African American author Brent Staples wrote in the *New York Times Book Review* that Naipaul suffered 'from expectations about what he *ought* to write, given that he is a brown man (of Indian descent) born into the brown and black society that is Trinidad' but that in his case 'a strictly racial reading amounts to no reading at all'. *A Way in the World* was 'a distinguished book even by Naipaulian standards, a bewitching piece of work by a mind at the peak of its abilities.'[85] In the *New Republic* Caryl Phillips, black British but born in St Kitts, gave a sympathetic review: 'In its deeply moving climax the novel seems to suggest that even Naipaul now realizes that to give up everything to be a writer, particularly the generosity of spirit that allows one to tolerate the foolishness often to be found in one's fellow man, is to commit an act of great folly.'[86]

*

A couple of months before the publication of *A Way in the World*, Vidia flew first class to America for the formal presentation of his archives to the University of Tulsa. The operation on the bone spurs on his back had been a success, and he was feeling fit and ambitious, his hair short and a new beard closely clipped. He submitted to a filmed interview with Professors George H. Gilpin Jr. and Hermione de Almeida, a pair of admiring academics from the university who were married to each other and had, with the help of a representative in London, secured the purchase of his papers.[87] The Bodleian Library at Oxford, hoping the archive might be deposited there free of charge out of gratitude and reverence, had been swiftly dismissed. Using impeccable logic, Gillon Aitken argued to various interested American institutions that the loss of the boxes at Ely's made the remaining material especially valuable: Tulsa, wealthy from oil, produced the money. Gillon sold the archive for $470,000, covering material to the end of 2002, with an additional $150,000 to become available for papers generated during the five years after that date, making a total of $620,000. Pat was a co-signatory to the legal agreement, which specified that 'my wife, Patricia Ann Hale Naipaul, agrees that all correspondence and related material in her possession are an integral part of the Archive according to the terms of this Agreement.'[88] Her diaries would go to Tulsa. The contents of the archive were to remain closed to public access indefinitely, bar the manuscripts and typescripts of Vidia's books, which were open to inspection by literary scholars.

During this period Vidia kept to himself, guarding himself, emerging occasionally to be interviewed by international publications. He would appear on television, looking grumpy, though speaking in a more demotic accent than he had in the 1960s. The themes chosen by reporters were familiar: his scope, his irascibility, his outsider status, his inscrutability, his deliberate childlessness, his Brahminical fastidiousness, his genius, his rudeness; Pat's silent presence. In 1993, the German magazine *Du* devoted a 100-page edition to him, illustrated with manuscript material and old family photographs. Awed by V.S. Naipaul's reputation for making trouble, journalists saw him as a challenge. 'I assumed at first that Sir Vidiadhar Surajprasad had servants,' wrote Zöe Heller in an *Independent on Sunday* profile in the same year. ' "The coffee will come," he said when I arrived at his flat in South Kensington. He gave a rather weary, papal wave in the direction of the kitchen. Then the telephone rang. "It will be answered. It will be answered. It will be answered." ' They discussed violent crime in Britain. 'Naipaul said: "I see that several generations of free milk and orange juice have led to an army of thugs." '[89] In an astute interview in *Publishers Weekly* by an old Oxford contemporary, John F. Baker, Vidia's public attitude was identified: 'For what strikes one most of all about Naipaul is the extraordinary force of his persona. It is an actorly one, enhanced by a remarkably deep and mellifluous voice, that seems to alternate constantly between sternness and playfulness. He says outrageous things very decisively, then seems to pause as if to weigh whether one is going to take them seriously or as a joke; and since levity always seems to lie close to his surface, the effect is of a hugely intelligent person playing sly games whose outcome only he can determine.'[90] Sometimes, he would be frank and revealing. In *Der Spiegel*, he said he had only voted once, in 1983, for Margaret Thatcher's Conservatives. 'Until I was in my forties, I was kind of an instinctive Labour Party man, but then intellectually I found them less and less attractive.' Asked how he dealt with 'carnal acts' in his fiction, he answered that he had initially been unable to write about sex: 'When I was young, you know, I was a great frequenter of prostitutes. I found them intensely stimulating. But what happened was that by the time I was in my mid-thirties, I began to feel depressed by sex with a prostitute. I felt cheated and frustrated.'[91]

Having broached the subject of prostitution to a German publication with no ill effect, Vidia was lulled into speaking about it again when he was interviewed at length by the *New Yorker* the following year. Two of his sentences ran around the world, chased by Tina Brown's publicity machine: 'So I became a great prostitute man, which, as you know, is highly unsatisfactory. It's the most unsatisfying form of sex.'[92] A man had admitted to having sex with a prostitute: it made the news in many countries. 'Naipaul Tells Dark Secrets of Sex Life,' wrote Geordie Greig in the *Sunday Times*. Speaking spontaneously, thinking only of himself, Vidia had failed to consider the consequences. 'I gave an interview to the *New Yorker*, to a nice man, Stephen Schiff, and I mentioned things I really never thought would come back to the house. I remember making a decision to tell Stephen Schiff about it. A simple decision. It all occurred in my head at the moment it was happening.'[93] For Pat, it was a devastation. Vidia's silent visits to prostitutes, starting decades before in Muswell Hill, had never been discussed between them. For Vidia, what he said to Schiff was a memory of old days before Margaret; for Pat, it was a gross revelation, and an insult to her status as his loving wife. 'I couldn't see that this would be front page news. I didn't think it would be like that. But that's how Pat [heard about] it. And she ran to get the paper. I told her, please don't get it. Please don't read it . . . She read it privately. Shortly after that she became ill again, and people say that this cancer business can come with great distress and grief. She was very upset. She was tearful and wounded.'[94]

There was more in the article. The *New Yorker* reported that in the 1970s, Vidia had met a woman, and she had become his lover. 'Her name was Margaret, and she was an Argentine of British descent, a slender, attractive married woman (with three children) who was about ten years younger than Naipaul, and several inches taller . . . she has often joined Naipaul during his travels.'[95] The revelation about Margaret did not upset Pat. The existence of a mistress had been widely known for years, even if it had never been noted in print before. It was the idea of her husband having plentiful, degraded sex with prostitutes, whores, hookers, tarts, that fed her imagination, and horrified her. The papers wanted more. 'Dear Lady Naipaul,' wrote Victoria Combe of the *Daily Telegraph*, 'We were wondering whether you would like to discuss some of the issues raised in the New Yorker magazine. We appreciate you may be reluctant to air your views in public but we would guarantee you a responsible interview.'[96] Pat kept silent, as she had always kept silent, but allowed the knowledge to eat away at her. Vidia had been 'a great prostitute man', and now all the world knew about it. 'I think that consumed her. I think she had all the relapses and everything after that. All the remission ended.' Pat's cancer was back, and would not go away. Vidia had to live with the responsibility of what he had done, and bear the blame for the rest of his days. 'She suffered. It could be said that I had killed her. It could be said. I feel a little bit that way.'[97]

CHAPTER TWENTY-FIVE

THE SECOND LADY NAIPAUL

AS HE APPROACHED THE AGE of retirement, Vidia felt compelled to go on writing. He collected notes, and even recorded his dreams, as writers are prone to in old age. In one, he was in an accountant's office in Germany discussing the oddities of German language usage; another time he was shouting in class, and being tested on his French vocabulary by his sister Mira. Or: 'I was in Queensgate with Helen Fraser. We were going to lunch. A bus came along. She ran to get it. I didn't run as fast (or as readily) as she. She made the bus. I didn't. And then there followed the trouble of looking for her in restaurants; and during this trouble I talked to Javed (of the Bombay Brasserie) of my problem.' At a publisher's office, he saw 'something scandalous' – a heap 'as big as a small van' of photocopied booklets. A fire was kindled. 'The booklets were critical of me & my work.' The dream was linked to people 'raking down the fire' onto a body, 'inspired by a brief glimpse of Foxe's Book of Martyrs'. It made Vidia think about eight-year-old Sewan attending Pa's cremation in Trinidad. 'I suppose it marked him for ever. Poor boy. All that grief to carry; all that terror.'[1]

In June 1994, unable to find the spark for a work of fiction, Vidia decided to write a short book about Brazil, Chile, Venezuela and Argentina. Gillon Aitken noted its proposed themes: 'Immense wealth, immense upheaval, oil and theft, degraded & ineducable population.'[2] V.S. Naipaul made an excursion to Brazil in August as a guest of the British Council and the Cultura Inglesa, to be feted and interviewed. He disliked the climate, and Pat was sent frequent faxes with peremptory instructions: 'Bolt should be replaced on gate only if the replacement is sturdy, if it fits, and if it is rust-proof. Send a copy of the letter from Tulsa to Gillon, to ask for his advice. I am off now for a day or two to an orange estate. Vidia.'[3] And what of his nephew Ved, he enquired: had he cleared his debts yet? A trip to Chile later in the year was called off when Pat had another relapse, and had to be admitted to hospital for surgery. In February 1995 Vidia went to Buckingham

Palace to watch the head of a teachers' union, the governor of Brixton prison, a black rugby player and the Duke of York's private secretary eat Terrine de Canard à l'Orange and Côtelettes d'Agneau Réforme. Also present at the luncheon were the Duke of Edinburgh and the Queen, who sat at Vidia's right hand drinking Chardonnay Currawong Creek. The author noted politely on his copy of the menu: 'A vegetarian (fish) meal was quietly offered to me.'[4]

He saw little of Margaret except when he was travelling and wanted company, but she continued to keep in touch by fax. Vidia's replies were rarely more than a sentence long, and usually unsigned: 'I will telephone you; but I don't want to know anything about Nobel Prizes – you must stop paying attention to those things.' Margaret sent occasional news from Argentina: her daughter Karin was getting married, her son Alexander had given her a fountain pen for Christmas, she had been to a dinner dance at a big hotel. Sometimes, in a reminder of old days, she would flatter him, telling him he was the Lion King and that she remembered him as a predatory animal who would savage her.[5]

By now, conscious that his stay in Brazil had yielded nothing, Vidia was anxious to begin another book. There were plenty of distractions should he want them, such as addressing the Association of Wessex Tourist Guides or attending a conference of Bhojpuri speakers in Uttar Pradesh. He even thought about accepting a residency at the University of Calgary. When he was made a Companion of Literature, he sent Tristram Powell to the Royal Society of Literature to collect a scroll on his behalf. He extended kindness to strangers. When Anthony Milne, a former journalist and clerk at the Red House who was working at Toys-R-Us in Swindon, told Vidia his thoughts about Guyana, he was invited to lunch. Vidia suggested he lacked 'an attitude' and proposed that Milne write about an '*idea*: this is how black racism, allied to a bogus Marxism, can wreck a country the size of Great Britain in twenty years. And that material becomes even more interesting still if you deliver it as a white West Indian, someone with a special interest and attitude to the place.' Milne wrote an admiring appraisal of V.S. Naipaul instead, and sent it to him. 'The piece won't do, and I am sure you know so, too. It is unfocused; it hops restlessly about from point to point; and it is shallow: it actually says nothing when it should say something. To be focused: before you write, decide what you are writing about, think about a rational progression of ideas – four or five, no more – and then write . . . What did we talk about at lunch? It says nothing to say that your host was charming . . . No more lessons. VSN.'[6] An attempt to beatify Vidia on French television induced cooperation followed by rage against a prolix producer. He told his publisher, Ivan Nabokov, 'I am leaving it to you to tell the French T.V. people that I don't wish to see any more of Josianne Maisse. After four months she has done almost nothing, & her verbiage has led to nothing except a request for an 8-hour interview, which exceeds in idiocy anything I have so far encountered. I feel greatly abused by the people who sent her. It was wrong of them to expose me to this degree of idleness and stupidity.'[7]

Vidia wanted to get to work. He decided to loop back on himself once more and write a reprise of *Among the Believers*. In a new global political climate, he would return to Iran, Indonesia, Malaysia and Pakistan to look at the future of Islamist ideology through the fate of the countries and personalities he had encountered in 1979. Once again, he would make a forceful rejection of the late twentieth-century academic convention that all cultures, peoples and belief systems are different but equal.

Gillon Aitken was drafted in to secure a magnificent advance. The idea was to make a deal which linked the new travel book, *Beyond Belief*, with an edition of the letters that Vidia and Pa had written to each other during his Oxford days. Gillon recalled, 'I was worried. I couldn't find the money. I did go back to Viking and they wouldn't be drawn, and then Reed made an offer which was no good. I tried HarperCollins, they didn't come though, I tried Cape, they didn't come through.' With no UK publisher prepared to make a substantial offer, Gillon's next plan was to recover the rights to Vidia's complete backlist, which André Deutsch had sold to Penguin, and secure a wider deal. 'I asked Cape for £1 million for *Beyond Belief*, *Letters Between a Father and Son* and twelve early titles. The plan didn't work, so I went next to Little, Brown and offered *Beyond Belief* and the letters, which was pretty make-weight because the letters were a questionable commercial project. So that was the package. They paid £225,000. I had to write Vidia a careful letter; he wasn't pleased.'[8] In America, Gillon had another cunning plan. Aided by Andrew Wylie, with whom he was in the process of parting professional company, he sold the *New Yorker* four long extracts from the unwritten book for $200,000. It turned out to be a bad deal for the magazine; Bill Buford of the *New Yorker* wanted the material to be rewritten, but Vidia refused and only a part was published. Another section ended up later in the *New York Review of Books*, producing more money. Next Gillon set to work on Sonny Mehta at Knopf: 'Vidia would like to contract for the US book publication rights, with an advance of $300,000 – no more, no less.'[9] It was an interesting approach to negotiation, and Mehta hesitated. Seven days after he had sent his first letter, Gillon withdrew from the negotiation, declaring that Mehta had taken too long to reach a decision. His plan to take his eminent client elsewhere did not proceed as smoothly as he had hoped, and he made a deal along similar lines with Mehta's senior colleague Harold Evans.

As soon as the contract was agreed, Vidia prepared to start his journey. A link with the past was broken in July 1995 when the last of his Hindi-speaking aunts died, Kalawatee Mausi, who used to take his mother to school. Kalawatee had been a Trinidad senator in the 1960s, and a political adviser to her brother Rudranath, and like all her sisters, a forceful presence. A month earlier, Pat's Auntie Lu had also died, at the age of ninety-three. There was business and paperwork to clear up too. The *New Yorker* was running extracts from his early correspondence with Paul Theroux. The famously persuasive Ismail Merchant, after years of trying, had concluded a contract to put *The Mystic Masseur* on the screen. 'I will do an excellent film from this wonderful work of yours,' he assured Vidia.[10] After negotiations the film rights were sold to Merchant Ivory Productions for $75,000, with a further $75,000 to be paid when filming commenced. It was the highest fee that Merchant Ivory had ever paid to adapt a book for a film.[11] Vidia would also receive 5 per cent of producer's net profits, but everyone knew that the industry's accounting procedures meant that no further money was likely to be paid. The result was a dire film, released in 2001, in which Om Puri as Ramlogan shifted between a Jamaican and an Indian accent.

Before leaving England for Indonesia, Vidia put together a 'travelling list'. In its care and restraint, in its honing, it reflected the man and the writer, who knew that he had to be preserved at all costs to do his work. Despite having a large share portfolio and a substantial six-figure sum in his offshore US-dollar account in Jersey, Vidia remained frugal in his spending. He did his own accounts and bookkeeping, with Pat's determined help.

Suits & trousers & jackets
Travel out in Simpson's grey
Pack – Simpson's beige lightweight

Jackets
Blue blazer (new or old)

Trousers
M&S cotton
BHS cotton
Oscar Jacobson charcoal lightweight worsted

Underclothes
Pants 4 prs
Socks 4 prs
Pyjama 1 pr
T-shirts 2
Sleeveless vests 2

Shirts
4 cotton (dress)
M&S leisure 2
Smedley shirts 2
Smedley roll-neck 3

Pullovers
1 cotton (BHS or M&S)
1 wool (M&S or Aquascutum)

Shorts
Bathing trunks
Exercise pants
Trainers
1 pr perhaps to be worn on journey

Diary
Notebooks
Paper
Computer & Disks
Ink cartridges
(Plug adaptor)

Medicines & Soaps
Ventolin 2
Becloforte 1

Antibiotics 2
Migraleve
Paracetamol & codeine
Celbutomol
Augmentin[12]

On 25 July 1995, Vidia flew out of Heathrow airport to Jakarta. More than two years later, writing in a private journal, he described his departure from his wife. 'I had embraced her – for the first time for many years – at the airport (in or near the Costa coffee shop: she complained later that the coffee had damaged her: a sign of her fatal illness, if only I knew); she had fallen into my arms; and I had felt how ill she was. She had telephoned the airline later to find out whether I had arrived. The plane had been delayed. So (when I got to Jakarta) we talked eventually, full of old love (though the other person was soon to arrive: the eternal lie of the situation).'[13]

As on his previous trips, Vidia asked other people to aid him, and in most cases they fell over themselves to do so. Margaret jumped on an aeroplane, and travelled loyally with him through Indonesia, being permitted to collect and file useful press cuttings. Publishers' staff in London and New York provided contacts and helpers. Ian Buruma recommended the journalist Ahmed Rashid in Pakistan, who produced a string of names and invited Vidia to stay at his house in Lahore. Bob Silvers found regional experts and their telephone numbers. Harry Evans sent a gigantic list of possibly interesting people. Rahul Singh located reporters and politicians in Jakarta. Once Vidia arrived in the relevant country, diplomats would arrange dinners and foreign correspondents would open their contacts books to him. He got in touch with many of the people he had met on his trip sixteen years earlier, and asked to see them. When a meeting went well, he responded warmly. To Dr Dewi Fortuna Anwar, an Indonesian academic and politician, he wrote: 'I want to thank you for sending me to your ancestral house in Padang. Your mother was the soul of courtesy and generosity; and the experience was an amazing and educational one for me. Everything was beautiful: the mountains, the plains, the rice-fields, the houses.'[14] As always, Vidia kept meticulous notes, and when he had time to spare he would type them up in order to make the process of writing the book easier. He travelled cautiously, guarding himself against possible asthma or back pain. By early September, he had completed his research in

Indonesia and returned to Wiltshire for a week to get ready for his next journey – to Iran. In October, following a trip to Persepolis, he found himself back in England preparing to fly to Lahore, where he was met at the airport by an enthusiastic Ahmed Rashid. November was spent in Pakistan, December in Malaysia, and by Christmas he had come back to Dairy Cottage, where Pat was dying. While he was in Indonesia, Vidia learned the word 'langsat' – a term used to describe someone with a perfect, fair complexion, named after the creamy colour of the langsat fruit.

In the finished book, which he wrote during the course of 1996 and early 1997, Vidia began with a prologue. 'This is a book about people. It is not a book of opinion. It is a book of stories. The stories were collected during five months of travel in 1995 in four non-Arab Muslim countries – Indonesia, Iran, Pakistan, Malaysia. So there is a context and a theme. Islam is in its origins an Arab religion. Everyone who is not an Arab who is a Muslim is a convert. Islam is not simply a matter of conscience or private belief. It makes great demands.' Then he crossed out the word 'great' and replaced it with 'imperial'.[15] When *Beyond Belief* was published, few reviewers would accept the claim that since it was a book about people, it was not a book of opinion. Vidia introduced many thoughts and concepts that would, after 11 September 2001, become better known: ritual purification, sacrifice, Islamic martyrs, mujahidin, *talebeh* or students (hence Taliban). Above all, he wrote about the idea that an individual's devotion to a perceived idea of Islamic teaching might push every other consideration aside, and lead him to unconscionable acts. Vidia's perception arose, as before, from the combination of his sharp eyes, a precisely developed control of his own talent and complete confidence in his ability to analyse a wider situation. A year earlier, he had written to a Tulsa oilman he met at dinner: 'totalitarianism has been the great curse of the century, and you know in your heart of hearts that every form of totalitarianism has pretended to have a core of virtuousness; this illusion of serving virtue makes us look away ... A writer who does this looking away ... is betraying his essence and cannot be a good writer. I cannot think of any intellectual self-violator who was or is a good writer. The good writers have always looked for truth. Nothing else is worthwhile, if you are a writer.'[16]

Working hard at the text, revising more than he had with *Among the Believers*, Vidia produced a long and thoughtful book. *Beyond Belief* concentrates on personal stories. Mr Jaffrey – last encountered in *Among the Believers* sitting behind a 'high standard typewriter' at the *Tehran Times* eating a dish of fried eggs' – had fled to Pakistan under suspicion of being an American spy, and died in 1990. The reader meets Iran's sinister hanging judge Ayatollah Khalkhalli, now 'very small, completely bald, baby-faced without his turban, head held down against his chest'; and Linus, the rural Indonesian poet with the handicapped sister 'dragging her slippered feet from a dark side room'; in Kuala Lumpur we revisit the Muslim youth worker Shafi, but he turns out to be an impostor, a man pretending to be Shafi 'out of pure idleness . . . to get a little attention'.[17] There are new characters too, like Shahbaz, the English public school-educated Pakistani with a tale of his time as a guerrilla fighter in Baluchistan. In Iran we hear the terrible story of Abbas, 'twenty-seven, and a war veteran', who left school to join a Martyr's Battalion in the Iran–Iraq war.[18] His first job was to wash the cartridge belts and harness straps of the dead, since there was a shortage of equipment; today he has a piece of artificial bone in his head and makes one-minute films. V.S. Naipaul's peerless eye does not remain closed for long. A Kentucky Fried Chicken outlet in old Tehran had been 'angrily re-lettered to Our Fried Chicken, with the face of the Southern colonel smudged and redrawn'; a carpet in a hotel lift 'was dirty and stained and didn't absolutely fit'; and a chambermaid has 'a definite smell from wearing so many clothes, some of them perhaps of synthetic material'.[19]

Michael Ignatieff in the *New York Times* thought that while Naipaul had drawn a sometimes distressing portrait, *Beyond Belief* was 'not anti-Islamic in any easy way, and it is unfailingly perceptive about how true believers handle the discordance between their dreams of godly life and ungodly reality . . . His informants have the vividness of characters in a good novel.'[20] Anatol Lieven was also impressed, writing in the *Financial Times* of the author's 'warm sympathy even for many of his Islamist subjects, a sympathy which gives this book its deeply moving quality . . . his most justifiably bitter criticisms of Islam relate to its treatment of women.'[21] A rare female reviewer, Geeta Doctor, wrote in the *Indian Review of Books* that Naipaul was too willing to opine and condemn: 'This is the sort of bashing of "otherness" that used to take place in the noonday of Communism.'[22] Robert Irwin in the *Guardian* felt the stress on the affect of Islam was overdone: 'Religion is ultimately responsible for the awful breakfast Naipaul is served in Tehran and more generally for shabby buildings, corrupt judges and street crime.'²³ In the *Observer*, Ian Jack noticed a shift in the author's approach to the act of writing: there was 'a sense of scraping away' as though he was on 'a search for some kind of purity, or a prophylactic against exhaustion.'²⁴ Sunil Khilnani declared in the *Sunday Telegraph* that *Beyond Belief* was 'the most achieved instance yet of a form refined by Naipaul since his turn away from the novel – declared by him to be historically outmoded.'²⁵ The most hostile review came from his old adversary Edward Said, in *Al-Ahram Weekly*. V.S. Naipaul was 'one of the truly celebrated, justly well-known figures in world literature today' but had squandered his gifts by writing a 'stupid' and 'boring' book. 'Somewhere along the way Naipaul, in my opinion, himself suffered a serious intellectual accident. His obsession with Islam caused him somehow to stop thinking, to become instead a kind of mental suicide compelled to repeat the same formula over and over. This is what I would call an intellectual catastrophe of the first order.'²⁶

In the *Sunday Times*, I wrote: 'The human encounters are described minutely, superbly, picking up inconsistencies in people's tales, catching the uncertainties and the nuances – how or why, for instance, a conversation changes course ... The difficulty comes with *Beyond Belief*'s general theme, as indicated in the curious subtitle, *Islamic Excursions Among the Converted Peoples*. Most of the converts in question changed faith somewhere between the seventh and eleventh century, yet Naipaul's sense of the past is so intense, so profound, that he sees them as rejectors of their indigenous belief, engaged in "a dreadful mangling of history", and suffering from resultant "neurosis". Conversion to Islam and the ensuing emphasis on foreign holy places is for him "the most uncompromising kind of imperialism". He does not consider the possibility that Islam might, over the centuries, have become an indigenous religion, while his claim that, "Everyone not an Arab who is a Muslim is a convert" might just as well be made about Christianity.' Despite my hesitations, I concluded, 'V.S. Naipaul has been writing now for nearly half a century. He has 23 books to his name – brilliant combinations of travel, fiction, history, politics, literary criticism and autobiography. It is a body of work of astonishing scope and subtlety, giving him a fair claim to be Britain's greatest living writer ... Although he often brings the reader to a moment of realisation elliptically, there is a candour to his writing, a constant precision at its heart. It is this quality of integrity – the close analysis of human conduct – that enables Naipaul's work to transcend the peculiarity of his general theories, as he narrates the extraordinary lives of ordinary people from his singular perspective.'[27] A decade later, I would not resile from this view.

*

When Vidia arrived in Indonesia in late July 1995, he knew Pat was seriously ill. A month earlier, in a chilling letter to his accountant Barry Kernon, he had written: 'Pat's personal papers (an important element of the archive) will be shipped on her death.'[28] A fortnight after he left England she was admitted to Chalybeate Hospital, and he sent her a fax with 'tremendous and enduring love'. As she prepared to visit the doctor with her part-time housekeeper Angela Cox, the Saab would not start and they had to call the AA breakdown service. When the mechanic arrived, he was unable to mend the car since Vidia, not Pat, was a member of the AA. The appropriately named Mr Sparke suggested that Pat sign the form instead, and for the first and last time, she forged her husband's signature, quite successfully.[29] After forty years, Vidia was again feeling the sort of intense emotion he had felt during their early courtship, and signed a fax with a farewell from those days, a reminder of little Sewan's line, 'I love you six.' He wrote to Pat: 'Very grieved to hear about so many things. Please let me know what you think I can do. With v. great love and gratitude for all that you are. V. SIX.' And Pat, being Pat, suggested there was nothing her husband should do except continue with his work. So he travelled to Bandung, telling her that the material was shaping up. 'I was visibly moved by the Fax,' wrote Pat, who had to rest for long stretches each morning and evening. 'I read it like lightning. It answered every need. You asked what you could do and that was it.'[30] Angela drove Pat to and from her appointments, and kept the house clean. She did not realize her employer was so ill. 'Mrs Naipaul was not a very open lady. She was very personal, and didn't discuss in great detail. I felt sorry for her that she was on her own so much, but Mr Naipaul was very supportive when he was at home. They had a great understanding of each other. It would have been nice if he could have been around a little more, but he was a very sensitive man, and he found it difficult to cope with being around. He was a gentleman, and always treated me with great respect.'[31]

The recreation of something like an old love – if on opposite sides of the world, divided by years of pain – put a stress on Vidia's relationship with Margaret, and filled him with guilt. One day when he telephoned Pat from the hotel in Jakarta, Margaret made a remark which stuck in his mind, and filled him with unexpressed, silent anger. 'Margaret said a few foolish things that made me react badly, quietly. Pat was in the hospital and I telephoned to find out how she was. I did it the next day and Margaret said, "Ummm, almost like old lovers," or, "It is almost like an affair," and I thought that was rather crass of her.' In his head, Vidia began to reject the mistress who had through decades of harassment chosen to stand by him, and even now was traipsing around Indonesian villages wearing an unappetizing red hat. Now that he might, if things went badly, have Margaret as his wife, he had a fateful, hateful, fatal sense that he did not want her in his life any more. It was unjust, but as ever Vidia presented himself as a figure controlled by irreducible needs. 'I feel that in all of this Margaret was badly treated. I feel this very much. But you know there is nothing I can do . . . I stayed with Margaret until she became middle-aged, almost an old lady.'[32]

When Margaret flew home from Indonesia, Vidia carried on to Iran and Pakistan. He had asked her to accompany him on the second leg of the trip, but she refused, saying she had never liked any of the Pakistanis she had met. On 26 October, two days after Vidia arrived in Lahore, his helper Ahmed Rashid took him to a party at the US consul general's house. Moving fast in Pakistan's cultural capital, Vidia had fixed to meet bureaucrats, military men, lawyers, politicians and editors. The evening at the diplomat's house was a typical occasion of its type, where the educated elite of a failing state discuss how best to spring the country from its present mess. Benazir Bhutto was running a corrupt and violent administration, but would Nawaz Sharif, or an unnamed military dictator, do any better? Vidia listened, saying little. Another guest was a tall, feisty, energetic, fearless, generous, dyslexic, emotional, fairly scandalous forty-two-year-old journalist, who wrote under the name 'Nadira'. When she arrived at the party at the end of a long day at the office, Ahmed Rashid asked if she would like to meet the famous writer. In her account, she saw a sorrowful looking man piling his plate high with salad in this land of vigorous meat eaters. 'I walked up to him and said: "Are you V.S. Naipaul?" And he said, "Yes." I looked at him, I wasn't smiling, I wasn't laughing, I just looked into his eyes and I said: "Can I kiss you?" And I kissed him on his cheek. I said: "A tribute to you. A tribute to you." Then he said we should sit down and he insisted I sit next to him . . . He wangled a dinner invitation out of me too, on that evening. I thought to myself, God, now I am stuck with this bloody dinner.'[33] Vidia's engagement diary records that they met nine times over the next fortnight: 'Nadira at hotel, to take me to dinner . . . 8.30 Nadira.'[34]

She became his subject.

> Vidia said to me that he needed a woman to talk about this society. He was staying in the Awari Hotel, close to my office on the Mall. He called me at my office. I thought, I'd better help him, he's a good man and he's among scoundrels. I fixed a ticket for him to go to Islamabad. I told Vidia everything . . . He reminded me of my father, in his precise use of language. I wasn't interested in him, believe me. I thought, this is a sick society, I'll tell him, I took him to meet my aunt and she said, 'Beta, tell him all about our lives.' I was harassed and chased and propositioned three times a day in Pakistan, that's the sort of place it is. I wanted him to look at us in the way he looked at the Indians in *An Area of Darkness*. My editor Khaled Ahmed, the editor of the *Nation*, used to give me Vidia's books and say, 'Read him, he's the best.' I had a copy of *A Million Mutinies* and I hadn't read it.[35]

So Nadira told Vidia her story. She was born in 1953 in Mombasa in Kenya, where her father, M.A. Alvi, was a banker. He came from an anglophile and well-connected Muslim family in Lahore, and her mother was a Pathan and an only child, most of whose family had been killed in the massacres at the time of Partition. Mr Alvi was a philanthropist, with a keen sense of honour, and he saw himself as a cut above the other Indian or Pakistani Muslims on the east coast of Africa. In Nadira's words: 'My grandfather was Dr. Hakim Haji Gulam Nabi Awan who was the royal physician to King George and many royal houses. He was a founder member of the Lahore Gymkhana and King Edward medical college. It is through him that I am related to the high and mighty of Pakistan. My father didn't look at people as worms, no matter how poor they were, but he wouldn't let us go to the houses of these low-grade Kashmiris or Punjabis. He would be shocked that I found happiness with an indentured labourer's grandson.' Nadira had four sisters and two brothers, and since she was the youngest girl, her upbringing was more progressive than her sisters' had been. She went to a British school in Dar es Salaam, until her father sent her to a convent in East Pakistan (later Bangladesh), where she was so unhappy that she came back to Kenya. It was a disjointed childhood, jumping between cultures.

Aged sixteen, she was dispatched to her father's family in Lahore and enrolled at Kinnaird College. She was shocked to be part of a monolithic Muslim society, and had to learn proper Urdu and Punjabi, and adjust her accent so as not to be teased by the other girls. In 1977 she married impulsively, to a country landowner in Bahawalpur, close to the border between Pakistan and India. There was a complication: he was already married to an English wife and had two children, so Nadira had to accommodate herself to living in a joint family as a junior wife, in feudal style. She had a daughter and a son, Maleeha and Nadir (known as Nonie), and by the time she met Vidia her marriage was finished. 'I had my children taken away and my life had become topsy-turvy.'[36] Unusually for a woman in Pakistan, Nadira was divorced and lived in her own household. She was above all a survivor, who lived on her wits. 'I was in control of my life. I had a servant who ran the house, my major domo. I told my unhappy girlfriends that I knew what it was to be a man. My friends helped me, women from the NGOs, from the human rights organizations. But I was vilified. When I went to a party, the men would come running over and the women would freeze.'[37]

Nadira was in a precarious position in a merciless society, and her vulnerability and nerve drew Vidia, just as it drew other men. She had a reputation as a newspaper columnist, first with 'The People's Platform' in which she gave voice to the views of the street on anything from religion to the military to democracy, and then with 'Letter from Bahawalpur' in the *Frontier Post*, and another column in *Dawn*. On television and in public forums, she spoke freely, sometimes too freely, and wrote in the press in imperfect English about the plight of individuals such as Bano, a rural woman who had been blinded in one eye by her in-laws and rejected by her own family: 'She belongs to a lower middle class family where girls are confined within the walls of the house once they reach puberty ... The limited amenities available such as education, medicine or even choice morsels of food, were always reserved for the men.'[38] During a debate at the Press Club, she was accused of blasphemy — a criminal offence in Pakistan — by a senior mullah. Nadira had given up her husband's surname 'Mustafa' on her divorce and reverted to her mother's surname 'Khannum' linked to her father's surname 'Alvi', but to make the point that Nadira Khannum Alvi was her own woman, her columns ran beneath her photograph and the single name 'Nadira'. To some, though, she was known as 'Nadaan'

Nadira, suggesting that she was an innocent abroad, unversed in the ways of the world. Why else would she take the risks she did? Her name was linked to a newspaper owner, a senior bureaucrat and columnist, a landowner (or 'prince', to use Nadira's word) in Punjab, and an alleged drug baron on the Afghan frontier. As Vidia quickly realized, she was without male protection in a feudal and patriarchal society. Nadira was under no illusions. She told him: 'My uncles and father are dead. My brother and nephew in the military wish to have nothing to do with me. My family has evaporated. So you are right I have no protection, but I have the pen. This is a good protection Vidia.'[39]

Nadira spoke freely to Vidia, holding back little. Then something strange happened: the writer, the writer who had guarded himself scrupulously since childhood, avoiding intimacy or revelation, began to speak. It was a partial account, but it came from deep inside him. He told Nadira about Pat, about Margaret, and about his family. He told her that his wife was dying and his mistress had hopes he could not fulfil. 'We were driving past the Gymkhana Club, and Vidia said, "I am a very passionate man." He told me he should never have married Pat, but that she was a great support to his work, that he was sexually deprived but Margaret had changed all that, and that he had come to the end of the road with Margaret but had carried on because it was convenient. I listened like a friend. He was very angry with Pat, he felt angry that she was dying and angry that she was not dying fast enough because he wanted to carry on with his life. He was dealing with the shock of her dying by being angry. Vidia can't cope with grief or pain or bad news: he shoots the messenger. I knew it was a dead marriage, so I didn't think it was strange that he was with me rather than Pat.'[40]

Things moved fast after this. Vidia wanted to see more of Pakistan, and Nadira thought he should visit the depths of the countryside. 'I said to him, "Do you want to see where my dreams were shattered?"' She took him to Bahawalpur, and as they gazed out over the moonlit desert at Lal Suhanra, Vidia said to her, 'I have never wanted children, but if I did I would want you as their mother.' From a man whose wife had been unable to conceive and whose mistress had been through several terminations, it was a strange remark to make to a woman who had been forcibly separated from her own children, but Nadira took it as a sincere compliment. She brought him to the provincial assembly and to meet friends and associates, and when he came to write a chapter on the region in *Beyond Belief*, it was full of vigorous stories, and filled with a sexual charge last encountered in *A Bend in the River*. 'A journalist from Bahawalpur who had got to know one of the women of the Nawab's harem told me ... "After his foreign trips he would enter the harem with tin trunks, and the women would go crazy. They had asked for chemises and chiffons and feathers, and they would fight for these things".'[41]

Nadira helped to arrange his journeys, telephoning her many friends and contacts. She sent him to see Minoo Bhandara, a Parsi newspaper columnist who ran Pakistan's only brewery, in Murree. 'Nadira phoned me. She said, "An Indian friend of mine will be coming. He's dark-skinned and you will like his company." I picked him up from the airport. He was standing there sullenly and I said, "Dr Livingstone, I presume?" He went, "Yes, yes, yes." I took him around for a few days. I had no idea he was romantically involved. Nadira was a good friend of mine, a journalistic butterfly. She was a chirpy little thing, bright, known to a lot of important people ... Naipaul didn't want to meet people socially. He told me he liked roaming around the countryside, seeing things. I mentioned that my sister was a novelist, Bapsi Sidhwa, but he wasn't interested. When I asked him who his favourite writers were he said, "My father." Later I sent a letter to him in England, but didn't get a reply. A friend of mine said maybe my letter contained grammatical mistakes ... I would credit him with seeing more than I did [about Pakistan] at that time. He saw political Islam getting stronger by the day.'[42]

The next stop was Karachi, where Nadira's friend Mazdak met them both at the airport. Vidia was dropped off at his hotel, and a few days later on 24 November, Mazdak gave a Thanksgiving dinner (his sister-in-law was American) to which the itinerant author was invited. When the party was coming to an end, Nadira heard that a girlfriend of Mazdak's had been present, and an argument began. While she was screaming at him at around 3 a.m., the telephone rang and a voice said, 'Is Margaret there? I have to speak to her.' 'Margaret who?' asked Mazdak, and Nadira snatched the telephone, realizing who was on the other end. 'Come now to the hotel, I need to talk to you,' said Vidia. She refused, but agreed to come at 8.30. Nadira went to bed, furious, and when she arrived at the hotel a few hours later, Vidia was still wearing his clothes from the night before. 'He looked wild. His hair was all over the place. I said, "Are you OK?" He asked me not to go, and then he said, "Will you consider one day being Lady Naipaul?" I knew Pat was dying and Margaret was finished ... It was not that I was trying to displace a dying woman and an old floozy. So I said, you must wait. I rang Mazdak at his office and said, "V.S. Naipaul has just asked me to marry him." Mazdak said, "I'm sorry, I can't match that offer." I said, "Well I'm not coming back, so kindly pack up all my stuff and send it here to the hotel." I stayed the night with Vidia [and] the phone rang in the hotel room. I answered it. A woman said, "Can I speak to V.S. Naipaul?" It was Pat. She said to him, "Was that Margaret?" and Vidia said, "No, no, it is someone else." About three days after that Vidia flew back to London. I said to him, "I'll only marry you if you come back, I want you to meet the people who are important in my life." I knew that Margaret was in London. I had asked him. But I don't know what he had said to her. He told me, "You're not to worry, you will not be dishonoured." I called the superintendent of police in Karachi, and he gave Vidia a police escort to the airport. Vidia tipped his hat as he was saying goodbye, and I thought that was so old-fashioned and so beautiful.'[43]

Vidia travelled swiftly to Malaysia, anxious that neither the prospect of looming death nor marriage should interfere with his work, and returned to Wiltshire for Christmas. Unsurprisingly, Pat was unable to give him the sort of welcome he sought. As he told his fiancée over the telephone, making long calls to Pakistan heedless for once of the expense, there was nobody to look after him.[44] 'His room wasn't done when he came back, and he caught a slight chill because there was no blanket. He is not a man to be inconvenienced. He got very irritated.'[45] Earlier that year, Pat had undergone surgery to her remaining breast and irradiation of her neck and armpit. In October, before Vidia went to Pakistan, she had had further radiotherapy and chemotherapy.[46] By Christmas, she was dying, and knew it. While Vidia was away during the summer she had telephoned his sister Mira in Florida. 'Pat didn't want to talk, she just asked to speak to Amar.'[47] The radiation oncologist came on the line, and was far from pessimistic when Pat told him of her condition. 'She asked about treatment and I gave her advice, communicated with the specialist,' Amar remembered later. Some progress was made in treating the cancer, and as the weeks passed Pat and Amar continued to talk on the telephone. But then: 'She refused to have further treatment. She was saying to me, "What do I have to live for?"

It was a passive decision, but a conscious decision, to choose her own death. She said she would rather that a younger person had the treatment.'[48]

Before flying to Malaysia at the start of December, Vidia had decided he would return to Pakistan in the new year. Ahmed Rashid played the 'pigeon' role previously filled by Menchi Sábat, receiving a fax and passing it on to Nadira. 'Dear Ahmed, This is for Nadira. Langsat: P[akistan] I[nternational] A[irlines] can do a business class flight London/Karachi/Lahore on 3 January.'[49] There was one difficulty: first he had to tell Margaret that their relationship was over. How was he to do it? Vidia spoke to her in Argentina by telephone twice in late December, and twice in early January. Then his calls ceased. 'I didn't tell Margaret I had met Nadira.'[50] By saying nothing, he had shelved the problem. His wife's deteriorating condition did not deter him: he flew east, and remained in Lahore for just over two weeks. This time, the news that V.S. Naipaul and 'Nadaan' Nadira of 'Letter from Bahawalpur' fame were holed up together in the Awari Hotel spread swiftly through Lahore. Minoo Bhandara heard the gossip: 'I asked, "Is V.S. Naipaul a bigamist?" And I was told, no, but his wife is going to die in the next couple of months, and then he's going to marry Nadira.'[51] For Vidia's wife-to-be, it was a time to cut old ties and introduce him to her friends and family. 'I was so much under his spell, he was so witty and funny. I was so in love. Nobody had given me that kind of attention and passion before. I felt protected. He was daddy, uncle, lover all rolled into one ... He was moved by the old yellow pencil marks I had made in my copy of *India: An Area of Darkness*. I was in love. Vidia was focusing on pulling the net. He bought me a ring – a lapis with two diamonds – and gave me some money. My daughter was happy but my son was devastated.'[52]

Vidia instructed his solicitor Michael Carey, 'worried about accidents', that Nadira was to be given £125,000 and the flat in Queen's Gate Terrace in the event of his sudden death. Back in London on 19 January, Vidia visited the dentist, suffering from nerve pain. On the same day, Pat went for her last meal at the Bombay Brasserie near the flat with Angela Cox, who had driven her up to London to meet her husband, now that he had returned from Pakistan after his important research. A few weeks earlier, Pat had seen Teresa Wells and confided in her that she was dying. She also told her that Vidia had met a new lover in Pakistan, with whom he wanted to spend his life. In

Teresa's words, 'Pat suggested that once she died it would be easier for them.'[53]

*

During the last days of January, Pat's condition deteriorated fast. With Vidia, she went for an appointment at Chalybeate Hospital, where the anaesthetist Dr Hamilton told him that she had liver cancer and only days to live. Pat lay in her little bed at Dairy Cottage, cared for by Angela, taking her medicines – temazepam, mystan, tranadol – and applying durogesic patches to relieve the pain. Sometimes, she would write notes, but could only manage a few lines. 'Hair Loss. Is it going to stop? Will it grow again. Thick so still, I think not too noticeable. But (upsetting me) brush, pull – handfulls slight despair ... Sunday. Pressure – liver/chest/lungs? Small pain (gone) within ribs to the side – left short breathed. Had to rest most of day ... Apologise for not cleaning teeth.'[54] On good days, she would come downstairs and talk to Vidia. 'She loved Africa, she loved India, she loved the Caribbean. In the last week of her life, I talked to her in that front room. She was sitting on this sofa, the same sofa, and I said, "Has it been reasonably all right?" She didn't ... although the idea was she didn't know she was dying and only I knew. She said that she loved meeting my family. That was marvellous. So that was a good time. And she loved India. She thought I was very hard on India when I was writing *An Area of Darkness* because she saw things about India which of course I, coming from the culture, couldn't see ... Even at the end when she was dying, I [told her] these are the notes about Indonesia, let me read them to you. I read them for too long. She was in great pain. She cried and then I stopped. I asked her opinion about certain things and she gave it. She always gave good advice, literary advice. She was always very good. A few days before her death she was able to judge it.'[55]

As Pat slipped towards the end, a nurse named Mary Boon was engaged to assist Angela. Vidia would walk the country lanes each morning. 'I fell into a great strange pattern, very upsetting because she was dying. She would sit in her room or sleep in the early morning and I would get up very early when it was still dark and go for long walks on the road. I would walk to the bridge, half an hour, and come back and it would be still dark. So it was a strange kind of house. Pat behaved beautifully when she was dying. The nurses and people who came to the house were wonderful. When we came here in 1982 ... I had such a clear vision of the hearse coming down the lane. I could imagine it. We had just moved in. I thought it might have been for me. I had that clear idea, that clear premonition of seeing the black hearse.'[56]

On 30 January, Vidia started to keep a journal. 'Pat, taking the now useless pills (freshly prescribed by Dr Hamilton) – "To be on the safe side." Talking of her illness and my sorrow: "These things happen." This morning, after I had brought up the fromage frais and honey in two cocottes – as she had asked for it – she didn't remember asking for it . . . Very slowly arranging spaces on her bedside table. Playing with the Kenya (1966) bark-cloth mat. Her bedside books were Ibn Battuta's travels in Africa and Asia (in the Routledge paperback). And Locke . . . And just two or three days ago – how this corruption has galloped within her – she talked about the unfairness of the reviews of [*The Information* by] Martin Amis.' It was the only thing Vidia knew: making notes, taking notes. 'This morning the poor darling had forgotten what the various pills in her bedside table were for . . . These things will torment me until the end . . . She to me: "How are you? Are you well? Are you doing your work?" Smiles and looks beautiful when I say yes. "How's your chest? It was the first thing I heard this morning." "But it didn't worry you?" "Too used to it." Smiling. So beautiful . . . I to her: "Are you content?" Yes. Would you say you have had a happy life? No direct answer. "It was perhaps my own fault" . . . The "patch" is working together with the Zudol tablets. She sleeps. But when she wakes up she feels "stunned" by what she has been through. Her bad – jaundiced – colour comes and goes. She is pure grace.' Vidia read some of *Nicholas Nickleby* and *The Pickwick Papers* to Pat, a book she had read to him in Bravington Road when they were both twenty-two and he was suffering from asthma. 'She kissed me when I arranged her to sleep. She held me and kissed me. Which she hadn't done for twenty years and more.'[57] He told her he had met Nadira in Pakistan, but not that he planned to marry. 'I left that out. Pat was too ill to react. I don't know how much she understood.'[58]

The following night, as Pat was being taken to the bathroom by Mary, 'She said, with a joke, "Let us hear no more of you now." Meaning that I was to go to sleep . . . Just now, about twenty minutes ago, when she appeared to open her eyes, and I spoke love to her, she raised her hand and actually stroked my face. Before that she had tried to talk – unsuccessfully.' In the morning he tried to help her out of bed to go and wash, but it was too painful for her to move. Angela helped. When Pat came back to bed, her legs were wet. 'I burst into tears for her sake. She began to talk. "Vidia, you are making a mistake. Vidia, you are making a mistake." "I always make mistakes" ... The words don't come. I get irritated. And then Angela tells me that she is distressed by my irritation; but the mistake all had to do perhaps with the bathroom ... I cried later. Pat then smiled and stroked my face encouragingly with her hand.' That night, Patricia Naipaul, née Hale, fell into a coma. Vidia removed her Cartier watch for fear it might be stolen by a passing health worker. The next morning, on Saturday, 3 February 1996, a little before seven o'clock, Pat passed away. 'Mary called me and took me in. Her hand cold and clammy. The moment of death. Her face much decayed. Unbearable ... Mary asked whether I wanted to be alone with her. I didn't ... The visiting sister: "Only the body's gone" – meaning that the rest of the person was in the memory.'[59]

Vidia did not know what to do. Having spent a lifetime shunning friends, he had no network of support. His wife was dead, at the age of sixty-three. He sent Angela to buy apples, carrots, prawns, sole and kippers. A few days earlier, Vidia had sent Paul Theroux a fax in Hawaii asking him to write an appreciation of Pat when the time came. 'I took her too much for granted,' he had written. Now, he wrote to Paul once more. 'The doctor came; and half an hour later the undertaker's assistant, very Dickensian; and Pat was taken out of her room by this assistant and the day nurse. I didn't watch. Just a week ago we had gone to Southampton to see the doctor. I felt relieved when she left. I telephoned some people. I even thought I would start working. But then I felt very tired, and it occurred to me to send this note to you.'[60] Paul's short, moving obituary was published in the *Daily Telegraph*, at Gillon Aitken's behest. 'As the first reader, highly intelligent, strong-willed and profoundly moral, Pat played an active part in Vidia's work. She understood that a writer needs a loyal opposition as much as praise ... "She is my heart," he told me once.'[61] A death notice appeared in the newspapers: 'Patricia Ann (Lady Naipaul). Wife of V.S. Naipaul ... after a long and wasting illness. Funeral at Salisbury Crematorium Thursday 8 February at 9.40 a.m.'[62]

Vidia telephoned Eleanor. 'He told me Pat had died, and I had to call back to ask when the funeral was: about half-past nine, I think, to deter people from coming. I went on my own. Vidia was very reserved. He shook hands, and afterwards I drove home.'[63] Three months earlier Eleanor had discovered that she and Pat had a half-sister, Jane, born to Ted and Vera in January 1971. Knowing that Pat was ill, waiting for the right moment, she had delayed telling her the news. And now her sister was gone. Ted Hale, in poor health, did not attend the cremation. Eleanor explained why: 'I only told my father about Pat after the funeral because I wasn't being encouraged to attend myself.'[64] Vidia spent £295 on a 'Fundamental coffin' and £15 on an urn. The event was attended by Vidia, Eleanor, Angela, Jenny, Nella and her husband Nigel, Tristram Powell, Margaret's sister Diana Stobart and a few others. It was a piercingly cold February day; snow lay on the ground. There were four wreaths by the coffin: two from different generations of Powells, one from Pat's childhood friend Sheila Rogers and her sister Peggy, and one from Jenny and Tarun. The service was momentary. There were no readings, or music, or an address. On the way out of Salisbury Crematorium. Vidia said to his brother-in-law Nigel, 'It was chaste, it was Quranic in its purity.'[65] Tristram Powell described the funeral as the most austere occasion he had ever attended: 'Vidia was in a controlled state, formal, under tremendous control. And in a way it was a rather powerful experience just by the sheer austerity of it ... Then everyone disappeared, and I was on my own waiting for a taxi to come and pick me up to go back to the station.'[66] Angela, although she had been employed by the Naipauls for ten years, was surprised that there were so few people present. 'But Mrs Naipaul was a very quiet lady.'[67]

Vidia could see no other way to do it. He and Pat had no religious faith, although she had been interested in the history of churches and cathedrals.

People have rebuked me about the funeral. Messages came back to me about the shabby way I did it. But I could do it only in that way, because there was only me. The nurses recommended Harrolds [undertakers], their funeral service and so I did that and they did it all for me. They sent the man in a rather dusty black coat. The coat should have been cleaned. I did nothing at all. The day after they took Pat out wrapped up (and I didn't look at her being taken out, I couldn't look at her dying because her mouth became open and I asked them to close it) I put an announcement in the papers, I think it would have been in the *Telegraph* – and the *Times* had it as well. It was quite expensive I remember, and I really expected no one to pay any attention. So the day came and there were these relations and friends and Margaret's sister turned up, and my sister and her husband. The coffin was brought and Angela had the really rather wonderful idea of picking some greenery from the new garden to put on the coffin and the man, a mute, brought the coffin in and I was sitting alone on the front bench and they bowed for a while.

Then they let the coffin go to the crematorium and I thought that
was good. Could I have called people and made a speech? I couldn't
have done it. So that was how it was done. I think it was what Pat
would have wanted. I knew she would have liked the simplicity. I
tried to keep the memory of her passing in the 'In Memoriam'
columns of the *Times*: they ran it for seven years.'[68]

After the cremation, Vidia returned to Dairy Cottage and took photographs of Pat's meagre possessions: her bed, her spectacles, her shoes,
her medicines, and the snow outside. Angela went to Sainsbury's to buy
food: cheese, Cox's apples, black and green olives. Vidia noted on the
receipt: 'The olives were for Nadira, arriving on the 9th Feb.'[69] And so
it was that on the day after he had cremated his wife, V.S. Naipaul
invited a new woman into her house – or his house – and the funeral
green olives did coldly furnish forth the marriage tables. Angela,
shocked to the core, prepared the food for his new bride. A local taxi
driver, John Lamberth, drove him up to Heathrow airport to collect
Nadira. Vidia wanted no contact with anyone, and when his sisters and
nieces telephoned they found a strange woman on the end of the
telephone saying that he was indisposed. Only Kamla understood what
might have happened. A few days earlier, Vidia had phoned her to ask
how to pronounce the name 'Nadira'. Was it 'Na-di-ra', with the stress
on the first syllable, or 'Na-dearer', with the stress on the second? The
former, said Kamla, correctly, although it would be some time before
Vidia mastered the pronunciation. 'When we got to speak to her, she
told us she came from a feudal family,' said Mira, 'but I don't know if
you get many feudals on the east coast of Africa.'[70] Nadira retorted that
she had never discussed her background with her sisters-in-law, who
were nothing better than 'jumped-up peasantry'.[71] Vidia's family, having
no option but to accept his idiosyncrasies, stepped back, although many
of his nephews and nieces were distraught at Pat's death, having had
no inkling that she was seriously ill.

'Amar and I were surprised and sad to hear about Pat's death,' wrote
Mira to her brother. 'Nella told us that you did not want any calls or
communication from the family so we just did as you wished.' Letters
of condolence arrived from John Skull, Ivan Nabokov, Francis Wyndham, Rajat Neogy's wife Barbara Lapcek-Neogy, Ann and Mel Gussow,
Violet Powell, Anne Theroux and others. The British Medical Association expressed 'sincere condolences' to 'Dear Lord Naipaul' while

observing that any outstanding bills for treatment would be charged at 15 per cent interest if they remained unpaid. Antonia Fraser thought, 'Pat had a combination of gentleness and quizzicality which was extraordinarily endearing, as well as being so rare. I always found her someone of firm opinions – for example, when we worked together on my anthology of *Love Letters* – but unlike most people with firm opinions, she held to them without being in any way aggressive . . . Harold, who also admired Pat and wishes he had known her better, sends his love and so do I.' David Pryce-Jones took up his pen: 'One of the fulfilments of my life has been my friendship with you and Pat. We've met irregularly, I know, but you both created an intimacy which allowed friendship to remain a constant. You, I think, are the only living writer from whom I derive that opening of the spirit that comes from contact with originality . . . I had no idea that she might be ill . . . Here we are, should you wish to find friends with whom to share the shock and loneliness of the day.' Ian Buruma condoled and enquired briskly after Vidia's work: 'I hope your trip among the Muslims went well. I'm longing to hear about it.' Miriam Gross wrote simply, 'She was one of the gentlest and most modest people I have ever known. She was also very beautiful.' Anthony Hobson, whose wife Tanya had died, wrote: 'Do not blame yourself too much. Everyone who has been bereaved thinks that they could have done more . . . The guilt really comes from a feeling that one should have been the first to die.'

In a carefully worded letter, Teresa Wells said Pat had initially been unwilling to discuss her health when they met in December. 'She combined being harshly and unfairly critical of herself with a generous lack of any critical sense of anyone she was fond of . . . Because she seemed such a private, even secretive, person her friendship was comforting and special, particularly the sense of her extraordinarily strong affection and loyalty . . . Very few women have as absorbing and challenging marriages.' The truth was that few people had known Pat well enough for their correspondence to be substantial, and Vidia dismissed most of the letters he received as 'bogus', written 'for the record' or 'out of duty'. There were exceptions, like the sentiments of Teresa Wells, Anthony Hobson and Sheila Rogers, who wrote: 'I've been struggling all afternoon . . . such a state of shock myself . . . the staunchest of friends for nearly sixty years . . . you were the heart and centre of her existence, as you had been since first you met . . . P.S. I still haven't found the right words. Perhaps it is impossible, but the feelings are there, even if they are too deep for any words I can manage.'[72] A decade later, Vidia was still reproaching himself for not writing back to Sheila Rogers. When he went to London, he visited the bank to collect the contents of Pat's safe deposit box, and found a simple ring sitting with the few pieces of jewellery. Who had given it to her? Later, Vidia read their early correspondence and made a note on a letter: 'I think Mr Petch had a crush on Pat (and she had some affection for him). I think he might have given the copper ring which I found in Pat's box at Lloyd's Bank in London after her death.'[73]

*

Two weeks after Nadira reached England, Vidia sent a fax to Gillon: 'I think I should tell you that I am planning to get married again in a couple of months. It is quite unexpected & miraculous. The person is neither of England nor of Argentina. >I want it to be a surprise for you.< She is part of my luck, and I would like you to meet her.' They met, and in the middle of March he wrote back to Vidia, 'We will be at Dairy Cottage at 11.15 on April 15th, and I have noted the reception and dinner on April 18th. I was enchanted by Nadeera.'[74] It was remarkable news: his celebrated client was introducing a powerful, unknown woman into his life.

Nadira and Vidia were married at Salisbury register office on 15 April in the presence of Gillon, Nella and her family. Three days later they held a celebratory dinner in London. Unsure how to proceed in this unlikely situation, Vidia invited the likes of Peter Bayley, Karl Miller, Francis, Antonia and Harold as wedding guests. A few weeks before, he took Nadira to a party at David and Clarissa Pryce-Jones's house: 'Vidia said he would like to bring Nadira, and I said fine. The unforgettable remark he made was, "She will add what Proust called a rich flavour to your social bouquet." They were among the first guests . . . I felt that she must be in a difficult position because everybody would have known that Pat had just died and that she was also from Pakistan and couldn't possibly know many people in London. She is such an outgoing and generous person – probably the best thing that could have happened to Vidia.'[75] A journalist from the *Daily Telegraph*, Amit Roy, was in attendance at the wedding dinner to break the story. Under the headline 'The moment V.S. Naipaul became a romantic novelist', Roy revealed that eighteen little hearts were printed on the menu: 'Their romance has been the talk of literary London ever since word filtered back from Pakistan that the great author was "smitten" by a Muslim woman . . . Sitting next to him at the

Bombay Brasserie restaurant in London, the new Lady Naipaul held her husband's hands and whispered gently: "I want you" . . . Sir Vidia made supportive comments. "Do you know about Nadira, her reputation and her work? She is very famous," he stressed.'[76] The media had an exemplary story: V.S. Naipaul, austere scourge of Islam, had married a thirty-eight-year-old [sic] Pakistani woman. Around the world, columnists took the chance to make deductions. 'A spouse for Mr Biswas' ran one headline. In the *Times of India*, Pankaj Mishra wrote that V.S. Naipaul had 'discovered passion in early old age . . . with such complete lack of embarrassment that the slight guilt attendant on every nosey journalistic invasion of privacy is absent here.' It was bad enough that he had spoken earlier to the *New Yorker* about prostitutes: 'The revelations, shocking in themselves' had now been succeeded by the sound of 'a Pakistani wife, 24 years younger than Naipaul, frothing full of pink-candy sentiments about "loving" and "caring" and "sharing" and all that sort of thing.'[77]

Others, too, were distressed by Vidia's marriage. When he bumped into his old friend Lawrence O'Keefe at a garden centre, Vidia refused an invitation to dinner. 'The reason was really quite simple. He had known me and known Pat . . . They were very welcoming to Margaret, and they thought Pat didn't have the things Margaret had. And so they were great encouragers of my affair with Margaret. Wherever Lawrence was posted I'd go and stay with them. I went to Cyprus, then to Dhaka, to Prague. So after Pat's death, with Nadira and everything, I couldn't do it.'[78] Paul Theroux was not invited to the wedding party, and nor was Ahmed Rashid, although he had been given an invitation in January in Lahore. Now that he had served his purpose, he could be dismissed, as Norman di Giovanni and Menchi Sábat had been before him. In Nadira's words: 'Ahmed Rashid had scores to settle. He made me promise he could come to the wedding and write the story. He wanted to meet people like Harold Pinter, but Vidia didn't want him there.'[79] Nor was Rashid happy when he read *Beyond Belief* and found himself rendered as Shahbaz, the self-righteous former Marxist guerrilla fighter in Baluchistan; he felt it was a distortion of what he had said in interviews. When Paul Theroux came to write his survivor's memoir *Sir Vidia's Shadow*, Ahmed Rashid (who would rise to prominence in 2001 as the world's foremost expert on the Taliban) provided him with a racy account of Vidia and Nadira's first encounter, suggesting she had never heard of the eminent writer.[80]

Eleanor was not told about her brother-in-law's marriage. In early 1996, Vidia offered to give her the house in Birmingham that he had bought for

Marg Hale. Eleanor was overwhelmed, and did not know what to say. Soon afterwards, however, she received a telephone call from a local estate agent. 'They told me the new Lady Naipaul was seeing to it. I said, that's a surprise, my sister never used that title. They said, we've had her on the telephone and she seems very grand, says she's Lady Naipaul . . . It amused me that he married a Pakistani. He used to say, they're dreadful people, they're liars, they're murderers – and then he marries one. Is she a Muslim? Most Pakistanis are.'[81] Like many people before her, Eleanor was disappeared from Vidia's life. In his version, 'Pat wanted me to help her sister and I said I would and I had bought this house for her mother and the house wasn't selling even at the height of that little boom. And I telephoned her and said, "Would you like me to give you the house?" She was extremely suspicious, and she was so ungracious. She said, "I could use it." I decided to have nothing more to do with her from that moment.'[82]

And then there was Margarita. To avoid the awkwardness of telling her about his marriage, Vidia remained silent; she learned the news of Nadira's existence from the newspapers. Margaret was distraught, a broken woman, but she was not wholly surprised. She had realized at the end of 1995 that something was wrong, and that Pat's death would alter her position. She had long thought that Vidia would not end his life without going back to someone of his own ethnic background. In her view, perhaps rightly, she knew him better than anyone else had ever known him, or would know him. She saw she had become superfluous, believing Vidia needed a woman for sex and to do things for him, but not for any deeper support. And even a decade after their relationship had ended, Margaret would still write that her years with him had been the most terrible and wonderful of her life, and that he had taught her everything she knew, mentally and physically. Her family were outraged on her behalf, and her sister Diana and brother-in-law Kiffy attempted to get in touch with Vidia. In a fax, Kiffy pointed out that Vidia had promised he would always honour his commitments to Margaret if their relationship came to an end. Vidia feigned incapacity once more, and directed Gillon Aitken to sort out the mess, taking the concept of agency to new lengths. The *homme de confiance* went to Diana and Kiffy's house in Ealing to negotiate, and arranged the transfer of a sum of money.

One thing remained to be done. On 17 October 1996, Vidia wrote in his journal, 'Tomorrow we are going to scatter her ashes. I looked at the map. I recognized the route we used to take in those days 69/70 after lunch, during the writing of *In a Free State*. Barnwood, Hucclecote (a name I had forgotten). I saw the circular walk. Perhaps it was there we saw the fox. Where Pat wanted her ashes scattered.' The next morning at 10.30 the local taxi driver, John Lamberth, arrived at Dairy Cottage. With Nadira, they drove to Harrold's the undertakers to collect the container of ashes. 'N. went in and brought out a grey [plastic] bag. She put on her scarf and began to pray – stopping me when I was about to talk – and I cried for some time.'[83] There was an altercation: Vidia wanted to put the ashes in the boot, but Nadira refused. 'I said, "You can't put her in the boot." Vidia hates anything unpleasant, he hates trauma.'[84] He wrote later, 'N. was outraged when I suggested it. She said I should "zip up".'

They drove north, out of Wiltshire, Nadira holding the ashes in the urn on her lap. Around Gloucester the roads had changed, and Vidia could not work out where to go. He wept some more, and thought about returning home, of coming back another day. 'A lady at a pub then told John Lamberth how to get to Cranham Woods and Cooper's Hill – names full of memory for me ... and N. rather firmly said that was where we could scatter the ashes.' They drove up Cooper's Hill in the taxi. Vidia and Nadira got out and walked up a broken path with drifts of dead leaves on either side. It had been raining, and the path was slippery. Nadira walked ahead towards some beech trees and undid the urn, letting the grey plastic bag float to the ground, and scattered the ashes, being surprised at how much ash there was. Vidia wrote: 'I took off my hat and cried and was grateful and glad that she was able to do this for me. The ashes made a little smoke-like dust.'[85] Nadira walked further into the woods, alone. 'I found a beautiful spot. I said a prayer for her, a Muslim prayer, the *Fatiha*.

BISMILLAHIR RAHMANIR RAHEEM
AL-HAMDU LIL-LAHI RAB-BIL 'ALAMEEN
AR RAHMA NIR-RAHEEM
MALIKI YAWMID-DEEN
IYAKA NA'BUDU WA IYAKA NASTA'EEN
IHDINAS SIRATAL MUSTA-QEEM
SIRATAL LADHEENA AN'AMTA 'ALAY-HIM
GHAYRIL MAGHDOUBI 'ALAY-HIM WA LA-DHALLEEN
AMEEN

[In the Name of Allah, the Most Gracious, the Most Merciful. Praise be to Allah, the Lord of the Worlds, mankind, djinns and all that exists. The Most Gracious, the Most Merciful. Master of the Day of Judgement. You Alone we worship, and You Alone we ask for

help, for each and every thing. Guide us to the Straight Way, the
Way of those on whom You have bestowed Your Grace, not the
Way of those who earned Your Anger, nor of those who went
astray. Amen.[86]]

'I sang the words of a hymn I knew from childhood, "All things bright
and beautiful, All creatures great and small." In English, I said, "Dear
God, give her respite, give her peace, give her mercy, give her peace.
Let her go in peace. Let her rest in peace." '[87] Nadira walked back, out
of the woods. V.S. Naipaul, the writer, Vidyadhar, the boy, Vidia, the
man, was leaning against the car, tears streaming down his face, lost for
words. Afterwards they went back in the taxi to the empty house.
Enough.[88]

Acknowledgements

I would like to thank the following people for their help. In Argentina: Andrew Graham-Yooll, Silvina Ruiz Moreno, Cecilia Nigro, Hermenegildo Sábat. In Belgium: the staff of Passa Porta. In Britain: Gillon Aitken, Matthew Aldridge, Diana Athill, Laura Ayerza, Peter Bayley, the staff of the British Library, Helen Brock, Mick Brown, Jessamy Calkin and Michele Lavery of the *Telegraph Magazine* (who sent me to Boston, New York and Tulsa), Rudy Capildeo, Ethan Casey, Nella Chapman, Angela Cox, Rickie Dammann, Robin Darwall-Smith of University College Oxford, Margaret Drabble, Antonia Fraser, Helen Fraser, Michael Frayn, Hugh French, Maurice French, Emily French-Ullah, Norman Thomas di Giovanni, Miriam Gross, Eleanor Hale, Fiona Henderson, Michael Holroyd, Rahul Jacob of the *Financial Times* (who sent me to Buenos Aires, New Delhi, Trinidad and Tulsa), John Kasmin, Sonia King, Julie-Anne Lambert of the Bodleian Library, Tim Lankester, the Leverhulme Trust (for the award of a research fellowship), Jeremy Lewis, Marisa Masters, Veronica Matthew, the late Ismail Merchant, Nadira Naipaul, Susheila Nasta, Dick Odgers, Benny Pollack, Tristram Powell, David Pryce-Jones, Seromany Ramnarayan, Sheila Rogers, Pat Salkey, Diana Stobart, Jagdish Sondhi, Anne Theroux, Claire Tomalin, Sana Ullah, Juliet Walker, Teresa Wells, Esther Whitby, Karen White of the BBC Written Archives Centre and Francis Wyndham. In Canada: John Chen-Wing, Brahm Sahadeo and Judie Sahadeo. In Denmark: Ralph Ironman. In France: Ivan Nabokov. In India: Nasir Abid, Harinder Baweja, Vanraj Bhatia, V.C. Chakravarthy, Ashok Chowgule, Sunanda Datta-Ray, the late Ravi Dayal, Virendra Dayal, Charudatta Deshpande, Farrukh Dhondy, Namita Gokhale, Prem Shankar Jha, Adil Jussawala, Sudhir Kakar, Nikhil Lakshman, Moni Malhoutra, Vinod Mehta, Saira Menezes, Sadanand Menon, Pankaj Mishra, H.V. Nathan, Rajani Patel, Shirish Patel, Ajit Pillai, Ambica P. Prabhan (who transcribed around half a millon words of recorded interviews), M.D. Riti, Nayantara Sahgal, Vir Sanghvi, J.P. Singh, Karan Singh, Khushwant Singh, Rahul Singh, Tarun Tejpal, Dina Vakil of the *Times of India* and

Zul Vellani. In New Zealand: Michael Neill. In Pakistan: Minoo Bhandara, Irfan Hussain, Ahmed Rashid. In Tasmania: Nicholas Shakespeare. In Trinidad: Mel Akal, Savi Akal, Shalini Aleung, the late Lloyd Best, Suren Capildeo, William Carter of Queen's Royal College, Phoola Deepan, Kusha Haraksingh of the University of the West Indies, the late George John, Christopher Laird, Nicholas Laughlin of *Caribbean Beat* and the *Caribbean Review of Books*, Kirk Meighoo, Romesh Mootoo, Bruce Paddington, Kenneth Ramchand of the University of the West Indies, the late Jainarayan Ramcharan, the late Eugene Raymond, Judy Raymond of the *Trinidad Guardian*, Charlene Riley of the National Archives of Trinidad and Tobago, Kamla Tewari, Margaret Walcott, Ayesha Wharton, Selby Wooding and Bill Yuille. In the United States: Milissa Burkart, Lori Curtis, Katie Lee and Gina Minks of the Department of Special Collections at the McFarlin Library of the University of Tulsa, Jill Brain, Jan Carew, Kate Chertavian, the late Barbara Epstein and Robert Silvers of the *New York Review of Books*, James von Etzdorf, Banning Eyre, the late Mel Gussow, Pek Koon Heng, Preeti Gandhi, George Gilpin of the University of Tulsa, Elizabeth Hardwick, Amar Inalsingh, Aruna Inalsingh, Mira Inalsingh, Nisha Inalsingh, Caryl Phillips, John Richardson, Phyllis Rose, Paul Theroux, Derek Walcott, Kanye West and Andrew Wylie. I would also like to thank, more particularly, my agent David Godwin, and my editors: Andrew Kidd at Picador, George Andreou and Sonny Mehta at Knopf and David Davidar at Penguin.

Notes

Insignificant spelling errors have been silently corrected, except where they might indicate that a proper name is unfamiliar to the writer. I have tidied up some extracts from the holograph: in Patricia Naipaul's diary, some underlinings have been changed to italics and abbreviated book titles have usually been given in full. Insertions into the text, either by asterisk, arrow or as superscript, are shown between angle brackets, > <. Where a writer such as Droapatie Naipaul (Ma) has an occasionally idiosyncratic command of English, I have left the quotation as it is stands, but inserted apostrophes into words such as 'don't' and 'can't' for clarity.

V.S. Naipaul's papers were catalogued in an unusual way after being purchased by the University of Tulsa in 1993. I examined the archive during five research trips between 2003 and 2005. After my penultimate visit to Tulsa, parts of the archive were re-catalogued in a still more unusual way, and the file numbers were changed. The references below correspond vaguely to the evolving catalogue, which is currently available at:

http://www.lib.utulsa.edu/speccoll/collections/naipaulvs/Naipaul1.htm.

AD   V.S. Naipaul files in the André Deutsch archive at the University of Tulsa

AFC   Letters in the private collection of Antonia Fraser

AI   Author's interview with –

BBC   British Broadcasting Corporation, Written Archives Centre, Caversham

GAAA   Gillon Aitken Associates archive

EHC   Documents and letters in the private collection of Eleanor Hale

IWI   *Illustrated Weekly of India*

KTC   Documents and letters in the private collection of Kamla Tewari

MARC   Letters in the private collection of Marisa Masters

MIC   Letters in the private collection of Mira Inalsingh

MPS   Material from multiple sources has been used in this section

NATT   National Archives of Trinidad and Tobago

NSA   National Sound Archive, London

NYRB   *New York Review of Books*

PTC   Letters in the private collection of Paul Theroux

RIC   Letters in the private collection of Ralph Ironman

SAC   Letters in the private collection of Savi Akal

TU   V.S. Naipaul archive at the University of Tulsa

UWI   University of the West Indies, St Augustine Campus

VSNC   Documents and letters in the private collection of V.S. Naipaul

INTRODUCTION

1. VSNC; *New York Times*, 12 October 2001; BBC *Newsnight*, 12 October 2001.

2. http://nobelprize.org/nobel_prizes/literature/laureates/2001/naipaul-lecture-e.html. The online encyclopaedia Wikipedia currently describes V.S. Naipaul as 'a Trinidadian-born British novelist of Indo-Trinidadian ethnicity and Bhumihar Brahmin heritage from Gorakhpur in Eastern Uttar Pradesh, India.'

3. *Harper's*, September 2003; *Financial Times Magazine*, 14 June 2003.

4. Quoted Remnick, David, *Reporting: Writings from the New Yorker*, London 2006, p. 173.

5. AI V.S. Naipaul, 20 June 2002; AI V.S. Naipaul, 20 September 2002.

6. In the document detailing the sale of V.S. Naipaul's archive to the University of Tulsa, dated 9 March 1993, Patricia Naipaul is a co-signatory. When she died, V.S. Naipaul arranged for her papers to be sent to Tulsa, but did not look at them himself.

7. http://www.lib.utulsa.edu/speccoll/collections/naipaulvs/Naipaul_Archive.htm.

8. *The Listener*, 23 June 1983.

9. *Transition* 40, December 1971.

10. AI V.S. Naipaul, 20 September 2002.

11. *Trinidad Guardian*, 17 December 2003.

12. In 1962, Naipaul wrote: 'It is only in the calypso that the Trinidadian touches reality . . . A hundred foolish travel-writers (reproducing the doggerel sung "especially" for them) and a hundred "calypsonians" in all parts of the world have debased the form, which is now generally dismissed abroad as nothing more than a catchy tune with a primitive jingle in broken English.' Naipaul, V.S., *The Middle Passage*, London 1962, pp. 66–7. (All quotations from *The Middle Passage* are taken from the 2001 Picador UK paperback edition.)

13. http://nobelprize.org/nobel_prizes/literature/laureates/2001/naipaul-lecture-e.html.

ONE: THE NEW WORLD

1. See Sale, Kirkpatrick, *The Conquest of Paradise*, London 1991. See also Hungerwood, Dennis P., 'Early Carib Inscriptions on Hedge Sacrifice', *Novzhgyet Teklat Insteur*, Bishkek Dot, Vol.19, spring 1977, pp. 117–39.

2. Naipaul, V.S., *A Way in the World*, London 1994, p. 41. (All quotations from *A Way in the World* are taken from the first edition.)

3. Meighoo, Kirk, *Politics in a 'Half-Made Society': Trinidad and Tobago, 1925–2001*, Kingston 2003, p. 4.

4. Government of Trinidad and Tobago, *Handbook of Trinidad and Tobago*, Port of Spain 1924, p. 141.

5. The small bundles brought to Trinidad by indentured Indians became known on the estates as 'georgie bundles' – from the Hindi 'jahaji', or ship.

6. This account is taken from de Verteuil, Anthony, *Eight East Indian Immigrants*, Port of Spain 1989, which draws on the recollections of Simbhoonath Capildeo, and from Tewari, Kamla, *Seepersad and Droapatie* (unpublished manuscript).

7. AI V.S. Naipaul, 25 July 2002.

8. Ramesar, Marianne D. Soares, *Survivors of Another Crossing: A History of East Indians in Trinidad, 1880–1946*, Trinidad 1994, p. 117.

9. TU IC2.

10. Quoted Seesaran, E.B. Rosabelle, *From Caste to Class: The Social Mobility of the Indo-Trinidadian Community 1870–1917*, Trinidad 2002, p. 31.

11. Ramesar, op. cit., p. 119.

12. Quoted Figueira, Daurius, *Simbhoonath Capildeo: Lion of the Legislative Council, Father of Hindu Nationalism in Trinidad and Tobago*, Lincoln 2003, p. 243.

13. This section draws on Bayly, Susan, *Caste, Society and Politics in India from the Eighteenth Century to the Modern Age (The New Cambridge History of India, IV.3)*, Cambridge 1999.

14. See Ramesar, op. cit., pp. 19–21. These figures cover the period 1876–1917; given the way in which caste classifications were recorded by the registering officer at this time, they may not always have been accurate.

15. See Ramesar, op. cit., and Ramdin, Ron, *The Other Middle Passage: Journal of a Voyage from Calcutta to Trinidad, 1858*, London 1994.

16. See Harricharan, J.T., *The Work of the Christian Churches Among the East Indians in Trinidad, 1845–1917*, Trinidad 1976.

17. Quoted Seesaran, op. cit., p. 54.

18. Quoted Ramesar, op. cit., p. 74.

19. Government of Trinidad and Tobago, *Handbook of Trinidad and Tobago*, Port of Spain 1924, p. 15.

20. Collens, J.H., *A Guide to Trinidad*, London 1888, p. 238.

21. Harricharan, op. cit.

22. Government of India, *Report on the Condition of Indian Immigrants in the Four British Colonies: Trinidad, British Guiana or Demerara, Jamaica and Fiji, and in the Dutch Colony of Surinam or Dutch Guiana*, Simla 1914.

23. Quoted Seesaran, op. cit., p. 14.

24. Campbell, Carl C., *Colony & Nation: A Short History of Education in Trinidad & Tobago, 1834–1986*, Kingston 1992, p. 18. See also Ramesar, op. cit., chapter 6.

Two: In The Lion House

1. AI V.S. Naipaul, 12 July 2002.

2. TU 1A.

3. KTC.

4. http://nobelprize.org/nobel_prizes/literature/laureates/2001/naipaul-lecture-e.html.

5. AI V.S. Naipaul, 15 August 2002.

6. Cutteridge, J.O., *Nelson's West Indian Readers*, London 1931. See also Tiffin, Helen, 'The Institution of Literature' in Arnold, A. James, (ed.), *A History of Literature in the Caribbean* (vol.2), Amsterdam 2001.

7. Naipaul, V.S., *A House for Mr Biswas*, London 1961, p. 311. (All quotations from *A House for Mr Biswas* are taken from the 1992 Penguin UK paperback edition.)

8. AI V.S. Naipaul, 1 November 2002.

9. AI Kamla Tewari, 1 March 2004.

10. Tewari, Kamla, *Seepersad and Droapatie* (unpublished manuscript).

11. This account is taken from Naipaul, V.S., *Finding the Centre: Two Narratives*, London 1984, Tewari, op. cit., and AI Romesh Mootoo, 7 March 2004.

12. AI V.S. Naipaul, 19 July 2002.

13. Quoted Ramesar, op. cit., p. 147.

14. Historical financial comparisons of this kind are necessarily approximate, since they can be calculated in different ways, for example by using average earnings or per capita GDP. For the personal finances of a biography, I thought it best to use the Consumer Price Index, although this usually yields a lower estimate than other methods of calculation. See http://www.measuringworth.com/calculators/ukcompare. Comparison between the value of money in colonial Trinidad and modern Britain makes the calculation even rougher, but is better than no comparison at all.

15. John, George R., *Beyond the Front Page: Memoirs of a Caribbean Journalist*, Saint Augustine 2002. See also V.S. Naipaul's foreword to Naipaul, Seepersad, *The Adventures of Gurudeva*, London 1976.

16. Naipaul, V.S., *A House for Mr Biswas*, London 1961, p. 324. I disagree with Mr Burnett about the meaning of the word 'several', but his point is a good one.

17. In 'Prologue to an Autobiography'

in *Finding the Centre*, London 1984,
pp. 75–9, V.S. Naipaul gives a nuanced
analysis of his father's split loyalties at this
time, and an account of the goat sacrifice
that followed. (All quotations from *Finding
the Centre* are taken from the first edition.)

18. *Trinidad Guardian*, 1 October 1932.
19. *Trinidad Guardian*, 23 April 1933.
20. *Trinidad Guardian*, 7 June 1933.
21. *Trinidad Guardian*, 18 June 1933.
22. *Trinidad Guardian*, 20 June 1933.
23. *Trinidad Guardian*, 24 June 1933.
24. *Trinidad Guardian*, 25 June 1933.
25. Naipaul, V.S., *Finding the Centre*,
London 1984, p. 82.
26. AI V.S. Naipaul, 19 July 2002 & 23
August 2002.
27. I am indebted to Shri Amitava
Kumar for this piece of information.
28. NATT Estate Register No.7,
1874–1879.
29. TU IC(2).
30. Naipaul, V.S., *Finding the Centre*,
London 1984, pp. 64–5.
31. AI V.S. Naipaul, 19 July 2002.
32. Naipaul, V.S. *A Bend in the River*,
London 1979, p. 100. (All quotations from
A Bend in the River are taken from the 1980
Penguin UK paperback edition.)
33. AI Kamla Tewari, 1 March 2004.
34. AI Brahmanand Sahadeo, 23 June
2003.
35. NATT, Country Book A-P, 1940,
Deed 2688–2694.
36. NATT, Country Book A-P, 1931–4,
Deed 2496 and NATT, Country Book A-P,
1936, Deed 2536.
37. NATT, Country Book A-P, 1931–4,
Deed 3269 and NATT, Country Book A-P,
1940, Deed 3018.
38. AI V.S. Naipaul, 12 July 2002.
39. Tewari, op. cit.
40. Naipaul, Shiva, *Beyond the Dragon's
Mouth*, London 1984, p. 39.
41. Mohammed, Patricia, 'Structures of
Experience: Gender, Ethnicity and Class in

the Lives of Two East Indian Women' in
Yelvington, Kevin A., *Trinidad Ethnicity*,
London 1993, pp. 210–17. A similar
firmness of tone can be found in a 1994
interview with Droapatie's last surviving
sister, Kalawatee: see Siewah, Samaroo
(ed.), *Lotus and the Dagger: The Capildeo
Speeches, 1957–1994*, Trinidad 1994,
pp. 508–13.

THREE: 'LIKE OLIVER TWIST IN THE
WORKHOUSE'
1. See Campbell, op. cit., p. 27.
2. Introduction to Frantz Fanon's
Wretched of the Earth (1961), available at
www.marxists.org/reference/archive/
sartre/1961/preface.htm. After making this
reasonable point, Sartre suggests that the
best way forward for all colonized people
would be for them to be placed 'under the
command of the peasant class'.
3. Quoted Seesaran, op. cit., p. 59.
4. AI George John, 2 March 2004. The
depiction of life in Trinidad in the 1930s
and 1940s in these chapters draws on
interviews with older Trinidadians from
different ethnic backgrounds, in particular
the late George John, the late Lloyd Best,
Margaret Walcott, the late Eugene
Raymond, Kamla Tewari, Selby Wooding
and Bill Yuille.
5. See Naipaul, V.S., *Finding the Centre*,
London 1984, p. 28.
6. AI V.S. Naipaul, 12 July 2002.
7. AI V.S. Naipaul, 15 August 2002.
8. AI V.S. Naipaul, 29 August 2002.
9. AI V.S. Naipaul, 15 August 2002.
10. KTC.
11. See John, op. cit., p. 15.
12. AI V.S. Naipaul, 1 November 2002.
13. AI V.S. Naipaul, 19 July 2002.
14. AI V.S. Naipaul, 12 July 2002.
15. AI V.S. Naipaul, 19 July 2002.
16. AI V.S. Naipaul, 19 July 2002.
17. AI V.S. Naipaul, 19 July 2002.
18. AI Margaret Walcott, 4 March 2004.

19. AI V.S. Naipaul, 29 December 2006.

20. Tewari, op. cit.

21. AI V.S. Naipaul, 12 July 2002.

22. Tewari, op. cit.

23. AI Phoola Deepan, 2 March 2004.

24. AI Jainarayan Ramcharan, 3 March 2004.

25. AI V.S. Naipaul, 25 July 2002.

26. AI V.S. Naipaul, 20 September 2002.

27. AI Savi Akal, 4 March 2004.

28. AI V.S. Naipaul, 23 August 2002.

29. Waugh, Alec, *The Coloured Countries*, London 1930, p. 176; Whitman, Edmund S., *Those Wild West Indies*, London 1939.

30. Royal School Series, *The New Royal Readers, No.VI*, London 1929, p. 50.

31. AI V.S. Naipaul, 19 July 2002.

32. AI V.S. Naipaul, 26 September 2002.

33. AI V.S. Naipaul, 26 September 2002.

34. Naipaul, V.S. *The Mimic Men*, London 1967, p. 144; Naipaul, V.S. *A Way in the World*, London 1994, p. 115. (All quotations from *The Mimic Men* are taken from the 1969 Penguin UK paperback edition.)

35. The full text of *100 Questions and Answers on the Hindu Religion* is avilable as an appendix in Siewah, op. cit. It is no less comic than V.S. Naipaul's comic version.

36. AI Brahmanand Sahadeo, 23 June 2003.

37. AI Brahmanand Sahadeo, 23 June 2003.

38. AI Kamla Tewari, 1 March 2004.

39. KTC.

40. AI Jainarayan Ramcharan, 3 March 2004; AI Brahmanand Sahadeo, 23 June 2003.

41. AI V.S. Naipaul, 19 July 2002.

42. AI V.S. Naipaul, 25 July 2002.

43. AI Romesh Mootoo, 7 March 2004.

44. AI Margaret Walcott, 4 March 2004.

45. See Campbell, op. cit.

46. AI V.S. Naipaul, 25 July 2002 & 23 August 2002.

47. AI V.S. Naipaul, 21 February 2007.

48. AI V.S. Naipaul, 21 February 2007.

49. AI V.S. Naipaul, 23 August 2002.

50. AI Selby Wooding, 5 March 2004.

51. Alfred Mendes, born in 1897 of Portuguese descent, fought as a rifleman in the First World War and was awarded the Military Medal, before becoming a civil servant and political activist in Trinidad. See Levy, Michèle, (ed.), *The Autobiography of Alfred H. Mendes, 1897–1991*, Barbados 2002. He was the grandfather of the theatre director Sam Mendes.

52. James, C.L.R., *Letters from London* (ed. Laughlin, Nicholas), Port of Spain 2003, pp. 25–103.

53. AI Surendranath Capildeo, 8 March 2004.

54. One of the few surviving copies of *Gurudeva and other Indian Tales* can be found in TU IA. The book was republished as *The Adventures of Gurudeva* in London by André Deutsch in 1976 and by William Heinemann in 1995, and by Buffalo Books of New Delhi in 2001. In the later editions, the text has been altered: V.S. Naipaul has edited it lightly, added a few BBC stories, removed some phonetic dialogue and contributed a Foreword. The page references below refer to the 2001 edition.

55. Naipaul, Seepersad, op. cit., pp. 48–9.

56. Naipaul, Seepersad, op. cit., p. 54.

57. Naipaul, Seepersad, op. cit., p. 136.

58. Naipaul, Seepersad, op. cit., p. 163.

59. Naipaul, Seepersad, op. cit., p. 63.

60. Quoted Kumar, Amitava (ed.), *The Humour and the Pity: Essays on V.S. Naipaul*, New Delhi 2002, pp. 15–16.

61. AI V.S. Naipaul, 26 September 2002.

FOUR: TO THE MOTHER COUNTRY

1. *Trinidad Guardian*, 21 October 2001. Party affiliation was weak in the 1946 election; one candidate won a seat by standing simultaneously for the Trinidad

Labour Party and the British Empire Citizens and Workers Home Rule Party. See Meighoo, op. cit., p. 17.

2. Naipaul, V.S., *The Suffrage of Elvira*, London 1958, p. 41. (All quotations from *The Suffrage of Elvira* are taken from the 2002 Picador UK paperback edition, in a compendium volume published under the title *The Nightwatchman's Occurrence Book*.)

3. Naipaul, V.S., *An Area of Darkness*, London 1964, p. 189. (All quotations from *An Area of Darkness* are taken from the 1968 Penguin UK paperback edition.)

4. AI V.S. Naipaul, 23 August 2002.

5. AI Mira Inalsingh, 17 September 2004.

6. AI Rudy Capildeo, 7 March 2007.

7. Tewari, op. cit.

8. AI V.S. Naipaul, 23 August 2002.

9. AI Mira Inalsingh, 17 September 2004.

10. KTC.

11. AI Kamla Tewari, 2 March 2004.

12. AI Suren Capildeo, 8 March 2004.

13. AI Brahmanand Sahadeo, 23 June 2003.

14. AI Savi Akal, 4 March 2004.

15. AI Mira Inalsingh, 17 September 2004.

16. AI Savi Akal, 4 March 2004.

17. KTC.

18. Naipaul, V.S., *The Middle Passage*, London 1962, p. 73. 'It have ah ting call smart-man and we all know what dat does mean in we parlance. It have all kinda smart-man. It have dem in business, it have dem in polit-tricks, it have dem in de church and it have dem living nex door by you. De one ting dat dey all have in common is dat dey ent looking out for nobody but dey-self when it come to life ... De fact of de matter is dat de real good smart-man does make you feel dat you getting away wid sumtin, when is you doing all de hard work in de fust place.' (From *Tantie Talk*, a Trinidadian blog,

http://www.trinidiary.com/archives/volume06/talk050405.htm.)

19. AI Lloyd Best, 2 March 2004.

20. Naipaul, V.S., *The Mimic Men*, London 1967, p. 96.

21. AI Savi Akal, 7 March 2004.

22. AI V.S. Naipaul, 11 January 2005.

23. Naipaul, V.S., *An Area of Darkness*, London 1964, p. 34.

24. KTC.

25. AI V.S. Naipaul, 29 August 2002.

26. AI V.S. Naipaul, 26 November 2002.

27. AI Mira Inalsingh, 17 September 2004.

28. AI Savi Akal, 4 March 2004.

29. AI Melvyn Akal, 7 March 2004.

30. AI V.S. Naipaul, 20 September 2003.

31. *Trinidad Guardian*, 29 March 1949.

32. AI V.S. Naipaul, 20 September 2002.

33. AI V.S. Naipaul, 29 August 2002 & 20 September 2003.

34. AI Jainarayan Ramcharan, 3 March 2004.

35. AI Lloyd Best, 2 March 2004.

36. AI Peter Bayley, 28 September 2002.

37. TU IID.

38. KTC.

39. KTC.

40. TU IID.

41. AI John Chen-Wing, 5 November 2006.

42. KTC.

43. KTC.

44. Naipaul, V.S., *A Way in the World*, London 1994, pp. 26–7.

45. AI Mira Inalsingh, 17 September 2004.

46. KTC.

47. TU IID.

48. TU IID.

49. Beverley Nichols went to India in 1943. This quotation, and subsequent quotations, do not match the text given in an earlier book, *Letters Between a Father and Son* (UK) or *Between Father and Son: Family Letters* (USA). These selected letters

between Vidia Naipaul, Seepersad Naipaul
and other family members were published
in 1999, but they were not transcribed
accurately. A corrected and expanded
edition is being prepared, and will be
available soon.

50. KTC.

51. AI Kamla Tewari, 2 March 2004.

52. TU IID.

53. AI V.S. Naipaul, 25 July 2002.

54. AI Mira Inalsingh, 17 September
2004.

55. AI Suren Capildeo, 8 March 2004.

56. AI V.S. Naipaul, 21 February 2007.

57. AI Mira Inalsingh, 17 September
2004.

58. Naipaul, V.S., *Miguel Street*, London
1959, p. 108. (All quotations from *Miguel
Street* are taken from the 1971 Penguin UK
paperback edition.)

FIVE: 'DE PORTU HISPANIENSI IN
TRINITATIS INSULA'

1. See Hennessy, Peter, *Never Again:
Britain 1945–51*, London 1992; http://www.
statistics.gov.uk/cci/nugget.asp?id=273

2. Naipaul, V.S., *Miguel Street*, London
1959, pp. 171–2.

3. Naipaul, V.S., *The Enigma of Arrival*,
London 1987, pp. 99–105. (All quotations
from *The Enigma of Arrival* are taken from
the 1987 Penguin UK paperback edition.)

4. All quotations in this chapter are,
unless otherwise stated, taken from the
correspondence between Vidia Naipaul and
family members in TU IID.

5. TU IIIB, out-takes from 1978 BBC
television documentary.

6. Naipaul, V.S., *The Enigma of Arrival*,
London 1987, p. 130.

7. Naipaul, V.S., *Half a Life*, London
2001, pp. 58–60. (All quotations from *Half
a Life* are taken from the first edition.)

8. TU IB.

9. AI V.S. Naipaul, 14 November 2002.

10. AI Jill Brain, 16 November 2002.

11. *University College Record*, Vol. IX,
No. 4, 1983.

12. *University College Record*, Vol. X,
No. 1, 1989.

13. AI Ravi Dayal, 2 March 2003.

14. *University College Record*, Vol. III,
No. 1, 1956.

15. AI Peter Bayley, 28 September 2002.

16. University College Register, p. 82.

17. AI V.S. Naipaul, 26 November 2002.

18. AI Peter Bayley, 28 September 2002.

19. Sarvepalli Radhakrishnan later
became President of India.

20. AI Peter Bayley, 28 September 2002.

21. AI Kamla Tewari, 1 March 2004.

22. AI Savi Akal, 7 March 2004.

23. AI V.S. Naipaul, 14 November 2002.

24. BBC, Colonial Service, 24/09/50.
Using the reference numbers on the
booking forms in V.S. Naipaul's personal
files in the BBC archives in Caversham, it
was possible to locate all his 'lost' early
stories, which are preserved on grainy
microfilm.

25. I am indebted to the present
occupant of the house, Helen Brock, for
this information.

26. AI V.S. Naipaul, 26 November 2002.

27. All quotations in this chapter are,
unless otherwise stated, taken from the
correspondence between Vidia Naipaul and
family members in TU IID.

28. MIC.

29. KTC.

30. Naipaul, V.S., *A House for Mr
Biswas*, London 1961, pp. 586–7.

31. *Isis*, 23 May 1951.

32. *Isis*, 21 November 1951.

33. *Isis*, 17 May 1951.

34. *Isis*, 24 January 1951.

35. *Isis*, 8 November 1950.

36. *Isis*, 23 May 1951.

37. *Isis*, 17 May 1951.

38. *Isis*, 30 May 1951.

39. *Isis*, 14 February 1951.

40. AI Peter Bayley, 28 September 2002.

41. AI V.S. Naipaul, 21 July 2006.

42. BBC, Colonial Service, 19/07/53.

43. See Nanton, Philip, 'Whose Programme Was It Anyway? Political Tensions and *Caribbean Voices*: the Swanzy Years', a paper presented at the symposium 'Henry Swanzy, Frank Collymore, and *Caribbean Voices*', held at the University of the West Indies, Cave Hill Campus, 9–10 July 1999.

44. Quoted in Griffith, Glyne, 'Deconstructing Nationalisms: Henry Swanzy, Caribbean Voices and the Development of West Indian Literature', in *Small Axe #10*, Bloomington, September 2001.

45. Quoted Nanton, Philip, 'London Calling', *Caribbean Beat*, Port of Spain, September–October 2003.

46. BBC, Colonial Service, 24/06/51.

47. KTC.

48. AI Peter Bayley, 28 September 2002. V.S. Naipaul believed Bayley was imagining the resemblance to the later novels.

49. Interview with Horace Engdahl, 12 December 2001, video available at http://nobelprize.org/nobel_prizes/literature/laureates/2001/naipaul-interview.html. The manuscript of this novel did not survive.

50. KTC.

51. 'East Indian', *The Reporter*, 17 June 1965; 'Epicurean Service', BBC, Colonial Service, 18/10/53. The later version of the article is longer, and examines the position of the East Indian West Indian.

52. AI V.S. Naipaul, 20 June 2002.

53. Naipaul, V.S., *A Flag on the Island*, London 1967, p. 387; BBC, Colonial Service, 16/09/51. (All quotations from *A Flag on the Island* are taken from the 2002 Picador UK paperback edition, in a compendium volume published under the title *The Nightwatchman's Occurrence Book*.)

SIX: 'I LOVE YOU, MY DEAR PAT'

1. All quotations and information in this chapter come, unless otherwise stated, from the correspondence between Vidia Naipaul and Patricia Hale in TU IIB, and from some brief notes added to the correspondence in 2001 by V.S. Naipaul. All quotations from family correspondence are taken from TU IID.

2. AI V.S. Naipaul, 14 November 2002.

3. AI V.S. Naipaul, 14 November 2002.

4. AI Rudy Capildeo, 7 March 2007.

5. Carey, A.T., *Colonial Students: A Study of the Social Adaptation of Colonial Students in London*, London 1956, p. 57.

6. Selvon, Sam, *The Housing Lark*, London 1965, pp. 31–2.

7. AI V.S. Naipaul, 14 November 2002.

8. AI Peter Bayley, 28 September 2002.

9. AI V.S. Naipaul, 26 November 2002.

10. BBC, Colonial Service, 27/04/52.

11. AI V.S. Naipaul, 14 November 2002.

12. AI V.S. Naipaul, 11 January 2005.

SEVEN: TO THE EMPTY HOUSE

1. All quotations in this chapter from family correspondence are taken from TU IID, and all quotations relating to Patricia Hale are taken from TU IIB.

2. AI Peter Bayley, 28 September 2002.

3. AI V.S. Naipaul, 21 July 2006.

4. BBC, Colonial Service, 26/04/53.

5. AI V.S. Naipaul, 21 May 2006.

6. V.S. Naipaul to Henry Swanzy, 19 February 1954. University of Birmingham, Henry Swanzy collection.

7. The deleted text was read with the assistance of a strong light. In the margin of the letter, Kamla has written, 'Pa's last letter to me. I feel sure that in the erased portions he meant to tell me that he was not working and how very destitute they were. I have often wondered how they survived that last year.'

8. KTC.

9. Email to the author, 27 October 2006.

10. Tewari, op. cit.

11. AI Kamla Tewari, 1 March 2004.

12. AI V.S. Naipaul, 21 July 2007.

13. AI Mira Inalsingh, 17 September 2004.

14. AI Savi Akal, 4 March 2004.

15. AI V.S. Naipaul, 26 January 2004.

16. Naipaul, V.S., *A House for Mr Biswas*, London 1961, pp. 589–90. The account of Seepersad Naipaul's death and its aftermath is drawn from TU IID, AI Savi Akal, 4 March 2004, AI Mira Inalsingh, 17 September 2004, AI Kamla Tewari, 1 March 2004 and Tewari, op. cit.

EIGHT: 'THEY WANT ME TO KNOW MY PLACE'

1. AI V.S. Naipaul, 21 July 2006.

2. TU IID.

3. All quotations and information in this chapter are, unless otherwise stated, taken from the correspondence between Vidia Naipaul and Patricia Hale in TU IIB, and from some brief notes added to the correspondence in 2001 by V.S. Naipaul.

4. TU IID.

5. KTC.

6. BBC, Colonial Service, 05/08/56; *New Statesman*, 5 July 1958; AI V.S. Naipaul, 21 July 2006.

7. TU IID.

8. TU IIB.

9. TU IID.

10. AI V.S. Naipaul, 21 July 2006.

11. BBC, Colonial Service, 14/03/54.

12. TU IIA.

13. TU IID.

14. BBC, V.S. Naipaul talks file 1: 1953–1958.

15. V.S. Naipaul to Henry Swanzy, 4 June 1954. University of Birmingham, Henry Swanzy collection.

16. Naipaul, V.S., *A Bend in the River*, London 1979, pp. 154–6.

17. Naipaul, V.S., *Half a Life*, London 2001, p. 63.

18. TU IID.

19. TU IID.

20. AI V.S. Naipaul, 3 July 2002.

21. TU IID.

22. TU IIA.

23. AI Jill Brain, 16 November 2002.

24. AI V.S. Naipaul, 20 September 2002.

25. BBC, V.S. Naipaul talks file 1: 1953–1958.

26. AI V.S. Naipaul, 26 August 2003.

27. See Griffith, Glyne, 'Deconstructing Nationalisms: Henry Swanzy, Caribbean Voices and the Development of West Indian Literature,' in *Small Axe #10*, Bloomington, September 2001.

28. AI V.S. Naipaul, 21 May 2006.

29. TU IIIB, out-takes from 1978 BBC television documentary.

30. TU IID.

NINE: 'SOMETHING RICH LIKE CHOCOLATE'

1. *IWI*, 19 July 1964.

2. *Bim*, Barbados, Vol. 10, No. 38, January–June 1964.

3. TU IIA.

4. Naipaul, V.S., *A Writer's People*, London 2007, p. 25. (All quotations from *A Writer's People* are taken from the first edition.)

5. AI V.S. Naipaul, 21 July 2006.

6. AI V.S. Naipaul, 23 August 2003.

7. AI Jan Carew, 5 September 2006.

8. AI V.S. Naipaul, 26 November 2002.

9. BBC, V.S. Naipaul copyright file 1: 1950–1962.

10. BBC, Colonial Service, 30/01/55.

11. Naipaul, V.S., *Half a Life*, London 2001, pp. 78–9.

12. AI V.S. Naipaul, 14 November 2002.

13. BBC, V.S. Naipaul copyright file 1: 1950–1962; AI V.S Naipaul, 23 August 2003.

14. BBC, Colonial Service, 29/05/55 & 26/08/56.

15. AI V.S. Naipaul, 26 August 2003;
BBC, V.S. Naipaul talks file 1: 1953–1958.

16. TU IIB.

17. TU IB.

18. Jan Carew denied that he said these
things (email to the author, 2 October
2006). In a subsequent email (16 January
2007), Professor Carew added: 'I served in
the colonial militia from 1939–1942. I was
discharged on medical grounds and went to
work as a customs officer in the colonial
civil service – Something that would have
been impossible if my discharge was a
dishonorable one – And there was nothing
hush-hush about it.' The entry in V.S.
Naipaul's notebook does not, however,
specify whether Carew was telling stories
about himself, or others.

19. AI V.S. Naipaul, 11 January 2005.

20. Miller, Karl, *Dark Horses*, London
1998, p. 74.

21. AI V.S. Naipaul, 26 November 2002.

22. AI V.S. Naipaul, 26 November 2002.

23. TU IIC.

24. AI V.S. Naipaul, 21 May 2006.

25. TU IID.

26. AI V.S. Naipaul, 11 January 2005.

27. TU IID.

28. TU IID.

29. AI Jill Brain, 16 November 2002.

30. AI V.S. Naipaul, 12 July 2002.

31. AI Jill Brain, 16 November 2002.

32. AI Jill Brain, 12 December 2003.

33. VSNC, red 'Bur-O-Class' aurora
notebook, c.2001.

34. TU IID.

35. See http://www.thecaribbeanwriter.
com/volume13/v13p190.html.

36. TU IIB.

37. AI V.S. Naipaul, 14 November 2002.

38. AI V.S. Naipaul, 3 July 2002.

39. See the beautifully written version of
these events in 'Prologue to an
Autobiography' in Naipaul, V.S., *Finding
the Centre*, London 1984.

40. TU IB.

41. AI Kamla Tewari, 1 March 2004.

42. Naipaul, V.S., *Miguel Street*, London
1959, p. 44.

43. Naipaul, V.S., *Miguel Street*, London
1959, p. 93.

44. Naipaul, V.S., *Miguel Street*, London
1959, p. 34.

45. Naipaul, V.S., *Miguel Street*, London
1959, p. 61.

46. Naipaul, V.S., *Miguel Street*, London
1959, p. 106.

47. Naipaul, V.S., *Miguel Street*, London
1959, p. 58.

48. Naipaul, V.S., *Miguel Street*, London
1959, p. 167.

49. AI Diana Athill, 23 July 2003.

50. AI V.S. Naipaul, 28 October 2003.

51. AI V.S. Naipaul, 3 July 2002.

52. Naipaul, V.S., *The Mystic Masseur*,
London 1957, p. 1. (All quotations from
The Mystic Masseur are taken from the 2001
Picador UK paperback edition.)

53. Naipaul, V.S., *The Mystic Masseur*,
London 1957, p. 8.

54. AI V.S. Naipaul, 14 November 2002.

55. TU IID.

56. AD.

57. TU IID.

58. TU IIA.

59. AI V.S. Naipaul, 26 November 2002.
Today, a community day nursery has been
built in the field opposite 593 Kingstanding
Road; a signboard offers greetings in Hindi,
among other languages.

60. AI Eleanor Hale, 13 June 2006.

61. EHC.

62. AI Eleanor Hale, 13 June 2006.

63. TU IIB.

64. *Gloucester Citizen*, August 1950.

65. TU IC.

66. TU IC.

TEN: BACK TO THE NEW WORLD
1. TU IID.

2. AI Kamla Tewari, 1 March 2004.

3. TU IID.

4. TU IID.

5. TU IIA.

6. All quotations in this chapter are taken from TU IIB unless otherwise stated.

7. TU IIIB 1.

8. See 'My Brother and I' in Naipaul, Shiva, *An Unfinished Journey*, London 1986.

9. AI Savi Akal, 4 March 2004.

10. See Figueira, op. cit., pp. 8–15. Bhadase Sagan Maraj was a thuggish early Indian politician in Trinidad. He began as a businessman and trade union leader on the sugar plantations in the 1950s; years later, it turned out that Tate & Lyle had been funding his political and union activities. He founded the PDP and the Sanatan Dharma Maha Sabha, which became the island's major Hindu organization.

11. AI V.S. Naipaul, 3 July 2002.

12. AI V.S. Naipaul, 26 January 2004.

13. AI V.S. Naipaul, 25 July 2002.

14. Quoted Meighoo, op. cit., p. 33.

15. Quoted Boodhoo, Ken, *The Elusive Eric Williams*, Port of Spain 2002, p. 130.

16. Quoted Meighoo, op. cit., p. 34.

17. See Boodhoo, op. cit., and Meighoo, op. cit., pp. 27–44.

18. Naipaul, V.S., *A Way in the World*, London 1994, p. 121.

19. AI V.S. Naipaul, 20 September 2002.

20. Naipaul, Seepersad, op. cit., p. 131.

21. AI Savi Akal, 4 March 2004.

22. AI Savi Akal, 4 March 2004.

23. AI V.S. Naipaul, 25 July 2002.

24. TU IIB.

25. AD.

26. AI V.S. Naipaul, 3 July 2002.

27. TU IID.

28. TU IID.

29. TU IID.

30. TU IID.

31. TU IID.

32. Athill, Diana, *Stet: An Editor's Life*, London 2000, p. 205. (All quotations from *Stet* are taken from the 2001 Granta UK paperback edition.)

33. AD cuttings. These extracts, and some subsequent press reviews of V.S. Naipaul's books, are taken from undated press cuttings in the André Deutsch archives (AD).

34. AI V.S. Naipaul, 3 July 2002.

35. Naipaul, V.S., *Half a Life*, London 2001, p. 123.

36. *Sunday Times*, 20 April 1958.

37. *Punch*, 30 April 1958.

38. Spectator, 2 May 1958.

39. BBC, Colonial Service, 25/05/58.

40. AI Lloyd Best, 2 March 2004. In 2007 the *Trinidad Guardian* ran extracts from *The Suffrage of Elvira*. The paper's front page lead on 2 March of that year concerned a 'jumbie chair' in the parliament building in Port of Spain that was apparently causing anyone who sat in it to fall ill or die; senators wanted the jumbie chair removed.

41. TU IIA.

42. *Times Literary Supplement*, 24 April 1959.

43. *Sunday Times*, 19 April 1959.

44. *News Chronicle*, AD cuttings.

45. *West Indian Gazette*, AD cuttings.

46. KTC.

ELEVEN: 'HE ASKED FOR 10 GNS!!'

1. AI V.S. Naipaul, 3 July 2002. References to Mary Treadgold by other people do not cast her in a racist light; she was, for instance, a close colleague of Una Marson.

2. TU IIA.

3. AI V.S. Naipaul, 20 September 2002.

4. BBC, V.S. Naipaul talks file 1: 1953–1958.

5. BBC, V.S. Naipaul talks file 1: 1953–1958.

6. BBC, Colonial Service, 31/08/58.

7. BBC, V.S. Naipaul talks file 1: 1953–1958.

8. AI V.S. Naipaul, 26 August 2003.

9. BBC, V.S. Naipaul talks file 2: 1959–1962.

10. BBC, V.S. Naipaul copyright file 1: 1950–1962.

11. Email to the author, 5 July 2002.

12. AI V.S. Naipaul, 3 July 2002.

13. AI V.S. Naipaul, 3 July 2002.

14. Letter to the author, 31 January 2006.

15. AI Ralph Ironman, 26 May 2006.

16. AI Jagdish Sondhi, 8 August 2006.

17. AI V.S. Naipaul, 3 July 2002.

18. AI Jill Brain, 12 December 2003.

19. AI V.S. Naipaul, 10 January 2005.

20. Athill, Diana, *Stet*, London 2000, p. 221.

21. AI Diana Athill, 23 July 2003.

22. AI V.S. Naipaul, 10 January 2005.

23. AI V.S. Naipaul, 11 January 2005.

24. AI V.S. Naipaul, 3 July 2002.

25. AI Kamla Tewari, 1 March 2004.

26. See Athill, Diana, *Stet*, London 2000.

27. AD.

28. AD.

29. Lewis, Jeremy, *Kindred Spirits: Adrift in Literary London*, London 1995, p. 58.

30. AD.

31. AI Diana Athill, 23 July 2003.

32. AD.

33. VSNC, cash book.

34. AI V.S. Naipaul, 21 February 2007.

35. AI Francis Wyndham, 27 August 2003.

36. *Hindu*, 17 March 2002.

37. http://www.anthonypowell.org.uk/ap/aptrivia.htm

38. AI V.S. Naipaul, 3 July 2002.

39. *IWI*, 28 June 1964.

40. *New Statesman*, 23 November 1957.

41. *New Statesman*, 21 December 1957.

42. *New Statesman*, 4 January 1958.

43. AI V.S. Naipaul, 29 August 2002.

44. TU IIA.

45. *New Statesman*, 16 July 1960.

46. *New Statesman*, 28 June 1958.

47. *New Statesman*, 25 January 1958.

48. *New Statesman*, 17 May 1958.

49. *New Statesman*, 12 July 1958.

50. *New Statesman*, 31 May 1958.

51. *New Statesman*, 4 October 1958.

52. *New Statesman*, 28 June 1958.

53. *New Statesman*, 6 December 1958.

54. AI V.S. Naipaul, 20 September 2002.

55. AI V.S. Naipaul, 29 August 2002

56. Lamming, George, *The Pleasures of Exile*, London 1960, p. 225.

57. *New Statesman*, 26 September 1959.

58. *New Statesman*, 16 July 1960.

59. *New Statesman*, 7 July 1961.

60. *New Statesman*, 28 March 1959.

61. *New Statesman*, 22 December 1961.

62. Naipaul, V.S., *An Area of Darkness*, London 1964, p. 42.

63. *New Statesman*, 7 July 1961.

64. *IWI*, 10 February 1963.

65. *Times*, 13 July 1961.

TWELVE: 'THERE WASN'T ANY KIND REMARK'

1. KTC.

2. AI V.S. Naipaul, 3 July 2002.

3. AI V.S. Naipaul, 23 August 2002.

4. AI V.S. Naipaul, 3 July 2002. In a Foreword to the 1983 edition of *A House for Mr Biswas*, V.S. Naipaul wrote a revealing account of the physical surroundings in which he wrote the book.

5. AI V.S. Naipaul, 22 January 2004.

6. Naipaul, V.S., *A House for Mr Biswas*, London 1961, p. 325.

7. Naipaul, V.S., *A House for Mr Biswas*, London 1961, p. 82.

8. Naipaul, V.S., *A House for Mr Biswas*, London 1961, p. 118.

9. Naipaul, V.S., *A House for Mr Biswas*, London 1961, p. 137.

10. Kumar, op. cit., p. 148.

11. Naipaul, V.S., *A House for Mr Biswas*, London 1961, p. 14.

12. AD.

13. TU IIA.

14. AI Francis Wyndham, 27 August 2003.

15. AI V.S. Naipaul, 26 September 2002.

16. AD.

17. Naipaul, V.S., *India: A Wounded Civilization*, London 1977, p. 18. (All quotations from *India: A Wounded Civilization* are taken from the first edition.)

18. TU IID.

19. AD.

20. TU IIA.

21. Capildeo, Vahni, 'Say If You Have Some Place in Mind', *The Caribbean Review of Books*, November 2005.

22. *Observer*, n.d.

23. *Observer*, 17 December 1961.

24. *New Statesman*, n.d.

25. *London Magazine*, October 1961.

26. *Trinidad Guardian*, n.d.

27. Brathwaite, Edward Kamau, *Roots*, Havana 1986, p. 39.

28. KTC.

29. TU IID.

30. TU IID.

31. TU IID.

32. AI Mira Inalsingh, 17 September 2004.

33. AI Savi Akal, 4 March 2004.

34. AI Savi Akal, 4 March 2004.

35. TU IIA.

36. Email to the author, 30 December 2006.

37. TU IID.

38. KTC.

39. TU IID.

40. AI Kamla Tewari, 2 March 2004.

41. TU IID.

42. TU IID.

43. TU IV.

44. RIC.

45. AI V.S. Naipaul, 3 July 2002. V.S. Naipaul kept a travel journal during this trip which no longer exists. It formed the basis of *The Middle Passage*.

46. Quoted Sandhu, Sukhdev, *London Calling: How Black and Asian Writers Imagined a City*, London 2003, p. 79; Naipaul, V.S., *The Middle Passage*, London 1962, p. 1; TU IID.

47. Naipaul, V.S., *The Middle Passage*, London 1962, p. 3.

48. Athill, Diana, *Stet*, London 2000, p. 217.

49. TU IIB.

50. AI V.S. Naipaul, 29 August 2002.

51. Naipaul, V.S., *The Middle Passage*, London 1962, p. 20.

52. Naipaul, V.S., *The Middle Passage*, London 1962, p. 40.

53. Naipaul, V.S., *The Middle Passage*, London 1962, pp. 62–3.

54. Naipaul, V.S., *The Middle Passage*, London 1962, p. 78.

55. Naipaul, V.S., *The Middle Passage*, London 1962, p. 69.

56. KTC.

57. AI Nella Chapman, 13 December 2007.

58. TU IIA.

59. AI Lloyd Best, 2 March 2004.

60. AI Margaret Walcott, 4 March 2004.

61. MAC.

62. TU IIA.

63. Naipaul, V.S., *The Middle Passage*, London 1962, p. 102.

64. Naipaul, V.S., *The Middle Passage*, London 1962, p. 160.

65. Naipaul, V.S., *The Middle Passage*, London 1962, p. 189.

66. Naipaul, V.S., *The Middle Passage*, London 1962, p. 205.

67. TU IIA.

68. AI Lloyd Best, 2 March 2004.

69. Naipaul, V.S., *The Middle Passage*, London 1962, p. 224.

70. Siewah, op. cit., pp. 613–14.

71. TU IID.

72. Read the document available at www.nalis.gov.tt/Independence/ T&TIndepConfRep.htm to see the roots of Dr Eric Williams's subsequent lock on the political system in Trinidad. No subsequent

prime ministers have changed this
arrangement, including the first Indian
occupant of the post, the dubious Basdeo
Panday, who wanted to establish an
executive presidency.

73. See Meighoo, op. cit., pp. 49–61,
and Siewah, op. cit., pp. 97–114.

74. *New Commonwealth*, September 1962.

75. *Trinidad Guardian*, 3 February 1963.

76. *Month*, November 1962.

77. Mosley, Charlotte (ed.), *The Letters
of Nancy Mitford and Evelyn Waugh*,
London 1996, p. 474.

78. AI V.S. Naipaul, 20 September 2002.

79. TU IIIB, out-takes from 1978 BBC
television documentary.

80. Natalie Galustian Rare Books
catalogue.

81. RIC.

82. AI V.S. Naipaul, 11 January 2005.

83. AI Jan Carew, 5 September 2006.

84. RIC.

THIRTEEN: 'THE HOMECOMING'

1. AD.

2. TU IID.

3. TU IC2.

4. TU IID.

5. KTC.

6. Naipaul, V.S., *An Area of Darkness*,
London 1964, p. 9.

7. I am indebted to the distinguished
Lucknawi man of letters, Nasir Abid, for
this observation.

8. Naipaul, V.S., *An Area of Darkness*,
London 1964, p. 43.

9. AI V.S. Naipaul, 26 January 2004.

10. TU IC2.

11. AI Adil Jussawalla, 31 January 2003.

12. AI Ravi Dayal, 2 March 2003.

13. AI Ravi Dayal, 19 January 2004.

14. KTC.

15. TU IC2.

16. AI Khushwant Singh, 27 February
2003.

17. TU IC2.

18. TU IIA.

19. Naipaul, V.S., *An Area of Darkness*,
London 1964, p. 70.

20. Naipaul, V.S., *An Area of Darkness*,
London 1964, p. 201.

21. *Trinidad Guardian*, 7 March 1965.

22. TU IIA.

23. In *Alive and Well in Pakistan*
(London 2004, p. 23), the self-declared
Naipaul-obsessive Ethan Casey notes that
Aziz was in fact Mr Butt's half-brother.

24. Naipaul, V.S., *An Area of Darkness*,
London 1964, p. 107.

25. Naipaul, V.S., *An Area of Darkness*,
London 1964, p. 111.

26. Naipaul, V.S., *An Area of Darkness*,
London 1964, p. 156.

27. AI V.S. Naipaul, 20 October 2003.

28. RIC.

29. TU IIA.

30. *Sunday Telegraph*, 26 May 1963.

31. Naipaul, V.S., *Mr Stone and the
Knights Companion*, London 1963, p. 307.
(All quotations from *Mr Stone and the
Knights Companion* are taken from the
2002 Picador UK paperback edition, in
a compendium volume published under
the title *The Nightwatchman's Occurrence
Book*.)

32. *New Statesman*, 31 May 1963.

33. *Sunday Telegraph*, 26 May 1963.

34. TU IIA.

35. TU IC2.

36. AI Karan Singh, 29 March 2003.

37. TU IC2.

38. TU IIB.

39. TU IC2.

40. Naipaul, V.S., *An Area of Darkness*,
London 1964, p. 162.

41. AI Zul Vellani, 30 January 2003.

42. AI V.S. Naipaul, 21 February 2007.

43. TU IID.

44. KTC.

45. TU IIB.

46. UWI, C.L.R. James Collection, Box 5, Folder 106. Thank you to Nicholas Laughlin for locating this letter.

47. RIC.

48. RIC.

49. AI Ravi Dayal, 2 March 2003.

50. AI Virendra Dayal, 28 March 2003.

51. Naipaul, V.S., *An Area of Darkness*, London 1964, p. 204.

52. TU IC2.

53. TU IIB.

54. TU IC2.

55. AI Khushwant Singh, 27 February 2003.

56. TU IID.

57. KTC.

58. AI Moni Malhoutra, 25 March 2003.

59. TU IC2.

60. TU IIB.

61. AD.

62. AD.

63. AI Vanraj Bhatia, 21 January 2003.

64. TU IIB.

65. TU IIA.

66. AI Moni Malhoutra, 25 March 2003.

67. TU IIB. Moni Malhoutra wrote an entertaining account of this adventure suggesting that V.S. Naipaul had narrowly avoided being eaten by a tiger. See 'Living Dangerously with V.S. Naipaul' in *First Proof: The Penguin Book of New Writing from India 1*, New Delhi 2005.

68. AI J.P. Singh, 19 January 2004.

69. TU IIB.

70. AI J.P. Singh, 19 January 2004.

71. TU IIB.

72. Naipaul, V.S., *An Area of Darkness*, London 1964, p. 260.

73. Naipaul, V.S., *An Area of Darkness*, London 1964, p. 263.

74. TU IIA.

75. TU IIB.

76. Letter in the private collection of Moni Malhoutra.

77. AI V.S. Naipaul, 26 January 2004.

FOURTEEN: 'LOVELY *VOGUE*, JUST BOUGHT'

1. Naipaul, V.S., *An Area of Darkness*, London 1964, p. 252.

2. TU IIA.

3. *Observer*, AD cuttings; *Times Literary Supplement*, 24 September 1964; *Daily Telegraph*, 17 September 1964; *New Statesman*, 11 September 1964.

4. Chandran, C. Sarat, 'Leveraging the Diaspora', newindpress.com, 9 February 2007.

5. AD.

6. Siewah, op. cit., pp. 189–90. Nissim Ezekiel's essay is available in Jussawalla, Adil, *New Writing in India*, London 1974.

7. Quoted Kumar, op. cit., p. 18.

8. *IWI*, 10 February 1963.

9. Naipaul's own copies of his 'Letters from London' were destroyed, and it was thought that no complete set of back issues of the *Illustrated Weekly of India* had survived. But I found a set on microfilm at the *Times of India* building in Mumbai.

10. *IWI*, 14 April 1963.

11. *IWI*, 12 May 1963.

12. *IWI*, 23 June 1963.

13. *IWI*, 28 July 1963.

14. *IWI*, 25 August 1963.

15. *IWI*, 29 September 1963.

16. *IWI*, 19 January 1964.

17. *IWI*, 27 December 1964.

18. AI V.S. Naipaul, 22 January 2007.

19. See Dhondy, Farrukh, *C.L.R. James: Cricket, the Caribbean, and World Revolution*, London 2001, & Dorn, Paul, *A Controversial Caribbean: C.L.R. James*, Spring 1995, http://www.runmuki.com/paul/CLR_James.html.

20. Naipaul, V.S., *A Writer's People*, London 2007, p. 12.

21. *IWI*, 28 July 1963.

22. *Encounter*, September 1963.

23. UWI, C.L.R. James Collection, Box 3, Folder 75.

24. UWI, C.L.R. James Collection, Box 5, Folder 106.

25. Quoted Dhondy, op. cit., p. 137.

26. KTC.

27. *New Statesman*, 28 October 1966.

28. *Spectator*, 16 October 1964.

29. *NYRB*, 4 March 1999.

30. KTC.

31. TU IIA.

32. KTC.

33. BBC, TVART 4. How prescient of Mr Burstall!

34. *Trinidadian*, February–March 1934.

35. NSA, NP346R.

36. See Hamner, Robert D. (ed.), *Critical Perspectives on V.S. Naipaul*, Washington, D.C. 1977, p. 147.

37. AI Pat Salkey, 11 April 2007.

38. Quoted Sandhu, op. cit., p. 97.

39. AI V.S. Naipaul, 21 February 2007.

40. Powell, Anthony, *Miscellaneous Verdicts: Writings on Writers 1946–1989*, London 1990, p. 391.

41. Quoted Stanford, Peter, *The Outcast's Outcast: A Biography of Lord Longford*, London 2003, p. 334.

42. Fraser, Antonia, and Pakenhams Elizabeth, Judith and Rachel, *The Pakenham Party Book*, London 1960, p. 40.

43. AI Antonia Fraser, 21 July 2003.

44. AFC.

45. AFC.

46. TU IIA.

47. AFC.

48. TU IIA.

49. Naipaul, V.S., *The Mystic Masseur*, London 1957, p. 195.

50. TU IIA.

51. AI V.S. Naipaul, 22 January 2004.

52. AI Francis Wyndham, 27 August 2003.

53. TU IV.

54. AI V.S. Naipaul, 22 January 2004.

55. *Trinidad Daily Mirror*, 7 March 1964.

56. Naipaul, Shiva, *Beyond the Dragon's Mouth*, London 1984, pp. 8–9.

57. Naipaul, Shiva, *An Unfinished Journey*, London 1986, p. 29. This page reference is from the 1988 edition.

58. AI Francis Wyndham, 27 August 2003.

59. KTC.

60. VSNC. Figures are missing for 1967.

61. AI V.S. Naipaul, 28 October 2003.

62. See Watson, Graham, *Book Society*, London 1980.

63. AI V.S. Naipaul, 26 September 2002 & 28 October 2003.

64. AI Richard Odgers, 13 December 2007.

65. AI V.S. Naipaul, 22 January 2004.

66. TU IIB.

67. SAC. V.S. Naipaul gave the early typescripts of *A Flag on the Island* to Savi and Mel Akal, having written it in their house.

68. Naipaul, V.S., *The Mimic Men*, London 1967, p. 216.

69. Naipaul, V.S., *The Mimic Men*, London 1967, p. 80.

70. *Observer*, 26 October 1969.

71. TU IIB.

72. *Trinidad Guardian*, 7 March 1965.

73. TU IIB.

74. AI V.S. Naipaul, 21 February 2007.

75. *Literary Review*, August 2001.

76. AI Mira Inalsingh, 17 September 2004.

77. AI Francis Wyndham, 27 August 2003.

78. AI Mira Inalsingh, 17 September 2004.

79. TU IID.

FIFTEEN: 'THE SCHINTSKY METHOD'

1. AI Paul Theroux, 21 September 2004.

2. AI V.S. Naipaul, 21 February 2007.

3. The early drafts of *The Mimic Men* survive in TU IB.

4. A note in TU IV by V.S. Naipaul dated 17 March 1995 reads: 'I borrowed the voice of the Trinidad minister (who wrote

the 1960 letter of invitation to me) for the colonial-politician narrator of *The Mimic Men* (1967). I knew his family as a child, and was to meet him in 1960 in Trinidad; but I borrowed the narrator's voice purely from this letter. I borrowed especially the word "interdigitating", which I had never heard before, but was trained by my Latin to understand.'

5. AD.

6. TU IIA.

7. AFC, 22 August 1966.

8. Email to the author, 28 September 2006.

9. Naipaul, V.S., *The Mimic Men*, London 1967, p. 11.

10. AI Jagdish Sondhi, 8 August 2006. The Sondhis were part of a small community of Indian and Pakistani professional families in Mombasa, mainly doctors, lawyers, bankers and architects, which included the Alvi family; Mr Alvi was the local president of the Muslim League. His daughter Nadira can be encountered in Chapter 25.

11. AFC, 9 June 1966.

12. AFC, 9 June 1966.

13. AD.

14. TU IIA.

15. TU IC.

16. TU IC2.

17. TU IIA. During the 1950s, Vidia had dealings with C. deGroot, the Commissioner for the West Indies, British Guiana and British Honduras in the United Kingdom.

18. AFC, 22 August 1966.

19. *Financial Times*, 4 May 1967.

20. AD, n.d.

21. *NYRB*, 11 April 1968.

22. *Kenyon Review*, November 1967.

23. Williams, Eric, *From Columbus to Castro: The History of the Caribbean 1492–1969*, London 1970, p. 502.

24. Michael Manley's letter was written in December 1977 while he was Jamaica's prime minister, and had been managing persistent violent unrest. John Hearne later described this period to Vidia as 'a six-year course of the very worst mimicry, fraudulent conversion of idealism and plain, degenerate buffoonery'. (TU IIA.)

25. TU IIA.

26. *Radio Times*, 24–30 March 1979.

27. TU IIA.

28. AD.

29. AI Francis Wyndham, 27 August 2003.

30. RIC.

31. AD.

32. AD. The final title was thought up by Piers Burnett of André Deutsch.

33. http://nobelprize.org/nobel_prizes/literature/laureates/2001/naipaul-lecture-e.html.

34. TU IIA.

35. *Guardian*, 20 November 1969.

36. Naipaul, V.S., *The Loss of El Dorado*, London 1969, p. 365. (All quotations from *The Loss of El Dorado* are taken from the 2001 Picador UK paperback edition.) In a letter to the Tulsa archivist Sid Huttner dated 10 July 1994, V.S. Naipaul wrote, 'The place was notorious; there were torture rooms. The young British governor who came out in 1810 changed all that. He made the Port of Spain jail part of the King's law. So there was an element of humanitarianism in the jail-gate legend, and it was an act of ignorance and vandalism on the part of independent Trinidad to take it down (apart, of course, from the great beauty of the Georgian cast-bronze lettering). I was told some years ago that the bronze letters have not been thrown away but are lying in some unknown cellar somewhere in Trinidad. The whole affair is full of ironies.'

37. *New Yorker*, 8 August 1970.

38. Quoted Hamner, op. cit., p. xxvii.

39. *Saturday Evening Post*, 3 June 1967.
40. TU IIA.
41. TU IIA.
42. AD.
43. TU IIB.
44. AI V.S. Naipaul, 1 November 2002.
45. TU IIA.
46. TU IIA.
47. TU IIA.
48. *Outlook India*, 4 October 1999.
49. TU IIB.
50. RIC.
51. PTC, 19 September 1967.
52. TU IIA.
53. TU IIA.
54. KTC.
55. KTC.
56. AI Peter Bayley, 28 September 2002.
57. KTC.
58. KTC.
59. AI Francis Wyndham, 27 August 2003.
60. AI David Pryce-Jones, 26 January 2005.
61. Email to the author, 28 September 2004.
62. TU IIA, 26 September 1966.
63. TU IIA, 6 November 1966.
64. TU IIA, 26 October 1966.
65. TU IIA, 30 October 1966.
66. TU IIA, 16 November 1968.
67. TU IIA, 26 October 1966.
68. TU IIA, 30 May 1967.
69. AI Paul Theroux, 21 September 2004.
70. PTC, 30 September 1966.
71. PTC, 18 October 1966.
72. PTC, 26 February 1967.
73. PTC, 21 February 1967.
74. AI V.S. Naipaul, 15 August 2002.
75. TU IIA, 22 July 1967.
76. TU IIA, 30 May 1967.
77. TU IIA, 25 October 1967.
78. TU IIA, 25 October 1967.
79. PTC, 16 November 1967.
80. PTC, 8 June 1968.
81. Email to the author, 31 May 2006; AI Anne Theroux, 3 June 2006.
82. TU IIA, 2 May 1970.
83. TU IIA, 18 December 1969.
84. TU IIA, 7 May 1969.
85. TU IIA, 18 December 1969.
86. PTC, 7 January 1970.
87. TU IIA, 2 May 1970.
88. TU IIA, 17 December 1970.

SIXTEEN: 'THE WORLD'

1. RIC.
2. AI Marisa Masters, 26 April 2004.
3. MARC.
4. PTC.
5. RIC.
6. AFC.
7. NSA, LP 34025, *The World at One*, 8 November 1968.
8. *Times*, 9 November 1968.
9. AI V.S. Naipaul, 26 January 2004.
10. AD.
11. AD. The phrase 'Black Power' would be taken up again in 2000 by followers of Robert Mugabe, when they invaded and occupied white-owned farms in Zimbabwe.
12. *NYRB*, 24 April 1969.
13. *Trinidad Guardian*, 28 November 1968.
14. TU IIIC.
15. Although V.S. Naipaul failed to listen to Dekker or Marley, they wrote on matching subjects. 'Emancipate yourself from mental slavery, None but ourselves can free our mind' sang Bob Marley in 'Redemption Song'.
16. TU IIA.
17. TU IIA.
18. AFC.
19. PTC.
20. AD.
21. AD.
22. *Telegraph Magazine*, April 1970.
23. AI Jill Brain, 12 December 2003.
24. AFC.

25. AI V.S. Naipaul, 26 January 2004.

26. TU IIA.

27. MARC.

28. TU IIA.

29. AI Marisa Masters, 26 April 2004.

30. Marisa Masters liked to collect the famous. When I interviewed her, she produced photographs of herself with, among others, Ivana Trump, Shere Hite and Mohamed al-Fayed.

31. AI Antonia Fraser, 21 July 2003.

32. AI Savi Akal, 4 March 2004.

33. AFC.

34. AFC.

35. TU IID.

36. PTC, 13 October 1970.

37. PTC, 26 May 1971.

38. TU IIA.

39. *Telegraph Magazine*, c.October 1972.

40. AI Eleanor Hale, 13 June 2006.

41. AI V.S. Naipaul, 26 January 2004.

42. KTC.

43. *Telegraph Magazine*, 10 December 1970.

44. Naipaul, V.S., *Magic Seeds*, London 2004, p. 267. (All quotations from *Magic Seeds* are taken from the first edition.)

45. Naipaul, V.S., *In a Free State*, London 1971, p. 26. (All quotations from *In a Free State* are taken from the 1973 Penguin UK paperback edition.)

46. Naipaul, V.S., *In a Free State*, London 1971, p. 29. No critic at the time of publication appears to have been aware that 'hubshi' was a term of abuse.

47. Naipaul, V.S., *In a Free State*, London 1971, p. 21. The narrative technique in this story leads to occasional absurdities. For instance: would an Indian (from India) think: 'A man came out from the kitchen with a tray. At first he looked like a fellow countryman, but in a second I could tell he was a stranger. "You are right," Priya said, when the stranger went back to the kitchen. "He is not of Bharat. He is a Mexican."'?

48. Naipaul, V.S., *In a Free State*, London 1971, p. 83.

49. AD.

50. AI V.S. Naipaul, 20 October 2003.

51. Naipaul, V.S., *In a Free State*, London 1971, pp. 104–7.

52. TU IIA.

53. TU IIA.

54. TU IIA.

55. AD.

56. TU IB.

57. *Times Educational Supplement*, 1 October 1971.

58. *NYRB*, 30 December 1971.

59. *New York Times Book Review*, 17 October 1971.

60. *Times*, October 1971.

61. MARC.

62. Theroux, Paul, *Sir Vidia's Shadow*, London 1998, p. 175. Stephen Tennant was in fact close to bankruptcy, and had to be bailed out from time to time by his brother.

63. RIC.

64. TU IID.

65. TU IID.

66. TU IB, *Black Power & National Reconstruction* by Lloyd Best.

67. *NYRB*, 3 September 1970.

68. TU IID.

69. *Sunday Times Magazine*, 12 May 1974 & 19 May 1974.

70. The ghost was Stephen John, author of *Roman Orgy*.

71. AI Farrukh Dhondy, 28 August 2004.

72. Lewis, op. cit., p. 72.

73. Athill, Diana, *Make Believe* (second edn.), London 2004, pp. 1–2.

74. Athill, Diana, *Make Believe* (second edn.), London 2004, pp. 5–6. I examine the story in more detail in an introduction to this edition of *Make Believe*.

75. TU IID.

76. KTC.

77. AD.

522 NOTES

78. NSA, *The Arts This Week*, 29 October 1970.

79. BBC, RCONT 20, V.S. Naipaul Copyright File.

80. MIC.

81. TU IIA.

82. TU IIA.

83. TU IIA.

84. AI Margaret Drabble, 13 May 2005.

85. TU IIA.

86. BBC, RCONT 20, V.S. Naipaul Copyright File.

87. TU IIA.

88. The original *Bad Sign, Good Sign* song can be heard at www.montynorman.com.

89. NSA, T34250, *A Word in Edgeways*, 15 October 1971.

90. NSA, *The Arts and Africa*, 17 December 1971.

91. NSA, M3033R, Radio 3, 29 January 1973.

92. *Business Standard*, 16 October 2001.

93. TU IIB.

94. TU IID.

95. AD.

96. Tewari, op. cit.

97. Cliff Lashley was later beaten to death in Kingston, though not at V.S. Naipaul's instigation.

98. AI Kenneth Ramchand, 5 March 2004.

99. AI V.S. Naipaul, 21 July 2006.

100. *Sunday Times Magazine*, 16 July 1972.

101. AI V.S. Naipaul, 2 October 2003.

102. KTC.

103. TU IID.

104. AD.

105. AD. The judges for the Booker Prize that year were Saul Bellow, John Fowles, Antonia Fraser, John Gross and Malcolm Muggeridge.

106. *New Statesman*, 1 December 1972.

107. TU IIA.

108. TU IIA.

109. TU IIA.

110. TU IIA.

SEVENTEEN: 'WITH THE AID OF A CUTLASS BLADE'

1. All quotations in this chapter are taken from Patricia Naipaul's diary in TU IC2, unless otherwise stated.

2. PTC, 3 February 1972.

3. AI Mel Akal, 4 March 2004.

4. Athill, Diana, *Make Believe* (second edn.), London 2004, pp. 51–3.

5. Athill, Diana, *Instead of a Letter* (second edn.), London 2001, pp. 18–156.

6. Note by V.S. Naipaul in TU IB dated 13 February 1995.

7. AD.

8. AD.

9. AD.

10. TU IB.

11. AI V.S. Naipaul, 21 May 2006.

12. AI V.S. Naipaul, 28 October 2003.

13. AI Robert Silvers, 19 November 2003.

14. TU IIA.

15. Naipaul, V.S., *The Mimic Men*, London 1967, p. 82.

16. AI Savi Akal, 4 March 2004.

17. See Luna, Félix, *A Short History of the Argentinians*, Buenos Aires 2000.

18. AI Hermenegildo Sábat, 2 November 2004.

19. TU IB.

20. *NYRB*, 10 August 1972.

21. See di Giovanni, Norman Thomas, *The Lesson of the Master: On Borges and His Work*, London 2003.

22. AI Norman Thomas di Giovanni, 22 June 2004.

23. TU IB.

24. TU IB.

25. *NYRB*, 19 October 1972.

26. AI Norman Thomas di Giovanni, 22 June 2004.

27. AI V.S. Naipaul, 27 October 2003.

28. TU IB.

EIGHTEEN: MARGARITA

1. AI Norman Thomas di Giovanni, 22 June 2004.
2. MPS.
3. AI Norman Thomas di Giovanni, 22 June 2004.
4. AI V.S. Naipaul, 27 October 2003.
5. AI Norman Thomas di Giovanni, 29 June 2004.
6. TU IIB.
7. AI V.S. Naipaul, 27 October 2003.
8. AI Norman Thomas di Giovanni, 22 June 2004.
9. AI V.S. Naipaul, 10 January 2005.
10. TU IC2. All subsequent quotations and information in the chapter relating to Patricia Naipaul are taken from her diary in TU IC2, unless otherwise stated.
11. AI Savi Akal, 4 March 2004.
12. TU IIA.
13. PTC, 6 June 1972.
14. PTC, 2 July 1972.
15. TU IC.
16. *NYRB*, 10 August 1972.
17. TU IB.
18. TU IB.
19. AI Hermenegildo Sábat, 2 November 2004.
20. *NYRB*, 10 August 1972.
21. AI Andrew Graham-Yooll, 3 November 2004.
22. MPS.
23. AI Hermenegildo Sábat, 2 November 2004.
24. AI Michael Neill, 28 August 2005.
25. *Wellington Dominion*, 26 July 1972.
26. TU IIB.
27. AI V.S. Naipaul, 1 November 2002.
28. AI Pek Koon Heng, 31 May 2006.
29. AI Michael Neill, 28 August 2005.
30. MPS.
31. AI V.S. Naipaul, 25 July 2002.
32. TU IIA.
33. Private collection.
34. SAC.
35. TU IB.

36. PTC, 10 September 1972.
37. PTC, 18 September 1972.
38. TU IIA.
39. TU IV.
40. PTC, 22 October 1972.
41. AI Norman Thomas di Giovanni, 29 June 2004.
42. TU IIA.
43. AI Diana Athill, 23 July 2003.
44. AI Marisa Masters, 26 April 2004.
45. AI V.S. Naipaul, 10 January 2005.
46. AI V.S. Naipaul, 8 December 2006.
47. TU IIA.
48. KTC.
49. TU IID.

NINETEEN: ENGLAND AND ARGENTINA

1. RIC.
2. AI Michael Frayn, 21 September 2007.
3. AI V.S. Naipaul, 10 January 2005.
4. MPS.
5. AI Savi Akal, 4 March 2004.
6. TU IID.
7. TU IIB.
8. TU IIB.
9. VSNC, Task memo book.
10. *NYRB*, 12 June 1980.
11. TU IIA.
12. Michell, John (ed.), *Souvenir Programme for the Official Lynching of Michael Abdul Malik with Poems, Stories, Sayings by the Condemned*, Cambridge 1973.
13. *Sunday Times Magazine*, 12 May 1974 & 19 May 1974. The complete text of the article, together with an important postscript written in 1979 after Abbott's execution (from which part of this quotation is taken), can be found in Naipaul, V.S, *The Writer and the World*, London 2002. See also Humphry, Derek, and Tindall, David, *False Messiah: The Story of Michael X*, London 1977.
14. AD.
15. AI V.S. Naipaul, 10 January 2005.
16. *NYRB*, 4 April 1974.
17. TU IIA.

18. TU IIA.

19. AI Andrew Graham-Yooll, 3 November 2004.

20. AI V.S. Naipaul, 28 October 2003.

21. AI V.S. Naipaul, 10 January 2005.

22. AI Savi Akal, 4 March 2004.

23. AI Savi Akal, 7 March 2004.

24. VSNC, Task memo book.

25. TU IC2. All subsequent quotations and information in the chapter relating to Patricia Naipaul are taken from her diary in TU IC2, unless otherwise stated.

26. TU IIA.

27. MARC.

28. AFC.

29. McKay, Peter, *Inside Private Eye*, London 1986, p. 142.

30. TU IIA.

31. Naipaul, V.S., *Guerrillas*, London 1975, pp. 12–15. (All quotations from *Guerrillas* are taken from the 1976 Penguin UK paperback edition.)

32. TU IB.

33. Naipaul, V.S., *Guerrillas*, London 1975, p. 253.

34. Naipaul, V.S., *Guerrillas*, London 1975, pp. 242–3.

TWENTY: THE MARRIAGE OF MANDRAX AND VALIUM

1. TU IC2. All subsequent quotations and information in the chapter relating to Patricia Naipaul are taken from her diary in TU IC2, unless otherwise stated.

2. AI Hermenegildo Sábat, 2 November 2004.

3. MPS.

4. TU IB, draft letter in 'Kamikaze in Montevideo' notebook.

5. *NYRB*, 17 October 1974.

6. *NYRB*, 28 November 1974.

7. AD.

8. AI Diana Athill, 23 July 2003.

9. TU IIA.

10. TU IIA.

11. TU IV.

12. TU IIA.

13. *Mother Jones*, August 1980.

14. *Caribbean Contact*, November 1975.

15. *Spectator*, 13 September 1975 & *Observer*, 14 September 1975.

16. *Listener*, 25 September 1975.

17. TU IIA.

18. TU IIB.

19. *NYRB*, 19 September 1974.

20. TU IB.

21. AI Andrew Graham-Yooll, 3 November 2004.

22. AI V.S. Naipaul, 10 January 2005.

23. AI V.S. Naipaul, 27 October 2003.

24. AI V.S. Naipaul, 10 January 2005.

25. Theroux, Paul, *Sir Vidia's Shadow*, London 1998, pp. 214–28.

26. AI Michael Neill, 28 August 2005. See also C.K. Stead's 'Diary' in *London Review of Books*, 27 April 2000.

27. AI Pek Koon Heng, 31 May 2006.

28. AI Antonia Fraser, 21 July 2003.

29. Reproduced with permission from the unpublished diary of Antonia Fraser, © Antonia Fraser.

30. *Telegraph Magazine*, 12 October 2002, out-takes from interview with Mick Brown.

31. *Atlantic Unbound*, 31 March 2004, www.theatlantic.com/doc/200403u/int2004-03-31.

32. See Theroux, Paul, *My Secret History: A Novel*, London 1989, pp. 277–99.

33. See Theroux, Paul, *My Other Life: A Novel*, London 1996, pp. 175–6. In *My Other Life*, he describes a dinner at his house in London with the writer Anthony Burgess and a bibliophilic fan, Lettfish, which provoked (the real) Anne Theroux to write a letter to the *New Yorker* magazine disassociating herself from fictional comments she was meant to have made. See Stinson, John J., 'Burgess as Fictional Character in Theroux and Byatt', in *Anthony Burgess Newsletter: Issue 2*, http://

bu.univ-angers.fr/EXTRANET/
AnthonyBURGESS/NL2Theroux.htm.

34. Theroux, Paul, *Sir Vidia's Shadow*,
London 1998, p. 24.

35. Theroux, Paul, *Sir Vidia's Shadow*,
London 1998, p. 88.

36. Theroux, Paul, *Sir Vidia's Shadow*,
London 1998, p. 51.

37. Theroux, Paul, *Sir Vidia's Shadow*,
London 1998, p. 144.

38. The administrator of the Booker
Prize, Martyn Goff, described Paul
Theroux's account of the selection of the
1979 winner as 'pure invention . . .
Theroux's account is a mile from the truth,
nor could any vote of his have decided the
outcome.' *Daily Telegraph*, 22 August 1998.

39. Theroux, Paul, *Sir Vidia's Shadow*,
London 1998, p. 39.

40. Paul Theroux confirmed this to me
during an interview, 21 September 2004.

41. See Theroux, Paul, *Sir Vidia's
Shadow*, London 1998, p. 213, and the same
text (from December 1971) in Jussawalla,
Feroza (ed.), *Conversations with V.S.
Naipaul*, Jackson 1997, p. 31. Theroux used
this quotation in his 1972 profile of V.S.
Naipaul in the *Telegraph Magazine*.

42. Theroux, Paul, *Sir Vidia's Shadow*,
London 1998, p. 253.

43. Theroux, Paul, *Sir Vidia's Shadow*,
London 1998, p. 358.

44. Theroux, Paul, *Sir Vidia's Shadow*,
London 1998, p. 51.

45. AI Lloyd Best, 2 March 2004.

46. AI Paul Theroux, 21 September
2004.

47. AI V.S. Naipaul, 15 August 2002.

48. AI Sheila Rogers, 12 December
2007.

49. See Powell, Tristram and Georgia
(eds.), *A Dedicated Fan: Julian Jebb
1934–1984*, London 1993.

50. AI Michael Holroyd, 13 May 2005.

51. AI Francis Wyndham, 27 August
2003.

52. AI Michael Neill, 28 August 2005.

53. *Time*, 11 August 1975.

54. *New Review*, November 1975.

55. AI David Pryce-Jones, 26 January
2005.

56. TU IIA.

57. AI Antonia Fraser, 21 July 2003.

58. TU IIA.

TWENTY-ONE: 'I WANT TO WIN AND
WIN AND WIN'

1. AI Antonia Fraser, 21 July 2003.

2. AI Marisa Masters, 26 April 2004.

3. AI John Kasmin, 26 July 2004.

4. AI David Pryce-Jones, 26 January
2005.

5. AI V.S. Naipaul, 10 January 2005.

6. *NYRB*, 26 June 1975.

7. TU IIA.

8. TU IB.

9. TU IB.

10. *NYRB*, 26 June 1975.

11. TU IB.

12. AI Prem Shankar Jha, 15 January
2004.

13. AI V.S. Naipaul, 1 November 2002.

14. AI Vinod Mehta, 16 December 2002.

15. AI V.S. Naipaul, 1 November 2002.

16. AI Ravi Dayal, 2 March 2003.

17. TU IB.

18. AI V.S. Naipaul, 26 January 2004.

19. AI Sudhir Kakar, 2 March 2003.

20. AI Rahul Singh, 23 May 2004.

21. AI Shirish Patel, 31 January 2003.

22. AI V.S. Naipaul, 20 September 2003.

23. *New Statesman*, n.d. (October 1977).

24. *Times*, n.d., *Spectator*, 22 October
1977, *New Statesman*, n.d., *Sunday
Telegraph*, 23 October 1977.

25. *New York Times*, 13 May 1979.

26. TU IIA.

27. Private collection, courtesy of Hugo
Vickers.

28. TU IIA.

29. AI V.S. Naipaul, 11 January 2005.

30. *NYRB*, 11 October 1979. This article was written in 1977, but published in 1979.

31. *NYRB*, 30 January 1992.

32. *New Statesman*, 4 July 1980.

33. Amis, Martin, *Experience*, London 2000, p. 263.

34. Naipaul, V.S., *The Return of Eva Perón*, London 1980, p. 5.

35. *Observer*, 29 June 1980; *Daily Telegraph*, AD cuttings.

36. AI V.S. Naipaul, 20 September 2002.

37. *Harpers & Queen*, July 1980.

38. *NYRB*, 12 June 1980.

39. AI V.S. Naipaul, 10 January 2005.

40. AI Kamla Tewari, 1 March 2004.

41. AI Mira Inalsingh, 17 September 2004.

42. AI Savi Akal, 4 March 2004.

43. AI Suren Capildeo, 8 March 2004.

44. AI V.S. Naipaul, 8 December 2006.

45. Part of the seminar is transcribed at www.pancaribbean.com/banyan/naipaul.htm. Banyan Productions date it to 1974, but it appears to be from 1977.

46. TU IIA.

47. TU IC2. All subsequent quotations and information in the chapter relating to Patricia Naipaul are taken from her diary in TU IC2, unless otherwise stated.

48. TU IB.

49. Naipaul, V.S., *A Bend in the River*, London 1979, p. 135.

50. AI V.S. Naipaul, 21 May 2006.

51. AI V.S. Naipaul, 29 December 2006.

52. Naipaul, V.S., *A Bend in the River*, London 1979, p. 99.

53. AI Savi Akal, 4 March 2004.

54. Naipaul, V.S., *A Bend in the River*, London 1979, pp. 159–61.

55. Naipaul, V.S., *A Bend in the River*, London 1979, pp. 180–2.

56. MPS.

57. AI V.S. Naipaul, 12 July 2002.

58. TU IC.

59. Naipaul, V.S., *A Bend in the River*, London 1979, p. 287.

TWENTY-TWO: A HOUSE FOR MR NAIPAUL

1. TU IIA.

2. AI Phyllis Rose, 18 September 2004.

3. TU IIA.

4. *Sunday Telegraph Magazine*, 23 September 1979. This profile, by Linda Blandford, gives an unusually perceptive insight into V.S. Naipaul's behaviour and state of mind.

5. TU IIA.

6. TU IID.

7. TU IIA, 12 September 1978.

8. AI Phyllis Rose, 18 September 2004.

9. *Wesleyan: The Wesleyan University Alumnus*, Spring 1981.

10. TU IIA.

11. AI John Richardson, 16 September 2004.

12. *Vogue (USA)*, August 1981.

13. AD.

14. TU IIA.

15. TU IIA.

16. Shiva had won the Winifred Holtby Award for *Fireflies*, which may have been an additional consideration when it came to rejecting the prize.

17. *New York Times Book Review*, 13 May 1979; *Chicago Tribune Book World*, 13 May 1979; *Times*, 9 December 1979; *Evening Standard*, 25 September 1979; *Spectator*, 1 December 1979; *Guardian*, 14 February 2004.

18. Naipaul, V.S., *A Bend in the River*, London 1979, p. 9.

19. *Nation*, 3 May 1980.

20. *Wesleyan: The Wesleyan University Alumnus*, Spring 1981.

21. *New York Times*, 13 May 1979.

22. *Newsweek*, 18 August 1980.

23. BBC Radio 4, 11 May 1980, sound recording available in TU IIIB.

24. TU IID.

25. AD.

26. AD.

27. AD.

28. AD.

29. AD.

30. TU IIA.

31. TU IIA.

32. TU IIA.

33. AI Gillon Aitken, 13 August 2003.

34. AI V.S. Naipaul, 26 September 2002.

35. VSNC, cashbook.

36. VSNC, notebook. These deductions are approximate; precise comparable figures are not available for the different decades.

37. PTC, 5 April 1981.

38. *Vogue (UK)*, c.September 1979.

39. MPS.

40. AI V.S. Naipaul, 29 December 2006.

41. MPS.

42. TU IIA.

43. AFC.

44. TU IIA.

45. TU IIB.

46. *Private Eye*, 3 August 1979.

47. AI Francis Wyndham, 27 August 2003.

48. TU IC2. All subsequent quotations and information in the chapter relating to Patricia Naipaul are taken from her diary in TU IC2, unless otherwise stated.

49. TU IIA.

50. AI V.S. Naipaul, 29 December 2006.

51. AI V.S. Naipaul, 11 January 2005.

52. TU IIA.

53. RIC.

54. VSNC, Task memo book.

55. Recording from 1980 in TU IIIB.

56. *Sunday Times*, 4 October 1981.

57. TU IIA.

58. TU IIA, 8 April 1981.

59. *Washington Post*, 11 October 1981; *Times*, 4 December 1981; *Newsweek*, 16 November 1981.

60. *New Statesman*, 16 October 1981; *NYRB*, 24 June 1982; *Hudson Review*, Summer 1982. See also Bawer, Bruce, *Civilization and V.S. Naipaul* in *Hudson Review*, Autumn 2002.

61. Naipaul, V.S., *Among the Believers*, London 1981, p. 89. (All quotations from *Among the Believers* are taken from the 1982 Penguin UK paperback edition.)

62. TU IB.

63. TU IIA.

64. *Business Standard*, 16 October 2001.

65. TU IB.

66. AI Eleanor Hale, 13 June 2006.

67. TU IC. On 13 December 1981, Pat wrote in her diary: 'Started Boswell's Life of Johnson yesterday. I don't really like biography as an art form, but impressed.'

68. AI Selby Wooding, 5 March 2004.

69. *Salmagundi*, Fall 1981, quoted in Jussawalla, Feroza (ed.), *Conversations with V.S. Naipaul*, Jackson 1997, p. 77. The most convincing academic study of Naipaul's work is Hayward, Helen, *The Enigma of V.S. Naipaul*, Oxford 2002.

70. AI V.S. Naipaul, 20 September 2002.

71. AI V.S. Naipaul, 2 October 2003.

72. AI V.S. Naipaul, 8 September 2007.

73. *New Yorker*, 23 May 1994.

74. Hare, David, *A Map of the World*, London 1982, pp. 17–20.

75. Available at http://social.chass. ncsu.edu/wyrick/DEBCLASS/walsp. htm. My shortest interview while researching this book was with Derek Walcott: 'I feel jaded with him, I get increasingly irritated by him, I don't want to talk about him, I don't want to add to the legend of Naipaul.' (AI Derek Walcott, 16 September 2004.)

76. TU IIA.

77. TU IIA.

78. TU unclassified papers.

79. *Frankfurter Allgemeine Zeitung Magazin*, 23 December 1983. These answers are taken from V.S. Naipaul's original submission, written in English.

80. TU IB.

81. AI V.S. Naipaul, 11 January 2005.

82. VPRO-TV, 18 April 1982, video

recording available in TU IIIB. The ticket was economy class. After the trip, Cees Noteboom was quoted in *Het Parool* saying, 'As a writer you know that when you take a trip like this, you will be confronted with a bunch of idiots. If you haven't got the patience for it, you shouldn't go.'

83. TU IB.

84. TU IIA. The Cambridge University regulations specified that the bonnet needed to be taken off and put on from time to time during the ceremony: 'At this point the recipient again puts on his bonnet. The recipient does not speak at any point and is guided throughout the proceedings by the Esquire Bedells.'

85. TU IID.

86. TU IIA.

87. TU IA.

88. *Vanity Fair*, April 1983. The article was illustrated with family archive photographs and a new portrait of V.S. Naipaul by the 'jumped-up' photographer Lord Snowdon.

89. TU IA.

90. MPS.

91. *Daily Mail*, 7 May 1982.

92. Naipaul, V.S., *Finding the Centre*, London 1984, pp. 116–17.

93. TU IB.

94. MPS.

95. TU IIA.

96. MPS.

97. *Harper's*, March 1984.

98. Tewari, op. cit.

99. *NYRB*, 25 October 1984.

100. Naipaul, V.S., *Finding the Centre*, London 1984, p. 9.

101. *Daily Telegraph*, 11 May 1984.

102. *Dublin Sunday Tribune*, 6 May 1984.

103. *Observer*, 6 May 1984.

TWENTY-THREE: 'UNDOING MY SEMI-COLONS'

1. TU IV.

2. TU IID

3. KTC.

4. *Globe & Mail Magazine*, December 1988.

5. *New Statesman*, 18 December 1998.

6. TU unclassified papers.

7. AI Shalini Aleung, 2 March 2004.

8. KTC.

9. AI Nisha Inalsingh, 17 September 2004.

10. AI V.S. Naipaul, 8 December 2006.

11. TU IID.

12. AI Gillon Aitken, 13 August 2003.

13. AI Mira Inalsingh, 17 September 2004.

14. Hilary Mantel was the first young winner of the Shiva Naipaul Memorial Prize.

15. AD.

16. *Spectator*, 24 August 1985.

17. Naipaul, Shiva, *Black and White*, London 1980, pp. 3–4.

18. Naipaul, Shiva, *North of South*, London 1978, p. 44.

19. TU IID.

20. AI Vinod Mehta, 16 December 2002.

21. AI Nikhil Lakshman, 31 January 2003.

22. AI V.S. Naipaul, 20 September 2002.

23. AI V.S. Naipaul, 22 January 2004.

24. AFC.

25. KTC.

26. TU IID.

27. TU unclassified papers.

28. TU IC2.

29. VSNC, Task memo book; TU IB.

30. AI V.S. Naipaul, 10 January 2005.

31. *NYRB*, 9 April 1987.

32. Naipaul, V.S., *The Enigma of Arrival*, London 1987, p. 42.

33. Naipaul, V.S., *The Enigma of Arrival*, London 1987, pp. 152–3.

34. Naipaul, V.S., *The Enigma of Arrival*, London 1987, pp. 63–4.

35. Naipaul, V.S., *The Enigma of Arrival*, London 1987, pp. 56 & 27.

36. Naipaul, V.S., *The Enigma of Arrival*, London 1987, p. 203.

37. Naipaul, V.S., *The Enigma of Arrival*, London 1987, p. 60.

38. Naipaul, V.S., *The Enigma of Arrival*, London 1987, p. 186.

39. Naipaul, V.S., *The Enigma of Arrival*, London 1987, p. 209.

40. Naipaul, V.S., *The Enigma of Arrival*, London 1987, p. 278.

41. Naipaul, V.S., *The Enigma of Arrival*, London 1987, p. 252.

42. TU IIA.

43. *New Criterion*, October 1987.

44. *Boston Review*, June 1987.

45. TU unclassified papers.

46. TU IIA.

47. TU unclassified papers.

48. Powell, Anthony, *Journals: 1987–1989*, London 1996, p. 31.

49. *Times Literary Supplement*, 28 August 1987.

50. *Guardian*, 13 March 1987. Salman Rushdie was perceptive about the absence of the word 'love' in *The Enigma of Arrival*; remember that during the writing of *A Bend in the River*, Pat had noted in her diary: 'Vidia is so proud of never using the word love.'

51. *South Bank Show*, 1988, recording available in TU IIIB.

52. http://nobelprize.org/nobel_prizes/literature/laureates/2001/press.html.

53. *New Republic*, 13 April 1987.

54. 'The Schooner "Flight"' is available at http://www.cs.rice.edu/~ssiyer/minstrels/txt/1041.txt.

55. MARC.

56. *Chicago Tribune*, 30 November 1986.

57. TU IIA.

58. GAAA.

59. AI V.S. Naipaul, 11 January 2005.

60. AI Norman Thomas di Giovanni, 29 June 2004.

61. VSNC.

62. *Atlanta Constitution*, 28 May 1987.

63. TU IIA.

64. Naipaul, V.S., *A Turn in the South*, London 1989, p. 119. (All quotations from *A Turn in the South* are taken from the 2003 Picador UK paperback edition.)

65. Naipaul, V.S., *A Turn in the South*, London 1989, p. 125.

66. TU IV.

67. Naipaul, V.S., *A Turn in the South*, London 1989, p. 226.

68. *NYRB*, 30 March 1989.

69. GAAA.

70. GAAA.

71. GAAA.

72. AI Gillon Aitken, 26 July 2004.

73. AI Francis Wyndham, 27 August 2003.

74. GAAA.

75. AI Helen Fraser, 12 December 2007.

76. GAAA.

77. TU unclassified papers.

78. GAAA.

79. Powell, Anthony, *Journals: 1990–1992*, London 1997, p. 194 & Powell, Anthony, *Journals: 1982–1986*, London 1995, p. 291.

80. The recipe involved mutton and curry powder served with fried banana and dried coconut, and is available at http://www.anthonypowell.org.uk/ap/apcurry.htm, should you wish to eat it. 'If eggs are used they should be hard-boiled and set in halves on the curry. Odds and ends of potatoes and vegetables may also be called into play, though the last should be used in moderation.' One of Anthony Powell's relations told me his famous curry was 'absolutely disgusting, but we had to pretend we liked it'.

81. Naipaul, V.S., *A Writer's People*, London 2007, pp. 34–8.

82. AI Helen Fraser, 12 December 2007.

83. Powell, Anthony, *Journals: 1982–1986*, London 1995, p. 20.

84. TU IIA.

85. Powell, Anthony, *Journals: 1987–1989*, London 1996, p. 155.

86. Powell, Anthony, *Journals: 1987–1989*, London 1996, p. 126.

87. Powell, Anthony, *Journals: 1982–1986*, London 1995, p. 77.

88. Powell, Anthony, *Journals: 1987–1989*, London 1996, p. 127.

89. Powell, Anthony, *Journals: 1982–1986*, London 1995, p. 236.

90. AI David Pryce-Jones, 6 January 2005.

91. AD.

92. Kitty Giles; Bobby says the same thing to Linda in *In a Free State*.

93. TU IC.

94. TU IC2.

95. TU IC.

96. AI V.S. Naipaul, 22 January 2004.

97. TU IIA.

98. TU IV.

99. The material that follows is taken from TU unclassified papers.

100. *Independent*, 17 March 1989. These statements were first made to a *Sunday Observer* reporter in Bombay.

101. *Times*, 18 August 1993.

TWENTY-FOUR: ARISE, SIR VIDIA

1. AI Ralph Ironman, 26 May 2006.

2. AI Moni Malhoutra, 25 March 2003.

3. GAAA.

4. Luxury hotels in India were still comparatively cheap in 1988–9; V.S. Naipaul's hotel bills for the trip totalled around £13,000.

5. AI Vinod Mehta, 16 December 2002.

6. Naipaul, V.S., *India: A Million Mutinies Now*, London 1990, p. 1. (All quotations from *India: A Million Mutinies Now* are taken from the 1991 Minerva UK paperback edition.)

7. Naipaul, V.S., *India: A Million Mutinies Now*, London 1990, p. 6.

8. Naipaul, V.S., *India: A Million Mutinies Now*, London 1990, p. 37.

9. Naipaul, V.S., *India: A Million Mutinies Now*, London 1990, p. 15 & p. 60.

10. AI Nikhil Lakshman, 31 January 2003.

11. AI Charudatta Deshpande, 30 January 2003. Vithal Chavan was murdered in the chawl by a rival gang a year later. He is called Mr Ghate in *India: A Million Mutinies Now*.

12. AI Sadanand Menon, 11 January 2004.

13. AI H.V. Nathan, 31 January 2003. H.V. Nathan was for many years the right-hand man to Murli Deora, who ran the Congress Party's operation in Bombay.

14. AI Nasir Abid, 16 January 2004.

15. AI Sadanand Menon, 11 January 2004.

16. TU unclassified papers.

17. AI Nasir Abid, 16 January 2004.

18. AI V.S. Naipaul, 26 January 2004. Harinder Baweja denies being small.

19. AI Harinder Baweja, 27 March 2007.

20. AI Malavika Sanghvi, 29 March 2003.

21. AI Vir Sanghvi, 29 March 2003.

22. AI Malavika Sanghvi, 29 March 2003.

23. *Time*, 10 July 1989.

24. AI Nasir Abid, 16 January 2004.

25. GAAA. This letter was written at the end of 1991.

26. *Literary Review*, September 1990.

27. *Tatler*, October 1990.

28. *Financial Times*, 20 October 1990.

29. *New York Times*, 30 December 1990.

30. *Sunday Telegraph*, 30 September 1990.

31. *NYRB*, 14 February 1991.

32. TU unclassified papers.

33. AI V.S. Naipaul, 8 September 2007.

34. Tewari, op. cit.

35. AI Kenneth Ramchand, 5 March 2004. This trip may have taken place in 1984, but for narrative purposes I have left it here.

36. *Trinidad Guardian*, 7 March 1990.

37. AI Margaret Walcott, 4 March 2004.

38. AI Nella Chapman, 13 December 2007.

39. TU unclassified papers.

40. TU unclassified papers.

41. TU unclassified papers.

42. TU unclassified papers.

43. TU unclassified papers.

44. TU IC2.

45. *Evening Standard*, 15 October 1993.

46. NYRB, 31 January 1991.

47. TU unclassified papers.

48. TU unclassified papers.

49. Meyers, Jeffrey, *Privileged Moments: Encounters with Writers*, London 2000, p. 101.

50. TU unclassified papers.

51. GAAA.

52. AI V.S. Naipaul, 26 September 2002.

53. *Times of India*, 18 July 1993.

54. AI V.S. Naipaul, 2 October 2003 & 20 September 2003.

55. TU IIA.

56. TU IIA.

57. AI Eleanor Hale, 13 June 2006.

58. From a biographer's point of view, the most significant loss was the early novels, the Oxford diaries, the travel journals and the letters from friends and associates. V.S. Naipaul said later: 'What the documents that were lost in the warehouse would have reported, even the little journals that I kept – scrappy things – was the rage I felt. That came from my own unhappiness. I was capable of immense anger. I used to get angry very easily. Not only with Pat. I always got in rages, and often in public, entering the BBC, on a railway station – great rage, half mad. In Waterloo or some other station, if something happened to irritate me, probably someone might say something and I would be very angry . . . I was on the edge of anger all the time, and I never wrote about it. I wrote about it only once

when I tried to define it in *An Area of Darkness* . . . I felt I was the defeated man, not seeing the way out. In a way, my father's rages had trained me for it, you understand. He was a great rager.' (AI V.S. Naipaul, 22 January 2004.)

59. AI V.S. Naipaul, 26 January 2004.

60. GAAA.

61. http://nobelprize.org/nobel_prizes/literature/laureates/1992/walcott-lecture.html.

62. TU IC2.

63. VSNC, purple Memorandum Book No 3. On the inside cover, V.S. Naipaul has written, 'An extraordinary, feeding little book. Always consulted by me during the writing of later books.'

64. VSNC, 'A Way in the World – notes 1990'.

65. TU unclassified papers.

66. Naipaul, V.S., *A Way in the World*, London 1994, p. 2.

67. Naipaul, V.S., *A Way in the World*, London 1994, p. 37.

68. Naipaul, V.S., *A Way in the World*, London 1994, p. 41.

69. Naipaul, V.S., *A Way in the World*, London 1994, p. 45.

70. Naipaul, V.S., *A Way in the World*, London 1994, p. 67.

71. Naipaul, V.S., *A Way in the World*, London 1994, p. 72.

72. Naipaul, V.S., *A Way in the World*, London 1994, p. 75.

73. Naipaul, V.S., *A Way in the World*, London 1994, pp. 77–94.

74. Calder Marshall, Arthur, *Glory Dead*, London 1939, p. 239.

75. Naipaul, V.S., *A Way in the World*, London 1994, p. 105.

76. Naipaul, V.S., *A Way in the World*, London 1994, p. 119.

77. Naipaul, V.S., *A Way in the World*, London 1994, p. 124.

78. Naipaul, V.S., *A Way in the World*, London 1994, p. 156.

79. Naipaul, V.S., *A Way in the World*, London 1994, p. 346.

80. Naipaul, V.S., *A Way in the World*, London 1994, pp. 367–8.

81. Naipaul, V.S., *A Way in the World*, London 1994, p. 369.

82. *Trinidad Guardian*, 26 June 1994.

83. *New York Times*, 17 May 1994.

84. *Sunday Times*, 8 May 1994.

85. *New York Times Book Review*, 22 May 1994.

86. *New Republic*, 13 June 1994.

87. TU IIIB.

88. GAAA.

89. *Independent on Sunday*, 28 March 1993.

90. *Publishers Weekly*, 6 June 1994.

91. *Der Spiegel*, 20 September 1993.

92. *New Yorker*, 23 May 1994.

93. AI V.S. Naipaul, 10 January 2005.

94. AI V.S. Naipaul, 11 January 2005.

95. *New Yorker*, 23 May 1994.

96. TU IIA.

97. AI V.S. Naipaul, 10 January 2005.

TWENTY-FIVE: THE SECOND LADY NAIPAUL

1. VSNC, small blue notebook.

2. GAAA.

3. VSNC.

4. VSNC.

5. MPS.

6. VSNC.

7. VSNC.

8. AI Gillon Aitken, 13 August 2003.

9. GAAA.

10. VSNC.

11. AI Ismail Merchant, 17 August 2004.

12. VSNC. V.S. Naipaul took eleven shirts with him, fifty-six fewer than Sir Francis Younghusband took to Tibet.

13. VSNC.

14. VSNC.

15. VSNC.

16. VSNC.

17. Naipaul, V.S., *Beyond Belief: Islamic Excursions Among the Converted Peoples*, London 1998, pp. 88, 222, 388–9. (All quotations from *Beyond Belief* are taken from the first edition.)

18. Naipaul, V.S., *Beyond Belief*, London 1998, p. 201.

19. Naipaul, V.S., *Beyond Belief*, London 1998, pp. 144 & 173–4.

20. *New York Times*, 7 June 1998.

21. *Financial Times*, 2 May 1998.

22. *Indian Review of Books*, 16 July 1998.

23. *Guardian*, n.d.

24. *Observer*, 3 May 1998.

25. *Sunday Telegraph*, 3 May 1998.

26. *Al-Ahram Weekly*, 6–12 August 1998.

27. *Sunday Times*, 3 May 1998.

28. GAAA.

29. VSNC.

30. TU IIB.

31. AI Angela Cox, 8 September 2007.

32. AI V.S. Naipaul, 27 October 2003 & 10 January 2005.

33. *Savvy*, January 2002.

34. VSNC.

35. AI Nadira Naipaul, 26 August 2007.

36. *Savvy*, January 2002.

37. This paragraph is based on AI Nadira Naipaul, 26 August 2007 and *Savvy*, January 2002.

38. *Frontier Post*, 13 February 1993.

39. *Savvy*, January 2002.

40. AI Nadira Naipaul, 26 August 2007.

41. Naipaul, V.S., *Beyond Belief*, London 1998, p. 355.

42. AI Minoo Bhandara, 2 September 2007.

43. AI Nadira Naipaul, 26 August 2007.

44. VSNC. His telephone bill for the quarter was £373.09, ten times its normal level.

45. AI Nadira Naipaul, 26 August 2007.

46. TU IV.

47. AI Mira Inalsingh, 17 September 2004.

48. AI Amar Inalsingh, 17 September 2004.

49. VSNC.

50. AI V.S. Naipaul, 8 September 2007.

51. AI Minoo Bhandara, 2 September 2007.

52. AI Nadira Naipaul, 26 August 2007.

53. AI Teresa Wells, 13 December 2007.

54. TU IV.

55. AI V.S. Naipaul, 26 January 2004.

56. AI V.S. Naipaul, 11 January 2005.

57. VSNC.

58. AI V.S. Naipaul, 8 September 2007.

59. VSNC.

60. PTC.

61. *Daily Telegraph*, 6 February 1996.

62. VSNC.

63. AI Eleanor Hale, 13 June 2006.

64. AI Eleanor Hale, 14 June 2006.

65. AI Nella Chapman, 13 December 2007.

66. AI Tristram Powell, 14 August 2003.

67. AI Angela Cox, 8 September 2007.

68. AI V.S. Naipaul, 11 January 2005.

69. VSNC.

70. AI Mira Inalsingh, 17 September 2004.

71. AI Nadira Naipaul, 7 January 2008.

72. VSNC.

73. TU IIB.

74. GAAA.

75. AI David Pryce-Jones, 26 January 2005.

76. *Daily Telegraph*, 20 April 1996.

77. *Times of India*, 23 June 1996.

78. AI V.S. Naipaul, 14 November 2002.

79. AI Nadira Naipaul, 26 August 2007.

80. Given his prominence as a writer on South Asia, it seems unlikely that Nadira Khannum Alvi had never heard of V.S. Naipaul, although it is possible that she had forgotten his name when Ahmed Rashid first mentioned his presence at the US consul general's house on 26 October 1995. A member of Nadira's family confirmed to me that she owned a well-thumbed copy of *India: An Area of Darkness*.

81. AI Eleanor Hale, 13 June 2006.

82. AI V.S. Naipaul, 11 January 2005.

83. VSNC.

84. AI Nadira Naipaul, 26 August 2007.

85. VSNC.

86. This translation of the *Fatiha* is not literal; it includes some extra words to make the sense clearer.

87. AI Nadira Naipaul, 26 August 2007.

88. For the moment.

Index

and other Indian Tales, 43–6, 173;
Ramdas And The Cow, 85; VSN's letters
to, 77–8, 80, 86, 87, 89, 93, 95, 97,
106–7, 114, 118–19
Naipaul, Shivadhar (Sewan, Shiva; brother
of VSN): childhood in Trinidad, 28, 48,
51, 89, 119, 125, 128, 169, 179, 251; at
QRC, 202–3; wins Island Scholarship,
251; in England, 251, 256, (at Oxford
University, 256, 270–1), 269, 270–1,
284, 293–4, 384, 398, 445; visits Turkey,
270; visits Kamla, 285; letters to VSN,
89, 119, 135, 165, 202–3, 205, 424; death
and tributes, 423, 425–6; memorial
service, 425; personality and writing,
423–5; Black and White, 398, 424; The
Chip-Chip Gatherers, 423; Fireflies,
293–4; North of South, 384, 424; VSN's
letters to, 228, 230
Naipaul, Tarun Shivaprasad (nephew of
VSN), 320, 384, 423, 425–6

NAIPAUL, VIDIADHAR (formerly Vidyadhar)
SURAJPRASAD: birth and name, ix, xiii, 8;
childhood in Trinidad, 14–17, 27–8,
47–53, 104; at QR College, 40, 41–2, 54,
55–8, 64, 74; awarded scholarship, 57–8;
applies to Oxford, 58–9; jobs in
Trinidad, 60; on departure of Kamla,
61–4; affair with Golden, 64; leaves
Trinidad, 64–6; journey to England,
67–8; first weeks in England, 68–71;
Oxford student, 72–84, 88–90, 91–108,
109–18; first BBC contributions, 84, 86;
vacation work on farm, 86–7; trip to
Paris, 87–8; to Spain, 94–5; courtship of
Pat Hale, 91–4, 96–7, 99–108, 109–13,
114–18, 122–3, 128–9, 133, 134–6,
137–42, 151–2; breakdown, 94–6;
suicide attempt, 105–6; jobs and search
for after graduation, 118, (on farm, 121),
122, 124, (in college library, 131),
132–4, (NPG, 137), 139–40; attempts
B.Litt., 123–4, 131; in Spain 1957,
128–9; with BBC Colonial Service,
142–3, 144–8, 183–5; marries Pat,

152–3; living apart, 153–7, 160–1;
Christmas with Pat's family, 161–2;
returns to Trinidad, 165–76; returns to
England, 177–8; works at C&CA,
185–7; book reviewing, 192–6; travels
in Caribbean, 1959, 206–11; in India
1962, 219–35, 237–8; writes regular
'Letter from London' 238–41; in New
York, 1965, 253; Trinidad, 254–5;
Uganda, 257–9; travels in Africa,
259–63; India, 1967, 267–8; Scotland,
277; Jamaica, 279–80; Belize, 280; New
York, 1969, 280–3; Canada, 283; living
in Gloucester, 284, 286–7, 290; moves to
Teasel Cottage, 290–2; in India, 296–7;
Caribbean, 297–9; wins Booker Prize,
299–300; in Trinidad, 1972, 301–5;
Argentina, 306, 307–10, 313; affair and
travels with Margaret Gooding, 310,
311–14, 317–18, 319–22, 323–8, 330,
333–6, 340–4, 349–50, 354–5, 362,
367–74, 379–81, 390, 392–3, 399, 409,
413, 416–17, 432–3, 435, 437, 447–52;
473, 477, 482 (ended, 488); in Trinidad,
314–15; New Zealand, 315–16, 318–19;
Morocco, 323; Scandinavia, 329–30;
Trinidad, 1973, 330; Uruguay, 335–6;
Argentina, 349; leaves Pat, 351–2; in
Zaire, 361, 368–9; in Spain, 1975, 369;
India, 369–74; Argentina, 1977, 376,
377–8; Trinidad, 379–81; at Wesleyan
University 390–4, 395, 396; buys Dairy
Cottage, 399; in Malaysia, 399;
Indonesia, 400–1; India, 1980, 401–2;
collapse, 402; moves to Dairy Cottage,
408; in New York, 413; Holland, 413;
Israel, 414; West Africa, 416; Grenada,
417; in Trinidad, 417–18; Dallas, 418;
Trinidad, 422; on death of brother,
425–6; in USA, 431–4; and Pat's illness,
442; in India, 446–53; US, 453;
Trinidad, 455–6, 457; Guyana, 457;
New York, 458; biographers proposed,
458–9; operation on spine, 459; in US
468; Brazil, 472; Indonesia, 477–8,
481–2; Pakistan, 482–7, 488; on Pat's